The American Law Institute

The American Law Institute

A Centennial History

Edited by
ANDREW S. GOLD AND ROBERT W. GORDON

OXFORD
UNIVERSITY PRESS

Oxford University Press is a department of the University of Oxford. It furthers the University's objective of excellence in research, scholarship, and education by publishing worldwide. Oxford is a registered trade mark of Oxford University Press in the UK and certain other countries.

Published in the United States of America by Oxford University Press
198 Madison Avenue, New York, NY 10016, United States of America.

CIP data is on file at the Library of Congress

ISBN 978–0–19–768534–1

DOI: 10.1093/oso/9780197685341.001.0001

Printed by Integrated Books International, United States of America

Note to Readers
This publication is designed to provide accurate and authoritative information in regard to the subject matter covered. It is based upon sources believed to be accurate and reliable and is intended to be current as of the time it was written. It is sold with the understanding that the publisher is not engaged in rendering legal, accounting, or other professional services. If legal advice or other expert assistance is required, the services of a competent professional person should be sought. Also, to confirm that the information has not been affected or changed by recent developments, traditional legal research techniques should be used, including checking primary sources where appropriate.

*(Based on the Declaration of Principles jointly adopted by a Committee of the
American Bar Association and a Committee of Publishers and Associations.)*

You may order this or any other Oxford University Press publication
by visiting the Oxford University Press website at www.oup.com.

Foreword

David F. Levi and Richard L. Revesz

Twenty-five years ago, in the foreword to the American Law Institute's (ALI's) 75th anniversary volume, then President Charles Alan Wright speculated that the ALI's 100th birthday might be a time of champagne and fireworks. The ALI's record over the last century of bringing together the legal profession's leading lights to help clarify and guide the law is, undoubtedly, worthy of celebration. But much as President Wright believed a quarter century ago, and like Director Herbert Wechsler thought a quarter century before him, we feel that a more restrained commemoration, reflecting the ALI's perpetual nature, is in order. In that spirit, we have commissioned this volume to look back at the ALI over its first 100 years. True to the ALI's commitment to open discussion, we have invited leading scholars to examine our history from their own perspectives, not those of the ALI or the Reporters. Indeed, Reporters and others who were involved in the projects discussed might not share the views expressed here, and in some cases will disagree with them. Nevertheless, the chapters capture important moments in the ALI's past and touch on fundamental themes and values that will continue to characterize the ALI well into the future.

One of those themes is the power of bringing a wide range of viewpoints and interests into conversation on complex questions. By design, the ALI is diverse in background and approach. Our membership includes practitioners, judges, and academics, drawn from the private and public sectors and across the political spectrum. They hail from all fifty states, the District of Columbia, all U.S. territories, and twenty-five countries outside of the United States. To some, our diversity might be seen as a hindrance, one that is unlikely to accomplish much in our polarized times. But as the last 100 years have shown, when found among people of good faith striving toward a common goal, such diversity of thought can lead to mutual education and moderation based on reasoned debate and discussion. The consensus-building process that has been central to the ALI's work has also been of great value to the ALI, as it has generated credibility for our projects and ensured that our work gets neither too far ahead of the law nor too far behind it.

Of course, the ALI's work has not been without controversy. A particular point of debate now, as at the time of the ALI's founding, has been what the ALI's projects are *for*. We endeavored to address this question in 2015, with the release of revisions to the ALI Style Manual designed to clarify the distinctions among these types of projects. The goal of our Restatements, which are primarily addressed to courts, has remained constant: in the words of the 1923 Report on the ALI's establishment, "to help make certain much that is now uncertain and to simplify unnecessary complexities, but also to promote those changes which will tend better to adapt the laws to the needs of life." Consistent with practices in effect since our founding, the Style Manual makes clear that Restatements need not adopt the majority rule in each instance, but, where they decline to do so, they "should say so explicitly and explain why." In light of their different purpose, Model and Uniform Codes are not subject to this limitation. As the Style Manual explains, Model and Uniform Codes are "addressed to legislatures, with a view toward legislative enactment" and "are written in prescriptive statutory language." Finally, Principles projects aim to articulate best practices for particular institutions or actors. They may be addressed to private entities (e.g., the Principles of the Law, Compliance and Enforcement for Organizations) or public institutions (e.g., Principles of the Law, Policing). In some cases, as the ALI Style Manual provides, Principles projects may be addressed to courts "when an area is so new that there is little established law," though we have not undertaken a project of this type in the last decade.

Beyond the projects that have characterized the ALI's work during its first century, the last several years have shown that the ALI's convening and consensus-building strengths have positioned it to address pressing issues in an age of hyperpolarization and gridlock. In April 2022, for instance, a bipartisan group of legal scholars, convened at the invitation of the ALI's leadership, announced a set of shared principles that might be used to guide possible efforts to reform the Electoral Count Act. And in May 2022, the ALI successfully completed the Principles of the Law of Policing, a project that engaged an extraordinary group of leaders from all levels of government, including police departments from across the country; advocacy organizations like the NAACP Legal Defense Fund and the Black Lives Matter movement; and members of the academy. The project offers clear, accessible guidance on police department policies and procedures and on urgent, difficult questions like the use of force. In taking up such projects, the ALI's adherence to its process and standards has allowed it to maintain and build the credibility that is central to its success.

Recent years have also seen the continuation and expansion of the ALI's work beyond the United States, a tradition that began in the mid-1940s with the ALI's Statement of Essential Human Rights. In 2011, drawing inspiration from the ALI, the European Law Institute (ELI) was formed as a forum for academics, judges, and practitioners to hold discussions, with the aim of analyzing legal developments and stimulating the evolution of European Union law. The ALI and ELI completed our first joint project, Principles for a Data Economy, in May 2022, and we look forward to continuing to collaborate with colleagues in Europe and across the globe on issues where joint efforts can advance our mission of clarifying, modernizing, and otherwise improving the law.

Finally, we would be remiss if we did not recognize those who have made the work of the ALI possible over the last century. Thank you to the Reporters, Advisers, Council Members, and Members Consultative Group participants, many of whom have dedicated their immense talents and years of their lives to the ALI's projects. Thank you further to our members, whose engagement at the Annual Meetings have proven invaluable, and to the donors whose support enables our work and helps to preserve our neutrality. Thank you to our remarkable predecessor Presidents and Directors. Lastly, thank you to the ALI's staff for their tireless efforts behind the scenes and without whom we could not function.

We want to end by expressing our deep appreciation to Professors Robert Gordon and Andrew Gold, for serving as the general editors of this important volume and to authors of each of the chapters. We have no doubt that these contributions will give rise to further robust debate about the nature of our work and result in making us a stronger institution.

Acknowledgments

In the course of putting together this Centennial History we have incurred many debts. We are especially grateful for the leadership of the American Law Institute's (ALI's) Director, Richard Revesz, who has kept close track of this project every step of the way and has been an unfailing source of encouragement, advice, and practical assistance. We are likewise indebted to the ALI's Deputy Directors, Stephanie Middleton and Eleanor Barrett, and to ALI fellows Ben Brady and Will Tadros. For help in locating photographs, we thank Sarah Oswald and Elizabeth Wittig of the Biddle Law Library at the University of Pennsylvania and the ALI's Chief Communications Director, Jennifer Morinigo. Our editorial advisory board, which overlapped substantially with our roster of authors, was very helpful in recommending topics and contributors, and in commenting on draft essays submitted to two day-long conferences of authors. David Seipp and Carol Lee both volunteered to comment extensively on many of the essays, improving them greatly as they did so. Edward Cooper and Guy Struve also contributed valuable comments.

A.S.G.
R.W.G.

Contents

Contributors

Kenneth S. Abraham
David and Mary Harrison Distinguished Professor of Law, University of Virginia

George A. Bermann
Gellhorn Professor of Law and Monnet Professor in European Union Law, Columbia University

William W. Bratton
Nicholas Gallicchio Professor of Law, Emeritus, University of Pennsylvania

Richard R.W. Brooks
Emilie M. Bullowa Professor of Law, New York University

Naomi R. Cahn
Justice Anthony M. Kennedy Distinguished Professor of Law and Nancy L. Buc '69 Research Professor in Democracy and Equity, University of Virginia

Deborah A. DeMott
Professor of Law, Duke University

Kimberly Kessler Ferzan
Earle Hepburn Professor of Law and Professor of Philosophy, University of Pennsylvania

Andrew S. Gold
Professor of law, Brooklyn Law School

John C.P. Goldberg
Carter Professor of General Jurisprudence Harvard University

Deborah Gordon
Associate Professor of Law, Drexel University

Robert W. Gordon
Professor of Law Emeritus, Stanford University; Chancellor Kent Professor of Law and Legal History, Emeritus, Yale University

David F. Levi
Levi Family Professor of Law and Judicial Studies and Dean Emeritus of the School of Law, Duke University; formerly Chief U.S. District Judge, Eastern District of California; President, American Law Institute

Linda C. McClain
Robert Kent Professor of Law, Boston University

Thomas W. Merrill
Charles Evans Hughes Professor of Law, Colombia University

Linda S. Mullenix
Morris & Rita Atlas Chair in Advocacy, University of Texas

Douglas NeJaime
Anne Urowsky Professor of Law, Yale University

Roberta Cooper Ramo
Partner, Modrall Sperling Law Firm; President Emerita and Council Life Member, American Law Institute

Richard L. Revesz
AnBryce Professor of Law and Dean Emeritus, New York University School of Law; Director, American Law Institute

Frederick Schauer
David and Mary Harrison Distinguished Professor of Law, University of Virginia

Robert E. Scott
Alfred McCormack Professor of Law, Emeritus and Director, Center for Contract and Economic Organization, Columbia University

David J. Seipp
Law Alumni Scholar Professor of Law, Boston University

Emily Sherwin
Frank B. Ingersoll Professor of Law, Cornell University

Henry E. Smith
Fessenden Professor of Law, Harvard University

Symeon C. Symeonides
Alex L. Parks Distinguished Research Professor and Dean Emeritus, College of Law, Willamette University

Allison Tait
Professor of Law, University of Richmond

W. Bradley Wendel
Edwin H. Woodruff Professor of Law, Cornell University

G. Edward White
David and Mary Harrison Distinguished Professor of Law, University of Virginia

Introduction to the Centennial History

Andrew S. Gold and Robert W. Gordon

I. Introduction

The American Law Institute (ALI) dates its formal founding to a meeting in Washington, D.C., on February 23, 1923, attended by an august array of judges, law teachers, and practitioners.[1] The meeting heard a "Report of the Committee on the Establishment of a Permanent Organization for the Improvement of the Law." The Committee was chaired by Elihu Root, the dean of the New York corporate bar, who had been McKinley's secretary of war and Theodore Roosevelt's secretary of state, and was dominated by northeastern corporate lawyers, professors from elite law schools, and high court judges. Its roster is a list of the leading moderate Progressive lawyers of the time: among them Judges Benjamin Cardozo, Learned Hand, and Julian Mack; Professors Arthur Corbin, Ernst Freund, Edmund Morgan, Roscoe Pound, John Henry Wigmore, and Samuel Williston; and practitioners such as Charles A. Boston, C.C. Burlingham, Charles Evans Hughes, Russell Leffingwell, and Victor Morawetz.

The intellectual godfathers of the new ALI had been Roscoe Pound, whose famous speech to the American Bar Association in 1906 had identified the "Causes of Popular Dissatisfaction with the Administration of Justice" as the law's complexity and uncertainty, and Wesley N. Hohfeld, a young law teacher who in 1914 urged the new profession of full-time law teachers to devote themselves, like German jurists, to systematic exposition of legal fields.[2] The call was taken up by an alliance of academic and practicing law reformers, and given shape, energy, and direction by the remarkable William Draper Lewis, a professor and former Dean of the University of Pennsylvania Law School[3] and the ALI's first Director from 1923 to 1947.

The Committee's report analyzed the "causes of uncertainty and complexity in the law" and proposed to create a new institute whose task would be the "restatement" of

---

[1] For detailed accounts of the founding, *see* Kenneth S. Abraham & G. Edward White, *The Work of the American Law Institute in Historical Context*, in this volume; N.E.H. Hull, *Restatement and Reform: A New Perspective on the Founding of the American Law Institute*, *in* THE AMERICAN LAW INSTITUTE: SEVENTY-FIFTH ANNIVERSARY, 1923–1998, at 49 (1998); John P. Frank, *The American Law Institute, 1923–1998, id.* at 3; G. Edward White, *The American Law Institute and the Triumph of Modernist Jurisprudence*, 15 L. & HIST. REV. 1 (1997); HERBERT F. GOODRICH & PAUL A. WOLKIN, THE STORY OF THE AMERICAN LAW INSTITUTE, 1923–1961 (1961); and William LaPiana, *"A Task of No Common Magnitude": The Founding of the American Law Institute*, 11 NOVA L. REV. 1085 (1987).

[2] Roscoe Pound, *The Causes of Popular Dissatisfaction with the Administration of Justice, Address Before the Annual Convention of the American Bar Association* (Aug. 29, 1906), 14 AM. LAW 445 (1996); Wesley N. Hohfeld, *A Vital School of Jurisprudence*, 14 AALSA HANDBOOK 76 (1913–1916)

[3] Lewis was also a legal Progressive. He had been an (unsuccessful) candidate for governor of Pennsylvania on the TR-Bull Moose ticket and was an early proponent of bringing empirical social sciences into the law school curriculum.

Andrew S. Gold and Robert W. Gordon, *Introduction to the Centennial History* In: *The American Law Institute*. Edited by: Andrew S. Gold and Robert W. Gordon, Oxford University Press. © Oxford University Press 2023. DOI: 10.1093/oso/9780197685341.003.0001

the law to promote greater uniformity, clarity, and systematic organization of case law in different fields. The report even went into detail about the organization of the new institute's work: the appointment of a Director and Council to select its projects, the assignment to each project of a Reporter drawn from the legal academy, advised by a body of experts, and the submission of ultimate products to the comments of members. Academics were the only branch of the profession who could put in the time necessary to draft Restatements,[4] but to ensure that their products were usable and acceptable to the profession, the practicing bar and bench would be engaged at every stage of drafting and review. Astonishingly, the broad outlines of this scheme have lasted to the present day.

The unusual form chosen for the new institute's projects, "Restatements" of the law, was not entirely novel. As David Seipp explains in his chapter for this volume,[5] the demand for concise and learned digests or abridgments of masses of common law cases has a long history, and something very like the ultimate form of the Restatements, code-like statements of legal rules that were not legislative codes, but designed for use as starting points for legal reasoning for common law courts, had been anticipated in the early nineteenth century by Justice Joseph Story. But nothing on the scale of the ALI's projects had ever been undertaken, outside of the great Roman and European codifications. The initial ALI Report outlined multiple aims for the Restatements:

> To promote the clarification and simplification of the law and its better adaptation to social needs, to secure the better administration of justice, and to encourage and carry on scholarly and scientific work.[6]

These aims were not always consistent with each other. To reduce complexity, and promote uniformity among jurisdictions, each Restatement sought to state a single version of each rule. This might be the rule adopted by a majority of jurisdictions, or what was, in the Reporters' judgment, the best rule. To reduce uncertainty caused by variations, or imprecision, in legal terminology across jurisdictions and legal fields, the Restatement aimed to promote adoption of uniform terminology, but also to be careful not to perplex practitioners with novel vocabularies. The most difficult challenge was to reduce uncertainty caused by lack of agreement on fundamental principles or conflicting social policies. The Report urged the ALI to stay away from legal fields riven by social, economic, or political controversy, yet still hoped it could provide guidance on how to adapt rapidly changing fields of law to social change.

As experience with restating the law was repeatedly to demonstrate, such conflicts of views were unavoidable. No field of law is immune from controversy, often of a

---

[4] The original plan was that each Restatement would be accompanied by a treatise written by the Reporter, which would include annotations to all the state cases. This plan actually worked only for the First Restatements of Contracts and of Conflict of Laws, whose Reporters had already written their treatises. *See* Abraham & White, *supra* note 1; and Deborah A. DeMott, *Restating the Law in the Shadow of Codes: The ALI in Its Formative Era*, in this volume.

[5] David J. Seipp, *The Need for Restatement of the Common Law: A Long Look Back*, in this volume.

[6] REPORT OF THE COMMITTEE ON THE ESTABLISHMENT OF A PERMANENT ORGANIZATION FOR THE IMPROVEMENT OF THE LAW PROPOSING THE ESTABLISHMENT OF AN AMERICAN LAW INSTITUTE (1923), *reprinted in* THE AMERICAN LAW INSTITUTE: SEVENTY-FIFTH ANNIVERSARY, *supra* note 1, at 173.

fundamental kind. Sometimes conflict was provoked by the critique of outsiders, like the first generation of Legal Realists. As the ALI's membership expanded to include more varied constituencies—and as many fields of practice segmented into champions for conflicting interests and client constituencies—and, among academics, for competing theoretical views—conflicts within the ALI itself were bound to proliferate, and sometimes threatened to sink projects altogether. As the essays in this volume show, intellectual disagreements have sometimes been tempered, but also sometimes amplified, by the strong personalities and convictions of individual Reporters. Among the more notable conflicts have been those provoked by projects on strict products liability, software contracts, family dissolution, aggregate litigation, the law governing lawyers, employment law, the death penalty, the defense of consent to sexual assault, and—in possibly the most bitter and long-lasting dispute—corporate governance.[7]

The ALI has weathered all these conflicts by developing strategies for managing them. The Legal Realist critiques of the 1920s were absorbed, and to some extent accommodated, in the series of Second Restatements beginning in 1952. The ALI overcame its initial resistance to codification and produced the Model Penal Code and Uniform Commercial Code. Another adjustment has been the conversion of potentially divisive Restatement projects to "Principles" projects, which explicitly recognize rapid change in social trends and conflicting interests and perspectives in legal fields, and try to anticipate and influence directions of change and to achieve compromises on conflicted issues. Yet another has been to include conflicting perspectives in early stages of the drafting process, to forestall last-minute sabotage. And still another has been the development of a strong institutional culture of civility and mutual respect.[8] Indeed a capacity for adaptation seems to have been the secret to the ALI's longevity. The ALI always had to struggle to obtain financing, solving the problem in its early years by obtaining a grant from the Carnegie Corporation (of which Root was a director), being creative in tapping new funding sources (including the New Deal's Works Progress Administration when the Carnegie money ran out, and eventually relying on a combination of member dues, foundation grants, and capital contributions of donors.[9] It has also modestly expanded, but considerably diversified, its membership. Its early members were virtually all establishment lawyers, white, male, and Protestant (and, like much of the elite bar of the 1920s and 30s, sometimes regrettably nativist in their prejudices). The ALI began with 308 members and set an initial membership limit at 500, raising it by degrees to 3,000 in 1994. The ALI today has 2,767 elected members, 1,686 life members, and a few other categories of membership for a total of 4,778 members. It remains an elite organization, representing about 0.37 percent of all American lawyers, and about 2 percent of the total membership of the American Bar Association. It is however considerably more diverse: 30 percent of the membership is now female, 15 percent is minorities, and women have been elected in equal numbers to classes in recent years. The current membership is split almost equally between academics (1,831) and private practitioners (1,731), and includes

---

[7] Many of these controversies are described in the present volume.

[8] See Roberta Cooper Ramo, *The American Law Institute at 100: A Three-Decade Personal Reflection*, in this volume.

[9] See DeMott, *supra* note 4.

654 judges, 145 government lawyers, 182 lawyers for nonprofit organizations, and 245 corporate in-house counsel.

II. Design of the Present Volume

It was decided early on in discussions between the editors and members of the ALI Council that we should not attempt to celebrate the Centennial with a comprehensive history of the ALI. Such a history would be a monumental undertaking requiring many years' labor and would run the risk of ending up as a spiritless catalogue of the ALI's impressively numerous projects.[10] We settled instead on commissioning a multi-author volume of essays on specific ALI undertakings, including some of the more important Restatements and Codes, and a sampling of Principles projects, as well as some additional essays on themes cutting across substantive fields of law, and essays treating of the ALI's institutional history. We created an editorial advisory committee of distinguished scholars and lawyers to propose subjects and recommend authors— and ultimately many of the advisers became our authors. We gave no instructions to the authors other than to engage with the intellectual substance of the ideas informing the ALI's projects, to feel free to be critical when warranted, and to try to assess what elements of the projects have turned out to have lasting influence and what may be learned even from apparent failures. The authors, as readers will see, approach the ALI and its works from a variety of perspectives. The resulting book is a window into the course of legal thought over a century.

III. Themes of This Collection

The chapters in this volume raise a host of interesting descriptive questions. Most fundamentally, what does it mean to restate the law? On one account, Restatements are a means of clarifying the law, and they operate to resolve unnecessary complexity and uncertainty found in the mass of common law precedents.[11] From another perspective, Restatements reconstruct common law doctrine, with Reporters acting analogously to appellate judges.[12] Sometimes, Restatements may reform the law's content while still respecting its conceptual structure, its architecture.[13] In certain cases, Restatements also support legal reform by anticipating where the path of the law is headed, even if that path is not yet prevalent in the courts. Alternatively, Restatements may seek to change the law more fundamentally, in which case Reporters could more closely resemble a council of revision or a regulatory agency.[14] This is a non-exhaustive list, but it indicates the variety of approaches that emerged over the past

---

[10] For a full inventory of both completed and ongoing projects, *see* the appendix to this volume.

[11] For discussion of this clarifying role, *see* Abraham & White, *supra* note 1.

[12] *See* John C.P. Goldberg, *Torts in the American Law Institute*, in this volume.

[13] *See* Andrew S. Gold & Henry E. Smith, *Restatements and the Common Law*, in this volume.

[14] *See* Goldberg, *supra* note 12.

century. These differing approaches also raise normative questions: What is the best way to go about restating? Does the answer vary with context?

The authority of Restatements is another common theme. When a Restatement of law is first published, it is not automatically binding in the way that a legal precedent is. Even so, Restatements may be adopted by state supreme courts, with the result that they then become legally binding. A prominent example is Section 402A of the Restatement (Second) of Torts, on products liability—this section has been adopted repeatedly by state courts. Note, however, that even where there is no formal adoption of a Restatement, a Restatement may still be highly influential. Is there a sense in which the more influential Restatements are law?[15] If so, their significance will be different from the significance of treatises and journal articles. Note also that the influence of Restatements also bears on how they are interpreted by the courts. If courts see certain Restatement provisions as canonical (for example, provisions in the Restatement of Contracts), then these Restatements will likewise be interpreted differently from other guiding legal texts.[16]

It is a short step from these questions to another inquiry: How does the existence of a Restatement change the path of the law? Does the Restatement project tend to moderate or slow reform, as some Legal Realists feared?[17] Or do Restatements speed up legal evolution? Perhaps both? The concern that Restatements will freeze prior law in place recedes to some extent when Restatements endorse legal reforms. Such Restatements may, of course, now freeze their reforms in place, but they are less likely to preserve an earlier common law status quo. That said, significant deviations from the common law could also affect the degree to which Restatements influence the law. Especially in contested areas of law, courts may react differently to a Restatement's guidance if it reconstructs existing law than if it alters the law's course more dramatically.[18] Still, such reactions should not obscure the general pattern of the Restatements' influence. The impacts of Restatements on the law are legion, sometimes as a direct consequence of legal adoption, and at other times through an indirect change in legal thought.[19]

Then again, it is not just the law that changes over time but also the Restatements themselves. Restatements have changed in response to a wide variety of inputs, ranging from changes in the underlying law that is to be restated, to changes in social views and practices, to changes in Reporters' viewpoints and predilections. Occasionally, the views of outside parties have also had an impact.[20] Whatever the source, certain

---

[15] For discussion of how Restatements may qualify as law, *see* Frederick Schauer, *The Restatements as Law*, in this volume.

[16] On the Restatement of Contracts as canonical, *see* Richard R.W. Brooks, *Canon and Fireworks: Reliance in the Restatements of Contracts and Reliance on Them*, in this volume.

[17] For discussion of the different ways in which Legal Realists critiqued the early Restatement projects, *see* Robert W. Gordon, *Restatements and Realists*, in this volume.

[18] *See* Goldberg, *supra* note 12.

[19] In this regard, it is noteworthy that the Restatement of Restitution offered an innovative *rationale* for the law. *See* Emily Sherwin, *A Short History of the Restatement of Restitution and Unjust Enrichment*, in this volume.

[20] As an example, consider the State Department's role in the development of the Restatement of the Foreign Relations Law of the United States. *See* George A. Bermann, *The International Law Profile of the ALI*, in this volume.

Restatements have evolved considerably from their initial version to subsequent versions. It is noteworthy that changes in the law are only one of the primary factors that have made a difference; changes in social norms have also played a role. Thus, the Restatement of Trusts has reflected shifts in understandings of the family.[21] Where the law has changed, it goes without saying that a subsequent Restatement may need to change with it, but legal change is but one basis for revision. Again, Restatements have evolved for many reasons, and the influences on this evolution are an important part of understanding the Restatements' significance.

The scope of topics covered within the Restatements is one of the more notable changes. Sometimes this is a matter of doctrinal scope, as with the Restatement of Property. Historically, Restatements of Property have only covered a subset of the law of property.[22] Several of the gaps have now been filled in, and the Restatement (Fourth) of Property, now in progress, is intended to cover substantially more territory than its predecessors. In other cases, the question is jurisdictional. Thus, Restatements are usually concerned with common law at the state law level, and not with international law (at least not directly). With the more recent Restatements of Conflict of Laws, and with the Restatement (Second) of Foreign Relations Law in the United States, international law has gained an increasingly prominent role.[23] A shift in coverage may also concern the type of law at issue. Classically, what is restated is the common law. Statutory material has been relevant to varying degrees over the past century, but restatement of statutory material has not been the norm.[24] With recent Restatement projects on corporate governance and on copyright, the proportion of statute-based law expanded considerably. Each of these changes bears on the import and influence of the Restatements.[25]

Yet restating the law is not the only important project that the ALI has undertaken over the past 100 years. There are also Principles projects, such as the Principles of Corporate Governance. Scope of coverage is again a noteworthy theme. Notwithstanding an overlap in subject matter, corporate governance concerns are not coextensive with corporate law.[26] The Principles of Corporate Governance were, nonetheless, an important influence on the direction corporate law would subsequently take. Indeed, they have paved the way for a forthcoming Restatement of the Law—Corporate Governance, now in progress. Likewise, the Principles of the Law of Family Dissolution have proven a substantial influence on the development of family law. Drafted during a time of flux, they have been an important source of dialogue among courts and legislatures, and also among advocates and academics.[27] So, too,

---

[21] *See* Naomi R. Cahn, Deborah Gordon, & Allison Tait, *The Restatements of Trusts—Revisited*, in this volume.

[22] *See* Thomas W. Merrill, *The Restatement of Property: The Curse of Incompleteness*, in this volume.

[23] *See* Symeon C. Symeonides, *Conflict of Laws in the ALI's First Century*, in this volume; Bermann, *supra* note 20.

[24] For discussion from the ALI's early history, *see* DeMott, *supra* note 4.

[25] Another important scope question concerns the choice to restate law and not related subject matters (such as ethical standards) that the law bears upon. *See* W. Bradley Wendel, *Constructing a Legal Field: The Restatement of the Law Governing Lawyers*, in this volume.

[26] *See* William W. Bratton, *Special Interests at the Gate: The ALI Corporate Governance Project, 1978–1992*, in this volume.

[27] *See* Linda C. McClain & Douglas NeJaime, *The ALI Principles of the Law of Family Dissolution: Addressing Family Inequality Through Functional Regulation*, in this volume.

the Principles of the Law of Aggregate Litigation have had an incremental impact on the law.[28]

In addition, the past century has seen full-scale codification projects, as exemplified by the Model Penal Code[29] and the Uniform Commercial Code (UCC).[30] Such projects have been very consequential, with wide adoption across the United States and dramatic effects on the law's content and uniformity. To the extent the early ALI was hesitant about codification—indeed, Restatements were historically seen as an alternative to codification—today's ALI is much more open to codification projects.[31] Many of the contemporary debates over these codes have concerned updating, rather than codification itself. For example, there have been debates over updates to the Model Penal Code's treatment of the death penalty.[32] In the UCC context, there have been debates over updates for computer information transactions.[33] In each case, the codes themselves are firmly established features of the legal landscape.

IV. Conclusion

A hundred years is a long life span for a law reform project. Most such projects terminate when they achieve their limited initial goals, they fail, or their members lose interest and their funding runs out. The ALI remains an enterprise in full vigor, with an enormous number of projects completed and an impressive array of projects in forward motion. The enterprise has never lacked for critics, beginning with the Legal Realists of the 1920s and 30s (and, although their critiques are not as well remembered, legal conservatives of the same era), but the ALI has survived by constant adaptation to change, accommodating the views of many of its critics, providing a medium for their resolution in its deliberative procedures, and simply updating Restatements (and launching new Principles projects) whenever the older ones are threatened with obsolescence. The ALI's projects are often the results of compromise, but have been saved from featureless blandness by the commanding intellectual gifts of their principal Reporters and the predominant good faith of dissenters. For a while in the 1980s and 90s, when the legal academy was experiencing the turn to interdisciplinary studies and what Judge Richard Posner has called "the decline of law as an autonomous discipline,"[34] it appeared that the ALI might run out of talent to manage its doctrinal projects. The threat was avoided as a series of enterprising and persuasive ALI leaders have recruited first-rate academics and lawyers to undertake and advise on

---

[28] See Linda S. Mullenix, *Aggregationists at the Barricades: Assessing the Impact of the Principles of the Law of Aggregate Litigation*, in this volume.

[29] See Kimberly Kessler Ferzan, *From Restatement to Model Penal Code: The Progress and Perils of Criminal Law Reform*, in this volume.

[30] See Robert E. Scott, *The Uniform Commercial Code and the Ongoing Quest for an Efficient and Fair Commercial Law*, in this volume.

[31] See DeMott, *supra* note 4. On debates over codification and the pre-history of the ALI, *see* Seipp, *supra* note 5.

[32] See Ferzan, *supra* note 29.

[33] See Scott, *supra* note 30.

[34] Richard A. Posner, *The Decline of Law as an Autonomous Discipline: 1962–1987*, 100 Harv. L. Rev. 761 (1987).

new projects, as these have incorporated insights from neighboring disciplines into the ALI's work, and as a fresh generation of scholars has revitalized doctrinal studies of private law.[35] The unique form of the Restatements—subject to much derision in the ALI's first decades—has proved remarkably durable. The Restatements have sought both to express concise versions of what their learned community of drafters consider the best examples of existing law, while also encouraging the law's evolution. The form offers practitioners and judges an overview of legal fields that is more accessible than masses of common law cases, and more flexible than legislation. The critiques of the First Restatements, that the barebones statements of rules, accompanied only by brief illustrations, provided too little in the way of clues to the sources of their authority, and too little commentary on their rationales, have been answered in late Restatements by more extensive commentary and annotations to cases.

Institutions that survive a long time have to avoid hardening into orthodoxy as the founding generation ages, or dissolving into factionalism as newcomers take their place. The culture of the American Law Institute, carefully curated by successive Presidents, Directors, and Councils, unafraid of controversy, but skillful in mediating it, has enabled it to flourish. Its membership, earnest, patient, thorough, and deliberative in its proceedings, has done the same.

---

[35] *See* ANDREW S. GOLD ET AL. (EDS.), THE OXFORD HANDBOOK OF THE NEW PRIVATE LAW (2020).

PART I
FOUNDING AND DEVELOPMENT
OF THE AMERICAN LAW
INSTITUTE

1

The American Law Institute at 100

A Three-Decade Personal Reflection

Roberta Cooper Ramo

I. Introduction

In celebration of the American Law Institute's (ALI's) 100th anniversary, in a volume of preeminent legal scholars outlining the impact of the ALI's work, I have been asked to share my personal experience over many decades as an ALI member and leader, and also to describe the culture that produces the work which continues to bind practicing lawyers, judges, and legal academics together, shoulders jointly to the wheel for years, to fulfill the mission of the ALI. I keep the Charter in my calendar:

> To promote the clarification and simplification of the law and its better adaptation to social needs, to secure the better administration of justice and to encourage and carry on scholarly and scientific legal work.

The exact time at which any of us writes influences our views. I write as the pandemic still rages and people threaten healthcare experts and school boards trying to protect them and their children. I write with the ravages of climate change impacting all of us, but its reality still denied by many. I write with people in the streets demonstrating for voting rights and in favor of and against the right for women to choose whether to bear children. In the face of upheaval in American society, I wonder if the ALI's founders foresaw the vital importance of the ALI's culture in allowing the organization to fulfill its mission in difficult times. Also, I write from the perspective of the first woman to be elected President of the ALI.

Looking back, and also thinking about the next century of ALI work, I suspect that the ALI's founding fathers (while there were no founding mothers, there were two women prosecutors from California in the early membership) would have been astonished to find that their impactful experiment in improving the justice system would be led by a woman from and in practice in Albuquerque, New Mexico. My perspective comes from many years on the Council and my service as ALI President for nine years and as Chair of the Council for three years. However, I also see the ALI through the perspective of being from and in New Mexico. From my office, I see the sunset and sometimes the sunrise, the Sandia Mountains, the New Mexico sky, and hot air balloons. In our firm's reception area, one is as likely to see someone in a cowboy hat and boots as in a suit. This is a different slice of practicing law in the vastness of the United States. Here too the work of the ALI betters the justice system from ranches to pueblos, from cities to villages, and in all of our courts. These observations

Roberta Cooper Ramo, *The American Law Institute at 100* In: *The American Law Institute*. Edited by: Andrew S. Gold and Robert W. Gordon, Oxford University Press. © Oxford University Press 2023. DOI: 10.1093/oso/9780197685341.003.0002

are not comprehensive but rather illustrative of the elements that make the ALI an American treasure.

In 1991, I was astonished to receive a letter inviting me to become an ALI member. The Restatements were important resources during my legal education at the University of Chicago Law School. I associated them with Professor Soia Mentschikoff and her work on the Uniform Commercial Code. Professor Mentschikoff was the only woman on the University of Chicago law faculty in the 1960s when I was a student. But gender had nothing to do with her Olympian presence as a teacher, a scholar, and a larger-than-life thinker. It was both thrilling and humbling to think about being invited to join an organization in which she had a major presence.

The letter inviting me to join ALI explained that one of the obligations of membership was attendance and participation at the Annual Meeting. I immediately made plans to attend in May 1992. The workings of the ALI were a mystery to me. Like many, I suspect, I thought that the Restatements came directly from Mount Olympus. It occurred to me that Soia Mentschikoff simply drafted all and threw them down to earth with the same great arm she showed throwing an eraser at a law student who gave a grievously wrong answer to an Article 9 question.

The 1992 Annual Meeting program and the speakers outlined were inspirational and intimidating: Chief Justice William Rehnquist and Justice Harry Blackmun, former Attorney General Elliot Richardson, Secretary of Labor Lynn Martin, and Director of Central Intelligence Robert Gates. Projects ranged from Taxation and Principles of Corporate Governance to Complex Litigation and the Law Governing Lawyers. When the materials started pouring in, I had no idea where to start or what I was expected to do. So I began with the Law Governing Lawyers, about which I thought I might know something, and, as a non-litigator, I kept going into the darkness of Complex Litigation.

The Annual Meeting in Washington, D.C., was in the two-story ballroom of the Mayflower Hotel. It looked like an opera house, with gold baroque details on the balcony and a stage. I knew some members from my involvement with the American Bar Association (ABA) and the joint committee of the ABA and the ALI sponsoring continuing legal education programs, and others from my time at the University of Chicago Law School.

Gerhard Casper, about to become president of Stanford, but known to me from his time as Dean of the University of Chicago Law School, came right over as I walked in. He welcomed me and introduced me all round to everyone who walked by as I found a seat. Every stranger I sat next to seemed to welcome seeing a new face as I found a seat each day. The chairs were small and balancing the drafts on laps a common challenge.

I do not recall having the courage to ask a question or make an observation. As each draft was brought to the floor, the combination of questions and comments by experts and nonexperts in each particular area of the law began to lay the foundation for my understanding of how the work actually got done.

Sitting there that first meeting, I came to realize that this combination of experts and nonexperts helped to make the work particularly impactful. The substance produced by the Reporters was expanded and edited by the Advisers and the Council. The final corrections, additions, and nuance came at the Annual Meeting from members working in the area and from those like me, who often knew very little about a particular Restatement. The vetting of an expert drafting by lawyers and judges, who would use the work, meant that the Black Letter, notes, and examples were accessible and understandable.

At some point in the conversation that first day, a white-haired man whom I vaguely recognized as the Treasurer went to the microphone to say to one set of Reporters that if they looked at a certain page and line, it was contradicted many pages later by a different page and line. After taking a moment to look at both entries, the Reporters smiled ruefully to acknowledge that Bennett Boskey was right as usual.

Such attention to detail, practicality, and substance was inspirational. As each project came to the floor, speaker after speaker set out contradictions they saw in the drafting, asked questions about the way the law was cited or the Black Letter or the Reporters' Notes were written, or suggested clearer ways to express the point. At the end of a discussion, the same white-haired man was recognized to make the motion the Chair called "the Boskey Motion." I had no idea what it was. It took years for me to understand its impact and its brilliance. The Boskey language is: "I move approval of this draft of (whatever the project is) subject to this discussion and the usual editorial prerogatives of the Reporters." The Boskey Motion allows the reporters to make edits to the text incorporating the discussion, without the need to bring the project back to the body or the Council, so long as the substance is not changed from what has been approved at the meeting.[1] This motion was repeated throughout the meeting at the conclusion of the discussion of each draft. I also realized I had been mispronouncing "prerogative" all of my life!

The Annual Meeting's lunches and dinners were an opportunity to sit and talk with icons of the law and with those like me who simply loved the law as a civil way our democratic country resolves conflict and clears up confusion. In a single meeting, I realized that I would/could be a better lawyer by preparing and participating in the work of the ALI. The honor was meaningful to me, the work transformative.

II. ALI Governance

With that first meeting, I was launched into the rhythm of the ALI. All successful organizations, especially nonprofit ones, have a rhythm to their work. If it is chaotic, the work doesn't get done, and in many cases, the organization ultimately collapses. If the culture becomes rigid, the work becomes less impactful and the organization may fail. Current times show the strength of the ALI. The remarkable leadership of President David Levi, Director Ricky Revesz, and Deputy Director Stephanie Middleton kept the ALI's work moving at its usual pace, if not quite its usual way, in the face of the halt to normal life brought by the plague of COVID-19.

Over those first few years as a member, I saw that the ALI rhythm is set by Council meetings in October and January, the Annual Meeting in May, and the steady march of project meetings. The intellectual work is sometimes hard, but never boring. Watching and participating in the conversations between academics, judges, and

---

[1] Michael Traynor, "That's Debatable": The ALI as a Public Policy Form, Part III: The Boskey Motion, The President's Letter, 25 A.L.I. Rep. 1 (Spring 2003).

practicing lawyers is like watching the very best artists collaborating in a jazz riff or even an opera or a Broadway musical. All this effort is made to improve the American justice system.

At this time, when it is hard to find or participate in a civil conversation about anything important, ALI conversations are grounded on four principles: establishing the facts of the law and the case law; drawing on diverse experience and outlook; civil, often intense, and far-ranging debate; and compromise. However, the word "compromise" may imply a kind of horse trading in which much is lost. The back-and-forth discussion and analysis of the language of the ALI's work clarifies and focuses on the end result.

The founders of the ALI recognized the need to unify, codify, and make the principles of law understandable in a country in which commerce was being nationalized by nationwide highways, railroads, telegraphs, and telephones. The founders conceived the idea of the Restatements of the Law on which the entire country could rely. The process they established was revolutionary. Judges, legal scholars, and practicing lawyers would work together to draft the Restatements. Simply restating the law was not enough. They also wanted to simplify and improve the law for the betterment of all who rely on the American justice system.

The national importance of the work of the ALI can be understood not just by counting citations but by looking at who has served on the Council and their dedication to the work.[2] The luckiest of breaks for me came when I was elected to the Council. I sit with icons of the law, some of whom I didn't know at first, but whom I came to admire without reservation as I listened to their ideas and their questions. Their work ethic and their quick thoughtful responses to the discussions with the Reporters are a pleasure to behold.

When I joined the Council there were no term limits. Council members left because they died, became a U.S. Supreme Court Justice (Justice Ginsburg and Justice Jackson), or for various reasons simply could not do the work of the Council along with their own professional work.

My chance came because New York Court of Appeals Chief Judge Judith Kaye (the first woman in that position)—who had taken Justice Ginsburg's place on Council when she joined the Supreme Court—found that the burden of her work kept her from being a full participant on the Council. I was elected to fill the vacant seat.

From that first Council meeting in December 1997 to today, the work and thought that the already incredibly busy Council members undertake under the brilliant leadership of the Director and the Deputy Director deserve gratitude from all for moving the American legal system forward in such an impactful way.

I joined the Council when Charles Alan Wright was the President. He was one of the most active U.S. Supreme Court advocates of his time. Notwithstanding his faculty position at the University of Texas Law School and the responsibilities of leading the ALI, he never stopped taking important legal issues to the U.S. Supreme Court.

---

[2] See AMERICAN LAW INSTITUTE, SEVENTY-FIFTH ANNIVERSARY, 1923–1998, at 325 (1998); AMERICAN LAW INSTITUTE, COUNCIL MEMBERS (2021), https://www.ali.org/about-ali/governance/officers-council/list-council-members/.

His service as President was a marker that the ALI's view of legal intellectuals broadened to parts west of the Mississippi and east of the California Coast.

There were few new members of the Council, and I had no idea what was expected of Council members. The agenda for the meeting in December 1997 came out, and I plunged into the drafts, making comments along the margins and calling the Council members whom I knew to ask questions about issues that I did not understand. Not only was there no orientation, there was a surprise at the first Council dinner I attended. It was held at the Century Association in New York. Dinner included spouses, but my darling husband was on call that week at home. The dinner was actually in the basement of the Century Association, a pool table pushed to one side. I assumed it was chosen as, rare in New York at that time, it did not discriminate in its membership. As dessert was being served, Charles Alan Wright went to the podium and after some remarks about issues of general interest that had come up during the Council meeting that day, said something like: "As everyone knows, it is a Council tradition that the newest member of the Council address us at dinner as way of introduction."

I certainly had not known that! I sat there for what must have seemed to everyone as a very long time, before I stood up to speak. I have only the slightest recollection of what I said. I noted what an honor it was to be among the Council members, and I do remember telling everyone what had happened when I told my husband that I had been nominated to join the Council. During my first year of law school, my husband, Barry Ramo, had once or twice come across the Midway from the University of Chicago Hospital, at which he was an intern, to sit in the back of a class or two. Civil Procedure was taught by the then new faculty member Geoffrey Hazard. Later, after some years on the Yale Law School faculty, Hazard had become the Director of the ALI. My husband knew that I had not exactly distinguished myself when Professor Hazard called on me unexpectedly in one class that he observed. When I called to tell Barry about my nomination, his first reaction was, "Does Geoffrey Hazard know about this?" I had to admit that I had no idea, but by the time I was standing before the Council as a new member, I had come to know that, to my complete surprise, he had been supportive of the idea.

An Albuquerque lawyer came over time to sit with Council colleagues I had not met before: former head of both the FBI and CIA and former federal judge William Webster; Chief Justice of the Massachusetts Supreme Court, Margaret Marshall; Conrad Harper, a well-known New York lawyer who had been Legal Adviser to the State Department; and storied New York lawyers Sheila Birnbaum, who often argued before the U.S. Supreme Court, and Martin Lipton, who was known even to me as a brilliant corporate tactician and the éminence grise behind many a New York City mayor. There was Michael Traynor, whose quiet knowledgeable comments about so many projects moved everything forward. Seth Waxman, former Solicitor General of the U.S. Supreme Court, is a full participant in ALI work. And I sat beside those I did know and so admired: Lloyd Cutler with whom I had worked on some international bar matters; Bob Stein, the longtime Dean of the University of Minnesota Law School who had become the Executive Director of the ABA and with whom I had worked hand in glove as President of the ABA; and a breathtaking group of other icons of the American legal world. All were clearly committed to the work, to the collaborative and respectful culture, and to one another as friends as well as colleagues.

The Council is composed of nationally important and distinguished lawyers, jurists, and scholars. While these individuals continue to do all manner of work from heading the CIA to serving on courts all over the United States, to working as general counsel of major institutions, presidents of universities and deans of law schools, lead counsel in major class action suits, and professors teaching and writing at law schools, all find the work of the ALI so meaningful that they come to the Council meetings and participate fully.[3] Watching, listening, and participating in the debate and discussion at the Council often leaves me awestruck.

"How do things get done?" Decades ago, William Hubbard,[4] my friend from South Carolina and new to the Council, whispered that question to me as we sat one afternoon in New York at the Fall Council meeting. I don't remember the particular issue that caused the question. But I do remember my answer: "I have no idea."

As we both sat and began some committee work and acted as Advisers, "how things get done" began to unfold. The Director brought ideas to a Program Committee.[5] If approved, the Program Committee brought proposals to the Council for debate, to be either accepted and moved forward or rejected or sent back for any number of reasons.

There was almost no turnover on the Council. This made increasing diversity more difficult. President Michael Traynor appointed Allen Black, a well-known Philadelphia lawyer, the Chair of something called the "Special Committee on Strategic Communication." Its task was to figure out how to diversify the membership with a focus on age, race, ethnicity, and gender. I was appointed to the Committee. We worked at making sure that our lists of able/outstanding women and people of color became an action list for the Membership Committee.

When I became President in 2008, I asked Judge Yvonne Gonzalez Rogers to chair the Membership Committee. In addition to gender and racial diversity, I was concerned that we were not nominating or attracting lawyers not in private practice, including public defenders, Legal Aid lawyers, prosecutors, and government and military lawyers. ALI member Helaine Barnett, then the President of the National Legal Services Corporation, agreed to chair an Ad Hoc Committee on Public Lawyer

---

[3] During my first year on the Council, the body included Kenneth S. Abraham, Shirley S. Abrahamson, Philip S. Anderson, Susan Frelich Appleton, Richard S. Arnold, Sheila L. Bimbaum, Allen D. Black, Bennett Boskey, Michael Boudin, William M. Burke, Hugh Calkins, Gerhard Casper, William T. Coleman Jr., Edward H. Cooper, N. Lee Cooper, Lloyd N. Cutler, George H.T. Dudley, Christine M. Durham, William H. Erickson, Thomas E. Fairchild, John P. Frank, George Clemon Freeman Jr., Paul L. Friedman, Antonio García-Padilla, Jaime S. Gorelick, Conrad K. Harper, D. Brock Homby, Vester T. Hughes Jr., Joseph F. Johnston, Mary Kay Kane, Nicholas deB. Katzenbach, Herma Hill Kay, Carolyn Dineen King, Pierre N. Leval, Edward Hirsch Levi, Betsy Levin, Hans A. Linde, Martin Lipton, Robert MacCrate, John W. Martin Jr., Hale McCown, John J. McKetta III, Vincent L. McKusick, Robert H. Mundheim, Roswell B. Perkins, Harvey S. Perlman, Ellen Ash Peters, Louis H. Pollak, Roberta Cooper Ramo, Ernest J. Sargeant, Mary M. Schroeder, Sherwin P. Simmons, Wm. Reece Smith Jr., Robert A. Stein, John T. Subak, Michael Traynor, Bill Wagner, Patricia M. Wald, Elizabeth Warren, William H. Webster, Lawrence E. Walsh, W. Herbert Wechsler, George Whittenburg, Herbret P. Wilkins, James H. Wilson Jr., John Minor Wisdmo, and Charles Alan Wright.

[4] Former President of the ABA, now Dean of University of South Carolina Law School.

[5] Now the Projects Committee.

Outreach to find ten to twenty lawyers from these sectors who would add an additional kind of diversity of experience to our membership.[6] They produced superb nominations, who as members make rich contributions to the ALI's work. In the process of looking at the work of the Barnett task force, we realized that participation in the ALI as a member was too expensive for many of the public interest lawyers we were seeking to recruit, as well as for many current members, including many judges. Yet coming to Annual Meetings and attending the lunches and dinners are a key part of building our culture.

As she came close to being a life member, Professor Susan Appleton suggested that we start a class gift campaign, and we did. Her wonderful idea produced the solution to the expense of participation. From the first class gift campaign chaired by Professor Appleton and Gregory P. Joseph to the present, the ALI has received $1.6 million in class gifts. Those funds are primarily used to reimburse ALI members who would not otherwise be able to afford full participation. It has made the diversity of our membership real and not aspirational.

President Traynor's egalitarian instincts and brave leadership focused on the issue of broadening the diversity of the Council. He noted that it was hard for us to work on the Nonprofit Organizations project and not look at whether our own governance met the times. He appointed a Special Committee on Governance, chaired by Robert Mundheim, on which I served, to determine such very basic issues as whether there should be term limits for Council members and for officers. Term limits for Council members had to be long enough to allow long-term projects to be completed. For officers, periodic turnover had to consider the need for steady long-term leadership which did not disrupt the success of the ALI. All of the recommendations for change were brought to the Council by a report from Chair Mundheim.

Voting against their own interests, but for the interest of the ALI, the Council passed a fifteen-year term limit for Council members, which was approved by membership at the 2007 Annual Meeting. The change allowed for the input and presence of those who became emeriti after fifteen years. It was agreed that emeriti would continue to have a voice, but not a vote at Council meetings. We could not lose the participation of Council members who had been there a long time and were still at the height of their productive professional lives. The Council also enacted term limits for officers and committee members. To ensure easy transitions and institutional memory, the immediate past President serves a three-year term as Chair of the Council. These changes have allowed the Council to become increasingly diverse in every way. Diversity of the membership adds depth and relevance to our work and remains an ongoing priority.

---

[6] Besides Chair Barnett, members included Kim J. Askew, Christine M. Durham, JoAnne A. Epps, Paul L. Friedman, Gail K. Hillebrand, Kathryn M. Kase, William J. Leahy, Margaret Colgate Love, Michael J. Marchand, Roberta Cooper Ramo, Zaldwaynaka Scott, Robert E. Stein, and Elizabeth S. Stong. The committee finished its work in 2011, and ALI was able to provide financial support for eleven public lawyer members to attend the 2011 Annual Meeting.

A. The Work

1. The Model Penal Code and the Death Penalty

A single issue, dealing with the language on the death penalty in the 1962 Model Penal Code, is an excellent example of ALI culture, governance, and the quality of thought and research that underlies our actions. Prior to the Annual Meeting in 2007, President Traynor received a call from two members, Professor Ellen Podgor and Professor Roger Clark. They noted that in the lengthy ongoing discussions of the sentencing portion of the Model Penal Code, the section concerning the death penalty was omitted from review. Both they and Michael Traynor knew this was intentional because the project had been approved to move forward without undertaking any work on the death penalty Section 210.6.

Professors Clark and Podgor gave President Traynor a heads-up that at the meeting they were going to move to eliminate the death penalty sections from the Model Penal Code and have the ALI take a position in opposition to the death penalty. Traynor responded that he would look at the governance aspects of their proposal and get back to them.

After discussion with ALI Director Lance Liebman and others, Traynor asked Clark and Podgor to defer the motion, but told them that he would ask a small group with diverse opinions and expertise on the death penalty to advise the Council on the matter. He also committed that the work would be done expeditiously. President Traynor sent a memo to the membership on May 10, 2007, outlining the issues arising from the Clark/Podgor motion, explaining the process that would go forward in response, and thanking them for their willingness to participate in the process.[7]

The 2007 Annual Meeting proceeded in just that fashion. The motion to have the ALI stand in opposition to the death penalty and remove Section 210.6 of the Model Penal Code was introduced by Professors Podgor and Clark. There was limited debate. In response to Michael Traynor's comments, Professors Podgor and Clark agreed to defer their motion. President Traynor noted that he would appoint a small group to advise the Program Committee and the Council on what, if anything, might be done about the death penalty sections of the Model Penal Code and the substance of the Podgor/Clark motion. He noted that the results of such study and discussion would be reported back to the Council and the membership. Michael Traynor is among the most thoughtful and kind lawyers, and, with a twinkle in his eye, he noted that it was likely that the next President (that would be me) would have the task of leading the substantive discussion of the membership on the issue.

Michael Traynor, with Director Liebman's advice, appointed a small committee chaired by Professor Daniel Meltzer of Harvard, also a member of the Council, to review the situation and report to the Program Committee. The Meltzer Committee met and produced a memo laying out three options: an ALI call for abolition of the death penalty in the United States, ALI's withdrawal of Section 210.6, or revision of Section 210.6.

---

[7] Memorandum to members of the ALI from President Michael Traynor, May 10, 2007.

To allow broad membership input, President Traynor and Director Liebman also established for the first time an online forum for discussion of this matter moderated by Council member Susan Appleton of Washington University Law School. This was the ALI's first foray into the world of the internet, which allowed for broader participation by members. After considering all of this feedback, the Program Committee and the Council decided to commission a white paper to inform their decision.

Lance Liebman constructed a working group that had knowledge, experience, and a diversity of views on death penalty law and practices. It was not possible to find an academic who thought that the death penalty should be maintained or was neutral. However, Professor Meltzer and Director Liebman agreed that Carol Steiker of Harvard Law School and her brother Jordon Steiker of the University of Texas Law School were highly regarded scholars in this area and could be trusted to do the work for a white paper that would be viewed as fair by both sides. The Steikers agreed to undertake this sensitive task.

Their paper was reviewed by a small group of state and federal judges including those who had presided over death penalty cases; prosecutors and defense lawyers; and academics who had studied the application of the death penalty and related issues such as whether the death penalty was a deterrent to crime.[8] In sterling ALI fashion, the paper was discussed, revised several times, and given to the Program Committee for its review and then to the Council prior to its December 2008 meeting.

The Program Committee met in November 2008 and agreed upon a set of recommendations to the Council: that Section 210.6 be removed, but that the ALI not take a position on capital punishment. At a December Council meeting, the Council discussed and accepted those recommendations. At the Annual Meeting in May 2009, my first as President, the issue of the death penalty was on the agenda for discussion and action by the membership. I was relieved that it wasn't up on the first day.

The thoughtful consideration and quality of discussion are to me a perfect example of what should happen when our American democracy must deal with passionately held views on both sides of a complicated, fraught issue.

The agenda for the Annual Meeting in May 2009 called for the discussion and action of the membership of the "Capital Punishment Report and Vote on Council Recommendation that ALI Withdraw Model Penal Code § 210.6" to begin on Tuesday, May 19, at 2 p.m. As I walked up to take my place on the dais, the importance of and passion about this issue were palpable. Every seat on the floor in the ballroom of the Mayflower was taken. People were crowded into every aisle and sitting on the stairs leading down to the floor of the ballroom. The balcony looked like an eighteenth-century portrait of an English court, where a crowd was waiting to watch a notorious case. People sat elbow to elbow on small uncomfortable chairs. Those lucky enough to get a seat against the outside railings upstairs had a bird's-eye view. I wondered if the fire marshal might make an appearance to shut us down. I worried about people falling all over one another to get to the microphones to speak.

---

[8] Participants included Nancy F. Atlas, Charles F. Baird, David O. Carter, Roger S. Clark, Christine M. Durham, Jaime Esparza, Jeffrey A. Fagan, James E. Ferguson II, Joseph L. Hoffmann, Kathryn M. Kase, Nancy J. King, Daniel J. Meltzer, William H. Pryor Jr., and Kevin R. Reitz.

Because of the complexity of what I suspected would be numerous motions and amendments, I asked Philip Anderson of Arkansas, longtime Council member and expert parliamentarian, to sit next to me and to advise me on parliamentary points. I gaveled the meeting to order and asked Judge Paul Friedman, Chair of the Program Committee, to inform the members of the work and activity on the death penalty section that had taken place since Professors Clark and Podgor had made their motion two years before and to report on the action of the Council.

After Judge Friedman gave his report explaining the Council action, it was moved and seconded that the action of the Council recommending to the membership the removal of the death penalty section of the Model Penal Code be approved by the membership.

The debate began. The issues were whether the ALI should, as the Council had voted, simply remove the death penalty section of the Model Penal Code; whether it should take a stand against the death penalty in the United States; and what, if anything, should be added to the language accompanying the removal of Section 210.6.

For almost three hours, the lines to speak at microphones were long. The debate was intense, often moving, but always respectful. The speakers ranged from academics who had a scholarly viewpoint on the issues to lawyers who represented clients in death penalty cases and judges who had presided over death penalty cases. Many pointed out that the death penalty was constitutional and asked how the ALI could thus weigh in against it. Many people suggested various ways to add language from the Steiker paper to the motion, and others favored the simple removal of the section as recommended by the Council.

Lawyers and judges were concerned that judges have an opportunity to abstain from a vote so that they were not compromised in any way going forward. A yellow tablet made its way from front to back and up the stairs (with someone holding it, although a floating yellow tablet has always seemed a good idea to me) so that all who felt the need to sign that they had abstained from the votes had that opportunity.

After many efforts at amendment of the original motion, the following amended motion passed with an overwhelming vote in favor: "For reasons stated in Part V of the Council's report to the membership, the ALI withdraws Section 210.6 of the Model Penal Code in light of the current intractable institutional and structural obstacles to ensuring a minimally adequate system for administering capital punishment."

The room broke into spontaneous and long applause. Perhaps the applause was just for the result, but I felt it was equally for the scholarship, the process, and the discussion. The members of the ALI discussed a highly charged issue and came to a compromise.

The motion that passed was substantively different from the Council's action, which had simply withdrawn Section 210.6 of the Model Penal Code. Under the ALI's bicameral process, any vote changing the substance of a Council-approved document at the Annual Meeting and must go back to the Council for review and action. In this rare instance, the action of the membership then made its way back to the agenda for the October Council meeting for action. After a brief discussion, the Council approved the motion passed by the members at the Annual Meeting. The ALI position on the death penalty became official. I will never forget my memories of that room and the words of so many.

2. The First Restatement of American Indian Law

An entirely different process brought the Restatement of American Indian Law into being. After I was nominated to be ALI's President Elect, I asked several of my partners who worked in Indian Law and Natural Resources to have lunch with me. I was curious to see if they thought that there were areas of the law in which the ALI had not worked that we should consider. I was thinking about both water law and Indian law. My partners explained to me why water law would not be a good field for a Restatement. They explained that there was "Western Water Law" and "Eastern Water Law" and never the twain would meet. But many agreed that something on Indian law would be very helpful at this time, especially Lynn Slade, an ALI member whose practice focused on Indian Law. Many of the tribes now had the resources to litigate issues of importance to them. At the same time, many more businesses across the United States were doing business on Indian land. The federal courts had many important cases concerning the tribes on their dockets.

I proposed to Director Liebman that we explore the possibility of doing work on Indian Law. In wonderful Liebman fashion, he was both doubtful and encouraging at the same time. At the 2011 Annual Meeting, Liebman noted during an informal meeting that one of the projects being considered was Indian Law. Professor Matthew Fletcher of Michigan State University Law School came to the microphone to voice his endorsement of that idea. On March 29, 2012, in Washington, D.C., we held an exploratory meeting of federal and state judges, tribal members, lawyers who represented the tribes and businesses doing business with tribes, academics who worked in the area, and lawyers in the relevant federal government agencies.

We asked Professor Fletcher to start the discussion with a presentation about the most basic issues and definitions of Indian Law. After a lively discussion of issues, which included the Indian lawyers and judges among us showing us a federal identity card that at least Lance Liebman and I had no idea even existed, the group concluded that the possibility of a Restatement of American Indian Law might very well be a good idea. The judges at the meeting were especially anxious to have something from the ALI to help them, as they were facing a wide variety of Indian law issues not previously litigated. Director Liebman asked Professors Fletcher and Wenona T. Singel, both tribal members who served as judges on various tribal courts, to draft a proposal that could be taken to the Program Committee.

The proposal was submitted to the Program Committee by Lance Liebman and then with Committee approval to the Council. There was some skepticism about the need for a restatement in this area and questions about whether this should be a project at all. But with Liebman's support, the Council approved moving forward with a Restatement and approved Professor Fletcher as Reporter, and Professor Singel and Kaighn Smith Jr., a lawyer practicing in the field, as Associate Reporters.

Before the proposal was approved, we had an information session before the opening of the 2012 Annual Meeting to present the basics of Indian Law to the members. I was expecting a few dozen at this early morning session. We walked in to find the entire room filled. ALI members were interested in something completely unknown to most of them and came to be educated. From there, the hard work began. Since none of the Reporters had been Reporters or even Advisers on ALI projects before, we invited them to some other project meetings so they could see how every Reporter had to be prepared for criticism coming in from all sides. The three Reporters, with solid Advisers, plunged in. Their work was aided by the *Handbook for Reporters*, which had been greatly influenced and clarified by the work of Council member Conrad Harper.[9]

Given the time that ALI projects take, the work went on as Lance Liebman retired and new Director Ricky Revesz took over. Behind the scenes, Deputy Director Stephanie Middleton acted as a critical bridge between Reporters, Council members still not sure we should move ahead on this project, and judges wondering why we were not moving more quickly. The project that began at a lunch in Albuquerque finished in the Annual Meeting on Zoom in 2021, with Secretary of the Interior Deb Haaland, a Laguna Pueblo Indian lawyer, awaiting her printed copy.

The need to clarify and simplify Indian Law in a Restatement is a recent tribute to the vibrancy and openness of the culture and the organization.

3. Principles Projects

Among the many important contributions under the leadership of Director Ricky Revesz (including finally getting the Bluebook to acknowledge ALI as the institutional author of our publications!) was a clarification of the difference between Restatements and Principles projects. Separate retreats of the ALI Executive and Projects Committees shortly after Revesz took office in 2014 noted the need to clarify what Principles projects were. When Director Revesz came to the directorship, there were several Principles projects already in process (and several already completed). The Principles of Aggregate Litigation completed under Lance Liebman's leadership was extremely influential as class actions became more ubiquitous in the United States. Many of the European countries looked at the project as they started thinking about litigation related to products liability and environmental issues.

The subjects of Principles projects ranged from Election Administration to Government Ethics, from Corporate Governance to Student Sexual Misconduct: Procedural Frameworks for Colleges and Universities. But there was some confusion about just what a "Principles" project was supposed to be. Before starting the Principles of Policing Project, Ricky Revesz suggested a clarification and definition of Principles projects that was accepted by the Projects Committee and the Council: "Principles are primarily addressed to legislatures, administrative agencies, or private actors. They can, however, be addressed to courts when an area is so new that there is little established law."[10]

A recently approved project on Principles for a Data Economy is a joint effort of the ALI and the European Law Institute. This is the third major project between the ALI and other countries Director Geoffrey Hazard had initiated two influential Principles projects in Transnational Civil Procedure and Transnational Insolvency that included the much used Principles of Cooperation among the NAFTA Countries.

---

[9] AMERICAN LAW INSTITUTE, CAPTURING THE VOICE OF THE AMERICAN LAW INSTITUTE: A HANDBOOK FOR ALI REPORTERS AND THOSE WHO REVIEW THEIR WORK (rev. ed. 2015), https://www.ali.org/publications/style-manual/.

[10] *Id.*, at 3–4.

The Policing Project was initiated by Director Revesz in a presentation to the Projects Committee and then the Council in 2015, after the killing of Michael Brown in Ferguson, Missouri, but well before the horrific murder of George Floyd and the others that followed as seen on cell-phone videos that left little doubt about the facts.

The involvement of non-lawyer police chiefs, community activists, elected officials, and social scientists in the Advisers group for this project was important in ensuring that the project would be useful to all stakeholders. Both the subject and the inclusion of non-lawyers provoked significant discussion at the Council. But the project was approved with a nontraditional group of Advisers and went forward with efficient speed. Its importance was magnified by the murder of George Floyd and other horrible incidents, now photographed and circulated on social media, which completely changed the broad public perception of improper use of police force. The Use of Force section gave police departments and those who governed them a helpful framework for rethinking their practices, and ALI made those sections freely available. The project has already been cited by the New Mexico Supreme Court in a recent decision about police power. Principles projects like the Policing Project and others are aimed at fulfilling our mission to improve the law.

B. Early Career Scholars

In the spring of 2007, as I approached becoming the President of the ALI, I asked Gerhard Casper if I could talk to him about his view of current issues facing the ALI and possible initiatives. Generous with his time as always, he agreed to spend an afternoon with me talking about the future. Among other challenges, I mentioned that for the last few years, we had apparently been having a problem attracting the best young scholars around the country to our work. He explained why that might be. It seemed that over the last decade there had been a decline in interest in law reform work. Gerhard suggested that we call a meeting, at a very nice place, and invite at our expense ten outstanding young legal scholars and ask them what we could do to make the ALI and its work important to them.

Happy to follow advice from Gerhard, President Traynor embraced the idea. Through a variety of sources, Lance Liebman suggested a list of selected young legal scholars from across the country, and we invited them at our expense to a weekend in Delaware. We also included three tenured professors: Susan Appleton, Kate Bartlett, and Steve Sugarman. Michael Traynor, Lance Liebman, Deputy Director Elena Capella, and I went to Delaware to hear what they had to say.[11]

It was a fascinating group and the discussion was illuminating. One of the bottom lines from these young scholars was that they didn't feel their deans gave any value to ALI work during the tenure process. When I asked what would change their minds, one of them said, "Give a Prize. Deans love prizes." So that is just what we proceeded to do.

---

[11] Young scholars in attendance included Rachel Barkow, Sarah H. Cleveland, Heather Gerken, Ellen D. Katz, Pauline Kim, Goodwin Liu, Barak D. Richman, Christopher Sprigman, Catherine T. Struve, George Triantis, and David A. Weisbach.

John Langbein of Yale led a committee that fleshed out what an award might look like. ALI Council member Harold Koh, then Dean of Yale Law School, hosted a small number of us, including Professor Langbein, to discuss it further. The Council approved the award. Despite skepticism all round, we plunged forward with what was then called the Young Scholars Medal, now the Early Career Scholars Medal. The idea was to give a cash award and also to give the winners a chance to address an Annual Meeting on a topic of their choice and to host a seminar in their area to discuss one or more issues, with experts from academia, the practicing bar, and judges.

Our first committee was chaired by Judge William Fletcher of the 9th Circuit. Thanks to the prodding of Lance Liebman the members of the committee had over seventy submissions to review. It turns out that being on this committee requires a significant commitment, because the submissions ran to hundreds of pages of law review articles, chapters in books, and occasionally a complete book itself! There have been twelve winners from nine law schools.[12] What I did not anticipate was the importance to our members of hearing the wide range of presentations by the winners over the years—from new takes on basic legal subjects to presentations that explained cutting edge issues about which our members were anxious to learn.

In the ten years that have followed, Justice Goodwin Liu and Justice Mariano-Florentino Cuéllar of the California Supreme Court and Judge Diane Wood of the U.S. 7th Circuit have each chaired the Early Career Scholars selection. The importance of the program has been recognized not only through the quality and quantity of nominations by law school deans but by being underwritten by a generous donor. But part of the quality and enthusiasm of the law school deans is their knowledge of Director Ricky Revesz, whose letter calling for nominations every two years has particular resonance with deans who know both his successful career as the Dean of NYU Law School and his brilliant scholarship and legal work related to the environment.

This small example illustrates the importance of the Director to the influence and continuing relevance of the ALI. The Directors I knew from Hazard to Liebman to Revesz—each used their unique skills to move the ALI upward. From the first Director to the current one—each in his own style keeps the quality of the work up to the high standard of our founders.[13]

---

[12] 2021 Recipients: Ashley S. Deeks (University of Virginia School of Law, now serving as White House Associate Counsel and Deputy Legal Adviser to the National Security Council) and Francis X. Shen (University of Minnesota Law School). 2019 Recipients: Michelle Wilde Anderson (Stanford Law School) and David Pozen (Columbia Law School). 2017 Recipients: Colleen V. Chien (Santa Clara University School of Law) and Daniel Schwarcz (University of Minnesota Law School). 2015 Recipients: Elizabeth Chamblee Burch (University of Georgia School of Law) and Michael Simkovic (Seton Hall Law School, now at the University of Southern California Gould School of Law). 2013 Recipients: Adam J. Levitin (Georgetown Law Center) and Amy B. Monahan (University of Minnesota Law School). 2011 Recipients: Oren Bar-Gill (New York University School of Law, now at Harvard Law School) and Jeanne C. Fromer (New York University School of Law).

[13] The following individuals have served as director of the ALI: William Draper Lewis (1923–1947), Herbert Funk Goodrich (1947–1962), Herbert Wechsler (1963–1984), Geoffrey C. Hazard Jr. (1984–1999), Lance Liebman (1999–2014), and Richard Revesz (2014–present).

III. Moving into the Second Century

As with many organizations during these last two years 2020 and 2021, it was hard to give up the in-person Annual Meeting with its opportunities to hear brilliant debate, see old friends, meet new ones, hear from nationally prominent jurists and lawyers, and participate in discussion. No Annual Meeting was held in 2020. The Annual Meeting in 2021 provided a brilliant example of civility in discussion in an unexpected virtual setting.

In too many meetings during the pandemic, not being in person somehow seemed to some people to give them permission to engage in racist, sexist, threatening rants. That behavior even became common during in-person encounters. But the ALI's culture of civil debate about even highly controversial questions never showed signs of weakening. Over one thousand members registered for the 2021 Annual Meeting, Zoomed in, participated, and voted to finalize four projects and approve parts of others. Facts were agreed upon. Questions about the correct interpretation of a case were either confirmed by Reporters or the Reporters agreed to look again and correct if necessary. The membership grappled with fraught issues of the time, like Sexual Assault in the Model Penal Code. They also approved the first Restatement of American Indian Law.

President David Levi, with Director Revesz and Deputy Director Middleton, invented and then realized an annual meeting when we could not be together but had to continue our work. Their leadership ensured that the important work of the ALI did not slow down, nor was the quality diminished.

For each and every one of us, meeting only online was necessary, productive, and unsatisfactory. For those of us who knew one another it was at least a chance to see and hear from those we knew on a smaller crowded screen. But it was not possible to welcome our new members in a personal way. The year 2022 is on the horizon, and we will invent new ways to get to know one another and do our work. Like Gerhard Casper at my first meeting, when we meet we will reach out to welcome new members. We will be grateful for the diversity of thought and views and experience of judges elected and appointed; Republicans, Democrats, and independents will sit side by side and speak and listen. Some compromises will continue to be recommended in advance and others will be cobbled together on the spot responding to the debate.

I cannot conclude without a word about being a woman lawyer, elected into the ALI, welcomed into the Council, and promoted to leadership. There were few women in my class at the University of Chicago Law School. The men at Chicago, including most of my classmates, went out of their way to treat us as fellows. Compared to what I heard from other law schools at the time and later, the atmosphere was remarkable because of the lack of sexism in the law school. There were no "ladies days" in classes. We were welcomed into study groups. When I could not find jobs each summer and as I was about to graduate, the Law School came forward to make sure I had a place to use and build my skills.

The rest of the world was not so welcoming. Law firms explained that they would never hire a woman. One offered me a job as a paralegal. A prominent fellowship was withdrawn because I was pregnant. In each case, wonderful men stepped up to fight for me or with me or to offer me jobs. This is important because in my world then, there were almost no women lawyers. When I first encountered a group of women lawyers at the ABA, it was a revelation. In meeting the women of the ALI, I found the full-throated participation of women a wonder.[14]

The reason I write about this in a chapter about the ALI is because from the very first meeting though my becoming President, the ALI was a place where I simply never felt sexism. It was completely remarkable and freeing. All around me were amazing women, judges, lawyers, and scholars. Also around me were amazing men, seeing me and the other women working with them as the equal assets that we are. Gerhard Casper, Conrad Harper, Bennet Boskey, Marty Lipton, Ken Frazier, Douglas Laycock, Paul Friedman; each Director I knew, from Hazard to Liebman to Revesz, and each President, from Perkins to Wright to Traynor and now to Levi, were and are eager to use the talents of all of us. Who cannot stand in awe of Council members Justice Ginsburg, Justice Ketanji Brown Jackson,[15] Shirley Hufstedler, Judith Kaye, Elizabeth Cabraser, Sheila Birnbaum, Carol Lee, Margaret Marshall, Diane Wood, Caroline King, Carolyn Lamm, Christine Durham, Marsha Simms, Yvonne Gonzales Rogers, Teresa Harmon, Mary Kay Kane, Mary Schroeder, Kim Askew, Patricia Millett, Lee Rosenthal, Patricia Wald. How diminished would the work be without them.[16]

Our picture for our 100th celebration will show a diverse group of men and women, of all the hues of the human spectrum. Those members in the picture represent an ALI that is now composed of judges, professors, and lawyers—including lawyers who are at the helms of our major law firms and corporations, but also the equally able lawyers who represent the poor, work as prosecutors and public defenders, labor in state and federal government, and serve our country in the armed services.

The rich diversity and devotion of our members and our leadership means that the ALI is vibrant and important as we round the corner of 100 years and look beyond. The Directors and the leadership are just willing to take up anything that meets our mission, as were our brilliant founders in 1923.

The ALI culture is honed by its leaders and enriched by its members as the organization faces new and unexpected challenges. The work has been vibrant for a century, and its value and relevance are evident. Our culture should ensure that on the 200th anniversary the ALI will stand as it does on its 100th—living up to its mission and striving to meet the challenges of the American democracy from 2023 to 2123.

---

[14] After one of the debates on the definition of consent in the Model Penal Code sexual assault provision, several women expressed concern that voice votes seemed out of balance because men's voices came more loudly. We then went to hand raising or standing to vote to make sure that bias was eliminated in the voting process.

[15] Justice Jackson is the second Council member lost to the U.S. Supreme Court, when she was confirmed by the U.S. Senate on April 7, 2022, and worn in on June 30, 2022.

[16] Shirley Hufstedler was the first woman elected to the Council in 1974. Pat Wald was the second in 1978. (Justice Ginsburg was elected at the same time.) Pat Wald also was the first female officer of the ALI, elected as second vice president in 1987 and then as first vice president beginning in 1993. The first African American on the Council was William T. Coleman Jr. in 1969.

2

The Need for Restatement of the Common Law

A Long Look Back

David J. Seipp[*]

The 100th birthday of the American Law Institute (ALI) prompts some thoughts about Anglo-American common law and its long history. The ALI has done much to preserve and to unify American common law, to improve and to reform it, to revere and to idealize it, principally by restating the common law. As a life member of the ALI and a historian of the early common law, I explore in this chapter some precursors of the Restatement idea. Why did the common law need restating? What was the predicament to which the ALI's founding in 1923 was the answer?

I. Joseph Story

Close to a century before 1923, Joseph Story saw the need and usefulness of an effort that resembled in important respects the work of the ALI. He was an associate justice of the U.S. Supreme Court, half of the Harvard law faculty, and author of treatises spanning commercial and constitutional law and equity jurisprudence. In an 1821 speech to Boston lawyers, Justice Story warned that the twenty-four states in the Union, all but Louisiana basing their jurisprudence on the common law, were rapidly diverging from one another, "perpetually receding farther and farther from our common standard," so that it was hopeless to expect any greater uniformity in the future.[1] He warned that there were already more than 150 volumes of reports of American court decisions,[2] with no end in sight, and he feared that American lawyers

---

[*] I thank and acknowledge my Boston University faculty colleagues, especially Kristin Collins, the careful eye of the inimitable Carol F. Lee, and excellent research assistance by Julien Gelly and Howard Chen. Throughout this chapter, spelling and punctuation of quotations have been modernized. Another perspective on Joseph Story's importance as a treatise writer and commissioner on codification, G. Blaine Baker, *Story'd Paradigms for the Nineteenth-Century Display of Anglo-American Legal Doctrine, in* LAW BOOKS IN ACTION: ESSAYS ON THE ANGLO-AMERICAN TREATISE TRADITION 82 (Angela Fernandez & Markus D. Dubber eds., 2012), reached my notice too late to be considered here.

[1] JOSEPH STORY, *Progress of Jurisprudence* (1821), *in* MISCELLANEOUS WRITINGS 198, 213 (William W. Story ed., 1852). Decades earlier, Justice Samuel Chase had written in *U.S. v. Worrall* that there was already "a great and essential diversity" between the versions of common law received and elaborated in the different American states, 2 U.S. (2 Dallas) 384, 394; 28 F. Cas. 774, 779 (C.C. D. Pa. 1798) (no. 16,766). These words were repeated by St. George Tucker in his influential 1803 edition of Blackstone's *Commentaries*, and by Peter Du Ponceau in an 1824 address.

[2] STORY, *supra* note 1, at 212.

David J. Seipp, *The Need for Restatement of the Common Law* In: *The American Law Institute.* Edited by: Andrew S. Gold and Robert W. Gordon, Oxford University Press. © Oxford University Press 2023. DOI: 10.1093/oso/9780197685341.003.0003

would be "buried alive in the labyrinths of the law."[3] The remedy Story proposed in 1821 was "a gradual digest ... of those portions of our jurisprudence, which, under the forming hand of the judiciary, shall from time to time acquire scientific accuracy. By thus reducing to a text the exact principles of the law, we shall, in a great measure, get rid of the necessity of appealing to volumes which contain jarring and discording opinions."[4] What Story imagined in 1821 was a code with legislative sanction. In 1825 he wrote to his friend Henry Wheaton, the Supreme Court reporter, "Half of our [legal profession's] time is now consumed in examining cases," but "[w]hat a great gain it would be for us to have a starting point—something irrevocably fixed as settled principle," because this "would greatly abridge the labors and exhausting researches of the profession," and "reduce to certainty, method, and exactness much of the law, already passed upon by judicial tribunals."[5]

Later, in January 1837, after Justice Story had begun teaching as Dane Professor at Harvard and had published the first four of his nine treatises on commercial and constitutional law, including an 1834 commentary on conflict of laws that highlighted diverging state doctrines,[5a] he chaired a commission to advise the Massachusetts legislature whether to codify Massachusetts law.[6] Story's commission cautiously recommended a partial codification, so long as it remained "a code of the common law of Massachusetts" and not a code of statute law. By this Story meant that the code he proposed "is to furnish the rules for decisions in courts of justice" directly and by analogy, "as a part of the common law."[7] Here is what Justice Story foresaw in his 1837 report:

> [I]t ought to be a perpetual index to the known law, gradually refining, enlarging, and qualifying its doctrines, and at the same time, bringing them together in a concise and positive form for public use.[8]
>
> [T]he reduction of the common law to a text should not be held to change the nature or character of the interpretation or application of its doctrines.[9]
>
> It will show what the existing law is, as far as it goes, in a clear and intelligible manner. It will have a tendency to suppress useless and expensive litigation. It will greatly abridge the labors of judges, as well as of the profession, by furnishing a

---

[3] *Id.* At 237. George Wickersham, the ALI's first President, quoted these words of Story to describe the predicament that American lawyers saw when the ALI was founded in 1923. *The American Law Institute and the Projected Restatement of the Common Law in America*, 43 L.Q. Rev. 449, 450–51, 456–57 (1927). Story's concern was shared by Caleb Cushing, a young Massachusetts lawyer and future U.S. Attorney General, in *Law Reports*, 18 N. Am. Rev. 371, 375–77 (1824).

[4] Story, *supra* note 1, at 237.

[5] Quoted in James McClellan, Joseph Story and the American Constitution 93 (1971).

[5a] Joseph Story, Commentaries on the Conflict of Laws, Foreign and Domestic (1834). Story considered this his best treatise, of greater interest than any other of his works, and Daniel Webster lauded it highly. G. Blaine Baker, *Story'd Paradigms for the Nineteenth-Century Display of Anglo-American Legal Doctrine, in* Law Books in Action: Essays on the Anglo-American Treatise Tradition 82, 84 (Angela Fernandez & Markus D. Dubber eds., 2012).

[6] Story was sole author of the commission's report. Charles M. Cook, The American Codification Movement: A Study of Antebellum Legal Reform 176 (1981). The other members, all Massachusetts lawyers, were Theron Metcalf, Story's Harvard colleague Simon Greenleaf, Charles Forbes, and Luther Cushing.

[7] Story, *Codification of the Common Law, in* Misc. Writings, *supra* note 1, at 698, 716.

[8] *Id.*

[9] *Id.* at 720.

starting point for future discussion, instead of imposing the necessity of constant researches through all the past annals of the law.[10]

It would almost supersede, in cases constantly arising, the necessity of daily consultation of authorities, spreading over centuries, and so numerous and various in
their application, as to task the time and diligence of the ablest lawyers to a most exhausting extent.[11]

When there was an opportunity to remedy any defects, rectify any anomalies, or correct any erroneous doctrine, Story recommended, this "ought to be done with a cautious and skillful hand, and with a deep sense of the delicacy of intermeddling with
established principles." No changes should be introduced "except such as have the
sanction of experience, and the support and approbation of enlightened judges and
jurists," with the aim being "to introduce harmony and consistency and simplicity into
the general system."[12]

Story's crucial recommendation was that the legislature should require the
code "to be interpreted and applied to future cases as a code of the common law of
Massachusetts and not as a code of mere positive or statute law."[13] This "reduction of
the common law to a text" thus should not be interpreted by courts as a statute, but
rather should be applied directly or by analogy "as a part of the common law." Its approval by the legislature "should not be held to change the nature or character of the
interpretation or application of its doctrines." Story wanted the benefits of codification
without what he saw as the defects of codification. If the legislature insisted on doing
something about the common law, let it help improve the way common law courts
went about their business, and otherwise have it stay away from the common law.

I have long been struck by how well these 1837 passages from Justice Story describe
the aims and methodology of Restatement projects that the ALI has undertaken for
the century now completed. A group of at least five drafters "of high standing in the
profession and otherwise suitably qualified," Story advised, "with all the aids which
can be obtained," especially with access to the most complete library of reported decisions, would take several years to complete the project for Story's recommended list
of subject areas including the law of persons, property, and contracts, commercial and
maritime law, and the law of crimes and evidence. These drafters "must have frequent
meetings for discussion and scrupulous review of the labors of each other."[14] In contrast, learned treatises by individual authors, even Story's own, would not have the
added scrutiny and input from the rest of the team of drafters.

Although they were charged to report on codification, Story and his fellow commissioners preferred that the results of the project not be enacted as statutes by the
legislature. No enactment could encompass "all of the diversities, ramifications, ex-
pansions, exceptions, and qualifications" of general principles "as they ought to be
applied ... to all future combinations of circumstances in the business of human

---

[10] *Id.* at 726.
[11] *Id.* at 730.
[12] *Id.* at 733.
[13] *Id.* at 716.
[14] *Id.* at 733.

life."[15] Story's vision in 1837 was a collaborative written formulation of common law principles and doctrines drafted with the aid of intensive researches into all available common law authorities, and somehow, despite legislative imprimatur, remaining for courts a part of the common law to be considered along with other sources of guidance. In other words, what we know today as Restatements.

The benefit most strenuously expressed by Justice Story for such a project, and at greatest length, was the enormous saving of time and effort by future judges, lawyers, treatise writers, law teachers, and law students, if such a distillation of common law could be produced. Returning to a point he made in 1821, Story observed that "the known rules and doctrines of the common law are spread over many ponderous volumes." Nowhere collected in concise and systematic form, they had to be gathered from many treatises "of very different merit and accuracy," from digests and abridgements, from books of practice, "and above all, from books of reports of adjudged cases, many hundreds of which now exist, and which require to be painfully and laboriously consulted in order to ascertain them" by those "who possess an ample library of law books" and who "devote their whole leisure to the purpose."[16]

Many lawsuits, Story wrote, arose when researches by one party's counsel failed to disclose some well-established exception to a leading rule. In such cases, a single line of text "properly and accurately prepared" might dissipate "every doubt and uncertainty."[17] In a vigorously contested lawsuit, "no counsellor would feel safe without a thorough examination of all the leading cases (even though they should spread over centuries), lest he should be surprised at argument by a loose dictum, a questionable authority, or an ambiguous statement, either distinguishing or controlling the case before him." This put busy lawyers "to the most severe studies," lest in the long array of cases to be cited "there should be some intimation which might injuriously affect the client's rights or remedy. And yet, it is not too much to say, that often a single page of a code would contain, in a clear and explicit statement, all that the researches of a week or even of a month would scarcely justify them in affirming with an unfaltering confidence."[18]

Moreover, many points in the common law, though "established by a considerable weight of judicial authority, were not absolutely beyond the reach of forensic controversy" when an opposing counsel's research could uncover some "diversities of judicial opinion" or "nice distinctions and difference" or "incidental dicta which serve greatly to perplex the inquiries of the ablest lawyers."[19] "Much of the time of courts of justice," Story added, "is consumed in arguments of this sort, where there are numerous cases, with some slight differences of circumstances, bearing on the same general rule, all of which may be required to be examined and distinguished." Story wrote that Lord

[15] *Id.* at 706.

[16] *Id.* at 722. In an early article, *Hoffman's Course of Legal Study*, 16 N. Am. Rev. 45, 63 (1817), Story had noted that "continual exertions to keep pace with the current of new opinions and doctrines" were "a task of vast labor and difficulty," *supra* note 1, at 79.

[17] Story, *supra* note 7, at 722–23.

[18] *Id.* at 723. George Wickersham in 1927 made the same point that lawyers needed to ransack thousands of precedents or even ten thousand cases to arrive at a conclusion such as the projected Restatements would provide, *supra* note 3, at 457, 461.

[19] Story, *supra* note 7, at 724.

Eldon once found upwards of three hundred cases bearing on a question in an equity case in England. "And yet it is not perhaps too much to say, that four or five lines of text ... stating the true general rule, deducible from the best of them, would at once have put aside the necessity of any further consideration of most of these cases."[20]

Young Boston lawyer Charles Sumner, the future Senator, predicted in a letter to Francis Lieber that this report, which would come "with the authority of Judge Story's name and with the cogency of his learning and reason," would mark a new era in the history of American law and would "have a very great influence throughout the country."[21] The *American Jurist* reprinted the report in full and announced that it was "received with much favor" in the state house.[22] Taking Story's hint, the Massachusetts senate resolved to reduce only criminal law to a code, but the state legislature ultimately refused to adopt even that.[23] According to one of his biographers, Story "more than any other man defeated the extreme proposals of the American codification movement."[24]

In Story's well-known *Swift v. Tyson* opinion in 1842, he applied his common law method of broad comparative research to find a general federal common law result at variance with applicable New York State court decisions.[25] It is easy to suppose that motives to advance institutional power or economic interests lay behind such a decision. Perhaps similar motives lay behind the agitation of Story and others in codification debates that raged throughout the nineteenth century. But the debates described in this chapter were conducted at such a high level of abstraction for such a long time that it becomes difficult to ascribe or indeed to imagine any immediate economic or political motivations behind them.[26]

I do not think that Story was trying to placate radical codifiers like Robert Rantoul by offering a half-measure that would be adapted to elite ends, though this was a familiar pattern in the history of law reform.[27] Story genuinely wanted a team of minds as brilliant as his to go through every case and to formulate every rule of law. His opinion in *Swift v. Tyson* was a demonstration, on the narrow point of law in that case, of his method of broad and deep research, which compilers of his ideal statement of common law would do for every doctrine. His solitary efforts in that regard in his nine treatises were said by Roscoe Pound in 1914 to have "restated" judge-made law and made it conveniently and authoritatively available for American lawyers.[28]

Story had previously written in an *Encyclopedia Americana* article on "Law, Legislation, Codes" first published in 1831 that "it would be no small gain to have a positive text, which should give, in such cases, the true rule, instead of leaving it open

---

[20] *Id.* at 725.
[21] Charles Sumner to Francis Lieber, Nov. 17, 1836, in 1 MEMOIR AND LETTERS OF CHARLES SUMNER 186 (Edward L. Pierce ed., 1893).
[22] *Codification of the Common Law of Massachusetts*, 17 AM. JURIST & L. MAG. 17–51 (1837); also 10 MONTHLY L. MAG. 59–72 (1841).
[23] Cook, *supra* note 6, at 179–81.
[24] GERALD T. DUNNE, JUSTICE JOSEPH STORY AND THE RISE OF THE SUPREME COURT 318 (1970).
[25] Swift v. Tyson, 41 U.S. 1 (1842).
[26] Robert W. Gordon, review of Charles M. Cook, *The American Codification Movement*, 36 VAND. L. REV. 431, 444–45 (1982).
[27] *Id.* at 454–57.
[28] Roscoe Pound, *The Place of Judge Story in the Making of American Law*, 48 AM. L. REV. 676, 693 (1914).

to conjecture and inference by feeble minds.... [T]he text may admit of very exact statement, but the commentaries necessary to deduce it, may be exceedingly elaborate.... It may require an analysis by the greatest minds to demonstrate; but, when once announced, it may be understood by the most common minds" and thereby replace many vast treatises with "but a few hundred pages."[29] "[T]here are many branches of the common law which can, without difficulty, be reduced to a positive text."[30] As a Supreme Court justice, law professor, and treatise writer, Story was well placed to envision the savings of time and effort that would be afforded by the project that he and his fellow commissioners proposed in 1837.

II. Pre-Story: Centuries of Unwritten Common Law

Joseph Story was led to his conclusions about the common law and the benefits of its clarification by his own practice, teaching, writing, and judicial experience, and also by his close familiarity with the sources of English common law going back to the twelfth and thirteenth centuries. Taking Story's long view of Anglo-American common law, some themes emerge that help explain why the common law needed the sort of treatment that Story's commission recommended, and why the greatest legal minds of previous centuries had not anticipated and completed this task.

Story referred several times in treatises, speeches, and articles to *Glanvil*, the oldest source in the common law tradition, a Latin treatise composed in the late 1180s. *Glanvil* began with an apology. Compared to the two bodies of written law, Roman and canon, that were beginning to be taught in Europe's first universities, what the English royal courts were doing was definitely not written, yet *Glanvil* stated, "although the laws of England are not written, it does not seem absurd to call them laws" (*leges*).[31] In the thirteenth century, the massive treatise *Bracton* described English royal court proceedings in a thoroughly Roman framework. Its authors, English judges and their clerks, aspired to the cosmopolitan status of classical Roman jurists and university doctors of law.[32] They imagined that their courts' judgments might continue thereafter to be generalized and rationalized within a Roman law framework of categories and principles, part of a pan-European *ius commune*.

But this Latin, Romanized treatise tradition did not survive into the following centuries. Instead, the Year Books, law French reports of courtroom argument and dialogue, accumulated in chronological order and became a new professional literature of a very different sort. Lawyers made and copied their Year Book manuscripts in order to preserve examples of good and bad pleading, not to record the making of law by judges. There was a common law of medieval England, but it remained essentially

---

[29] 7 Encyclopaedia Americana 590 (1831); *later edition reprinted in* The Unsigned Essays of Supreme Court Justice Joseph Story: Early American Views of Law 229 (Valerie Horowitz ed., 2015).

[30] *Id.* at 232.

[31] The Treatise on the Laws and Customs of England Commonly Called Glanvil 2 (G.D.G. Hall ed. & trans., 1965).

[32] *See* Thomas J. McSweeney, Priests of the Law: Roman Law and the Making of the Common Law's First Professionals 4–7, 82, 97, 240 (2019).

unwritten, embodied in no particular text. Before 1480, a king's justice, Thomas Littleton, composed a law French treatise on English land law, *New Tenures*. He updated and reorganized an old ragbag of chapters about different types of landholding and transformed it into a brilliant multidimensional exposition of different estates in land in order of duration, different services for land in order of status, different ways of holding land jointly, and different ways of acquiring land. Written for his son, his book was eagerly seized upon by young aspiring lawyers. It was one of the first law books printed in England. Littleton cited very few Year Book cases in the book, though later printers added more.

Although it has been hard for modern legal historians to accept, medieval English courts were set up to avoid the elaboration of legal doctrine by judges. Judges presided over a dispute resolution process that was designed to ensure that juries made all the hard decisions. Judges themselves were not eager to make law. Year Book cases were almost never cited as precedent in later Year Books. Instead, in nearly every Year Book case, lawyers and judges posed hypothetical arguments and appealed to a common set of assumptions. This set of shared assumptions, a loose oral consensus about what was and was not agreed upon as law, was the unwritten common law. J.H. Baker set this out well in *The Law's Two Bodies*:

> The conceptual framework which was handed on by tradition, whether or not it was reflected in the reported cases in year books, is best described by the lawyers' own phrase, *common erudition*, common learning.... The phrase was in use by the 1440s, and we find the Latin *communis opinio* in earlier year books. "Erudition" is something learned, acquired as a student. Presumably the whole body of common learning, as an ideal conception, should have been comprehensive and coherent, like the learning so neatly displayed in Littleton, in contrast with the mass of disjointed and heavily abbreviated snippets jumbled up in the year books. Yet it would be a myth to suppose that a complete corpus of coherent common-law doctrine ever reposed in all the legal minds of the time.[33]

A.W.B. Simpson encapsulated this older English conception of common law as "a body of practices observed and ideas received" by lawyers and judges, which existed "only in the sense that they are acted upon within the legal profession" rather than a body of rules transmitted in particular decisions.[34] It was much easier for a tightly knit English legal profession to operate within this framework about which they all informally agreed, precisely because that agreement was never set down in writing. When judges disagreed, they adjourned the case until either they came to a unanimous view or the parties withdrew, settled, or died.

Sixteenth-century English lawyers were more insistent than their medieval predecessors that their reports of cases contain the resolutions of the court, constituting the reasons for their judgment. Sixteenth-century judges were more willing to decide important cases by majority vote. Early in the reign of Henry VIII, lawyer Anthony

---

[33] J.H. Baker, The Law's Two Bodies 67 (2001).
[34] A.W.B. Simpson, *The Common Law and Legal Theory, in* Oxford Essays in Jurisprudence: Second Series 77, 94 (1973).

Fitzherbert, later one of Henry's justices, performed the monumental task of collecting 14,837 excerpts of Year Book cases dating from 1217 to 1505, sorting them under 263 headings in 1,212 printed pages, an estimated 2.25 million words of law French and Latin. *La Graunde Abridgement* was a testament to the importance that English lawyers placed on their reports. When those trained in Roman law showed off their bound volumes of written law, English lawyers could match them, at least in volume, with Fitzherbert's abridgement. The abridgement entries remained, however, in Baker's words, "a mass of disjointed and heavily abbreviated snippets," just slightly better organized.[35] Fitzherbert had piled cases under headings in no discernible order, more than nine hundred under a single heading "Writ." Abridgements like Fitzherbert's were larger, printed versions of commonplace books, which were manuscripts that many lawyers had kept as their own memory aids since the fifteenth century, with similar sets of alphabetical headings under which they could note what they read or heard in court. Story wrote disparagingly about "the dust and the cobwebs of antiquated lore ... in the unfashionable pages of the Year Books,"[36] their "dry severity," and "the painful digestion" of the early abridgements.[37]

Edward Coke, defender of the common law against the divine right of Stuart kings, acquired instant authority for his thirteen volumes of *Reports* collected from 1600 to 1616 and four volumes of *Institutes of the Laws of England*, some not published until after his death in 1634. With commanding authority, however, did not come orderly exposition. Coke's gloss on Littleton's *Tenures*, the first volume of Coke's *Institutes*, hung Coke's own rambling, stream-of-consciousness commentary upon every word and phrase of Littleton's lucid text. As Baker puts it, Coke was "constantly wandering off at tangents," "oblivious to the disorder, writing like a helpful old wizard anxious to pass on all his secrets before he died, but not quite sure where to begin or end."[38] Like most aspiring lawyers, Story, when he began to read law, was "hurried at once onto the intricate, crabbed, and obsolete learning of Coke on Littleton."[39] "I took it up, and after trying it day after day with very little success, I sat myself down and wept bitterly. My tears dropped down upon the book, and stained its pages."[40] In it, Story read that Coke regarded Littleton's text as "the most perfect and absolute work that was ever written in any human science,"[41] but the state in which Coke left this treatise in 1628 did not present common law learning in a useful, accessible way.

A contemporary of Coke, Thomas Ashe, a briefless barrister at Gray's Inn, published his *Promptuarie, ou Repertory Generall* in 1614.[42] This was a vast index to Year Book cases, statutes, treatises, and early modern reports such as Coke's. Unlike earlier abridgements, Ashe listed only citations to these sources, not excerpts. Ashe put these citations under 739 alphabetical main headings, far more than any abridgement, and

---

[35] BAKER, *supra* note 33, at 67.

[36] Story, *Chancery Jurisdiction* (1820), *in* MISC. WRITINGS, *supra* note 1, at 149.

[37] Story, *Value and Importance of Legal Studies* (1829), in *id.* at 524.

[38] J.H. BAKER, INTRODUCTION TO ENGLISH LEGAL HISTORY 200 (5th ed. 2019).

[39] Story, *Autobiography* (1831), *in* MISC. WRITINGS, *supra* note 1, at 19.

[40] *Id.* at 20.

[41] EDWARD COKE, THE FIRST PART OF THE INSTITUTES OF THE LAWS OF ENGLAND, OR, A COMMENTARY ON LITTLETON [v] (5th ed. 1656) (preface).

[42] THOMAS ASHE, PROMPTUARIE, OU REPERTORY GENERALL (1614) (Lawbook Exchange reprint, 2017) (with introduction by David J. Seipp).

under at least 22,527 subheadings, all in law French, that further dissected and analyzed the subject matter of each of these main headings and cross-referenced each other. Cross-references allowed multiple points of entry, leading eventually to a useful list of citations. I estimate that Ashe listed 140,000 to 150,000 citations in all. This finding aid was the only true, detailed index of early English common law.

Nevertheless, Ashe's *Promptuarie* was never reprinted, very rarely mentioned in print by any lawyer at the time or by scholars since. The wording of Ashe's subheadings contributed to the work's failure. Almost all were phrased in law French as questions, and most ended with an equivocal "or not." One rarely finds among these subheadings a definitive statement of law. Story, so widely read that he knew of "Ashe's Repertory," seemed offended in 1825 that Ashe "does nothing more than put one upon inquiry, and condescends not to select a single proposition asserted by the cases."[43] . Ashe reflected an older, traditional view of English common law as a vast expanse of open-ended questions, of possible arguments, clever distinctions, and potential analogies.[44] From the standpoint of Ashe's principal sources, the Year Books, and the reasons these earliest law reporters created them, Ashe had it right. The sources Ashe indexed simply did not lend themselves to the sort of orderly written compilation of definitive law that Story envisaged two centuries later.

A modern Restatement puts in written form what are deemed settled points of law, intended to be persuasive in themselves, and intended also to derive persuasiveness from the ALI's authorship, through the reputation it has gained from previous Restatements. Unlike ALI's Restatements, Fitzherbert's massive abridgement added no new written formulations of law, but made it easier to cite the words of old cases. Inclusion of a case in his abridgement did not enhance its underlying authority or persuasiveness, even after Fitzherbert became a justice. Ashe deliberately avoided stating any affirmative propositions of law in his massive index of early common law, and his name would have added no persuasiveness or authority if he had. Closer to the Restatement form, Coke ventured his own written formulations of English law, and his overweening reputation among English lawyers served as its own recommendation. But instead of striving for order and clarity, Coke seemed to delight in complexity and disorder. He hinted at a universe of particular "nice" points of law that could all be known, but perhaps only by him.

Another contemporary of Coke and Ashe, Francis Bacon, played the most enigmatic role in this question of whether English common law could ever take written form. He was either the originator and inspiration of later efforts to rationalize and clarify English common law, or entirely irrelevant to them. Bacon was a lawyer fully familiar with the same legal sources so profusely strewn by Coke and so exhaustively indexed by Ashe. Throughout a thirty-year campaign to get a royal reward, first from Elizabeth I and then from James I, to match his undoubted intellectual talents, Bacon

---

[43] Story, *Digests of the Common Law* (1826), *in* MISC. WRITINGS, *supra* note 1, at 324–25.

[44] In more recent times, controversy arose over whether the common law ideally consisted of a body of rules (Story's view) or whether it was much more open-ended (Ashe's view). Gordon, *supra* note 26, at 458. J.H. Baker seemed to agree with Story that even medieval lawyers must have imagined an ideal body of rules and principles, BAKER, *supra* note 33, at 3, 68–69.

repeatedly proposed, from 1593 to 1623, that he should be given resources to plan and oversee a compilation of the laws of the realm.

The common law, he complained, "which is no text law," was thereby "subject to great uncertainties, and variety of opinion," whereby judges had too much discretion, and "the ignorant lawyer shrouds his ignorance of law in that doubts are so frequent and many."[45] The greatest benefit a monarch could confer on the kingdom, Bacon wrote, would be that the many books of case reports might be "reduced to fewer volumes and clearer resolutions."[46] To that end, he urged that obsolete and repetitive cases, those that merely posed idle queries, and those tediously, obscurely, or erroneously reported should all be eliminated,[47] while judicial statements worth preserving would be preserved verbatim.

The new writings of his own that Bacon sought to add were "maxims" of law that he "gathered and extracted out of the harmony and congruity of cases, and are such as the wisest and deepest sort of lawyers have in judgment and use, though they be not able many times to express and set them down."[48] Twenty-five of these he sent to Elizabeth I, set forth in pithy Latin, followed by an English explanation "with a clear and perspicuous exposition; breaking them into cases, and opening their sense and use and limiting them with distinctions; and sometimes showing the reasons above whereupon they depend, and the affinity they have with other rules"[49] and with "their limits and exclusions duly assigned."[50] Bacon said he had another three hundred maxims "made useful by good differences, amplifications, and limitations, warranted by good authorities, and this not by raising up on quotations and references, but by discourse and deducement in a just tractate."[51] When Coke's *Reports* and Bacon's *Maxims* "shall come to posterity," Bacon hoped there would be no question "who was the greater lawyer."[52] No trace of these further maxims has survived, and none of his law reform proposals was ever adopted.

Daniel Coquillette has noted that Bacon's project "bears an uncanny resemblance to modern restatements."[53] Judge Carl McGowan remarked at the ALI's fiftieth anniversary that Bacon's maxims, with "each rule stated separately and followed by lengthy explication and example," anticipated by four hundred years "the best ALI manner."[54] There are resemblances between Francis Bacon's bids for royal patronage through law reform and the work of the ALI, but not, I contend, a direct line of influence. Bacon's final plan, set out in Latin aphorisms in 1623, owed more to the model of the Roman law Digest than to the needs of English common law. Bacon, like the author of the

---

[45] FRANCIS BACON, *A Proposition to his Majesty... Touching the Compiling and Amendment of the Laws of England* (1616), *in* LAW TRACTS 5, 9 (2d ed. 1741). I have cited Bacon's words to sources known to have been accessible in Joseph Story's time.

[46] 16:2 WORKS OF BACON xvii, 1 (Basil Montagu ed., 1834), note CC to *Life* (1593 speech in Parliament).

[47] *Id.*

[48] BACON, *The Maxims of the Law, in* LAW TRACTS, *supra* note 45, at 30.

[49] *Id.* at 34.

[50] *Id.* at 30.

[51] BACON, *1616 Proposition, supra* note 45, at 12–13.

[52] *Id.* at 13.

[53] DANIEL R. COQUILLETTE, FRANCIS BACON 101 (1992).

[54] ALI, 50TH ANNIVERSARY VOLUME 285 (1973). Unlike the ALI enterprise, however, Bacon deliberately left his maxims "distinct and disjointed," so that the judicial mind could flit from one to another and put them to uses quite different from their original purposes and applications. BACON, *supra* note 45, at 31.

Glanvil treatise more than four centuries earlier, seemed embarrassed that in direct comparison to Roman law, English common law remained unwritten. To produce this new digest would be "heroical," he wrote, and its authors would be "ranked among legislators and the restorers of states."[55] Unlike Story, who in 1837 tolerated the prospect of legislative enactment of a concise written text of common law as a necessary evil, but would put interpretive rules in force to keep the result a part of the common law, Bacon in 1623 regarded it as appropriate and desirable for the king and Parliament to enact a compilation of the common law. He died in 1626, leaving only fragments of the philosophical and legal systems he had imagined.

Why was Francis Bacon not the focus of attention as the originator of the Restatement idea? Story had high regard for Bacon as a great philosopher, a genius of the English Enlightenment, and as a literary stylist. Bacon's *Law Tracts*, which included the preface to his *Maxims* and his 1616 proposal to recompile England's laws, was on Story's approved list of treatises.[56] Story advised Harvard law students to innovate in law "greatly but quietly, and by degrees scarce to be perceived," quoting one of Bacon's essays.[57] But Story made no reference to Bacon nor copied any of his language when he recommended an expert reduction of parts of American common law to written texts.

Perhaps Story ignored Bacon's proposals to clarify the common law because Story was solidly part of a Whig tradition in Anglo-American law that had long sidelined Bacon. In the great contest between absolute monarchy and the common law, Bacon was on the wrong side. He could be suspected of a creeping Romanism unwelcome to most common lawyers. Yet Bacon remained one of the most quotable legal authors in bar association speeches, and his contributions to the ideas that went into the ALI were noted by Judge Cardozo in 1924,[58] Professor Goodhart in 1948,[59] and Judge McGowan in 1973.[60] Bacon sought to eliminate those bits of the old law that had ceased to be useful, in marked contrast to Coke, who cherished and celebrated the complexity of law in all its particulars.

Between Bacon's death and Story's report, efforts continued in the direction of writing the common law or replacing it with a written text. The lifting of press censorship from 1640 to 1660 allowed the printing of a strong outpouring of antilegalist discontent that had probably always been roiling, but had been largely lost to history, alongside the slow, technical, and expensive common law.[61] Radical reformers sought to uproot the common law entirely and replace it with a single book that would fit in a pocket and could be understood by anyone.[62] New England colonies, for a time, did just this.[63] William Sheppard, a lawyer allied to the Commonwealth cause, also

---

[55] *De Augmentis*, Aphorism 59, *in* 7 WORKS OF BACON 273 (1815 ed.). A later translation was "and reformers of law."

[56] Story, *Course of Legal Study* (1817), *in* MISC. WRITINGS, *supra* note 16, at 76.

[57] Story, *Value and Importance of Legal Studies* (1829), *in id.* at 516, quoting *On Innovations* in FRANCIS BACON, ESSAYS MORAL, ECONOMIC, AND POLITICAL 91, 21 (1807).

[58] BENJAMIN N. CARDOZO, THE GROWTH OF THE LAW 4 n.4 (1924).

[59] Arthur L. Goodhart, *English Contributions to the Philosophy of Law*, 48 COLUM. L. REV. 671, 676 (1948).

[60] McGowan, in ALI, 50TH ANNIVERSARY VOLUME, *supra* note 54, at 285.

[61] Gordon, *supra* note 26, at 452–53.

[62] BARBARA J. SHAPIRO, LAW REFORM IN EARLY MODERN ENGLAND, 1500–1740, at 115 (2019).

[63] *Id.* at 118.

thought he could reduce all of English law to "one plain, complete, and methodical treatise or abridgment" to which all disputes would be referred, so that what was currently obscure in English law could become "clear and certain" and in accord with natural law and reason. Sheppard would have this book "subscribe[d] for the settled law" by the judges (suggesting that he was a more moderate reformer) and confirmed by Parliament.[64] He produced *An Epitome of All the Common and Statutes Laws of This Nation Now in Force* (1656), dedicated to Cromwell, with over 1,100 pages digesting as much of English law as he could, in English. After the Restoration, Sheppard was far too associated with Cromwell and the regicides to have his broadest efforts be taken seriously by lawyers.

Matthew Hale, a moderate law reformer during the Commonwealth and Chief Justice from 1671, added an unsigned preface in 1668 to an abridgement by Henry Rolle, one of his predecessors. Rolle's abridgement had added analytic subheadings like those pioneered by Ashe. In the preface, Hale wrote that the common laws of England were "vast and comprehensive" and consisted "of infinite particulars."[65] Hale wished for "some complete *Corpus Juris Communis* ... extracted out of the many books of our English laws for the public use and for the contracting of the laws into a narrower compass and method, at least for ordinary study."[66] This would require "many industrious and judicious hands and heads to assist in it" over a long time.[67] Hale bemoaned that university graduates "not much acquainted with the study of the common law of England" harbored a prejudice that the common law lacked "method, order, and apt distributions." Showing that familiar defensiveness, he conceded that those trained in Roman law considered their own written texts "much more methodical and orderly than the common law."[68] He insisted, however, that the common law too could be reduced "into a competent method, as to the general heads thereof." What Hale seems to have had had in mind in this preface was not a single written text agreed by the profession, but merely that "every student does or may easily form unto himself a general digestion of the law, accommodate[d] to his memory and use"[69] under topic headings "like common boxes in which many particulars are placed." Roman law, Hale said, did little more than this.[70] What Hale described here were the old commonplace books still maintained by many lawyers, in which they jotted down points of law under a conventional shared set of alphabetical headings. Nineteenth-century versions of this organizing mode, often called digests, would continue this development begun by the early abridgements.

Among writings found at Hale's death was his own short *Analysis of the Law*, first published in 1713 and later appended to his *History of the Common Law*. It was an attempt to reduce "the several titles of the law into distribution and heads according to an analytical method." He confessed having failed in the first few tries, but thought it "not altogether impossible" to reach "a tolerable method or distribution." He settled

---

[64] WILLIAM SHEPPARD, ENGLAND'S BALME 6 (1656).

[65] [Matthew Hale,] Preface to HENRY ROLLE, UN ABRIDGMENT [iii] (1668).

[66] *Id.* at [v].

[67] *Id.*

[68] *Id.* at [vi].

[69] *Id.* at [vii].

[70] *Id.* at [viii].

on rights, wrongs, and remedies as his main divisions of common law, although he incorporated parts of the Roman divisions of law into persons, things, and actions. He subdivided the civil part of the law into fifty-four sections, each an outline in two to four pages. In another volume, published in 1736, he subdivided the criminal law and treated it in detail. It is easy to see the progression from Hale's analysis to Blackstone's division of his four volumes, published from 1765 to 1769, into rights of persons, rights of things, private wrongs and public wrongs. Blackstone's polite and mostly admiring description of English law was not regarded in England as a comprehensive reduction of the whole of common law to writing—far too much was left out—but in the United States it might be regarded otherwise.

One Oxford student who attended Blackstone's lectures, the basis for his *Commentaries*, was Jeremy Bentham. Bentham thereafter devoted his life to refuting the nonsense he heard from Blackstone. For Bentham, only replacement of the common law by a written, enacted code would suffice. Bentham wrote a letter to President James Madison in 1811, and circulated it in 1817 to governors of the twenty American states. Bentham's letter excoriated the common law as a "shapeless mass of merely conjectural and essentially uncognizable matter ... matter without mind, work without an author,"[71] a "species of mock-law,"[72] a "prodigious mass of rubbish,"[73] "excrementitious matter,"[74] "confused, indeterminate, inadequate, ill-adapted, and inconsistent."[75] Yet after all this thundering, Bentham added that "the collection of English reports of adjudged cases, on adding to them the abridgements and treatises, by which a sort of order, such as it is, has been given to their contents" would be "a stock of materials which is beyond all price" and "ready in hand ... to the composition of a complete body of law"[76] in the form of a code by the right drafter, that is, Bentham, which would be enacted by a legislature. After war between their two countries ended, Madison politely declined.[77]

Bentham inspired fervent disciples in England and America, and provoked equally fierce detractors. He started fights over codification that would continue throughout the nineteenth century. Story, no Benthamite, tried to skirt carefully the drive for codification, but the concerns he voiced in his 1837 report had been shared by earlier American jurists. Zephaniah Swift, a congressman and later Chief Justice of Connecticut, published *A System of the Laws of the State of Connecticut* in 1795. On its first page he claimed that "no country is favored with a more perspicuous code" but complained that "in no country is it more arduous and difficult to obtain a systematic understanding of the law."[78] It was "surrounded by such thick clouds of technical

---

[71] JEREMY BENTHAM, PAPERS RELATIVE TO CODIFICATION 30 (1817), much emphasis omitted.

[72] *Id.* at 34.

[73] *Id.* at 35.

[74] *Id.* at 36.

[75] *Id.* at 37.

[76] *Id.*

[77] STEVEN J. MACIAS, LEGAL SCIENCE IN THE EARLY REPUBLIC 51 (2016). Not opposed in principle to codes, Madison advised a South Carolina lawyer in 1828 that he saw "no insuperable difficulty in classifying and defining every portion of [the state's common] law, provided the terms employed be at once sufficiently general and sufficiently technical." *Letter to Thomas S. Grimké, Jan. 15, 1828, in* 9 THE WRITINGS OF JAMES MADISON 298, 299 (Gaillard Hunt ed., 1910).

[78] 1 ZEPHANIAH SWIFT, A SYSTEM OF THE LAWS OF THE STATE OF CONNECTICUT 1 (1795).

jargon and abstruse learning that it is inaccessible to the mass of the people." Swift wanted to reform Connecticut law suitably for a republican form of government and make it available to all.[79]

Story's distinctive term "a code of the common law," meaning doctrines reduced to a concise and positive text approved by the legislature but "as a part of the common law" and not as a code of statute law, may have been suggested by a very different and older usage of that phrase in the first volume of New York Chancellor James Kent's influential *Commentaries on American Law*, published in 1826. Describing "unwritten or common law," he wrote that a "great proportion of the rules and maxims, which constitute the immense code of the common law, grew into use by gradual adoption and received, from time to time, the sanction of the courts of justice, without any legislative act or interference."[80] This "code" was not only unenacted, it was unwritten. It was not any particular lawyer's collection of rules and maxims, Kent wrote, but rather, quoting Hale, it was "the wisdom, counsel, experience, and observation of many ages of wise and observing men."[81] "The best evidence of the common law is to be found in the decisions of the courts of justices."[82]

Kent shared Story's worry that the explosion of law reports and treatises threatened to overwhelm the legal profession of the 1820s.[83] "The period anticipated by Lord Bacon seems now to have arrived," Kent wrote, and "a new digest of the whole body of the American common law ... , rejecting everything that is obsolete and inapplicable to our institutions, would be an immense public blessing."[84] Kent thus meant "code of common law" only in the sense of an imaginary code of timeless wisdom, which harkened back to the lawyers' oral consensus of premodern England, always incapable of reduction to writing. Kent's mention of a "new digest" at the end of this passage was the already familiar sort of digest or treatise or abridgement by an individual compiler such as Story or Swift or himself, offered as a guide to the law through the commercial marketplace of law publishing. Story's vision in 1837 was a very different one—a new text produced by a team of experts designated, perhaps, by a legislature, but then left as "part of the common law."

III. Post-Story: Writing the Unwritten Law

After Story's report in 1837, each year American lawyers faced hundreds of new reported decisions in their own states and thousands nationwide. Keeping track of the enormous volume of case law or finding what was needed to answer any individual question of law posed all the problems that Story had described in 1837, on an ever-magnified scale. New proponents and opponents of codification continued to wage state-by-state battles, and continued to elaborate their arguments.

---

[79] *Id.* at 4.
[80] 1 JAMES KENT, COMMENTARIES ON AMERICAN LAW 439 (1st ed. 1826).
[81] *Id.* at 439–40, quoting [Hale,] *supra* note 65, at [iii].
[82] 1 KENT, *supra* note 80, at 440.
[83] *Id.* at 441.
[84] *Id.* at 442.

David Dudley Field began his efforts to codify New York law in 1839, and became the most prominent and powerful advocate for codification in the United States. Many in the legal profession passionately opposed his and other efforts toward codification. Some opponents of codification, like Story, were happy to suggest written texts of common law as acceptable solutions to the law's uncertainty and inaccessibility, so long as these were not enacted as codes by legislatures. Others opposed even this, maintaining that the essence of the common law was that it must remain unwritten.

Memorable lines from the poet Tennyson about the difficulty of mastering "the lawless science of our law, that codeless myriad of precedent, that wilderness of single instances"[85] were widely quoted by proponents of codification, but could be met by opponents' insistence that the essence of the common law method lay in this very feature of the common law. On this view, the decision of every new case should draw upon everything, all previous decided cases and all the inchoate, unarticulated principles behind them, unmediated by the scribblings of any meddling text writer. In 1870, Boston lawyer Oliver Wendell Holmes Jr. quoted T.E. Holland's remark that "the old-fashioned English lawyer's idea of a satisfactory body of law was a chaos with a full index."[86]

Earlier that same year Holmes published his first scholarly article, unsigned, in which he made his case against codification. He thought "a philosophically arranged *corpus juris*," "a connected publication of the whole of the law," would be possible, but it would require the coordination of more than one author, perhaps at government expense. The importance of such a "well-arranged body of the law," Holmes considered, "cannot be overrated," so long as it was "made and expressed in language sanctioned by the assent of courts, or tested by the scrutiny of a committee of lawyers," and so long as "the code is not law," but was "only intended to declare the judicial rule," "a mere text-book recommended by the government as containing all at present known on the subject."[87] Here Holmes joined Story in the wish for something better than English lawyers' chaos with a full index, but rather a nonstatutory written formulation of common law, intended to persuade courts and lawyers of its reliability and usefulness.

Beginning in the 1880s, many of the lawyers most active in bar associations, founders of large law firms, along with academics from the growing number of law schools and prominent judges joined a public debate about codification and the nature of the common law. Had they not been spurred on by the relentless efforts of Field through nearly fifty years of agitation for his codes, these grandees of the legal profession would almost certainly not have taken time from their busy careers to address such extremely broad matters as the nature of common law and the future of the American legal system. And without this ferment of agitation about the common law, the path of least resistance would have been to let commercial legal publishers address

---

[85] ALFRED TENNYSON, AYLMER'S FIELD ll. 435–37 (1864).

[86] [Holmes,] Review of T.E. Holland, *Essays upon the Form of the Law*, 5 AM. L. REV. 114, 114 (1870).

[87] [Holmes,] *Codes, and the Arrangement of the Law*, 5 AM. L. REV. 1, 2–3 (1870). John Ruggles Strong, son of the lawyer-diarist George Templeton Strong, also recommended "that the Legislature appoint a commission of eminent gentlemen of the bar to prepare systematic and simple statements or text books" rather than codify the law. AN ANALYSIS OF THE REPLY OF MR. DAVID DUDLEY FIELD TO THE BAR ASSOCIATION OF THE CITY OF NEW-YORK 9 (1881).

the growing difficulties that American lawyers faced in finding their law. There might have been no ALI.

Frederic Coudert, eldest of the brothers whose New York firm was then one of the largest in the country, wrote in 1893 that Edward Coke "would have regarded with abhorrence the attempt to imprison the common law in a dungeon of epigrams and to substitute treacherous and insufficient words for living principles."[88] This same anti-codification preference for principles over words was given much fuller support and explanation in the pamphlets and speeches of James C. Carter, another leading New York lawyer and founder of the firm that became Carter, Ledyard, and Milburn. Beginning in 1884 in a report to the New York City bar and continuing in works published in 1889, 1890, and 1907,[89] Carter gave the name "unwritten law" to the whole field of private law and identified "written law" as the form appropriate only to public law. Private law applied "a national standard or ideal of justice to human affairs" through "unwritten rules sanctioned by the courts." Until particular facts were found by a court and matched to those of a prior precedent or otherwise resolved, the law as to these facts was necessarily "uncertain."[90] But this was a feature of the common law, in Carter's mind, not a defect.

Rules of law written by judges in their decisions of cases, Carter explained, were "provisional" only, applied to the particular facts of that case, and subject always to modification and adaptation in future cases "as justice or expediency may dictate."[91] Judges should not presume to pronounce what rules would be followed in cases not before them. Even when deciding an entirely new case, the judge's role was "to apply the existing standard of justice" to the new fact situation, "by ascertaining the conclusion to which right reason, aided by rules already established, leads."[92] "The unwritten law, bound by no rigid form of words, ... can address itself without embarrassment to the simple office of applying the standard of justice to the particular case."[93]

The common law, Carter noted, had not been "set down in any book in orderly and scientific form, but must be gathered piecemeal from a vast mass of judicial decisions upon particular cases."[94] This was a cause of serious complaint, he added, only among professors of law, whose duty was to teach it and lecture about it, not among lawyers and judges. If human affairs were "regulated by a wise and cultivated body of legal rules" that could be learned by the legal profession sufficiently to enable it to give "trustworthy advice and guidance," then "the mere circumstance that such rules cannot be found set down in words and arranged in orderly and systematic form is not, of itself, a very serious matter."[95]

---

[88] Frederic R. Coudert, Shall Our Law Be Codified?, 156 N. AM. REV. 204 (1893).

[89] JAMES C. CARTER, THE PROPOSED CODIFICATION OF OUR COMMON LAW: A PAPER PRESENTED AT THE REQUEST OF THE COMMITTEE OF THE BAR ASSOCIATION OF THE CITY OF NEW YORK (1884); THE PROVINCES OF THE WRITTEN AND THE UNWRITTEN LAW (1889) (address to Virginia State Bar Association); The Ideal and the Actual in the Law, 13 ANN. REP. A.B.A. 217 (1890); LAW: ITS ORIGIN, GROWTH AND FUNCTION (1907) (lectures intended for Harvard Law School).

[90] PROPOSED CODIFICATION, supra note 89, at 13. What Carter meant by a "national standard or ideal of justice" is more fully set forth in id. at 40–41.

[91] Id. at 25–26.

[92] Id. at 30.

[93] Id. at 37.

[94] Id. at 72.

[95] Id. at 72–73.

When law was set down in words, Carter wrote, then disputes became "about words." "The question of what is right or wrong, just or unjust, is irrelevant and out of place. The only question is what has been written." When courts administered the unwritten law, on the other hand, they applied "the national standard of justice ... something which cannot be embodied in written rule, or set down in any form of words." This was something judges knew and felt based on the totality of their familiarity with the law, morality, and culture of the community of which they were a part. Their judgments were scrutinized by the profession, the public, and the press.[96] Unless state-by-state codification interfered, Carter predicted, the states' judiciaries would eventually "approach to unity" because right, reason, and justice were everywhere the same and the "reciprocal influence of the intellectual and legal cultures of independent states ... tends to bring all private law to a unity."[97]

If Carter's main line of arguments supported the notion that common law could not and should not be written down, he switched course in the middle of his report to sound more like Story in 1837 or Holmes in 1870. Carter recommended that "some competent hand or hands should be found who would compose a correct treatise upon the whole body of law, in which all the knowledge relating to it should be arranged in a concise, scientific and orderly form." He immediately added that this new treatise would "not require legislation," and in fact, "legislation is wholly out of place" for such a work, as outlandish as a legislature enacting an authoritative treatise on chemistry.[98] Roman jurists had never asked for their writings to have the force of statutes,[99] and "[a]ll that has ever been done in the way of reducing the body of our own law to a concise, scientific, and orderly system has been accomplished, not by legislative intervention, but by individual genius and labor. All that shall ever be achieved in this direction," he predicted, "will be the fruit of the same species of effort." True law stood not because of binding force but "by reason of the inherent power of truth itself when once clearly exposed to intellectual recognition."[100] In a passage that would be often quoted in the first two decades of the twentieth century, Carter wrote in 1884:

[A] statement in the manner of a digest, and in analytical and systematic form of the whole unwritten law, expressed in accurate, scientific language ... would, by facilitating, save labor.[101]

Such a work, well executed, would be the *vade mecum* of every lawyer and judge. It would be the one indispensable tool of his art. Fortune and fame sufficient to satisfy any measure of avarice would be the sure reward of the man or the men who should succeed in conferring such a boon upon his fellows.... [S]tatutory enactment would not, in any degree, be necessary to its value. It could proudly dispense with any legislative sanction whatever.[102]

---

[96] *Id.* at 86.
[97] *Id.* at 91–92.
[98] *Id.* at 73.
[99] *Id.* at 74.
[100] *Id.* at 75.
[101] *Id.* at 96–97. Carter repeated this point in PROVINCES (1889), *supra* note 89, at 22–24.
[102] PROPOSED CODIFICATION, *supra* note 89, at 97. On the other hand, Carter also wrote in the same speech that lawyers felt that "the abstract statements of teachers and textbooks, even the best, make little impression upon the mind," compared with the living law of actual cases in the reports. *Id.* at. 76.

Again, the foreshadowing of the aims and ambitions of the ALI comes through in such a passage.

Carter was the primary opponent of codification in New York and in the nation, and his views have engaged the interest of legal historians more than a century after his death. He can be seen as ferociously conservative, harshly critical of any legislation straying into the domain of private law. Some of his ideas about the common law, such as his denial that judges ever "make law," seem quaint today. Aniceto Masferrer has shown that Carter's characterizations of Field's code and of European experience with codes were unfair and misleading.[103] But as Lewis Grossman has pointed out, there is much in Carter's description of how judges decided cases that seems to have run contrary to the formalist orthodoxy of his times and to have anticipated the legal realists of decades later.[104]

Another notable lawyer of Carter's time, John F. Dillon, formerly an Iowa judge, then in practice in New York and teaching at Columbia and Yale, joined in the debate and popularized the term "restatement" to describe what should be done to the whole of the law or large parts of it. Dillon told the American Bar Association (ABA) in 1886 and the Academy of Political Science in 1887 that there would come a stage in legal history when "laws become 'so voluminous and vast' that an authoritative and systematic recompilation or restatement of them" became necessary "to the end that they may be accessible ... to those whose business it is to advise concerning them, and to those whose duty it is to administer and apply them.... Our judiciary law, which embraces that of England, now runs back through six centuries, without revision or authoritative restatement."[105] Dillon tried to avoid taking sides on the heated issue of codification, but his word "authoritative" seems to imply statutory force. In any case he recommended "the composition" from case reports "of a complete body of law" all of which would be cast "into a new mould and into a new arrangement based upon logical principles rather than the usual existing divisions and titles in the law. This is the ideal code of the future ... the sound and true solution of the difficulties that confront us." He expected it would happen in the next fifty years.[106] And in 1894, Dillon wrote that "the work of jurists and legislators during the next century will be preeminently the work of systematic restatement, probably in sections, of the body of our jurisprudence. Call it a code, or what you will, this work must be done."[107]

Justice Holmes said in 1886 at Harvard, "The law has got to be stated over again," so that "in fifty years we shall have it in a form of which no man could have dreamed fifty years ago."[108] He said in 1897 at Boston University, "It is a great mistake to be

---

[103] Aniceto Masferrer, *Defense of the Common Law Against Postbellum American Codification: Reasonable and Fallacious Argumentation*, 50 AM. J. LEGAL HIST. 355, 393–95 (2008).

[104] Lewis A. Grossman, *Langdell Upside-Down: James Coolidge Carter and the Anticlassical Jurisprudence of Anticodification*, 19 YALE J. L. & HUM. 149, 201–17 (2007).

[105] John F. Dillon, *Law Reports and Law Reporting*, 9 ANN. REP. A.B.A. 257, 261 (1886); *Our Legal Chaos*, 2 POL. SCI. Q. 91, 99–100 (1887); LAWS AND JURISPRUDENCE OF ENGLAND AND AMERICA: BEING A SERIES OF LECTURES DELIVERED BEFORE YALE UNIVERSITY 269–70 (1894). Dillon had said much the same in his annual address, *American Institutions and Laws*, 7 ANN. REP. A.B.A. 203, 229–30 (1884), using the word "statement" instead of "restatement."

[106] *Legal Chaos, supra* note 105, at 104.

[107] LAWS AND JURISPRUDENCE, *supra* note 105, at 386.

[108] *The Use of Law Schools, in* OLIVER WENDELL HOLMES, COLLECTED LEGAL PAPERS 35, 42 (1920). Holmes was praising Joseph Story's contribution to the development of American law half a century earlier.

frightened by the ever-increasing number of reports. The reports of a given jurisdiction in the course of a generation take up pretty much the whole body of the law and restate it from the present point of view. We could reconstruct the corpus from them if all that went before were burned."[109] In Holmes's use of the term, "restatement" of the law was what judges did in every written decision.[110] Dillon considered "essential" all ten thousand volumes of accumulated case reports, while Holmes seemed to have been willing to pitch all but the newest few hundred volumes into the furnace.

Another set of actors in this post-Story story leading up to the Restatements were the commercial enterprises supplying those case reports to America's lawyers. In 1876, John B. West in St. Paul began selling excerpts of Minnesota state court opinions well before bound volumes from the official state reporters appeared. He quickly shifted to full texts of opinions and just as quickly expanded to several neighboring states in a Northwestern Reporter. By 1887, West Publishing had a Federal Reporter and seven regional reporters in a national reporting system covering the entire country, with a uniform format and rapid delivery of advance sheets to customers.[111] West had many competitors, protected its copyrights vigorously against them, drove some out of business, and acquired others. Two competitors, Lawyer's Co-Operative Publishing Co. of Rochester, New York, and Bancroft-Whitney of San Francisco, offered the profession their alternative of selective reporting only of the "significant" state court decisions, omitting those of mere local interest, with winnowing done by the publisher's editorial staff. West, in contrast, printed every case deemed by the state courts worthy of publication,[112] including those Lawyer's Co-op considered "repetitive, irrelevant, and precedentially valueless."[113] Lawyers voted with their pocketbooks in favor of West's all-inclusive reporting. As Story observed in 1837, any case might contain a point that could someday tip the balance in some future courtroom argument, and Coke had said much the same in 1628.[114] So lawyers felt the need to have access to them all. But how could they find what they were looking for?

Nineteenth-century lawyers relied on digests to get access to all the cases they might need in their work. State courts' official reporters added headnotes when they issued opinions, and West included these along with indexing. Before West entered the field, a number of east coast law publishers began publishing digests, successors to the abridgements of Fitzherbert, Rolle, and others in England. In sets of alphabetical or logically sequenced topics, usually with analytical subdivisions within each topic, American digest-makers used the court's headnotes or compiled their own brief statements of points of law decided by courts, with citations so that lawyers could find the full opinions.[115] Nathan Dane's *General Digest and Abridgement of American Law*

---

[109] *The Path of the Law*, 1 Bos. L. Sch. Mag. 1, 2 (Feb. 1897); 10 Harv. L. Rev. 457, 458 (Mar. 1897); Collected Legal Papers, *supra* note 108, at 167, 169.

[110] Holmes later enjoyed Brandeis's remark about the newly founded ALI, "Why, I am restating the law every day." Letter to Frederick Pollock, Feb. 24, 1923, 2 Holmes-Pollock Letters 124 (Mark DeWolfe Howe ed., 1941).

[111] Erwin C. Surrency, A History of American Law Publishing 49–51 (1990).

[112] *Id.* at 54–55.

[113] Thomas A. Wroxland, *Forever Associated with the Practice of Law: The Early History of the West Publishing Company*, 5 Legal Reference Services Q. 115, 123 (1985).

[114] Story, *supra* note 18; Coke, *supra* note 41, at fol. 9a ("there is no knowledge, case, or point in law, seem it of never so little account, but will stand our student in stead at one time or other").

[115] Surrency, *supra* note 111, at 111–15.

(1823–1829) was profitable enough for Dane to donate a professorship for Story at Harvard.[116]

The most famous digesters of American law after Dane were brothers Benjamin and Austin Abbott. Begun in 1860, their digest of New York cases and statutes from 1794 onward was widely acknowledged far superior to any previous work of the kind. Austin kept up Abbott's New York Digest, updating it with new cases every year, and that enterprise survives today as *West's New York Digest 4th*. Benjamin Abbott next took up in 1867 a *National Digest* of federal law. In 1870, he began a new series of an established venture published by Little, Brown & Co. in Boston since 1847, a *United States Digest* of all state and federal court decisions since 1790. Starting by comparing the various treatises, the Abbotts spent several years drawing up outlines of every branch of law, noting what was included within each topic and what excluded. Theirs were more extensive analyses of the law than any earlier or competing digest or abridgement.[117] Benjamin Abbott explained that his ten overarching categories for the *United States Digest*—persons, corporations, property, contracts, wrongs, crimes, remedies, evidence, and government—were divided and subdivided down to the level of specific topics under which a paragraph for each decided case would be included.[118]

West Publishing Co. acquired Abbott's *United States Digest* from Little, Brown in 1889 and renamed it *American Digest* from 1890 onward. It also hired John A. Mallory, editor of a competing *Complete Digest*, to continue and build on Abbott's improvements in law digesting. West introduced numbering of its 65,000 sections under 430 topics within seven broad categories, all settled upon by Abbott and Mallory, scope notes, and cross-references. It developed its trademark key symbol, and marketed very heavily the West Key Number system, starting in 1909.

West advertised: "Every point in every case will be keyed to the American Digest System, connected automatically and immediately by a simple and positive annotation with all past and future decisions on the same point." Key numbers, such as *Negligence § 42* or *Homicide § 142* "point out the topic and section in the American Digest System where complete lists of authorities may be secured and the latest cases always found." "The Key-Number Annotation is permanent, perpetual, and always up to date, … keeps pace with the decisions. Used exclusively in the National Reporter System and the American Digest System." "Through this orderly arrangement every case becomes available when needed as an authority in your daily practice." It was "the greatest labor saving device ever devised to relieve the overworked lawyer from the drudgery of case hunting" and would "conserve your time, your nervous energy, and your money, and will enable you to 'get there' with the authorities." "Our Reporters become more valuable as they get older, as their annotations then make available thousands of cases in point which were not yet decided when the Reporters were published." "The only perfect system by which a lawyer can use the latest case as an index to all earlier cases on the same point." Uniform, permanent Key numbers would lead,

---

[116] Erwin C. Surrency, review of Sutherland, *The Law at Harvard*, 13 AM. J. LEG. HIST. 91, 91–92 (1969).
[117] SURRENCY, *supra* note 111, at 115–16.
[118] Benjamin Vaughan Abbott, *Uniform Indexes*, 22 ALBANY L.J. 179–80 (1880).

through the fifty-volume *Century Digest* (1897–1904), back to all previous American cases beginning with 1658. All this for only $4 a year for monthly digest updates.[119]

West realized the power of making its key number system dominant within the legal profession, as it had done with its national reporter system. This meant not keeping it "exclusive" to West publications. With encouragement from the ABA, West licensed its key number indexing system to nearly every independently published state digest.[120] It also invited treatise and textbook writers to include West key numbers, so that readers could be led to all past and future cases making the same point. One of the difficulties that Story depicted in 1837, the hopeless searching through thousands of case reports for relevant cases, was made much easier for lawyers by means of these digests. West provided a single nationwide system so that lawyers would not have to learn the indexing choices of different compilers. As Frederick Hicks commented in 1923, "the multiplicity of decided cases" meant that "the common law would long ago have broken down" if not for West's finding aids.[121] Many late twentieth-century critics thought that West also put a circa 1880 straitjacket on the searchable topics by which law could be imagined.[122] The company was understandably slow and sparing in introducing new topics to its permanent, uniform system. Lawyers in the early twentieth century were dubious that West's hired employees had the requisite legal acumen to encapsulate holdings of judicial decisions accurately and to slot them correctly in the appropriate pigeonholes. The words of headnote writers were imperfect guides, and researchers still had to read aggregated paragraphs case by case, but some of the difficulty of finding which cases to read in full had been alleviated. Market forces had given U.S. lawyers a reporting system that provided everything, and a digesting system that gave them a standardized way of finding them.

With law publishing dominated by a single commercial competitor, and active professional bar associations joined by an Association of American Law Schools in 1900, the stage was set for a final episode that moved Story's dream of an expert, well-vetted but nonstatutory written statement of common law to its moment of realization in 1923. This episode started in 1888 with a letter from Henry Terry, a New York lawyer teaching law in Japan, to the ABA, urging that it seek proposals for a "complete scientific arrangement of the whole body" of the law, "generally accepted by the courts, the bar and the writers of treatises and digests, and in that sense authoritative."[123] The ABA set up a special committee on classification of law that would last until 1925. Terry had his own proposed classification of all of law, but so did James DeWitt Andrews, a Chicago lawyer and legal author who moved his practice to New York in 1903. Andrews chaired the ABA committee from 1901 to 1908, launched a major

---

[119] Advertisements from 1909 and 1910 issues of *Law and Commerce, National Corporation Reporter*, and *West Publishing Company's Docket*. In 1912 West's descriptive word index invited lawyers to match the facts of their case to any previously decided case.

[120] SURRENCY, *supra* note 111, at 123–24.

[121] FREDERICK C. HICKS, MATERIALS AND METHODS OF LEGAL RESEARCH WITH BIBLIOGRAPHICAL MANUAL 251 (1923).

[122] Views of Berring, Katsh, Delgado, Stefancic, and others are well summarized in Richard A. Danner, *Legal Information and the Development of American Law: Writings on the Form and Structure of the Published Law*, DUKE L. SCH. FAC. SCHOLARSHIP SERIES, paper 84 (2007).

[123] Letter from Henry T. Terry, Aug. 1888, in 12 ANN. REP. A.B.A. 9, 19 (1888) (report of secretary Edward Hinckley).

effort in 1910 to organize a joint effort of top legal scholars, lawyers, and judges to compile a *Corpus Juris* embodying all of American law, and established in 1913 an American Academy of Jurisprudence with eminent members to pursue this project jointly with the ABA.[124]

Andrews and his supporters, among them Philadelphia lawyer Lucius Hugh Alexander, proposed their *Corpus Juris* as a superior alternative to existing treatises, commercial digests, and West's system of arrangement and analysis of the law, whose employees they considered second- or third-rate. They envisioned highly centralized executive and editorial control over the large group of experts who would do the writing. Advisory groups consisting of recognized experts in each field would thoroughly examine and revise drafts. They importuned every notable judge, law school dean, and bar leader in the country for endorsements, which they publicized.

Andrews published his views in the *Yale Law Journal*.[125] Dean John H. Wigmore of Northwestern, though exactly the sort of eminent ally Andrews and his group sought, did everything he could to squelch this proposal. He wrote in "forceful dissent" that Andrews's idea was "untimely" in 1910 because just then U.S. law was in flux, "passing through a period of radical changes," "unsound" because fifty independent sovereign bodies of common law varied at many points, and "futile" because there were not enough scholars equal to the task.[126] Andrews fought on and started to organize his American Academy of Jurisprudence to make a "scientific and concise statement of the entire body of American law."[127]

Leader of the bar and former Secretary of State Elihu Root gave the restatement idea a boost in his ABA presidential address in 1916, by endorsing lawyers who had been "urging the organization of a definite and specific movement for the restatement of our law, for a new American Corpus Juris Civilis. They are quite right. It ought to be done."[128] Part of Root's message in 1916 was that practitioners, not academics, should do this work. This was probably because the Association of American Law Schools just a year before had set up a committee on a center for law and jurisprudence. In 1922, that committee would call for another committee on the establishment of a

---

[124] *See* Richard A. Danner, *James DeWitt Andrews: Classifying the Law in the Early 20th Century*, 36 LEGAL REFERENCE SERVICES Q. 113, 116, 121–55 (2017).

[125] James DeWitt Andrews, *The Next Great Step in Jurisprudence*, 19 YALE L.J. 485 (1910).

[126] Letter from John H. Wigmore, 22 GREEN BAG 428, 428 (1910).

[127] *Movement for Uniform Laws*, WICHITA DAILY TIMES, Dec. 15, 1911, at 9. Doubts about this Academy of Jurisprudence may have moved the AALS to explore establishment of a "national center for study of law and jurisprudence" in 1915, 15 A.A.L.S. PROC. 23, 30–31 (1915), and a "juristic center" in 1916, 16 *id.* at 180, 181–82 (1916), sometimes also called an "academy of legal science," 8 A.B.A. J. 393, 395 (1922), and an "organization for the improvement of law" in 1922, 19 A.A.L.S. PROC. 37, 38 (1922), and for Judge Cardozo to call for a "ministry of justice" in 1921, *A Ministry of Justice*, 35 HARV. L. REV. 113, 117 (1921), to provide "restatement" intended to "stimulate and free" judges. It seems that "American law institute" might have been one of the few word combinations still unused in 1923, although an "American Institute of Law," a correspondence school, was founded by the American Law Book Co. in New York in 1909 under the deanship of Charles Hepburn, secretary of the ABA section of legal education. Charles M. Hepburn, *A New Development in Legal Education*, 2 AM. L. SCH. NEWS 285, 285–88, 302 (1909). He reported to the ABA that it lasted only one year. 41 PROC. A.B.A. 412, 430 (1918).

[128] Elihu Root, *Address of the President*, 30 ANN. REP. A.B.A. 355, 365 (1916). Root had struck a somewhat different note speaking to the New York State Bar Association in 1911, that "restating settled law in new forms" by judges in their written opinions, "however well it is done, complicates rather than simplifies the administration of law." *The Reform of Procedure*, 23 GREEN BAG 111, 118 (1911).

permanent organization for the improvement of the law, which in turn led directly to the creation of the ALI. The ABA set up a second committee on classification and restatement of the law in 1917, but they reported in 1919 that any effort toward restatement would be premature. Andrews was still trying to organize something he was now calling a *Codex Library*, but the ABA withdrew all support from his project in 1923 and instead backed the newly formed ALI.[129] What brought together the ABA and leading law school deans in 1923, more than anything else, might have been their shared perception that James DeWitt Andrews and his Academy of Jurisprudence should not be entrusted with the task of classifying and restating American law.

Since it was first mentioned by Dillon in 1886 and particularly from 1914 onward, the word "restatement" had grown increasingly prominent in the dialogue of codifiers, classifiers, and law reformers. It was a word sufficiently imprecise to paper over the sharp differences between conservative bar association stalwarts, Langdellian formalists such as Joseph Beale, progressive reformers led by Roscoe Pound, and proto-realist successors of Wesley N. Hohfeld. The ALI's guiding spirit, University of Pennsylvania Dean William Draper Lewis, secured the backing of Elihu Root, ensuring not only support of the organized bar but also substantial seed money from the Carnegie Foundation, for an ALI in which the work of drafting would be borne principally by law professors with input at every stage from practitioners and judges.[130]

IV. Conclusion

Joseph Story is at the center in this account of the long development of an idea that the common law could be written down in an influential but nonstatutory form. Story's deep knowledge of the history of English common law reached back to centuries in which it would have been unthinkable among English lawyers and judges to want or expect a single written text of their amorphous consensus set of rules, practices, and guiding principles. The common law was in their collective heads, and that's where it should stay.

Succeeding generations were more willing to search through the published reports of arguments and judgments, until by Story's time the accumulation of case reports seemed too cumbersome for lawyers to endure. Nevertheless, even fifty years after Story's 1837 report, with tens of thousands more decisions added to the mix, prominent lawyers still insisted that American common law must remain essentially "unwritten." Judges could decide each new dispute based on their general awareness of the body of previous decisions, with the prior cases that contending counsel brought to their attention, and with the results of the judges' own research. Commercial law publishers helped the profession feel that even though they could not possibly read every new case decision, they could, at a manageable price, find the ones they needed from the vast library of volumes. For most American lawyers, codification was a step too far.

---

[129] Danner, *supra* note 124, at 146–55.
[130] N.E.H. Hull, *Restatement and Reform: A New Perspective on the Origins of the American Law Institute*, 8 LAW & HIST. REV. 55, 74–76 (1990).

Story's elegant solution was to thread the needle. A collective, focused effort by just the sort of eminent practitioners, judges, and law teachers whom a well-advised legislature would select to draft a code should work together and arrive at an agreed text on so much of the common law as appeared to have reached some settled consensus about what it was or should be. Such a text's authority would depend entirely on its persuasiveness as advice to judges and the legal profession, not at all on statutory enactment. The ALI Restatements have sought to embody Story's vision.

Jeremy Bentham would have had none of this. He made it clear that he wanted to replace the common law. Later proponents of codification always had to answer accusations that they, like Bentham, wanted to supplant entirely the tradition and system of the good old common law. Story wanted to save the common law, to save it from its own shortcomings. The ALI has done more than any other organization of which I am aware to keep the common law of the United States more clear, more unified, and more humane. I hope that this prequel to the storied history of the ALI—a prequel storied in its own way—begins to explain why the work of restating the common law has been so necessary, was so long seen to be necessary, and why nevertheless it was put off for so long. I hope this helps to make the case that, whether or not the past century of Restatements have been the most perfect and absolute work that was ever written in any human science, whether or not they have preserved and unified our national common law, American law is better with the ALI than without it.

3

The Work of the American Law Institute in Historical Context

Kenneth S. Abraham and G. Edward White

I. Introduction

This chapter examines the intellectual and social contexts in which the ALI has operated and how they have influenced the course the ALI and its projects have taken,
during the 100 years of its history. Our aim is to situate the central preoccupations
of the ALI at various times in the larger culture of the American legal profession and
the social forces that influence American law. From its origins, the ALI has been a
self-consciously elite organization, operating under the premise that a collection
of distinguished individuals drawn from the practicing bar, the judiciary, and the
legal academy can make significant contributions to the growth and development of
American law. But despite that stance, the ALI has not been free from pressures emanating from the broader legal profession and, beyond that, from American society as a
whole. Indeed, one of the themes of this chapter is the ALI's inability, despite its strong
commitment to professional independence from outside influences in its mission
to improve the state of American law, to be completely immune to those pressures,
which—especially during the last fifty years—have regularly affected its work.

II. Intellectual Origins

On February 23, 1923, a group of judges, practicing lawyers, and law professors met
in Washington, D.C., to hear a report of a committee established by the Association
of American Law Schools a year earlier.[1] The committee recommended the establishment of a "Permanent Organization for the Improvement of the Law," to be called
the "American Law Institute."[2] The formation of that organization was in response
to a perceived "general dissatisfaction with the administration of justice," which was

---

[1] The AALS meeting which voted to create the committee was held in December 1921, and the committee
came into being in May 1922. 1 PROCEEDINGS OF THE AMERICAN LAW INSTITUTE 2–3 (1923). With the exception of Council Minutes, which are deposited in the archives of the ALI and on file with the authors,
the ALI documents we cite in this chapter, including the PROCEEDINGS, cited *supra*, are available in the
HeinOnline "American Law Institute Library," mainly in the "Restatements and Principles," "Codifications
and Studies," and "Special Publications" subdirectories. We will not encumber footnotes, however, with
HeinOnline references. For more on the founding, *see* N.E.H. Hull, *Restatement and Reform: A New
Perspective on the Origins of the American Law Institute*, 8 LAW & HIST. REV. 55, 74 (1990).

[2] 1 PROCEEDINGS OF THE AMERICAN LAW INSTITUTE, *supra* note 1, at 1.

Kenneth S. Abraham and G. Edward White, *The Work of the American Law Institute in Historical Context* In: *The American
Law Institute*. Edited by: Andrew S. Gold and Robert W. Gordon, Oxford University Press. © Oxford University Press 2023.
DOI: 10.1093/oso/9780197685341.003.0004

thought to "breed ... disrespect for law."[3] That dissatisfaction was associated with "[t]wo chief defects in American law ... its uncertainty and its complexity."[4]

A portion of the report was devoted to analyzing the sources of uncertainty and complexity in greater detail,[5] but an introductory section summarized them. "Uncertainty" was associated with "lack of agreement among the members of the legal profession on the fundamental principles of the common law, lack of precision in the use of legal terms, conflicting and badly drawn statutory provisions, attempts to distinguished between two cases in which the facts present no distinction in the legal principle applicable, the great volume of recorded decisions, the ignorance of judges and lawyers and the number and nature of novel legal cases." "Complexity" was associated with "the complexity of the conditions of life, the lack of systematic development of the law, and the unnecessary multiplication of administrative provisions."[6]

The committee report concluded that "lack of agreement among lawyers concerning the fundamental principles of the common law" was "the most potent cause of uncertainty," and that complexity primarily manifested itself in "the unnecessary and harmful variation in the law of the different states" and "the lack of precision in the use of legal terms."[7] "Fortunately," the report concluded, "these two causes of uncertainty and complexity are precisely those over which the legal profession has the greatest control." The fact that "lawyers have so far failed to appreciate the extent of the resulting evil, or to recognize the responsibility of the profession to improve conditions" was "the sole reason why today these defects loom so large."[8]

The solution, the report argued, was to undertake the "restatement" of the fields of the common law. A Restatement was to differ from existing compilations, encyclopedias, and treatises addressing common law subjects. Encyclopedias were mere summaries of the decisions of courts, and to a limited extent of statutes, without an effort to "point out conflicts and uncertainties that do not lie on the surface," or "to make a critical analysis of the law," or "to enter upon a learned discussion of what is or ought to be the law." The same could be said of most treatises, where "the author's point of approach is usually that of a photographer, "placing before the reader the law as announced by the courts" without adding any "critical" or "constructive" comments about its content.[9]

The Restatements the committee contemplated were to be different. They were "not only to ... help make certain much of which is now uncertain and to simplify unnecessary complexities" but also "to promote those changes which will tend better to adapt the laws to the needs of life." Restatements were to be "analytical," "critical," and "constructive." "Analytical" meant "a division of topics based on a definite classification of the law that was the result of thorough study by a group of individuals qualified by their studies and their intellectual attainments." "Critical" meant that the "reason for the law as it is should be set forth," or "where it is uncertain the reasons for

[3] Id.
[4] Id. at 6.
[5] Id. at 66–96.
[6] Id.
[7] Id. at 10.
[8] Id. at 11–12.
[9] Id. at 12–13.

each suggested solution of the problem should be carefully considered "by means of "a thorough examination of legal theory." And by "constructive," the committee report meant to convey that the Restatements "should also take account of situations not yet discussed by courts or dealt with by legislatures but which are likely to cause litigation in the future."[10]

The committee report then turned to the form of Restatements. They were to be composed of statements of "principles of law," comparable to statutory provisions but less detailed, accompanied by "discussion of legal problems, authorities, and reasons" associated with the principles.[11] The latter discussion was to be separated from the portions of Restatements setting forth legal principles and was to "contain a complete citation of authorities, decisions, treatises, and articles."[12]

Restatements were not expected to be adopted as statutes by state legislatures, or if they were, with the "proviso that they shall have the force of principles enunciated as the basis of decisions of the highest court of the state, the courts having power to declare modifications and exceptions."[13] The committee had a "reasonable assurance" that a Restatement's promulgation of principles in a common law field would "be given by courts ... approximately such authority as is now afforded a prior decision of the highest court of the jurisdiction"[14]

The last topics addressed by the committee report (other than an estimate of the costs of undertaking Restatements)[15] were the selection of individuals to be engaged in producing Restatement volumes and the process by which those volumes would be produced. Those individuals were initially called Reporters and Critics for individual Restatements. Those individuals had already been designated (all of them being members of the committee itself), and additional discussions between Reporters and Critics took place in the summer and fall of 1922.[16] Initially conflict of laws, torts (perhaps first concentrating on negligence), and business associations were chosen as the common law fields first signaled out as desirous of restatement. Conflict of laws was described as a subject in which "[g]reat confusion exist[ed]." "Torts" was characterized as having "developed unsystematically and ... therefore full of the evil of uncertainty," particularly with respect to negligence, where "the over-elaboration of rules pertaining to what constitutes due care has unnecessarily complicated the law and made a new emphasis on simply fundamental principles important." And the law of business corporations was also uncertain because of "confusion and conflict in regard to the legal character of the [business] association," and "real differences of opinion as to the correct statement of the fundamental principles applicable to the solution of the more difficult problems presented."[17]

In considering the process by which Restatements in those three subjects should be produced, the committee noted the experiences of the National Conference of

[10] *Id.* at 14–15.
[11] *Id.* at 19.
[12] *Id.* at 21–22.
[13] *Id.* at 24.
[14] *Id.* at 25.
[15] *Id.* at 57–63.
[16] *Id.* at 3.
[17] *Id.* at 45.

Commissioners on Uniform State Laws, which had been in existence since the last decade of the nineteenth century. The process by which uniform state laws were enacted, although more elaborate than the one endorsed by the committee, emphasized "the combination of three stages": the "appointment of one person" to be responsible for "the production of a definite draft"; the "submission of this draft to a group of experts on the subject, the experts having authority to make any change no matter how extensive"; and "the submission by the experts of a statement of law satisfactory to them to a larger body of judges, lawyers, and law teachers, who taken as a whole represent wide and varied experience."[18]

As the process for producing Restatements evolved in the ALI, it would consist of a fourth stage. Reporters would submit tentative drafts to their Advisers, who would suggest revisions, and revised drafts would then be submitted to the ALI's Council, defined by the committee report as a body of twenty-one persons having "full power of management" of the ALI's affairs, with the proviso that "any legal work done under the direction of the Institute, before being published as an official publication of the Institute, should be submitted to a meeting of members ... for their several criticisms or expressions of opinions."[19] The committee report did not specify how large that membership should be, but recommended that, in addition to the Chief Justice and Associate Justices of the Supreme Court of the United States, the senior judge of each of the federal Circuit Courts of Appeal, the chief judges of all the highest courts of each state, the deans of each law school belonging to the AALS, and various other officials of legal organizations and law societies, "between one and two hundred other persons selected because of their high professional standing and their known interest in constructive work for the improvement of the law" should be invited to the February 23, 1923, meeting.[20]

The committee also stated some guidelines for selecting Reporters and Advisers for Restatements. It anticipated that initially there would be three Reporters and three "committees of experts," to be composed of "at least five and not more than ten persons."[21] It also anticipated that "the reporters and experts will be drawn mainly from the faculties of the law schools," although it added that it would be "most desirable" for persons from other sectors of the legal profession to serve on the committees reviewing drafts of Restatements.[22]

The committee producing the report which resulted in the creation of the ALI at the February 23, 1923, meeting was composed of some of the most visible members of the early twentieth-century legal profession. Among the judicial members of the committee were Benjamin Cardozo, Learned Hand, Julian Mack, Harlan Fiske Stone, and Cuthbert Pound. The practitioner members were overwhelmingly from cities in the northeast, and its academic members exclusively from elite law schools. It was a conspicuously elitist body.[23]

---

[18] *Id.* at 50.
[19] *Id.* at 40.
[20] *Id.* at 38.
[21] *Id.* at 51–52.
[22] *Id.* at 53.
[23] Representatives from the legal academy included Joseph Beale, Arthur Corbin, Ernst Freund, William Draper Lewis, Edmund Morgan, Roscoe Pound, Harlan Fiske Stone, John Wigmore, and Samuel Williston. The practitioners included not only Elihu Root as Chair and George Wickersham as Vice Chair, but Henry

The Restatements needed funding, and here the ALI called upon the Carnegie Foundation, one of the philanthropic organizations that had emerged in the early twentieth century as some of the individuals who had accumulated great wealth in the last decades of the previous century, such as John D. Rockefeller, Andrew Mellon, and Andrew Carnegie, sought ways to dispose of some of that wealth in ways that minimized their exposure to income taxation.[24] The creation of tax-exempt foundations with educational or philanthropic missions was a convenient way of accomplishing that purpose. One of the founders of the ALI, Elihu Root, was on the board of the Carnegie Foundation and helped facilitate a substantial grant from that institution to the ALI to help launch the Restatements.

Not all of the committee's expectations materialized in the early years of the ALI. The Business Associations Restatement was not included in the series of First Restatements, among other things because the changing content of the field and the emergence of governmental regulation made the content of any established principles in the area uncertain. Contracts, Agency, and Property were quickly added to the list of fields subject to restatement, accompanying Torts and Conflicts. Academics dominated the Reporters and Advisers of First Restatements, and the number of Advisers remained comparatively small, ranging between three or four per Restatement. The committee report anticipated that Reporters would spend most of their time drafting Restatements, but all continued to teach during the gestation process. Although the Council, whose first membership consisted of Cardozo, Hand, Stone, and a number of visible practitioners, would play a substantial role in the generation of Restatements, the membership at large did not, at least through the appearance of the First Restatements.

Historians have disagreed about how to characterize the ideological stance of the ALI at its inception, and those disagreements seem understandable when the jurisprudential goals of the founders of the ALI are identified.[25] On the one hand the founders' search for "certainty" in the attempted reconciliation of multiple common law decisions in multiple jurisdictions might be seen as a deeply conservative project, since it amounted to the boiling down of those decisions to a set of black-letter propositions that, once articulated in Restatements, were expected to remain in place over time.[26] The "certainty" produced by Restatements was apparently thought to be connected to the capacity of their black-letter rules to endure. That conception of the course of common law fields over time comes close to equating doctrinal certainty with doctrinal stasis.

Bates, Charles Boston, Charles Burlingham, Frederic Coudert, John W. Davis, William Guthrie, James Hall, Edward McGuire, John Milburn, Andrew Montague, Victor Morawetz, George Welwood Murray, Thomas Parkinson, James Reynolds, and Henry Taft.

[24] On the emergence of philanthropic institutions in early twentieth-century America, *see* OLIVIER ZUNZ, PHILANTHROPY IN AMERICA: A HISTORY (2014).

[25] *Cf.* WILLIAM TWINING, KARL LLEWELLYN AND THE REALIST MOVEMENT 275–76 (1973); ROBERT STEVENS, LAW SCHOOL: LEGAL EDUCATION IN AMERICA FROM THE 1850S TO THE 1980S, at 133–35 (1983); LAURA KALMAN, LEGAL REALISM AT YALE 1927–1960 (1986); NEIL DUXBURY, PATTERNS OF AMERICAN JURISPRUDENCE 24, 59–60 (1995), treating the ALI as a conservative effort to shore up traditional American jurisprudence, with Hull, *supra* note 1, treating it as a "progressive" reformist institution.

[26] *See* Duxbury, *supra* note 25.

On the other hand, Benjamin Cardozo, in setting forth his expectations for the ALI and its Restatements in a series of lectures entitled *The Growth of the Law* in 1924, maintained that although "the law's uncertainties are to be corrected ... so also are its deformities," and that "Restatement must include revision when the vestiges of organs, atrophied by disease, will become centers of infection if left within the social body." Cardozo fully expected that "Restatement will clear the ground of debris. It will enable us to reckon our gains and losses, strike a balance, and start afresh."[27] The ALI, in that sense, was to be an instrument of law reform. It was to be a "progressive" institution in the early twentieth-century sense of that term, one that elites employed to ensure that as modern American society changed, changes were equated with "progress," the process by which people informed by "scientific" knowledge made the present a qualitative improvement over the past and paved the way for further improvement in the future.[28]

So perhaps the best way to describe the ALI's ideological orientation at its origins is as a distinctive combination of "conservative" and "progressive" jurisprudence, its Restatements seeking to produce an authoritative synthesis of black-letter propositions that could be expected to remain in place over time, and also seeking, in the course of that synthesis, to engage in the "critical" and "constructive" discarding of unsound doctrinal "debris," thereby reforming the common law in the process.

The outstanding characteristic of the ALI on its formation in 1923, however, was not its jurisprudential ideology. Rather, it was its distinctive social and epistemological orientation. The founders were convinced that the state of American common law could be "improved"—made less uncertain and more doctrinally sound—simply though a combination of hard work and cooperative participation by distinguished lawyers charged with the task of "restating" the governing principles of common law fields. The authority of the Restatements, the ALI founders believed, would come from the social and professional stature of those selected to work on them and to oversee that work. Trained intellects, particularly those engaged in scholarship in common law fields in American law schools, could be expected to discern the doctrinal propositions governing a common law field and to set them forth in an articulate and persuasive fashion. If some of those propositions amounted to academic glosses on scattered judicial decisions, and injected aspirational reformist elements into a black-letter synthesis, so much the better: the profession was reaping the benefits of the labors of distinguished jurists.

It was this epistemological assumption—that highly educated legal academics, judges, and practitioners could improve the state of American common law merely by applying their talents to the derivation and application of black-letter principles—which was to stick in the craw of reviewers of the first set of Restatements when they were eventually published in the 1930s, unaccompanied by any of the ALI-sponsored treatises that were originally envisioned but fell by the wayside. But before turning to the critical reaction to the First Restatements, we want to conclude this snapshot of the ALI at its origins by briefly describing the process by which Restatements were

---

[27] BENJAMIN N. CARDOZO, THE GROWTH OF THE LAW 18–19 (1924).

[28] *See generally* LEWIS L. GOULD, AMERICA IN THE PROGRESSIVE ERA (2000); WALTER NUGENT, PROGRESSIVISM: A VERY SHORT INTRODUCTION (2010).

generated in the interval between the formation of the ALI and the publication of the First Restatement, that of Contracts, in 1932.

At the outset, Cardozo and the other founders of the ALI anticipated that Restatements, featuring encapsulations of black-letter doctrinal propositions, would be accompanied by treatises, apparently written by the Reporters for each of the Restatements.[29] The treatises would elucidate upon, justify, and apply the doctrinal principles governing common law fields. But as the First Restatements went through successive drafts in the ALI's process of producing them, the anticipated treatises disappeared from the project. There were two reasons for that development. First, some of the Reporters, such as Samuel Williston, Francis Bohlen, and Joseph Henry Beale, had already published treatises on the subject of their Restatement volumes, and declined to produce additional ones on the ground that such an effort would be not only time-consuming but largely superfluous. Second, ALI leadership concluded that publishing treatises as well as Restatement volumes would be a considerable additional expense for the ALI, and the content of the treatises would not be of abiding interest for most of the ALI's members.[30]

As the First Restatements went through drafts in which the Reporters submitted portions of them to Advisers and other interested members, black-letter propositions were frequently accompanied by commentary and citations to cases. From the outset of the Restatement project, it was anticipated that the commentary and cases citations would appear in the final versions of Restatements. But when the First Restatements were eventually published between 1932 and 1937, the commentary and case citations were not included: the volumes were almost exclusively collections of black-letter doctrinal principles and. Illustrations, containing no commentary or case citations.[31]

In light of the strongly critical reaction to the First Restatements that we describe later, in which reviewers suggested that their collections of black-letter principles were sufficiently abstract as to be meaningless, the ALI's decision not to prepare treatises, and not to include commentary and case citations in the Restatement volumes may appear myopic. But, as we will see, that interpretation was largely driven by the shift in American jurisprudence that was taking place at the very same time the First Restatements were being prepared. That shift eventually abandoned a distinction which was fundamental to traditional late nineteenth- and early twentieth-century conceptions of law and judging, that between the authority of legal sources, which was treated as resting on timeless, foundational principles of law, and the authority of interpreters of those sources (judges, legislators, and executive officials), which rested only on the offices they held. Although being a legislator or an executive official gave those individuals certain "lawmaking" powers, being a judge did not. The only authority judges had was that of their office, to discern existing legal principles and

---

[29] In his *Growth of the Law* lectures in 1924 Cardozo said that "[a]ccompanying each restatement ... will be a treatise, which is to consist of a complete exposition of the present condition of the law and a full citation of authorities." The treatises were "to analyze and discuss all the legal problems presented and justify the statement of the law set forth in the principles" CARDOZO, *supra* note 27, at 7.

[30] For more detail, *see* Deborah A. DeMott, *Restating the Law in the Shadow of Codes: The ALI in Its Formative Era*, in this volume; G. EDWARD WHITE, THE CONSTITUTION AND THE NEW DEAL 187–88 (2000); Charles Clark, *The Restatement of the Law of Contracts*, 42 YALE L. J. 643, 649–52 (1933).

[31] WHITE, *supra* note 30, at 188.

apply them to cases. The idea, animating the First Restatements, that fundamental legal principles could be collected, and that those principles were independent of the judicial decisions embodying them, followed from traditional conceptions of law and judging.[32] The appearance of the First Restatements demonstrated that those conceptions had come under pressure.

III. Reaction to the First Restatements

As the first set of Restatements was being prepared between 1923 and 1932, a jurisprudential movement was emerging in some American law schools that would eventually be identified by two of its adherents in 1930 as "Realism."[33] The Realist movement would establish itself on two prominent law faculties, Yale and Columbia, in the late 1920s and 1930s, spread to other institutions, and by the United States' entry into World War II in 1941 would become a mainstream jurisprudential perspective in the American legal academy.[34] The advent of Realism would stimulate a series of critical reviews of the First Restatement volumes by academics who had each endorsed, in differing ways, the underlying assumptions of the Realist movement.

Two of those assumptions gave Realism its distinctive cast. One was that the traditional distinction between the authority of sources of law and that of their interpreters was meaningless. When Karl Llewellyn and Jerome Frank published works in the early 1930s expressing dissatisfaction with established understandings of the law, they emphasized the unintelligibility of what Llewellyn called "traditional prescriptive rules."[35] Frank maintained that a belief that "the announced rules are the paramount thing in the law" was a "phantasy."[36]

The other defining characteristic of Realism was the insistence of its adherents that legal doctrines could not be understood in the abstract. Rather, that legal doctrines were invariably products of their social context, and that context constantly changed. Therefore, the "the law" at any one time was the sum of decisions and policies responding to on-the-ground developments in society at large. It followed from those two features of Realism that the collections of black-letter principles offered in Restatements, accompanied only by occasional illustrations and bereft of other

---

[32] In emphasizing the ALI founders' concern with "uncertainty" in common law subjects we are not intending to suggest that the concern originated primarily from traditional attitudes about law and judging, although those attitudes may have reflexively influenced the thinking of some founders. In our view, "uncertainty" was a more practical concern, based on the proliferation of common law decisions in the late nineteenth and early twentieth centuries and the appearance of numerous decisions that were inconsistent with one another and lacked intelligible rationales. The Restatements were to synthesize the principles undergirding common law decisions so as to render them more consistent and intelligible.

[33] See KALMAN, *supra* note 25, at 3–44.

[34] On the emergence of Realism in American law schools, *see* TWINING, *supra* note 24; KALMAN, *supra* note 25; JOHN HENRY SCHLEGEL, AMERICAN LEGAL REALISM AND EMPIRICAL SOCIAL SCIENCE (1995). For further detail on the Realists' critiques of the Restatements, *see* Robert W. Gordon, *Restatements and Realists*, in this volume.

[35] Karl Llewellyn, *Some Realism About Realism—Responding to Dean Pound*, 44 HARV. L. REV. 1222, 1237 (1931).

[36] Karl Llewellyn, *A Realistic Jurisprudence—The Next Step*, 30 COLUM. L. REV. 431 (1930); JEROME FRANK, LAW AND THE MODERN MIND 147 (1930).

commentary, would be regarded by Realists as exactly the wrong way to give an account of a common law subject.

The result was that between 1933 and 1937 most of the Restatements which were published in that period were subjected to severe criticism in law reviews by scholars whose jurisprudential views generally accorded with Realism. Similar language marked virtually all the reviews of Restatements. In his review of the Restatement of Contracts, Charles Clark, himself an Adviser for the Restatement of Property, called the black-letter form of the Restatements "an unreality" because "the black letter statements are not understandable ... without interpretation or background against which meaning can be discovered." He added that the "general purpose" of the Restatements, that of "clarification and simplification" of common law subjects, was "certainly fallacious" since "[o]ur civilization is complex and our law, if it is to keep abreast of business and social life, cannot be simple."[37]

Leon Green had a similar reaction to the Restatement of Torts, which was published in 1935. He described that Restatement as consisting of "overelaborated [doctrinal] generalizations," when tort law was better organized around "functional" lines, reflecting the social interests at stake in tort cases and the entities that served as plaintiffs and defendants. Tort decisions, Green felt, were produced by a combination of their fact patterns, their social contexts, and the inclinations of the judges who decided them. The Restatement of Torts emphasized none of those factors.[38]

Ernest Lorenzen took a comparable approach in his review of the Restatement of Conflicts of Law. He described the approach taken in that volume by Reporter Beale as resting on "the old rationalistic absolutist conception of law," which had inclined Beale to think of the common law as a "body of scientific principle" which remained "unchanged" despite misconceptions and misstatements of it by courts in particular jurisdictions, resulting in "errors." Lorenzen characterized Beale's conception of the common law as "now generally discredited." In his view the subject of conflict of laws was not a collection of "unchanged" rules or all-encompassing principles, but the aggregate of particular judicial decisions in which the choice to apply the laws of one state or another was made by human actors weighing social interests.[39]

In a 1937 review of the Restatement of Property, Myers McDougal listed some common features of the reviews of other Restatement volumes. Among those were "naivete in fundamental assumptions," centering on the assumption that "certainty is obtainable and obtainable by high abstractions" and was "more important than flexibility," and the related assumption that "the defects of 'the law' can be cured by restating it as it is." Other failings of the Restatements were "the omission of historical, economic, and sociological backgrounds" to the doctrines being collected and "a failure to study the social consequences of institutions and doctrines." There was also "the omission of supporting authorities, reasoned discussion, and contrast of conflicting opinion" in the Restatements, as well as "the use of 'doctrinal' rather than

[37] Charles Clark, *The Restatement of the Law of Contracts*, 42 YALE L.J. 643, 653, 655 (1932).
[38] Leon Green, *The Torts Restatement*, 29 ILL. L. REV. 582, 584–85, 592 (1935).
[39] Ernest G. Lorenzen & Raymond J. Heilman, *The Restatement of the Conflict of Laws*, 83 U. PA. L. REV. 555, 336 (1935).

'factual' classifications" of common law subjects. Those assumptions, in McDougal's view, were "little short of fantastic."[40]

McDougal's summary of the common objections of critics to the Restatements revealed how thoroughgoing their jurisprudential estrangement from the ALI's Restatement project was. They were not merely suggesting that the methodology employed in Restatement volumes was flawed. They were asserting that the starting jurisprudential assumptions of the entire project were wrongheaded because a search for essentialist common law principles was bound to fail. "Law" was not a body of those principles but the aggregate of legal decisions made by officials in changing social contexts.

Although the reaction of these leading legal scholars was critical, the profession at large was more supportive. Lawyers seemed to consult Restatements in doing their research and commonly cited Restatements in their briefs and arguments, since the courts were receptive to them. By 1961, the Restatements had been cited over 29,000 times in the state and federal courts.[41] The ALI and its Restatements were a fixture on the American legal scene. The Restatements, with whatever flaws they had in the view of their academic critics, were a success in the world of law in practice.

IV. The Second Restatements, the ALI, and Changes in the Legal Profession, 1940–1970

From its origins, the ALI had sought to ground the authority of its declarations about the state of the law on the distinguished status, and therefore the authoritativeness, of its members. The Restatements had been drafted by academic experts in common law fields who had been advised by other experts, drawn from the judiciary and the bar as well as the legal academy. And, as the critics of the first set of Restatements had pointed out, those volumes were intended to produce "certainty" in the understanding of common law subjects through a discerning collection of the doctrinal principles governing them. It must have been disheartening for those engaged with the production of the First Restatements to learn that at least one sector of the legal profession, academics at elite law schools, was not inclined to find much certainty, or even much intelligibility, in those volumes.

What at first seemed the radical implication of Legal Realism for Restatements, however, slowly evolved into a recognition that the black-letter-only format of the First Restatements had failed to recognize that certainty was not the only value Restatements could supply. Restatements, in modified format, had the potential to be a resource for lawyers and judges, beyond their mere statement of rules, in a variety of ways. Commentary following black-letter rules could explain and elaborate in ways that provided perspective and an understanding of the rules' purposes that would be useful to lawyers, judges, and academics. In addition, within decades of their completion, the law on many of the issues they addressed had often developed and changed.

---

[40] Myers McDougal, *Book Review*, 32 ILL. L. REV. 509, 510, 513 (1937).
[41] HERBERT F. GOODRICH & PAUL A. WOLKIN, THE STORY OF THE AMERICAN LAW INSTITUTE 1923–61, at 39 (1961).

An ALI committee chaired by Judge Learned Hand recommended, therefore, that a second set of Restatements, not limited to black-letter statements, be commissioned.[42]

As Reporters and Advisers to the Second Restatements were assigned in the 1950s, in all the common law fields covered by the First Restatements, and some additional ones,[43] two matters became clear. First, the individuals who would be directly involved in the drafting of those Restatements had all entered the legal academy during the period in which Realism became the mainstream jurisprudential perspective in the American law schools, and to some extent in the legal profession at large.[44] The Restatements they prepared would reflect that point of view.

Second, the Second Restatements were going to contain more instances in which Reporters and Advisers had disagreed on the application of a black-letter provision to a particular issue, that disagreement being signified by a "caveat" indicating that the Restatement was not taking a definitive position on the matter. In introducing commentary and signaling occasional disagreements in the process of restating the principles governing common law fields, the ALI was following through on an assumption which had animated Hand's committee. That assumption was that the restatement of common law rules necessarily involved an evaluation of their current social utility and desirability. The introduction of commentary was also a response to the criticism of the First Restatements as conveying an illusion of certainty in the promulgation of black-letter rules.[45]

Put another way, the Second Restatements were going to be more open about the policy dimensions of common law rules and more aspirational in their reformist thrust. Hand's committee had distinguished between rules that were "founded on historical facts," and although "unjustified by any principles of justice," might be left in place "because of the desirability of certainty" and "rules that were "insupportable in principle and evil in action."[46] The latter were to be excised in the Second Restatement. Herbert Wechsler, after becoming Director of the ALI in 1964, made it plain that his goal for the Second Restatements was that they serve as a "modest but essential aid in the improved analysis, clarification, unification, growth, and adaptation of the common law."[47] By that comment Wechsler meant that he was entirely prepared to fuse normative and declarative elements in the Second Restatements. In 1968, in response to a memorandum by two ALI members expressing "grave concern that the Institute is in the process of abandoning the long tradition that it undertakes in the Restatement to express established law, as distinguished from the law that a majority of those attending think ought to be, or will at some time in the future be, established by the courts," Wechsler said that "if we ask ourselves what the courts will do," we could

---

[42] *Id* at 11–12.

[43] New Restatements were initiated in Trusts and Foreign Relations law. *Id.* at 12–14.

[44] The second-generation Reporters included Robert Braucher as the Reporter for the Restatement of Contracts; William Prosser for that of Torts; James Casner for Landlord and Tenant (the Restatement of Property having been divided into that subject and others, such as donative transfers, estates in land, and servitudes); Willis Reese for Conflict of Laws; and Warren Seavey, who had replaced Floyd Mechem as the Reporter for the Restatement of Agency on the latter's death in 1928, remaining as Reporter for the Second Restatement of that subject.

[45] John P. Frank, *The American Law Institute, 1923–1998*, 26 HOFSTRA L. REV. 615, 623 (1998).

[46] Hand, quoted in *id.* at 623.

[47] Herbert Wechsler, *Restatements and Legal Change*, 13 ST. LOUIS U. L. REV. 185, 192 (1968).

not "divorce our answers wholly from our view of what they ought to do." He added that when he had presented the "grave concern" memorandum and his response to the Council at a March 1968 meeting, it had unanimously endorsed his position.[48] The Second Restatements were thus to differ from the First not only in their greater emphasis on commentary and division on some doctrinal issues, but on adopting, interstitially, a reformist posture.

As those Restatements were being prepared in the 1960s,[49] changes were taking place within the American legal profession which would affect not only the composition of the ALI's membership but its internal deliberations as well. Beginning in the mid-1960s, post-undergraduate American higher education underwent a decisive shift in its orientation. The 1950s and early 1960s had been a period of considerable growth in higher education at both the undergraduate and graduate levels, as with the prosperity that followed the end of World War II and incentives such as the G.I. bill for returning veterans to attend colleges more and more American families came to believe that obtaining higher education decrees was a prerequisite for business, professional, and financial success. College enrollments dramatically increased, and with them the number of new faculty positions. The effect was to create a favorable market for undergraduates to pursue graduate training in the arts and sciences, which was required for faculty positions.[50]

By the mid-1960s, the number of faculty positions in arts and sciences departments had expanded considerably. Then two developments occurred that suddenly diminished the job prospects for persons pursuing Ph.D. degrees in the arts and sciences. With the Vietnam War expanding and a greater emphasis on spending on scientific and technological projects triggered by the space race and the Cold War, the federal government's budgetary priorities shifted, and federal funding for most departments in arts and sciences was cut. This meant that fewer scholarships and fellowships were available for graduate programs in the arts and sciences, making them more expensive to undertake. And at the other end of the process for graduate students, available positions in arts and sciences departments shrunk, partly because there was less funding for new positions and partly because a surge of faculty hiring in the 1950s and early 1960s had resulted in fewer vacancies.[51]

As a consequence of those developments, more undergraduate students began applying to law and medical schools rather than graduate programs. Law schools, whose size was less constrained by the costs of offering an educational experience than medical schools, particularly benefited from the trend, and both proliferated and expanded, including admitting roughly twice as many women in 1982 as had been admitted in 1970. In addition, the American economy experienced a period of general, if uneven, growth in the last decades of the twentieth century, and law firms expanded

---

[48] *Id.* at 190–91.

[49] The Second Restatement of Agency was the first of its cohorts to be published, in 1958, doubtless because its Reporter, Warren Seavey, had been the Reporter for the First Restatement from 1928 until its publication in 1933. The other Second Restatements were completed in the 1960s.

[50] For more detail, *see* G. EDWARD WHITE, LAW IN AMERICAN HISTORY: VOLUME III, 1930–2000, at 368–71 (2019).

[51] *Id.* at 368–69.

as well. There were more places in law schools, more law graduates entering the job market, and more places for junior associates in firms.

The economics of medium- and large-size law firms in the late twentieth century made it cost-efficient for their partners to have a large number of junior and senior associates, working on salaries but billing hours at higher rates than their pay scales, but less cost-efficient for them to have large numbers of partners who pooled their assets. Over time the expectations that associates at large- and medium-size firms would be promoted to partner dwindled. With the market for law jobs still flush, disappointed candidates for partnerships increasingly elected to leave their firms for one of two alternatives. One was to form smaller, specialized firms, concentrating on particular types of legal business, often along with associates from their existing firm or disappointed candidates in other firms.

The other option was to work for established corporate clients of their former firms as "in-house counsels." As corporations grew in size along with the rest of the economy in the late twentieth century, they had an increasing amount of legal business that did not involve litigation: the ordinary legal dimensions of business transactions and consultations about prospective business ventures. Corporations found it efficient not to outsource routine legal matters to firms but to retain their own lawyers on a salaried basis. Law firms, faced with a glut of associates seeking partnerships, also found it desirable to recommend disappointed aspirants to corporations they regularly represented. The arrangement served to cement relations between firms and their corporate clients and to make it likely that the firms would be retained should corporations not be able to address legal matters in house.

When in-house counsel applicants for membership in the ALI came to be proposed in the late twentieth century, the initial reaction of the membership was skeptical on the ground that the ALI was designed to be a nonpartisan institution, dedicated to "improving" the law without regard to political goals or consequences. Eventually in-house counsel were deemed eligible for admission to the ALI under the proviso that in the course of the ALI's deliberations, members should "check their clients at the door."[52] That caveat proved difficult to adhere to and to enforce,[53] and it pertained not only to in-house counsel but to members of "boutique" firms who regularly represented certain types of clients. By the late twentieth century the practitioner sector of the ALI, once composed almost exclusively of members in elite firms engaging in general practice, had come to include more persons who regularly represented, or worked for, firms with distinct economic and social agendas. Meetings of the ALI membership increasingly came to include debates among "interested" members, often reflecting the views of their regular clients or their corporate employers.

Two incidents involving William Prosser and the Second Restatement of Torts can serve to illustrate the atmospheric change that began to take place within the ALI in

---

[52] Frank, *supra* note 45, at 629. A rule of the Council provided that "[m]embers should speak and vote on the basis of their personal and professional convictions and experience without regard to client interests of self-interest. It is improper under Institute principles for a member to represent a client in Institute proceedings." Quoted in *id.*

[53] As Frank put it, "This is not always as easy as it sounds. Some projects may affect clearly definable economic interests, and those economic interests may wish very strongly to mold in their behalf the projects that may affect those interests." *Id.*

the late 1960s, as the first effects of the developments within the American legal profession previously sketched came to be felt by the ALI.

The first incident was from the interval between 1960 and 1965, when Prosser, as Reporter for the Second Restatement of Torts, was preparing its text. In the early 1960s, Prosser had published two articles on what he called the "assault" upon and "fall" of the "citadel" of privity in defective products cases.[54] As early as the 1941 edition of his Torts treatise, Prosser had been an advocate for extending the liability of manufacturers of defective products beyond those with whom they were in "privity"—contractual relations—to include users or consumers injured by defects.[55] He also believed that using a standard of strict liability, rather than employing negligence coupled with *res ipsa loquitur*, was a more desirable way of dealing with injuries caused by defective products.[56] Prosser's approach had been endorsed by Justice Roger Traynor of the California Supreme Court in a 1944 concurring opinion in a case where the explosion from a soft drink bottle, caused by a defect not discoverable on inspection, had injured a waitress.[57] And by 1963 a majority of the California Supreme Court had endorsed strict liability for manufacturing defects in products.[58] But at that point most other courts continued to treat defective product injuries as governed by a negligence standard.

Prosser's articles nonetheless asserted that there was a "trend" in the direction of strict liability for product defects and that subsequently the citadel of privity had been breached, with the strict liability of manufacturers for product defects extending beyond retailers to users and consumers. Buoyed by that conviction, Prosser drafted a new section of the Second Restatement of Torts, 402A, which stated that where a product defect made it "unreasonably dangerous" to users or consumers, strict liability would govern. He secured the approval of his Advisers, the Council, and ultimately the membership of the ALI for 402A, even though comparatively few courts adopted it after its passage, some declining to accept the "unreasonably dangerous" limitation on liability and others choosing to maintain negligence as the governing standard for defective product injuries.

The ALI's adoption of 402A, which took place in 1965, illustrated the weight afforded to Reporters in the process of drafting Restatements. By the time his articles on the citadel of privity appeared, Prosser was the leading Torts scholar in the nation, being the author not only of an authoritative treatise but the most widely adopted Torts casebook. He had also been the dean of the University of California at Berkeley's law school since 1948, and in that capacity exercised considerable authority and brooked little opposition. In considering the largely aspirational change Prosser sought to initiate in Section 402A, the ALI was readily prepared to defer to his authority.[59]

---

[54] William L. Prosser, *The Assault Upon the Citadel*, 69 YALE. L.J. 1099 (1960); William L. Prosser, *The Fall of the Citadel*, 50 MINN. L. REV. 791 (1966).

[55] WILLIAM L. PROSSER, HANDBOOK OF THE LAW OF TORTS 688–92 (1941).

[56] *Id.* at 689.

[57] Escola v. Coca-Cola Bottling Co., 150 P.2d 436 (Cal. 1944).

[58] Greenman v. Yuba Power Co., 59 Cal.2d. 57 (1963).

[59] *See* for an account of the adoption of Section 402A, John C.P. Goldberg, *Torts in the American Law Institute*, in this volume.

In the mid-1960s, the changes in the American legal profession and the membership of the ALI were only beginning to take shape. But by 1970, when Prosser introduced two other sections of the Second Restatement of Torts, on public and private nuisance, the composition of the ALI had begun to change, as had the ideological orientation of some of its academic members, and those changes had begun to reflect themselves in the membership's reaction to Restatement drafts.

A prime example involved the material on nuisance. At the 1969 Annual Meeting Prosser had secured membership approval for Section 821B of the Second Restatement, on public nuisance. The section defined a public nuisance as an "unreasonable interference" with a "right common to the general public," and included among considerations for whether the interference was "unreasonable" its "continuing nature" or whether it had been "proscribed by a statute, ordinance, or administrative regulation." At the Annual Meeting the following year, he introduced Section 821D, on private nuisance, defining that tort as an intentional, and unreasonable, invasion of an interest in land. In doing so he set forth the previously approved Section 821B, on public nuisance, as a reference.

Prosser's presentation to the ALI membership of the new Section 821D, along with the previously approved Section 821B, evoked two quite disparate proposals, from the floor, both directed at the public nuisance section.[60] One proposal was to withdraw tort law entirely from the treatment of public nuisances, replacing it with environmental regulation. The other was to greatly expand the role of tort law in policing public nuisances, specifically air and water pollution. The responses signaled that the ALI membership had become polarized on the issue of particulate emissions by corporate entities, possibly because members were reflecting the various interests of their clients or employers. A motion to recommit Section 821B to Prosser for revision was approved by the membership, without a clear indication of the direction such a revision should take.[61]

Meanwhile, at the same Annual Meeting, Prosser's draft of Section 821D, which had distinguished between "intentional" and "unintentional" private nuisances, treating the latter as being governed by negligence law but requiring that the former be not just intentional but "unreasonable" to make out an action, was challenged by Professors Robert Keeton and Fleming James. These two torts scholars urged that "intentional" private nuisances be actionable whether they were "unreasonable" or not, in effect subjecting them to a form of strict liability. Prosser defended his treatment, but the membership ultimately voted to have him revise the section along the lines Keeton and James had suggested.

The episode represented a striking contrast to the ALI membership's response to Section 402A five years earlier. In that episode the membership had deferred to Prosser, even when he produced a section with little case support that was largely based on his own views. In 1970 the membership not only rebuffed Prosser on Section 821D, but retrospectively adopted a motion to recommit Section 821B to Prosser for unspecified revisions, although this section had been approved a year earlier. We

---

[60] For more detail, see John W. Wade, *William Prosser: Some Impressions and Recollections*, 60 CAL. L. REV. 1255, 1258–60 (1972).

[61] *See id.* at 1259.

cannot be sure exactly what was driving the change: Keeton and James's proposal to reconsider 821B would not have been understood as ideologically driven, but it nonetheless reflected an expanded theory of private nuisance liability which may have appealed to sectors of the membership. In any event, Prosser, who rarely took kindly to challenges to his authority—he resigned the deanship of Berkeley in the middle of the 1960–1961 academic year after the university sought to initiate a *pro forma* review of his position, even though he was sixty-two at the time and would have been required to retire at sixty-five—signaled after the nuisance episode that he was going to retire as Reporter of the Second Restatement, and did so over the summer of 1970.[62] The institution to which Prosser had presented his sections on nuisance was not the quite the same as the one that had approved his draft of Section 402A.

V. The Second Half-Century:
Diversification, Polarization, and Revitalization

Three themes dominate our account of the ALI's second half-century. First, the projects and subject matter of the ALI's work diversified, to include not only new Restatements but also other types of projects and the consideration of subjects outside the common law. Second, some projects and some of the ALI's work became controversial, with interests from both inside and outside the ALI reflecting a polarization of views. Third, toward the end of the period, there was increased involvement not only by the practicing bar but also by faculty at elite law schools, replicating in many ways the involvement of prestigious law professors at the time of the ALI's founding.

A. Corporate Governance and the Beginnings
of Increased Polarization

For roughly its first fifty years, most of the ALI's work had been Restatements, although it also produced the Uniform Commercial Code, the Model Penal Code, and a number of studies and special publications that were neither restatements nor codes.[63] In the late 1970s, however, it began a project in a different form that would produce the most heated controversy it had ever experienced: Corporate Governance.[64]

Beginning in the late 1960s, a number of controversies implicating corporate governance and corporate social responsibility erupted. Incidents such as Dow Chemical's manufacture of napalm gas used for defoliation during the Vietnam war and the secret corporate contributions to President Richard Nixon's re-election campaign that became connected to the Watergate scandal stimulated broad concern about the weak supervisory role played by corporate boards of directors in the governance of public

---

[62] *Id.* at 1260.

[63] GOODRICH & WOLKIN, *supra* note 38, at 19–31.

[64] For a full account of the Corporate Governance project, *see* William W. Bratton, *Special Interests at the Gate: The ALI Corporate Governance Project, 1978–1992*, in this volume.

corporations. By the late 1970s, legislation addressing the issue had been introduced in the U.S. Congress.

It was in this context that the ALI decided to undertake a project on Corporate Governance. From the outset there was recognition that the project would not be a pure Restatement, because it would not only be restating some corporate law, but also expressly considering reforming the law where necessary. The first draft of the project reflected this approach. It was called the project "Principles of Corporate Governance and Structure: Restatement and Recommendations."[65] Clearly this was to be more than a mere Restatement, although exactly how was yet to be determined.

The first draft, produced in 1981, proposed changes to rules that, among other things, would have increased the responsibilities and potential civil liabilities of corporate directors.[66] For example, the draft proposed what came very close to being a simple negligence standard for directors' liability for breach of their duty of care—breach of which could be the subject of derivative suits by shareholders against a director. This would have supplanted the "business judgment" rule, which eventually was understood to subject directors to liability only for gross negligence (or worse).

The draft produced considerable public criticism. Walter Wriston, CEO of Citicorp, was quoted in the New York Times as saying, "[w]e don't require four law professors to tell us how to run our business."[67] The Business Roundtable argued that "the proposed Restatement" was an "attempt to impose an additional and unnecessary layer of regulation on United States corporations," ignoring "the realities of competition and the marketplace...."[68] Partly in response to such criticism, the Corporate Governance project evolved. In a subsequent draft it was renamed "Principles of Corporate Governance: Analysis and Recommendations."[69] Removal of the name "Restatement" from the title took away some of the significance that Restatements carried, but several years of controversy followed nonetheless, with many of the corporate lawyers who were members leveling strong criticism at successive drafts. Eventually the project was approved, but not without leaving scars from the polarization that had accompanied it.

A lesson was apparently learned. The name "Principles" would come to designate ALI projects that attempted not only to state the law but also to express judgments about the wisdom of existing law and make proposals for reforming it. Several important projects over the next three decades would be designated "Principles," and finally in 2015, under Director Richard Revesz, the distinction between Restatements and Principles was formalized and broadened. Restatements now speak primarily to courts; Principles projects do not.[70]

---

[65] Principles of Corporate Governance and Structure: Restatement and Recommendations, Advisory Group Draft No. 1 (1981).

[66] For an extended analysis, including an account of the criticism the project received, see Joel Seligman, A Sheep in Wolf's Clothing: The American Law Institute Principles of Corporate Governance Project, 55 GEO. WASH. L. REV. 325 (1987).

[67] Tamar Lewin, The Corporate Reform Furor, N.Y. TIMES, June 10, 1982, at D1.

[68] Statement of the Business Roundtable on the American Law Institute's Proposed "Principles of Corporate Governance and Structure: Restatement and Recommendations" 33 (Feb. 1983).

[69] Principles of Corporate Governance: Analysis and Recommendations, Advisory Group No. 5 (1983).

[70] AMERICAN LAW INSTITUTE, CAPTURING THE VOICE OF THE AMERICAN LAW INSTITUTE 4, 13 (2015) ("Revised Style Manual").

B. Enterprise Responsibility for Personal Injury

Tort liability, a traditional subject of the ALI's work, took a new turn in the late 1970s. A "crisis" in the availability and affordability of medical malpractice liability insurance was followed by the rise of "mass" torts involving defective products and drugs, such as asbestos, the Dalkon Shield, and breast implants. A second "crisis" involving a broader range of defendants and purchasers of liability insurance arose in the mid-1980s. Whether the traditional tort system, designed primarily to handle sporadic accidents, was an adequate and sensible mechanism for handling these new forms of tort liability was a question at the forefront of public policy debates.

It was in this context that the Council approved a project that was initially termed "Compensation and Liability for Product and Process Injuries."[71] The project was never expected to be in the form of a Restatement or Principles. It had five Reporters and no Advisers, but there were two "Council Liaisons" often present at meetings of the Reporters, apparently to ensure that work of the project did not get into the kind of trouble that had recently befallen Corporate Governance. The purpose of the project was to address and assess the fundamental features of the tort system that had produced the recent and ongoing controversy.

The Reporters at first produced working papers on aspects of the tort system, such as workplace, medical, and product-related injury and liability insurance.[72] They also considered the fundamental purposes of the tort system—compensation, deterrence, and redress of social grievances. In due course, the project prepared drafts that included possible reforms to the system, some of them fundamental, such as no-fault in the area of medical injuries, proportional liability for injuries whose causes were uncertain, and reform of the law of damages.

As the project neared completion, it adopted a new name—"Enterprise Responsibility for Personal Injury"—and its Reporters began participating in meetings with Advisers that functioned much like the meetings of Restatement and Principles projects.[73] The ALI found that the project was controversial. The tort law world is divided into plaintiffs' and defense counsel, and drafts of the Enterprise Responsibility project were criticized from both sides. Plaintiffs' counsel objected to such proposed restrictions on liability as the abolition of the collateral source rule and the potential move to enterprise-based medical liability or medical no-fault. Defense counsel objected, among other things, to the consideration of proportional liability.

Periodic reports to the Council on the status and progress of the project had revealed not only that it was controversial but also that it was unclear how it could be put into a form susceptible to approval by the membership at the Annual Meeting. Director Geoffrey Hazard noted the possibility that Enterprise Responsibility project would simply be denominated a report "to" the ALI rather than "by" the ALI and could be serve as the intellectual basis for turning to a Third Restatement of Torts, beginning

---

[71] Report to the Council, Compensation and Liability for Product and Process Injuries 1 (Nov. 11, 1986).
[72] *Id.*
[73] *See* 1 REPORTERS STUDY, ENTERPRISE RESPONSIBILITY FOR PERSONAL INJURY (Apr. 15, 1991).

with products liability; he also suggested that it could be termed a "reporters study" that required no vote.[74]

The project's two-volume study was presented to the Annual Meeting in May 1991, with prior indication that it was for discussion only and would not be voted upon.[75] The same kind of heated debate that the project had undergone in smaller, prior meetings ensued on the floor. It appears that over the following summer, perhaps after receiving further criticism of the project, and perhaps even as some form of political compromise, the Director decided that the work of the project should not continue in some new or additional form. At its October 1991 meeting, the Council approved his recommendation that the ALI turn to a Restatement (Third) of Torts focusing initially on products liability.[76]

C. Into the Twenty-First Century: Intermittent Polarization

An additional consideration helps fill out the context in which the extended controversies over Corporate Governance and Enterprise Responsibility occurred. Opposition to the Corporate Governance project at the Annual Meetings, where projects are discussed and must be adopted by vote, was sometimes voiced by members who represented publicly traded corporations whose interests could have been affected by the project's recommendations. The ALI has no conflict-of-interest rules for members voting on project proposals. We have seen that there is an express rule, more in the form of a strong admonition that is not accompanied by an enforcement mechanism, that members are to "check their clients at the door." Undoubtedly some of the members were urged by their clients to oppose proposals made by the project. But it is also the case that in a career of representing a particular point of view, lawyers come to internalize that point of view and believe in it. Separating the two influences may be impossible.[77]

In the ensuing years, intermittent division along partisan lines became even more evident. The Enterprise Responsibility project was subjected to considerable partisan criticism, which may well have influenced the termination of the project at an earlier point than would otherwise have been the case. Partisan division of this sort has become fairly routine in the last few decades. This has been the case predominantly in fields of law in which the bar itself is divided by reference to the set of interests that a lawyer typically represents. In torts, lawyers tend to represent plaintiffs or defendants exclusively; in employment law, the division is between those who represent labor and those who represent management; in insurance law, between those who represent

[74] American Law Institute, Minutes of the One Hundred Ninety-Ninth Meeting of the Council (Dec. 5–7, 1990).

[75] *See* Enterprise Responsibility for Personal Injury, Unedited Transcript of Discussion of Reporters Study at Annual Meeting 39.

[76] American Law Institute, Minutes of the Two Hundred Second Meeting of the Council (Oct. 24–26, 1991).

[77] John Frank, a longtime member of the Council writing in 1998, recognized that the "two areas" in which pressures from economic interests affected the content of Institute projects were "Corporate Governance and Products Liability." Frank, *supra* note 45, at 629.

policyholders and those who represent insurers. Projects in which the bar is divided in this manner—whether Restatements or Principles—tend to be more polarized than when there are no evident "sides" divided by particular interests. For example, lawyers who practice Family, Property, and Agency law tend not to represent particular interests in these fields exclusively, and projects in those areas have been less controversial.

The ALI has come to recognize that projects in which partisan divisions can be anticipated require that the Reporters not be strongly identified with a particular point of view, and that the lawyers who serve as Advisers be representative of each side of the division within that field. Partly for this reason, the size of Advisers' groups has increased, and "Members Consultative Groups" were added, often with participation by both groups at in-person meetings. This approach may sometimes have diluted the depth of deliberation that takes place at meetings. But the approach not only helps to ensure that there is a full airing of differing points of view as drafts are prepared but also reduces the risk that particular interests will feel that those whose views they share have not been involved in the process. In the experience of one of the authors (Abraham), the expression of different points of view frequently and properly influences the choices the Reporters make.

In addition, interest groups sometimes lobby the Council, through the submission of memoranda or letters commenting on a draft that the Council is considering. And there is still heated debate at Annual Meetings, because no amount of attention to process can dissolve intense substantive disagreement. But debate tends to be more focused on substance, and less on process, than might be the case if the approach of ensuring the representation of different points of view at earlier stages were not taken. Nonetheless, on occasion partisanship definitely affects the flavor of the process, and sometimes continues after a Restatement or Principles project is complete.

D. The Revitalized Work of Recent Decades

The last two decades have witnessed a number of important changes in the profile of the ALI and its work. First, membership has diversified. The increase in the number of women in the legal profession that began in the 1970s eventually led to an increase in the number of women who were elected to membership in the ALI. An emphasis on identifying qualified people of color for membership also bore fruit. Second, the sheer volume of work has increased. Since 1990, roughly thirty-five major projects have been initiated, involving Restatements, Principles, and Codifications and Studies. The majority have been completed. That is a bit more than one new project per year. Since each project takes an average of about eight to ten years from beginning to end, this means that at any given time there is a considerable amount of work taking place. In recent years, the number of ongoing projects has increased to between fifteen and twenty at any one time. That is a practical limit, given the number of meetings of Advisers and Members Consultative Groups that are required during the course of the year, as well as the amount of time that can be devoted to any given project's work at Council Meetings and at the Annual Meeting.

This increase in activity and productivity has certainly been influenced by the leadership and energy of Directors Geoffrey Hazard, Lance Liebman, and Richard Revesz, along with the Presidents who have been in charge during this period, Roswell Perkins, Charles Alan Wright, Michael Traynor, Roberta Ramo, and David Levi. But it is also a result of the second important factor influencing the ALI's profile: the accelerating pace of legal change and of the rise of new legal issues and new areas of law to which the ALI has sought to make a contribution. The center of gravity of the ALI's work, until the last few decades, were the First and Second Restatements of traditional common law subjects. That work has continued to this day, in the Third Restatements of Torts, Agency, Property, and Trusts.

A considerable portion of the ALI's work over the last two decades, however, has focused on new subjects or subjects previously considered of secondary importance. Successive Directors (with the advice of the Council's program committee and the Council itself) have been the principal influence on what projects are undertaken and the form that a project takes. An increasing portion of the projects has been normative, addressed to institutions other than the courts in the form of Principles, or both. Thus, there have been or are in process Restatements of the Law of Charitable Non-Profit Organizations; Children and the Law; the U.S. Law of International Commercial and Investor-State Arbitration; the Law of American Indians; and Liability Insurance Law. There have been projects on the Principles of Aggregate Litigation; Compliance, Risk Management, and Enforcement for Corporations, Non-Profits, and Other Organizations; Data Privacy; Election Law; Government Ethics; Policing; Student Sexual Misconduct: Procedural Frameworks for Colleges and Universities; Transnational Civil Procedure. And there have been other projects revising the Model Penal Code provisions on Sentencing, and on Sexual Assault and Related Offenses; and a project on World Trade Law: The World Trade Organization. As recently as thirty years ago, few of those subjects would even have been on the legal horizon as subject matters suitable for an ALI project. And even for those that were on the horizon, many involved in the ALI would not have considered them appropriate subjects of attention by the ALI. That has all changed. The changing nature of law has necessitated a change in the nature of the ALI's work.

A third factor contributing to a change in the ALI's profile over the past several decades has been the increased involvement of practicing lawyers and academics, as compared to the situation between roughly 1980 and 2000. The revolution in the size and competitiveness of law firms between 1980 and 2000, with its accompanying pressure on bringing in and maintaining business, meant that the typical law firm partner often could not afford the time necessary to be involved in the work of such organizations as the ALI. The ALI recognized this phenomenon, creating regional advisory groups to identify promising potential ALI members and then recommend and recruit them. In addition, over a period of years after 2000, President Roberta Ramo visited many of the managing partners of the Big Law 200 firms to encourage them to support greater involvement of their partners in the ALI. These efforts bore fruit in the form of increased membership and more geographical, gender, and racial diversity in membership. In addition, greater attention to those forms of diversity has meant that the membership of the Council—subject to term limits beginning after about 2010— is also much more diverse than it had been.

This is not the place to pat the ALI on the back for those efforts, for it is still an elite organization, with both the strengths and weaknesses of that sort of group. Change in the makeup in the membership and Council, however, has influenced the legal subjects that each entity found important, interesting, and in need of attention. That changed not only the subjects that were selected as projects but also the level of involvement by the members in those projects. If debates at the Annual Meeting sometimes now look a bit more like debates in a legislature than they once did, at least part of the reason is not merely increased partisanship but also increased intellectual involvement on the part of those attending.

The increased involvement of academics in the work of the ALI has taken a different form. We referred earlier to the increasing disconnect between the work of practicing lawyers and the preoccupations of law professors, beginning in the late 1960s, when professors at elite, and eventually many other law schools, began to shift their attention away from traditional doctrinal scholarship. The pool of qualified law professors who would be interested in serving as Reporters or Advisers to ALI projects probably shrunk accordingly. Exactly when this trend bottomed out is not entirely clear. In the 1980s and 90s, involvement of academics was still substantial, but interest in the ALI at the elite law schools was probably at an all-time low.

On the initiative of Director Lance Liebman and Deputy Director Stephanie Middleton, in 2007, the ALI held an informal conference of selected law school junior faculty to get feedback about their interest in the ALI and what could be done to encourage it. One of the new programs that grew out of this conference were the junior faculty scholarship awards now made annually. Law school deans make nominations, and the two winners are each invited to make presentations at the Annual Meeting. Each winner also holds a one-day conference at the ALI's expense on a subject of their choice. The awards have raised the profile of the ALI among junior faculty at American law schools.

But more importantly, in the last decade there clearly has been increased involvement by senior law school faculty in the work of the ALI, including some of the leading legal scholars in the country. Part of the reason is that the subjects chosen for ALI projects—many of them not involving traditional legal subjects, as we noted earlier—are of greater interest than the common law subjects that were once the core of the ALI's focus. Part of the reason is the sheer persuasiveness of the last two Directors, Lance Liebman and Richard Revesz. An additional part may come from the increased interest on the part of law school faculty in taking legal doctrine seriously, as evidenced by the advent of programs and publications addressing what has sometimes been called "the new private law."[78] And a final part may be the level of energy and productivity of many prominent law professors, who now commonly publish several law review articles each year and find it feasible not only to be legal scholars but also to be involved simultaneously as ALI Reporters and Advisers. Whatever the explanations, faculty from Harvard, Yale, Chicago, Columbia, Michigan, Penn, Virginia, NYU, Duke, Berkeley, and UCLA, among others, have recently been or are now serving as Reporters. And faculty from those and many other law schools commonly serve as project Advisers. The result is that the work products of the ALI are informed by the scholarship of these individuals. Conversely, it seems likely that these scholars'

---

[78] See THE OXFORD HANDBOOK OF THE NEW PRIVATE LAW (Andrew S. Gold et al. eds., 2020); John C.P. Goldberg, *Introduction: Pragmatism and Private Law*, 125 HARV. L. REV. 1640 (2012).

publications are at least sometimes informed by their work on ALI projects. The gap between what goes on in law schools and what goes on in the work of the ALI is therefore probably narrowing.

VI. Conclusion

The intellectual evolution of the American Law Institute has paralleled the evolution of American law in the century of its existence. The First Restatements reflected the idea that certainty could be obtained by the exercise of intelligent deliberation and articulation of black-letter rules by sophisticated legal thinkers. That idea was met with skepticism by the legal Realists, even while the Restatements themselves were proving useful in the world of practice and adjudication. The Second Restatements took account of the Realist critique, adding commentary and reflecting a recognition of uncertainty where it existed, while maintaining the black-letter approach that had proved attractive to the bar and the bench.

Changes in the legal profession and in society at large have led over time to changes in the composition of the ALI, and in retrospect inevitably to polarization over the substance of some ALI projects, notably Corporate Governance and Enterprise Responsibility for Personal Injury, and certain of the Third Restatements as well. The ALI has learned to deal with such polarization, at times even taking advantage of it, both in the selection of projects and in the evolution of their substance as they move toward completion.

At the same time, the ALI's membership and leadership have become more diverse, while involvement of elite lawyers and professors from top-tier law schools, which had declined late in the twentieth century, has increased in recent decades. This increased diversity and involvement is the product of both active recruiting by ALI leadership and the rebirth of interest in legal doctrine on the part of an important segment of legal scholars.

It is no surprise that the ALI's intellectual evolution has followed this course, for otherwise it would have either withered away or become an outlier in American law. Instead, the ALI has changed with the times, both intellectually and organizationally, encountering pitfalls, obstacles, and criticism, but adhering to its original mission of improving the law through the production of work that is the result of intellectual efforts by a combination of lawyers, judges, and legal scholars. If this form of sustained intellectual interaction is not completely unique in American law, it is certainly highly distinctive.

4

Restating the Law in the Shadow of Codes

The ALI in Its Formative Era

Deborah A. DeMott[*]

I. Introduction

For institutions as for individuals, success over time can smooth out narratives of the past, expunging the memory of consequential events and choices made along the way. This chapter recounts the early history of the American Law Institute (ALI) from 1923 to 1945, emphasizing the significance of legislative codification to the ALI's ongoing definition of itself and its mission. This history is more complex than appears from some accounts, not the least because institutional necessities, including funding, shaped the ALI's work over time. Likewise, experience sharpened internal insight into what made (and continues to make) the ALI distinctively valuable. Signal elements of the Restatement—the ALI's principal accomplishment during this era—departed from the project's initial plan. Successfully executing the Restatement required ongoing processes to determine its form, staffing, substantive coverage, and internal organization. Framing the Restatement project as a rejoinder to codification casts new light on both the endurance and fragility of what it accomplished. The point of undertaking the Restatement—intended as an authoritative treatment of private-law subjects within the common law—may have been staving off an intrusion of codification into the common law's domain. If so, the ALI's embrace in the early 1940s of the project that culminated in the Uniform Commercial Code (UCC) appears an about-face that redefined itself and its work or mission. Looking inside the ALI through its surviving records illuminates these dimensions of its early history, including its resilience and evolution into an established institution.

As seen by the ALI's organizers—legal academics, judges, and members of elite segments within the bar—American law in the 1920s was in lamentable shape, in particular its perceived core of general private-law doctrine. Addressing the ALI's 1923 organizational meeting, Elihu Root noted prolixity and variation in legal doctrine: "[W]hatever authority might be found for one view of the law upon any topic, other authorities could be found for a different view...."[1] A profusion of statutory

[*] David F. Cavers Professor of Law, Duke University School of Law. For access to materials from ALI's archive, I am grateful to Sarah Oswald, Gabriella Femenia, and their colleagues in the Biddle Law Library, University of Pennsylvania Law School, which holds the archive. For help locating other materials, I thank Michael McArthur and Jennifer Behrens, Goodson Law Library, Duke Law School. The chapter benefited from discussions at a faculty workshop, Duke Law School and the editorial conference for the volume; comments from Andrew Gold, Carol Lee, and David Seipp helped as well. I served as the sole Reporter for the Restatement (Third) of Agency (2006).

[1] *Proceedings at the Organization of the Institute*, 1 A.L.I. PROC., Part II 48 (1923).

Deborah A. DeMott, *Restating the Law in the Shadow of Codes* In: *The American Law Institute*. Edited by: Andrew S. Gold and Robert W. Gordon, Oxford University Press. © Oxford University Press 2023. DOI: 10.1093/oso/9780197685341.003.0005

enactments prior to World War I compounded the challenges,[2] and state-by-state enactments of uniform statutes did not eliminate the risk of divergent judicial interpretations.[3] Additionally, in the judgment of Roscoe Pound, the last quarter of the nineteenth century represented "the nadir of American law-book writing," in which authors "assumed to find a rule for everywhere in a common-law decision anywhere."[4] Within a market for law books that operated nationwide by the end of the nineteenth century, authors' incentives aligned with their publishers to produce books that mostly indexed and detailed published decisions.[5] In a more recent assessment, "in the end the treatises recreated complexity," written as most law books were for a lawyers' market that sought shortcuts to precedents and potential arguments but not a text amenable to reading as a coherent whole.[6] Nor was the overall result by the 1920s—understood in today's terms as an epistemic crisis—believed to be resolvable through legislative codification of private-law doctrine. Indeed, although the Restatement represented an oft-repeated commitment to furnishing an authoritative account of "the law as we find it,"[7] it did not address codified doctrine from the seven states that had enacted general civil codes, most notably California.

Drafted neither as a statute for legislative enactment nor as a treatise or digest, the Restatement's authority initially turned on its form and its authorship. As an institutional author, the ALI comprised the well-regarded academics who served as Reporters for each subject, the intense scrutiny brought to bear on draft texts by cohorts of expert Advisers, and the distinguished generalist members of the governing Council, culminating in a vote taken by the ALI's broader elected membership at an Annual Meeting. The hoped-for result would constitute a "prima facie basis" for judicial action, drafted in the style of a well-drawn statute[8] and gathering authority through judicial and professional reception over time.[9] If successful, the Restatement would also keep control over private law within the judiciary, guided by "the craftsmen of the

---

[2] *Id.* at 49 (reporting 62,000 distinct statutory enactments in the five years preceding 1914).

[3] *Id.* at 57 (delegate notes "multiplicity" of judicial constructions of uniform state laws, in particular Negotiable Instruments Law) (W.H. Washington).

[4] ROSCOE POUND, THE FORMATIVE ERA OF AMERICAN LAW 159 (1938). In Richard Brooks's assessment, "What appeared as complexity was actually just data, lots of data (i.e. observations) which tended to overwhelm users accustomed to working with smaller samples." Richard R.W. Brooks, *Canon and Fireworks: Reliance in the Restatements of Contracts and Reliance on Them,* in this volume at 109. The problem, in other words, was epistemic and not (or not necessarily) ontological.

[5] *Id.* at 158. For more on the evolution of commercial law-book publishing in the United States, *see* David J. Seipp, *The Need for Restatement of the Common Law: A Long Look Back,* in this volume.

[6] Angela Fernandez & Markus D. Dubber, *Introduction, in* LAW BOOKS IN ACTION 10 (Angela Fernandez & Markus D. Dubber eds., 2012). Positioned within a broader history, the early treatise writers "were, in a sense, on the defensive," given the revolution in America, and thus "anxious" to demonstrate that their enterprise was respectable, by making "extensive use of English materials" in light of limited indigenous material. JOHN H. LANGBEIN ET AL., HISTORY OF THE COMMON LAW: THE DEVELOPMENT OF ANGLO-AMERICAN LEGAL INSTITUTIONS 847 (2009). In David Seipp's account, had the attention of the grandees of the legal profession not been drawn by public debates about the common law, "the path of least resistance" would have left to commercial publishers the task of addressing the epistemic problem confronted by lawyers. Seipp, *supra* note 5 at 41.

[7] For this phrase, *see, e.g.,* 5 A.L.I. PROC. 191 (1927) ("we must state the law as we find it") (J.W. Beale in response to G.B. Rose).

[8] *Proceedings at the Organization, supra* note 1, at 50 (E. Root).

[9] *Id.*

profession...."[10] Additional elements of form mattered. Despite its detailed articulation, ideally the Restatement would be relatively concise among its era's law books. For Joseph W. Beale (the Reporter for Conflict of Laws), a desirable form would be "a little compact book so that it could be carried about, a vest-pocket edition."[11]

And what larger objective motivated this undertaking? The elaborate report submitted to the ALI's 1923 organizational meeting advanced two arguments—not entirely consistent with each other—championing a detailed articulation of the common law over codification: (1) as models, European civil codes and their American counterparts were drafted in unacceptably general language that left too much room for judicial discretion;[12] and (2) by preserving the common law's flexibility, the Restatement would avoid undue rigidity.[13] The second rationale—ensuring flexibility—dominates retrospective accounts of the Restatement's objective.[14] And the ALI's leadership articulated a self-definition for the ALI that underpinned its emergence as a self-perpetuating and distinctly valuable institution. Its multistage deliberative processes, focused on texts drafted with care and expertise, came to define it as an institution more than (or at least as much as) the subject matter or form of its projects.[15]

Like many complex institutions that evolve over time, the ALI responded in its early years to contingencies and crises. In particular, its ongoing relationship with the Carnegie Corporation of New York—which funded the Restatement project—became delicate at times and required difficult choices, some of which shaped the substantive content of the Restatement. Additionally, making the Restatement broadly available meant that the ALI accommodated the commercial demands of the

---

[10] *Id.* at 112–13 (commending "the method of sympathetic usage"; to give work "force and power," it "must be such as to commend itself to the craftsmen of the profession.") (J.W. Davis).

[11] 2 A.L.I. Proc. 56 (1924) (J.W. Beale).

[12] *Report of the Committee on the Establishment of a Permanent Organization for the Improvement of the Law Proposing the Establishment of an American Law Institute*, 1 A.L.I. Proc. 20–21 [hereinafter *1923 Report*] ("The statement of principles should be much more complete than that found in European Continental Codes ... the court ... has a much wider discretion than judges of our own courts" in applying a code, given "the detail in which the law is set forth in prior decisions."). For a rich account of the place of the Restatement project in movements toward codification, *see* Nathan M. Crystal, *Codification and the Rise of the Restatement Movement*, 54 Wash. L. Rev. 239 (1979). On the history and present status of codification in one state (Montana), *see* Andrew P. Morriss et al., *Debating the Field Civil Code 105 Years Late*, 61 Mont. L. Rev. 371 (2000). On the contrasting history in California, *see* Bartholomew Lee, *The Civil Law and Field's Civil Code in Common-Law California—A Note on What Might Have Been*, 5 West. Leg. Hist. 13 (Winter/Spring 1992).

[13] *Id.* at 232 (enactment of principles in legislative codification "would sacrifice either "its flexibility or its fullness of detail ... [w]e fear that if the law stated in this detail were given the rigidity of a statute, injustice would result in many cases presenting unforeseen facts.")

[14] *See, e.g.*, John P. Frank, *The American Law Institute: 1923–1998*, in The American Law Institute: Seventy-Fifth Anniversary 1923–1998, at 3, 11 (1998) ("the goal was to maintain the flexibility of the common law"). On the evolution of the ALI's recognition of the values served by Restatements, as well as changes in the law following completion of the First Restatement, *see* Kenneth S. Abraham & G. Edward White, *The Work of the American Law Institute in Historical Context*, in this volume.

[15] 5 A.L.I. Proc. 55 (1929) (although ALI's "primary object" was "to secure an organization by which an orderly statement of our common law could be produced," it was "still more important" that "the legal profession has learned to organize itself for the constructive improvement of justice in this country") (W.D. Lewis); 10 A.L.I. Proc. 31 (1932), at 31 ("we have in the course of our labors [on the Restatement] developed a technique which we find useful in applying to the study of criminal procedure.") (G.W. Wickersham); Michael Traynor, *The First Restatements and the View of the American Law Institute, Then and Now*, 32 S. Ill. U. L.J. 145, 164 (2007) ("The Institute's strengths are its members and its established processes, stature, independence, and dedication to quality.").

law-book trade and its sales practices. The content of what was published reflects this accommodation. For several states, the ALI published comprehensive Annotations to pre-Restatement cases, which required central coordination. It also required funding and staffing, which came in part through state affiliates of the Works Progress Administration (WPA) and other federal relief programs that funded projects sponsored by state bar associations to employ indigent lawyers during the hard days of the 1930s. Separately, publishing the Annotations—seen as necessary to a viable market for the Restatement—implied that the Restatement's own ex cathedra authority might not always suffice. Additionally, the relatively advanced ages of several of the initial Reporters had substantive consequences. Among them, the death of Floyd Mechem— the initial Reporter for Agency—led to postmortem revisions of a basic doctrinal formulation previously approved by the ALI's Council and members.

Messy episodes like these early in the ALI's history mostly stem from challenges that confronted it as a new private-sector institution dedicated to producing authoritative legal texts. And what was to be done when ALI's commitment to restating "the law as we find it" met precedents followed in a majority of jurisdictions that contemporary lawyers and judges found "barbarous"?[16] During this era, the Restatement—by design not drafted for legislatively enacted codification—was not a mechanism for straightforward change in legal doctrine. By the end of the era recounted in this chapter, the UCC embodied a formal capacity to effect doctrinal change within the province of private law.[17] But other developments underscored the value of the Restatement itself. In particular, by heightening the salience of "local law" in *Erie Railroad Co. v. Tompkins*[18] for common-law cases in federal court, the Court in 1938 assured the collateral consequence of additional impact for the Restatement by directing federal courts to follow local law, or so the ALI's leadership believed. The Restatement would be "especially" salient when the Annotations for a particular state evidenced a close correspondence with Restatement provisions.[19]

The remainder of the chapter proceeds as follows. Section II opens with an account of the initial plan for the Restatement's form and structure and then explores how and why aspects of the initial plan changed over the course of the project. Mutability to this degree appears atypical of projects for legislative codification in which basic issues may be resolved early on. Section III turns to the Reporters for the first Restatement, relationships between their work for the ALI and the individually authored treatises they wrote, and the fortuities that almost inevitably followed. For two subjects (Agency and Contracts), Reporters' treatises preceded work on the Restatement; for

---

[16] *E.g.*, 5 A.L.I. Proc. 324 ("barbarous" rule that marriage terminates authority previously conferred by a woman on an agent) & *id.* at 325 ("I think that there are still several [states] that have the common law rule) (Mechem); 11 A.L.I. Proc. 90 (1933) ("a relic of remote barbarism" that principal's death terminates agent's authority without notice); 12 AL.I. Proc. 295 (1935) ("more or less of a barbarous" rule in Restitution limiting action to covenants in deed when payment made for deed to which transferor had no title) (Seavey); 14 A.L.I. Proc. 90 (1937) (civil action of criminal conversation founded in "entirely archaic barbarous concept of our marriage relation") (Bohlen).

[17] This era in the ALI's history also included work on statutes. These projects—most notably a Code of Criminal Procedure—are beyond the scope of this chapter.

[18] 304 U.S. 64 (1938).

[19] Minutes of the Council [hereinafter CO] Feb. 21–23 1940, at 38 (in *Erie* the Court "unintentionally no doubt" made Restatement "all the more important") (H.F. Goodrich).

Conflict of Laws and Trusts, the Reporters published their treatises midstream. At the risk of overemphasizing individual idiosyncrasies, the section argues that the Reporters' own treatises shaped the Restatement project itself, not just in doctrinal formulation, but sometimes in defining the coverage of Restatements of individual subjects. Likewise, early choices carried ongoing consequences; some Restatement projects overshadowed the scope of other projects, while Reporters' deaths and illnesses had substantive and organizational consequences. The focus shifts in section IV to the ALI itself as it evolved into an institution with a distinct role and mission, one capable of ongoing existence and identified as more than the author of the Restatement. Reaching that point required, among other things, surmounting "the publishing problem"[20] that the Restatement itself posed as well as developing a mature plan for funding independent of particular projects. It also required a substantive agenda capable of sustaining engagement over time, a need met by the UCC and later by the Model Penal Code.[21] A brief conclusion sums up.

II. The Restatement as Planned and How It Evolved: From the Ex Cathedra Text, Past the Treatises, to the Annotations

As described to attendees at the ALI's organizational meeting in 1923, the Restatement over time would "tend to assert itself and confirm itself and to gather authority as time goes on."[22] And mostly it did, but with departures in form and substance from the initial plan, complicated by persistent overoptimism about the time, effort, and funding required to meet commitments. To differentiate the Restatement from treatises written by authors who wrote as mere "photographers" of case citations,[23] the text of the Restatement would be a "direct and simple statement of the law as the Institute declares it,"[24] backed by the ALI's reputation. The text would not cite cases, not even cases supporting the outcome on hypothetical facts stated in an illustration. As work adopted and promulgated[25] by the ALI, the coherence and structure of the text stating authoritative rules—formally reinforced by its bold-face type—would do the work, while also bearing formal similarity to legislatively enacted codifications, whether in Europe or the United States.[26] Accompanying each Restatement—even if not as portable as Joseph Beale hoped—a separate treatise, with the Reporter (not the ALI) as author, would explain the reasoning.[27]

---

[20] CO, May 10–13, 1939, at 10 (H.F. Goodrich).

[21] The Model Penal Code project, begun in 1962, is beyond the scope of this chapter. On the Model Penal Code, *see* Kimberly Kessler Ferzan, *From Restatement to Model Penal Code: The Progress and Perils of Criminal Law Reform*, in this volume.

[22] *Proceedings at the Organization, supra* note 1, at 51 (E. Root).

[23] *1923 Report, supra* note 12, at 20.

[24] 2 A.L.I. PROC. 36 (1924) (W.D. Lewis).

[25] Not "published." Restatements are published by American Law Institute Publishers (ALIP), a separate and still extant entity traceable to a partnership between ALI and two law-book publishers. The ALI holds the copyright. *See infra* text accompanying note 139.

[26] On the significance of form for private codification projects, *see* NILS JANSEN, THE MAKING OF LEGAL AUTHORITY 107–27 (2010).

[27] 2 A.L.I. PROC. 37 (1924) (W.D. Lewis).

The Carnegie Corporation of New York funded the Restatement project.[28] The project, which began in 1923 with an estimated duration of ten years, lasted through 1944.[29] Some subjects had a sole Reporter throughout (Agency, Contracts, Conflict of Laws, Security, and Trusts) or a small team (Judgments and Restitution).[30] Torts and Property, respectively published in four and five volumes, had multiple reporters focused on discrete topics. The ALI began but discontinued Restatement projects in Business Associations and Sales of Land (or "Vendor and Purchaser").[31] By 1930, the Director (William Draper Lewis) had identified a list of additional subjects tentatively believed suitable for coverage in the Restatement, including Public Utilities and Sales of Chattels,[32] for a total of approximately twenty-two titles. Its cost implications doomed this expansion. But although Restatement work "could go on indefinitely," Lewis also noted in 1930 that it was timely to "visualiz[e] the Restatement as a completed whole,"[33] which implicitly assigned even greater importance to transsubstantive matters like consistent terminology and comprehensive indexing. By 1935, the Council's Executive Committee prepared a report on the ALI's future, addressing the content of an "ideal Restatement," which formed the premise of a final grant application to the Carnegie Corporation. The funding that resulted enabled the completion of the multivolume Restatements of Property and Torts, but forced a choice between two other subjects: Business Associations and Security.[34] The choice was Security.[35]

---

[28] Carnegie's initial grant in 1923 of $1,075,000 to support the Restatement project was later augmented for a total of $2,419,196.90, plus $25,000 toward support of the organization itself and $10,000 to support the "local annotations" project. See William Draper Lewis, "How We Did It," in HISTORY OF THE AMERICAN LAW INSTITUTE AND THE FIRST RESTATEMENT OF LAW 5 (1945). Overall through 1948, the Carnegie Corporation's committed grants to the ALI add up to more than $2.7 million. Richard L. Revesz, The Continuing Support of Our Founding Donor, ALI ADVISER, Apr. 20, 2021. Elihu Root, prominent in the ALI's founding, was a trustee of the Carnegie Corporation from 1919 until his death in 1937. Root succeeded Andrew Carnegie as the Corporation's president in 1911, serving until 1919, and had represented Andrew Carnegie as a private lawyer. For specifics of the ALI's ongoing relationship with the Carnegie Corporation, see infra text accompanying notes 155–65. On Root's role in securing the grant and his mentorship of William Draper Lewis, the ALI's initial Director, see N.E.H. Hull, Back to the "Future of the Institute": William Draper Lewis's Vision of the ALI's Mission During Its First Twenty-five Years and the Implications for the Institute's Seventy-Fifth Anniversary, in THE AMERICAN LAW INSTITUTE: SEVENTY-FIFTH ANNIVERSARY 105, 115 (1998).

[29] 2 A.L.I. PROC. 19 (1924). Adjusting for interim inflation, in today's dollars Carnegie's support would be more than $43 million. Revesz, supra note 28.

[30] Austin W. Scott and Warren A. Seavey were the Reporters for both; Erwin N. Griswold served as Assistant Reporter for Judgments. Seavey succeeded Floyd R. Mechem as the sole Reporter for Agency; Scott was the sole Reporter for Trusts.

[31] Samuel Williston, the Reporter, took on this subject following completion of the Contracts Restatement. Williston's separate commitment to edit the Annotations, see infra text accompanying notes 67 and 131, slowed his work on Sales of Land. He resigned from the project due to poor health. Minutes of the Executive Committee of the Council [hereinafter EC], Feb. 1, 1936, at 3.

[32] 9 A.L.I. PROC. 52 (1930) (W.D. Lewis). The additional estimated cost was $1.5 million.

[33] Id.

[34] Report of the Executive Committee to the Council on the Future of the Institute, 12 A.L.I. PROC. APPX. 409–30 (1935). As defined in the report, "Security" concerns "the law relating to all transactions in which the performance of a promise by a principal is secured either by the promise of another or by an interest in land, chattels, or choses in action." Id. at 416.

[35] Lewis, the Reporter for the discontinued Restatement of Business Associations, explained the situation otherwise in his retrospective account: looking at the subjects covered by the Restatement, a knowledgeable reader may wonder at the omission of "the common law partnership and the Law of Corporations ... The

When funding ran short to complete that Restatement, a further choice followed, as between suretyship and mortgages (suretyship won).[36]

The ALI's distinctive processes helped assure quality but did not come for free. Each Restatement had its distinct cohort of Advisers[37] who met with the Reporter and Director Lewis when the Reporter had a draft of new material and, sometimes and in smaller groups, to consider revisions to draft material. Advisers' meetings, or "Conferences," could run over several days, especially in the summer. Like the Reporters, Advisers received payment for their work. The carefully detailed documentation of this group work is an indication of its seriousness for the participants and the ALI itself. The ALI dispatched a stenographer (usually Louise C. Peters) to each meeting who took minutes; on-site or back at ALI headquarters in Philadelphia she transcribed and typed them up, using onion skin and carbon paper sets, for distribution to each Restatement's Advisers and Reporter.[38] Given the meetings integral to each group's work, projects with multiple distinct groups had cost implications; as of 1933, the Torts project cost more than any other over the preceding two years.[39] Additionally, Property and Torts took longer to complete than did other subjects.

Present at almost all of these meetings (and many others as well), and crucial to coordination, quality control, and enforcing consistency in usage and recurrent definitions, Director Lewis "lived a peripatetic life," in the assessment of Samuel Williston, the Reporter for Contracts.[40] In summer time, Lewis convened meetings at his summer home in Maine, housing meetings from 1930 onward in a "portable

---

reason for the omission was that corporations have their origin in statutory enactment. There was a fear that if undertaken the work could not be successfully carried on; that a considerable portion of our funds might therefore be wasted." Lewis, *supra* note 28, at 22. To be sure, these considerations might have prompted the choice of Security. Lewis's work as Reporter concluded with draft provisions on the creation of shares presented to the Annual Meeting in 1932. CO, Dec. 14–16, 1932, at 24. Discontinuing the Business Associations project responded to the overall demands on Lewis: "The increasing pressure of my work as Director necessarily made the work proceed very slowly...." *Id.* at 25. Nonetheless, Lewis remained "convinced that it is possible for the Institute to do most valuable constructive legal work by producing a comparatively short statement on Corporations for Profit...." *Id.*

[36] CO, Feb. 21–25, 1939, at 22.

[37] For Property and Torts, the composition of each cohort varied by volume and subject-matter divisions within volumes.

[38] EC, Oct. 22, 1926, at 4 (describing post-conference process). Louise C. Peters, the ALI employee who "took the majority of the stenographic notes" at these meetings, plus (unaided) all discussions at Annual Meetings from 1929 to 1942, resigned as of December 1944. EC, Nov. 28, 1944, at 2. This occasion marks the formal acknowledgment in ALI's internal minutes of her work and its importance. ("In looking back over our work on the Restatement ... we realize that what Mrs. Peters has done for the Institute has been an essential element in its success.") Apart from Peters and her colleagues in support roles at ALI headquarters, the first woman to play an acknowledged role in ALI's work is Soia Mentschikoff, appointed as a Legal Assistant to the UCC's Chief Reporter Karl Llewellyn in 1942 (EC, Dec. 19, 1942, at 38) and, in 1944, Assistant Reporter on the UCC's Sales article (CO, Feb. 22, 1944, at 2).

[39] CO, Dec. 14–16, 1932, at 31 (for current year, estimated cost of $21,900).

[40] SAMUEL WILLISTON, LIFE AND LAW: AN AUTOBIOGRAPHY 313 (1940, reprint ed. 1998) ("He attended the conferences on every subject, so that he was away from his Philadelphia home a large part of the time."). Lewis may have welcomed his travels. Reporting on his train trip to Seattle in summer 1928 for an ABA meeting, he applauded the "Canadian Pacific route," on which "one can get a compartment or drawing room without extra train fare, so I was able to put in four undisturbed good days" of work. EC, Oct. 20, 1928, at 14.

house" constructed at ALI's expense.[41] In general, the progress of the Restatement as a singular work produced through discrete projects—several conducted at the same time—required ongoing mechanisms to further coherence. Although the ALI was aware of the importance of consistent terminology from the start,[42] and despite the impact of Lewis's pervasive presence, occasional meetings among multiple Reporters proved necessary to "smooth out differences" among their formulations.[43] Not all differences in definition were resolvable this way. The initial Reporter for Torts (Francis Bohlen) "reserved the right to question" the Agency draft's definition of "independent contractor" when the question became important to the Torts Restatement.[44] And some pervasive terms and concepts (like "notice") were "troublesome."[45]

The original plan coupled each Restatement with a separate explanatory treatise written by the Reporter as its author to contain citations to case authority and, when the cases diverged, explain the route taken by the Restatement. Treatise drafts would accompany Restatement drafts for review by each project's Advisers and at Annual Meetings; both would be published simultaneously. The treatise component of the plan required arrangements in 1923 with publishers for the two Reporters who had already published definitive treatises—Floyd R. Mechem (Agency) and Williston (Contracts)—because the Restatement treatises were likely to be based on their prior publications.[46] Beale, yet to publish his treatise on Conflict of Laws, had it well underway. In exchange for $4,000 in 1923, he transferred rights to his work-in-progress to the ALI. Beale surrendered his accumulated treatise materials to Lewis, who had them inventoried and then transferred custody back to Beale, with the materials to remain in a steel cabinet to be purchased by Lewis, except when Beale used the materials for ALI purposes.[47] By 1925, work on the treatises had been reduced relative to work on the Restatements themselves[48] and unresolved questions remained, including the extent to which the treatises would be sufficiently standardized.[49] Not all reporters cooperated with the treatise component of the initial plan; Mechem submitted no material for a treatise to accompanying the Restatement volume on Agency.[50] At the end of 1925, the Council confined work to the Restatement itself, with treatises to provide

---

[41] CO, May 7, 1930, at 7 ("The Director is authorized to have erected a portable house with a room approximately 12 X 15 feet, at a cost not exceeding $1000 for use as a conference room at Northeast Harbor, Maine …"). The cost for the portable house was charged against the general administration account as an item of "Office Furniture and Equipment." For ten years, Williston spent a week at Lewis's property each summer. WILLISTON, *supra* note 40, at 313. He reports the presence of two "portable houses … placed among the trees on the shore" of a sound. *Id.*

[42] *E.g.*, 4 A.L.I. PROC. APPX 46 (1926) (important that recurrently occurring words and expressions "stand for the same thing throughout") (W.D. Lewis).

[43] *E.g.*, EC May 2, 1931, at 5 ("labor" of Beale "at least technically concluded" following conference to "smooth out differences" with Agency and Torts Restatements).

[44] EC, Oct. 14, 1927, 6 A.L.I. PROC. 92–93. This subsequent inquiry does not appear to have happened. *See* text *infra* accompanying note 109.

[45] CO, Apr. 28–May 1, 1926, *in* 4 A.L.I. PROC. 22 (1926).

[46] EC, May 19, 1923, *in* 1 A.L.I. PROC. 37.

[47] EC, June 29, 1923, *in* 2 A.L.I. PROC. 118–19. The cabinet was to bear the ALI's name.

[48] CO, Apr. 30–May 1, 1925, *in* 3 A.L.I. PROC. 38.

[49] 2 A.L.I. PROC. 44–45 (noting likelihood that treatises will vary).

[50] CO, Dec. 16–19, 1925 at 20. Mechem may have viewed such a treatise as unnecessary because his two-volume work, published in 1914, was readily available. For more on Mechem's treatise, *see infra* text accompanying notes 89–90, 92–96, and 113.

explanatory material but not comprehensively to parallel Restatement provisions.[51] Likely not coincidentally, the same meeting noted that three of the Reporters were over the age of sixty[52] as well as the costs entailed by a commitment to publish the treatises. Although minutes from ALI's internal meetings do not reveal whether Beale returned the $4,000 when his treatise materials (and the rights to them) were returned to him in 1933,[53] his salary in that period is noticeably less than the amounts authorized for other Reporters.[54]

John Frank's retrospective assessment is convincing: the plan for simultaneous treatises was "a pie-in-the sky concept," feasible only for Reporters who had already written a treatise or had one well underway, while "for a Reporter who did not already have his treatise in his pocket ... the task was simply impossible."[55] As a consequence, beginning in 1932 with the publication of Contracts, the Restatements were "authoritative without authorities," comprising succinctly written doctrinal articulation and brief commentary.[56] Periodically, the Council requested more from Reporters— lists of authorities for their Advisers, explanatory notes—but no consistent practice emerged. By the time the Council and its Executive Committee took up the question of publishing explanatory notes, it was too late for Contracts (already published) and unrealistic for Agency, which was headed toward a firm deadline for publication.[57]

Formally, the Restatements resembled legislatively enacted codifications of doctrine, testing the power of ex cathedra text.[58] Perhaps this outcome was welcome at the time.[59] Two decades later, discussion at the 1953 Annual Meeting turned to a draft definition of charitable trusts that chose between two different lines of authority, prompting a member's request that the text acknowledge the choice. The ALI's President (George Wharton Pepper) responded: "There has been a change of thought on that subject during the life of the Institute. At the start, it was thought to be wise to secure for the black letter ... a certain ex cathedra authority to suppress any mention of competing doctrines or dissent or any question of authorities which would raise a question about the soundness" of the Restatement's doctrinal formulation.[60] With time, "we have become more realistic...."[61] Three years later, the ALI's Director

---

[51] CO, Dec. 16–19, 1925, 3 A.L.I. PROC. 409–10.

[52] Id. at 409, noted in Frank, supra note 14, at 15.

[53] CO, Mar. 6, 1929, at 7 (Beale "anxious to make an arrangement with a publisher for the publication of his treatise...").

[54] Compare EC Oct. 18, 1930 ($2,500 Reporter's salary for Conflict of Laws; $5,000 salary for Reporters for Agency and Contracts), with CO, Dec. 5, 1924 ($5,000 salary for Reporters for Conflict of Laws, Contracts, and Torts).

[55] Frank, supra note 14, at 14–15.

[56] Id. at 14.

[57] EC, Dec. 1, 1933, at 5 (For Beale and the Conflicts Restatement, unclear whether it would be "fair" to ask him; Herbert Goodrich, also working on Conflicts, was too busy.) Perhaps not "fair" because the ALI's relationship with Beale likely soured when the Council took charge of a draft. EC Oct. 20, 1933 at 5 ("careful scrutiny" given to draft by Council; "more than a mere courtesy due Mr. Beale" to send him a copy of the results with an "opportunity ... to make any observation thereon he desires").

[58] 2 A.L.I. PROC. 37 (1924) (noting that Restatements would be characterized by some as "speaking 'ex cathedra'") (W.D. Lewis).

[59] The "poverty of references" in Restatement drafts attracted external criticism. 5 A.L.I. PROC. 106 (1927) (G.W. Wickersham).

[60] 30 A.L.I. PROC. 50 (1953).

[61] Id.

(Herbert F. Goodrich, who succeeded Lewis) stated he saw "no profit at all in discussing whether" the initial Restatements would have been better had they been less ex cathedra.[62]

Qualifying the claim that the Restatements spoke ex cathedra, as early as 1927 Lewis acknowledged that "somebody is going to get out annotations to these Restatements. That is bound to come."[63] Leaving their production to commercial law-book publishers would be unsatisfactory, Lewis argued. Authors engaged to research and write annotations would be insufficiently familiar with the ALI's terminology, while commercial publishers' incentives would not further simplification as opposed to multiplying citations.[64] Better then to encourage state bar associations, working in conjunction with the ALI, to sponsor the production of "local annotations" summarizing state-law cases keyed to Restatement provisions. Along with precluding efforts from commercial publishers, the local-annotations project had additional motivations. For the Restatement to gather authority through judicial citations and its use by lawyers, more familiarity with its substance within state bars could only help. Working on annotations served as a commitment device that bonded lawyers to the Restatement, while the availability of annotations helped sales of Restatement volumes in a state, as ALI's publishing partners emphasized.[65] Moreover, the Annotations responded to lawyers' skepticism. The ALI's President (George W. Wickersham) told the 1935 Annual Meeting that "the force of habit of the American legal mind," even when confronted by statements of the law produced by the best legal minds, is to "desire[] to go back through the welter of cases and put himself in the position of those who produced these formulations of the law," to confirm their accuracy.[66] Additionally, lawyers may have been skeptical because they understood that their professional obligations to clients required caution in relying on a novel secondary resource like the Restatement.

Although the ALI distanced itself from formal authorship of the Annotations, it published them and worked to maintain quality. Production of Annotations always lagged the Restatement volumes. Goodrich served as the designated liaison with state bar associations, which varied in keenness and capacity to undertake the project. Samuel Williston (his work on the Contracts Restatement concluded), edited the Annotations and was praised for his tact in working with their authors.[67] The annotators' work necessarily involved a great deal of drudgery, requiring proceeding page-by-page through the digests for particular subjects, sometimes aided by lists of cases furnished by Reporters.[68] But annotation work also required imagination and

---

[62] 33 A.L.I. PROC. 43 (1957) (H.F. Goodrich) ("The Restatement appeared.... It has been successful and it has had a very great influence on the development of the law").

[63] Minutes of Conference of Co-operating Committees of Bar Associations and Specially Invited Persons, Oct. 27, 1927, in 6 A.L.I. PROC. 53.

[64] Id. at 54.

[65] For more, see infra text accompanying notes 140–43.

[66] 12 A.L.I. PROC. 49 (1935) (G.W. Wickersham).

[67] CO, Dec. 18–21, 1933, at 56 (lauding Williston's "gracious urbanity" as editor in ironing out problems) (H.F. Goodrich).

[68] CO, May 8, 1935, at 15 ("The work itself is unmitigated drudgery") (H.F. Goodrich). To be sure, legal scholarship in this era—including that conducted by Restatement Reporters and treatise authors—required stamina in light of the then-available research methodologies.

intellectual agility to organize relevant cases by Restatement sections and then draft a concise and accurate summary of each case.[69]

As a consequence, staffing the Annotations remained a challenge throughout, as did funding.[70] Despite an initial failure to interest the Carnegie Corporation in making an additional grant toward the costs, Carnegie eventually contributed.[71] The ALI itself funded some of the work, as did its publishing venture, American Law Institute Publishers (ALIP).[72] Further support during the Depression of the 1930s came through projects sponsored by state affiliates of federal relief programs—including the WPA and the Civil Works Administration (CWA)—directed toward employing indigent lawyers. In 1934, Lewis and Goodrich traveled to Washington, D.C., to urge the CWA program administrator to extend a Minnesota program to other states.[73] In time, federal relief support ended;[74] by 1943, as law professors and young lawyers joined the war agencies and military services, Goodrich thought the outlook for more annotations in the immediate future was "not very good."[75] And thus the program of local annotations ended. By this time judicial citations to the Restatement itself sufficed to populate a separate book of annotations, *The Restatement in the Courts*, produced by the ALI's own staff and organized state by state.[76]

III. Early Choices and Later Fortuity: Reporters, Their Treatises, and Restatement Projects over Time

The ALI's ongoing challenge of securing the Restatement's identity and authority, tied to but distinct from the Reporters, stemmed from its ambition to produce authoritative legal texts as a private-sector organization. Lewis emphasized to the 1927 Annual Meeting that the Restatements represented "distinctly group work," noting that some Advisers had effectively become Reporters' collaborators,[77] and later reinforcing the point at the 1934 Annual Meeting by characterizing the Restatements as a "group project."[78] To be sure, much work *was* done within groups of Advisers and with Lewis—all those meetings and successive drafts—but each Restatement volume was also personalized to its respective Reporter. Seen in retrospect, Reporters who undertook a Restatement with a treatise already published or well underway were "essentially codifying the treatises with the Restatements...."[79] On the other hand, two large

---

[69] EC, Apr. 10, 1934, at 5.

[70] By 1940, in order to "round out" an Annotations program, Goodrich urged focusing on states that combined extensive territory with light accumulations of cases plus directly employing "a competent person to produce as much manuscript as possible" to be reviewed by the local bar association. EC, Dec. 21, 1940, at 26.

[71] Lewis, *supra* note 28, at 5.

[72] For more on ALIP, *see infra* text accompanying notes 140–44.

[73] EC, Feb. 10, 1934, at 5. Lewis's retrospective account of producing and funding the Annotations does not mention WPA and other relief programs as sources of support. Lewis, *supra* note 28, at 12–13.

[74] CO, Feb. 23–26, 1943, at 13.

[75] CO, Feb. 23–26, 1943, at 47.

[76] *See, e.g.,* CO, Feb. 23, 1943, at 37 (purchasers of year's Restatement volume to receive paperbound supplement to *The Restatement in the Courts*).

[77] 4 A.L.I. PROC. APPX. 37 (1926).

[78] 11 A.L.I. PROC. 329 (1934).

[79] Frank, *supra* note 14, at 14–15.

Restatement projects (Torts and Property) undertaken by Reporters without a treatise of their own—or even a comprehensive contemporary work by another author— took much longer to complete. No doubt this was due in part to the scope of Property and Torts as subjects, but the absence of an already elaborated analytic structure to serve as a starting point cannot have helped. Relatedly, the coverage of the Property Restatement remained an open question from its start in 1926 well into the 1930s.[80]

Additionally, in defending their drafts before the ALI's membership in successive Annual Meetings, the Reporters visibly personified each Restatement volume, which muddled distinctions between their authority as Reporters, which was derivative of the ALI's, and their stature based on their own publications, including their treatises. In turn, by defining the field for inquiry, the Reporters' treatises likely shaped the results when "the law as we find it" underwent restatement. Separately, proceeding simultaneously with multiple Restatement projects—some later discontinued—had implications for the coverage of individual Restatements. And death and illness among the ranks of Reporters inevitably shaped the projects.

No doubt it came as welcome news to the Executive Committee in 1923 that Samuel Williston was, not just willing, but "anxious" to undertake the work of Reporter for the Restatement of Contracts.[81] Published in three substantive volumes in 1920, Williston's *The Law of Contracts* was well received by practicing lawyers and the judiciary, following Williston's 1909 treatise on the law of sales of goods.[82] Beginning in 1902, at the request of the Commissioners on Uniform State Laws, Williston drafted the Negotiable Instruments Law[83] and the Uniform Sales Act (1906).[84] Beyond Williston's professional stature, in the assessment of the ALI's Council's Executive Committee, his treatise on contract law, which "exhaustively set forth" the law, tended to clarify it,[85] with the consequence that "[i]t will make the task of restating the law … far simpler that it would otherwise be."[86] And work could proceed expeditiously; Williston anticipated when appointed in 1923 that a draft of a "considerable part" of the Contracts Restatement could be ready for consideration at the ALI's Annual Meeting tentatively scheduled for February 1925.[87] Likewise, when Floyd Mechem was designated the Reporter for the Restatement of Agency, the Executive Committee acknowledged his stature as "the one person pre-eminently fitted" to serve.[88] His treatise was "accorded an authority by the courts unexcelled if indeed equaled by that accorded to any other legal treatise."[89] Published in 1914, Mechem's second edition remains the last treatise on agency law in the United States of comparable depth and scope.[90]

---

[80] *Report on Future of Institute, supra* note 34, at 418–19.

[81] EC, May 5, 1923, *in* 1 A.L.I. PROC. 62 (1923).

[82] WILLISTON, *supra* note 40, at 263–64.

[83] *Id.* at 219. *See also* SAMUEL WILLISTON, THE LAW GOVERNING SALES OF GOODS AT COMMON LAW AND UNDER THE UNIFORM SALES ACT (1909) (post–Sales Act treatise).

[84] WILLISTON, *supra* note 40, at 222.

[85] EC, May 19, 1923 at 62 (statement of Council to Carnegie Corporation).

[86] *Id.*

[87] *1923 Report, supra* note 12, at 93–94.

[88] *1923 Report, supra* note 12, at 97–98.

[89] *Id.*

[90] *See* FLOYD R. MECHEM, A TREATISE ON THE LAW OF AGENCY: INCLUDING NOT ONLY A DISCUSSION OF THE GENERAL SUBJECT BUT ALSO SEPARATE CHAPTERS ON ATTORNEYS AUCTIONEERS BROKERS AND FACTORS (2d ed. 1914). For more on Mechem himself and his successor, Warren A. Seavey, *see* Deborah

The relationship between the Restatements and the Reporters' treatises can be characterized in substantive terms, as "codifying" legal doctrine as stated in the treatises into Restatement form.[91] Focusing on the Mechem and Williston treatises suggests an additional relationship that also shaped the Restatements for Agency and Contracts, as Reporters' prior publications (regardless of format) likely shaped other volumes as well: the Reporters' treatises defined the scope of inquiry into the law, a prerequisite to "restating the law as we find it." Exhaustive treatments of their subjects the treatises undoubtedly were, but only within the ambit defined by the author. For both treatises, that was the common law, mostly from the United States but with due regard for English precedents. Neither treatise inquired into doctrine as codified in the civil code states in the United States, paralleling its omission from the Restatements. This approach carried pitfalls, as an example from Agency demonstrates.

In fairness, Mechem's treatise acknowledges early on that "several states have statutory statements of the law of agency as part of a general code."[92] An Appendix to Mechem's second volume, preceding the Table of Cases and Index, contains verbatim the language of the Codes' agency law provisions. However, doctrinal analysis in the body of the treatise does not address the Code provisions, just as they go unmentioned in the Restatement. Most of the time, the omissions are of no moment because the substance of the Code provisions falls in line with the Restatement's formulations.

But not always. In the Restatement, section 138 defines a power given as security, that is, "the power to affect the legal relations of another, created in the form of an agency authority, but held for the benefit of the power holder or a third person and given to secure the performance of a duty or to protect a title. ..."[93] Unlike actual authority in an agency relationship, a power given as security cannot be terminated through revocation by its creator.[94] Powers given as security are valuable in many commercial contexts because they are less fragile than authority in common law agency relationships.[95] Neither Section 138 nor the counterpart treatment in Mechem's treatise[96] acknowledges that the California Civil Code defines an irrevocable power "given as security" substantially more narrowly, by requiring that such a power be "coupled with an interest in the subject matter of the agency."[97] As a consequence, irrevocability requires that the power holder possess a proprietary interest in the "subject matter of the agency"; and the power must be held by the person who holds the interest, not another person or an affiliated entity.[98] The California Annotations to the Restatement

A. DeMott, *The First Restatement of Agency: What Was the Agenda?*, 32 So. Ill. U. L.J. 17 (2007) [hereinafter DeMott, *The First Restatement*]; Deborah A. DeMott, *The Contours and Composition of Agency Doctrine: Perspectives from History and Theory on Inherent Agency Power*, 2014 Univ. Ill. L. Rev. 1813 [hereinafter DeMott, *Inherent Agency Power*].

[91] Frank, *supra* note 14, at 14–15.
[92] Mechem, *supra* note 90, vol. 1, at 11. On the Codes and other precursors to the Restatement, *see* Seipp, *supra* note 5.
[93] Restatement of Agency § 138 (1933).
[94] *Id.* § 139.
[95] For a contemporary account of powers given as security and irrevocable proxies to exercise voting rights in securities or membership interests, *see* Restatement (Third) of Agency §3.12 (2005).
[96] Mechem, *supra* note 90, at 405–19.
[97] Cal. Civ. Code § 2359.
[98] *See* Pacific Landmark Hotel, Ltd. v. Marriott Hotels, Inc., 23 Cal. Rptr. 2d 555, 561 (Cal. App. 1993).

of Agency—published in 1937, four years in the Restatement's wake—note the discrepancy, commenting that "[t]he [California] cases leave serious doubt as to whether [the Code provision] is the equivalent of 'powers given as security' as used in Section 138."[99] Thus, relying solely on the Restatement's articulation of "the law as we find it" could be perilous, especially for lawyers unfamiliar with local law.

The perceived linkage between Reporters' treatises and their Restatements may be closest for Conflict of Laws. Beale's three-volume treatise on Conflict of Laws,[100] published in 1935, and the one-volume Restatement, published in 1934, were often reviewed together.[101] Overall, Goodrich told the Council, the Restatement "has been pretty well received"; reviewers who entirely rejected Beale's approach "were unhappy" with the Restatement, while those "more thorough[ly] Bealian than Mr. Beale himself" were displeased by instances in which the Restatement "departed from the Reporter's theory."[102] Writing retrospectively in 1945, Lewis nominated one subject by name for "revision with advantage" in work to succeed the first Restatement: Conflict of Laws.[103] Change in the law itself, of course, could warrant revision; but it would also serve to distance the ALI from Beale as an individual author.[104]

Early on, the Executive Committee recognized the "practical advantage" in having work on Agency, Contracts, and Torts proceed at the same time to enable frequent conferences among Reporters, given Agency's "intimate[]" connection to the other subjects.[105] Although contemporaneous work on all three subjects (plus others) facilitated overall coherence within the Restatement, it also led to midstream relocations of topics as well as overhang effects given the sequencing and pace of work within each project. For example, as between Torts and Agency, at the 1925 Annual Meeting Lewis noted that "we have had to decide under which subject shall be treated the liability of the master to the servant for the master's or the fellow servant's negligent act."[106] At least tentatively, this issue (addressed in the fellow servant rule) went to Torts.[107] But the Agency Restatement, notwithstanding internal upheavals of its own, proceeded on schedule to final publication in 1933, and included the fellow servant rule.[108] And

---

[99] I CALIFORNIA ANNOTATIONS TO THE RESTATEMENT OF THE LAW OF AGENCY 108 (1937). *See also* Hawkins v. Daniel, 273 A. 3d 792, 810 n. 21 (Del Ch. 2022) (noting disparity between California and common law rule in dispute concerning irrevocable proxy; Delaware follows common law rule).

[100] JOSEPH W. BEALE, A TREATISE ON THE CONFLICT OF LAWS, 3 vols. (1st ed. 1935). Beale also published a one-volume work in 1916. *See* Joseph W. Beale, A TREATISE ON THE CONFLICT OF LAWS OR PRIVATE INTERNATIONAL LAW (1916).

[101] CO, Feb. 12, 1936, at 25 (Goodrich).

[102] *Id.* at 25–27. On Beale's theory itself and the Restatement, *see* Symeon C. Symeonides, *Conflict of Laws in the ALI's First Century*, in this volume.

[103] Lewis, *supra* note 28, at 21.

[104] Beale died on January 20, 1943. The Council statement memorializing him acknowledges that it was a "foregone conclusion" that Conflicts would be a subject included in the Restatement and that Beale would serve as Reporter, combining "wide knowledge of the decisions" with a "clear concept of the subject as a whole." CO, Feb. 23, 1943, at 8.

[105] *1923 Report, supra* note 12, at 97.

[106] 3 A.L.I. PROC. at 126–27 (1925).

[107] *Id.* at 127.

[108] RESTATEMENT OF AGENCY § 474 (1933) (subject to exceptions, "the master is not liable to his servant who, while acting within the scope of his employment or in connection therewith, is injured solely by the negligence of a fellow servant in the performance of acts not involving the performance of the master's nondelegable duties....").

neither Bohlen nor a fellow Torts Reporter appears to have pursued Bohlen's stated concern, noted earlier, about the definition of "independent contractor" in drafts of the Agency Restatement.[109]

The Torts Restatement took much longer to complete. Bohlen's incapacitation from mid-1937 onward led to delays and required reorganizing the work, including adding a fifth working group.[110] As it happens, the Reporter helming that group—Seavey—served throughout as an Adviser to the Torts Restatement, in addition to his work on Agency as an Adviser and then the Reporter, a further connection between the projects that may have diminished the significance of situating individual topics. When Lewis explained the ongoing reorganization of work on Torts to the Executive Committee, he noted that Seavey had been asked to suggest additional Torts topics for inclusion (Seavey served as the Reporter for the Division covering Miscellaneous Rules). For Lewis, "among [Seavey's] good qualities is fertility in the suggestion of situations which may arise in any field of law in which he is dealing,"[111] a trait relevant to Seavey's recurrent presence in multiple working groups.

Although the Agency Restatement includes topics earlier allocated to Torts, it also omits some that strike contemporary readers by their absence. Most prominent are situations in which an agent represents, not an individual person as principal, but an entity of some sort. This omission—which persists in Restatement of Agency (Second) (1958)—attracted inquiry at the 1926 Annual Meeting. In response to a member who questioned why the draft did not cover the appointment of an agent for a corporation, Mechem replied, "that was thought to belong in Mr. Lewis's Business Associations...."[112] The coexistence of that project (discontinued in 1933) likely asserted an overhang effect on Agency's coverage. But the overhang may not entirely explain the omission. Mechem's treatise itself does not deal with corporate officers or, for the most part, with the implications when an agent represents a principal that is not an individual.[113] Thus, and independently of any overhang over Agency asserted by the Business Associations project, the Reporter's treatise likely circumscribed the ambit of inquiry to exclude instances of agency relationships outside the treatise.

Additionally, up until the final draft submitted to the ALI's members in 1933, the Agency Restatement defined apparent authority as did Mechem's treatise, as a power to affect the principal's legal relations when a principal negligently causes a third party to believe the agent possesses authority, entirely distinct from the agent's actual authority that the principal intentionally confers on the agent.[114] Based on his treatise, for Mechem apparent authority bore a close relationship to deceit or fraud as a basis

---

[109] See supra text accompanying note 44.

[110] CO, Feb. 22–26, 1938 at 17. On the ALI's relationship with Bohlen after this point, see infra note 159. Seavey served as sole Reporter for Chapter 47 (Damages) and for Divisions 11 (Miscellaneous Rules) and 12 (Defenses Applicable Against All Tort Claims).

[111] EC, Apr. 30, 1938, at 3.

[112] 4 A.L.I. PROC. APPX. at 162 (1926).

[113] Not that corporations go entirely unmentioned. See, e.g., MECHEM, supra note 90, at § 130 (noting that private corporations have power to appoint agents; "[t]he existence of the agency and the effect of the agent's acts ... are subject to the same rules which apply to individuals.").

[114] MECHEM, supra note 90, at 514. The treatise illustrates this with a diagram featuring concentric circles, with "Declared or Express Authority" at its core. Id. at 515. Never do (or could) the lines defining the circles intersect.

for a principal's liability to a third party;[115] an agent acted with apparent authority only when the principal's manifestations to the third party concerning the agent's authority diverged from those made to the agent. Requiring divergent manifestations to agent and third party excluded the possibility—known as "lingering apparent authority"— that an agent might appear to have authority following the principal's revocation of authority when the third party lacked notice of the revocation. It also excluded the possibility that an agent might act throughout with *both* actual and apparent authority but the third party could prove the presence of apparent authority much more readily on the basis of manifestations made to it, not internal manifestations as between principal and agent.[116]

Floyd Mechem died in December 1928; Seavey's appointment as the successor Reporter rapidly followed.[117] Seavey, an Adviser from the project's beginning, had become increasingly dominant within the Agency group.[118] The final draft of the Agency Restatement presented to 1933 Annual Meeting redid the basic definition of apparent authority.[119] Defending the final draft, Seavey said of Mechem, "I do not think he quite appreciated at the time the consequences" of his definition of apparent authority.[120] Nor, it seems, did anyone else at that earlier time.[121]

Finally, individuals who served as Reporters themselves—and distinct from their Restatements once published—changed over time in many ways, occasionally distancing them from the ALI and its evolving mission. In his autobiography, published in 1940 when he was seventy-nine years old, Samuel Williston wrote in a mellow tone of codification: "It is certainly probable that at least the partial codification which we already have will be extended to other subjects."[122] The Restatement itself "can serve as a foundation for a code which would surely be superior to anything which could be struck off as an original enactment."[123] One year later, Williston's tone was not mellow when he dispatched written objections focused on the UCC project that the ALI was about to undertake jointly with the National Conference of Commissioners on Uniform State Laws (NCCUSL). Focused on a revision of the Uniform Sales Act, the proposal, in Williston's assessment, contemplated a lengthy process of state-by-state enactment, followed by uncertainty: "Even if the substance of the old rules is preserved, if they are stated in a statute in new words, litigation is invited.... Amendments

---

[115] *Id.* at 512.

[116] For this rationale, *see* RESTATEMENT (THIRD) OF AGENCY § 2.03 cmt. c. (2006).

[117] EC, Dec. 19–22, 1928, at 2 & 27 (acknowledging Mechem's death and appointing Seavey as successor Reporter).

[118] For examples, *see* DeMott, *Inherent Agency Power, supra* note 90, at 1823–24.

[119] *Compare* RESTATEMENT OF AGENCY § 8 ("Apparent authority is the power of an apparent agent to affect the legal relations of an apparent principal with respect to a third person by acts done in accordance with such principal's manifestations of consent to such third person that such agent shall act as his agent") (1933), *with* RESTATEMENT OF AGENCY § 10 ("Apparent authority is the result of the manifestation by one person of consent that another shall act as his agent, made to a third person, where such manifestation differs from that made to the purported agent") (Tentative Draft No. 1 1926).

[120] 11 A.L.I. PROC. at 79–80 (1933) (discussing revision to Section 8). No comments came from the floor.

[121] When Mechem presented the draft—155 sections long—to the 1926 Annual Meeting, no questions or comments from the floor concerned the definition of apparent authority. 6 A.L.I. PROC. APPX. 152–53. Efforts to date to locate a set of minutes from the relevant Advisers' Conference have failed.

[122] WILLISTON, *supra* note 40, at 316.

[123] *Id.*

should, therefore, never be made without real necessity."[124] Distributed at two successive meetings of the Executive Committee,[125] Williston's objections did not dissuade its members from proceeding. His 1941 objections precede, by almost a decade, Williston's published denunciation of the Code—by that time in full draft form—in particular Article 2 codifying the law on sales of goods.[126] Although prior scholarship dates Williston's opposition to 1950,[127] he stated his position and elaborated his grounds to the ALI's Director and Executive Committee in 1941.

In Williston's published assessment, the UCC draft contained provisions "not only iconoclastic but open to criticisms I regard as so fundamental as to preclude the desirability" of enacting Article 2, if not the entire Code.[128] To be sure, Article 2 would also supersede the Uniform Sales Act (drafted by Williston) but it would also represent "the codification of a large portion of the law, where provisions are expressed in novel phraseology" repealing "statutes that have had years of judicial construction...."[129] For William Twining, Williston's published critique is "a typical example of a conservative defense of the *status quo*."[130] But Williston's history within the ALI is also relevant to understanding his opposition. After all, sequencing the Contracts volume first, with Williston as its Reporter, was seen as crucial to the success of the larger Restatement venture. And notwithstanding his advanced age, Williston soldiered on through 1943 to edit the Annotations, again lending his stature and seasoned judgment to a project crucial to the Restatement's credibility and commercial prospects.[131]

But Williston's opposition to the UCC project failed to persuade the ALI's leadership. Might Williston's opposition also have anticipated the ALI's evolution into sponsorship of a large-scale codification of private law, as well as the specifics of Article 2? After all, introducing new terminology to govern "a large portion of the law" and revamping its substance is just what a code can accomplish. When the ALI's Executive Committee received Williston's 1941 objections, the challenge of articulating an

---

[124] EC, Aug. 29–30, 1941, App. A headed "MEMORANDUM OF ARGUMENTS PART IV In re CODE OF COMMERCIAL LAW." This text, typed on onionskin paper, does not identify the author, but that it is Williston is evident from the minutes themselves. The format implies that Lewis's practice was to have material he received retyped for distribution. The next item in Appendix A is a letter to Lewis from Schnader, *see infra* text accompanying note 166, dated August 22, 1941, reporting the "particularly good news" that Karl Llewellyn was "highly enthusiastic" about the Code as a joint project of ALI and NCCUSL.

[125] EC, May 2, 1942, at 10, referring to distribution of Williston's "objections" at meeting and at Executive Committee meeting on Aug. 29–30, 1941.

[126] Samuel Williston, *The Law of Sales in the Proposed Uniform Commercial Code*, 63 HARV. L. REV. 562 (1950).

[127] *See, e.g.*, Robert L. Flores, *Risk of Loss in Sales: A Missing Chapter in the History of the UCC: Through Llewellyn to Williston and a Bit Beyond*, 27 PAC. L.J. 161, 166 (1996) (Williston's "famed opposition to the Code came in 1950, when he was nearly ninety years old").

[128] Williston, *supra* note 126, at 562.

[129] *Id.* at 562.

[130] WILLIAM TWINING, KARL LLEWELLYN AND THE REALIST MOVEMENT 287 (2d ed. 2012). And "Williston lived a long time ..." Mark L. Movsesian, *Rediscovering Williston*, 62 WASH. & LEE L. REV. 207, 223 (2005).

[131] EC, June 18, 1943, at 9 (Williston to supervise and edit state Annotations through December 1, 1943, at a salary not to exceed $500). When Reporters were asked in the mid-1930s to identify candidates for statutory fixes, Williston singled out some prospects from Contracts. *See Report on Future of Institute, supra* note 34, at 426 (noting that Williston had already drafted a proposed Uniform Written Obligations Act and a draft statute allocating risk of loss in contracts to sell real property to the seller unless the buyer is in possession).

agenda for the ALI's future work, beyond completing the Restatement, loomed large. Director Lewis was aware by then that Karl Llewellyn—Reporter for NCCUSL's revision project for the Uniform Sales Act—was enthusiastic about linking in the ALI. William Schnader, NCCUSL's president,[132] announcing Llewellyn's enthusiasm to Lewis, went further, observing that "the Institute's participation in this job is necessary to really round out the Institute's work on the Restatement."[133] In short, perhaps Williston's institutional affinity for the ALI went only so far.[134]

IV. The American Law Institute as an Ongoing Institution: From the "Publishing Problem" of the Restatements to Institutional Stability

Early on, the ALI's leadership recognized both that an annual membership meeting was imperative and that the agenda of the meeting must include "matters of first importance" for discussion.[135] Once the ALI introduced dues for members, the significance of the content of the annual agenda went beyond sustaining members' engagement with the ALI's work. The Restatement itself had succeeded by the mid-1930s on many criteria: increasing acceptance by courts, as evidenced by citations in published opinions, plus mostly favorable reviews and strong sales of its individual volumes. The volumes published by 1935 sold in numbers "far larger than ... any other legal text book...."[136] Contracts alone, Lewis announced in 1934, had the greatest sales volume for any law book;[137] to his professed surprise, one year following its publication, Agency's sales equaled those of the Contracts volume at the same point.[138] Toward the end of the decade, as the Restatement was still far from completion and money was tight for the ALI and its projects, the Restatement itself (notwithstanding its sales) was central to the ALI's financial woes. And apart from funding issues, what could sustain the ALI as an institution going forward following the completion of the Restatement? Restatements of additional subjects? Revisions to already published volumes, like Conflict of Laws? Further work on criminal-justice statutes? Their individual importance undeniable, a steady diet of these possibilities could fall short of the ambition represented by a commitment to work on "matters of first importance."

From its start in 1923, the ALI was clear that it would hold the copyright to its publications; the title page would give Reporters "due credit."[139] But the ALI itself would

---

[132] *See infra* text accompanying notes 166–69.

[133] EC, Aug. 29–30, 1941, App. A (letter dated Aug. 22, 1941 to Lewis from Schnader).

[134] Nor was Williston the only prominent participant to defect when the ALI's evolution became unacceptable. For William Prosser, the Reporter for Restatement (Second) of Torts, the ALI to which he presented a draft in 1969 "was not quite the same" as it had been in 1965 when the ALI adopted Prosser's draft section on products liability. Confronted by the success of a motion at the 1969 Annual Meeting directing him to revise the draft's treatment of private nuisance, Prosser retired as Reporter soon after. Abraham & White, *supra* note 14, at 66.

[135] *1923 Report, supra* note 12, at 93.

[136] *Report on Future of the Institute, supra* note 34, at 412.

[137] 11 A.L.I. PROC. 329 (1934).

[138] "We were, of course, aware of the singular fact that many lawyers do not regard the law of Agency with equal seriousness...." *Id.*

[139] CO, May 19, 1923, 1 A.L.I. PROC. 28 (Council Resolution 31).

not serve as the publisher. It formed a partnership for that purpose with two commercial publishers (West Publishing Co. and Lawyers' Co-Op Publishing). With Goodrich as ALI's representative, the board of ALIP met for the first time in 1932 and entered into publication contracts for the Contracts and Agency volumes.[140] Timed for September publication in 1932 and 1933 (and thus the prospect of law school usage), Contracts and Agency set a pattern to be followed for the remainder of the volumes. This consisted of staggering the release of individual volumes at predictable intervals,[141] a pace that would not swamp the market. ALI's partners, grounded in their commercial experience, shaped some ALIP decisions; neither ALI members nor judges received complimentary copies of Restatement volumes, and no price discount was offered to members.[142] ALI's partners in ALIP also underscored the importance of a firm commitment to publishing a volume per year, as Goodrich duly communicated to the Executive Committee.[143] A reliable publication schedule mattered to law book dealers, whose representatives (including their traveling sales forces) needed books to sell to their customers on a predictable basis. A reliable publication schedule also helped to secure much-prized standing orders to purchase successive Restatement volumes.[144]

ALI's partners in ALIP also emphasized the importance of the Annotations to making the Restatement volumes marketable. As Goodrich summarized the stakes for the Council in 1934, doing state annotations—to pre-Restatement cases keyed to numbered Restatement provisions—represented a "gigantic task," but the success of the work on the Restatement depended on it "to no slight degree."[145] As detailed earlier, viewed on an intellectual plane, the Annotations were important to overcoming lawyers' skepticism; on the plane of commercial publishing, the Annotations were crucial to selling Restatement volumes into a lawyers' market that valued case citations. Sales in states with Annotations for Contracts and then Agency greatly exceeded sales in states with no Annotations,[146] although ALIP charged more for Restatement volumes packaged with Annotations.[147]

The Annotations also made the Restatement "a publishing problem," in Goodrich's assessment. Having encouraged state bar associations to cooperate with it in producing Annotations, the ALI had "a strong moral obligation" to publish them.[148] Restatement volumes themselves had been priced with the objective of attaining maximum circulation, as well as the "friendly" support of the law book trade.[149] The inaugural Contracts volume was priced to sell, "as low as it was safe to make it," but

---

[140] CO, Feb. 25–27, 1932, at 10.

[141] 11 A.L.I. PROC. 326 (1934).

[142] CO, Dec. 14–16, 1932, at 38.

[143] EC, Apr. 17, 1943, at 11 ("very unfortunate if the Institute should fail in this connection," comment occasioned by potential delay in scheduled publication of a Property volume).

[144] Standing orders were prized because they secured future sales without additional marketing effort on a per-volume basis. Internal shorthand termed the business they represented the "S.O.B." list, which carried "no sinister significance." EC, Oct. 22, 1932, at 20 (H.F. Goodrich).

[145] CO, Dec. 18–21, 1933, at 17.

[146] Id. at 54 (sales in "Annotations" states "far outstrip" sales in other states) (H.F. Goodrich).

[147] See infra note 150.

[148] CO, May 10–13, 1939, at 11.

[149] Id. at 10.

"complicated by the Annotations problem" because their potential market was mostly limited to single states, which varied in market size, all to be sold at the same uniform price.[150] To produce the Annotations required the ALI's support, while publishing them represented a net loss to be carried by the Restatement given the pricing structure. And, Goodrich informed the Council in 1939, it was unanswerable whether "the enterprise" was profitable at that time.[151]

Over time, as the annual march of Restatement volumes continued and the Annotations program ended, ALIP became profitable, paying ALI $10,000 as its share of profits in 1944.[152] By that time, the ALI's overall financial condition—along with questions about its substantive program going forward—had compelled a series of decisions about itself. Writing on the occasion of the ALI's 75th anniversary in 1998, John Frank reassured readers that it was "thoroughly solvent," its condition of being "adequately but not excessively financed"[153] funded through a combination of membership dues and contributions, publication sales and revenues, grants for projects, and investment income.[154] These indicia of financial stability and continuity for a private-sector institution did not typify the ALI's early years. In addition to limited revenue stemming from publications, the ALI lacked an endowment and did not charge its members dues or seek financial contributions from them.

Delicate episodes in the ALI's ongoing relationship with the Carnegie Corporation shaped the ALI's resolution of issues central to its ongoing existence, beginning with how to fund its own operations, including its central office and the costs associated with holding Annual Meetings.[155] Throughout the relationship, Carnegie exercised active oversight. In 1930, it directed an inquiry into whether improvements might be made in the economy and efficiency with which Restatement work proceeded;[156] the amount of its initial appropriation would be exhausted by the end of 1931.[157] Satisfied by the investigation's findings,[158] Carnegie funding continued. In 1933, Carnegie asked whether it might be possible to reduce the salaries paid to Reporters.[159]

---

[150] EC, Oct. 22, 1932, at 19–20. The Contracts volume was priced at $6, with an additional charge of $3 for Annotations for a particular state, bound with the Restatement volume as a pocket part. When separately bound, the Annotations cost $1 more.

[151] CO, May 10–13, 1939, at 12.

[152] EC June 10, 1944, at 3 ($10,000 payable by ALIP to ALI upon receipt to be credited to Maintenance Fund, which supported central operation).

[153] Frank, supra note 14, at 27.

[154] Id. at 28.

[155] The Carnegie Corporation now characterizes its grant-making during this period as "marked by a certain eclecticism and perseverance in its chosen causes." See https://www.carnegie.org/about/our-history/past-presidents/#keppel (last visited July 8, 2022).

[156] CO, Feb. 22–24, 1930, at 25–26.

[157] 8 A.L.I. Proc. 53 (1930). On the magnitude of Carnegie's financial support, see supra text accompanying notes 28–29.

[158] CO Dec. 18–21, 1930, at 20–21 (reason to believe ALI was "doing the work economically and efficiently").

[159] EC, Oct. 20, 1933, at 25. Following Bohlen's incapacitation in 1937, he was paid for his ongoing availability to consult with other Reporters from his home, up through the end of 1938, with the approval of Carnegie's president. EC, June 9, 1938 at 11. Ingrid K. Bohlen, Francis Bohlen's wife, wrote a letter dated December 26, 1938, stating gratitude for "ALI's generosity in keeping up these monthly payments for so many months after all hope of activity on Mr. Bohlen's part was gone." She reported that Bohlen was unable to write and had not dictated the letter. Lewis read Mrs. Bohlen's letter to the Council. CO, Feb. 22–25, 1939, at 59. Memorializing his lifelong friend, Lewis wrote after Bohlen's death that "[h]e lost health and fortune

A special committee appointed by the Executive Committee, including the President (George Wharton Pepper), conceded that at the outset Reporters' salaries may have been "overgenerous";[160] but by 1933, to cut Reporters' pay risked "dampened enthusiasm" for the task just when the pressures on Reporters were most intense.[161] By 1938, Carnegie determined it would not fund either an endowment for ALI or the extension of the Restatement beyond the subjects included in its prior agreement.[162] Facing a projected deficit for 1938, the ALI sold securities it held.[163] Carnegie's final grant in 1940 enabled the completion of the Judgments volume of the Restatement and the continuation of ALI's central-office operations through June 30, 1941.[164] The grant came coupled with the condition that ALI secure funding for its ongoing operations as a going concern from its members through membership dues or members' contributions.[165]

Separately, sustaining its members' engagement and justifying the ALI's ongoing existence required an agenda of "matters of the first importance." Although various topics and projects were under discussion, the ALI embraced the UCC project in 1942. William A. Schnader—NCCUSL's president and a member of ALI's Council—wrote in fall 1941 inviting ALI's cooperation "in the production of a Uniform Commercial Code," a project NCCUSL already had underway.[166] In winter 1942, Schnader spoke to the Council at length about the proposed code and the ALI's participation; a majority of the Council gave their unqualified support.[167] Fundraising began, backstopped by Schnader personally and his law firm.[168] The Council accepted the proposal in May 1942, subject to funding, and elected the Reporter (Karl N. Llewellyn) a member of the ALI.[169]

At the 1942 Annual Meeting, Lewis told the members that "the law relating to one commercial subject can be solved in a more satisfactory manner if it is dealt with as part of a complete code, rather than if it is treated separately."[170] Lewis also noted the

---

at practically the same time." William Draper Lewis, *Francis Hermann Bohlen*, 91 U. PENN. L. REV. 377, 379 (1943).

[160] The rate was $5,000/year.

[161] EC, Oct. 20, 1933, at 25 (concluding that any cut of over 10% would be "unthinkable" and a 10% cut would save only $2,500 overall).

[162] CO, Feb. 22–26, 1938, at 5.

[163] CO, Feb. 22–26, 1938, at 7 ($10,000 in bonds).

[164] CO, Feb. 21–23, 1940, at 7.

[165] EC, Oct. 26, 1940 at 22. Annual dues ($10) began in 1941. EC, Feb. 17, 1941, at 4.

[166] EC, Nov. 1, 1941, at 5. That summer, Schnader wrote to Lewis of Llewellyn's enthusiasm for ALI's involvement. *See supra* text accompanying note 133. Earlier, in 1935, ALI and NCCUSL entered into a co-operation agreement for statutory projects of potential interest to both organizations. EC, Dec. 17, 1935, at 7. The relationship encompassed a proposed statute on Aeronautical Flight. The Council decided not to submit the draft statute to the Annual Meeting because the statute "involve[d] matters of controversial public policy affecting a growing industry," as opposed to obvious defects in substantive law; the cost of any further consideration would need to be met from sources other than the Carnegie grant. CO, May 11–14, 1938, at 14.

[167] CO, Feb. 24–27, 1942, at 36. One member (Daniel M. Kirby) was "willing to co-operate should the Institute take the work, [but] felt it was embarking in the field of legislation with which he had no experience, but that if the Institute did proceed with this work it should change its flag." *Id.*

[168] EC, May 2, 1942, at 9–10.

[169] CO, May 11–15, 1942, at 2–3.

[170] 19 A.L.I. PROC. 47 (1942).

hoped-for growth postwar in trade between the United States and "nations south of us ... [e]ach of which has its code of commercial law."[171] As a consequence, legislative codification became the form for a significant portion of the ALI's work going forward, notwithstanding the objections to the UCC project expressed by Samuel Williston. Likewise, ALI's geographical orientation, as Lewis made explicit, shifted in a cosmopolitan direction to encompass Code jurisdictions, away from the sole focus on English common law antecedents[172] and their legacy in the United States.

V. Conclusion

Viewed from today's vantage point, the Restatement succeeded, but the story is messier, one overall shaped by resilience in light of contingencies of all sorts. That there is no general civil code for the United States—and none waits in the offing—could mean the Restatement succeeded in staving off an intrusion of codification, leaving the United States a "common-law" country. But the ALI itself evolved into an institutional champion of codification by embracing the UCC as a code encompassing a major swath of economic activity, albeit not a "complete code" in the terminology Lewis used in 1942.[173] Additionally, multiple relationships emerged between Restatements in particular subjects and statutes. For example, innovative provisions in the UCC's Article Two shaped the content of the Second Restatement of Contracts.[174] And the successive Restatements of Trusts furnished language that trusts legislation directly incorporated, with Restatement (Third) of Trusts and the Uniform Trust Code " 'drafted in close coordination.' "[175]

Separately, uncertainty about what the law may be on any particular point of private law does not beset contemporary lawyers with epistemic anxiety. To be sure, the Restatement helps as a well-organized secondary authority but so do dramatic advances in the technology of legal research that would have mitigated the drudgery required to produce the Annotations. Restoring a fuller history for the ALI's early era does not diminish the magnitude of its accomplishment, but it underscores that what then mattered so much—the assumed opposition of the common law and legislative codification—carries lower stakes now, accustomed as we are to working in a legal milieu in which they coexist.

The fuller history demonstrates that the both the Restatement and the institution that produced it were works in progress during the ALI's early era, as was the form of

---

[171] Id.

[172] For Williston, Article 2 of the Code was additionally problematic because it broke from the English statutory precedent, the 1893 Sales of Goods Act, which had served as his model in drafting the Uniform Sales Act. Williston, *supra* note 126, at 563–64.

[173] The UCC excludes important commercial-law topics; for example, Section 9-109(a)(1) makes its application to collateral effective only for security interests in personal property and fixtures. More generally, Section 1-103(a) expressly embraces "principles of law and equity" not displaced by particular Code provisions. Thanks to Steven Schwarcz for raising these points.

[174] Robert E. Scott, *The Uniform Commercial Code and the Ongoing Quest for an Efficient and Fair Commercial Law*, in this volume.

[175] Naomi R. Cahn, Deborah Gordon, & Allison Tait, *The Restatements of Trusts—Revisited*, in this volume, at 153.

its work. Additionally, paradox is a recurrent element in the story of the ALI and the defining accomplishment of its early era. An exemplar of ex cathedra text emerged—unaccompanied by the treatises contemplated by the original plan—but that text partnered with case annotations in several states—the Annotations—themselves necessitated by the demands that commercial publishing imposed on an organization at least partially rooted in disdain for law books that catered to a lawyers' market. A private-sector institution, which some hoped would keep control over private law with "craftsmen of the profession," turned to public relief programs of the New Deal to complete its work. And the Reporters, crucial to the ALI's institutional authorship of the Restatement, were not themselves entirely submerged as authors within it. All considered, perhaps it's a lesser paradox that an institution cast as a defender of the common law realm of private law came to champion extensive codification. Finally, by informing our understanding of the ALI as an institution, as well as the evolution of its work, the fuller history demonstrates the value of maintaining and preserving archival resources. From its early days onward, likely the ALI's leadership varied in awareness that the ALI might (and should) become a subject of historical inquiry; although the eyes of history could always explore yet more material, enough survives to tell a somewhat messier story.

PART II
RESTATEMENTS

5

Canon and Fireworks

Reliance in the Restatements of Contracts and Reliance on Them

Richard R. W. Brooks[*]

A Voice: "What is the law?"

I. Introduction

That voice asking "what is the law"—a voice resident inside the head of every lawyer and a regular visitor to laypeople everywhere—on May 1, 1925, called out loudly from a Washington, D.C., ballroom. It was regarding "the sort of question on which lawyers do differ every time it comes up," said Mr. Lewis, who had been reading aloud draft sections of what would become the Restatement of Contracts at the Annual Meeting of the recently formed American Law Institute (ALI).[1] There were differing opinions about what the law was or should be streaming in from the ALI Council and the Advisers and the Associate Reporters for the nascent restatement. It was from this confluence of competing visions of the law that the voice shouted: "What is the law?"[2] Not what was the law or what should be the law, the voice pointedly demanded of Mr. Lewis, but what *is* the law? To which Mr. Lewis, looking to the man next to him, said, "I rather have the habit, when it comes to saying what the law is all over the United States, of leaning on my friend Williston."[3]

It was the great fortune of William Draper Lewis, Director of the ALI, to have been sitting next to Samuel Williston, his friend and more importantly the unquestioned authority on the U.S. common law of contracts. Williston knew the answer, of course, but the bigger problem was that most lawyers, judges, law teachers, and laypeople

[*] New York University School of Law. This chapter has been greatly improved by my reading the thoughtful writings of Barbara Black, Moshe Halbertal, and David Seipp, and even more so by the insightful and generous comments they have each shared with me. I am also indebted to Andrew Gold and Robert Gordon for their many suggestions and countless tolerances. Thanks also to Deborah DeMott, John Goldberg, Robert Scott, and the many participants at the ALI conferences in the spring and summer of 2022 who read and helped me revise early drafts. Christine Park, an extraordinary librarian at NYU Law School, deserves more credit than space will allow here, and my sincere appreciation to Omar Andron, Amelia Goldberg, Travis Long, and Cara Maines for their research and reading assistance.

[1] *Minutes of the Third Annual Meeting Held at Washington, D.C.—May 1 and 2, 1925*, 3 A.L.I. Proc. 82, at 198.

[2] *A Voice: What Is the Law?*, 3 A.L.I. Proc. 82 (1925), at 199.

[3] *Id.*

didn't have Lewis's good fortune. They had no comparable authority ready at hand that could clarify and state the law currently throughout the country. It was this void that the restatements project was meant to fill, to create an authoritative source that anyone could turn to when beginning an inquiry into the common law, the common law across the entire United States. Now on the 100th year following the ALI's launch of its ambitious project to restate the sprawling common law of the states, it is noteworthy the degree to which legal education and practice has come to rely on the Restatements (First and Second) of Contracts.[4] As the first published Restatement of Law and one of the ALI's most high-profile projects, the ways in which the Restatements of Contracts have been received, described, and criticized reveal much about the ALI's history and its aspirations. A number of these aspirations, perhaps unsurprisingly, have fallen short, but the first Restaters could hardly have imagined the influence that their Restatement would come to exert on the course of contract law over the next century.

There were, to be sure, high expectations of the project from the start. "Its objective is nothing less than the restatement of our common law," wrote one contemporaneous observer, while another gushed that it was "the most authoritative effort in two thousand years to summarize and state existing legal principles."[5] An audacious assertion, tending on overstatement and revealing a common law conceit, eliding, for instance, the great law projects commissioned by emperors Justinian and Napoleon on the principles of Roman and civil law. A more reserved expression of the Restatement's aspirations and objectives is found in its introductory comments:

> [T]o promote the clarification and simplification of the law and its better adaptation
> to social needs, to secure the better administration of justice and to carry on scholarly
> and scientific legal work.[6]

Taking a more distant assessment of the Restatement's own stated ambition, it's difficult to deny its success as measured by the degree to which it has become a source of reliance for anyone commencing a search for the U.S. common law of contracts. From first-year law students to scholars and practicing lawyers, as well as judges and other arbiters sitting in domestic and foreign tribunals, they all turn to the Restatements of Contracts as their point of departure for finding the basic principles of our contract doctrine. It is no exaggeration to say that the Restatements of Contracts have achieved the status of a canon. Not a canon in some loose or metaphorical sense, but in the most authentic sense of the term: a body of texts through and around which knowledge of the common law of promissory exchange is acquired, debated, and refined.

Asserting that the Restatements of Contracts are canonical is not meant to draw allusions to sacred texts. Quite the opposite. These texts are avowedly profane—designed

---

[4] The plural "Restatements of Contracts" (or simply "Restatements") will be used here in reference to both Restatements (First and Second) of Contracts. The singular "Restatement of Contracts" (or simply "Restatement") will refer to the Restatement (First) of Contracts.

[5] Charles E. Clark, *The Restatement of the Law of Contracts*, 42 YALE L.J. 643, at 644, n.2 and accompanying text (1933) (quoting "From 'Radio Program of the American Bar Association' announcing President Wickersham's address on May 7, 1933, on 'Restating the Law; an Attempt at Simplification.'"

[6] RESTATEMENT (FIRST) OF CONTRACTS, Introduction (1932) (referring to "[t]he object of the Institute as expressed in its charter.").

and intended for practical people dealing with everyday legal issues as they unfold in courtrooms, boardrooms, law classrooms, or anywhere else in our earthbound world.[7] At the same time, however, the Restatements were never meant to be a mere collection of rules for reference and rote learning. At the launch of the first meeting where the ALI membership would discuss and debate early drafts of the contracts Restatement, the Vice President of the ALI, Benjamin Cardozo, shared with the audience the charge that had been given to Williston and his fellow Reporters. He summed it up in three sentences, each of substantially increasing length and content: "Be bold. Be ever bold. Be not too bold."[8] They were encouraged to speak definitively and firmly when restating what they took to be the established rules and doctrines of contract law.[9] Furthermore, they were not to hold back stating when, in their judgment, the law was not yet settled or unclear.[10] Most importantly, and exposing them to greatest risk, they were tasked to go beyond isolated cases in search of controlling principals of law across the whole country and then restate them not too boldly as vague abstractions but rather precisely as defensible propositions.[11] In that task, even at this early date in their venture, Cardozo felt they had already braved ground where others "made wary by many an ambush" would not think to tread. "By the form and method chosen, the framers of the restatement have courted danger and defied it."[12] They were, however, just beginning, and many questions remained. One above all others.

What is it to restate the law? Surely it is not the mundane task of inscribing legal text onto pages bound in sumptuous red leather volumes or in other encasements like the stele of Hammurabi's Code now standing regally in the Louvre, commanding attention and nothing else.[13] To restate the law is not to pronounce a code or to procure an artifact.[14] Reviewing in 1933 the recently published Restatement, Edwin Patterson presciently described its chief and continuing value as offering a "framework for

---

[7] "It is intended for the use of practical people," proclaimed Samuel Williston, the Reporter of the Restatement of Contracts, in his opening comments before the first ALI meeting discussing the project. 3 A.L.I. PROC. 82, at 160.

[8] *Id.* at 106.

[9] "[L]et us give definiteness and fixity of outline where there is definiteness and fixity in the law as it exists or where argument so preponderates that a choice is fairly safe." *Id.*

[10] "Let us not hesitate, however, in other situations to say in all frankness that the problem is yet unsolved, and while indicating competing considerations either way, to leave the answer to the years." *Id.*

[11] "It is hard enough," Cardozo said of the judicial task, "to declare the rights and wrongs engendered by a concrete situation." *Id.* at 99. "It is harder still when, abandoning particulars, we must announce in magisterial tones the rationalizing principle in which particulars are enveloped, the co-ordinating rule under which they are subsumed." *Id.* at 99.

[12] *Id.* "In the fierce light that beats upon these categorical propositions, standing stark and unprotected in the open, there is room for truth and for error, but seldom for half truth or truth unwilling to declare itself." *Id.*

[13] The first Restatement was "[b]eautifully bound in red leather in two volumes," observed then Dean Clark of the Yale Law School, "with a price appropriate to its sumptuous setting." Clark, *supra* note 5, at 643.

[14] "'Restatement' does not mean merely the putting of an old rule into new words; so far as old rules still prevail, it is generally wise to retain the old words thereof. It means the discovery and statement of the rules of uniformity as they exist today." Arthur L. Corbin, *Restatement of the Law of Contracts*, 14(10) A.B.A. J. 602, 603 (1928). Williston echoed the statement: "I quite agree that old language should be used if it can be used without sacrifice of accuracy." 3 A.L.I. PROC. 82, at 180. However, when old language misses the mark, a Restatement will often require more than repackaging of judicial statements; it often entails a search and synthesis of statements that have eluded prior expressions of the law, even in cases where judges otherwise apply the rules correctly. *See infra* note 44 and accompanying text.

discussions of case-law and in formulating a large number of broad propositions which gain meaning not from the concreteness or precision of their terms as much as from their relations to other propositions in the set."[15] Meaning here is gained not from stated propositions of law, suggested Patterson, but in situating, discussing, and ultimately in restating them.

Active readers of Restatements are themselves restating law. That is its value. Those propositions appearing in its texts are not to be relied on as if they were incontrovertible statements of fact. "Dogmatic statements wherever they are found, in court opinions, in learned treatises, in official 'Restatements,' cannot be relied on," cautioned Corbin.[16] Restatements are *just* restatements of law, which when done well are the principal mode of discovery and learning in the common law. To restate the law is an attempt to refine prior statements of the common law and thereby to improve our knowledge of it, which will invite further restatements of later stated law since no law can be perfectly stated. Restating the law is an ongoing endeavor, as argued in the first half of this chapter, and in this endeavor the Restatements have become an indispensable guide, a canon for framing discussion and debate among seasoned practitioners and serious students of law as well as those just starting to discover the U.S. common law of contracts. They rely *on* the Restatements in the way readers of other canonical texts engage and learn from those sources, even if only to contest them.[17]

In the second half of this chapter, attention is turned to the subject of reliance *in* the Restatements. That numerous doctrines of reliance can be found throughout both the First and Second Restatements of Contracts is unsurprising. Reliance is everywhere in contract, so readily observable it is easily taken for granted or as often overlooked. Throughout history, reliance has "furnished an indispensable factual core" for enforcing contracts, both formal and informal.[18] Samuel Williston was well aware of this history, an awareness bolstered further by his fellow Reporters and reflected in their work on the Restatement. Appreciation of reliance as a traditional and continuing basis for enforcing promises which are at their core contractual, regrettably, has been displaced in sensational and still-ongoing debates over the more peripheral matter of reliance on gratuitous promises. To some extent it was only natural that attention would be drawn to the exotic "promissory estoppel" as it was predominantly viewed. Though the Reporters did not use the term in stating the black-letter doctrine (originally in Section 88), its debut at the Mayflower Hotel in 1926 was undoubtedly the cause célèbre at the fourth Annual Meeting of the ALI. In the following years it remained the center of conversation as it was largely anticipated to be the Restatement's

---

[15] Edwin W. Patterson, *The Restatement of the Law of Contracts*, 33 COLUM. L. REV. 397, at 402 (1933).

[16] *Corbin on Contracts*, §78 (1963), at 335.

[17] Relying *on* the Restatements does not imply deferring to (or not doubting or questioning) the bold statements that the Reporters were encourage to make, yet notwithstanding Corbin's caution, there may still be too much of that sort of reliance. *See* Shyamkrishna Balganesh, *Relying on Restatements*. 122 COLUM. L. REV. 2119 (2022) (critiquing reliance by courts on the Restatements broadly, and in specific cases, in their use of restatement black letter and other texts in legal reasoning reflected in published opinions). As Balganesh notes, reliance doesn't require deference, but failing to rely, for instance, by not reading or referencing the Restatements in some contexts may raise eyebrows, as Fred Schauer suggests in his chapter, precisely because of its canonical status. Frederick Schauer, *The Restatements as Law*, in this volume.

[18] Lon L. Fuller & William R. Perdue Jr., *The Reliance Interest in Contract Damages: 1*, 46 YALE L.J. 56, at 67 (1936).

most novel contribution. Yet some others saw it as more anomaly than novelty.[19] That distinction mattered little to most observers. Discussion of promissory estoppel seemed to draw nearly all attention away from the extensive manner in which the Restatement recognized and continued to build on more traditional notions of reliance as a basis of contractual liability.

When the promissory estoppel doctrine was finally published in the 1932 Restatement (by then as Section 90) it had no official comments and only a few illustrations, which only further added to its mystique. During the lead up to its publication, however, it had "already become somewhat famous," wrote Charles Clark, "as representing some modification of the ancient rules of consideration."[20] With the spotlight trained on the controversy of enforcing relied-upon gratuitous promises as contracts under Section 90, the more traditional reliance doctrines for contract enforcement were obscured.[21] Those older reliance doctrines now out of view, it became easier for a relatively new doctrine of consideration ("enshrined" in Section 75) to assume the mantle as the "ancient" rule. In the way these two rules, Sections 90 and 75, engaged with one another (not in the schizophrenic or combustible "matter and anti-matter" manner that Grant Gilmore suggested), they have conspired to obscure the centrality of reliance as a once and continuing core independent ground for contract enforcement, as well as a once and continuing core basis of consideration.[22]

Traditionally, consideration was observed in actions recognizing a benefit granted to a promisor from a promisee's reliance (debt) or a detriment suffered by a promisee in relying reasonably on a promise (assumpsit). Reliance was for centuries intricately part and parcel of the consideration doctrine until a distinctly American theory sought to limit consideration to bargains made irrespective of reliance. After noting the revolutionary nature of this bargain theory, which would become "enshrined" in Section 75 of the Restatement, Gilmore quipped "[t]here is never any point in arguing with a successful revolution."[23] There's a hint of redundancy here, like that expressed in "sufficient consideration." Comment a of Section 71 of the Restatement (Second) tells us if

---

[19] "A so-called 'promissory, estoppel,' although not so termed, was held sufficient by Lord Mansfield and his fellow judges as far back as the year 1765. (Pillans v. Van Mierop, 3 Burr. 1663.) Such a doctrine may be an anomaly; it is not a novelty." Allegheny Coll. v. National Chautauqua County Bank of Jamestown, 246 N.Y. 369, 159, at 178 (1927) (Kellogg, J. (dissenting)).

[20] Clark, *supra* note 5, at 656.

[21] It is important to emphasize that Section 90 (in its peculiar form) was what was novel or whatnot, rather than the notion of gratuitous promises being enforced through estoppel or reliance, especially but not only in the case of charitable subscriptions. This point is elaborated further in section III.C of this chapter.

[22] GRANT GILMORE, DEATH OF CONTRACT 60–61 (1974).

[23] *Id.* at 21. Gilmore was making a more subtle point with the usage, which he had earlier elaborated elsewhere:

> There is no point in arguing with a revolution. It may be that whatever can be pulled down ought to be pulled down; if it is no longer strong enough to withstand assault, it should be replaced by something that is. In this sense any successful revolution is self-justifying: by its success it has revealed the inadequacies of what it has replaced. We may have a romantic attachment to the old regime but we should not let it cloud our thought about present reality.

Grant Gilmore, *Products Liability: A Commentary*, 38 U. CHI. L. REV. 103, 116 (1970).

it's sufficient then it's consideration, and if it's not, it's not.[24] Similarly, it is only called a revolution when it's successful, and when it's not, it's not. In the latter case it's merely a rebellion or less. How successful was the rebellious "bargain for" requirement before it was enshrined in the Restatement? Citing Langdell's 1880 treatise for a statement of the theory, Patterson wrote (in 1933) that while judicial holdouts remained, "[t]he bargained-for test of consideration long ago established its supremacy in academic circles," but there too, in fact, the circle was less complete than he suggested.[25]

Speaking before the Commissioners on Uniform State Laws in 1925, the same year Section 75 was first presented at the ALI Annual Meeting, Williston spoke with frustration about the "considerable number" of faculty, including notables at Harvard and Yale, who continued to resist the bargained-for consideration doctrine:

> There are a considerable number of men teaching law who denounce the doctrine of consideration with all their force. Wherever they get a chance to hit it, they hit it, for instance Dean Pound of Harvard and Professor Corbin of Yale.[26]

Dean Pound and Professor Corbin were indeed hitting against consideration, at least in the bargained-for form that Williston defended, and so were many others engaged in the battle over the role of reliance in the doctrine. These battles were ongoing and reflected in debates in the academy and at the ALI meetings. Defenders of reliance as a substitute or support for consideration made their strongest arguments in cases of half-completed exchanges and in other situations where reliance without enforcement would appear to sanction injustice. In cases of wholly executory agreements, however, there was no actual reliance to entangle the pure bargain theory. Yet, here too reliance could support the bargain theory. "To say that each promise is given in reliance upon the other would not seem to be stretching legal theory too far," as Harriman suggested; it is not implausible to say that "the consideration must be an act done in reliance on the promise[.]"[27] Bargain theorists were not amused.

When Williston presented Section 75 to the ALI membership in 1925, there was significant resistance in the audience and no doubt among some Reporters. But it went through, and its victory signaled doom to some defenders of reliance.[28] "It once seemed a great achievement to 'reduce' consideration to the formula of bargained-for detriment to the promisee [yet] thus 'reduced,'" as Karl Llewellyn warned, "[t]he principle threatened in addition all enforcement based on subsequent reliance."[29] In

---

[24] "Thus 'consideration' refers to an element of exchange which is sufficient to satisfy the legal requirement; the word 'sufficient' would be redundant and is not used." RESTATEMENT (SECOND) OF CONTRACTS § 71 cmt. a.

[25] Patterson, *supra* note 15, at 416.

[26] *Proceedings, 35 Handbook of the National Conference of Commissioners on Uniform State Laws and Proceedings of the Annual Conference Meeting* 56 (1925), at 308.

[27] EDWARD AVERY HARRIMAN, ELEMENTS OF THE LAW OF CONTRACTS (1896) at 80–81 (section entitled "*Consideration Must Be Furnished in Reliance on the Promise.*").

[28] Comment b of Section 75 would later clarify the Reporters' intent to eliminate reliance as a form of consideration in favor of the bargained-for requirement alone. "The fact that the promisee relies on the promise to his injury, or the promisor gains some advantage therefrom, does not establish consideration without the element of bargain or agreed exchange." RESTATEMENT (FIRST) OF CONTRACTS § 75 [Definition of Consideration] cmt. b (1932).

[29] Karl N. Llewellyn, *The Rule of Law in Our Case-Law*, 47 YALE L.J. 1243, at 1262 (1938).

the following year, as is well known, the Reporters filled a number of the gaps created by strict adherence to the bargain theory with a set of black-letter rules designed to enforce contracts absent consideration, most notably Section 90 (erstwhile Section 88 in 1926).[30] What was less well known and noted, however, are the numerous reliance-based doctrines in the Restatement, such as Section 45, operating at the core of contract law, not displaced by the bargain theory, but soon to be overshadowed by the novel reliance doctrine in Section 90. The central aim of the second half of this chapter is to reveal this broader scope of reliance in the Restatements and the distortion of reliance caused by Section 90's doctrine of promissory estoppel.

II. Reliance *on* the Restatements

It is a peculiar feature of complex societies that seemingly intractable problems are often met with too many answers rather than too few. "The world is saturated with deity and with law," wrote Ralph Waldo Emerson, an overabundance of authorities rendering "the Law"—the true law, already elusive enough—all the more difficult to find in a crowded field of imperators and impersonators.[31] Amid all the hubbub, the allure of simplicity, that is to say simplicity for its own sake, can become an attractive distraction, or worse, a delusive one, taking attention away from the practical demands of finding law or laws appropriate to the states and conditions in which real-world controversies arise and persist. That was the sober assessment made by Charles Clark, then Dean of the Yale Law School, about the Reporters of the First Restatement. They lost sight of the actual law, he concluded, in their search for a simplistic fantasy.

Grasping for "*the law*'—the 'common' non-statutory law—of our forty-eight states, our territories and our federal system," the first Restaters extended their reach impossibly and in consequence fell, as Clark put it, for a "delusive simplification." Not one to mince words, he summed up their Restatement in no uncertain terms: "[T]he resulting statement is the law nowhere and in its unreality only deludes and misleads."[32] A harsh judgment to be sure, but not entirely untrue. It was half true. Contract law in no jurisdiction matched the assembled whole of the restated law.[33] That part, the first

---

[30] "[S]ome informal promises are enforceable without the element of bargain. These fall and are placed in the category of contracts which are binding without assent or consideration (see §§85–94)." RESTATEMENT (FIRST) OF CONTRACTS § 75 [Definition of Consideration] cmt. b (1932).

[31] Ralph Waldo Emerson, "Montaigne; or the Skeptic" (1850). On the elusiveness of "the Law," Emerson writes:

> [T]he prized reality, *the Law*, is apprehended, now and then, for a serene and profound moment amidst the hubbub of cares and works which have no direct bearing on it;—is then lost for months or years, and again found for an interval, to be lost again.

Id. (emphasis added).

[32] Clark, *supra* note 5, at 643, 654 (emphasis added). "It is either a generality so obvious as immediately to be accepted, or so vague as not to offend, or of such antiquity as to be unchallenged as a statement of past history." *Id.* "With one leg it steps forward; with the other it goes backward. It is caught between stating the law which should be and the law which is and often ends by stating only the law that was." *Id.* at 643, 656.

[33] Some of the mismatch was due to gaps in previously stated laws. "The 'law,' then, is to be restated as a whole because so great a part of that law is now inadequately stated by earlier jurists." Corbin, *supra* note 14, at 602, 603. But gaps in the statement of existing law were only part of the story. In many instances the "restated" law contravened existing law in a number jurisdictions and sometimes even most jurisdictions, as may be said, for instance, of Section 90 (promissory estoppel).

part of Clark's judgment, is correct and apparent by inspecting the Black Letter against case law then in any state. However, the second part, wherein he asserts that the stated law "only deludes and misleads," cannot be established by merely inspecting the doctrine. To assess a text's delusive quality one would have to consider its purpose along with the knowledge and beliefs of those engaged with it.

Texts are not only informative or merely for the purpose to elucidate or delude. Texts are also performative, and often they perform valuable functions irrespective of their truth-value. A text may be solemnly recited, read aloud, whispered, worshiped, revered, banned, or burned in protest. These and any number of other activities are the things people do with and to texts. Texts also do things with and to people, about which anyone who has ever been moved by a piece of writing can attest. Most profoundly, perhaps, a text can coordinate a community's beliefs, expectations, and practices. An inscribed creation myth or other records of fiction received as fact, such as what Lon Fuller called the "beneficial illusion"—the belief in a "time immemorial" common law identifiable from written judicial opinions—can be a "valuable social myth," but it is "valuable only so long as it is believed in."[34] There is an argument in favor of adherence to this illusion, to which some ALI members apparently did. To be clear, however, Williston and his Associate Reporters were neither self-delusional nor believed in a singular and true common law of the then forty-eight states and territories. Even his greatest detractors did "not criticize Williston because he suffers from the delusion that there is 'an existing law' of contracts to state."[35] Still, an endeavor to restate the law requires a belief that there is law out there to be restated. "In undertaking to draft a formal Restatement of any branch of the law, there is involved an assumption that *a* common law exists," Corbin conceded, but that is not to say he embraced the fantasy that *the* common law exists.[36] He was of course aware of the rumors:

> Doubtless it has been a common assumption that the common law is a set of definite rules of conduct handed down by our remote ancestors, complete and perfect and capable of being applied in all jurisdictions in any conceivable situation, however new and unprecedented, originating perhaps with some divine lawgiver when the world began.[37]

Corbin, speaking for himself and some of his fellow Reporters, was candid with the academy, bar and bench regarding their disbelief about anyone locating *the* common law. "No student of the law can find any such set of rules; and the Committee on Contracts is not finding or 'restating' any such rules."[38] What, then, was the

---

[34] Lon L. Fuller, *Williston on Contracts*, 18 N.C. L. Rev. 1, at 14 (1939). Striking an ambivalently pessimistic note about the continuing faith of this social myth, Fuller continued, "[t]here are numerous signs that this faith is crumbling in this country I confess, a considerable measure of wishful thinking in this hope-expressed-as-prophecy." *Id.* at 14–15.

[35] *Id.* at 1, 13 (referring to Cook's review of Williston's (1939) revised edition of treatise on contracts).

[36] Corbin, *supra* note 14, at 602 (emphasis added).

[37] *Id.*

[38] *Id.* In all fairness to Clark, he was not the only serious scholar who felt the Restatement of Contracts betrayed the Reporters' claim that they were not promoting the illusion that they had found and restated *the* common law. Edwin Patterson, in a thoughtful and less critical review than Clark's, points to the same issue. Patterson, *supra* note 15, at 397, 399.

Committee on Contracts up to in its restatement of the law? An answer to this question is prompted by recalling our departing observation about the peculiar feature of complex societies: the Reporters saw in their society not one common law but in fact many, too many for its own good, too many for a nation that had in just over a century "grown almost inconceivably complex, politically, socially and economically."[39] Simplicity in the form of hard and fast rules was not what they needed or achieved, but rather something more of a "common standard" in the words of Justice Story, or a canon, in its traditional meaning of a "common measure," or simply a "common law."

A.   A Common Law from Complexity

Two seemingly contradictory views, each one widely shared and firmly held, grounded the ALI's founding and function. On the one hand were sweeping claims of variability and uncertainty in the American common law. Recalling in 1923 the reasons for the creation of the ALI, Elihu Root pointed to a then "increasing complexity and confusion of the substantive law," yet still "growing worse from year to year" and "tend[ing] to create a situation where the law was becoming guesswork."[40] On the other hand were confident assertions of uniformity in this same body of law, a belief in "the fact that the law of contracts of so many jurisdictions is so nearly identical that the Restatement is possible."[41] Together these views appear paradoxical. There was enough variability in the law to create widespread confusion and, at the same time, enough uniformity in the same body of law to eliminate confusion by simply restating the law. Like all good paradoxes, the contradiction here was more apparent than real, although the answer to the puzzle itself was not quite so apparent.

Legal uniformity, if it was present, should have implied an absence of variability, uncertainty, and confusion, and yet in the early twentieth century all three appeared rampant. As did the appearance of complexity, which counterintuitively provided an opportunity, the very possibility that a restatement could redress the seemingly conflicting and confusing statements of existing law. What appeared as complexity was actually just data, lots of data (i.e., observations), which tended to overwhelm users accustomed to working with smaller samples. "In spite of complexity," Corbin noted (he might have better said *because* of it), one could observe "there is in fact a high degree of uniformity";[42] that uniformity, however, was hidden within an ever expanding complex of stated rules and doctrines in "thousands of new decisions annually added to our already bursting storehouses." These storehouses of judicial opinions and other writings were "making it continually more difficult to understand, to state, and to teach the common law."[43] While many seasoned lawyers, sophisticated jurists and learned law faculty saw no clear path, short of a legislative code, to cut through

---

[39] Arthur L. Corbin, *Restatement of the Law of Contracts*, 14 A.B.A.J. 602 (1928).

[40] Elihu Root, *Address of Elihu Root in Presenting the Report of the Committee*, 1 A.L.I. Proc. 48–49 (1923).

[41] Judson A. Crane, *Contracts Restatement*, 81 U. Pa. L. Rev. 806, at 816 (1932–1933).

[42] Corbin, *supra* note 14, at 602, 603.

[43] Arthur L. Corbin, *The Restatement of the Common Law by the American Law Institute*, 15 Iowa L. Rev. 19 (1929). Andrew S. Gold & Henry E. Smith, *Restatements and the Common Law*, in this volume.

the thicket of conflicting rules and doctrines, the ALI's restatements project shined a hopeful light on one approach toward a common law.

Securing a common law from within this thicket, a guide through the complexity, assuming one exists, required a tripartite endeavor: first, underlying legal principle from case law ("the soul of the decision") must be found,[44] then it must be clearly restated,[45] and finally it must be made commonly known.[46] For the first part, the Committee's search for uniformity was, said Corbin, no different from the process of discovery in physics or chemistry. He departed, however, with a reference to history and politics. "History repeats itself," not only in political events, Corbin wrote, but also in "judicial and administrative conduct."[47] All common law results from this aspect of repetition and "consistency in judicial and administrative conduct."[48] A statement of the common law in this light is just an expression "of uniformity in the past sequence of events, based upon the recorded observation of those events."[49] With an ever increasing number of observations over novel events, previously stated law may be usefully restated to incorporate insights gleaned from more recent observations. Seeing legal uniformity in this regard, more as patterns of legal *regularity*, the search for common law appears comparable to the identification of laws in the physical sciences:

> The stated laws of physics and chemistry have continually had to be *restated* in the light of wider observation and more nearly correct analysis. In the same way and for exactly the same reasons, we have had a continuous series of restatements of the common law, from the very earliest times of which we have a record down to the present.[50]

A restatement of common law is not a product but rather a process, a sempiternal process of discovery and reiteration. What's ancient here is not the law itself, as if sourced from some purported, perhaps divine, ancestral lawgiver, but the ritual of restating observed regularities of legal statements even as, indeed especially as, social practice changes over time. In producing the Restatement (First) of Contracts, the Reporters saw themselves as undertaking "merely the latest of these restatements," dating back to the earliest attempts to recapitulate the common law. Others, however, saw the

---

[44] "At the beginning there has been need to gather from the pronouncements of the courts the principle or the rule implicit in their judgments, to find the soul of the decision beneath its integument of clay." Benjamin N. Cardozo, 3 A.L.I. PROC. 82, at 98.

[45] Recall Corbin's early rejection of a restatement as simply putting "an old rule into new words" (*see supra* note 14). Looking back, several decades later, Corbin elaborated:

> The Restatement was not and could not be a mere rewording of the rules and principles that had previously been stated in other words, a mere putting of "old wine in new bottles." The work required a "choice" among varied and conflicting rules and principles, the abandonment of some and the substitution of new ones in new words.

Arthur L. Corbin, *Sixty-Eight Years at Law*, 13 U. KAN. L. REV. 183, at 186 (1964).

[46] *See infra* note 84 and accompanying text.

[47] *Id.*

[48] *Id.* "Its rules and principles are statements in words of this uniformity and consistency. *Id.*

[49] *Id.*

[50] *Id.* (emphasis added).

endeavor as an existential threat to the law they sought to capture in the bound volumes of the Restatement. In fixing the common law of contracts onto the pages within those volumes, many feared the Reporters would deprive the law of its vigor and versatility, its valued and venerated capacity to spontaneously adapt to changing social needs and practices.[51]

B. A Folk Theorem of Fixed Codes

By setting out to provide a written statement of the common law of contracts, the first Restaters open themselves up to well-rehearsed charges of distorting legal command by reducing it to writing. As David Seipp reveals in his informative contribution to this volume, Dean Clark was retelling an age-old warning when he cautioned that "stating law as an existing thing inevitably takes away life and vitality of the statement[.]"[52] It was a senescent warning echoed in wider principles of uncertainty in the physical and social sciences: that is, uncertainty tends to result from efforts to record the current position of moving objects, regardless of whether those objects are particles or the practices of an evolving society and the laws governing it. In the way that measuring the position of protons by hitting them with light is said to shift their course and momentum, it may be said that writing down an ever-evolving common law will alter or arrest the development of rules and doctrines intended to change with society.[53] Moreover, as the societal rate of change increases—which well describes the fifty-year period in the wake of the American Civil War and its abruptly concluded Reconstruction—so too must the law, and hence the risk of uncertainty in relying on previously written statements of its content. In periods of rapid social change it may then be predicted that the cost of relying on written law would become more apparent, or maybe it is only or mostly the fear of it that grows in appearance.

In either case, during the half-century spanning the Gilded Age and the Progressive Era, the "folkways and mores" of civil and commercial society appeared to "have changed constantly," observed Corbin, and with that "change, the law of Contracts has perforce also changed."[54] Civil and commercial society were in all likelihood aided, or

---

[51] Cardozo himself, "at least in some of the preliminary drafts," perceived the threat "in a certain search and seeking now and again for definiteness and assurance and finality in fields where definiteness and assurance and finality must be left to the agency of time." Cardozo, *Minutes of the Third Annual Meeting Held at Washington, D.C. May 1 and 2*, 1925, 3 A.L.I. PROC. 82, at 99.

[52] Clark, *supra* note 5 at 657.

[53] Measurement effects and uncertainty regarding protons in contrast to cultural practices are, to be sure, subject to distinct theories (Heisenberg and Hawthorne, to give names to two), and these distinctions should not be obscured too much in the analogy. *See* Werner Heisenberg, *The Physical Content of Quantum Kinematics and Mechanics* (1927), *in* QUANTUM THEORY AND MEASUREMENT 62 (J.A. Wheeler & W.H. Zurek eds., 1983); HENRY A. LANDSBERGER, HAWTHORNE REVISITED (1958). Heisenberg's uncertainty principle was at the time familiar to legal scholars and to lay readers. "[P]hysicists, indeed have just announced the Principle of Uncertainty or Indeterminacy," proclaimed Jerome Frank in 1930. "Even in physics and chemistry, where a high degree of quantitative exactness is possible, modern leaders of thought are recognizing that finality and ultimate precision are not to be attained." LAW AND THE MODERN MIND 7 (1930). *See also*, Percy Williams Bridgman, *The New Vision of Science*, HARPER'S MAGAZINE, Mar. 1929, at 443. I thank David Seipp for this reference.

[54] Corbin, *supra* note 14, at 602.

at least not initially hindered, by the capacity of the common law to adjust during this period of constant change. At some point, however, particularly as economic and social exchange increased across the forty-eight states, each with its own common law, what may have been appreciated as a benefit of the law's adaptability was increasingly seen as burdensome inconstancy, complexity, or confusion. Clarity was called for, but no one wanted stifle the law's adaptive capacity.

How is it possible to produce a clear written statement of the law that is at once in line with current practice and allows for its spontaneous change over time? "It is impossible," wrote Henry Maine in *Ancient Law*, "to suppose that the customs of any race or tribe remained unaltered during the whole of the long—in some instances the immense—interval between their declaration by a patriarchal monarch and their publication in writing."[55] Here oral societies are said to have a distinct advantage in keeping law and social practice apace: "in societies without writing, even where courts exist, there is no effective distinction between 'law' and 'custom,'" argued Jack Goody, and in "consequence the sources of law see to it that a relatively close link is maintained with the other aspects of the social system."[56] Writings create a wedge between law and custom, or so it is claimed when custom changes while law is seen as fixed in writings.

But what about those writings comprising the common law? Implicit in the age-old worry about authoritative statements of law expressed in written codes is the notion that this worry does not apply to the published judicial opinions constituting the "unwritten" common law. Judicial constraint from the precedential writings of earlier judges, *stare decisis*, is supposed to be a celebrated feature of the common law. Common law judges, however, restrained by precedent, are seldom trapped by their own written verbal expressions. To them "even the sureness about what the precise authoritative words are," as Karl Llewellyn wrote, "is almost wholly lacking."[57] Whether spoken or written, "the verbal form of a rule of case-law is rarely fixed," and therefore law's capacity for spontaneous adjustment to societal demands is still preserved in written judicial opinions.[58]

Something essential changes, according to Maine, when rules and doctrines existing in case law are codified by legislatures. "A new era begins," he asserted in characteristically sweeping tones, when law is legislated. "When primitive law has once been embodied in a Code, there is an end to what may be called its spontaneous development."[59] Maine was hardly the first to express this conjecture about written codes—so

---

[55] Henry Sumner Maine, ANCIENT LAW (1861), at 21.

[56] JACK GOODY, THE LOGIC OF WRITING AND THE ORGANIZATION OF SOCIETY (1986), 135–136.

[57] Llewellyn, *supra* note 29, at 1243, 1243–44.

[58] *Id.* at 1244. "The same judge who announces 'a rule' as 'long-established and clear' will often enough phrase 'it' three different ways in the same opinion. In the very fact that this does not startle us lies a key to the degree of implicit fluidity of case-law rules." *Id.* Cardozo was an escape artist in this regard and proud of it. "Those of us whose lives have been spent on the bench or at the bar," as he noted, "know the value of the veiled phrase, the blurred edge, the uncertain line." 3 A.L.I. PROC. 82, at 106. "Well, I am strong for them even now, at least in their proper places, or rather, I ought to say, for reservations and limitations which will preserve whatever of value there may be in impressionistic forms and phrases." *Id.*

[59] Maine, *supra* note 55, at 21. While Maine was onto something, Goody suggested, he didn't entirely grasp the dynamic that he was attempting to describe. "Though Maine points to the problem, he does not fully appreciate that the spontaneous development on which he comments is the imperceptible process of adjustment of norms that constantly takes place in oral societies in response to external pressures or internal forces. The process is imperceptible because norms have only a verbal, an oral existence, so that rules

old it can only be called a folk conjecture—asserting that law's ability to adjust to custom and social practice is constrained when a written code defining it comes into existence.[60] Whatever the truth of this conjecture regarding legislative code, it is important to recall that Restatements were never intended to take form as statutes, precisely for the reasons of maintaining the common law's flexibility.[61] While the ALI sought from the Restatement "a definiteness of form approaching the pronouncements of a statute," as its Vice President, Benjamin Cardozo, told the membership at the ALI's third Annual Meeting, it did not envision a formal code of the common law of contracts;[62] not even one as modest as Joseph Story's "code of the common law," subject to legislative approval but "not as a code of statute law[.]"[63] Years later, when the ALI would eventually lend its weight in producing a code intended for legislative approval, its membership still sought to preserve the flexible principles of law and equity originating in common law, unless specifically displaced by the legislation.[64]

A fixed statutory code was never in store for the restatements project, which was meant to be closer to Chancellor James Kent's vision, described by Seipp, of a flexible "immense code of the common law," reliant only on "the sanction of the courts of justice, without any legislative act or interference."[65] Capturing this elusive flexible code was a long-held ambition of Cardozo,[66] and he imagined that it would be the crowing achieving of the restatements project. "We are now to see whether our law has found a medium of expression that will solve or help to solve the age-long problem of uniting flexibility to certainty[,]" as he described the challenge and the hope of the endeavor.[67] Addressing the ever-present worry that a code (a "form forever fixed"), even one existing in the virtuous form he imagined for the restatements, would constrain the common law's growth and development, Cardozo reminded his audience of the

that are not longer applicable tend to slip out of the memory store." Goody, *supra* note 56, at 139. *Cf.* John Gardner, who argues that even a written constitution will necessarily have gaps and ambiguities, like all real-world written legal contracts, conventions and codes, which inevitably will be addressed through judicial interpretation and thus preserve the law's capacity for spontaneous development overtime as disputes arise. John Gardner, *Can There Be a Written Constitution?*, in OXFORD STUDIES IN PHILOSOPHY OF LAW (Leslie Green & Brian Leiter eds., 2011). I am grateful to Andrew Gold for bringing Gardner's chapter to my attention.

[60] "Henceforward the changes effected in it, if effected at all, are effected deliberately and from without.... Wherever, after this epoch, we trace the course of legal modification we are able to attribute it to the conscious desire of improvement, or at all events of compassing objects other than those which were aimed at in the primitive times." Maine, *supra* note 55, at 21–22.

[61] "It was emphatically concluded that the Restatements should not be adopted as statutes; the goal was to maintain the flexibility of the common law." *The American Law Institute, Seventy-Fifth Anniversary 1923–1998*, July 6, 1998 (President's Foreword), at 11. On codification and the common law, after and before the ALI's incorporation, *see* the thoughtful historical accounts in this volume by Deborah A. DeMott, *Restating the Law in the Shadow of Codes: The ALI in Its Formative Era*, in this volume; and David J. Seipp, *The Need for Restatement of the Common Law: A Long Look Back*, in this volume; as well as Nathan M. Crystal, *Codification and the Rise of the Restatement Movement*, 54 WASH. L. REV. 239 (1979).

[62] 3 A.L.I. PROC. 82, at 100.

[63] Seipp, *supra* note 61.

[64] U.C.C. §1-103(3)(b).

[65] Seipp, *supra* note 61. "Kent thus meant 'code of common law' only in the sense of an imaginary code of timeless wisdom, which harkened back to the lawyers' oral consensus of premodern England, always incapable of reduction to writing." *Id.*

[66] *See* discussion in Gold & Smith, *supra* note 43.

[67] 3 A.L.I. PROC. 82, at 100.

retained capacity always possessed by judges and lawyers, as arbiters and advocates, to shape the law.[68]

C. A Canon of U.S. Contract Law

A "canon" originally signified a measuring rod.[69] Today a canon is most commonly understood as a generally agreed upon, though not necessarily uncontested, collection of texts establishing a standard or measure of value of something worthy of study. By this definition, the texts contained in the Restatements surely comprise a canon of the American common law of contracts. To say these texts consist in a canon, however, is not to claim they began as such. Writings tend to acquire canonical status over time— some faster than others and rarely any expectantly so when first written. Yet the ALI's Committee on Contracts expected the Restatement to be an object of study and criticism:

> As time goes on, the work of the present Committee, in the final form that is adopted by the Institute, will be subjected to the test of criticism by the judges as they apply the law to new issues and by law professors and students as they engage in legal research.[70]

That they expected their restatement to be studied and criticized, however, does not mean they were self-consciously engaged in creating a canon. They were almost certainly not thinking in those terms. Williston, Corbin, and the Advisers and other members on the Committee, though all scholars of law, did not perceive themselves as undertaking an academic or hermeneutic project.[71] Although "hailed, for better or for worse, as a professorial product,"[72] their Restatement was meant to deal with everyday lawyerly concerns and problems caused by legal uncertainty,[73] which during "the Roaring Twenties" were increasingly brought to light "by the rapidity and complexity of modern life,"[74] and "the largeness of the sphere which is occupied in it by Contract."[75]

---

[68] Cardozo, 3 A.L.I. Proc. 82, at 100. "[S]omething will have to be left, even when the restatement is completed, to those tentative gropings, those cautious experiments, those provisional hypotheses, that are part of the judicial process." *Id.* "Many of the rules and principles to be extracted from the enormous body of our case law are there in the opinions, not as precepts explicitly avowed, but as assumptions, presuppositions, things felt rather than perceived." *Id.*

[69] Derived from the Greek word *kanōn* meaning originally a straight bar, "perhaps from *kanna* 'reed' (see cane (n.))." *See* https://www.etymonline.com/word/canon.

[70] Corbin, *supra* note 14, at 602, 604.

[71] The ALI's Committee on Contracts included Samuel Williston, Harvard University, Reporter; Arthur L. Corbin, Yale University, Special Adviser, and Reporter for Chapter on Remedies; Merton L. Ferson, University of Cincinnati; Dudley O. McGovney, University of California; William H. Page, University of Wisconsin; George J. Thompson, Cornell University; William E. McCurdy, Harvard University, Legal Assistant; Zechariah Chafee Jr., Harvard University, Adviser for Sections relating to Specific Performance; Edgar N. Durfee, University of Michigan, Adviser for Sections relating to Specific Performance; and William Draper Lewis, Director, Chairman Ex Officio. Restatement (First) of Contracts Committee (1932).

[72] Patterson, *supra* note 15, at 397, 398.

[73] "It is this complexity and uncertainty that has called the American Law Institute into being, and with which the various committees 'restating' the law must deal." Corbin, *supra* note 14, at 602, 603.

[74] Corbin, *supra* note 43, at 19.

[75] Maine, *supra* note 55, at 304.

There was simply too much law—too many competing rules and doctrines generating needless complexity and hindering contractual coordination. Hence, the first and principal task of the Committee presented itself immediately. "It is the making of a *selection* among competing rules and doctrines."[76] By selecting and making salient *one* set of rules and doctrines among the many competing alternatives (even an arbitrary selection), the Committee could establish focal points for contracting laypersons, lawyers, judges, faculty, and students of contract law.[77] To all these actors the Restatement of Contracts proposed a body of law on which they could rely, which is not to say they would necessarily defer to the Committee's selections.[78] Jurisdictional differences would still be observed, but over time those differences would recede or else stand as chosen departures from the orienting positions taken in the Restatement. No greater law, legislation or authority was required to rule over the complex mix of competing statements of the common law. One statement, a Restatement, just needed to rise above the din.

Announcing one set of black-letter rules, doctrines, and an established lexicon could, by itself, eliminate much unnecessary guesswork in the law. In the absence of a single national or uniform law, a singled out statement of law (i.e., a "restatement") abstracted from the multiplicity of state common law offered a serviceable second-best solution to the problem of too much law. Anything is sometimes better than everything. But it wasn't just anything that was selected for restatement. Criteria for selection into the Restatement of Contracts relied heavily on the weight of authority,[79] among other prudential considerations such as consistency and simplicity.[80] Contemporary law and economics scholars may be surprised by the extent to which the Committee's selections were guided, or at least so claimed, by considerations of efficiency,[81] "and by the generally accepted notions of social and economic welfare."[82] Broad social and economic considerations undoubtedly captured some committee

---

[76] Corbin, *supra* note 14, at 602, 603.

[77] After noting the difficulties faced by teachers and students of the law due to the diversity and disorganization of common law pronouncements, Corbin wrote:

> To the same extent and for the same reasons the work of the practicing lawyer in advising clients and the work of the judges in deciding cases were becoming increasingly difficult. Necessarily, this situation was reflected in the published opinions of the judges. Uncertainty of mind produced confused reasoning and actual conflict in decision. Legal terminology, always shifty and inexact as in the case of all the other branches of social science, became more and more inefficient in obtaining clarity of expression and more unsatisfactory to everybody concerned[.]

Corbin, *supra* note 43, at 19.

[78] No court would or was expected to "blindly follow the Restatement where in a particular jurisdiction a contrary rule has been adopted by a considerable body of decisions." Crane, *supra* note 41, at 807. *See* discussion in Schauer, *supra* note 17.

[79] "In general, this is determined by what has long been appealed to by courts and writers as the Weight of Authority." Corbin, *supra* note 14, at 602, 603. "Obviously some propositions of law must be rejected in favor of others with which they are inconsistent; the 'weight of authority' test can be applied. The draftsmen of the Restatement were experts in applying this test. Other propositions of law, seemingly diverse, may be capable of translation into common terms." Patterson, *supra* note 15, at 397, at 399.

[80] Specifically, "consistency of a rule with other accepted rules in related branches of law [and] simplicity of construction and ease of application." Corbin, *supra* note 14, at 602, 603.

[81] "The best evidence as to the efficiency of a rule is to be found in the number and the types of cases in which it has been applied." *Id.*

[82] *Id.*

members' attention,[83] but the Committee as a whole trained its focus on the more mundane problem of legal uncertainty caused by the complexity and multiplicity of common laws across the states.

Restating the common law effectively as common knowledge,[84] even at the risk of fostering the illusion of a singular law,[85] was seen as an expedient solution to the problem of legal uncertainty.[86] In addressing one problem, however, the Restatement was said to introduce other, potentially more insidious, threats to the common law. By providing a snapshot of the law at a given point in time, the Restatement, critics warned, would ossify the law, or worse, "restate" what was never the law or "only the law that was."[87] None of these worries, however, are unique to the Restatement. They may be said of any text asserting revelations about the common law, including the multitudes of judicial opinions comprising the "unwritten" common law. "Restatement," as Edwin Patterson reminds us, "presupposes that there has already been a statement of the law in authoritative form."[88] Cardozo's efforts to distinguish the judicial process from that of the Reporters' ("the difficulty of the [latter] process is multiplied many fold") is less a distinction of kind than of degrees (as John Goldberg agues in his chapter in this volume) between written judicial statements and reportorial restatements.[89]

---

[83] "While it is not the function of the present Committee to try to reform the ways of business or the mores of existing society, it will indeed be well if the Institute is able in the future to keep selected Committees at work on scientific and unbiased research into the bases of human behavior and the *efficiency* of legal rules and judicial administration." *Id.* at 604 (emphasis added).

[84] Specifically, "common knowledge" in the sense of shared information that's known to be known among those who know or should know, which a prominent Restatement was meant to achieve. Common knowledge here recalls the shared consensus that Baker refers to as "common erudition" or "common learning" of the unwritten common law among early English lawyers. *See* Seipp, *supra* note 61 (quoting J.H. BAKER, THE LAW'S TWO BODIES 67 (2001); and citing A.W.B. Simpson, *The Common Law and Legal Theory, in* OXFORD ESSAYS IN JURISPRUDENCE: SECOND SERIES 77, 94 (1973)). Wide *public* distribution was key to the success of the Restatement of Contracts becoming common knowledge, but it needn't have met the more technical definition often used in game theory: wherein something is common knowledge between or among persons, if each person knows that thing and knows the others also know it, and they all know that they all know it, and they all know that they all know that they all know it, and so on *ad infinitum*. *See, e.g.*, Robert Aumann, *Agreeing to Disagree*, 4 ANNALS OF STATISTICS 1236–39 (1976); Paul Milgrom, *An Axiomatic Characterization of Common Knowledge*, 49 ECONOMETRICA 219–22 (1981); John Geanakoplos, *Common Knowledge*, 6(4) J. ECON. PERSP. 53–82 (1992); Robin Cubitt & Robert Sugden, *Common Knowledge, Salience and Convention: A Reconstruction of David Lewis's Game Theory*, 19 ECON. & PHIL. 175–210 (2003).

[85] "The assertion (in the preface) that it is 'the product of expert opinion' seems to imply that there are no divergent expert opinions. This is contrary to fact.—The illusion that 'the law' can be found in one and only one set of authoritative propositions is not wholly dispelled." Patterson, *supra* note 15, at 397, 399.

[86] None of the Reporters appeared subject to the impossible illusion that they could rid the law of uncertainty, least of all perhaps Corbin, as he revealed to Robert Braucher three decades after the Restatement's publication. "I have read all the contract cases for the last 12 years; and I know that 'certainty' does not exist and the illusion perpetrates injustice." *Letter from Arthur L. Corbin to Robert Braucher (Nov. 13, 1961) (Robert Braucher Papers, Harvard Law School Library, MS Box 17, Folder 7), in* Joseph Perillo, *Twelve Letters from Arthur L. Corbin to Robert Braucher Annotated*, 50 WASH. & LEE L. REV. 755 (1993), at 758.

[87] Clark, *supra* note 5, at 643, 656.

[88] Patterson, *supra* note 15, at 397, 399.

[89] 3 A.L.I. PROC. 82, at 99. Additionally, casebook editors or treatise writers, particularly ones as influential as Williston, Corbin, and Farnsworth were, may just as easily be seen as undertaking the task of restating the law, not in their respective roles as Reporters, but as editors and writers of law books. *See, e.g.*, Fuller's comments on Williston as a legal text writer: "By insisting upon judging the text writer strictly in terms of his avowed purpose, that of stating 'the law', we are hard at work to eliminate from the positivistic

Restatements did not introduce the phenomenon of the common law being fixed in written form; the American common law of contracts was only ever "unwritten" in the sense of there being no single authoritative document, like the so-called "unwritten British constitution."[90] Nonetheless the Restatement did claim a novel form of authority over the common law, one that signaled a subtle change in approach and deference to judicial statements of law, whether individually received or collected in casebooks and case reporters, or summarized in digests and treatises. Here, then, was the underlying worry about the Restatement. Concern over the Restatement of Contracts was not principally a matter of its being a written statement of the common law, of which there were volumes. Rather, it was its presentation as an authoritative collection of the law, which is to say, a canon, approved by a self-selected body of legal elites and curated exclusively by law school professors.[91] "This deference to academic authority in the face of a juridical tradition which nominally denies authoritative status to the doctrines of the unofficial expert" was not lost on careful observers.[92] Patterson observed a shift away from established common law principles "in the direction of the continental juristic tradition" found in civil law countries.[93] Looking in retrospect, others have identified this moment as a time when "leading academics in the field of contracts sought to reassert their influence over the bar."[94]

"Be bold," you may recall Cardozo saying to the Reporters in his opening remarks at the ALI annual meeting about "the high emprise on which the *scholars* of the Institute have ventured."[95] "But not too bold." He offered that closing comment no doubt more to assuage the practitioners in the audience than to restrain the academics on the committee. Even the choice of the term "Restatement," suggested Patterson, seems "happily calculated to allay the suspicion that any modification has been made in the pre-existing law."[96] Other prepublication assurances were also offered as a show of

philosophy all the little covert tolerances and inconsistencies which have made it a workable system in the past." Fuller, *supra* note 34, at 1, 14.

[90] Speaking of "the British constitution, for example, it is said that 'much (indeed, nearly all) of the constitution is written, somewhere.'" Mark D. Walters, *The Unwritten Constitution as a Legal Concept, in* PHILOSOPHICAL FOUNDATIONS OF CONSTITUTIONAL LAW 33 (David Dyzenhaus & Malcolm Thorburn eds., 2016) (quoting A. TOMKINS, PUBLIC LAW 7 (2003) [check quote].

[91] More than any single commentary or treatise could possibly claim, the Restatement of Contracts (under the auspices of the ALI) asserted the collected wisdom and authority of the nation's legal elite, including its most prominent treatise writers who, notwithstanding their prominence, could never accomplish alone the combined authority assembled by the ALI.

[92] Patterson, *supra* note 15, at 397, 398.

[93] *Id.* "[A]cademic determinism rather than economic determinism accounts for the form and content of the Restatement." *Id.*

[94] E.A. Farnsworth, *Contracts Scholarship in the Age of Anthology*, 85 MICH. L. REV. 1406, at 1425 (1987). "In his 1929 lectures at Virginia, Williston recalled that Lord Coke had thought it 'the part of a good judge to magnify his office' and likened professors to judges in this regard. 'So I make no apology for taking an enlarged view of the office of those who have followed the same occupation as my own.'" *Id.* "Thus began," as Teeven wrote, "a process modeled on the civil law practice of academics drafting legislative solutions." Kevin M. Teeven, *Origins of Promissory Estoppel: Justifiable Reliance and Commercial Uncertainty before Williston's Restatement*, 34 U. MEM. L. REV. 499, at 510 (2004).

[95] *Id.* (emphasis added).

[96] *Id.* at 399. "It is compatible with the tradition that courts merely find the law and that expert opinion is repetitive rather than creative." *Id.*

the Reporters' humility and restraint in their determination of the common law.[97] Writing in the journal of the American Bar Association, Corbin sought to assure practitioners that "no Committee is competent to pass a final judgment upon such matters of policy," and yet, wrote Corbin, to do its work the Committee on Contracts is "compelled to pass judgment and to make a selection."[98]

Passing judgment and making a selection are the first steps toward creating a canon. Sealing the selection, however imperfectly, completes the canon. Though canons are often said to be either sealed or open,[99] this suggests more of a firm theoretical dichotomy than the fluid gradations actually observed in practice.[100] Every canon is to some extent sealed, including the Restatement, and since sealing indicates a further shift toward scholarly interpretive authority,[101] further assurances to counter the appearance or degree of the sealing may have been expected and were, in any case, offered: "The Committee on Contracts does not labor under the delusion that it has attained perfection. Its work must be subjected to *constant* revision in the future."[102] A published Restatement is not a sealed crypt for dead law, but nor can it be constantly revised.[103]

Has the Restatement offered our common law of contracts that elusive "medium of expression" which allow us to "solve or help to solve the age-long problem of uniting flexibility to certainty," which Cardozo predicted or hoped for? It has certainly not solved that age-long problem and has probably caused a few new ones, but it has

---

[97] Corbin provided an extraordinary disclaimer regarding the Reporters' then-ongoing work on the Restatement of Contracts:

> Its authors have only limited time, energy and wisdom. They have not yet had sufficient education. They have lacked a close association on the Committee with selected lawyers and judges who could have given criticism based upon ripe experience in the creation and application of the law. They have not had the time or energy required for adequate research into the mountainous mass of case material for the solving of many knotty points of substantive law. Their economic training is faulty and their knowledge of social conditions is not sufficiently wide and deep. They have not had sufficient experience in other branches of the law, although they are aware that "the law is a seamless web" that renders defective service when it is rent into separate parts.

Corbin, *supra* note 14, at 602, 604.

[98] *Id.* at 602, 603.

[99] "An example of an open canon is a system of legislation that permits the addition of new laws whose legal status will be as binding as the existing law.... In a sealed canon, by contrast, the status of the textual elements is exclusive, and no new texts of equal importance may be added." MOSHE HALBERTAL, PEOPLE OF THE BOOK: CANON, MEANING, AND AUTHORITY (1997) at 16. "The Bible is the most prominent example of a sealed and exclusive canon." *Id.*

[100] No canon can be entirely open (without barriers to entry and exit a canon cannot truly exist and persist over time) nor is any completely sealed (writings within a supposedly sealed canon may become apocryphal or otherwise lose their canonical status).

[101] "The moment the text was sealed, authority was removed from the writers of the text and transferred to its interpreters." HALBERTAL, *supra* note 99, at 19. "Unlike the authority of the priest" or of judges, to quote and paraphrase Halbertal, "that of the scholar does not rest on a monopoly over ritual. Priestly [or judicial] authority rests on the claim that a certain group has the exclusive right to perform a variety of rituals. The expert's authority is derived not from his exclusive role in the ritual but from his skills as interpreter of the sealed text." *Id.*, at 23.

[102] Corbin, *supra* note 14, at 602, 604 (emphasis added). "There will be new developments in Contract law, just as there have been in the past. The Restatement is long and complex; but there will arise cases that it does not cover. All this will require periodical revision of the Restatement." *Id.* Note the subtle change from "constant revision" to "periodic revision."

[103] Though Corbin claimed, and who's to doubt, that he did exactly that with "one man revision" of the first Restatement of Contracts. *See* Perillo *supra* note 86.

almost just as assuredly helped to solve a number of the problems which it was meant to address. Moreover even in its too bold, too definitive, and too dogmatic statements against which Corbin cautions us not to rely, the Restatements have been a useful point of reference and departure for argument and *restatement*, correctly understood. For example, during the long fifty-year period after the First Restatement and before the Second, the former was constantly debated and challenged by scholars on the one hand, while it no doubt offered a comforting source of certainty (even if a false comfort) for practitioners and students of the law on the other hand.[104] Both the challenges and the sense of certainty were valued products of the Restatement (First) and beneficial for the Restatement (Second). The Restatements of Contracts has been an unmitigated success as a canon on which we have relied for almost a century to discern, debate, and derive principles, rules, and doctrines of our common law of contracts. We learn not from the stated law, but from restating the law.

III. Reliance *in* the Restatements

Contract theory has long held a particular attraction for scholars, including for a number of the Reporters on ALI's exclusively academic Committee and Contracts. As lead Reporter, however, Williston made clear that the Committee did not see itself as tasked with addressing abstract arguments on the bases of contract liability.[105] This of course was very much in line with Williston's scholarly approach to contracts.[106] "Williston was not a particularly profound, or what you might call an adventurous, thinker," wrote Barbara Black, "and furthermore he understood a Restatement to be [just] a restatement."[107] With Williston at the helm, the Reporters took a pragmatic approach to the law, which is not to suggest that they were entirely unconcerned with considerations of morality and justice as bases for contract. They were, however, less

---

[104] "The Restatement offered opportunity for the products of the class-room and the law review to reach a wider audience." Patterson, *supra* note 15, at 397, 399. On the scholarly challengers, *see* Robert W. Gordon, *Restatements and Realists*, in this volume, and *infra* notes 152–56 and accompanying text. For a more recent challenge from the perspective of too much judicial deference on current Restatements, *see* Balganesh, *supra* note 17.

[105] In his opening comments at 1925 ALI Annual Meetings, where drafts of the Restatement were first presented to the whole membership, Williston stressed that "[t]he endeavor in this Restatement is to restate the law as it is, ... for the use of practical people" who are more concerned with "ordinary legal terminology" and "what practical consequences will follow from a certain state of facts than a philosophic analysis of legal relations." *Minutes of the Third Annual Meeting Held at Washington, D.C., May 1 and 2, 1925,* 3 A.L.I. PROC. 82, at 159. "One of the first things the Reporter had to consider in reference to this restatement," said Williston referring to himself in third-person, "was to decide on the desirability of adopting a Hohfeldian analytical form in stating the law," he said in response to Walter Cook, who suggested a more theoretical (Hohfeldian) characterization of promise, contract, and breach Sections 1 and 2: "I feel satisfied that to make the restatement in that form would make it unintelligible to a large part of the Bar and Bench and destroy its practical value." *Id.* at 168.

[106] "What may be called the bases of contract liability," wrote Lon Fuller, are nowhere "critically examined" in Williston's expansive treatise. Fuller, *supra* note 34, at 1, 9. Assessing Williston's multivolume treatise from the perspective of legal and social theory, Lawrence Friedman described it as designed to exclude such considerations: "volume after volume, solid, closely knit, fully armored against the intrusion of any ethical, economic, or social notions whatsoever." LAWRENCE FRIEDMAN, HISTORY OF AMERICAN LAW (2d ed. 1985) at 626.

[107] Barbara Aronstein Black, "Samuel Williston at the ALI: Promissory Estoppel" at 22.

concerned with abstract moral principles than enforcing conventional morality and preventing "practical injustice" in promissory exchanges, which to them, though not for all the same reasons, clearly required enforcement of justified reliance on contractual bargains.[108]

A. Interesting but Practically Unimportant

Relying by performing one's side of a bargain provided the essential basis for enforcing exchanges through actions in *debt*, one of the three common law actions from which our modern law of contracts derives. These half-completed exchanges argued Fuller and Purdue, facilitated not only the enforcement of informal exchanges but probably also "originally furnished an indispensable factual core for most formal contracts."[109] Actions in assumpsit, another leg of the three-footed stool on which contract law historically stood, also initially found their footing in reliance, a fact of which Williston was well aware.[110] He clearly recognized and endorsed reliance as one of the original bases for enforcing "real contracts" along with other bargain-based promissory exchanges constituting then contemporary contract doctrine.[111] No doubt so did a majority of the ALI membership that gathered in 1925 for the ALI's third Annual Meeting to discuss and debate the first draft of the Restatement. Whatever else that may have been controversial at this meeting, reliance as a traditional basis for enforcement *bargain promises* was not among them. That enforceable promises justify reliance and vice versa (i.e., that justified reliance made promises enforceable)

---

[108] 3 A.L.I. PROC. 82, at 201. Notwithstanding recent efforts to rehabilitate Williston's approach (at least concerning damages) as more theoretical than previously received—some commentators situating him as a "promise theorist," others as a "reliance theorist"—Black resisted both revisionists' views in favor of Williston's practical "passion" for protecting reliance:

> [I]n my reading of Williston, the driving force here was his profound disapproval of those who induce reliance through promise and fail to keep their promises. As I have noted elsewhere, it was to protection of reliance that such passion as Williston had about contracts attached. No doubt Williston did think that keeping one's promise was the honorable thing to do, but his concern was not primarily with the morality, far less the sanctity, of promise, but with the harm done those who justifiably rely on promises.

Black, *supra* note 107, at 20. On revival of Williston's jurisprudence, *see* Williston Mark L. Movsesian, *Rediscovering Williston*, 62 WASH. & LEE L. REV. 207 (2005).

[109] Fuller & Perdue, *supra* note 18, at 52, 67. "A difficulty in identifying the 'ultimate' motives for enforcing contracts exists even as to the earliest stages of legal history," yet, wrote Fuller and Purdue, "a place of favor was accorded what may be called the *real* contract, the 'delivery-promise,' or the half-completed exchange." *Id.*

[110] "The gist of the action of assumpsit," wrote Williston, "consisted in undertaking to do something and injuring the plaintiff by inducing him to rely on this undertaking." SAMUEL WILLISTON, THE LAW OF CONTRACTS, vol. 1, § 138, at 305 (1920). The third leg of the stool, of course, was actions of *covenant*, whereby written agreements became enforceable once sealed and delivered.

[111] As Williston observed in his 1920 treatise:

> [I]t may fairly be argued that the fundamental basis of simple contracts historically was action in justifiable reliance on a promise—rather than the more modern notion of purchase of a promise for a price, and that it is a consistent development from this early basis to define valid consideration as any legal benefit to the promisor or legal detriment to the promise given or suffered by the latter in reasonable reliance on the promise.

Id. at § 139, at 313 (1920).

were broadly shared sentiments among the participants at the meeting. It was simply a matter of practical justice, a long-established norm in contract law. To the extent there was any controversy over justified reliance, it concerned more issues at the periphery, or beyond the bounds, of what Williston took be the settled law of contracts. Fissures here were immediately revealed once Benjamin Cardozo opened the meetings and invited comments on the draft:[112]

> JUDGE CARDOZO: We will now take up the restatement of the law of contracts section by section. We will take up first section 1. Are there any special suggestions with reference to section 1?

Cardozo had already alerted the audience (in his welcoming remarks) that determinations involving the choice "between the objective and the subjective conception of a contract" lay "latent in the preliminary chapters" of the draft Restatement.[113] They weren't so latent to anyone paying attention, and nor were they trivial matters, as the choice between objective and subjective conceptions of contract, then highly debated, implicated numerous core doctrines—including, to start, the creation and definition of contract obligation. Whether and to what extent reliance, when justified, creates obligations that are distinctly contractual were first-order questions asked from the start of the Reporters' introduction to the ALI membership.

> VICTOR MORAWETZ (New York): [T]here is a rule of law which is based on justice[:] that if a person by words or acts expresses to another person that he enters into a contract, then the person to whom this expression is conveyed, unless he has knowledge to the contrary, is *entitled to rely* on it[.][114]

As Morawetz continued to expound on his position, the moderator, Cardozo, interrupted him, saying, "The inexorable clock warns me that your time has more than expired." However, a "motion, numerously seconded," was then quickly approved, allowing Morawetz to continue. Many in the audience were sympathetic to his position. Williston on the podium was not.

> MR. WILLISTON: It is, of course, possible to state the law, and the law is sometimes today stated as Mr. Morawetz states it[:] if parties express to one another such words or perform such acts as indicate an intent to make a contract, they shall then not be allowed to state what their actual intent was; that is, the *formation of contracts becomes a branch of the law of estoppel.*[115]

---

[112] 3 A.L.I. PROC. 82, at 160. Following Cardozo's invitation "for suggestions with reference to section 1," the minutes note that Director Lewis read Section 1 aloud: "A contract is a promise or a set of promises for breach of which the law gives a remedy or the performance of which the law in some indirect way recognizes as a duty." *Id.*

[113] *Id.* at 106–07.

[114] *Id.* at 162–63 (emphasis added).

[115] *Id.* at 165 (emphasis added).

Williston continued with a conciliatory nod toward Morawetz's account, "Mr. Morawetz and I both agree that is a contract," before abruptly disparaging the subjectivist camp as purveyors of fiction. They were all "talking fiction," he said, "and I should like to stop talking fiction."[116] Claiming "the real truth" consists in the facts of what people "say, and what they do," Williston concluded in a tone so triumphant one could almost hear him from the pages of the meeting minutes: "[T]he restatement is intended to state the actual facts (applause)."[117] Applause notwithstanding, many in the audience, including Julius Cohen, were considerably less confident than Williston in separating the facts from the fictions that create *contract* obligation:

> JULIUS HENRY COHEN (New York): Those statements of fact upon which most of us rely upon the theory of estoppel, to prevent the other from contesting them, are quite often as important as the definitive obligations assumed by the parties. Now, how do those things fall either in your definition or Mr. Morawetz's definition?[118]
>
> MR. WILLISTON: If they simply make a statement that they are true, then it is within the doctrine of estoppel; I should define estoppel as a misrepresentation of fact on which the other party justifiably relies, and I do not in my treatment make offers or promises the basis of estoppel.[119]

On what bases did Williston formulate his thoughts and treatment of offers and promises if not, at least in part, based on notions of estoppel? Section 45 (unilateral offers) and Section 90 (promissory estoppel), among a number of other reliance-based doctrines that Williston, himself, shepherded through the process for inclusion into the First Restatement, raise the question of whether he was working from a theory of reliance which he considered to be wholly distinct from estoppel. Insight into the question may be gleaned from a review by Lon Fuller of Williston's revised treatise published roughly five years after the Restatement.[120] In his review, Fuller shares a personal exchange with Williston wherein he "asked Professor Williston why the Restatement of Contracts did not include the subject of estoppel in pais."[121] Williston's response was unsatisfying and left Fuller inquiring further about reliance and estoppel more broadly,[122] and what specific roles they play in contract creation. Williston eventually conceded "that 'reasonable reliance' is 'doubtless' one 'juristic' reason for 'the recognition of contractual obligations,' but went on to say," in a revealing admission to Fuller, that "a contractual obligation 'is a right-duty relation, and the reasons why the relation is created are interesting but practically unimportant.'"[123]

It seems, then, that as far as Williston was concerned—while there may be some underlying theory or theories that account for both estoppel in pais and the various

---

[116] *Id.* at 165–66.
[117] *Id.* at 166.
[118] *Id.*
[119] *Id.*
[120] Fuller, *supra* note 34, at 1.
[121] *Id.* at 3, n.3.
[122] "This raises the question, what will the American Law Institute do with the notion of estoppel in pais? Are we to have a special *Restatement of Estoppel*, or, a *Miscellaneous Restatement?*" *Id.* (emphasis original).
[123] Fuller, *supra* note 34, at 1, 4–5, n.5.

reliance-based contract doctrines which he endorsed—neither theory nor estoppel were the business of the Restatement of Contracts. Williston saw estoppel as something "other," a category entirely distinct from contract, and being a committed categorizer, as Black observed, "for him the category, once assigned, did dictate quite a lot."[124] Moreover, he had no interest in any theory confounding the practical aims of the Restatement (a great disappointment to the many admirers of Hohfeld's analytical framework in the ALI). Williston acknowledged the weight of authority for reliance as a justification for contract enforcement. And that was enough for him. He didn't need abstractions or theories to inform him further. Nor was he welcoming of them. "I do not care in what way you may make your true contracts,"[125] he stated bluntly "wherever a promise is binding, it is a contract."[126]

Williston's deep commitment to the weight of judicial authority, particularly when it came to restating the law, would not allow him to shy away from accepting reliance as a broad basis of contract enforcement. Hence, it's easy to see reliance running throughout the Restatement, but it runs wild with no overarching theory to discipline it.[127] Theories might have been offered to inform and organize restatements of the law regarding contractual reliance, if not estoppel. They were, presumably, either not considered or rejected by Williston, no doubt, both for prudential and personal reasons. "Original § 90," as Gilmore said in his inimitable way, "was exposed to the world naked of Comment,"[128] and while the absence of explanation may have been tactical or compelled by exigencies,[129] presenting promissory estoppel without

---

[124] Black, *supra* note 107, at 22. Farnsworth earlier made a similar observation: "In Williston's thinking, liability based on reliance on a gratuitous promise was, like liability based on a gratuitous undertaking, entirely distinct from liability based on bargain." Farnsworth, *supra* note 94 at 1457. Reliance on a bargain promise, however, was very much within his category of cognizably contract liability. Before Farnsworth, Fuller similarly commented on Williston's fixed categorization of "contract," a term one might view as "merely a convenient description for a set of related problems, possessing no definite boundary, but shading off imperceptibly into the law of tort, property, quasi-contract, and procedure on all sides." Fuller, *supra* note 34, at 1, 2.

Williston, however, "has no such conception of contracts."

> For him a contract liability is something different in kind from all other kinds of liability, as different from a tort liability, let us say, as a covenant was different from assumpsit for seventeenth-century lawyers.

Id.

[125] 4 A.L.I. Proc. 6, at 94.

[126] *Id.* at 102.

[127] "Whether through misunderstanding or through deliberate choice, the reliance theory has been applied by courts down to the present day, and has found its way into scholarly treatises. The Restatement, by *rejecting the theory but accepting its results*, has made room in contract law for familial and other noncommercial promises which cannot be squeezed into the bargain category." Patterson, *supra* note 15, at 416–17 (emphasis added).

[128] GILMORE, *supra* note 22, at 71. "In the laconic style that marked the first Restatement, Williston provided no commentary except for four illustrations [and moreover] the first Restatement has no Reporter's notes to give us the inspiration of its illustration." E. Allan Farnsworth, *Contracts during the Half-Century between Restatements*, 30 CLEV. ST. L. REV. 371, at 373 (1981).

[129] Frank, commenting on the general absence of "Explanatory Notes" in the early Restatements, recalled a letter by Cardozo suggesting such exigencies regarding the Restatement of Contract:

> In December 1932, Justice Cardozo, by then on the Supreme Court of the United States, wrote Director Lewis[:] "I confess that the absence of explanatory notes will to my thinking detract greatly from the value of the Restatement. It is plain that you had no alternative in the case of the contracts, but I hope that the decision is not a final one as to other branches of the law."

comment or context of its fit within a broader conception of contractual reliance only made it stand out more, loom larger, overshadowing the thicket of reliance in the rest of the Restatement.

B. Reliance Before and Beyond Promissory Estoppel

Reliance is so explicit in much of the Restatements that a simple tally of the term (in the Black Letter, comments, illustrations, and Reporter's Notes) is enough to convey its salience beyond promissory estoppel.[130] While the tally is significant, it still under-counts the weight of reliance in the Restatements. For instance, "reliance" is not mentioned in the black-letter Section 90 (nor is "promissory estoppel" for that matter). In the Second Restatement, Sections 86 and 87 also deal significantly with matters of reliance, but the term does not show up in a black-letter search of those sections. Moreover, inspecting the published Restatements doesn't capture the pervasiveness of "reliance" in the background debates and discussions at the ALI meetings. Take, for example, Section 35 (reliance after an offeror's death)[131] or Section 42 (reliance and offeree's knowledge of revocation).[132] In some instances previously contentious issues of reliance seem to have been worked out so completely before the ALI meetings that the official records show little trace of their prior significance. That was the case with Section 45 (on unilateral offers). After Cardozo invited suggestions what we see is pretty pedantic:[133]

JUDGE CARDOZO: Are there any suggestions as to Section 43? Section 44? Section 45?
MR. WILLIS: I wonder if there is not an inaccuracy in Section 45 [which] says the of-feror is bound by a contract. I wonder if that is not misleading [to say "contract"].
MR. WILLISTON: I call an irrevocable offer a contract....

John P. Frank, *The American Law Institute: 1923–1998*, in THE AMERICAN LAW INSTITUTE SEVENTY-FIFTH ANNIVERSARY, 1923–1998 15 (1998). Earlier in the project, Cardozo anticipated that the treatises, which did not materialize, would offer the explanatory accounts. "Undoubtedly, much may be done in the treatises supporting the restatements, with their more discursive methods, to mark the tendencies and directions that will determine growth hereafter." 3 A.L.I. PROC. 82, at 106.

[130] For example, "reliance" (or one of its derivatives, such as "rely," "relying," "relies," and so on) appears in seventeen black-letter sections of the First Restatement (i.e., §§ 143, 162, 196, 224, 297, 306, 308, 319, 323, 347, 381, 415, 422, 472, 597) and in thirty-five black-letter sections of the Second Restatement (i.e., §§ 34, 89, 94, 129, 139, 149, 150, 158, 164, 165, 166, 168, 169, 170 171, 172, 175, 177, 230, 256, 272, 311, 323, 344, 345, 349, 351, 370, 373, 374, 376, 377, 378, 381, 382).
[131] Williston reading aloud Oliphant's written objections questioning Section 35's rule terminating an offer on the death of the offeror: "Why shift these losses to another who has acted in reasonable reliance upon the dead man's assurance." 3 A.L.I. PROC. 82, at 198.
[132] Williston clarifying the distinction between knowledge and reliable information: "So we have Section 42. The distinction between knowledge and reliable information is pretty hard to draw. I suppose to make it applicable you must have the facts showing the offeror's change of mind and you must have such informa-tion of those facts as a reasonable offeree would be justified in relying upon. That is the idea." 3 *Id.* at 203.
[133] *Id.* at 204. The entirety of the discussion is contained on two pages, 204–05, including the reading of the black letter: "Section 45. If an offer for a unilateral contract is made, and part of the performance re-quested in the offer is given or tendered by the offeree in response thereto, the offeror is bound by a contract, liability upon which is conditional on the completion by the offeree of the requested performance within the time stated in the offer, or, if no time was there stated, within a reasonable time."

MR. WILLIS: I beg your pardon, you do not want to call this an irrevocable offer, do you?

MR. WILLISTON: That is what you called it, did you not?

MR. WILLIS: Oh, no.

MR. WILLISTON: You stated the power to revoke is destroyed.

MR. WILLIS: It becomes irrevocable-

MR. WILLISTON: All right. When it becomes irrevocable it is an irrevocable offer.

MR. WILLIS: But it does not seem to me that that is so; it seems to me that a contract is one thing and an irrevocable offer is another.

MR. WILLISTON: We are apart on that. An irrevocable is not *the* contract which the offer proposes, but being a binding promise, it is a contract.

JUDGE CARDOZO: Is there anything else under that section? Is there anything under Section 46? Section 47? Section 48? Section 49? Section 50? Section 51?

That was all that was said concerning Section 45. Lost in this anodyne exchange were any remnants of the contentious debate, only several years earlier, concerning the effect of reliance on a unilateral offer. It occurred in what Allan Farnsworth, Reporter for the Restatement (Second) of Contracts, called "the first great debate on contract law" wherein "[t]he battle was fought and won in the pages of the law reviews."[134] On one side of the debate, formalists maintained that an offeree's reliance by commencing to perform following a unilateral offer had no effect on the offeror's power to revoke it. Moreover, they argued, there would be no injustice in the offeror's revocation of the offer because the offeree knew or should have known the terms of its acceptance. Adherents to this classically Langdellian position included Maurice Wormers, who gave first-year contracts teachers the chestnut of the overtaking Brooklyn Bridge revocation hypothetical,[135] and notably Williston.[136] Arguing on the other side against the injustice of revocation post commencement and for the imposition of some duty founded on various theories of reliance and estoppel were Dudley McGovney, Clarence Ashley, and notably Corbin.[137] Given the significance of the adherents on each side and the amplitude of quarrel, not to mention its recency, it is perhaps surprising to hear no hint of this "great debate on contract law" in the discussion of Section 45.

McGovney and Corbin, in their writings and perhaps more so in their roles as Associate Reporters to Williston, appear to have persuaded him, or maybe it was

---

[134] *See* Farnsworth, *supra* note 94, at 1452, and E. Allan Farnsworth, *Casebooks and Scholarship: Confessions of an American Opinion Clipper*, 42 SW. L.J. 903, 913 (1988).

[135] "Suppose A says to B, 'I will give you $100 if you walk across the Brooklyn Bridge,' ... B starts to walk [and gets] about one-half of the way across. At that moment A overtakes B and says to him, 'I withdraw my offer.'" No problem, said Wormers; A owes no duty to B from the latter's reliance. I. Maurice Wormser, *The True Conception of Unilateral Contracts*, 26 YALE L.J. 136, at 136-37 (1916).

[136] *See* Farnsworth, *supra* note 94, at 1449-1454.

[137] D.O. McGovney, *Irrevocable Offers*, 27 HARV. L. REV. 644, 655, 663 (1914); Clarence D. Ashley, *Offers Calling for a Consideration Other Than a Counter Promise*, 23 HARV. L. REV. 159, 161, 166 (1910); Arthur L. Corbin, *Offer and Acceptance, and Some of the Resulting Legal Relations*, 26 YALE L.J. 169, 191-92 (1917). "During the second decade of the twentieth century, several academics began to write in support of the increasing instances of judicial relief given unilateral offerees on account of reliance hardship." Teeven, *supra* note 94, at 558.

Ashley or someone else.[138] In any event, Williston abandoned his opposition to partial reliance affecting unilateral offers sometime before the 1925 ALI meeting where Section 45 (reflecting the position of McGovney and Corbin) was presented to the membership with little fanfare.[139] Other well-known accounts of Corbin's influence on Williston's embrace of reliance in the context of promissory estoppel—from Grant Gilmore's early musings to Barbara Black's most recent telling—add weight to the undergirding presence of reliance in the Restatements. But one needn't look to Section 90 (especially as it tends to distort the larger view) to appreciate the extensive bases of reliance in the Restatements. Reliance is observable in the Restatement's treatment of offers and acceptances, consideration and moral obligation, construction and interpretation, modification and waivers, avoidance and excuses, enforcement (e.g., statute of frauds) and remedies, just to name the most obvious areas.[140] Furthermore, although the discussion here has for the most part focused on the Restatement (First) of Contracts, the scope of reliance has only increased with the Restatement (Second) of Contracts, as indicated in footnote 135.[141]

C. The Costs of Canonization

Samuel Williston gets more blame and more credit for promissory estoppel than he deserves. He is said to have coined the term in 1920.[142] But earlier usage by others is not hard to find.[143] He is said to have provided the first substantial treatment of the doctrine in Section 139 of his treatise. But, again, it is easy to discover substantive entries in cases and earlier treatises, so long as the search terms are not restricted

---

[138] Given the competing claims by various observers, some well known and others obscure, Farnsworth's restrained conclusion is well taken: "What role, if any, it played in Corbin's attempt to push Williston in the direction of recognizing reliance must be left to surmise." Farnsworth, *supra* note 94, at 1462.

[139] "Between the publication of Williston's treatise in 1921 and the first Restatement draft in 1925, Williston changed his position regarding irrevocable unilateral offers after he joined forces on the Restatement drafting committee with Yale law professors Corbin and McGovney, two of the four drafters active on the project." Teeven, *supra* note 94, at 563. "Wormser also eventually switched his position." David G. Epstein & Yvette Joy Liebesman, *Bearded Ladies Walking on the Brooklyn Bridge*, 59 ARK. L. REV. 267, at 279 (2006).

[140] Less obvious but no less important are reliance claims doing work in risk assignments, pre-contractual and post-contractual obligations, as well as in related areas of law, "ancillary" to but supporting "traditional contract law," such as torts (e.g., deceit), property (equitable servitudes), remedies (latches), and restitution to name a few.

[141] Limitations of space prohibit elaboration on reliance in the later Restatements. *See*, however, Charles L. Knapp, *Reliance in the Revised Restatement: The Proliferation of Promissory Estoppel*, 81 COLUM. L. REV. 52 (1981); Joseph M. Perillo, *Restitution in the Second Restatement of Contracts*, 81 COLUM. L. REV. 37, 40 (1981); RICHARD R.W. BROOKS, RELIANCE IN ECONOMICS AND LAW (2022).

[142] *See, e.g.*, Benjamin F. Boyer, *Promissory Estoppel: Requirements and Limitations of the Doctrine*, 98 U. PA. L. REV. 459 (1950), 459. Williston himself may have cultivated the impression of his coinage. At the ALI, he insisted on the usage (to set it apart from estoppel proper) and he made regular reference to his use of the term in his 1920 treatise: "I rather insist on the use of the word promissory in front of it, if you are going to talk about estoppel" 4 A.L.I. PROC. 6 at 97; "I have used the word estoppel in connection with this sort of case in my treatises" *Id.*; "I have in my treatise used the term "promissory estoppel" for this sort of case"; *id.* at 90.

[143] "A promissory estoppel cannot exist," plaintiffs in error argued before the U.S. Supreme Court in 1889. *See* "Brief of George Hoardly for Plaintiffs in Error," October Term 1898, Sup. Ct. of U.S., at 58, in *Tracy v. Tuffly*, 134 U.S. 206 (1890). Argued November 22, 25, 1889. Decided March 3, 1890.

to "promissory estoppel."[144] Looking only at the Reporters, Williston may have been second or later to have a substantive discussion on promissory estoppel as a substitute for consideration. Corbin, who apparently disfavored the term as too vacuous, roundly addressed reliance as an alternative to consideration in his 1919 edition of *Anson's* treatise.[145] Three years earlier, whether he welcomed the title or not, Corbin chaired a round table discussion on "Promissory estoppel as a substitute for consideration" at the 1916 Annual Meeting of the American Association of Law Schools.[146] "Is § 90 of the Contracts Restatement, or § 45, 'new' doctrine?" posed Llewellyn, rhetorically questioning what he dubbed "the caseless Restatement of the Law of Contract."[147] "The cases say: Both are rather belated *explicit* doctrine."[148] Promissory estoppel, in name and form, was not unexplored territory when Williston reach it, but nor he did leave it unaltered.

Neither courts nor commentators have ever abandoned the ancient grounds of reliance for enforcing promises as contracts. Those grounds remained well trodden through the 1920s, though they had become overgrown with entangled doctrines originally spun from equity or at law. Some clearing was called for, exactly the sort of task the Reporters set out for themselves, and it was here that Williston, in cahoots Corbin and other Associate Reporters, left their distinctive mark by cutting back, pruning, and altering the growth of the old reliance doctrine with the introduction of Section 90. It has been suggested that the Reporters merely elevated an existing doctrine—a minority view, though we were assured, a "respectable" one.[149] But that is not all they did. "By deliberately choosing to *canonize* a minority view," they concocted "promissory estoppels," as Patterson put it.[150] Yet there was something off about it, like an "s" attached to the end of "estoppel," rendering it unfamiliar though

---

[144] "The label 'promissory estoppel' supplied catchy phraseology for the open recognition of a ground that had largely been smuggled in either under the doctrine of consideration or as a form of equitable relief." Teeven, *supra* note 94, 499, 526.

[145] "Indeed, there are many cases justifying the statement that consideration may consist of acts in reliance upon a promise even though they were not specified as the agreed equivalent and inducement, provided the promisor ought to have foreseen that such action would take place and the promisee reasonably believes it to be desired." WILLIAM R. ANSON, PRINCIPLES OF THE ENGLISH LAW OF CONTRACT (Arthur L. Corbin ed., 3d Am. ed. 1919) at 124, n. 1. "Corbin objected to the term on the ground that estoppel was too widely and loosely used to be of much value." Jay M. Feinman, *Promissory Estoppel and Judicial Method*, 97 HARV. L. REV. 678, n.1 (1984).

[146] "Round Table Conferences," *Association of American Law Schools. Proceedings of the Annual Meeting 1916* (1916). The general topic of the Roundtable was "Consideration," with special reference to "Promissory estoppel as a substitute for consideration (Reliance on a promise as opposed to reliance on a statement of fact.)" Dudley McGovney (another Reporter on Contracts) chaired the AALS Contracts Round Table the year before, in 1915, and one would imagine he also participated in the 1916 Round Table, particularly since "Irrevocable offers" was the second general topic slated for discussion that year, a topic of great interest to McGovney as well as Corbin.

[147] Llewellyn, *supra* note 29, at 1243 n.25, 1252, & 1269.

[148] *Id.* n.25, at 1252 (emphasis original).

[149] "The recognition of promissory estoppels involved … the adoption of a substantial and respectable minority view." Patterson, *supra* note 15, at 415–16. That was the only minority position taken by Williston &c., according to John Frank. "Most of the time the Restatements reflect the majority view; the only exception in the first Restatement of Contracts was §90, which adopted the minority view on promissory estoppel." John P. Frank, *The American Law Institute: 1923–1998, in* THE AMERICAN LAW INSTITUTE SEVENTY-FIFTH ANNIVERSARY, 1923–1998, at 17–18 (1998).

[150] Patterson, *supra* note 15, at 415–16 (emphasis added).

not entirely unrecognizable. The same may be said of the doctrine after the Reporters fashioned it for inclusion in their Restatement.

A purportedly modest doctrine initially looked at askance, Section 90 has become what's mostly seen as the central reliance justification for enforcing contracts today. While it has not usurped the status of "bargained-for consideration," as some observers predicted, Section 90's impact on reliance has been remarkable. Not that the Reporters planned or hoped for this extraordinary outcome. They were not seeking radical change nor were they acting with abandon—"members of the American Law Institute," Gilmore once remarked, "are not revolutionaries in their habits of thought or ways of living"—just the opposite.[151] They feared that by placing the doctrine (unaltered and unrestrained) into the Restatement, courts would, with the imprimatur of the ALI, become too liberal in their use of reliance to enforce promises. It was this prospective abandon of judges that they sought to constrain, judges who might look for and find liberal license in reading the unaffected doctrine in the Restatement. Responding to worries that Section 90 would open up for enforcement "a Pandora's box of casual and gratuitous promises," they confined and contorted the doctrine, cutting its applicability by adding constraints not found in the cases.[152] An enfeebled doctrine was proffered, not just a marginal one; it was a reliance doctrine in much reduced form.

Williston did not simply elevate a then extant minority view reliance. He couldn't even if he wanted to, because members of a significant faction within the ALI—those who had been taught to embrace the narrow view of contracts based almost exclusively on the bargain theory advanced by Langdell, then by Holmes and later by Williston himself (more so in earlier years)—would not sit for it. "For minds that resisted the leap expressed in Restatement section 45," as Farnsworth observed regarding debates a decade earlier, "the leap expressed in section 90 was inconceivable."[153] To win their support, Williston "conjured up a limitation on the basic promissory estoppel action," as Black observed, adding a clause restricting its use only in cases of unavoidable injustice.[154] Additional restraints were imposed by qualifiers in the black letter.[155] Williston further "dampened expectations by saying that section 90 does not assert a 'sweeping rule' that reliance is sufficient support for a promise."[156] Distortion of a doctrine, by dampening or otherwise altering its prior or primary or plain meaning, is sometimes a cost that must be borne for it to gain admission to a canon. Contract's traditional reliance doctrine and promissory estoppel bore that cost when Section 90 was canonized in the Restatement.[157]

---

[151] GILMORE, *supra* note 22, at 68.

[152] Patterson, *supra* note 15, at 417.

[153] Farnsworth, *supra* note 94, at 1454. "This heresy did not occur to the antebellum mind, trained in the orthodoxy that a promise needed consideration or a seal to be binding. Nor did it occur to Langdell or other contracts scholars of his century." *Id.*

[154] Black, *supra* note 107, at 17. The clause "instructs a court that it need not, and indeed may not, enforce such a promise if the injustice which has motivated adoption of the broad principle of promissory estoppel can be avoided in some other way." *Id.*

[155] Such "qualifications placed upon the rule" included "should reasonably expect," "substantial," and "if injustice can be avoided only." Patterson, *supra* note 15, at 417.

[156] Teeven, *supra* note 94, at 245 (quoting § 90 (Proposed Final Draft No. 1 (1928))).

[157] Indeed, both the traditional doctrines of reliance and consideration suffered the costs of distortion and effacement as a consequence of Sections 90 and 75 canonization in the Restatement.

Moshe Halbertal provides a wonderful illustration of this phenomenon in his description of the price paid by Ecclesiastes for entry into the biblical canon.[158] In its earlier form, the Book of Ecclesiastes "contains more than a hint of heresy": God is omnipotent but arbitrary; good men perish, and bad ones sometimes prevail.[159] Hence the text recommends, "do not overdo goodness and do not act the wise man to excess."[160] Its original ending closed with the nihilistic summation: "Utter futility— ... All is futile."[161] Reading Ecclesiastes in its original form raised the same question for the exegetes that Estoppel, unadorned, appeared to have raised for the Reporters. "Is all restraint to be removed?"[162] Ecclesiastes' original hedonistic message had to be reinterpreted and restated to become part of "the body of the Scriptures."[163] As Halbertal concluded: "The book of Ecclesiastes thus pays dearly for the everlasting fame it wins by being canonized; renown comes at the expense of distortion and effacement of its unique and radical message."[164] In the case of Section 90's canonization, it was not only the more liberal promissory estoppel doctrine in case law that suffered, but also traditional notions of reliance in contracts more broadly.

It turned out, as they would later realize, that Williston and his fellow Reporters pushed for too much restraint in their desire to suppress the hedonistic impulses they feared would arise in judges sensing unwarranted liberty from an unfettered statement of the doctrine. In the wake of Section 90's official release in 1932, courts and scholarly commentary appeared to have largely accepted the restrictions placed on the prior doctrine. In the first prominent case mentioning Section 90, *James Baird Co. v. Gimbel Bros., Inc.* (1933), Learned Hand delivered his much-cited opinion holding that in the context of commercial bargains, "[t]here is no room in such a situation for the doctrine of 'promissory estoppel.' "[165] A number of courts followed Hand's lead in embracing this restrictive view of Section 90, as did many law professors, at least at first.[166] There was and remains, however, some room to debate whether (in addition to the restrictions and qualifications mentioned in footnotes 155 and 156) the Reporters

---

[158] "A case in point is the book of Ecclesiastes, whose composition has been dated to the third century BCE and whose text reflects a deeply skeptical position typical of early Hellenistic philosophy." HALBERTAL, *supra* note 99, at 23.

[159] *Id.*

[160] *Id.* at 23–24.

[161] *Id.* at 26.

[162] *Id.* at 25 (quoting The Midrash).

[163] *Id.* at 24. "The accommodation of the text to the canon was made possible not only by reinterpretation but by additions to the text itself." *Id.* at 26. "Paradoxically, then, the canonization of a work sometimes serves to suppress its most plausible readings. Because the canonization of a book is in fact the canonization of a very specific reading of it, one must make certain the reader does indeed read it that way." *Id.*

[164] *Id.* at 25.

[165] James Baird Co. v. Gimbel Bros., 64 F.2d 344, 346 (2d Cir. 1933). "Hand seemed to approach the Restatement's promissory estoppel doctrine as if it had wiped the slate clean of prior justifiable reliance decisions in New York." Teeven, *supra* note 94, at 538.

[166] "Between Restatements," wrote Farnsworth, "section 90 received virtually unanimous judicial and academic approval." Farnsworth, *supra* note 128, at 371, 374. The claim of virtual unanimity of approval for Section 90 among judges and scholars in the half century between 1932 and 1981 is demonstrably false. There were mixed academic reviews for Section 90 even in the earliest assessments, as the 1933 articles written by Clark and Patterson illustrate. *See* Clark, *supra* note 5, and Patterson, *supra* note 15. Nonetheless, there was early considerable academic support following *Baird Co. v. Gimbel Bros.* for the Restatement's restricted view. *See, e.g.,* Warren L. Shattuck, *Gratuitous Promises—A New Writ?*, 35 MICH. L. REV. 908, 943–44 (1937); Boyer, *supra* note 142, at 652; Teeven, *supra* note 94, at 538–39.

intended to limit the doctrine to gratuitous promises in line with Hand's reading of it and as indicated in ALI debates where Hand was present and engaged in the discussion,[167] or whether they envisioned it would apply also to commercial exchanges as is consistent with the Black Letter and the plain fact that the Reporters knew the original doctrine was not limited to gratuitous promises.[168] All of this remains part of the enduring attraction and distraction of the canonized doctrine of Section 90.

There is, of course, no good reason to believe that the Reporters were of one mind regarding this aspect of the doctrine, and perhaps the equivocal Black Letter and absence of official commentary on Section 90 were meant to give cover to their differences of opinion.[169] Corbin and Williston are famed for their diverging views and it should surprise no one to discover that their opinions diverged here too. Section 90's whole appearance, on closer inspection, looks less mysterious and more like a product of strategic ambiguity. In any event, whatever they may have sought beforehand, after seeing Hand's narrow view take hold and harden its grip on the reach of justifiable reliance, it seems that Corbin and Williston had finally come to agree "that they had been too restrained in their description of the scope of promissory liability," as Teeven suggested. "Consequently, they tried to modulate the restricted view of promissory estoppel held by Hand and other judges by encouraging a more expansive application."[170] But the die was cast, or more precisely, the canon was sealed with the publication of the Restatement (First), not to be reopened until the Second. At that moment the Restatement's framers lost their special power to influence the doctrine's meaning. They then became merely readers and interpreters, like those on the bench, in the bar, and in the academy, which is to say they then became simply "restaters" but not without the restater's power.[171]

---

[167] Barbara Black persuasively supports the view that the Reporters firmly intended to limit Section 90's applicability to noncommercial promises:

> As the Reporter said, "there is simply a gratuitous promise which the promisor knows is gratuitous and which the promisee knows is gratuitous." There is no bargain, no deal, no exchange, just a promise and reliance. As Learned Hand, an active member of the ALI, wrote to Sir Frederick Pollock about the impetus behind the future Section 90, the Restaters had noticed that modern measures meant to apply to, and to simplify, commercial law had had an unintended effect on personal law, that is, that they made gratuitous-but-relied-upon promises unenforceable. Said Hand: "This the Restaters set out to correct."

Black, *supra* note 107, at 7.

[168] Kevin Teeven presents a good case for this position:

> The generalized language in section 90 was open to the possibility of commercial promises being covered; Williston certainly knew that commercial promisees had received reliance relief because many of the unannotated cases included in his treatise's footnotes involved commercial promises. He left the actual scope of section 90 up in the air for the reader of the published version in 1932 since, unlike many of the Restatement's sections, he provided no comments or reporter's notes.

Teeven, *supra* note 94, at 532.

[169] As Patterson noted the Restatement presented material as though it is "the product of expert opinion" and in deriving that product "there are no divergent expert opinions." Patterson, *supra* note 15, at 399.

[170] Teeven, *supra* note 94, at 539. "In Williston's second edition of his treatise in 1936, he criticized Hand's limited interpretation of section 90[.]" *Id.* And in his subsequent treatise, Corbin also cautioned dogmatic and restrictive readings of doctrines that would limit the grounds of enforcement based on justifiable reliance.

[171] "After the act of canonization the expositor is no longer called upon to justify his views," as "[t]he reader, more than the text itself, becomes the bearer of authority." HALBERTAL, *supra* note 99, at 24.

IV. Conclusion

Speaking to the Harvard Law School Association in 1888, Oliver Wendell Holmes, Jr. predicted that "[t]he law has got to be stated over again, and I venture to say that in fifty years we shall have it in a form of which no man could have dreamed fifty years ago."[172] It would take slightly less than fifty years following Holmes's speech for the law of contracts to be stated over again in the form of a Restatement, an accomplishment that is looking back, as he suggested, few would have imagined in the 1830s. Is this Restatement and the larger continuing restatement project still worthy of wonder today, in 2023?

"Champagne and fireworks may well be appropriate in 2023 when we complete our first century," said Charles Alan Wright, President of the ALI in 1998 when the ALI commemorated its 75th anniversary.[173] Over its 100-year history the ALI, like all institutions that survive so long, has had successes and failures. How ought the Restatements of Contracts be measured on the scales of success and failure? One might say pragmatically, as the Chinese premier Zhou Enlai is said to have responded in 1972 when asked about the impact of the French Revolution: "Too early to say." France, of course, has had several significant revolutions, and apparently the premier was referring to the more recent uprising in May 1968, and not the one that began nearly two centuries earlier in May 1789. We needn't equivocate, however, in assessing the impact of the Restatements of Contracts in one essential regard. The Restatements are unquestionably the principal source for discovery of the U.S. common law of contracts on which anyone seeking to learn the law relies. In this regard, for achieving its canonical status, it is not too soon to pop the corks and light the fireworks.

---

[172] OLIVER WENDELL HOLMES, JR., THE USE OF LAW SCHOOLS (Oration before the Harvard Law School Association, at Cambridge, November 5, 1888, on the 250th Anniversary of Harvard University).

[173] CHARLES ALAN WRIGHT, PRESIDENT, ALI, THE AMERICAN LAW INSTITUTE, SEVENTY-FIFTH ANNIVERSARY 1923–1998 (July 6, 1998), (President's Foreword), at vii.

IV. Conclusion

6

Conflict of Laws in the ALI's First Century

Symeon C. Symeonides

I. Introduction

The law of Conflict of Laws has been the beneficiary of the American Law Institute's (ALI's) attention since its founding a century ago. Conflicts was one of the first three subjects that the ALI decided to restate.[1] After the first Conflicts Restatement of 1934,[2] the ALI produced the Second Restatement in 1969[3] and is currently drafting a third.[4] In the interim, the ALI carried out several other related projects. They include two proposed federal statutes on recognition of foreign judgments and complex litigation, respectively,[5] several studies and sets of principles,[6] as well as other Restatements on subjects related to Conflicts, such as foreign relations and international commercial arbitration.[7]

Because of the space limitations of this volume, this brief chapter is limited to the Conflicts Restatements. It is further limited to their choice-of-law segments, which have been the most consequential. The discussion begins with, and focuses more on, the flawed but formative first Restatement.

---

[1] The other two subjects were torts (1934), and business associations. The business associations Restatement was later abandoned and was replaced by the Restatement of Contracts (1932), Agency (1933), and Property (1937).

[2] *See* RESTATEMENT OF THE LAW: CONFLICT OF LAWS (1934) [hereinafter First Restatement].

[3] *See* RESTATEMENT OF THE LAW SECOND: CONFLICT OF LAWS 2ND (1971) [hereinafter Second Restatement].

[4] At the time of this writing, the latest draft is RESTATEMENT OF THE LAW THIRD: CONFLICT OF LAWS (Tentative Draft No. 3, Mar. 2022). It was approved by the ALI membership in May 2022.

[5] *See* AMERICAN LAW INSTITUTE, RECOGNITION AND ENFORCEMENT OF FOREIGN JUDGMENTS: ANALYSIS AND PROPOSED FEDERAL STATUTE (2006, discussed in George A. Bermann, *The International Law Profile of the ALI*, in this volume; AMERICAN LAW INSTITUTE, COMPLEX LITIGATION: STATUTORY RECOMMENDATIONS AND ANALYSIS (1994), discussed in Linda S. Mullenix, *Aggregationists at the Barricades: Assessing the Impact of the Principles of the Law of Aggregate Litigation*, in this volume.

[6] *See, e.g.,* AMERICAN LAW INSTITUTE, STUDY OF THE DIVISION OF JURISDICTION BETWEEN STATE AND FEDERAL COURTS (1969); AMERICAN LAW INSTITUTE, ALI/UNIDROIT PRINCIPLES OF TRANSNATIONAL CIVIL PROCEDURE (2004); AMERICAN LAW INSTITUTE, INTELLECTUAL PROPERTY: PRINCIPLES GOVERNING JURISDICTION, CHOICE OF LAW, AND JUDGMENTS IN TRANSNATIONAL DISPUTES (2008); AMERICAN LAW INSTITUTE, TRANSNATIONAL INSOLVENCY: GLOBAL PRINCIPLES FOR COOPERATION IN INTERNATIONAL INSOLVENCY CASES (2012).

[7] *See* RESTATEMENT (SECOND) OF FOREIGN RELATIONS LAW OF THE UNITED STATES (1965); RESTATEMENT (THIRD) OF FOREIGN RELATIONS LAW OF THE UNITED STATES (Revised) (1987); RESTATEMENT (FOURTH) OF FOREIGN RELATIONS LAW OF THE UNITED STATES (2018); RESTATEMENT OF THE U.S. LAW OF INTERNATIONAL COMMERCIAL AND INVESTOR-STATE ARBITRATION (Proposed Final Draft 2019). For a discussion of these restatements, as well as other ALI projects on international law, *see* Bermann, *supra* note 5.

Symeon C. Symeonides, *Conflict of Laws in the ALI's First Century* In: *The American Law Institute*. Edited by: Andrew S. Gold and Robert W. Gordon, Oxford University Press. © Oxford University Press 2023. DOI: 10.1093/oso/9780197685341.003.0007

II. The First Conflicts Restatement

The ALI explained its decision to include Conflicts in the first installment of restatements by referring to "[t]he great confusion existing in the subject of the conflict of laws ... and the importance of the subject in view of our Federal system with its forty-eight states, each with its own law."[8] These are valid reasons, to be sure. But perhaps a weightier reason was the role of Professor Joseph H. Beale, a dominant academic figure at the time, who, along with a handful of others, was instrumental in the ALI's founding.[9]

A. Joseph H. Beale (1861–1943)

In turn, the inclusion of Conflicts law inevitably led to Beale's appointment as Reporter because he was then the indisputable leader in the field.[10] In fact, Beale had put Conflicts law on the map. He was the first to teach Conflicts in any American law school, in 1893,[11] and the first to publish a Conflicts casebook, in 1900–1902,[12] which was subsequently adopted in most other law schools. The third volume included a summary of Beale's conception of Conflicts law and became the foundation of his three-volume treatise,[13] which the Restatement followed in structure, sequence, and substance.

Beale's treatise was characterized as "authoritative and epoch-making,"[14] "the best work yet produced on either English or American conflict of laws,[15] the "most

---

[8] *The Topics Which the Institute May First Undertake to Restate,* 1 A.L.I. PROC. 43, 45 (1923).

[9] The idea of establishing what later became the ALI was first proposed at the 1914 Annual Meeting of the Association of American Law Schools (AALS) when Beale was AALS president. He then appointed and chaired an AALS committee to explore the idea of establishing "a permanent organization for the improvement of the law." In 1921, the AALS endorsed that idea in a formal resolution, which was implemented two years later after the decisive involvement of some leading personalities of the bar. For a detailed documentation of this process and Beale's role in it, *see* N.E.H. Hull, *Restatement and Reform: A New Perspective on the Origins of the American Law Institute,* 8 LAW & HIST. REV. 55 (1990).

[10] For an account of Beale's illustrious career, *see* Symeon C. Symeonides, *The First Conflicts Restatement Through the Eyes of Old: As Bad as Its Reputation?,* 32 S. ILL. U. L.J. 39 (2007). This chapter draws from that article.

[11] Thereafter, Beale taught and published in almost every subject in the curriculum and left his mark upon many of them—he produced ten casebooks, eight textbooks, eighty-six law review articles, and fifty book reviews. He was well versed in the European legal literature, even though he believed it to be unhelpful for American Conflicts law. He translated Bartolus from Latin and another work from German, and spoke French and Spanish. *See id.* at 41–43.

[12] *See* JOSEPH H. BEALE, COLLECTION OF CASES ON THE CONFLICT OF LAWS, 3 vols. (1900–1902). This book contained four hundred American and English cases and seventy foreign cases translated into English. The only casebook published before then was JOHN W. DWYER, CASES ON PRIVATE INTERNATIONAL LAW (1899), which included only forty cases. The next Conflicts casebook appeared in 1909. *See* ERNEST G. LORENZEN, CASES ON THE CONFLICT OF LAWS, SELECTED FROM DECISIONS OF ENGLISH AND AMERICAN COURTS (1909).

[13] *See* JOSEPH H. BEALE, A TREATISE ON THE CONFLICT OF LAWS, 3 vols. (1st ed. 1935). An intermediate one-volume version appeared in 1916. *See* JOSEPH H. BEALE, A TREATISE ON THE CONFLICT OF LAWS OR PRIVATE INTERNATIONAL LAW, vol. I, pt.1 (1916).

[14] Arthur Leon Harding, *Joseph Henry Beale: Pioneer,* 2 Mo. L. REV. 131, 131 (1937).

[15] Frederick J. de Sloovère, *On Looking into Mr. Beale's Conflict of Laws,* 13 N.Y.U. L. Q. REV. 333, 368 (1936).

elaborate collection of cases ... which has ever been made,"[16] and "the only collection of American Conflict of Laws cases remotely approaching completeness."[17] Even David F. Cavers, one of Beale's most severe critics,[18] acknowledged that the treatise was "a remarkable feat of systematization ... establish[ing] order out of the chaos."[19] Indeed, in the eyes of his contemporaries, Beale was the great systematizer of American Conflicts law.[20] His treatise eclipsed even Joseph Story's seminal *Commentaries*, which had guided the development of American Conflicts law for more than a century.[21] Since the last edition of the *Commentaries*, the case law had grown significantly and in different directions, and no writer other than Beale attempted to collect or systematize it.[22]

B. Beale's Control of the Drafting Process

Beale dominated the process of drafting the first Restatement from the beginning to the end. Given Beale's personality and stature, this was predictable, but it was made easier by the fact that six of the ten Advisers to the Reporter were Beale's former students—only two of the ten had taught Conflicts, and nine of them belonged to the same jurisprudential school as Beale.[23] Beale's drafts came directly from his treatise, then in draft form itself, which was "required reading" for the Advisers.[24] The drafts sailed through the meetings of the Advisers,[25] then the Council, and then the ALI membership without any changes affecting the Restatement's fundamental premises.

---

[16] Henry L. McClintock, *Beale on the Conflict of Laws*, 84 U. PA. L. REV. 309, 309 (1936).

[17] Harding, *supra* note 14, at 159.

[18] *See* David F. Cavers, *A Critique of the Choice-of-Law Problem*, 47 HARV. L. REV. 173 (1933).

[19] David F. Cavers, *Book Review* (reviewing WALTER W. COOK, THE LOGICAL AND LEGAL BASES OF THE CONFLICT OF LAWS), 56 HARV. L. REV. 1170, 1172 (1943).

[20] *See* de Sloovère, *supra* note 15, at 370 ("Beale has brought this subject to the fore in this country almost single handed.... He has systematized the thinking in a field which ... was chaotic. He has laid the foundation for future development; and he has accurately brought this mass of conflicting materials, conflicting theories, and inconsistent rules and doctrines, by the sheer power of his analytical thinking and legal ability, into a consistent, rational and independent whole.").

[21] *See* JOSEPH STORY, COMMENTARIES ON THE CONFLICT OF LAWS, FOREIGN AND DOMESTIC, IN REGARD TO CONTRACTS, RIGHTS, AND REMEDIES, AND ESPECIALLY IN REGARD TO MARRIAGES, DIVORCES, WILLS, SUCCESSIONS, AND JUDGMENTS (1st ed. 1834).

[22] The only other American Conflicts books published since Story's *Commentaries* were FRANCIS WHARTON, A TREATISE ON THE CONFLICT OF LAWS, OR PRIVATE INTERNATIONAL LAW: A COMPARATIVE VIEW OF ANGLO-AMERICAN, ROMAN, GERMAN, AND FRENCH JURISPRUDENCE (1872), and RALEIGH C. MINOR, CONFLICT OF LAWS OR PRIVATE INTERNATIONAL LAW (1901). They were neither comprehensive nor systematic. *See* Symeonides, *supra* note 10, at 44–45.

[23] For the specifics, *see* Symeonides, *supra* note 10, at 66–67. The only exception was Joseph W. Bingham who was a legal realist, but perhaps because he was one of Beale's students, he expressed only minor disagreements with Beale and even chastised other realists for their rudeness toward him. *See* Joseph W. Bingham, *The American Law Institute vs. The Supreme Court: In the Matter of Haddock v. Haddock*, 21 CORNELL L.Q. 393, 434–35 (1936). Ernest Lorenzen, who was also a legal realist, served as Adviser only in the first year and resigned after "wag[ing] his share of the battle with a royal good will." Herbert F. Goodrich, *Institute Bards and Yale Reviewers*, 84 U. PA. L. REV. 449, 456 (1936).

[24] *See* Symeonides, *supra* note 10, at 67. The ALI authorized payment of $4,000 to Beale for "his assignment to the Institute of all unpublished material written or collected by him bearing on the topic Conflict of Laws." *Minutes of the Second Meeting of the Council*, 1 A.L.I. PROC. 28, 37 (1923) (May 19, 1923).

[25] For the Advisers' method of work and their reliance on Beale's treatise, *see* *Minutes of the Seventh Meeting of the Council*, 2 A.L.I. PROC. 241, 245–46 (1924).

When the first Conflicts Restatement was submitted for discussion to the ALI membership at its annual two-day meetings, it had to compete for time with the other three Restatements and several other projects underway in the 1920s. The Conflicts Restatement was discussed at eight Annual Meetings in two-hour sessions in 1925, 1927–1932, and 1934. A review of the minutes of these sessions shows that, on average, the membership spent less than two minutes per Restatement section, with some sections taking much more time and some sections not being discussed at all.[26]

Lack of adequate time for a thorough discussion has been a perpetual problem at ALI Annual Meetings.[27] For this and other reasons, the Annual Meetings process unintentionally "leave[s] the cards in the hands of the original reporter."[28] To be sure, before a draft makes it to the ALI Annual Meetings, it goes through several layers of scrutiny in front of smaller and more invested groups, especially the all-important ALI Council. However, judging from the final product, such scrutiny was either absent or too lenient in the case of the first Conflicts Restatement. Large sections of Beale's treatise found their way into the proposed final drafts, and as described later, they remained unchallenged at the Annual Meetings.

C. No Challenge to the Fundamentals

For example, one would expect to see long discussions of Beale's two overarching principles—territoriality and vested rights. Territoriality was the starting premise of much of the case law at that time, but it was not the all-encompassing, inexorable principle that Beale made it out to be.[29] Yet nobody raised this general question at the ALI meetings, even though some narrower questions indicate that the questioners, unlike Beale, did not accept territoriality wholesale. Similarly, Beale never had to defend his version of the vested rights theory, which had some support in the case law but was the target of serious academic criticism outside the ALI.[30]

The failure to question the Restatement's fundamental premises was directly connected to the fact that, as explained later, Beale's critics were absent from the ALI meetings. However, other, more mundane factors such as the timing and sequence of discussion also played a role. As is normal for works of such length, the Restatement was presented at the Annual Meetings not as a single whole, but in several pieces (drafts). The sequence of presentation depended on which drafts were ready first rather than on which were foundational. For example, the first draft presented at

---

[26] The minutes of these sessions, in most instances taken verbatim, occupy 486 small-size pages of the ALI Proceedings, averaging 333 words each. *See* 3 A.L.I. PROC. 222, 222–81 (1925); 5 A.L.I. PROC.139, 139–283 (1927); 6 A.L.I. PROC. 454, 454–78 (1928); 7 A.L.I. PROC. 68, 68–90 (1929); 8 A.L.I. PROC. 164, 164–99 (1930); 9 A.L.I. PROC.127, 127–77 (1930–31); 10 A.L.I. PROC. 70, 70–101 (1932); 11 A.L.I. PROC. 357, 357–410 (1934). Considering that the Restatement consists of 625 sections, this averaged to less than a page per section, including the text of some of the proposed sections.

[27] The problem has become much worse in the last thirty years; it demands the Council's urgent attention.

[28] Hessel E. Yntema, *The Restatement of the Law of Conflict of Laws*, 36 COLUM. L. REV. 183, 195 (1936).

[29] For a discussion of this issue, including a comparison of the relevant sections of Beale's treatise and the First Restatement, *see* Symeonides, *supra* note 10, at 57–59.

[30] *See id.* at 60–62.

an Annual Meeting was the draft on domicile,[31] a concept that, despite its practical importance, does not lend itself to an in-depth discussion of the grand principles of Conflicts law.

D. No Discussion of the *Lex Loci Delicti* Rule

Today's readers would be very surprised to learn that the all-important *lex loci delicti* rule for torts, which later became the main target of the choice-of-law revolution,[32] received no discussion time at the Annual Meetings—zero. While this rule was consistent with the case law of that time, Beale's reformulation of it was much more rigid, especially with his addition of certain subrules such as the "last event" subrule.[33] The only questions asked of Beale were stylistic. The whole discussion of the chapter on Wrongs took less than two hours, and more than half of that time was devoted to a discussion of a single rather unimportant section on ship collisions.[34]

E. The Absence of Academic Critics

Beale's main contemporary critics were three well-known legal realists: Walter W. Cook (1873–1943), Ernest G. Lorenzen (1876–1951), and Hessel E. Yntema (1891–1966).[35] Cook and Lorenzen were members of the ALI, but Yntema was not. Lorenzen was one of the Beale's initial Advisers, but he resigned before the first draft was presented to the ALI in 1925.[36] Cook attended the 1925 meeting and was asked by ALI Director William D. Lewis to explain his misgivings about Beale's definition of domicile. Cook was reluctant to do so, saying that he would not have enough time to explain his position and that he would prefer to address the Council at a later time. Judge Cardozo, who chaired the meeting as ALI Vice President, encouraged Cook to "state in general [his] position without developing it at this time."[37] Cook spoke briefly yet eloquently and tried to explain that a single, all-encompassing definition of domicile could not be valid nor helpful for all purposes.[38] Instead of personally responding,

---

[31] *See Minutes of the Third Annual Meeting Held at Washington, D.C., May 1 and 2, 1925*, 3 A.L.I. Proc. 82 (1925).

[32] *See* Symeon C. Symeonides, The American Choice-of-Law Revolution: Past, Present and Future 37–43 (2006).

[33] *See* Restatement § 377 ("The place of wrong is in the state where the last event necessary to make the actor liable for an alleged tort takes place.").

[34] *See* Joseph H. Beale, *Discussion of Conflict of Laws Proposed—Final Draft No. 3*, 10 A.L.I. Proc. 70, 70–101 (1931–1932).

[35] A fourth critic, David F. Cavers (1903–1988), who was one of Beale's students, was too young to be a member of the ALI before the Restatement's promulgation (Cavers graduated from law school in 1926). Cavers published his influential *Critique*, *supra* note 18, in 1933, by which time the Restatement was essentially finished, although it was not promulgated until 1934. A few other academic members of the ALI attended the Conflicts meetings but, apparently, none of them were Conflicts specialists.

[36] *See supra* note 23.

[37] Joseph H. Beale, *Discussion of the Tentative Draft, Conflict of Laws, Restatement No. 1*, 3 A.L.I. Proc. 226 (1925).

[38] *See id.* at 226–29. Cook made the same points with regard to domicile as he did later in his widely admired article on substance and procedure—namely, that one could not intelligently determine whether a

Beale asked his assistant, Austin W. Scott, to reply. Scott's reply was substantive and respectful, but essentially dismissive. As far as can be ascertained, Cook did not attend another ALI meeting discussing the Conflicts Restatement. There is also no record of Lorenzen or Yntema attending any of those meetings.[39] The absence of Beale's academic critics from the ALI meetings made passage of his proposals all the more likely.

It is not suggested here that academics have the monopoly on knowledge or wisdom, or that only they can be effective critics. In fact, the judges and attorneys who attended the Conflicts meetings asked Beale some excellent questions. However, most of the questions were practical, technical, or stylistic, and often drawn from the questioner's prior experience with individual cases. As useful as those questions are, they rarely affect a Restatement's foundation and orientation. In a field like Conflicts law, which was then quite young and even today is perceived as esoteric, few attorneys or judges build enough experience to confidently challenge the Reporter's general premises.

F. Beale Was Dominant and Unyielding

The setting of the ALI Annual Meetings gave Beale a distinct advantage. Even before he was appointed Reporter, he was the dominant and perhaps the most respected figure in American Conflicts law. He had mastered the case law and obviously knew his own drafts. As one observer noted at the time, "no writer has read so many cases ... than [Beale]."[40] He could therefore easily answer most of the questions asked by ALI members who, as Yntema noted, did not have "the advantage of the materials upon which the draft is based, and normally [were] without the time and incentive necessary to prepare an exhaustive critique."[41]

Beale used the Reporter's high pedestal to his advantage, and he rarely gave an inch—even when the questioners clearly had the better side of the argument. As Dean Erwin Griswold wrote in Beale's obituary, "[Beale] would not yield a bit from [his position], even when his opponents forced him into extreme conclusions."[42] Griswold tells of an incident in the classroom in which Beale told a student that there was no state in the Union that followed the view that the student advocated. The student replied with a citation of a Massachusetts case, to which Beale replied: "That's not a *state*; it's a *Commonwealth*. Next case."[43]

The ALI minutes do not contain such a colorful an exchange, but the discussion of party autonomy comes close. Party autonomy stands for the proposition that, subject

---

rule is procedural or substantive without reference to the context and purposes of the rule in question. *See* Walter W. Cook, *"Substance" and "Procedure" in the Conflict of Laws*, 42 YALE L.J. 333 (1933).

[39] Judge Learned Hand, who had developed a "local law theory" similar to Cook's and was a member of the ALI Council, attended many of the Annual Meetings and occasionally spoke. However, he did not challenge Beale.

[40] de Sloovère, *supra* note 15, at 368–69.

[41] Yntema, *supra* note 28, at 196.

[42] Erwin N. Griswold, *Mr. Beale and the Conflict of Laws*, 56 HARV. L. REV. 690, 694 (1943).

[43] *Id.* at 693.

to certain exceptions and limitations, contracting parties should be allowed to select in advance the law that will govern their contract.[44] This principle, which is now universal, was recognized by American transactional and judicial practice as early as 1825.[45] Yet Beale chose to ignore it because it did not fit into his territorialist conception of Conflicts law and his general "theological" view[46] that "[l]egal thinkers who are not judges" such as "teachers of law" had every right to posit what the law should be.[47] He later stated that he "felt entirely ready to adopt legal principles which have not the sanction of judicial decision, because he has had for many years the training of the teacher" and to draw from "his own knowledge of the subject and to a small extent . . . his conjectures as to the future development of the law."[48]

On this subject, Beale's view was that party autonomy amounted to "permission to the parties to do a legislative act" and that placing "so extraordinarily a power in the hands of any two individuals is absolutely anomalous."[49] Ignoring all the good reasons for which legislatures may choose to grant—and have granted— such a permission,[50] Beale proposed for the Restatement an inexorable *lex loci contractus* rule, mandating the application of the law of the state in which the contract was made.[51] During the discussion of this subject at the 1928 Annual Meeting, Beale candidly admitted that his proposed rule was "opposed to a majority of the cases,"[52] but claimed that this was inevitable because the case law was split in four different directions.

---

[44] *See* Symeon C. Symeonides, *The Scope and Limits of Party Autonomy in International Contracts: A Comparative Analysis, in* PRIVATE INTERNATIONAL LAW: CONTEMPORARY CHALLENGES AND CONTINUING RELEVANCE 101 (Franco Ferrari & Diego P. Fernández Arroyo eds., 2019).

[45] *See* Symeon C. Symeonides, *The Story of Party Autonomy, in* CHOICE OF LAW IN INTERNATIONAL COMMERCIAL CONTRACTS 129 (D. Girsberger, T. Kadner Graziano, & J.L. Neals eds., 2021).

[46] According to a contemporary commentator who was not otherwise a Beale critic, Beale's writings "justifie[d] the frequent charge of his critics that Professor Beale is a theologian." Henry L. McClintock, *Beale on the Conflict of Laws*, 84 U. PA. L. REV. 309, 317 (1936). The commentator noted that, in Beale's treatise:

> Principles and rules are stated dogmatically, without any doubt as to their accuracy and validity. Cases which are not in accord with those principles are wrong. Theological also is the reliance upon theoretical reasoning, rather than practical. The discussion of almost every topic begins with the postulating of abstract principles by which the cases which are later stated are to be tested.

Id. See also Pierre Schlag, *Law as the Continuation of God by Other Means*, 85 CAL. L. REV. 427, 429 (1997) (describing some of Beale's statements as "worthy of God himself.").

[47] 1 JOSEPH H. BEALE, A TREATISE ON THE CONFLICT OF LAWS 40 (1935).

[48] *Id.* at 29.

[49] Joseph H. Beale, *What Law Governs the Validity of a Contract (Part 3)*, 23 HARV. L. REV. 260, 260–61 (1909). *See also* JOSEPH H. BEALE, TREATISE ON THE CONFLICTS OF LAWS 1080 (1935) ("at their will . . . [parties] can free themselves from the power of the law which would otherwise apply to their acts."). In fairness to Beale, other writers of that period, including legal realists such as Lorenzen and Judge Learned Hand, took the same position against party autonomy. *See* Ernest G. Lorenzen, *Validity and Effect of Contracts in the Conflict of Laws*, 30 YALE L.J. 655, 658 (1921); E. Gerli & Co. v. Cunard S.S. Co., 48 F.2d 115, 117 (2d Cir. 1931) (Hand, J.). *See also* RALEIGH C. MINOR, CONFLICT OF LAWS OR PRIVATE INTERNATIONAL LAW 401, 401–02 (1901). *But see* WALTER W. COOK, THE LOGICAL AND LEGAL BASES OF THE CONFLICT OF LAWS 389–432 (1942).

[50] According to a recent survey, 153 of the 161 countries surveyed endorse party autonomy. The remaining holdouts are Bolivia, Colombia, Cuba, Eritrea, Nepal, Saudi Arabia, UAE, and Zimbabwe. See Symeon C. Symeonides, *Law Applicable to Contracts, in* A GUIDE TO GLOBAL PRIVATE INTERNATIONAL LAW 191, 192 (P. Beaumont & J. Holliday eds., 2022).

[51] *See* RESTATEMENT § 332.

[52] Joseph H. Beale, *Discussion of Conflict of Laws Tentative Draft No. 4*, 6 A.L.I. PROC. 454, 458 (1927–1928).

ALI members asked Beale several questions of the type today's Conflicts teachers ask students in debunking the *lex loci contractus* rule. Beale's answers were no more than sophistries clothed in Cambridge English. One member posed a hypothetical scenario in which two New York merchants, who happened to ride on the same train through the Hudson Tube to New Jersey, entered into a contract by exchanging the magic words a few seconds after the train crossed into New Jersey.[53] Beale responded with his own hypothetical case in which two Englishmen traveling on a steamer bound for New York entered into a contract as soon as the steamer entered New York waters. The contract was for the sale of liquor, which was then prohibited by the Eighteenth Amendment of the U.S. Constitution. "It would hardly be claimed, would it," said Beale triumphantly, "that it is a valid contract because the parties really must have intended that the law of their own country should govern them?"[54] Of course, as with so many of Beale's arguments, this was based on premises that were by no means inevitable. Besides conveniently choosing a topic (liquor prohibition) that involved a strong New York and U.S. public policy, Beale's answer assumed that the contract would be performed in New York and that the eventual dispute would be decided by either a New York court or another court that also subscribed to the inexorable *lex loci* rule that Beale had just proposed.

Beale's other answers were not much better.[55] For example, he claimed that the principle of party autonomy (which was then known as the doctrine of the parties' intention) would lead to uncertainty because it would often be difficult to ascertain the parties' intent. When asked about situations in which the parties clearly stated their common intent in the contract, Beale replied with answers that assumed that the parties were attempting to evade a fundamental policy of the *locus contractus*. When asked about situations in which no fundamental policy was involved, he replied that "the man is not yet born who is wise enough"[56] to inventory all gradations of public policy. The discussion was obviously hopeless. Judge Edward R. Finch, an ALI member, presciently warned Beale:

[Y]ou will never be able to hold your courts to that sort of a rule [*i.e.*, the *lex loci contractus*]. You can lay it down, but human nature is not so constituted that you can make a court adopt a general rule which will do injustice in a majority of the cases coming with it.[57]

History proved Judge Finch right and Beale terribly wrong.

[53] *See id.* at 460–61.
[54] *Id.* at 462.
[55] *See id.* 460–71.
[56] *Id.* at 462 ("[T]he man is not yet born who is wise enough to say ... whether the foreign law really is to be obeyed" and "whether [its] provisions are matters of such interest to the state that passed them that they would be enforced or are not.").
[57] *Id.* at 466.

G. The End Product

As Thurman W. Arnold observed, "[a] stream can rise no higher than its source."[58] Considering Beale's personality and doctrinaire philosophy, as well as the process that gave birth to the first Restatement, it is not surprising that it was a mirror image of Beale's treatise.[59] Beale's Restatement was, in many respects, a *pre*-statement that was conceived and executed not through induction from the cases but through deduction from general principles that sprang almost exclusively from Beale's head, in the same manner as Athena sprang fully formed from the cranium of Zeus. Neither these principles nor their implementation stood the test of time.

Academic criticisms immediately followed the Restatement's promulgation in 1934[60] and have intensified in subsequent years. Eventually, the Restatement became the favorite punching bag of virtually all academic writers and Conflicts teachers. Indeed, the Restatement was an easy target, rife as it was with flaws.

But, in the tradition of saying good things first,[61] let us also recognize some of the Restatement's positive contributions. They include the following:

(1) The first Restatement raised the level of awareness about, and knowledge of, Conflicts law among the members of the bar and the bench. Because of the Restatement, the "pedagogical neglect"[62] of Conflicts law that ALI Director William D. Lewis noted in his introduction to the Restatement gave way to a renewed interest in Conflicts law. Conflicts law gained its rightful place in the curriculum of all American law schools, and this, in turn, made possible the renaissance of American Conflicts law during the next generation.

(2) The Restatement facilitated the unification of American Conflicts law which had grown unevenly and in different directions in the various states. For the first time, it became possible to speak of a single American Conflicts law, despite some remaining but rather small variations from state to state.

---

[58] Thurman W. Arnold, *Institute Priests and Yale Observers: A Reply to Dean Goodrich*, 84 U. PA. L. REV. 811, 817 (1936).

[59] *See id.* at 824 (stating that "nothing else would have been possible in the intellectual atmosphere of the day").

[60] For a list of contemporaneous critiques, *see* Symeonides, *supra* note 10, at 75 n.180.

[61] In the same tradition, *some* good things *can* be said about Beale himself. In my article cited *supra* at note 10, I tried to examine the First Restatement and Beale himself "Through the Eyes of Old" and to determine whether they were "As Bad as [their] Reputation." My conclusions about the Restatement are restated in this chapter. For my conclusions about Beale, *see* Symeonides, *supra* note 10, 46–54, *et passim*. In general, Beale was a more complex person than his critics' descriptions suggest. For example, Jerome Frank's characterization of Beale as the "the right wing of the right wing" (*quoted in* LAURA KALMAN, LEGAL REALISM AT YALE: 1927–1960, at 26 (1986), was accurate in some respects but it overlooked the fact that Beale took some progressive positions. Among them was his opposition to a "rule of validation" in loan contracts because it would unduly favor powerful money lenders, his strong support for the admission of women at the Harvard Law School and his leading role in establishing the ill-fated Cambridge Law School for Women at Radcliff. Likewise, some statements in Beale's treatise (*see, e.g.*, 1 JOSEPH H. BEALE, A TREATISE ON THE CONFLICT OF LAWS 50 (1935)) suggest that, despite his own rigid Restatement rules, he understood the perpetual tension between the need for certainty and the need for flexibility in the law. He simply thought that, at that point in the development of American conflicts law, certainty was far more important than flexibility.

[62] *See* William D. Lewis, *Introduction* to RESTATEMENT OF CONFLICT OF LAWS, at xiii–xiv (1934).

(3) The Restatement was a comprehensive and complete *system*. It provided a thorough, organized, and disciplined network of bilateral, fixed, neutral, and detailed choice-of-law rules designed to provide solutions for all possible conflicts situations. This was the first time such a comprehensive and complete work on Conflicts law had been produced on American soil or indeed elsewhere. It was, as a contemporary author noted, "a system, something tangible out of the chaos of cases."[63]

(4) The Restatement was nonparochial, even if it was not particularly internationalist. Unlike many American approaches proposed since then (but not before), the Restatement did not give preference to the forum state *qua forum*. The Restatement purported to be, and in many respects was, impartial vis-à-vis forum and foreign law.[64] Its explicit aspiration was to eliminate (or at least reduce) forum-shopping and to foster interstate and international decisional uniformity by ensuring that a case would be decided in the same way regardless of where it was litigated. That this aspiration has never been fully realized is another matter.

Unfortunately, the first Restatement's flaws vastly outnumbered its good qualities. The list of flaws is too long to detail here, and the literature documenting them is too extensive to warrant exposition. The following are simply some of the most general—and most serious—defects:

(1) The first Restatement was a system of detailed, mechanical, and rigid rules that: (a) completely sacrificed flexibility on the altar of ostensible certainty and predictability, which eventually proved illusory; (b) ignored the lessons of experience in the pursuit of an ill-conceived theoretical purity; and (c) eliminated judicial discretion while purporting to be a distillation of the courts' experience.[65]

(2) Like Beale's treatise, the Restatement relied exclusively and excessively on two principles: territoriality and vested rights. It deduced virtually all its rules from these principles, while disregarding contrary case law. Beale saw the world as a neatly laid-out, black-and-white chessboard in which the critical event would always occur entirely in either a black or a white square. Reality is never so simple. Beale never accepted the proposition that, in some cases, for some issues, the law of a person's home state may have a legitimate claim of application (personality principle), even if the dispute is triggered by events occurring in another state. Beale thought that territoriality was the modern and personality the medieval principle. Had he been a better student of history or a better comparativist, he would have realized that any system that completely banishes either one of these two grand principles will inevitably run into an impasse and

---

[63] de Sloovère, *supra* note 15, at 345.

[64] *But see* Louise Weinberg, *Theory Wars in the Conflict of Laws*, 103 MICH. L. REV. 1631, 1645 (2005) (describing the Restatement's approach as "at least superficially 'neutral,' striking with even-handed ferocity now at plaintiffs, now at defendants").

[65] *See* Ernest G. Lorenzen & Raymond J. Heilman, *The Restatement of the Conflict of Laws*, 83 U. PA. L. REV. 555, at 588 (1935) ("Beale's system ... is more rigid in theory than that of any foreign country. It is also more rigid than the Anglo-American decisions upon which it is supposed to rest.").

that one should strive for the golden mean.[66] However, Beale was incapable of compromise, and he was too powerful in the ALI to be forced to accept any.

(3) The Restatement's choice-of-*law* rules—despite that label—were not designed to choose among conflicting *laws*. Instead, they pre-allocated "legislative jurisdiction" to a particular state[67] based solely on a single, predesignated, territorial contact. Subject only to limited exceptions, the law of the state with the designated contact applied almost automatically, regardless of its content, its underlying policy, or the substantive quality of the solution it would bring to the case at hand. All that mattered was whether that state had the specified contact— even if its presence there was entirely fortuitous, and even if that state had no real interest in the outcome of the case. As David Cavers observed as early as 1933, the Restatement was not much different from a slot machine programmed to find the "right" state in a "blindfolded" and random fashion.[68] Indeed, the Restatement's goal was to find what it considered the spatially appropriate law ("conflicts justice") rather than to ensure a substantively appropriate result in the particular case ("material justice").[69] It did not occur to Beale that, in order to intelligently resolve any conflict, one must first ascertain what the conflict is about and what the conflicting objectives and claims are. In turn, this requires looking into the content of the potentially conflicting laws, identifying their purposes or policies, and proceeding from there.

None of the preceding flaws are newly discovered; they are not the result of hindsight. All of them were identified by Beale's contemporary American critics, and many of the same points were prominent in the European legal literature of the early twentieth century. Nor is it accurate to blame the first Restatement's flaws on the case law that Beale purported to restate. Indeed, in many cases, Beale chose to ignore the case law when it did not fit his territorialist scheme, such as when he refused to accept the principle of party autonomy in multistate contracts.

III. The Aftermath

Despite its many flaws, the first Restatement was adopted with varying degrees of enthusiasm in virtually all states in the United States, thus unifying American Conflicts law for the first time.[70] If success is to be measured in numbers, one could conclude that the Restatement succeeded—initially. However, this initial success was hardly a validation of the Restatement's quality. American courts initially accepted the

---

[66] For a discussion of this point, *see* Symeon C. Symeonides, *Territoriality and Personality in Tort Conflicts*, *in* INTERCONTINENTAL COOPERATION THROUGH PRIVATE INTERNATIONAL LAW: ESSAYS IN MEMORY OF PETER NYGH 401 (T. Einhorn & K. Siehr eds., 2004).

[67] For a thorough discussion of this "jurisdiction-selecting" feature of the First Restatement, *see* Cavers, *supra* note 18.

[68] *See id.* at 191–92.

[69] For a comparative discussion of these concepts, *see* SYMEON C. SYMEONIDES, PRIVATE INTERNATIONAL LAW: IDEALISM, PRAGMATISM, ECLECTICISM 161–220 (2021).

[70] *See* SYMEONIDES, *supra* note 32, at 10–11, 37.

Restatement because it was the only game in town and because it was comprehensive and complete. Most courts encounter conflicts cases only infrequently and thus do not have the opportunity or the incentive to develop the necessary expertise. "Judicial experience with any given choice-of-law problem is usually more episodic than with analogous domestic-law problems."[71] In turn, this lack of judicial expertise makes resort to an authoritative document like a Restatement—which bears the prestigious imprimatur of the ALI—far more attractive, if not inevitable.

In any event, the courts' allegiance to the first Restatement was not as deep as the initial numbers suggested. As Cavers predicted, "neither [Beale's] Treatise nor [his] Restatement can mechanize judgment."[72] The Restatement's tendency to produce arbitrary results led many courts to employ evasive tactics or "escape devices," such as characterization, *renvoi*, and the public policy exception.[73] These covert and frequent deviations soon became overt rejections of the Restatement's dictates.

The first overt abandonment of the Restatement occurred in 1954, when the New York Court of Appeals rejected the *lex loci contractus* rule in *Auten v. Auten*.[74] The same court rejected the *lex loci delicti* rule in the seminal 1963 case *Babcock v. Jackson*.[75] These two decisions marked the beginning of the so-called choice-of-law "revolution," which lasted for more than a generation.[76] The quoted term is obviously hyperbolic. But it does convey the radicality of this movement and its unwillingness to consider the possibility that, as bad as they were, the first Restatement's rules could be repaired.[77] In fact, the leader of the revolution, Brainerd Currie, went as far as to denounce not only the rules of the first Restatement but *all* choice-of-law rules in general.[78] Eventually, the revolution prevailed in the majority of states.

Today, only nine states follow the first Restatement in tort conflicts and only eleven do so in contract conflicts.[79] However, the first Restatement commanded a majority of states for fifty years in contract conflicts (until 1984) and forty-five years in tort conflicts (until 1979).[80] This is not a bad record for such a flawed document.

[71] Arthur T. von Mehren, *Recent Trends in Choice-of-Law Methodology*, 60 CORNELL L. REV. 927, 966 (1975). *See also* Russell J. Weintraub, *The Restatement Third of Conflict of Laws: An Idea Whose Time Has Not Come*, 75 IND. L.J. 679, 680 (2000) ("[A]ll courts, but especially state courts, encounter choice-of-law problems haphazardly at infrequent intervals.").

[72] David F. Cavers, *Restatement of the Law of Conflict of Laws*, 44 YALE L. J. 1478, 1482 (1935).

[73] *See* SYMEON C. SYMEONIDES, THE OXFORD COMMENTARIES ON AMERICAN LAW: CHOICE OF LAW 65–86 (2016); SYMEON C. SYMEONIDES & WENDY C. PERDUE, CONFLICT OF LAWS: AMERICAN, COMPARATIVE, INTERNATIONAL 53–116 (4th ed. 2019).

[74] 124 N.E.2d 99 (N.Y. 1954).

[75] 191 N.E.2d 279 (N.Y. 1963).

[76] For comprehensive documentation and discussion, *see* SYMEONIDES, *supra* note 32.

[77] By contrast, other countries chose evolution over revolution. They repaired rather than abandon their old choice-of-law rules by introducing exceptions that lead to results similar to those that American courts have reach decades after the revolution. *See* Symeon C. Symeonides, *The American Revolution and the European Evolution in Choice of Law: Reciprocal Lessons*, 82 TUL. L. REV. 1741 (2008).

[78] *See* BRAINERD CURRIE, SELECTED ESSAYS ON THE CONFLICT OF LAWS 180 (1963) ("The [traditional] rules . . . have not worked and cannot be made to work. . . . But the root of the trouble goes deeper. In attempting to use rules we encounter difficulties that stem not from the fact that the particular rules are bad . . . but rather from the fact that we have such rules at all."). *See also id.* at 183 ("We would be better off without choice-of-law rules.").

[79] *See* SYMEON C. SYMEONIDES, CHOICE OF LAW IN PRACTICE: A TWENTY-YEAR REPORT FROM THE TRENCHES 31–34 (2020).

[80] *See* Symeon C. Symeonides, *The Choice-of-Law Revolution Fifty Years after Currie: An End and a Beginning*, 2015 U. ILL. L. REV. 1847, 1870, 1876 (2015).

In turn, this pinpoints the heavy responsibility of those who command the bully pulpit of the ALI. The ALI is a victim of its own success in that even bad Restatements can gain lasting judicial following. This should serve as a reminder to the ALI leadership, both in choosing Reporters and in overseeing the process of completing a Restatement. In the case of the first Conflicts Restatement, the ALI leadership cannot be blamed for choosing Beale as the Reporter because, as noted earlier, he was the unquestionable leader of the field at that time. However, the ALI deserves blame for giving Beale so much deference thereafter, specifically by: (1) surrounding Beale with a small group of only loyal Advisers, and (2) passively watching the migration of virtually all Beale's ideas from his treatise to the first Restatement. The result was a virtual petrification of American Conflicts law which, in turn, brought the choice-of-law revolution.

IV. The Second Conflicts Restatement

A. Lessons Learned: Starting on the Right Foot

To its credit, the ALI did not wait for the revolution to spread before beginning work on a new Restatement. The drafting of what became the Second Restatement began in 1953, one year before *Auten*, when the academic criticisms of the first Restatement had made only marginal inroads in judicial opinions. The ALI's early response was not only appropriate but also politically smart. For example, by releasing the Second Restatement drafts, the ALI provided a moderate outlet to those courts that were growing impatient with the first Restatement but hesitated to join the revolution's radical avant-garde led by Brainerd Currie.[81]

More than anything, the ALI deserves praise for both its choice of a new Reporter, Willis L.M. Reese, and the process that produced the Second Restatement. Neither could be more different than those of the first Restatement, and herein lies the proof that the ALI had learned its lesson. The drafting process provided many opportunities for internal and external criticisms.[82] More importantly, Reese did not have an ego problem—aside from being brilliant and knowledgeable (both of which are necessary attributes for any Reporter). Unlike Beale, Reese genuinely welcomed criticisms of his drafts and took account of these criticisms in his subsequent drafts. A perusal of the successive versions of what eventually became the all-important Section 6 of the Second Restatement reveals the evolution in Reese's own thinking and the extent to which he took account of criticisms. So much so that, in the end, the Second

---

[81] Before 1966, when the Second Restatement drafts became available, three states had abandoned the *lex loci delicti* rule and all opted for interest analysis. Between 1966 and 1969 (the year of the Second Restatement's promulgation), fourteen states abandoned the *lex loci* rule and nine of them adopted the Second Restatement. After 1969, twenty-five states abandoned the *lex loci* rule, and eighteen of them adopted the Second Restatement. For documentation, *see* Symeonides, *supra* note 80, at 1871–75; Symeonides, *supra* note 32, at 41, 46, 96–97.

[82] Unlike the First Restatement, in which Beale was assisted by only ten Advisers, six of whom were his former students (*see supra* text at note 23), the ALI appointed sixteen Advisers of diverse perspectives for the Second Restatement—eight professors, five practitioners, and three judges.

Restatement was criticized for being too wishy-washy and eclectic, and for trying too hard to please too many people.[83]

B. The Contrast with the First Restatement

As ALI Director Herbert Weschler noted in his introduction, the Second Restatement "present[ed] a striking contrast to the first Restatement in which dogma was so thoroughly enshrined."[84] In all material respects, such as "basic analysis and technique, [and] in the position taken on a host of issues," the Second Restatement was "a fresh treatment of the subject."[85]

Most of the substantive changes were limited to tort and contract conflicts, in which the first Restatement had proved a total failure. The Second Restatement replaced the rigid *lex loci delicti* and *lex loci contractus* rules with flexible issue-oriented and policy-sensitive rules.[86] However, as important as those changes were, the changes in methodology and jurisprudential philosophy were far more dramatic. The latter changes are crystallized in the all-important Section 6 of the Second Restatement, which enunciates its basic approach.[87]

Unlike the first Restatement, which chose in advance the applicable law based on the location of a single territorial contact, the Second Restatement relegates the choice to the court and simply posits the goal for the court's choice: to choose the law of the state that, with regard to the disputed issue, has "the most significant relationship" to the parties and the dispute. In doing so, the court is to consider *all* relevant contacts— not just one—but also the principles articulated in Section 6(2). These principles are quoted in full in the following because they exemplify the differences not only from the first Restatement but also from other modern approaches. The principles are:

(a) the needs of the interstate and international systems;
(b) the relevant policies of the forum;
(c) the relevant policies of other interested states and the relative interests of those states in the determination of the particular issue;
(d) the protection of justified expectations;
(e) the basic policies underlying the particular field of law;
(f) certainty, predictability and uniformity of result; and

---

[83] *See, e.g.*, ALBERT A. EHRENZWEIG, PRIVATE INTERNATIONAL LAW 67 (1967) ("[T]he [American Law] Institute, caught between its fundamentalist heritage and realist skepticism, has sought a compromise between the Revolution and the Establishment in Anarchy and Counter-revolution."). For a summary of other criticisms, *see* Symeon C. Symeonides, *The Judicial Acceptance of the Second Conflicts Restatement: A Mixed Blessing*, 56 MD. L. REV. 1248, 1249–50 (1997).

[84] Herbert Weschler, *Introduction* to RESTATEMENT (SECOND) OF CONFLICT OF LAWS, vii (1971).

[85] *Id.*

[86] In contract conflicts, the most significant change was the strong endorsement of party autonomy in § 187. This is the Second Restatement's most popular section—it is followed even in states that do not otherwise follow its other sections. *See* PETER HAY, PATRICK BORCHERS, SYMEON SYMEONIDES, & CHRISTOPHER A. WHYTOCK, CONFLICTS OF LAW 1008 (6th ed. 2018).

[87] That approach is then implemented in subsequent sections of the Second Restatement, most of which refer back to Section 6.

(g)   ease in the determination and application of the law to be applied.[88]

It is not a coincidence that certainty, predictability, and uniformity, along with administrability, which were the supreme goals of the first Restatement, are placed at the bottom of this list. The Second Restatement recognized that uniformity had proved illusory and, although it was still a laudable goal, the choice-of-law process should not neglect other goals, such the relevant policies of the involved states or the protection of justified expectations. Certainty and administrability were also worth pursuing, but not at the expense of other values such as the need to aim for the most appropriate result for the particular case. Such a result is more likely to be achieved if the court is free to consider all relevant contacts and factors rather than being bound to a predesignated result that depended on a single territorial contact or a questionable doctrine like vested rights. In the perennial tension between legal certainty and predictability on the one hand and flexibility and aptness on the other hand,[89] the Second Restatement consciously and clearly opted for the latter.

The reference to the policies of the involved states in Paragraphs (b) and (c) of Section 6(2) signifies another major shift from the first Restatement's territorialist, content-blind *state* selection to the Second Restatement's content-oriented *law* selection that is based on the relevant policies of the involved states and their interests in applying their laws. This shift from territorialism to policy analysis was one of the revolution's major breakthroughs,[90] which the Second Restatement wisely incorporated.

At the same time, the Second Restatement wisely disassociated itself from the revolution's more radical approaches, such as Robert Leflar's better-law approach[91] and Brainerd Currie's governmental interest analysis.[92] The better-law criterion, which is prominent in Leflar's list of five choice-influencing considerations, is noticeably absent from the list of Section 6(2), although the two lists are otherwise similar. Likewise, the list of Section 6(2) factors is different from and far broader than the policies relied upon by Currie's analysis, which was tainted by a pervasive protectionism of the forum's interest.[93] By placing "the needs of the interstate and international systems" at the top of the Section 6(2) list, the Second Restatement signals its denunciation of such protectionism.[94]

One of the criticisms of the Second Restatement concerns its excessive flexibility and, consequently, its malleability. Indeed, only in property and successions does the Second Restatement identify a priori the state of the most significant relationship.[95]

---

[88] RESTATEMENT (SECOND) § 6(2).

[89] *See* SYMEONIDES, *supra* note 69, at 254–64.

[90] *See* SYMEONIDES, *supra* note 32, at 382–88.

[91] *See* Robert A. Leflar, *Choice-Influencing Considerations in Conflicts Law*, 41 NYU L. REV. 367 (1966).

[92] *See* CURRIE, *supra* note 78.

[93] *See* SYMEONIDES, *supra* note 32, at 21–22.

[94] *See* RESTATEMENT (SECOND) § 6 cmt. d ("[T]he most important function of choice-of-law rules is to make the interstate and international systems work well[,] ... to further harmonious relations between states and to facilitate commercial intercourse between them.").

[95] *See* RESTATEMENT (SECOND) §§ 223, 225–32 (*inter vivos* transactions involving land); §§ 236, 239–42 (succession to land); §§ 260–65 (succession to movables); §§ 245–55 (*inter vivos* transactions involving movables). *See also* the unilateral choice-of-law rules contained in §§ 285 (divorce), 286 (nullity of marriage), and 289 (adoption).

In all other areas of Conflicts law, the Second Restatement's black-letter sections are tentative and equivocal. For some cases, the Second Restatement provides presumptive rules stating that State X is the state of the most significant relationship, unless it appears that, in the particular case, another state has a more significant relationship.[96] The "unless" clause is repeated throughout the Second Restatement.[97] In other cases, the presumptive rules are no more than mere pointers stating that courts will "usually" apply the law of State X.[98] In the remaining and most difficult cases, the Second Restatement does not even attempt to enunciate presumptive rules. It simply provides a nonexclusive, nonhierarchical list of the factual contacts that the court should "take[] into account" in choosing the applicable law "under the principles stated in § 6."[99]

However, the Second Restatement's excessive flexibility proved to be a strength rather than a weakness. As documented elsewhere, this flexibility was the main reason for the Restatement's eventual popularity among judges.[100] Judges like to have as much flexibility as possible, and the Second Restatement provided plenty. Although, in the beginning, the Second Restatement was just one of several modern approaches vying for the allegiance of American courts, it gradually gained acceptance in a plurality of U.S. jurisdictions. Today, it is followed in twenty-five states in tort conflicts and twenty-four in contract conflicts.[101]

In any event, the political climate during the Second Restatement's drafting did not favor hard and fast rules. The spectacular failure of the first Restatement's wrong-headed rules engendered intense skepticism of all rules, as Currie's categorical denouncement exemplifies.[102] Faced with this reality, Willis Reese and his fellow drafters of the Second Restatement turned necessity into virtue. As explained later, they concluded that the formulation of rules should be deferred for a later time and that, in the meantime, the Second Restatement should serve as a transitional document that would guide American Conflicts law from revolution to maturity and eventual recast in a Third Restatement.

C. A Transitional Document

As noted earlier, the drafting of the Second Restatement began in 1953, at the dawn of the choice-of-law revolution, and was completed in 1969 during the revolution's early stages. As Reese wrote, this was a period of "turmoil and crisis ... when rival theories were being fiercely debated, and when serious doubt was expressed about the

---

[96] For example, all ten of the Restatement sections for different types of torts conclude with the "unless" escape clause. *See, e.g., id.* § 152.

[97] *See, e.g., id.* §§ 146–51, 153–55, and 175. In contract conflicts, the "unless" clause appears in most of the sections devoted to particular contracts. *See, e.g.,* §§ 189–93, 196.

[98] For example, in tort conflicts, eleven of the nineteen sections devoted to specific tort issues conclude with the adage that the applicable law will "usually be the local law of the state where the injury occurred."

[99] *See, e.g., id.* §§ 145, 188.

[100] *See* Symeonides, *supra* note 83, at 1269–72.

[101] *See* SYMEONIDES, *supra* note 79, at 33–34.

[102] *See supra* note 78.

practicality, and indeed the desirability, of having any rules at all."[103] "Attempting to 'restate' the law of choice of law" at that time "was analogous to trying to write a history of World War II during the Battle of Stalingrad."[104] There was no way to know where or how far the revolution would go. This is why Reese viewed the Second Restatement as "a transitional work."[105] His answer to the grand dilemma of "rules or approach"[106] was in favor of rules—but not for his time. Although he believed that "the formulation of rules should be as much an objective in choice of law as it is in other areas of law,"[107] he concluded that, at least in tort and contract conflicts, it would be premature and unwise to adopt definitive rules.[108] This is why, in these two areas, the Second Restatement attempted no more than to "provide formulations that were ... broad enough to permit further development in the law."[109] Reese retained the firm hope, however, that these broad formulations would provide guidance and room for judicial testing and experimentation and, in due time, would permit the formulation of "more definite"[110] or "precise"[111] rules.

Reasonable minds may differ on whether Reese's decision to move so far away from rules in the certainty-versus-flexibility spectrum was necessary, or whether a middle ground was possible. But Reese's hope did materialize. Guided by the Second Restatement's "broad formulations," courts began converging around similar and often identical results in certain patterns of cases, especially in tort conflicts. In fact, as the revolution's initial fervor began to subside, the same convergence occurred among courts that followed other modern approaches. These developments have been documented in detail elsewhere.[112] Encouraged by this convergence, two states undertook the previously unthinkable task of enacting choice-of-law statutes that codified these results, in 1991,[113] 2001,[114] and 2009.[115]

---

[103] Willis L.M. Reese, *The Second Restatement of Conflict of Laws Revisited*, 34 MERCER L. REV. 501, 518–19 (1983).

[104] William M. Richman & William L. Reynolds, *Prolegomenon to an Empirical Restatement of Conflicts*, 75 IND. L.J. 417, 417 (2000).

[105] Reese, *supra* note 103, at 519.

[106] Willis L.M. Reese, *Choice of Law: Rules or Approach*, 57 CORNELL L.Q. 315 (1972).

[107] Willis L.M. Reese, *General Course on Private International Law*, 150 RECUEIL DES COURS 1, 61 (1976 II).

[108] *See* Reese, *supra* note 103, at 518.

[109] *Id.* at 519.

[110] *Id.* at 518 (stating that torts and contract conflicts were not yet susceptible to "hard and fast rules," but expressing the hope that "it will be possible to state more definite rules at some time in the future"); *see also id.* at 508.

[111] Reese, *supra* note 107, at 62 (stating that the conflicts experience since the revolution had "reached the stage where most areas of choice of law can be covered by general principles which are subject to imprecise exceptions. We should press on, however, beyond these principles to the development, as soon as our knowledge permits, of precise rules.").

[112] *See* SYMEONIDES, *supra* note 32, at 207, 259, 346, 435; SYMEONIDES, *supra* note 73, at 200, 208, 210, 216, 223, 227–28, 247–48, 268.

[113] *See* the Louisiana choice-of-law codification (LA. CIV. CODE arts. 3515–49 (1991)), discussed in Symeon C. Symeonides, *The Conflicts Book of the Louisiana Civil Code: Civilian, American, or Original?*, 83 TUL. L. REV. 1041 (2009).

[114] *See* Oregon's statute for contract conflicts (OR. REV. STAT. §§ 15.300–15.380), discussed in Symeon C. Symeonides, *Oregon's Choice-of-Law Codification for Contract Conflicts: An Exegesis*, 44 WILLAMETTE L. REV. 205 (2007).

[115] *See* Oregon's statute for tort conflicts (OR. REV. STAT. §§ 15.400–15.460), discussed in Symeon C. Symeonides, *Oregon's New Choice-of-Law Codification for Tort Conflicts: An Exegesis*, 88 OR. L. REV. 963 (2009).

V. The Third Restatement

In 2014, after several pleas for a new Restatement,[116] the ALI decided to begin work on the Third Restatement and entrusted the reportership to three highly accomplished Conflicts scholars.[117] The Reporters have since produced several drafts,[118] two of which made it to the ALI Annual Meeting and were approved by the membership in 2021 and 2022.[119]

Writing separately, the Chief Reporter, Professor Kermit Roosevelt, described as follows the attributes of the rules that should be included in the Third Restatement:

> The rules should be narrow, with a flexible residual approach handling cases not governed by rule. They should be sensitive to the content of laws and the policies of affected states. They should be derived from the practice of courts. They should have escape clauses that allow departure in case of serious error. Both the rules and the escape clauses should be derived from an overarching methodology that allows users of the rules to understand what they were designed to achieve and, correlatively, to identify instances in which they fail to achieve those ends.[120]

The preceding description gives every reason to hope that, this time, the ALI may find the golden mean between the two extremes—the inflexible dogmatic rules of the First Restatement and the excessively open-ended pointers of the Second Restatement.

VI. Conclusions

Indeed, looking back at the ALI's first century, it seems that the quest for the golden mean characterizes the ALI's engagement with Conflicts law. The ALI started on the wrong foot by entrusting the reportership of the first Restatement to a highly respected but dogmatic scholar who had enough influence to win adoption of his proposals virtually without modification. The result was a comprehensive, systematic, and doctrinally pure set of rules that unified American Conflicts law and raised its profile among the members of the bench and the bar. Unfortunately, these rules were wrong-headed and had the propensity to produce arbitrary results.

---

[116] *See, e.g.,* Symeonides, *supra* note 83, at 1280; Symeon C. Symeonides, *The Need for a Third Conflicts Restatement (And a Proposal for Tort Conflicts),* 75 IND. L.J. 437 (2000); Symeon C. Symeonides, *A New Conflicts Restatement: Why Not?,* 5 J. PRIV. INT'L L. 383 (2009); Symposium: *Preparing for the Next Century—A New Restatement of Conflicts,* 75 IND. L.J. 399–686 (2000).

[117] Professor Kermit Roosevelt III of the University of Pennsylvania is the Reporter, and Professors Laura E. Little (Temple University) and Christopher A. Whytock (U.C. Irvine) are Associate Reporters.

[118] For an approving discussion of their first draft on tort conflicts, *see* Symeon C. Symeonides, *The Third Conflicts Restatement's First Draft on Tort Conflicts,* 92 TUL. L. REV. 1 (2017).

[119] *See* RESTATEMENT (THIRD) OF CONFLICT OF LAWS (Tentative Draft No. 2, Mar. 25, 2021); RESTATEMENT (THIRD) OF CONFLICT OF LAWS (Tentative Draft No. 3, Mar. 2022).

[120] Kermit Roosevelt III, *Certainty Versus Flexibility in the Conflict of Laws, in* PRIVATE INTERNATIONAL LAW: CONTEMPORARY CHALLENGES AND CONTINUING RELEVANCE 6, 25 (Franco Ferrari & Diego P. Fernández Arroyo eds., 2019). As evidence that such rules are feasible, Roosevelt noted that the rules of the Louisiana codification possess these attributes.

The choice-of-law revolution was a reaction to the shoddy quality and inflexibility of these rules. Perhaps it was an overreaction in the sense that bad rules, especially when they are not statutory, can be modified rather than demolished. However, unlike other countries which chose reform and evolution,[121] revolution appeared to be the only option in the United States. Be that as it may, a strong anti-rule sentiment was prevalent when the ALI began work on the Second Restatement.

This time, the ALI started on the right foot by entrusting the reportership to Willis Reese. Reese was a brilliant scholar, but, more importantly, he was a non-dogmatic, open-minded, and collaborative consensus seeker. In contrast to the First Restatement, which was the work of a single man, the Second Restatement was a collective product incorporating a broad array of views from both within and outside the ALI. Unlike the First Restatement, whose rules resembled a straitjacket, the Second Restatement moved to the other extreme by avoiding hard and fast rules and providing formulae that were too open-ended and equivocal. This was partly by necessity—due to the strong anti-rule climate that prevailed at that time—and partly by design—because of Reese's assessment that rules were premature at that time given the lack of judicial experience with the new approaches.

Forty-five years later, there was more than enough accumulation of such experience to support a new restatement. Again, the ALI made the right choice by appointing as Chief Reporter a scholar who believes that new choice-of-law rules (different from those of the First Restatement) are necessary and feasible, and has articulated the right vision about the essential attributes of those rules.[122] If this vision is implemented, the ALI will begin its second century by successfully completing its quest for the golden mean.

[121] *See* Symeonides, *supra* note 77.
[122] *See supra* text at note 120.

7

The Restatements of Trusts—Revisited

Naomi R. Cahn, Deborah Gordon, and Allison Tait

A trust is one of several juridical devices whereby one person is enabled to deal with property for the benefit of another person.[1]

I. Introduction

The Restatement of Trusts was one of the first of the American Law Institute's (ALI's) projects, and that Restatement, along with its two successors, has profoundly influenced both the common law and statutes in the field. Courts routinely refer to the Restatement in decisions on trusts,[2] and the Restatement has served as a "storehouse for legislative drafters," with provisions incorporated directly into many state statutes.[3] That influence has continued throughout the almost first century since the project started. Indeed, the Uniform Trust Code (UTC), enacted in approximately two-thirds of states in some form, mentions the Restatement over three hundred times and, in its prefatory note, observes that the UTC "was drafted in close coordination" with the Restatement (Third);[4] this coordination is highly unusual among the various Restatements. The trust Restatements have also deeply influenced the Uniform Prudent Investor Act, now in effect in forty-six states.[5]

The Carnegie Corporation provided funding to the ALI, with a particular interest in a property Restatement,[6] and the Restatement of Trusts developed directly out of concern for the unwieldy scope of drafting a Restatement of Property. Because trusts

---

[1] RESTATEMENT OF THE LAW, TRUSTS, Introductory Note (1935).

[2] Robert H. Sitkoff & Max M. Schanzenbach, *Jurisdictional Competition for Trust Funds: An Empirical Analysis of Perpetuities and Taxes*, 115 YALE L.J. 356, 373 (2005) (noting "little variation in state law" before 1986, as states typically cited the Restatement as well as treatises by Scott and Bogert); Lawrence W. Waggoner, *What's in the Third and Final Volume of the New Restatement of Property That Estate Planners Should Know About*, 38 ACTEC L.J. 23, 24 (2012) ("When it comes to litigation, the courts pay attention to the Restatement and usually follow it"); Jeffrey N. Gordon, *The Puzzling Persistence of the Constrained Prudent Man Rule*, 62 N.Y.U. L. REV. 52, 58 (1987) ("Scott's work has played a pivotal role in the legal understanding of the trustee's investment management duties").

[3] John H. Langbein, *Why Did Trust Law Become Statute in the United States?*, 58 ALA. L. REV. 1069, 1081 (2007) [hereinafter *Trust Law*]; *see* John H. Langbein, *The Uniform Trust Code: Codification of the Law of Trusts in the United States*, 15 TR. L. INT'L 66 (2001).

[4] UNIF. TR. CODE Prefatory Note 4 (UNIF. L. COMM'N 2003), https://www.uniformlaws.org/HigherLogic/System/DownloadDocumentFile.ashx?DocumentFileKey=6bae0bb2-00ea-8080-d084-5be9ef7bbc66.

[5] UNIF. PRU. INV. ACT (UNIF. L. COMM'N 1994), https://www.uniformlaws.org/committees/community-home?communitykey=58f87d0a-3617-4635-a2af-9a4d02d119c9.

[6] Minutes of the Twelfth Meeting of the Council—Dec. 17–20, 1926, 4 A.L.I. PROC. 96105 (out of Property); 103–04 (Carnegie).

Naomi R. Cahn, Deborah Gordon, and Allison Tait, *The Restatements of Trusts—Revisited* In: *The American Law Institute*. Edited by: Andrew S. Gold and Robert W. Gordon, Oxford University Press. © Oxford University Press 2023.
DOI: 10.1093/oso/9780197685341.003.0008

were initially developed as a means to transfer real property, when land was the primary form for wealth—and indeed, nineteenth-century trust treatises focused on land[7]—the Trusts project was seen as a "branch" of the property project.[8] Wills and intestate succession, which are often taught with trusts in law school courses, remained part of the Restatement of Property.[9] There are arguments that it might have been more "systematic"[10] to keep trusts in the property Restatement, given that, like wills and intestate succession, they all involve gratuitous, and frequently intergenerational, transfers of property.[11]

As this chapter traces, the three trust Restatements reflect the development of the "modern trust," which, whether private or charitable, holds a variety of financial interests not solely or typically land. The three Restatements also reflect economic, social, and cultural changes that have occurred over the last century. We focus, in particular, on three issues in this development: who were the people using trusts and how; what role did "public policy" play in this private area; and how have trustees' investment duties shifted. For example, the First Restatement, drafted between 1928 and 1935, did not recognize the modern inter vivos revocable trust. Under that Restatement, a trust could be created by "a declaration by the owner of property that he holds it as trustee for another person."[12] By the Restatement (Third), the method of creation had become a gender-neutral "declaration by an owner of property that he or she holds that property as trustee for one or more persons."[13] Not until the Third Restatement is there a section on the Creation of Inter Vivos Trusts, along with recognition that they

---

[7] Langbein, *Trust Law, supra* note 3, at 1072.

[8] Proceedings, May 12, 1927, 5 A.L.I. PROC. 82(1), 110, 110; *see also* 1926 minutes, *supra* note 6, at 105 ("while the topic 'Trusts' is part of the law of Real Property, it is, from the point of view of the Restatement a related but independent Subject the law of which should be restated by those who have made a special study of it.").

[9] *See* Thomas W. Merrill, *The Restatement of Property: The Curse of Incompleteness*, this volume ("wills and intestate succession are included under the umbrella of the Restatement of Property, whereas trusts are subject to a separate restatement, even though, from the perspective of modern legal practice and law school curricula, it would make more sense to cover both topics in a single restatement, e.g., 'Trusts and Estates.'").

[10] *See* Andrew S. Gold & Henry E. Smith, *Restatements and the Common Law*, this volume (describing systemic or "architectural" approach to law and Restatements). One also might wonder if treating these two subjects together would have provided the ALI with any economic advantage. *See* Deborah A. DeMott, *Restating the Law in the Shadow of Codes: The ALI in Its Formative Era*, this volume (describing importance of Restatement sales to ALI funding).

[11] There are arguments in favor of both placements. Wills and trusts do seem to be part of property, given that they dispose of property and definitions of property are integral to what can be disposed of in wills. Intestacy could have been placed with family, given that much of intestacy law depends on definitions of family. In fact, there might well be arguments for a separate Wills and Intestacy Restatement that would deal with disposition of property at death. As discussed later, there were contemporaneous arguments that the ALI should not develop a Restatement of Trusts at all. *See infra* note 33.

[12] RESTATEMENT (FIRST) OF TRUSTS § 17 (1935). Although the First Restatement did not contemplate or provide for the *modern* inter vivos revocable trust, it did allow in Section 17 and some other sections for the creation of a trust inter vivos. *See, e.g., id.* § 58. An inter vivos trust at that time would have to comply with Wills Act formalities and if "he retains such complete dominion over the property that no substantial interest is created in the intended beneficiaries until the death of the settlor, and the disposition is therefore a testamentary disposition and is invalid" unless the settlor complies with testamentary formalities. *Id.* § 57 cmt. h. While a settlor could expressly provide for revocability, it was not presumed. *Id.* § 330.

[13] RESTATEMENT (THIRD) OF TRUSTS § 10 (2003).

need not comply with the requirements of the Wills Act.[14] This iterative process of understanding the trust, then, demonstrated how the trust generally, and the revocable trust in particular, has become a flexible means of managing property inter vivos and therefore available to broader groups of users.

After providing a brief history of the trust Restatements, this chapter then turns to trace the preceding three through lines identified: first, it threads together how the three Restatements address the question of shifting social and legal norms, including how diverse populations across the wealth spectrum engage with wealth transfer through trusts; second, the chapter focuses on the "public policy" provision in each of the three trust Restatements and tracks that provision's focus on gender roles, marriage, religion, and "detriment to community"; and third, it traces provisions relating to trustees' fiduciary responsibilities to beneficiaries, primarily decisions about investments. As this chapter celebrates the positive impact of the Restatements of Trusts on the development of trust law, the chapter also provides suggestions for a Restatement (Fourth) of Trusts that, as has been true of the previous Restatements, would reflect the many developments in trust law since the Restatement (Third). In so doing, this chapter also steps back to provide a tempered critique of the role of trusts in perpetuating inequality, albeit with an understanding that the goal of the Restatement is not to transform the law but rather to reflect its development.

Ultimately, the questions raised in this chapter suggest that it is not too early to start envisioning and framing a Restatement (Fourth) of Trusts.

II. History of Restatements of Trusts

When work on the Restatement of Trusts was undertaken in 1927, it was the seventh such project of the new ALI, and publication of the Restatement of Trusts in 1935 meant that they were among the first ten volumes of Restatements issued.[15] The Restatement (First) was issued in two volumes, with 460 sections. Austin Wakeman Scott, who taught Felix Frankfurter and many other legal luminaries at Harvard Law School, was the Reporter for the first two Restatements of Trust—as well as the Restatement of Restitution.[16] As Lance Liebman noted in the Foreword to the Restatement (Third) of Trusts, "[f]or half a century, Austin Wakeman Scott was the great American scholar of the law of trusts. Professor Scott was reported to have said: 'To be great, a law professor must complete a Restatement.'"[17] By his own lights, he is then doubly great, in the trusts Restatement domain alone.

---

[14] RESTATEMENT (THIRD) OF TRUSTS, Part 2, Chap. 5, Introductory Note ("The answer given to that question in this Restatement (and also, now, quite consistently given in the case law, despite often awkward rationale) is 'no.'"). The Second Restatement includes a Topic on The Creation of Testamentary Trusts (topic 11), but not on the Creation of Inter Vivos trusts.

[15] RESTATEMENT (FIRST) OF TRUSTS, Introduction (1935).

[16] 2008 A.L.I. PROC. 160 ("He was as important a figure as anyone, and if you want to have the sense of tradition, Professor Scott taught civil procedure to Felix Frankfurter"). As "a law student, [Scott] married the daughter of the President of Harvard University." 2015 A.L.I. PROC. 3. Scott is also widely known for his treatise on Trusts, which was published in 1939 with a second edition published around the same time as the Restatement (Second).

[17] RESTATEMENT (THIRD) OF TRUSTS, Foreword (2003).

During the drafting process, Scott described the initial decision-making on the scope of the Restatement (First).[18] As he explained, the Reporter and Advisers decided to develop a Restatement on express trusts first, and then, after the completion of that project, to undertake constructive trusts; he was sensitive to the "confusion" that had resulted from treating express and implied contracts together.[19] Nonetheless, an early draft of the Restatement noted that the "Subject of Trusts" as handled in the Restatement included charitable, resulting, and constructive trusts.[20] And Scott was careful to point out that, notwithstanding the potential broad scope of the term "trust," the volume would not treat "all kinds of situations where one person deals with property for the benefit of another," because some such circumstances would be dealt with elsewhere, such as through the already-existing project on a Restatement of Agency.[21]

Scott shaped the Restatements in a series of ways. As a first example, he viewed trusts as donative, rather than contractual arrangements; this perspective was not inevitable, given the views of other, contemporaneous scholars.[22] That decision has meant that a trust is viewed by many in the nature of a unilateral transaction, with the donor's intent controlling, rather than as a bilateral agreement, in which a trustee has some power.[23] Second, even though the original Restatement was slated to include "express private trusts," charitable trusts, resulting trusts, and, as described earlier, constructive trusts,[24] the last became part of the Restatement of Restitution, courtesy of what was probably a Harvard Law School hallway conversation.[25] The first Restatement did include Chapter 11, "Charitable Trusts," with more than fifty sections, and Chapter 12, "Resulting Trusts," with almost sixty sections,[26] although the ALI did not publish its

---

[18] *See generally* Austin W. Scott, *The Restatement of the Law of Trusts*, 31 COLUM. L. REV. 1266 (1931).

[19] *Id.* at 1267.

[20] *Id.* n.3.

[21] *Id.* at 1267.

[22] John H. Langbein, *The Contractarian Basis of the Law of Trusts*, 105 YALE L.J. 625, 644 (1995) (observing that Scott "got it wrong, but had the fortitude to write his error into the Restatement of Trusts" and citing Scott's earlier discussion of this issue: Austin Wakeman Scott, *Nature of Rights of the Cestui Que Trust*, 17 COLUM. L. REV. 269, 269–70 (1917)). Langbein's view has highly influenced many scholars. *See, e.g.,* Robert Sitkoff, *An Agency Costs Theory of Trust Law*, 89 CORNELL L. REV. 621, 628–31 (2004); Henry Hansmann & Ugo Mattei, *The Functions of Trust Law: A Comparative Legal and Economic Analysis*, 73 N.Y.U. L. REV. 434, 471 (1998). Some also see this as "a larger exercise within academia to view all relationships generally as a species of contract." Frederick R. Franke Jr., *Resisting the Contractarian Insurgency: The Uniform Trust Code, Fiduciary Duty, and Good Faith in Contract*, 36 ACTEC L.J. 517, 520 (2010).

[23] Langbein, *supra* note 22, at 652 ("On [] matters [relating to the trustee's role], the trustee's reasonable understanding of the deal should be as relevant as the settlor's."); *id.* at 671 ("The conventional account of the trust that we find in the second Restatement and in the treatises simply does not give due weight to the bedrock elements of contractarian principle that inform the norms of trust law, namely, consensual formation and consensual terms. Trusts are deals."). Thus, for example, Langbein argues that the duty of loyalty is "overbroad," given the "deal" the settlor believed they were making. *Id.* at 665.

[24] Austin W. Scott, *The Restatement of the Law of Trusts*, 16 A.B.A. J. 496, 497 (1930). For resulting trusts, *see* Austin W. Scott, *Discussion of Trusts, Tent. Draft No. 5*, 11 A.L.I. PROC. 589, 589 (1934).

[25] 2000 A.L.I. PROC. 226 ("Austin Scott, who, of course, was at work on the Restatement of Trusts, had planned in his Table of Contents, somewhere way at the end, Chapter 9 or Chapter 10, the last one was going to be called 'Constructive Trusts.' Well, at some point—I assume it was chatting with each other in the corridors at the Harvard Law School"). The rules applicable to resulting trusts were set out in Sections 404–60 of the First Restatement.

[26] RESTATEMENT (FIRST) OF TRUSTS, Chapters 11, 12, § 358 (1935).

first Restatement on Charitable Organizations until 2021.[27] Third, Scott's impact as the Reporter meant that commercial trusts were excluded from the Restatement,[28] notwithstanding that the "1920s saw a miniature boom in writings about business trusts in law reviews, practice manuals, and treatises."[29]

Furthermore, in seeking to articulate the law of trusts, the Restatement distinctly pushed the law in certain directions. For example, Scott noted that "[t]here is among the courts a difference of opinion" on whether "the wife or children" of a trust benefi-ciary can reach into a spendthrift trust.[30] In a 1936 *Harvard Law Review* article, Scott seemed somewhat skeptical about the ability of a settlor to insulate beneficiaries from all claims, finding spendthrift clauses "hardly applicable" to a wife, and "wholly inap-plicable" to children.[31] Indeed, he had expressed similar skepticism long before he be-came the Reporter, noting that spendthrift trusts allowed the "creat[ion of] a favored class of persons who can live in idleness and in comfort or even in luxury without paying their debts," and that, rather than a promising "reform," the spendthrift trust "seems to violate the sound principles of personal responsibility upon which the doc-trines of the common law are based."[32]

While the Restatement of Trusts may have been one of the earliest of the Restatement projects, it was not uncontroversial as a project. In a 1931 *Columbia Law Review* article—published midway through the drafting of the Restatement—Yale law professor Thurman Arnold suggested that, rather than a Restatement of Trusts, the cases might instead be better sorted into a "restatement of the law of future interests, others in a restatement of the law of the administration of insolvent estates, others in a restatement of equitable remedies for fraud."[33] Moreover, notwithstanding Scott's "unquestioned skill," Arnold concluded that it was precisely Scott's skill that illus-trated "the attempt to restate trusts as a philosophy is the best proof that it cannot be done."[34] Scott quickly responded that, much as he "welcomed Arnold's criticisms," all through his article were "to be found certain assumptions as to the Restatement which are not warranted by the Restatement itself."[35] Arnold's criticisms did not stop the project. Instead, the First Restatement has profoundly affected American law, and its impact is difficult to overstate. Within two years of its completion by the ALI in 1935,

---

[27] RESTATEMENT OF THE LAW, CHARITABLE NONPROFIT ORGANIZATIONS (2021), https://www.ali. org/publications/show/charitable-nonprofit-organizations/ RESTATEMENT OF THE LAW, CHARITABLE NONPROFIT ORGANIZATIONS, Introduction (Tentative Draft No. 3, 2019) ("Although some of the American Law Institute's projects, most notably the Restatements of Trusts, include Sections that address charities or mention nonprofits generally, none addresses the topic in an organized or comprehensive manner.").

[28] *E.g.*, RESTATEMENT (SECOND) OF TRUSTS § 1 cmt. b (1959). "Austin W. Scott, the reporter, excluded commercial trusts from the Restatement on the ground that 'many of the rules' of trust law are inappli-cable in commercial settings." John H. Langbein, *The Secret Life of the Trust: The Trust as an Instrument of Commerce*, 107 YALE L.J. 165, 166 (1997).

[29] John Morley, *The Common Law Corporation: The Power of the Trust in Anglo-American Business History*, 116 COLUM. L. REV. 2145, 2166 (2016) (citing sources).

[30] Austin W. Scott, *Reception by the Courts of the Resettlement of Trusts*, 23 A.B.A. J. 443, 444 (1937).

[31] Austin Wakeman Scott, *Fifty Years of Trusts*, 50 HARV. L. REV. 60, 69–70 (1936).

[32] Austin W. Scott, *The Trust as an Instrument of Law Reform*, 31 YALE L.J. 457, 466 (1922).

[33] Thurman Arnold, *The Restatement of the Law of Trusts*, 31 COLUM. L. REV. 800, 801 (1931).

[34] *Id.* at 823.

[35] Austin Wakeman Scott, *The Restatement of the Law of Trusts*, 31 COLUM. L. REV. 1266, 1268 (1931).

the Restatement had been either cited or quoted by the Supreme Court of the United States as well as by both supreme and appellate courts in a majority of states.[36]

The Restatement (Second) of Trusts, drafted between 1953 and 1959, was prompted by a second grant from the Mellon Trust, designed to ensure that the Restatements remained current.[37] With Scott once again at the helm, the Restatement (Second) did not make substantial changes to the First Restatement.[38] In his first Council draft in 1953, Scott predicted that "a considerable part of the material [for the second restatement] will not be affected, and the fundamental principles are unchanged."[39] It did, however, "provide fuller explanations for conclusions reached" so as to "give all possible aid to the practitioner, the judge and the law student."[40] As the introduction acknowledged, "[t]here will not be very much here which is contrary to what was said in the First Edition. But there is much more said here than was said in the First Edition," offering recognition that the field of trusts was quickly expanding in new and unanticipated directions.[41] One reason for the Restatement (Second) was to "integrate the material in the Restatement of the various Subjects," such as the Restatements of Property and Restitution, "neither of which had been adopted at the time of the adoption of the Restatement of Trusts."[42]

The Restatement (Third) of Trusts was drafted between 1994 and 2003, a period when United States trust law and other related laws addressing donative transfers were undergoing "rigorous, comprehensive reexamination."[43] Perhaps due in part to its close association with the new UTC, which was drafted during the same time period, the Restatement (Third) turned out to be more progressive and substantially longer than the previous versions. According to critics, this Restatement, more so than either of the previous Restatements, was often less about clarifying rules than moving them forward.[44] Edward Halbach, described as the "contemporary master of the law

---

[36] Scott, *supra* note 30, at 443.

[37] Herbert F. Goodrich, *Introduction*, RESTATEMENT (SECOND) OF TRUSTS vii (1959).

[38] *Id.*

[39] RESTATEMENT, SECOND, TRUSTS COUNCIL DRAFT 1 (Jan. 26, 1953), *available at* https://heinonline-org.proxy01.its.virginia.edu/HOL/Page?collection=ali&handle=hein.ali/resect1020&id=3&men_tab=srch results (Austin W. Scott General Note to the Council).

[40] *Id.*

[41] *Id.*

[42] *Id.* at 2.

[43] Edward C. Halbach Jr., *Uniform Acts, Restatements, and Trends in American Trust Law at Century's End*, 88 CAL. L. REV. 1877, 1881 (2000). The Restatement (Third) of Trusts was drafted hand in hand with the UTC and with the Restatement (Third) Property: Wills & Other Donative Transfers. *See* John H. Langbein, *Major Reforms of the Property Restatement and the Uniform Probate Code: Reformation, Harmless Error, and Nonprobate Transfers*, 38 ACTEC L.J. 1, 2 (2012).

[44] For critiques of rules announced in the Third Restatement that deviated from common law, *see, e.g.*, Mark Merric & Steven J. Oshins, *Effect of the UTC on the Asset Protection of Spendthrift Trusts*, 31 EST. PLAN. 375 (2004) (critiquing UTC and Restatement (Third) for eliminating common law distinction between support and discretionary trusts); Frances H. Foster, *Privacy and the Elusive Quest for Uniformity in the Law of Trusts*, 38 ARIZ. ST. L.J. 713, 767 (2006) (criticizing disclosure rules in Restatement and UTC); 12 DEL. CODE § 3315(a) (2008) ("Where discretion is conferred upon the fiduciary with respect to the exercise of a power, its exercise by the fiduciary shall be considered to be proper unless the court determines that the discretion has been abused within the meaning of § 187 of the Restatement (Second) of Trusts, not §§ 50 and 60 of the Restatement (Third) of Trusts."); *see also* Richard Thomson, *Too Much for Too Little: The Restatement's Measure of Damages Where the Trustee Sells a Trust Asset for an Insufficient Price*, 96 MINN. L. REV. 2144, 2144 (2012) (criticizing measure of damages in Restatement (Third) § 205 cmt. d for a negligent, albeit authorized, sale of a trust asset as potentially leading to "incongruently large [damages] compared with the duty to which the beneficiaries are entitled").

of trusts," inherited (so to speak) the Reporter position held by Scott for the first two Restatements,[45] and he spent approximately twenty years, aided by numerous others, putting together the four volumes that make up the Restatement (Third) of Trusts.[46] The Foreword, written by then Director of the ALI Lance Liebman, makes the ALI's gratitude to Halbach for this enormous undertaking feel palpable.[47] The drafting of the Restatement (Third) officially started in 1994, but from 1987 to 1992, Halbach also worked on a Restatement of the Prudent Investor Rule, described in its Foreword as "a project in its own right and ... a partial revision of the Restatement Second of Trusts."[48] This volume, which covered modern investing rules and "related rules concerning the conduct of a trustee in the management of a trust," eventually became part of the main volume of Restatement (Third).[49] Halbach describes the goal of this interim volume as permitting trustees "to act in enlightened ways."[50]

Over time, then, the Restatements did significant work both in describing the state of trust law and providing some aspirational points of focus. Shaped quite dramatically by two men, Scott and Halbach, these first three Restatements reflected the law—both as it was and could be—and also the preferences and philosophies of these two formative authors. In this way, the Restatements were significant for what subjects they discussed as much as for what subjects remained untouched.

III. Pulling Threads from the First Through the Third Restatements of Trusts

The attempt to provide black-letter law in the trusts context initially spanned 460 provisions (reduced by the Restatement (Third) to 111 sections). This section focuses on three aspects of the Trust Restatements that reflect how economic, social, and cultural developments outside of trust law have profoundly affected trust law and how it was restated over the years.

A. The Trajectory of Trust Users: Who Are the Settlors, Beneficiaries, and Trustees?

Drafted between 1927 and 1935, the Restatement (First) of Trusts reflected its time period in the ways it described and illustrated how and by whom trusts were created and used. Employing all masculine pronouns,[51] featuring the "prudent man" as

---

[45] Lance Liebman, *Foreword*, RESTATEMENT (THIRD) OF TRUSTS ix (2003).

[46] *See id.* ("highly qualified Advisers gave the Reporters constructive criticism, as did our committed Members Consultative Group, our Council and our membership"); *see also infra* note 79 (discussing Advisers).

[47] Liebman, *supra* note 45, at ix–x.

[48] Geoffrey C. Hazard Jr., *Foreword*, RESTATEMENT (THIRD) OF TRUSTS: PRUDENT INVESTOR RULE (1990).

[49] RESTATEMENT (THIRD) TRUSTS, Chapter 17 (2003).

[50] Edward C. Halbach Jr., Organizational Meeting, Philadelphia, Dec. 18, Prelim. Draft 1 (Dec. 8, 1987) of the RESTATEMENT (THIRD) OF TRUSTS: PRUDENT INVESTOR RULE (1987).

[51] RESTATEMENT (FIRST) OF TRUSTS § 2 & cmt. b (1935) (defining a trust, as a "fiduciary relationship with respect to property" and explaining that a person in that fiduciary relation may not delegate "*his* duties as

trustee,[52] and providing illustrations of its rules that involved primarily male actors,[53] the Restatement showed in multiple ways that trusts were created, used, and administered primarily by and for men.

In the spendthrift trust provisions, for example, the Reporters recognize that "certain classes of claimants" are excepted from the rules that protect property held in a spendthrift trust, but they contemplate that it will always be a husband's interest in the trust that his "wife or child" might seek for support or "the wife for alimony."[54] In other words, when marriages ended, the spouse seeking support was imagined as exclusively female and the person from whom support was sought exclusively male. The Restatement (Second) contained the same language and examples,[55] with one anomalous exception.[56] This default to the male as the only relevant property owners and managers was quite clearly reflective of the economic and social reality of the times in terms of naturalized gender roles and who held and controlled the wealth in families. These assumptions also reflect the legal realities of the relevant time period; it was not until 1979 in *Orr v. Orr* that the Supreme Court found unconstitutional a spousal support statute that granted support only to women upon divorce and not to men.[57] Where this language failed was in any attempt to recognize the idiosyncratic ways in which women inherited and managed wealth even at the time.[58] Instead, the language reflected exclusionary tropes about women and their relationship (or nonrelationship) to money.

fiduciary" and "*he* is under a duty not to profit at the expense of the other [nor] ... enter into competition with him without his consent." (emphasis added)).

[52] *Id.* § 227 ("In making investments of trust funds the trustee is under a duty to the beneficiary ... (a) in the absence of provisions in the terms of the trust or of a statute otherwise providing, to make such investments and only such investments as a prudent man would make of his own property having primarily in view the preservation of the estate and the amount and regularity of the income to be derived.").

[53] In Section 18, "Capacity of Settlor, Declaration of Trust," "a person" has capacity to create a trust "by declaring himself trustee of property." *Id.* § 18. Comment a explains that "certain classes of human beings," which includes "married women at common law" together with "infants" and "insane persons," lack the "full capacity" possessed by "other human beings." *See also* § 350 cmt. a (Creation of a Charitable Trust, Capacity of the Settlor). The illustration shows how a "human being" with "full capacity" manifests that intent. *Id.* § 24 cmt. b ("A, the owner of Blackacre, devises it to B with a direction in the will that B pay the net income thereof to C during C's life and that on C's death he convey Blackacre to D.").

[54] *Id.* § 157.

[55] *See, e.g.*, RESTATEMENT (SECOND) OF TRUSTS §§ 2, 18, 24, 41, 43, 44, 45, 74, 157, 350 (1959).

[56] In the section on "Tentative Trusts of a Savings Deposit," the surviving spouse claiming an elective share in a (male) depositor's account is referred to by both genders. *See id.* § 58 cmt. e ("e. Restrictions on testamentary disposition. Although the surviving spouse in claiming *his or her* statutory distributive share of the estate of the decedent is not entitled to include in the estate property transferred during his lifetime by the decedent in trust for himself for life with remainder to others, ... the surviving spouse of a person who makes a savings deposit upon a tentative trust can include the deposit in computing the share to which such surviving spouse is entitled."). This change appears first in the 1948 Supplement.

[57] Orr v. Orr, 440 U.S. 268, 268 (1979).

[58] *See* Lena Edlund & Wojciech Kopczuk, *Women, Wealth, and Mobility*, 99 AM. ECON. REV. 146 (2009) (describing an empirical study of women and wealth from nineteenth century to present); *see also* Sarah C. Haan, *Corporate Governance and the Feminization of Capital*, 74 STAN. L. REV. 515, 522 (2022) (noting that by 1929, women owned the majority of shares in some of the country's largest corporations; *see generally* MARY SYDNEY BRANCH, WOMEN AND WEALTH: A STUDY OF THE ECONOMIC STATUS OF AMERICAN WOMEN (1934) (statistical study showing status of women as taxpayers and controllers of wealth).

As is clear from these provisions, women—at least married women—are not completely absent from the first two trust Restatements. Indeed, the Reporters of both volumes include sections that explicitly address married women's capacity to be trust beneficiaries[59] and to serve as trustees.[60] But women are not the primary actors in any examples, with the exception of provisions on dower, curtesy, and coverture, where they by definition share the stage.[61] And while married women are singled out and widows receive a nod,[62] single women are virtually invisible. Accordingly, while women themselves are mostly background characters, gender is nevertheless omnipresent in the Restatements, being quietly produced with each illustration and each elision.

Produced similarly through absence is race. Any vocabulary relating to race appears to be textually absent from the first two trust Restatements. The sole exception is a comment in the cy pres provisions[63] and some state annotations discussing cases on race.[64] And although the race of the actors in the illustrations is never specified, the vast majority of national wealth was held by white people during the relevant drafting periods.[65] This default form of identity in the Restatements, it is worth noting, was reflective of the composition of Reporters and Advisers for the first two Restatements who were all men and, from what we can tell, mostly white.[66]

In terms of human relationships, the Restatements of Trusts also reflect and reinforce the prevailing hetero-normative vision of a family at the time of drafting. Consequently, both the First and Second Restatements contain no references to same-sex relationships. As indicated, the words "wife" and "husband" appear frequently, the

[59] RESTATEMENT (FIRST) OF TRUSTS § 118 ("The Beneficiary, Married Women") (1935).

[60] Id. § 90 & cmt. b ("The Trustee, Married Women") (limiting married woman's capacity to serve as trustee to property she would have the capacity to deal with if it were owned by her outright, so nothing that would involve "making conveyances and contracts which are neither void nor voidable").

[61] Id. §§ 144, 145, 146.

[62] Id. § 25, cmt. b, illus. 4 ("A devises and bequeaths all his property to B, his wife, "desiring her to give all her estate at her death to my relations." Since the expression of desire applies not only to A's property, but also to B's property as to which A had no power to create a trust, he does not presumably intend to create a trust as to his property. In the absence of other evidence, B is entitled beneficially to the property and does not take it in trust") (emphasis added). Although § 57, cmt. c, does acknowledge that even if a statute entitles "the wife of a testator" to a portion of the estate, "a married man" could avoid this claim by transferring "his property inter vivos in trust even though he reserves a life estate and power to revoke or modify." RESTATEMENT (FIRST) OF TRUSTS § 57 ("Restrictions on testamentary disposition") (1935).

[63] RESTATEMENT (FIRST) OF TRUSTS § 399 ("Cy Pres"), cmt. h (1935) ("Thus, where a testator, who died before slavery was abolished in the United States, bequeathed money in trust to be expended for the circulation of books and delivery of lectures or otherwise as in the judgment of the trustee would create a public sentiment that would put an end to negro slavery in the United States, and slavery in the United States was abolished by an amendment to the Constitution, the court may direct the application of the bequest to the promotion of the interests of former slaves.").

[64] See, e.g., RESTATEMENT (FIRST) OF TRUSTS, Trust State Annotations: Florida, Maryland, Arkansas.

[65] In 1930, for example, the racial wealth gap was 9–1, and in 1950 it was 7–1. Ellora Derenoncourt et al., Wealth of Two Nations: The U.S. Racial Wealth Gap, 1860–2020, National Bureau of Economic Research, Working Paper 30101 (2022), available at https://repec.cepr.org/repec/cpr/ceprdp/DP17328.pdf. For discussions of the racial wealth gap, and its history, see also, e.g., Danaya C. Wright, The Demographics of Intergenerational Transmission of Wealth: An Empirical Study of Testacy and Intestacy on Family Property, 88 U.M.K.C. L. REV. 665, 670–72 (2019); Palma Joy Strand, Inheriting Inequality: Wealth, Race, and the Laws of Succession, 89 OR. L. REV. 453, 458–63 (2010).

[66] To clarify, we have not found any information that any of them were not white. RESTATEMENT (FIRST) OF TRUSTS x–xi (1935); RESTATEMENT (SECOND) OF TRUSTS iii (1959).

words "partner" (as in intimate partner) and "companion," unsurprisingly, do not;[67] there are several references to "cohabitation" but only in the context of it being illegal.[68] A family in the Restatements of Trusts looks like this:

> The "family" of a designated person may be construed to include himself and his wife and children or such children or other relatives or other person as are living with him . . .[69]

Perhaps even more so than with race and gender, the failure to recognize same-sex relationships is to be expected given the underground and illegal nature of same-sex relationships.[70] Nevertheless with probate cases like *In re Will of Kaufmann* in 1965, questions about same-sex partners and inheritance mechanisms were already present on court dockets by the time of the Restatement (Second).[71] Moreover, as with race and gender, the silence around sexual preference in family formation accomplished substantive work in reflecting—and reifying—the norm of the heterosexual marital family.[72]

The Restatement (Third) reflects a significant shift in how, for, and by whom trusts were used, though some of the social assumptions that pervade the first two Restatements do still exist. For example, the Restatement (Third) is noticeably more inclusive with respect to gender than its predecessors. Starting with the definition of "fiduciary relation" in Section 2, the masculine pronouns are exchanged for a more gender-neutral approach, so that "a person in a fiduciary relation to another is under a duty to act for the benefit of the other" and "not to profit at the expense of the other" or compete "without the latter's consent."[73] The Restatement (Third)'s illustrations contemplate a broader array of family members creating, administering, and benefiting from trusts, with "examples of a fairly representative but far from exhaustive array of express private trusts" including male and female settlors, trustees, and beneficiaries.[74] Of course, the families in the illustrations still consist of two different-sex

---

[67] Even the word "spouse" appears in only eleven sections in the Restatement (First). *See* RESTATEMENT (FIRST) OF TRUSTS §§ 62, 74, 144, 145, 146, 170, 238, 239, 289, 407, and 408 (1935).

[68] *Id.* §§ 290 cmt. a, 293 cmt. c, 294.

[69] *Id.* § 120 cmt. b ("Members of a Definite Class"); *see also, e.g., id.* § 161 ("Inseparable Interests"), illus. 1 ("A bequeaths Blackacre to B in trust to provide a home for C and his family. C has a wife and two children. C's creditors cannot reach his interest under the trust."); § 362 cmt. b ("Restrictions upon the Creation of Charitable Trusts") ("Usually the invalidity of the disposition is made dependent on the survival of certain members of his family, such as his wife or child, descendant of a child or parent."). The first two trust Restatements did recognize that not all families live in harmony and that marriages may end before death. *See, e.g., id.* § 26.

[70] An illegality that persisted in some states until *Lawrence v. Texas*, 539 U.S. 558, 578 (2003), in 2003 with respect to intimate relationships and until *Obergefell v. Hodges*, 576 U.S. 644, 675 (2015), in 2015 with respect to marriage.

[71] *In re* Kaufmann's Will, 20 A.D.2d 464, 474 (N.Y. App. Div. 1964), *aff'd*, 205 N.E.2d 864 (1965).

[72] The question of the role of Restatements in reifying the heteronormative family also emerges in the contribution of Linda C. McClain and Douglas NeJaime, *The ALI Principles of the Law of Family Dissolution: Addressing Family Inequality Through Functional Regulation*, in this volume.

[73] Obergefell v. Hodges, 576 U.S. 644, 675 (2015).

[74] RESTATEMENT (THIRD) OF TRUSTS § 2 (2003); *see also, e.g., id.* § 11 ("a person has capacity to create a revocable inter vivos trust by transfer to another or by declaration to the same extent that the person has capacity to create a trust by will."); § 17 (a trust is created by "a declaration by an owner of property that he or she holds that property as trustee for one or more persons").

parents. These families seek to keep their property in the family, to give to their children equally, to care for elderly siblings and ancestors suffering from poverty and bad health, and to donate to "worthy charities in the community."[75] Not only is the couple a heteronormative one but it is clear that the family is also well resourced.

This is not to say that the drafters did not consider changing social and cultural dynamics. John Langbein, who served as an Adviser on this volume and also as the Reporter for Restatement (Third) of Property: Wills and Donative Transfers (and an ex officio member of the UTC Drafting Committee), echoed Halbach's view of the period during which both Restatements and the Uniform laws were drafted as a "cycle of renewal."[76] Langbein supplied additional reasons for revisions in these volumes as "changes in reproductive technology," a gerontological revolution, changes in gender relations and concerns about gender equity, and changes in theory and practice of investment.[77] He described the drafting process as "deeply inclusive,"[78] although representation on the drafting committees of women and people of color does not appear to differ significantly from earlier Restatements.[79]

The Restatement (Third)'s major contribution to making trust planning more accessible was to recognize the broader role of revocable trusts and their interplay with other planning.[80] This contribution had less to do with race and gender than it did categories of wealth and class. In a symposium piece about the state of twentieth-century law, Halbach explained that many of the changes seen in the Restatement (Third) came about because trusts were being used by "broader segments of society than in the past, and with greater diversity of objectives ... but increasingly without aid of legal counsel."[81] Moreover, donors were living longer, and thus experiencing "substantial periods of diminished physical or mental health."[82] Accordingly, an explicit goal of the Restatement (Third) was to make trusts more "user-friendly" and "flexible," so accessible to the "ordinary person."[83] The Reporters explain that "widespread legislative and judicial endorsement" and "popular interest" have together established the revocable trust "in American law as a socially useful and successful device for property management, especially late in life, and for the disposition of property (outright or in further trust) following the settlor's death."[84] Section 25 therefore recognizes revocable trusts as nontestamentary[85] but nevertheless "subject to substantive restrictions on testation ... and other rules applicable to testamentary dispositions,"[86] such

---

[75] *Id.* § 13.
[76] Langbein, *supra* note 43, at 5.
[77] *Id.* at 5.
[78] *Id.* at 6–7.
[79] By the Third Restatement, Halbach was aided by four male associate reporters; three women accompanied the twenty men who served as Advisers. *See* RESTATEMENT (THIRD) OF TRUSTS, Vol. 1, at v–vii (2003); RESTATEMENT (THIRD) OF TRUSTS Vol. 3, at v–ix (2007); RESTATEMENT (THIRD) OF TRUSTS Vol. 4, at v–ix (2012). Similar demographics attend the 1992 Restatement (Third) of Trusts: Prudent Investor Rule volume, for which Halbach was also the reporter. Both volumes increased participation through large "consultative groups."
[80] RESTATEMENT (THIRD) OF TRUSTS § 25 cmt. a (2003); *see also* § 19 ("Pour-Over Disposition by Will").
[81] Halbach, *supra* note 43, at 1883.
[82] *Id.*
[83] Halbach, *supra* note 43, at 1881, 1883; *see also* RESTATEMENT (THIRD) OF TRUSTS, Foreword ix (2003).
[84] *Id.* § 25 cmt. a.
[85] *Id.* § 25 (1) & (2).
[86] *Id.* § 25(2).

as the spousal elective share, claims by estate creditors, and revocation-on-divorce rules.[87] With respect to creditor provisions, the Restatement (Third) substantially re-worked the rules on discretionary and spendthrift trusts to address what happens to a beneficiary who is a settlor or who may become a settlor.[88]

As these provisions relate to beneficiary rights—here, the use of trusts to shield beneficiaries from the claims of creditors—the Reporters of the Restatement (Third) sought to strike a balance between the settlor's powers to control property and cred-itors' rights. First, in addition to the long-recognized exception for spousal and child support claims, the Reporters spent time discussing an exception for tort creditors, recognizing that this exception had been recommended early on, had not gained sig-nificant traction, but had been recognized in at least one case that "may prove to be in-fluential elsewhere."[89] Second, the Reporters affirmed the long-standing common law rule that creditors could reach the interests of any beneficiary who was also a settlor of the trust.[90] In both cases, these rules "reflect a general acceptance of a fundamental common-law principle that a property owner, being free either to bestow property rights and benefits upon others or to withhold them, can bestow those rights and benefits through the trust device with the settlor's chosen conditions and restraints so long as those conditions and restraints are not, in the conventional terminology of trust law, unlawful or contrary to public policy."[91]

B. The Trajectory of Public Policy in the Restatements

Within the trust Restatements, the authors traditionally cabined public policy in a separate section, identifying and discussing particular policy issues that have re-mained remarkably similar over time, albeit with certain modifications and ampli-fications. The Restatement (First) set forth the parameters that defined public policy in Section 62, stating in broad strokes that a trust or trust provision was invalid if it tended to induce the commission of illegal or immoral acts or acts against "public policy." The Reporters furnished an example of "tending to induce the commission of illegal acts" in a trust established to pay the fines of a group of people "engaged in the commission of criminal acts." A private trust, the Reporters explained, might also be invalid on the grounds of inducing the commission of an immoral act if the trust had as its purpose the provisioning of a nonmarital ("illegitimate") child.[92]

---

[87] *Id.* § 25 cmts. d, e; *see also id.* §§ 34.1(3), 34.3(3), 55.

[88] *See id.* at § 58 cmts. e & f; § 60 cmts. e & g.

[89] *Id.* § 59 Reporter's Note to cmt. a at 400 (citing *Sligh v. First Nat'l Bank*, 704 So. 2d 1020 (Miss. 1997)); *see* Thomas P. Gallanis, *The New Direction of American Trust Law*, 97 IOWA L. REV. 215, 221–22 (2011).

[90] *Id.* § 58(2), 60 cmt. f.

[91] RESTATEMENT (THIRD) OF TRUSTS, Introductory Note 4012 (2003).

[92] The Reporters also noted: "Whether such provisions are invalid depends upon the conceptions of public policy which are prevalent in the community at the time of the creation of the trust." What is meant by "public policy" in a particular community at a particular time raises a host of questions that are beyond the scope of this chapter but that we hope to explore in the future. *See* Lawrence v. Texas, 539 U.S. 558, 560 (2003) ("The fact that a State's governing majority has traditionally viewed a particular practice as immoral is not a sufficient reason for upholding a law prohibiting a practice."). *But cf.* Nathan Oman, *Private Law and Local Custom, in* THE OXFORD HANDBOOK OF THE NEW PRIVATE LAW 159, 172–74 (Andrew S. Gold et al. eds., 2020) (describing the local character of the common law).

In terms of "public policy," the Reporters identified two thematic strands in the comments. One strand of public policy concern centered on family relationships and the maintenance of nuclear, marital families.[93] From this perspective, trusts or trust provisions that restrained marriage, encouraged divorce, or encouraged the neglect of parental duties might be judicially determined to be invalid on public policy grounds. The other strand involved trusts and trust provisions that violated perpetuities, or otherwise restrained alienation (discussed earlier), and therefore facilitated accumulations. The Reporters did not specify or elaborate on the policy objectives that subtended these categories but nevertheless listed such trusts and trust provisions as being against public policy. As with some of the other textual examples given elsewhere, the authors revealed as much through their silence as through their direct explanations, perhaps assuming their objectives to be self-evident.

The Restatement (Second) of Trusts reiterated the same categories in its discussion of public policy,[94] retaining a public policy emphasis on the importance of financial support within the marital family and the role of rules restraining perpetuities. Accordingly, the examples of "inducement of criminal or tortious acts" describes invalid trust provisions as those providing for payment of money to a "person" "if he should secure a divorce from his spouse by perjury or other improper means" or "if he should violate his duty to support his children, or should violate a public duty, such as the duty to serve in the armed forces of the nation if he is conscripted."[95] Similar language appears in the examples offered for trusts "encouraging immorality." One example of a trust provision encouraging "immorality" is a provision that encourages the beneficiary to produce "an illegitimate child."[96] Taking a step away from the self-assuredness of the Restatement (First), however, the Restatement (Second) declined to provide too much specific guidance for fear of treading on particularized "conceptions of public policy which are prevalent in the community"[97]:

> Owing to the changing character of ideas of morality, especially in regard to the relations of the sexes and religious matters, and owing to the diversity of ideas in different communities, it is inadvisable, if not impossible, to make categorical statements on these matters.

This nod to the variety and mutability of cultural norms was a shift in direction and tone from the previous Restatement and gestured to an understanding of the difficulties of universal pronouncements in the context of mores and morals, creating space for productive ambiguity in future iterations.

In addition to the categories culled from the Restatement (First), the Restatement (Second) Reporters added one new category: "Disposition of property detrimental to the community."[98] Here, the Reporter remarked:

---

[93] Two other scenarios the Reporters envisioned as contra public policy were the restraint of religious freedom and restraining a beneficiary from performing public duties.

[94] RESTATEMENT (SECOND) OF TRUSTS § 62 (1959); RESTATEMENT (THIRD) OF TRUSTS § 29 (2003).

[95] RESTATEMENT (SECOND) OF TRUSTS § 62 cmt. b (1959).

[96] *Id.* § 62 cmt. c.

[97] *Id.* § 62 cmt. d.

[98] *Id.* § 62.

A provision in the terms of the trust is invalid if performance of the provision would be injurious to the community as well as to the beneficiary. Thus, if a testator devises land in trust for a long period and directs that no building shall be erected upon any part of the land of more than three stories in height, and the land is situated in the heart of the business district of a city, the enforcement of the provision may be so harmful to the community, as well as to the beneficiaries of the trust, that it is against public policy to enforce it.

The example clearly involves a trust provision that impairs efficient use of the property in a profit-maximization community of business interests and therefore fails to speak to either larger societal interests or inequality concerns. Nevertheless, the new category recognized that there could be interests at stake other than the beneficiaries' interests, providing a pivot point for future iterations.

Moving to the Restatement (Third), Section 29 ("Purposes and Provisions That Are Unlawful or Against Public Policy"), sounded the same categories and assumptions as previous Restatements.[99] That is to say, Section 29 reiterated that an intended trust or trust provision was invalid if it was "unlawful or its performance calls for the commission of a criminal or tortious act," if it violates the relevant perpetuities period, or if it is contrary to "public policy." In the commentary about what kinds of trusts or trust provisions would be invalid on grounds of calling "for the commission of a criminal or tortious act," the Reporter included a new example concerning fraudulent transfer. The example runs as follows: "[T]he owner of property might transfer it to another who agrees to hold it in trust for the transferor or another with the purpose being to conceal the interest of the transferor or other person, not merely for reasons of privacy but in order to mislead the government or others with respect to the true beneficial interests in the property."[100] This recognition of the ways in which trusts could be used to "mislead" the government or other creditors such as a divorcing spouse is a notable first in the public policy section.

Outside of trusts that deal in and tend to encourage illegality and fraud, the same strands appear in the discussion of public policy: the regulation of family relationships and the violation of perpetuities rules.[101] In the context of family relationships, new commentary identified trusts or trust provisions that discourage "a person from living with or caring for a parent or child or from social interaction with siblings" as being against public policy. In addition, the Reporter also added that trusts or trust provisions were against public policy to the extent they mandated certain career choices and penalized beneficiaries for acting outside of very narrow parameters with respect to career choices. This example was new in the sense that it took work and

---

[99] RESTATEMENT (THIRD) OF TRUSTS § 29 (2003).

[100] Id.

[101] The Restatement (Third) did not directly address the increase in jurisdictions' recognition of perpetual trusts. See Jesse Dukeminier & James E. Krier, The Rise of the Perpetual Trust, 50 UCLA L. REV. 1303, 1343 (2003) (observing that the Restatement (Third) of Trusts, ch. 13, introductory note, "dodges the issue" of perpetual trusts by writing: "It is worth noting, however, that this section [on modification and termination of trusts] applies in the common-law context and that different issues—and different planning and drafting considerations—may arise with respect to trusts of indefinite duration in jurisdictions that have adopted legislation to abolish the rule against perpetuities.").

career choices seriously as something that trust settlors might choose to control and manipulate, something the previous iterations had not done.

More broadly, the "General Comments" to Section 29(c), addressing trusts that are "contrary" to public policy, explained that a trust provision that induces beneficiaries "to exercise or not exercise fundamental rights that seriously affect their personal interests and lives" may be invalid even if a settlor could have made such gifts during life. Speaking broadly to this idea of finding the appropriate level of settlor control within the public policy framework, the Reporter wrote:

> The private trust is tolerated, even treasured, in the common-law world for the flexibility it offers to property owners in planning and designing diverse beneficial interests and financial protections over time, individually tailored as the particular property owner deems best to the varied needs, abilities, and circumstances of particular family members and others whom the owner chooses to benefit. Yet these societal and individual advantages are properly to be balanced against other social values and the effects of deadhand control on the subsequent conduct or personal freedoms of others, and also against the burdens a former owner's unrestrained dispositions might place on courts to interpret and enforce individualized interests and conditions.

The Reporter made no comment on what "other social values" might come into play or factor into the calculus of public policy pertaining to trust regulation and the regulation of dead-hand control. Nevertheless, adverting to such a balancing act and recognizing the possibility of myriad and competing interests was a step toward mitigating settlor control when exercised as a mode of social control over a beneficiary such as conditioning distribution on the religion, race, or gender of a beneficiary's spouse.

C. The Trajectory of Trustee Investment Duties

Trustees are required, pursuant to the duty of loyalty, to act in the sole interests of beneficiaries and, pursuant to the duty of care, to manage trust investments prudently; those duties have been consistent themes throughout the trust Restatements. In the Restatement (First), this was phrased as a trustee being "under a duty to the beneficiary to administer the trust solely in the interest of the beneficiary,"[102] and to make investments (in the absence of contrary terms in the trust) "as a prudent man would make of his own property having primarily in view the preservation of the estate and the amount and regularity of the income to be derived."[103] While the comments noted that out-of-state investments were "not necessarily improper," the Reporters also noted that purchasing stock was permissible "if prudent men in the community are accustomed to invest in such shares when making an investment of their savings with a view to their safety."[104] These provisions, remained the same in the Restatement

---

[102] RESTATEMENT (FIRST) OF TRUSTS § 170 (1935).
[103] Id. § 227(a).
[104] Id. § 227, cmts. k, l.

(Second),[105] although the comments recognized that attitudes had changed toward interstate—and international—investments and that states' statutes had become more likely to allow investments in common stock.[106]

In between the most recent two Restatements was the interim Restatement of the Prudent Investor Rule, which was described as both "a project in its own right" as well as a "partial revision of the Restatement Second of Trusts."[107] The basic statement of the duty remained the same, although the investment standard had become gender neutral; the trustee's duty "to the beneficiaries [is] to invest and manage the funds as a prudent investor would ..."[108] Yet as the project was being drafted, Halbach noted that he needed "to decide how and where to treat issues about social influence on investment decisions," suggesting that they might be beyond the basic description of loyalty or could be "slipped" into the commentary on loyalty in Section 227.[109] He did, indeed, "slip" them into the commentary on loyalty, noting that the minimal common law involving "social investing" was not helpful.[110] He reminded readers of the importance of acting to further the trust purposes and with a mindset contemplated by the settlor.[111]

In Restatement (Third), a trustee still "has a duty to administer the trust solely in the interest of the beneficiaries,"[112] and "to invest and manage the funds of the trust as a prudent investor would, in light of the purposes, terms, distribution requirements, and other circumstances of the trust."[113] The Reporters provide more clarity on the issue of "social investing,"[114] language that did not appear in earlier Restatements.[115] This prohibition on investing in ways that might "advance" a trustee's "personal views concerning social or political issues or causes" could mean that any consideration of factors other than what is in the beneficiary's sole interest—even if consideration of such factors might ultimately benefit the beneficiary—would be impermissible because there would be a "mixed motive."[116] Section 87 provides additional support for that position, as the comments note that a trustee might abuse their power when acting from an "improper," albeit not "dishonest motive, such as when the act is undertaken in good faith but for a purpose other than to further the purposes of

---

[105] RESTATEMENT (SECOND) OF TRUSTS §§ 170, 227 (1959).

[106] Id. § 227, cmts. l, m.

[107] Hazard, supra note 48, at ix.

[108] RESTATEMENT (THIRD) OF TRUSTS: PRUDENT INVESTOR RULE § 227 (1987).

[109] Memo from Edward C. Halbach, Jr., Second Expanded Draft of "Prudent Investor Rule" and Related and Affected Sections for Discussion, June 2–3, at iii, iv, in RESTATEMENT OF THE LAW TRUSTS: PRUDENT INVESTOR RULE Prelim. Draft No. 4 (Aug. 15, 1989).

[110] RESTATEMENT (THIRD) OF TRUSTS: PRUDENT INVESTOR RULE § 227 cmt. c.

[111] Id.

[112] RESTATEMENT (THIRD) OF TRUSTS § 78 (2007).

[113] Id. § 90; see Susan Gary, Best Interests in the Long Term: Fiduciary Duties and ESG Integration, 90 COLO. L. REV. 731, 785 et seq. (2019).

[114] Thus, for example, in managing the investments of a trust, the trustee's decisions ordinarily must not be motivated by a purpose of advancing or expressing the trustee's personal views concerning social or political issues or causes." RESTATEMENT (THIRD) OF TRUSTS § 90 cmt. c (2007).

[115] For example, it is not in Section 170 (Duty of Loyalty), 187 (Control of Discretionary Powers), or 227 (General Standard of Prudent Investment) of the Restatement (Second) of Trusts.

[116] Max M. Schanzenbach & Robert H. Sitkoff, Reconciling Fiduciary Duty and Social Conscience: The Law and Economics of ESG Investing by a Trustee, 72 STAN. L. REV. 381, 413 (2020).

the trust."[117] These provisions could be seen as part of the move toward shareholder wealth maximization, also evidenced in the opposition that Employee Retirement Income Security Act (ERISA) managers have faced in considering Environmental, Social, and Governance (ESG) investing.[118]

While the parameters of the Prudent Investor Rule have changed, from an emphasis on preserving the corpus and ensuring income in the first two Restatements to "liberating expert trustees to pursue challenging, rewarding nontraditional strategies, when appropriate to the particular trust, to providing unsophisticated trustees with reasonably clear guidance"[119] in Restatement (Third), the "sole interest" standard and "no further inquiry" rule has remained consistent.[120]

IV. "A Cycle of Renewal": Envisioning the Fourth Restatement

Moving from one version of the Restatement to the next, what has come into increasingly sharp focus is the extent to which reform is, for the most part, effectuated in response to new developments in social outlook, wealth management, laws outside of the trust area (such as civil rights), and public policy. Part of the "cycle of renewal"[121] is recognizing what was previously absent and making space for such matters within new discussions. Accordingly, the remainder of this chapter focuses on a few potential areas for reform, recognizing that the work of the Reporters will lie in not only keeping pace with public understandings of concepts like family and gender but also

---

[117] RESTATEMENT (THIRD) § 87 cmt. c; *see* Schanzenbach & Sitkoff, *supra* note 116, at 414 ("If a trustee could not consistent with the terms of the trust make an outright distribution to achieve the same collateral environmental benefit, then the trustee ought not be allowed to circumvent that limit by pursuing the same purpose via the trust's investment program.").

[118] Christopher M. Bruner, *Corporate Governance Reform and the Sustainability Imperative*, 131 YALE L.J. 1217, 1243 (2022); *see* Quinn Curtis et. al., *Do ESG Mutual Funds Deliver on Their Promises?*, 120 MICH. L. REV. 393, 396 (2021) (noting that the Department of Labor adopted an ERISA rule in late 2020 "that may deter 401(k) plans from offering ESG funds"); Schanzenbach & Sitkoff, *supra* note 116, at 403–04 (noting Supreme Court precedent that ERISA investments must be made by focusing solely on financial benefit). *But see* Abbye Atkinson, *Commodifying Marginalization*, 71 DUKE L.J. 773 (2022) (noting the importance of considering the impact of investments on pension fund beneficiaries); Gary, *supra* note 113, at 798 (a prudent investor is increasingly advised to consider ESG factors).

[119] Edward C. Halbach Jr., *Trust Investment Law in the Third Restatement*, 27 REAL PROP. PROB. & TR. J. 407, 411 (First and Second Restatements), 415 (1992).

[120] The UTC diverged from the Restatement by changing the "no further inquiry" rule into a presumption, which a trustee could rebut by showing an absence of conflict. *See* UTC § 802(c); *see also* John H. Langbein, *Questioning the Trust Law Duty of Loyalty: Sole Interest or Best Interest?*, 114 YALE L.J. 929, 944 (2005) (arguing that the "no further inquiry" rule is a relic and prevents trustees from engaging in transactions that will benefit both the trust and its beneficiaries, reflecting his contrarian view of trusts); Melanie B. Leslie, *In Defense of the No Further Inquiry Rule: A Response to Professor John Langbein*, 47 WM. & MARY L. REV. 541 (2005) (arguing that "best interests" standard would impose the risk of serious harm on beneficiaries). Although drafted in tandem and sharing many provisions, the UTC and Restatement (Third) do diverge at times. *See, e.g.*, Philip J. Ruce, *The Trustee and the Remainderman: The Trustee's Duty to Inform*, 46 REAL PROP. TR. & EST. L.J. 173, 185–192 (2011) (describing differences between UTC and Restatement in defining beneficiaries entitled to information from a trustee); Daniel B. Kelly, *Restricting Testamentary Freedom: Ex Ante Versus Ex Post Justifications*, 82 FORDHAM L. REV. 1125, 1179 (2013) (describing differences in modification and termination provisions).

[121] Langbein, *supra* note 43, at 5; text accompanying *supra* note 79.

in recognizing the ubiquitous presence of public policy concerns throughout the Restatement. Even as the Restatement of Trusts was shaped by its Reporters to be flexible, they recognized the need to draw on court decisions and statutes, "seeking a seamless statement of the best principles of American trust law and offering intellectual guidance" to state legislatures, courts, and estate planners.[122] The following three sets of suggestions, centered on calibrating the interests of trust settlors and beneficiaries with the social and democratic good of the relevant communities and larger collectives, take seriously this charge to state "best principles" and "offer[] intellectual guidance," although we recognize that some are aspirational, rather than summaries of current developments.

A. Recognizing New Populations and Uses

Historically—and in the social imagination—it is clear that trusts have been and continue to be primarily the tools of the wealthy,[123] even as they have come to be easier to create, understand, use, and administer. As a result, discussing how a Restatement (Fourth) might address a more diverse set of users is, in itself, a challenge; any discussion of wealth transmission affects a much narrower section of society than does a discussion of wealth generation, for example.[124] Nonetheless, a new Restatement might build on the idea of growing access to revocable trusts as highly utilized estate planning devices by expanding on how trusts are being used as management vehicles for incapacity, for special needs, and even as a way to hold fractionalized property.[125] In addition, a Restatement (Fourth) might take a position on the increase of Domestic Asset Protection Trusts (DAPTs), previously mentioned only in the comments to Restatement (Third), Section 60 (Transfer or Attachment of Discretionary Interests). Since the last Restatement, this form of trust, which allows an individual to create a trust for their own benefit and shield the property in that trust from creditors, has become even more prevalent as at least nineteen states have authorized them through new legislation.[126] Although the Restatement (Third) disapproves of the comparable

---

[122] Liebman, *supra* note 45.

[123] RAY D. MADOFF, IMMORTALITY AND THE LAW: THE RISING POWER OF THE AMERICAN DEAD 80 (2010) ("[A]s a practical matter, [generation-skipping trusts] were *only* available to those families wealthy enough to keep their assets locked up in trust); Stewart E. Sterk, *Trust Decanting: A Critical Perspective*, 38 CARDOZO L. REV. 1993, 1994 (2017) ("Poor people do not create trusts."); *see also* Alison A. Tait, *High-Wealth Exceptionalism*, 71 ALA. L. REV. 981, 995–1000 (2020) (describing how private trust companies enhance the wealth of high-net-worth families); Felix Chang, *Asymmetries in the Generation and Transmission of Wealth*, 79 OHIO ST. L.J. 73, 74–75 (2018); Iris J. Goodwin, *How the Rich Stay Rich: Using a Family Trust Company to Secure a Family Fortune*, 40 SETON HALL L. REV. 467, 467–78 (2010); Carla Spivack, *Beware the Asset Protection Trust*, 5 EUR. J. PROP. L. 1–26 (2016); Carla Spivack, *Democracy and Trusts*, 42 ACTEC L.J. 311, 339 (2017); Kent Schenkel, *Exposing the Hocus Pocus of Trusts*, 45 AKRON L. REV. 63, 64 (2012).

[124] Naomi R. Cahn, *Dismantling the Trusts & Estates Canon*, 2019 WIS. L. REV. 165 (2019).

[125] Caitlin Henderson, Note, *Heirs Property in Georgia: Common Issues, Current State of the Law, and Further Solutions*, 55 GA. L. REV. 875, 898 (2021) (discussing family land trusts as a way to remedy heirs property).

[126] David G. Shaftel, *Twelfth ACTEC Comparison of the Domestic Asset Protection Trust Statutes* (2019), https://www.actec.org/assets/1/6/Shaftel-Comparison-of-the-Domestic-Asset-Protection-Trust-Statutes.pdf?hssc=1.

vehicle, a self-settled spendthrift trust,[127] a Restatement (Fourth) will have to decide how to address DAPTs and similar trusts[128] and the enhanced asset protection that they offer. Related doctrines, such as trust "decanting," directed trusts, and trust protectors, all of which together tend to increase wealth disparities, have also become pivotal topics in the trust landscape,[129] and it will be crucial for the Reporters to craft appropriate provisions addressing these trust law developments.

Perhaps as an easier task for the future Reporters, there are a number of areas in which a new Restatement could revise material based on the use of gendered language and social constructs, especially around families. For example, by examining and reimagining how gender and race manifest in the rules and illustrations, the Reporters could use their expressive powers to show that diverse populations engage with trusts.[130]

B. Public Policy Concerns and New Trust Law Developments

Looking ahead and envisioning a Restatement (Fourth), there are multiple ways in which the Reporters could build on the foundations laid out in previous versions, amplifying and expanding the connections between trust regulation and public policy. Even focusing solely on the specific public policy sections found in the previous Restatement—Section 62 in the First and Second, Section 29 in the Third—there is ample room for expanding to recognize existing developments.

Consider "illegal" trust terms, such as the fraudulent transfer example given in Restatement (Third). The rules on fraudulent transfer are one of the few tools that govern transfers into trusts, and future Reporters might want to analyze how such rules facilitate public policy goals related to tax collection, creditor rights, and family support debts. This analysis would align with new and continuing developments in trust law across the states, discussed in the previous section.[131] Similarly, with the category of perpetuities, the Reporters should take into account new legislative activity expanding perpetuities periods. Perpetuities violations have been considered a public policy violation in all previous versions of the Restatement, but the Reporters have never explicitly articulated the policy rationales that make the Rule Against Perpetuities so fundamental. With almost a dozen states having fully abolished the

---

[127] RESTATEMENT (THIRD) OF TRUSTS § 58 (2007).

[128] See, e.g., 2022 Fla. Sess. Law Serv. Ch. 2022-101 (West) (authorizing spousal limited access trusts (SLATs) that provide substantial asset protection benefits to donor spouse).

[129] See Sterk, supra note 123, at 2028–32 (describing social costs of decanting); see generally Tait, supra note 123 (describing how high-wealth families use trust and financial rules to preserve their wealth).

[130] See, e.g., E. Gary Spitko, The Expressive Function of Succession Law and the Merits of Non-Marital Inclusion, 41 ARIZ. L. REV. 1063, 1077–80 (1999) (describing expressive function of intestacy law); Leeford Tritt, Technical Correction or Tectonic Shift: Competing Default Rule Theories Under the New Uniform Probate Code, 61 ALA. L. REV. 273, 294–95 (2010) (same).

[131] For a sampling of commentary, see John K. Eason, Home from the Islands: Domestic Asset Protection Trust Alternatives Impact Traditional Estate and Gift Tax Planning Considerations, 52 FLA. L. REV. 41, 53 (2000); Adam Hirsch, Fear Not the Asset Protection Trust, 27 CARDOZO L. REV. 2685 (2005–2006); Stewart Sterk, Asset Protection Trusts: Trust Law's Race to the Bottom, 85 CORNELL L. REV. 1035, 1048 (2000); Ritchie W. Taylor, Domestic Asset Protection Trusts: The "Estate Planning Tool of the Decade" or a Charlatan?, 13 BYU J. PUB. L. 163, 167 (2013).

Rule Against Perpetuities[132] and even more having extended the perpetuities period to anything from 365 to 1,000 years,[133] Reporters may be called upon, in order to capture these developments, to take a stance on how these developments sit with the traditional framing of perpetuities within the Restatements.[134]

Finally, Reporters for any future Restatement have the capacity to use the public policy power to effectuate antidiscrimination norms. Previous Restatements have all addressed within the public policy section the extent to which trusts or trust provisions may place conditions on a beneficiary's religious faith and practice.[135] This concern could provide the impetus for amplification around the topic of discriminatory conditions within trusts. Recognizing that these kinds of public policy limits are the only mechanism through which to address and combat discrimination in trusts and trust provisions, the Reporters might include policy statements about other forms of discrimination, such as by stating explicitly that trusts or trust provisions that place conditions based on race, gender, age, ability, or ethnicity presumptively violate public policy. The list might even include gender identity.[136] Developing this more expansive framework in the public policy sections will not only move the Restatement toward a more robust understanding of antidiscrimination but also will help address concerns, stated elsewhere in this chapter, about the silence around the production of gender and race within the Restatements.

C. Reconceptualizing Fiduciary Responsibilities

While the obligation of a trustee to act in the sole interest of the beneficiaries remains firmly entrenched,[137] an example of the property rather than "contractarian" focus on

---

[132] A growing number of states—at least seventeen—allow for self-settled DAPTs. Those states are Alaska, Delaware, Hawaii, Michigan, Mississippi, Missouri, Nevada, New Hampshire, Ohio, Oklahoma, Rhode Island, South Dakota, Tennessee, Utah, Virginia, West Virginia, and Wyoming.

[133] Some states have repealed the rule against perpetuities (Alaska, Delaware, Idaho, Kentucky, New Jersey, Pennsylvania, Rhode Island, and South Dakota). Other states have adopted longer fixed periods for the rule against perpetuities, sometimes only for certain types of property, including Alabama, Arizona, Colorado, Delaware (110 years for real property held in trust), Florida, Nevada, Tennessee, Utah, and Washington. About a third of states have retained the rule against perpetuities but allow certain trusts to continue without application of the rule (Arizona, District of Columbia, Hawaii, Illinois, Maine, Maryland, Michigan, Missouri, Nebraska, New Hampshire, New Jersey, North Carolina, North Dakota, Ohio, Oklahoma, Virginia, and Wyoming). Howard Zaritsky, *The Rule Against Perpetuities, 50-State ACTEC Survey*, available at https://www.actec.org/assets/1/6/Zaritsky_RAP_Survey.pdf?hssc=1 (last visited Aug. 25, 2022).

[134] *See* Jesse Dukeminier & James Krier, *The Rise of the Perpetual Trust*, 50 UCLA L. Rev. 1303 (2002–2003); Mary Louise Fellows, *Why the Generation-Skipping Transfer Tax Sparked Perpetual Trusts*, 27 Cardozo L. Rev. 2511 (2005–2006); Max Schanzenbach & Robert Sitkoff, *Perpetuities or Taxes—Explaining the Rise of the Perpetual Trust*, 27 Cardozo L. Rev. 2465 (2005–2006); Lawrence Waggoner, *Effectively Curbing the GST Exemption for Perpetual Trusts*, 135(10) Tax Notes (June 2012).

[135] A trust provision is ordinarily invalid if its "enforcement would tend to restrain the religious freedom of the beneficiary by offering a financial inducement to embrace or reject a particular faith or set of beliefs concerning religion. Illustrative is a provision granting or terminating a beneficial interest only if the beneficiary should adopt or abandon a particular religious faith." Restatement (Third) of Trusts § 29 (2003).

[136] *See* Bostock v. Clayton County, 140 S. Ct. 1731 (2020).

[137] Langbein, *supra* note 120, at 943 (arguing that the sole interest test should be replaced by the best interest test).

fiduciary obligations, the development of ESG investing provides a distinct set of additional challenges to the meaning of "sole interest" and of "prudence." If a beneficiary's sole interest is defined as maximizing financial returns, albeit through prudent investing, then any attention to ESG investing might be seen as a distraction (at best) or, as discussed earlier, as a potential violation of the duty of loyalty. Indeed, pressure by beneficiaries or regulatory bodies to engage in ESG investing could be deemed as violating the duty of loyalty in requiring a trustee to consider "collateral benefits to third parties."[138] Alternative, less draconian views of compliance with the duty of loyalty might make ESG considerations permissible under certain circumstances,[139] given that they are already becoming factors in other types of investment management and so could become part of acting as a prudent investor would.[140] Perhaps ESG considerations "should" be part of any investment analysis.[141] They might even be required, but only when such an investment strategy enhances the long-term value of a company,[142] and can thus be viewed in the beneficiary's sole interest.

Yet, despite the fact that these debates are heatedly taking place across investment offices, the special demands of ESG investing have not yet been addressed by the Restatement. A Restatement (Fourth) could do so, guided by the efforts of some states to require trustees to consider beneficiaries' interests in ESG investing as a modification of the Prudent Investor Rule.[143] For example, in Delaware, the code states: "when considering the needs of the beneficiaries, the fiduciary may take into account the financial needs of the beneficiaries as well as the beneficiaries' personal values, including the beneficiaries' desire to engage in sustainable investing strategies that align with the beneficiaries' social, environmental, governance or other values or beliefs of the beneficiaries."[144] Delaware also provides for the enforceability of a trust term that directs a "sustainable or socially responsible investment strateg[y] ... with or without

---

[138] Schanzenbach and Sitkoff distinguish between "risk-return ESG," which focuses on improving returns by using ESG metrics to improve return while minimizing risk (a fossil-fuel share company has stock prices that are artificially inflated because of inadequate accounting for regulatory risks), and "collateral benefits" ESG, which focuses on "providing a benefit to a third party or otherwise for moral or ethical reasons." Schanzenbach & Sitkoff, *supra* note 134, at 397–98. They agree with the Restatement approach in which "collateral benefits ESG investing would 'ordinarily' violate the sole interest rule," which does not allow for the trustee to motivated by the trustee's own views. *Id.* at 412.

[139] "[I]n general, ESG investing is permissible for a trustee of a pension, charity, or trust subject to American trust fiduciary law if: (1) the trustee reasonably concludes that the ESG investment program will benefit the beneficiary directly by improving risk-adjusted return; and (2) the trustee's exclusive motive for adopting the ESG investment program is to obtain this direct benefit." *Id.* at 385–86.

[140] Jane Gorham Ditelberg, *Investing in and for the Future: ESG Investing for Trust Assets Under the Prudent Investor Rule*, 47 ACTEC L.J. 23, 24 (2021)

[141] Gary, *supra* note 113, at 799 ("As long as a strategy does not involve sacrificing financial returns, then even if the duty of loyalty is defined as the duty to act solely in the financial interests of the beneficiaries, the duty of loyalty is not compromised by a direction to invest using a strategy that incorporates ESG criteria").

[142] "[W]e argue that the fiduciary duty (of loyalty) should be extended and declared publicly by our policymakers to require that institutional investors take equality factors into account." Anat Alon-Beck et al., *No More Old Boys' Club: Institutional Investors' Fiduciary Duty to Advance Board Gender Diversity*, 55 U.C. DAVIS L. REV. 445, 481 (2021) (advocating such a duty for institutional investors). "We believe that this suggested extension is consistent with a director's fiduciary duties, as long as the decision positively contributes to the financial growth and overall long-term value creation of the company." *Id.* at 484.

[143] Ditelberg, *supra* note 140, at 25.

[144] DEL. CODE ANN. TIT. 12, § 3302(a) (2018)(emphasis is new language); Ditelberg, *supra* note 140, at 25 (noting that Georgia adopts a similar approach); *see also* Schanzenbach & Sitkoff, *supra* note 134, at 387 (nothing that Delaware was the first state to address ESG considerations in its trust code).

regard to investment performance";[145] it allows a trustee to consider an investment that "sacrifices returns to achieve a benefit for a third party or for moral or ethical reasons."[146] Again, in order to better reflect what is happening within trust companies and what is being discussed among trustees, a Fourth Restatement will want to recognize these developments and fold them into new discussions.

V. Conclusion

The Restatements of Trusts have achieved the goals set forth in the ALI's 1923 Certificate of Incorporation: "to promote the clarification and simplification of the law and its better adaptation to social needs, to secure the better administration of justice, and to encourage and carry on scholarly and scientific legal work."[147] The Restatements of Trusts helped to institutionalize a relatively new field of law.[148]

Today, while the core elements of trust law are reflected in the Restatement (Third) and the widely adopted UTC, broader questions about the role of trusts are becoming more important in an era of increasing social and economic inequality. On the one hand, Norman Dacey's popularization of the revocable trust,[149] the development of "Totten trusts,"[150] and the growing use of trusts in planning for incapacity show the increasing potential reach of trusts as mechanisms for making trusts available to a broader group of people. On the other hand, dynasty trusts and domestic asset protection trusts show the ongoing role of trusts in sheltering wealth, conditions attached to trusts and trust provisions demonstrate the continuing challenge of combatting discrimination, and questions around ESG investing reveal new opportunities to consider the good of multiple stakeholders. The role of trusts in fostering economic inequality may not be an issue that should be addressed in a Restatement, but it is certainly a fundamental question raised by the Restatement's clarification of the law.

---

[145] DEL. CODE ANN. TIT. 12, § 3303(a)(4).

[146] Schanzenbach & Sitkoff, *supra* note 134, at 418.

[147] AMERICAN LAW INSTITUTE, CAPTURING THE VOICE OF THE AMERICAN LAW INSTITUTE: A HANDBOOK FOR ALI REPORTERS AND THOSE WHO REVIEW THEIR WORK 1 (rev. ed. 2015) (quoting original Certificate).

[148] *See* Scott, *supra* note 31, at 60 (Harvard first offered trusts as a course in 1882).

[149] *See* John H. Langbein, *The Nonprobate Revolution and the Future of the Law of Succession*, 97 HARV. L. REV. 1108, 1113 (1984).

[150] *Id.*

8

Torts in the American Law Institute

*John C.P. Goldberg**

I. Introduction

From its inception, the American Law Institute (ALI) has devoted much attention to tort law. This attention has come in different forms or modes. I label these, respectively: "ALI in the Mode of Appellate Court," "ALI in the Mode of Law Reform Commission," and "ALI in the Mode of Think Tank."

The members of this trio can be placed along a spectrum of ambitiousness with respect to law reform. None is *un*ambitious. But Appellate Court Mode is more tethered to doctrine, while Think Tank Mode is largely untethered. Law Reform Commission Mode lies in between.

One might suppose that the promise of the ALI—which enables leading academics, in consultation with representatives of the bench and bar, to undertake long-term, large-scale research projects—resides in work at the more ambitious end of this spectrum. However, based on an admittedly impressionistic survey, I will suggest that, in the domain of tort law, the ALI has had important successes when proceeding in Appellate Court Mode, and that it has courted trouble when operating in the other modes.[1]

II. ALI in the Mode of Appellate Court

It is not easy to pin down what it means to "restate" the law. In fact, "restatement" probably has meant different things at different times in the ALI's history.[2] However,

---

* Carter Professor of General Jurisprudence, Harvard Law School. As an Associate Reporter for the Fourth Property Restatement, I am among those responsible for drafting provisions on property torts that are slated to appear in that Restatement and the Third Torts Restatement. Having experienced the work involved, I hope that what follows, even when critical, conveys my admiration for all those who have served as Reporters. And I acknowledge that one who bears petards may find himself hoisted by them.

Thanks to Ken Abraham, Jonathan Cardi, Deborah DeMott, Kim Ferzan, Andrew Gold, Bob Gordon, Mike Green, Leslie Kendrick, Carol Lee, Linda McClain, Tom Merrill, Doug NeJaime, Tony Sebok, David Seipp, Rob Sitkoff, Henry Smith, Guy Struve, Brad Wendell, Ted White, and Ben Zipursky for very helpful comments, and to Riva Yeo for excellent research assistance. Remaining errors are mine.

[1] Because of space limitations, my survey omits discussion of some relatively well-known episodes. One of these—the adoption of the Second Restatement's public nuisance provisions—is mentioned elsewhere in this volume. *See* Kenneth S. Abraham & G. Edward White, *The Work of the American Law Institute in Historical Context*, in this volume]. Whether the pattern I purport to find generalizes to the ALI's engagement with other areas of law is beyond the scope of this project.

[2] *See generally* Deborah A. DeMott, *Restating the Law in the Shadow of Codes: The ALI in Its Formative Era*, in this volume (identifying the distinctive assumptions underlying the initial Restatement projects).

at least since the second round of Restatements, the term has invoked a "constructivist" form of legal analysis. Reporters and their Advisers start with the content, categories, and concepts of decisional law, then seek to untangle confusions, iron out inconsistencies, and update outmoded doctrines. Because modifications are inevitable and desirable, because of conflicts among and ambiguities within judicial decisions, and because of the need to adjust legal rules to reflect changing conditions and norms, mere case-counting or taxonomy cannot suffice. Yet if all goes well, the analysis remains tethered to extant law rather than freestanding—it is a *re*construction.

As even this minimalist sketch indicates, restatement-as-reconstruction assumes a position in jurisprudence. For example, it requires a rejection of the vulgar Legal Realist claim that application of common law involves an unmediated reaction between the particular facts of individual cases and the interpreter's psychological makeup or policy commitments. Interpretation-as-reconstruction also stands apart from the later Ronald Dworkin's strongly moralistic account.[3] While the Reporters for the ALI's torts projects have undoubtedly kept an eye on moral principles and sentiments as they have gone about their work, I doubt they have understood their task to be that of producing the morally best version of tort law (whatever that might be).

This is not the occasion for a defense of reconstructive methodology. Instead, it will suffice to point to the long-standing practice of common law adjudication as evidence of the viability of a middle path between vulgar Realism and strong moralism.[4] At least among Anglo-American lawyers, it is standard to suppose that the best versions of common law adjudication aspire to articulate concepts and doctrines clearly and accurately, and to place them appropriately within a complex and (one hopes) mostly coherent web.[5]

Of course the ALI is not literally a court. Nonetheless, it sometimes operates like a court, an aspiration stated in one of its internal guidance documents:

> A Restatement ... assumes the perspective of a common-law court, attentive to and respectful of precedent, but not bound by precedent that is inappropriate or inconsistent with the law as a whole. Faced with such a precedent, a ... Reporter is not compelled to adhere to what Herbert Wechsler called "a preponderating balance of authority" but is instead expected to propose the better rule and the rationale for choosing it. A significant contribution of the Restatements has also been anticipation of the direction in which the law is tending and expression of that development in a manner consistent with previously established principles.[6]

---

[3] RONALD DWORKIN, LAW'S EMPIRE 240–58 (1986).

[4] *See* JOHN C.P. GOLDBERG & BENJAMIN C. ZIPURSKY, RECOGNIZING WRONGS 232–59 (2020) (sketching a constructivist approach to the adjudication of tort cases). This is not to deny—though it is to decline to credit—long-standing expressions of skepticism about courts' use of common law reasoning. For a recent and influential iteration, *see* ANTONIN SCALIA: A MATTER OF INTERPRETATION 3–9 (new ed. 1997). It is perhaps no accident that Justice Scalia would later provide an offhand disparagement of one Restatement that has come to serve as something of a rallying cry for lawyers and judges anxious to find reasons to ignore them. Kansas v. Nebraska, 574 U.S. 445, 475–76 (2015) (Scalia, J. concurring in part and dissenting in part).

[5] *See generally* Andrew S. Gold & Henry E. Smith, *Restatements in the Common Law*, in this volume (explaining the importance of systematicity to common-law reasoning).

[6] AMERICAN LAW INSTITUTE, STYLE MANUAL, at 5 [hereinafter STYLE MANUAL].

In sum, by design, there is a strong resemblance between how our best appellate courts, operating in the synthetic manner of a Benjamin Cardozo, decide common law cases and the processes that, ideally, are to be followed by Restatement Reporters and Advisers.[7] Both gather the relevant legal materials, consider actual and hypothetical cases, and attempt to organize them in a way that is coherent and pragmatically workable. Neither has the "competence ... or authority to make major innovations in matters of public policy."[8]

A skeptic of the analogy on offer will have no trouble identifying differences between ALI Reporters and appellate judges. In deciding individual cases, judges probably are at liberty to pursue a more localized coherence: coherence, say, within a corner of contract or property law. Reporters, by contrast, must aim for coherence across entire areas of law and perhaps across several areas (such as contract, property, restitution, and tort). Reporters also are not bound in the same ways as courts are by legal rules of *stare decisis*. However, these differences are matters of degree, not kind.

In principle, courts should be mindful of how a decision in a particular case sits within the larger body of law of which it is a part, and whether it runs afoul of rules or principles found in adjacent bodies of law.[9] Moreover, Reporters operate under an institutional counterpart to the legal rule of *stare decisis*—they must work with extant case law, and (at least in an other-things-equal sense) must attend to relevant prior Restatements. They also frequently benefit from previous Restatements and judicial decisions applying the provisions of those Restatements, as well as an extensive process of commentary and critique from ALI members with substantial practice-based and academic expertise.[10] For these reasons, the notion of the torts Restatements, or portions of them, operating in the manner of appellate decisions seems apt.

The following four provisions, some of which have been revised across multiple Restatements, attest to the value of the appellate-court approach just outlined. Some have involved primarily consolidation and clarification, others greater innovation. Even the latter, I would suggest, are instances of the ALI fashioning legal content as does an appellate court—their success owes more than a little to their having been crafted to fit within the overall architecture of tort law.

A. Negligence Per Se

Although the doctrine of negligence per se is well settled, its legitimacy and contours were being debated at the time the first Restatement of Torts was published. Dean

---

[7] Here I reject the contention of Grant Gilmore and others that Cardozo was a closeted Realist. John C.P. Goldberg, *Book Review: The Life of the Law*, 51 STANFORD L. REV. 1419 (1999); John C.P. Goldberg, *Note: Community and the Common Law Judge: Reconstructing Cardozo's Theoretical Writings*, 65 N.Y.U. L. Rev. 1324 (1990); *cf.* Gold & Smith, *supra* note 5.

[8] STYLE MANUAL, *supra* note 6, at 6.

[9] For example, as noted later, some courts have recognized claims by disappointed heirs on terms that have generated problematic conflicts between the law of tort and the law of restitution. *See infra* text accompanying notes 69–74.

[10] When operating well, the ALI's exhaustive production process can provide Reporters with better informed and more constructive feedback than an appellate court judge typically stands to receive from appellate counsel, *amici*, and colleagues.

Thayer had published a defense of the doctrine in 1914.[11] Six years later, Cardozo offered a characteristically forceful articulation.[12] As he explained, when a legislature sets a standard of conduct that specifies the care that certain actors owe to members of a class of potential victims, letting jurors substitute their own standard would be akin to allowing them to play the role of a monarch who enjoys a "dispensing power" to waive, at her pleasure, generally applicable legislative requirements.

Not all were persuaded. Georgetown Professor Charles Lowndes published a 1932 article arguing that, in negligence cases, it is exclusively the province of the jury to determine whether a defendant has failed to act prudently.[13] On this basis, he maintained that both less and more should be made of statutory violations than is done under negligence per se doctrine. On his view, evidence that the defendant committed a statutory offense should be merely probative (not dispositive) of whether the defendant acted negligently. Yet a negligence plaintiff should be allowed to offer evidence of *any* such offence by the defendant. The latter contention was a pointed rejection of the idea—associated at the time with *Gorris v. Scott*—that a statutory standard should control the breach issue in a negligence case only if the statute was enacted to protect persons such as the plaintiff (the *protected-class* condition) from an incident of the sort in which the plaintiff was injured (the *covered-scenario* condition).[14] Although more open than Lowndes to the use of negligence per se, Clarence Morris joined him in criticizing both the protected-class and covered-scenario conditions.[15]

Assuming that criticisms of this sort were being voiced a few years earlier, they did not dissuade Reporter Francis Bohlen from including Section 286 in the First Restatement. It provides:

The violation of a legislative enactment by doing a prohibited act, or by failing to do a required act, makes the actor liable for an invasion of an interest of another if:
(a) the intent of the enactment is exclusively or in part to protect an interest of the other as an individual; and
(b) the interest invaded is one which the enactment is intended to protect; and,
(c) where the enactment is intended to protect an interest from a particular hazard, the invasion of the interests results from that hazard; and,
(d) the violation is a legal cause of the invasion, and the other has not so conducted himself as to disable himself from maintaining an action.[16]

---

[11] Ezra Ripley Thayer, *Public Wrong and Private Action*, 27 HARV. L. REV. 317 (1914).

[12] Martin v. Herzog, 126 N.E. 814 (N.Y. 1920).

[13] Charles L.B. Lowndes, *Civil Liability Created by Criminal Legislation*, 16 MINN. L. REV. 361 (1932).

[14] *Id.* at 375–76 (discussing *Gorris v. Scott*, 9 L.R. Ex. 125 (1874)). *Gorris* held that a shipowner's violation of a statutory requirement to keep sheep in pens, which was enacted to prevent the spread of disease, could not be invoked to establish the shipowner's negligent failure to prevent them from being washed overboard in a storm. Lowndes maintained that the significance of any statutory violation for a negligence case is its demonstration of the defendant's culpability, which the jury was entitled to consider irrespective of whether the protected-class and covered-scenario conditions were met.

[15] Clarence Morris, *The Relation of Criminal Statutes to Tort Liability*, 46 HARV. L. REV. 453 (1933). Morris regarded these aspects of the doctrine as artificial because he thought it unlikely that legislators thought about which classes of person a statute was intended to protect or what sorts of injuries they were being protected against. *Id.* at 475–77.

[16] RESTATEMENT OF TORTS § 286 (1934). A draft of this provision seems first to have appeared as Section 176. RESTATEMENT OF TORTS § 176, at 64–65 (Tent. Draft No. 4, Apr. 6, 1929). It was presented to the

Section 286's use of the phrase "makes the actor liable" indicates its endorsement of negligence per se. Its requirement that the statute be for the protection of an interest that is alleged by the plaintiff to have been invaded—presumably, in most cases, the interest in freedom from bodily harm—further clarifies that the doctrine applies only for some statutes, that is, those enacted to protect individuals from certain kinds of injuries at the hands of others. Finally, in Section 286(c), Bohlen appears to have adopted a compromise position on the *Gorris* issue: whether the protected-class and covered-scenario conditions would limit the application of the doctrine would depend on how best to interpret the statute the defendant was alleged to have violated.[17]

Subsequent Restatements have reaffirmed and improved on Bohlen's initial formulation.[18] Section 286 in the Second Restatement, drafted by William Prosser, appropriately adopts a more stringent position than Bohlen's in stating that a statutory violation can serve as the basis for a negligence per se jury instruction *only* if the court finds that the purpose of the statute is:

(a) to protect a class of persons which included the one whose interest is invaded, and

(b) to protect the particular interest which is invaded, and

(c) to protect that interest against the kind of harm which has resulted, and

(d) to protect that interest against the particular hazard from which the harm results.[19]

This rendition identifies the protected-class and covered-scenario conditions as necessary for the issuance of an instruction to the jury that it must find a breach of the duty of care if it finds that the defendant's conduct amounted to an (unexcused) statutory violation. Less helpful, however, are Section 286's superfluous subsections (b) and (c). Section 14 of the Physical and Emotional Harm provisions of the Third Torts Restatement, drafted by Gary Schwartz, thus made further improvements by eliminating them:

An actor is negligent if, without excuse, the actor violates a statute that is designed to protect against the type of accident the actor's conduct causes, and if the accident victim is with the class of persons the statute is designed to protect.[20]

---

membership that same year. 7 AMERICAN LAW INSTITUTE, PROCEEDINGS OF ANNUAL MEETING 174–76 (May 9, 1929).

[17] *See id.* § 286(c) cmts. e & h.

[18] One need not share Leon Green's view that a torts Restatement ought to organize the law around its application to particular industries or activities to accept his criticisms of the First Restatement's organization and its deployment of overly elaborate or otherwise inartfully drafted provisions. Leon Green, *The Torts Restatement*, 29 ILL. L. REV. 582, 585–88, 591–96 (1935). At the same time, it is important to acknowledge, as Green did, the immensity of the challenge that Bohlen faced in starting the project from scratch. *Id.* at 607 n.33.

[19] RESTATEMENT (SECOND) OF TORTS § 286 (1965).

[20] RESTATEMENT (THIRD) OF TORTS: LIABILITY FOR PHYSICAL AND EMOTIONAL HARM § 14 (2010).

Section 14 is particularly effective because it specifies the conditions for the application of the negligence per se doctrine so as to render it consonant with the analytically relational nature of the wrong of legal negligence (and all other torts). Negligence consists of an actor proximately causing injury to another by acting imprudently toward the other. The legal duty not to injure another through carelessness is relational in structure: it is a duty owed *to persons such as the victim.* It is also a qualified duty—one that does not require the actor to avoid injuring, full stop, nor even to avoid injuring by careless conduct. Rather, it is a duty to avoid injuring the victim through carelessness toward the victim that ripens into an injury of the sort that rendered the conduct careless. Thus, to be apt for use in determining whether negligence has been committed, a statute's standard of conduct must be tort-like (relational) in its structure: it must identify a duty owed by persons such as the defendant to avoid injuring persons such as the plaintiff through the right sort of injury-producing scenario. In this sense, Section 14 meshes elegantly with the general contours of tort law.

B. Rescue Doctrine

Another success story from the torts Restatements consists of Reporter William Prosser's introduction of Section 314A in the Second Restatement. Section 314, which of course immediately precedes it, contains what is commonly (if misleadingly) described as negligence law's "no-duty-to-rescue" rule. That section states: "The fact that the actor realizes or should realize that action on his part is necessary for another's aid or protection does not of itself impose upon him a duty to take such action."[21] Section 314A then qualifies this "rule" by identifying "Special Relations" that generate affirmative duties to protect or rescue.[22] Among these are the duty of a common carrier to provide first aid to a passenger who it knows or has reason to know is ill or injured, and similar duties running between innkeeper and guests, employer and employees, and a business open to the public and invitees on the business's premises.

Several features of Section 314A are worth highlighting. First, it nicely corrects for a deficiency in the first torts Restatement's treatment of affirmative duties. The first Restatement contains no counterpart to Section 314A, and instead moved directly from Section 314's "no-duty" rule to Sections 315–320. Each of the latter black-letter provisions identifies instances in which an actor's relation to *a third-party actor* (for example, the relation of a parent to a minor child) generates a duty of care to potential victims of the third-party's misfeasance. Thus, in all of the affirmative-duty scenarios covered by these provisions, liability still requires *misfeasance*—the wrongful injuring of plaintiff by the third-party—with the question in most of these cases being whether the defendant, *along with* the third party, can be held responsible. Missing from this presentation is 314A's crucial observation that there can be negligence liability for *genuine nonfeasance*—that there are duties to protect or rescue that arise in certain

---

[21] RESTATEMENT (SECOND) OF TORTS § 314 (1965).
[22] *Id.* § 314A.

situations that have nothing to do with a duty to prevent a third party from injuring another.[23]

More fundamentally, the Second Restatement's immediate juxtaposition of Section 314's negative proposition with Section 314A's recognition of affirmative duties helpfully wards off a familiar but misleading understanding of this aspect of negligence law—one that instructors often understandably exploit in their torts classes for pedagogic effect. Consider in this regard the following alternative descriptions of negligence law's treatment of affirmative duties:

1. Negligence law contains a general rule of no duty to rescue. Thus, even if a person encounters a stranger who is in dire need, and even if that person can easily and safely provide help, he or she is at liberty callously to watch the other person suffer or even die. However, there are exceptions when the defendant and the plaintiff are in a certain kind of special relationship, as in the case of parents who are obligated to take steps to rescue their minor children.

2. Negligence law contains a general rule stating that a person does not incur a duty to take steps to protect or rescue another just because well positioned to do so. Thus, an actor who happens to come upon a stranger in need of assistance is not legally obligated to emulate the Good Samaritan. In part because of worries about their ability to draw lines between rescues that are easy and rescues that are not easy, courts maintain that they are prepared to apply this rule even to cases in which the actor's failure to provide assistance is atrocious. However, it doesn't take a lot beyond the ability to provide aid to generate a legal duty to aid. If a plane or train passenger succumbs to illness while in transit, the carrier is legally obligated to provide first aid. Likewise, if a customer faints while on the premises of a business, it is legally obligated to provide assistance, and is subject to liability for any aggravation of the customer's injuries resulting from its failure.

The difference between these two descriptions is not night-and-day. But it is also not trivial. The former depicts negligence law as affirmatively embracing the morally callous baseline rule that there is no duty to rescue, then begrudgingly recognizing affirmative duties for persons in a limited set of normatively "thick" special relationships. The latter does not recognize a rule of no-duty to rescue—it instead more modestly observes that the presence of certain conditions is insufficient to generate such a duty. It then explains that there are times when not much is required beyond the ability to rescue to generate a duty to rescue. The issue under Section 314A is the terms on which the defendant and plaintiff interact or transact with one another on a given occasion, not whether they enjoy an ongoing relationship. (Think here of the store employee who is obligated to provide first aid to a stricken shopper.) The first description of this corner of negligence law invites the traditional characterization and condemnation of tort law as committed to starkly libertarian and atomistic notions of "every man for himself." The second, while hardly immunizing negligence law

---

[23] Sections 321–325 cover affirmative duties based on the defendant's having placed the plaintiff in peril or having voluntarily undertaken to assist the plaintiff.

from criticism, offers a more palatable account. The addition of Section 314A to the Second Restatement—accurately, in my view—moves the presentation of negligence law closer to the second depiction.[24]

One final point about Section 314A is worth mentioning. In the ALI meeting at which it was discussed, Prosser was quite candid with his audience that the section's recognition, in particular, of a duty owed by businesses to invitees was on the doctrinal frontier. He conceded that there were few decisions directly on point, and only one in which a state high court had ruled for the plaintiff.[25] He defended it nonetheless, observing that there were no rulings denying the existence of such a duty, and that this application of the special-relations rule was principled, in that businesses open to the public were situated in relation to their on-premises customers comparably to the way in which innkeepers are situated to their guests and carriers to their passengers (both a type of interaction or relation for which a duty to assist was well established). The ensuing discussion among ALI members offered interesting reflections on what it means to "restate" the common law of torts when there is little authority directly on point.[26] For his part, Prosser aptly conveyed the sense that restating the law includes making judgments about the direction the law is heading in light of the principles embedded in it, and hence that an extension of the law from within the law's own vocabulary and framework can legitimately count as "restating" it. As with the articulation of the requirements for negligence per se, here the relevant Restatement provisions reflect an interpretation of cases from within a holistic account of tort law that takes account of its embedded principles and its connections to prevailing social mores. That they do so has presumably helped to ensure their general acceptance by courts.

C. Intentional Infliction of Emotional Distress and Privacy Torts

In contrast to his treatment of negligence per se (discussed earlier), Bohlen's decision to rely on elaborate catalogs of "interests" to provide an overarching framework for the First Restatement was arguably more external imposition than reconstruction.[27] Perhaps unsurprisingly, it caused some problems that later Reporters, operating in the mode of an appellate court, would have to address.

---

[24] The Third Torts Restatement arguably takes a slight step backward in identifying in tort law a "principle" and "rule" of no duty to rescue that is subject to isolated exceptions. RESTATEMENT (THIRD) OF TORTS: LIABILITY FOR PHYSICAL AND EMOTIONAL HARM § 37 cmt. b (2010).

[25] AMERICAN LAW INSTITUTE, 37 PROCEEDINGS OF ANNUAL MEETING 159, 175 (May 19, 1960) (discussing *L.S. Ayres Co. v. Hicks*, 40 N.E. 2d 334 (Ind. 1942)). Prosser further acknowledged that even *Ayres* could be interpreted to have rested its holding on an alternative ground. *Id.*

[26] *Id.* at 175–90.

[27] *See* KENNETH S. ABRAHAM & G. EDWARD WHITE, TORT LAW AND THE CONSTRUCTION OF SOCIAL CHANGE 76–81 (2022) (discussing how interest analysis figured prominently in Bohlen's initial work on the Restatement, then faded in importance as the work proceeded); Michael D. Green, *Professor Francis Hermann Bohlen, in* SCHOLARS OF TORT LAW 133, 135–36 (James Goudkamp & Donal Nolan eds., 2019) (discussing the novelty of Bohlen's organizational scheme). For some purposes, there is value in grouping the recognized torts around certain interests or aspects of human well-being. Such an undertaking seems less promising as an organizing framework for a treatise written for judges who analyze cases on a wrong-by-wrong basis. It is thus no surprise that Bohlen's catalog of interests has played little role in subsequent Restatements and are rarely discussed by court decisions invoking the Torts Restatements.

In first presenting his plans for the torts Restatement to the ALI membership, Bohlen explained that, for practical reasons, he would "begin with the more primitive forms of interest, invasions of which were first redressed by the action of Trespass, the wrongs which are usually called assault and battery and false imprisonment."[28] In contrast, to the burgeoning and harder-to-corral field of accident law, intentional tort law was, according to Bohlen, settled, self-contained, and more than a little backward:

> The various interests which those wrongs offended were, on the whole, interests which were very dear to primitive men, interests of personal dignity rather than in material things. A savage man is dignified, he values his dignity, perhaps not more than we should, but more than we do. Those wrongs which affect those interests concern interests which have less value to us today than they had originally.[29]

In short, intentional tort law was a good place to start because it could be "compared to the withered branches of a tree. One is fond of the tree and likes its shape and leaves the dead limbs there, but they do not bear new branches, new leaves, or fruit."[30]

Twenty-three years later, Reporter Laurence Eldredge presented to the ALI a set of proposed amendments demonstrating that Bohlen's pronouncement of the death of intentional tort law was not true to the cases.[31] Indeed, Eldredge had to explain that Bohlen's project had twice gone astray in its very first provision. Comment a to Section 1 had stated that the interest in "emotional tranquility" receives little or no protection in tort law.[32] Comment e to the same section had said something similar about the interest in privacy.[33] Even before 1947, both statements were indefensible interpretations of doctrine. As Eldredge noted, a provision at the back end of the First Restatement—Section 867—which had been approved by the ALI in 1939, stated that liability would attach for certain privacy invasions.[34] And among the sections now in need of amendment was Section 46, which, as originally adopted in 1934, had stated a blanket rule of no liability for pure emotional distress.[35] Thus Eldredge unveiled a

---

[28] AMERICAN LAW INSTITUTE, 2 PROCEEDINGS OF ANNUAL MEETING 73 (Feb. 23, 1924).

[29] Id. at 74.

[30] Id. Within a year, Cardozo, who served as an Adviser for the Torts Restatement, was commenting that the law of battery, assault and false imprisonment had proven richer and more complicated than he and others working on the project had expected. Benjamin N. Cardozo, Law and Literature, in SELECTED WRITINGS OF BENJAMIN NATHAN CARDOZO 401–02 (Margaret Hall ed., 1947).

[31] KEEPING THE RESTATEMENT UP-TO-DATE: TORTS 12–13 (June 1947).

[32] RESTATEMENT OF TORTS § 1 cmt. a (1934).

[33] Id. § 1 cmt. e.

[34] Id. § 867 cmt. d. The section's Black Letter does not include an intent element: liability is predicated on "unreasonably and seriously interfer[ing] with another's interest in not having his affairs known to others or his likeness exhibited to the public." Id. § 867. However, it is clear from commentary and illustrations that the section primarily, if not exclusively, contemplated liability for intentional rather than accidental disclosures.

[35] Id. § 46. Section 46 recognized two exceptions: suits for assault that amounted to claims for distress over having been threatened with imminent physical harm (arguably not a necessary exception given that assaults involve the violation of the plaintiff's right to be free of such threats irrespective of whether they are distress-inducing) and claims by passengers subjected to insulting conduct by employees of common carriers. The content of Section 46 was presented to the ALI's membership as Sections 45A–45C of Proposed Final Draft No. 1 at its 1934 Meeting. See AMERICAN LAW INSTITUTE, 11 AMERICAN LAW INSTITUTE PROCEEDINGS 478–79 (June 30, 1934) (transcript of proceedings of May 11, 1934).

new Section 46, which recognized the tort of intentional infliction of severe emotional distress.[36] Bohlen (along with Oliver Wendell Holmes Jr. and others of his generation) had gone wrong in supposing that modernity was marked by the transition from *homo dignitas* to *homo materialis*.

Scholarly work by Eldredge and others, which had located intentional infliction of emotional distress (IIED) within the interstices of decisions nominally applying the law of battery, defamation, and other torts, has long been taken to exemplify a way in which the common law's reconstructive method permits and indeed encourages an incremental, synthetic form of innovation.[37] And indeed their analyses advanced the work of the courts in a manner similar to the way in which Cardozo in *MacPherson v. Buick* had rationalized and advanced prior decisional law that had specified the scope of manufacturer negligence liability for injuries caused by products.[38] Notably, there appears to have been little pushback against the recognition of IIED. And even though courts have tended to be cautious in applying this tort, especially when it seems to threaten free speech rights,[39] there does not appear to be significant sentiment suggesting that its recognition was a wrong turn.

Much the same can I think be said about the Second Restatement's treatment of privacy. In identifying four distinct privacy torts, Prosser of course famously elaborated upon Section 867 of the First Restatement.[40] Since then, the courts have wrestled with the extent to which evolving conceptions of free speech preclude liability for giving publicity to private facts, and have come to different conclusions about whether to recognize the false light tort.[41] Others have argued that Prosser's collection of privacy torts fails to cover important forms of wrongful privacy invasion.[42] These qualifications notwithstanding, there seems to be widespread acceptance of Eldredge's 1947 contention that invasions of privacy have a comfortable spot in the stable of modern torts. And in this sense the First and Second Restatements can be adjudged successful for having rightly rejected Bohlen's initial supposition that accident law is where the action is in modern tort law.

---

[36] RESTATEMENT OF TORTS, Supplement § 46 (1948).

[37] Eldredge appended to the text of the proposed new Section 46 citations to supporting case law, as well as articles by himself, Herbert Goodrich, Calvert Magruder, and William Prosser. KEEPING THE RESTATEMENT UP-TO-DATE: TORTS, *supra* note 31, at 12–13.

[38] 111 N.E. 1050 (N.Y. 1916); *see* John C.P. Goldberg & Benjamin C. Zipursky, *The Myths of* MacPherson, 9 J. TORT LAW 91, 104–12 (2016) (explaining the ways in which *MacPherson* was an accretive decision).

[39] Snyder v. Phelps, 562 U.S. 443 (2011); Hustler Magazine v. Falwell, 485 U.S. 46 (1988).

[40] William L. Prosser, *Privacy*, 48 CAL. L. REV. 383 (1960); RESTATEMENT (SECOND) OF TORTS § 652A (1977).

[41] *Compare* Godbehere v. Phoenix Newspapers, Inc., 783 P.2d 781, 788–89 (Ariz. 1989) (recognizing false light and noting that "additional protection for free speech comes from the principle that protection for privacy interests generally applies only to private matters"), *with* Lake v. Wal-Mart Stores, Inc., 582 N.W.2d 231, 235–36 (Minn. 1998) (declining to recognize false light, citing concerns that it "inhibits free speech").

[42] *See, e.g.,* Neil M. Richards & Daniel J. Solove, *Prosser's Privacy Law: A Mixed Legacy*, 98 CAL. L. REV. 1887 (2010) (stating that although Prosser "certainly gave tort privacy an order and legitimacy that it had previously lacked, he also stunted its development in ways that limited its ability to adapt to the problems of the Information Age"); Robert M. Connallon, *An Integrative Alternative for America's Privacy Torts*, 38 GOLDEN GATE U.L. REV. 71, 74 (2007) (arguing that Prosser's four-tort structure has "had the practical effect [of] limiting privacy-tort protections to acts that fall within the parameters established by the four torts, and excluding those that fall outside that structure").

D. Defect-Based Liability for Product-Related Injuries

Probably no torts-related Restatement provision has received more attention than Section 402A of the Second Restatement, which recognizes liability for injuries caused by defective products irrespective of negligence and without regard to warranty.[43] While often held out as a paradigmatic illustration of an aggressively revisionary Restatement provision—and hence one that, in the terms of my typology, might exemplify the ALI acting the mode of a law reform commission—my inclination is to treat it as an instance of the ALI acting in the mode of appellate court. Obviously, the proper characterization depends on an understanding of Section 402A's relation to the case law of the time, properly interpreted. Here, I an offer an account that falls between the two extremes famously offered by George Priest in successive articles.

Initially, Priest presented Section 402A as the imposition on an unsuspecting legal world of a radical reimagining of tort law as "enterprise liability."[44] On this rendering, the provision, though drafted by Prosser, was the brainchild of Friedrich Kessler and Fleming James, who had argued that negligence law's dominance in the domain of accidents should give way to a broad regime of strict liability as a second-best form of insurance coverage for certain accident victims. Prosser's role, on this account, was to put enough of a doctrinal veneer on Kessler's and James's revolutionary agenda to get it through the ALI. According to Priest, the revolutionaries succeeded—so much so that, by the late 1970s, products liability law had ceased to be genuine tort law (that is, law for the redress of legal wrongs) and was instead operating as an ersatz compensation scheme.

Four years later, responding to criticism from Gary Schwartz, Priest offered a very different narrative.[45] He conceded that his initial thesis had hinged on a highly improbable claim: namely, that the doctrinally oriented, theory-skeptical, politically above-it-all Prosser had done the bidding of high-theory, programmatic reformers.[46] Section 402A, as now described by Priest, was not a Trojan Horse but an ordinary farm animal: it aimed mainly to clear away technical rules of warranty law that had sometimes defeated meritorious claims for injuries caused by adulterated foods and other products with "manufacturing defects."[47] On this rendering, the provision was never meant to endorse strict liability for what today are called "design defects"—those were to be handled by negligence law. With Section 402A now recast as a modest bit of doctrinal housecleaning, Priest could readily explain why Prosser and the ALI had adopted it. In turn, he recharacterized what he took to be the disastrous expansion of products liability in the 1970s as a hijacking rather than the realization of its aspirations. Prosser and the ALI had stuck to their doctrinal knitting; it was progressive

---

[43] RESTATEMENT (SECOND) OF TORTS § 402A (1965).

[44] George L. Priest, *The Invention of Enterprise Liability: A Critical History of the Intellectual Foundations of Modern Tort Law*, 14 J. LEG. STUDIES 461, 517 (1985).

[45] George L. Priest, *Strict Products Liability: The Original Intent*, 10 CARDOZO L. REV. 2301, 2302 (1989).

[46] John C.P. Goldberg, *William L. Prosser*, in THE YALE BIOGRAPHICAL DICTIONARY OF AMERICAN LAW 439–41 (Roger K. Newman ed., 2009).

[47] Priest, *supra* note 45, at 2301 n.* (noting that Schwartz's critique encouraged him to reconsider the topic).

courts that had later legislated from the bench to transform products liability law into an ill-conceived social insurance scheme.[48]

As Mike Green has demonstrated, Priest's second narrative overcorrects for the errors of the first.[49] Section 402A contemplated strict liability across a range of cases, including some design defect cases. As such, it was no less a piece of doctrinal reconstruction than was Section 314A's recognition of a duty to rescue owed by businesses to stricken customers (discussed above). On the train of doctrine, Sections 314A and 402A were both closer to the locomotive than the caboose.[50] But neither was fabricated. Rather, they involved reasonable efforts by Prosser and the ALI to gauge where the law was and where it was heading, no doubt mindful that their efforts would, in Heisenberg-like fashion, affect the very developments they sought to predict. Already in 1941, in the first edition of his own torts treatise, Prosser was emphasizing that the negligence doctrine of *res ipsa loquitur*, when combined with broad jury discretion to determine the breach issue, allowed for defect-based liability in practice, and also that warranty law could produce the same effect, particularly for food products.[51] Twenty-five years later, by which time the landmark *Henningsen* and *Greenman* decisions had been handed down,[52] he offered an interpretation of negligence and warranty law—one that was indeed informed by a practical concern that doctrinal formalities had too often hamstrung tort law in its efforts to encourage safer products and provide compensation to injured consumers—that supported a legal duty, owed by commercial sellers, to avoid injuring consumers by sending dangerously defective products into the world.[53] This novel duty would of course be difficult for sellers to comply with perfectly. But its demandingness did not distinguish it dramatically from well-established tort duties.[54]

Equally wanting is Priest's supposition that the subsequent judicial development of products liability law took it outside the realm of tort, understood as a law of rights, wrongs, and remedies, thereby converting it into an insurance scheme.[55] Underlying this characterization is the thought that "strict liability" stands in sharp opposition to "negligence," with only the latter cogently grounding liability in wrongdoing. But it is

---

[48] *Id.* at 2301.

[49] Michael D. Green, *The Unappreciated Congruity of the Second and Third Torts Restatements on Design Defects*, 74 BROOK. L. REV. 807, 813–31 (2009); *accord*, Kenneth S. Abraham, *Prosser's The Fall of the Citadel*, 100 MINN. L. REV. 1823, 1842–43 (2016).

[50] *Cf.* Lawrence G. Sager, *The Incorrigible Constitution*, 65 N.Y.U. L. REV. 893, 926 n.96 (1990) (quoting and criticizing Bruce Ackerman's metaphoric contention that, when it comes to developing U.S. constitutional law, judges "'sit[] in the caboose, looking backward'").

[51] WILLIAM L. PROSSER, HANDBOOK OF THE LAW OF TORTS 683–85, 688–93 (1941).

[52] Henningsen v. Bloomfield Motors, 161 A.2d 69 (N.J. 1961); Greenman v. Yuba Power Prods., Inc., 377 P.2d 897 (Cal. 1963).

[53] *See* Abraham, *supra* note 49, at 1836–37, 1843 (emphasizing that Prosser's treatment of products liability reflected his general hostility toward technical limitations on liability that hampered tort law's ability to promote goals such as deterrence and compensation). Section 402A's criteria for defectiveness—that the product must pose a danger that the ordinary consumer would not expect it to pose—aptly drew on both warranty and negligence precedents. *See* GOLDBERG & ZIPURSKY, *supra* note 4, at 307–12.

[54] *Id.* at 192–97, 302–19.

[55] Priest is not alone in supposing that modern products liability marks the recognition of a distinct conception of liability that has nothing to do with enabling victims of a legal wrong to obtain recourse from those who have wronged them. *See, e.g.*, Gregory Keating, *Products Liability as Enterprise Liability*, 10 J. TORT L. 41 (2017).

false to suppose that strict products liability is necessarily liability without wrongful conduct. When a commercial seller sends a dangerously defective product into the world, and a risk of injury associated with that danger is realized in personal injury, the seller can be deemed—in a meaningful, nontrivial sense—to have wrongfully injured the victim. The invocation of compensation and deterrence as reasons (among several) *for judicial recognition of a new wrong* is a far cry from maintaining that tort law should be scrapped in favor of a different kind of law that severs liability from wrongdoing just because it promises to better provide compensation or deterrence.[56] Thus it is no surprise that Prosser and the ALI were comfortable producing Section 402A even granted its revisionary attributes. As noted earlier, they also approved Sections 314A, and Sections 46 and 652A, which were similarly revisionary. Nor is it a surprise that subsequent empirical studies—much to the surprise of some academics who had mistakenly imagined a vast gulf between negligence liability and strict products liability—have confirmed what Prosser expected: Section 402A's strictness has made a difference at the margin, but hardly revolutionized the terms on which businesses are held liable to persons injured by their products.[57]

---

[56] GOLDBERG & ZIPURSKY, *supra* note 4, at 195–96.

[57] *See* John C.P. Goldberg & Benjamin C. Zipursky, *The Easy Case for Products Liability: A Response to Professors Polinsky and Shavell*, 123 HARV. L. REV. 1919, 1933–34 (2010) (noting the relevant studies); William L. Prosser, *Strict Liability to the Consumer in California*, 18 HASTINGS L.J. 9, 52 (1966) (suggesting that the differences between proof requirements for negligence and strict products liability claims are sufficiently modest that "the alarm voiced by a good many manufacturers over the prospect of a vast increase in liability appears to be quite unfounded.") Business interests indeed voiced alarm over Section 402A and have criticized strict products liability law ever since. But this hardly establishes that the adoption of strict products liability marked a substantive-law revolution. (Businesses and their insurers have reason to resist even modest pro-liability changes in the law, especially if the scope of the change is uncertain or might prompt further pro-liability changes.) To the extent there was in fact an explosion of liability for product-related injuries in the 1970s, it probably had less to do with changes in substantive tort law and more to do with the rise of the consumer movement (and with it, growing skepticism that firms adequately attend to consumer safety), the recognition that certain products were causing harm on a mass scale (particularly asbestos), and the development of aggregate litigation techniques and a well-funded mass-tort plaintiffs' bar.

It is worth mentioning in this context a controversial aspect of Section 402A, namely, its statement, in a comment to the Black Letter, that "[g]ood tobacco is not unreasonably dangerous [and thus not defective] merely because the effects of smoking may be harmful...." RESTATEMENT (SECOND) OF TORTS § 402A cmt. i. Some have suggested this was an unprincipled exemption secured through the improper means of a December 1961 backroom meeting between Prosser and tobacco-industry lawyers. *See* Elizabeth Laposata, Richard Barnes, & Stanton Glantz, *Tobacco Industry's Influence on the American Law Institute's Restatements of Torts and Implications for its Conflict of Interest Policies*, 98 IOWA L. REV. 1, 9–30 (2012).

The premise for this suggestion—namely, that because such products pose significant health risks, they fall within the black-letter definition of a defective product—is dubious. Keith N. Hylton, *Lobbying and the Restatement of Torts*, JOTWELL, Apr. 3, 2013, https://torts.jotwell.com/lobbying-and-the-restatement-of-torts/ (last visited June 21, 2002) (explaining why, under then-prevailing conceptions of defectiveness, products posing well-known health risks tended not to be deemed defective). Also underwhelming as evidence of an unprincipled change of position is the fact that, during the 1961 ALI Annual Meeting (which preceded Prosser's meeting with tobacco industry lawyers), Prosser made no comment about, and thus seemed to accept, a member's remark that tobacco, along with boneless chicken, fell within the scope of 402A. Laposata, Barnes, & Glantz, *supra*, at 16–17. The remark in question seems merely to have asserted that a given tobacco product—like a given piece of chicken—*could be* the basis for a strict products liability claim *if it were adulterated, spoiled, or otherwise contained a defect*. Thus, Prosser's silence, even if properly construed as agreement, was consistent with Comment i being revised to specify that *good* tobacco is not unreasonably dangerous.

The allegation of improper means—which stands apart from the question of whether ordinary tobacco products should have been deemed defective under the terms of Section 402A—raises issues beyond the scope of this chapter as to how the ALI receives input from interested parties. For a discussion of some

A few remarks on the relation of Section 402A to the products liability provisions of the Third Torts Restatement will serve as a coda to this section. As is well known, Reporters James Henderson and Aaron Twerski overtly aimed to return important categories of product-related tort claims—namely, those for design defect and failure-to-warn—to a negligence standard. These efforts generated substantially controversy within the ALI. Professor Benjamin Zipursky and I have suggested that the revamping of design defect law in Section 2(b) of the Products Liability portion of the Third Restatement marked a departure from the principles underlying Section 402A.[58] And several prominent court decisions have declined to adopt Section 2(b) and have arguably adhered to Section 402A or something close to it, although other prominent decisions have embraced Section 2(b).[59] Whether this provision is an instance in which the ALI proceeded too aggressively—what this chapter refers to as the ALI acting in the mode of a law reform commission—has been the subject of an extensive debate that requires more attention than it can be given in this brief overview.[60]

III. ALI in the Mode of Law Revision Commission

Like the ALI, the Uniform Law Commission (ULC)[61] and foreign counterparts such as the Law Commission of the United Kingdom[62] are comprised of lawyers, judges, and academics and pursue law reform projects, usually with input from interested parties.[63] The work of these entities frequently involves drafting comprehensive model statutes that aim to present a body of law systematically while also "making interstitial reforms in places where improvement appear[s] to be needed."[64] In torts, unlike in areas such as criminal and commercial law, the ALI has not been in the business of producing comprehensive draft legislation. Thus, in describing the ALI as having sometimes proceeded in the mode of a law reform commission when addressing tort

of these issues, *see* Jeffrey W. Stempel, *Legal Ethics and Law Reform Advocacy*, 10 St. Mary's J. Legal Malpractice & Ethics 244 (2020).

[58] Goldberg & Zipursky, *supra* note 4, at 302–19. *But see* Green, *supra* note 49 (arguing to the contrary).

[59] Ford Motor Co. v. Trejo, 402 P.3d 649, 653–57 (Nev. 2017) (retaining a "consumer expectations" test for design defect derived from Section 402A and citing decisions from other states' courts that have rejected or embraced Section 2(b)).

[60] *Compare* James A. Henderson Jr. & Aaron D. Twerski, *Achieving Consensus on Defective Product Design*, 83 Cornell L. Rev. 867 (1998) (arguing that Section 2(b) was well-supported by prevailing doctrine), *with* David G. Owen, *Defectiveness Restated: Exploding the "Strict" Products Liability Myth*, 1996 U. Ill. L. Rev. 743 (arguing that case law recognized different conceptions of design defect and that Section 2(b) should have more overtly embraced a negligence framework), *with* Marshall S. Shapo, *A New Legislation: Remarks on the Draft Restatement of Products Liability*, 30 U. Mich. J.L. Reform 215, 218 (1997) (arguing that the Restatement (Third) of Torts is not a description of the existing law, but rather is the creation of drafters who acted as "a sounding board for essentially political discussion").

[61] http://uniformlaws.org/home (last visited Aug. 20, 2022).

[62] https://www.lawcom.gov.uk/ (last visited Aug. 20, 2022).

[63] For an overview of the ULC's process, *see* Gregory A. Elinson & Robert H. Sitkoff, *When a Statute Comes with a User's Manual: Reconciling Textualism and Uniform Acts*, 71 Emory L.J. 1073, 1083–97 (2022).

[64] John H. Langbein, *The Uniform Trust Code: Codification of the Law of Trusts in the United States*, 15 Trust Law Int'l 66, 66 (2001) (characterizing the ULC's Uniform Trust Code); *see also* 2021 Uniform Law Commission Annual Report https://www.uniformlaws.org/viewdocument/annual-report (listing Commission activities) (last visited Aug. 20, 2022).

law, I mean to focus on its attempts at "interstitial reforms." Though localized, law re-vision conducted in this mode, as contrasted to reconstruction in the manner of an appellate court, affords drafters more leeway to depart from case results and settled judicial usage.

At times, Restatement provisions bearing on tort law have been of this more adven-turous sort. Roughly speaking, the message from the ALI carried by these is roughly as follows: "We find this part of judge-made law too problematic to be salvageable on its own terms, and therefore submit that it ought to be rewritten along the fol-lowing lines." While a recommendation of this sort is not the equivalent of de novo lawmaking, it is more aggressive than common law reconstruction—more a teardown than a remodeling. This approach offers the prospect of uprooting "rotten," confused doctrine, thereby freeing courts to reason more soundly. But it also creates a risk that Reporters' well-intentioned efforts will introduce neologisms and novel rules that generate confusion or point in a problematic direction. This section identifies several instances in which downside risks such as these have been, or may be, realized.[65]

A. Prima Facie Tort and Interference with Inheritance

As the First Torts Restatement was wrapping up in the late 1930s, Warren Seavey and others added some concluding provisions. Included among these was Section 870, which stated:

> A person who does any tortious act for the purpose of causing harm to another or to his things or the pecuniary interests of another is liable to the other for such harm if it results, except where the harm results from an outside force the risk of which is not increased by the defendant's act.[66]

Doctrinally, this generic provision came out of nowhere. Instead, its roots can be found in Holmes's dubious theoretical claim that tort law had settled on the general principle of prima facie liability for any foreseeably caused "temporal damage."[67] True to this broad conception of liability, Section 870 included an illustration sug-gesting that it would be tortious for an actor intentionally to interfere with another's inheritance.[68]

---

[65] Though of course problematic in some ways (what law reform efforts are not?), the ALI's Commission-style efforts at comprehensive model acts, including the MPC and the UCC, have arguably been more suc-cessful. Kimberly Kessler Ferzan, *From Restatement to Model Penal Code: The Progress and Perils of Criminal Law Reform*, in this volume; Robert E. Scott, *The Uniform Commercial Code and the Ongoing Quest for an Efficient and Fair Commercial Law*, in this volume.

[66] RESTATEMENT OF TORTS § 870 (1939).

[67] Oliver W. Holmes Jr., *Privilege, Malice, and Intent*, 8 HARV. L. REV. 1, 1 (1894); Patrick J. Kelley, *The First Restatement of Torts: Reform by Descriptive Theory*, 32 S. ILL. U. L.J. 93, 121 (2007); Kenneth J. Vandevelde, *A History of Prima Facie Tort: The Origins of a General Theory of Intentional Tort*, 19 HOFSTRA L. REV. 447, 492–93 (1990).

[68] John C.P. Goldberg & Robert Sitkoff, *Torts and Estates: Remedying Wrongful Interference with Inheritance*, 65 STAN. L. REV. 335, 357 (2013).

Prosser and John Wade further developed and refined the Section 870 framework, adding to the Second Restatement a specific provision—Section 774B—addressing tortious interference with inheritance or gift:

> One who by fraud, duress or other tortious means intentionally prevents another from receiving from a third person an inheritance or gift that he would have otherwise have received is subject to liability to the other for loss of the inheritance or gift.[69]

As evidenced by the Section's misdescription of "duress" as "tortious,"[70] Section 774B was no more grounded in case law than Section 870 of the First Restatement had been. Indeed, as Prosser and Wade conceded, the main support for this provision consisted of decisions that allowed beneficiaries to recover in *restitution*, not tort.[71] In short, the interference-with-inheritance provision ran roughshod over a long-standing divide between two distinct domains of private law—unjust enrichment and tort—and it invited courts to do the same.[72] Predictably, Section 774B has generated considerable confusion. Worse, it has produced inconsistent treatment of identical claims, with outcomes depending on whether lawyers and courts fashion the disappointed beneficiary's claim as sounding in restitution or in tort.[73] As such, it attests to the risk of the ALI operating in the mode of a law reform commission.[74]

---

[69] RESTATEMENT (SECOND) OF TORTS § 774B (1979).

[70] "Duress" is not the name of a tort, injuring someone by placing them under duress is not of itself tortious, and duress is not a recognized excuse to tort liability.

[71] Goldberg & Sitkoff, *supra* note 68, at 360. Moreover, there were a few prominent cases that had refused to recognize tort liability for interference with inheritance. *Id.* at 355–59. On the "forgetting" of restitution by mid-twentieth-century legal academics in the United States, *see* Emily Sherwin, *A Short History of the Restatement of Restitution and Unjust Enrichment*, in this volume.

[72] Goldberg & Sitkoff, *supra* note 68, 360–61, 393–94.

[73] *Id.* at 365–79. On the problematic tendency of modern courts to collapse equity into tort, *see* John C.P. Goldberg & Henry E. Smith, *Wrongful Fusion: Equity and Tort*, in EQUITY AND LAW: FUSION AND FISSION 309 (John C.P. Goldberg, Peter Turner, & Henry E. Smith eds., 2019).

[74] Partly out of recognition of the problems associated with Section 774B, the Third Restatement has adopted a new formulation that limits the availability of this cause of action to instances in which relief through probate and restitution is unavailable. RESTATEMENT (THIRD) OF TORTS: LIABILITY FOR ECONOMIC HARM § 19(2) cmt. f (2020).

A perhaps illuminating contrast to Sections 870 and 774B is the "purposeful infliction of bodily harm" provision of the Intentional Torts to Persons portion of the Third Restatement. RESTATEMENT (THIRD) OF TORTS: INTENTIONAL TORTS TO PERSONS § 4 (T.D. No. 4, Apr. 1, 2019); *id.* § 104 (T.D. No. 1, Apr. 8, 2015). It allows for liability when an actor specifically sets out to cause and succeeds in causing another to suffer bodily harm by means other than the sort of touching or threatening that would give rise to liability for battery or assault. Reporters Kenneth Simons and Jonathan Cardi acknowledged the lack of directly on-point precedents for this provision. However, they also maintained—convincingly, in my view—that there was a great deal of indirect support for it (comparable to the support for the First Restatement's recognition of IIED, discussed earlier). And they were careful to fashion it as a narrow gap-filling tort rather than as a general theory or principle of liability in the manner of Section 870, or as a direct competitor to another body of law in the manner of Section 774B.

B. The Suppression of Duty in Negligence

Section 281 of the Second Torts Restatement, which revised Section 281 of the First Restatement, defined the elements of negligence as follows:

> The actor is liable for an invasion of an interest of another, if:
> (a) the interest invaded is protected against unintentional invasion, and
> (b) the conduct of the actor is negligent with respect to the other, or a class of persons within which he included, and
> (c) the actor's conduct is a legal cause of the invasion, and
> (d) the other has not so conducted himself as to disable himself from bringing an action for such invasion.[75]

As is explained in Reporter's Notes, Subsection 281(b)'s reference to conduct that is "negligent with respect to the other" is a statement of the *Palsgraf* principle.[76] As applied in a standard physical-injury case, this principle holds that the plaintiff must prove that the defendant's conduct was careless *as to the physical well-being of a person situated as was the plaintiff in relation to the defendant's conduct*. Carelessness as to a differently situated potential victim does not suffice. More generally, Section 281, although retaining the language of "interests" favored by Bohlen, indicates that negligence consists of an actor breaching a duty owed to each member of a class of persons, according to which the duty-bearer must avoid injuring such a person by means of conduct that is careless as to her.[77]

In an early draft of the Third Restatement's negligence provisions, Reporter Gary Schwartz adopted a plan that would have departed dramatically from predecessor Restatements and from case law.[78] Section 3 of the draft stated that "[a]n actor is subject to liability for negligent conduct that is a legal cause of physical harm …"; Section 6 then added that "[e]ven if the defendant's negligent conduct is the legal cause of the plaintiff's physical harm, the (defendant) is not liable for that harm if the court determines that the defendant owes no duty to the plaintiff."[79] The *Palsgraf* principle is nowhere to be found in this formulation. More fundamentally, Section 6 obscures the

---

[75] RESTATEMENT (SECOND) OF TORTS § 286 (1965).

[76] Palsgraf v. Long Island R.R., 162 N.E. 99, 100 (N.Y. 1928) ("The plaintiff sues in her own right for a wrong personal to her, and not as the vicarious beneficiary of a breach of duty to another."). Comment c and Illustration 1, which is based on *Palsgraf*, make clear that Section 281(b) endorses the *Palsgraf* principle, as does the fact that Section 281(b)'s requirement is articulated separately from Section 281(c)'s further requirement of "legal cause."

[77] While both the Second and First Restatements regarded negligence liability as requiring the defendant to breach a duty of care owed to the plaintiff, they also maintained that the duty in question was a duty to act in a certain manner, not a duty to avoid causing injury by so acting, apparently on the assumption that it is incoherent or inappropriate for legal duties to be specified in a way that includes not just a description of how an actor must conduct herself but also a description of a type of result that must be avoided or achieved. *Id.* at cmt. e; RESTATEMENT OF TORTS § 4 cmt. a (1934). For a critique of this line of thought, *see* GOLDBERG & ZIPURSKY, *supra* note 4, at 183–88.

[78] John C.P. Goldberg & Benjamin C. Zipursky, *The* Restatement (Third) *and the Place of Duty in Negligence Law*, 54 VAND. L. REV. 657 (2001). In fairness, Harvey Perlman, who was at the time working on an alternative version of the Restatement, proposed a vastly more radical departure. *Id.* at 687–92.

[79] John C.P. Goldberg, *Introduction, The Restatement (Third) of Torts: General Principles and the John W. Wade Conference*, 54 VAND. L. REV. 639, 653 (2001) (reproducing draft Sections 3 and 6).

Hohfeldian duty-right pairing at the core of negligence.[80] Although the term "duty" appeared in draft Section 6, it is used entirely negatively ("no duty"), thus implying that duty questions in negligence are exclusively concerned with the contours of a Hohfeldian immunity rather than a genuine legal obligation.

After some pushback from membership, Schwartz's successors—Mike Green and Bill Powers—rewrote the Third Restatement's negligence formulation to be more accommodating of the traditional and still-prevailing view among courts that negligence consists of the breach of a duty of care owed to a person such as the plaintiff that proximately causes harm to the plaintiff. As finally adopted, Sections 6 and 7 of the Physical and Emotional Harm provisions of the Third Restatement thus read as follows:

§ 6. Liability for Negligence Causing Physical Harm.
  An actor whose negligence is a factual cause of physical harm is subject to liability for any such harm within the scope of liability, unless the court determines that the ordinary duty of care is inapplicable.

§ 7. Duty.
(a) An actor ordinarily has a duty to exercise reasonable care when the actor's conduct creates a risk of physical harm.
(b) In exceptional cases, when an articulated countervailing principle or policy warrants denying or limiting liability in a particular class of cases, a court may decide that the defendant has no duty or that the ordinary duty of reasonable care requires modification.[81]

As in Schwartz's draft, the final iteration of Section 6 places duty at the back end of its formulation, preceded by an "unless" clause. In this respect, it also creates the impression that duty questions are questions about exemptions or immunities from liability that, in the first instance, is predicated simply on carelessness that injures, irrespective of whether such conduct is plausibly described as a breach of a duty of care owed to a person such as the plaintiff. However, unlike Schwartz's draft, Sections 6 and 7 in their final form make reference to negligence law's "duty of care" in a way that acknowledges it is a genuine obligation. Furthermore, Comment a to Section 6 acknowledges that duty is an element or component of the tort.[82]

The Third Restatement's treatment of the duty element of negligence is aggressively revisionary. It posits a general rule according to which an actor is subject to liability whenever the actor's conduct "creates a risk" of physical harm that is unreasonable, and that risk is realized. Obscured is the notion of the tort as built around a relational obligation—a duty owed to members of a class of persons—or any sort of obligation at all. The presentation of negligence on a liability-rule model is then reinforced by presenting cases in which duty is at issue as exclusively concerned with the question of whether to recognize a policy- or principle-based immunity or exemption from

---

[80] Ernest J. Weinrib, *The Passing of Palsgraf?*, 54 VAND. L. REV. 803 (2001).
[81] RESTATEMENT (THIRD) OF TORTS: LIABILITY FOR PHYSICAL AND EMOTIONAL HARM §§ 6 & 7 (2010).
[82] *Id.* § 6 cmt. a.

liability. Here, the Reporters were not merely operating on the doctrinal frontier, with relatively little case support: they proceeded in a manner that ran contrary to standard judicial usage.[83] What could warrant such a bold stance?

The primary justification offered by the Reporters was pragmatic. The suppression of duty in its obligation sense was necessary, they claimed, to solve a problem plaguing the adjudication of negligence suits. The problem, they maintained, is the tendency of courts to invade the province of the jury by addressing fact-intensive questions about whether a defendant had in a given situation taken sufficient care (the breach issue) as if they were questions about whether the defendant owed any care at all (the duty issue). And more often than not, they added, this error occurs because courts have long treated an actor's ability reasonably to *foresee* that its conduct might harm a person such as the plaintiff as relevant *both* to the duty and breach issues.

To combat this problem, the Reporters adopted a two-pronged attack: they downplayed prevailing judicial understandings of the role of duty in negligence, then instructed courts to abandon the "widespread" practice of treating foreseeability as relevant to the duty issue.[84] If the significance of duty to negligence is downplayed, and if foreseeability considerations are eliminated from duty analysis, they reasoned, courts will be less prone to mistake breach arguments for duty arguments, and hence less prone erroneously to grant defense motions for judgment as a matter of law on no-duty grounds when the issue at hand really is the fact-intensive, jury question of breach.[85]

The duty component of negligence has long been a source of confusion, and one may doubt whether the topic is neatly resolvable within a set of Restatement provisions on negligence.[86] And it is certainly appropriate for Reporters to treat the reduction of confusion as a ground for contemplating significant departures from ordinary judicial usage. Nonetheless, it is worth asking whether the benefits promised by this departure justify it. Of particular concern is the possible failure of the Reporters to appreciate that their strategy for solving the perceived problem of judges treating no-breach arguments as no-duty arguments generates a countervailing risk of judicial error. In particular, the suppression of duty, combined with the banishment of foreseeability considerations in duty analysis, may cause judges to lose sight of the moral center of the negligence tort, and to do so in ways that may portend a contraction of negligence liability running directly contrary to the Reporters' aspirations of leaving more cases for resolution by juries.

---

[83] Goldberg & Zipursky, *supra* note 78, at 658 n.1.

[84] *See generally* W. Jonathan Cardi, *Purging Foreseeability*, 58 VAND. L. REV. 739 (2005) (developing this line of reasoning). Until recently, almost every state explicitly maintained that foreseeability of (some) harm to persons such as the plaintiff is central to the analysis of duty issues. Quisenberry v. Huntington Ingalls Inc., 818 S.E.2d 805, 812 (Va. 2018) (citing Benjamin C. Zipursky, *Foreseeability in Breach, Duty and Proximate Cause*, 44 WAKE FOREST L. REV. 1247, 1258 (2009)).

[85] A.W. v. Lancaster County School Dist. 0001, 784 N.W.2d 907 (Neb. 2010), is an example of a negligence decisions that plays out as the Reporters hoped. The court eschewed foreseeability analysis in the course of declining the defendant's invitation to issue a no-duty ruling and instead determined that the case should be submitted to the jury on the issue of breach.

[86] *But see* Goldberg & Zipursky, *supra* note 78, at 737–50 (proposing provisions on negligence and duty suitable for use in a Torts Restatement).

Consider in this regard the opinion of the Arizona Supreme Court in *Quiroz v. ALCOA, Inc.*[87] It ruled, on no-duty grounds, that an employer could not be held liable for the death of its employee's son, which resulted from the son's exposure to asbestos fibers that the father had carried home on his work clothes. On the merits, the issue in *Quiroz* is difficult and has split courts around the country. My focus is instead on the court's reasoning.

Following the lead of commentary to Section 7, the Court deemed *irrelevant* to the duty issue the question of whether harm to an employee's family member was a reasonably foreseeable consequence of the employer operating its business as it did. Yet, whereas the Reporters sought to eliminate inquiries into foreseeability as an aspect of duty analysis to *discourage* no-duty rulings, the *Quiroz* court went in the opposite direction. Having eliminated foreseeability of harm to a person such as the plaintiff as a ground for recognizing a duty of care owed to the plaintiff, the Court concluded that there are only two grounds for deeming an actor to owe such a duty: (1) if the defendant and the plaintiff are in the right kind of robust "special relationship" at the time of the injury, or (2) if a relationship of care has been "created by public policy" *as evidenced by legislation.*[88] In short, the Restatement-driven excision of foreseeability from duty, which was meant to shift decision-making power from judges to juries, is invoked in *Quiroz* in a manner that suggests a dramatic narrowing of negligence liability. Under the law of Arizona today, *the fact that harm to a person such as the plaintiff was readily foreseeable to the defendant at the time of acting provides no reason for a court to deem the defendant to have owed it to the plaintiff to take care not to injure the plaintiff!*

Defenders of the Third Restatement's negligence provisions will respond that it is unfair to lay blame for *Quiroz*'s suspect reasoning at the feet of those provisions. As noted, Sections 6 and 7(a) dispense with foreseeability as a component of duty to ensure that juries rather than judges decide a broader range of negligence cases. And indeed, the Arizona court's extraordinary claim that there can be no negligence liability absent a legislative basis or a preexisting special relationship between defendant and plaintiff runs directly counter to Section 7(a), which states that there is (ordinarily) a basis for negligence liability whenever an actor acts so as to create a risk of physical harm to anyone. But this envisioned defense is not entirely compelling. The concept of risk-creation is hardly without ambiguity. Is the employer in *Quiroz* best characterized as having created the risk of the son's asbestos exposure or of having failed to protect the son from such exposure? And if the answer to this question is definitively that the employer created the risk then a different problem emerges, for the default rule of Sections 6 and 7 is now revealed to be extraordinarily—and, inevitably for some courts, alarmingly—broad relative to the doctrine that was supposedly being restated. Thus, it was hardly unpredictable that there would be courts unmoved by the Reporters' ambitions to reduce their role in the resolution of negligence cases, and that would find in the Restatement's unmooring of negligence from notions of

---

[87] 416 P.3d 824 (Ariz. 2018).

[88] *Id.* at 830 (noting that courts usually should recognize a public-policy–based duty of care only on the basis of legislative recognition of such a duty).

obligation and foreseeability a means not only of limiting the tort's reach, but of reanimating mid-nineteenth-century conceptions of the proper grounds for and scope of liability.

Time will tell, but *Quiroz* may prove to be an early indication that Sections 6 and 7 will attest to hazards that attend the ALI acting as a law reform commission.[89] With good intentions, Reporters have obscured what, for more than a century, had served as negligence law's moral center, as well as an important engine for its expansion. Decisions such as *Heaven v. Pender*, *MacPherson v. Buick*, and *Donoghue v. Stevenson* are landmarks precisely because of their insistence that older limitations on liability, especially the notorious privity rule, had given way to a broad duty of care grounded in a moral principle of foreseeability. According to *Heaven's* rendering, "whenever one person is by circumstances placed in such a position with regard to another that every one of ordinary sense who did think would at once recognise that if he did not use ordinary care and skill in his own conduct with regard to those circumstances he would cause dangers of injury to the person or property of the other, a duty arises to use ordinary care and skill to avoid such danger."[90] In suppressing the sense in which duty questions in negligence really are about the obligations we owe one another, and in cleaving duty from foreseeability, the Reporters seem to have assumed that courts would continue to accept the broad notion of duty articulated by these decisions even after it was detached from its moral underpinnings. That assumption, alas, may prove to be unfounded.

C. Legal Cause and Scope of Liability

One of the great achievements of the Physical and Emotional Harm component of the Third Torts Restatement is its untangling of the mess generated by the causation provisions of its predecessors. Unfortunately, it also needlessly perpetuates a mistake born of a law-revision-commission approach that was taken in the First Restatement and carried over to the Second.

Bohlen and Prosser did lawyers and courts no favors by introducing the locution of "legal cause" to address long-standing confusions concerning causation in tort cases. Reporters Green and Powers were thus wise to discard that language. Also helpful is their sharp (perhaps, from a purely theoretical perspective, artificially sharp) demarcation between issues of "factual" causation—whether the defendant's tortious conduct had something to do with the plaintiff being injured—from the "proximate cause" issue of whether the defendant's tortious conduct contributed to the plaintiff's injury in a manner so haphazard or attenuated as to relieve the defendant of responsibility.[91] Finally, they are to be commended for providing a crisp, workable rendering

---

[89] The Third Restatement's treatment of duty prompted the Chief Justice of the Virginia Supreme Court in a recent dissent (joined by two colleagues) to advocate a similar approach to the one adopted in *Quiroz*. *Quisenberry*, 818 S.E.2d at 817 (Va. 2018) (Lemons, C.J., dissenting).

[90] Heaven v. Pender, 11 Q.B.D. 503, 509 (Eng. C.A. 1883) (Brett, J.).

[91] RESTATEMENT (THIRD) OF TORTS: LIABILITY FOR PHYSICAL AND EMOTIONAL HARM §§ 26, 29 (2010).

of the "risk rule" formulation of proximate cause developed by Joseph Bingham, Warren Seavey, Leon Green, Robert Keeton, and others.[92]

Although in these respects admirable, the Third Restatement at the same time ignored one important lesson of the "legal cause" debacle by insisting that the phrase "proximate cause" be expunged from tort parlance. Thus, in place of "legal cause," the Reporters offered their own neologism: "scope of liability."[93] Indeed, Section 29, the central "proximate cause" provision of the Third Restatement, bears a still more enigmatic title: "Limitations on Liability for Tortious Conduct."[94]

It is of course possible that this usage will improve judicial decision-making, but there are reasons for skepticism. For one thing, the phrase "limitations on liability for tortious conduct" is nearly empty. Every recognized element and defense to a claim for negligence is a "limitation[] on liability." Section 29's title thus fails to inform the reader why it is a stand-alone section. The *effect* of the section's rule is to spare certain actors from liability they would face in its absence. But the reason for presenting it as a separate section is not merely to describe a set of results but to identify the grounds for them. A related problem with the phrase "limitations on liability" is that it is so broad as to invite confusion between rules that define the tort of negligence and rules, such as the eggshell skull rule, that determine what a successful plaintiff stands to recover by way of compensatory damages. Indeed, the Reporters concede that, in their (heterodox) view, the eggshell skull rule conflicts with their rendering of the "scope of liability" limitation.[95]

The proximate cause requirement is a substantive aspect of negligence (and products liability). Negligence consists of an actor breaching a duty owed to another to avoid injuring them through conduct that is careless as to them. Built into the relevant notion of "injuring" is the idea that an actor has not committed negligence when her careless conduct haphazardly harms the plaintiff, or contributes to harming the plaintiff merely by enabling another, independent actor to intentionally and wrongfully injure the plaintiff (i.e., where the actor is not acting in concert with the injurer and has affirmative duty to protect persons such as the plaintiff from wrongful injury by someone such as the injurer). Because careless conduct that causes harm in these ways does not involve a realization of a risk that rendered the defendant's conduct wrongful as to the plaintiff, no legal wrong has been committed, and hence there is no more basis for liability than if the actor's careless conduct had had no effect on the plaintiff. By contrast, when there is a realization of the risk (and the other elements of negligence are met and no defenses are available), the actor is subject to liability, and in an amount that corresponds, typically, to what the plaintiff has lost, irrespective of the foreseeability of the extent of loss. There is nothing contradictory about any of this: the inclusion of the risk rule as part of the definition of the wrong of negligence by no means entails the adoption, as a remedial rule, that victims of that wrong can

---

[92] *Id.* § 29.
[93] *Id.* ch. 6 (Special Note on Proximate Cause).
[94] *Id.* § 29.
[95] *Id.* § 29 cmt. p.

only recover damages that were reasonably foreseeable to the defendant when acting carelessly.[96]

It is true that the phrase "proximate cause" does not perfectly capture these limitations on negligence liability and thus can be expected to produce confusion in case law (as it does in the classroom). But use of that phrase is well settled, and even though it comes in different formulations, all express the same core idea that purely haphazard causation of injury is not, in negligence, a basis for responsibility. Moreover, the ALI has learned from experience that the substitution of a different phrase that has no basis in ordinary legal usage is unlikely to improve the situation. It seems quite possible that the same may prove true of the Third Restatement's effort to render "proximate cause" more tractable by giving it a nondescription—by presenting it as an undefined limitation on liability.

D. Design Defect and Prescription Drugs

I conclude this portion of my analysis with a brief mention of an instance in which ALI Reporters seemingly self-consciously adopted the posture of a law reform commission. It involves Section 6 of the Products Liability provisions of Third Restatement. Subsection 6(c) provides:

> A prescription drug or medical device is not reasonably safe due to defective design if the foreseeable risks of harm posed by the drug or medical device are sufficiently great in relation to its foreseeable therapeutic benefits that reasonable health-care providers, knowing of such foreseeable risks and therapeutic benefits, would not prescribe the drug or medical device for any class of patients.[97]

Only a drug or device that should never be provided to any patient, no matter what her circumstances, can be deemed defectively designed. This is tantamount to saying that, so far as tort law is concerned, no drug or medical device can be so deemed.

As is acknowledged in the Reporters' Notes, there was and is substantial case law rejecting the idea that manufacturers of prescription drugs and medical devices enjoy what amounts to a complete immunity from design defect liability.[98] Nonetheless, Section 6(c) was proffered on the basis of two rationales: (1) that drugs and devices that might help at least one person should be available, with their risks managed by holding manufacturers and physicians to their duties properly to warn or instruct users;[99] and (2) drugs and devices, unlike many other products, require regulatory approval to which courts owe deference.[100]

---

[96] John C.P. Goldberg & Benjamin C. Zipursky, Vosburg v. Baxendale: *Recourse in Tort and Contract*, in CIVIL WRONGS AND JUSTICE IN PRIVATE LAW 463, 471–74 (Paul B. Miller & John Oberdiek eds., 2020).

[97] RESTATEMENT (THIRD) OF TORTS: PRODUCTS LIABILITY § 6 (1998).

[98] *Id.* § 6 (Reporters' Note to cmt. f).

[99] Elsewhere, however, the same Restatement notes that duties to warn are hardly perfect substitutes for duties to design properly. *Id.* § 2 cmt. l.

[100] *Id.* § 6 cmt. b.

The second rationale flies in the face of the traditional rule of tort law that statutory and regulatory standards set floors, not ceilings. True, by virtue of the operation of the Constitution's Supremacy Clause, *federal* legislation and regulations can sometimes operate as a ceiling by preempting state tort law. But the Reporters were not charged with restating the federal common law of preemption. Indeed, it would have been entirely inappropriate for the Reporters silently to incorporate an account of the pre-emptive effect of federal law into their characterization of state products liability law.

The first rationale is no more convincing. It is one thing to say that courts have been, and should be, cautious about deeming drugs and medical devices defectively designed given that they receive some regulatory scrutiny for safety and that many have potential value beyond that provided by an ordinary consumer product. But it is hardly the case that prescription drugs and medical devices are uniform in this regard: many are not so much lifesaving as life-improving or lifestyle-improving.[101] Moreover, in some cases—and particularly with respect to certain medical devices— better designs are often available, which is why, in some cases, manufacturers have responded to product liability litigation by redesigning their products.[102]

In its departure from doctrine and its determination to immunize manufacturers of drugs and devices from design defect liability, Section 6(c) provides another cau-tionary example of the ALI acting as a law reform commission.[103]

IV. ALI in the Mode of Think Tank

Restatement Reporters have from time to time proposed retail-level innovations in the law of torts. Appropriately, however, they have demurred when it comes to whole-sale law reform. It is one thing to take the incremental step from negligence and war-ranty liability to strict products liability, or to replace the phrase "proximate cause" with "scope of liability." It is quite another to advocate that tort law, or some portion of it, be replaced by an accident compensation scheme or a regulatory mechanism for deterring accidents.

The latter approach was on display in the 1991 Reporters' Study: Enterprise Liability for Personal Injury. Originally titled "Compensation and Liability for Product and Process Injuries," this project was green-lighted by the ALI Council in 1986. Led at first by Professor Richard Stewart then by Professor Paul Weiler and featuring several

---

[101] *See, e.g.*, Freeman v. Hoffman-La Roche, Inc., 618 N.W.2d 827 (Neb. 2000) (declining to follow Section 6(c)'s test for design defect in a case in which the plaintiff alleged that the defendant's acne medi-cation was defectively designed in that it caused her to suffer severe adverse health effects). My point is not to get on a high horse about the different kinds of benefits drugs or medical devices provide, but to explain why Section 6(c) is substantially overbroad relative to one of its stated rationales.

[102] Under Section 6(e), so long as a drug or device with a more dangerous design would be prescribed to one class of user (perhaps, for example, because it is relatively cheap), the existence of an alternative and safer design would not suffice to establish that the more dangerous version is defective under Section 6(c). George W. Conk, *Is There a Design Defect in the Restatement (Third) of Torts: Products Liability?*, 109 YALE L.J. 1087, 1116 (2000) (making this point in connection with a discussion of alternative polio vaccines).

[103] For a charitable treatment of Section 6(c) that nonetheless critiques its inclusion of medical devices, *see* 1 DAVID G. OWEN & MARY J. DAVIS, OWEN & DAVIS ON PRODUCTS LIABILITY § 8:27 (4th ed. May 2021 update).

prominent scholars in the role of Reporters, the project consciously aimed for a different kind of contribution than is typically provided by ALI Restatements, or even by the Model Penal Code.[104] A brief comparison between an early memorandum to the Council from Professor Stewart, on the one hand, and the introduction to the final Reporter's Study, on the other, demonstrates that, in fewer than five years, the project evolved in interesting ways.

Professor Stewart's 1986 memorandum laid out the project's initial premise. Echoing Bohlen's comments from sixty years earlier, it maintained that the important and interesting parts of tort law are those that address personal injuries resulting from "enterprise activity," that is, injuries suffered in employment settings, as well as injuries caused by products, medical malpractice, and toxic exposures.[105] As applied to enterprise activity, tort is to be evaluated in terms of its social benefits and costs. On the upside, it has the potential to compensate injury victims for losses, enhance safety through the deterrent effect of potential liability, and issue condemnations of undesirable conduct in the service of "cathartic and educative functions."[106] On the downside are the costs of the litigation system to the government and parties, the costs associated with lost productivity because of overdeterrence, and the "cost" of inconsistent or arbitrary outcomes.[107] On balance, the supposition of the memorandum is that tort law delivers few goods at significant costs. As a practical matter, the report concedes the political untenability of tort's outright replacement by schemes modeled on workers' compensation systems or automobile no-fault, by use of contract terms to better allocate risks between firms and the public, and by the implementation of regulatory systems that better incentivize socially desirable behavior. And it acknowledges that there is some value in "maintaining a residual privately-initiated system of remedies to deal with serious problems that other institutions have not adequately resolved."[108] Nonetheless, it clearly contemplates substantial reforms, with tort law left to play only a gap-filling role in responding to the problem of enterprise-based, accidentally caused injuries.

Now turn to the 1991 Reporters' Study. It commences with a somewhat sheepish confession: the project had been prompted by a false alarm. The immediate impetus for the Study was "a major crisis in [the U.S.] tort litigation/liability insurance system" marked by steep increases in insurance premiums.[109] At least according to "popular impression," this crisis was attributable to an "explosion" in tort claims and damage awards.[110] Thus, the project was a response to "the prevailing sentiment ... that

---

[104] It appears that at least some ALI members contemplated that the Study would serve as a framing exercise for the then-anticipated Third Torts Restatement, and that, as the project neared completion, Restatement-like meetings were held among the Reporters and a group of Advisers. *See* Abraham & White, *supra* note 1.

[105] RICHARD B. STEWART, REPORT ON THE PROJECT ON ENTERPRISE PERSONAL INJURIES (Nov. 11, 1986).

[106] *Id.* at 5. Of these, the last is deemed the least important, given that the basis for enterprise liability had, according to Stewart, increasingly shifted away from notions of fault or wrongdoing.

[107] *Id.* at 5–6.

[108] *Id.* at 14.

[109] 1 REPORTERS STUDY, ENTERPRISE RESPONSIBILITY FOR PERSONAL INJURY 3 (Apr. 15, 1991). No doubt the study itself was not merely a response to the perceived insurance crisis, but also an effort by the ALI to experiment with ways in which it might contribute to law reform, particularly at a moment in time when there was skepticism in the legal academy about the value of doctrinal analysis and thus about the value of Restatements as traditionally understood. Abraham & White, *supra* note 1.

[110] REPORTERS STUDY, *supra* note 109, at 3.

something was seriously amiss in the tort regime."[111] As it turns out, "popular impression" and "prevailing sentiment" were, um, wrong. The insurance crisis had rapidly dissipated.[112] And further analysis indicated "that there never was a true general explosion in tort litigation, or at least that any incipient trend has definitely subsided."[113] Nonetheless, in the spirit of not letting a *perceived* crisis go to waste, the project had continued with the aim of addressing other putative failings of tort law as a system for addressing accidental personal injuries and possible alternatives.

On the "what is to be done?" question, the study likewise offers a vastly more circumspect tone than Stewart's 1986 memorandum. While still focusing on compensation and deterrence, it adds "corrective justice," along with "social grievance redress" as among tort law's possible functions.[114] And, although continuing to convey the sense that tort law has proven itself to be an inept and expensive method for delivering certain goods,[115] the study makes a point of emphasizing that alternative systems are likely to suffer from comparable problems.[116] It thus concludes with the sensible if bland suggestion that policymakers must carefully assess the costs and benefits associated with different mechanisms for addressing the social problem of injuries resulting from enterprise activity.[117]

What explains the evolution of the enterprise liability project? And what lessons does it hold for today? As for explanations, there are probably several. The project was launched without a clear understanding of its mission, or what sort of work-product it would ultimately generate. And, as it developed, it apparently became controversial within the ALI, with the final report bearing the signs of being a compromise document.[118] At the same time, one should also credit the Reporters for coming to acknowledge the enormous complexity of the task they had set for themselves, as well as the ease with which the messy business of tort law can be condemned so long as one does not give equally unsparing attention to the "alternatives." Poorly executed comparative institutional analysis juxtaposes warts-and-all apples against air-brushed oranges.[119] By contrast, when macro-level comparisons are done well, they tend to highlight difficult-to-weigh trade-offs, which in turn tends to generate a sensible-if-not-hugely-helpful suggestion for further analysis.

None of this is to deny that there is something to be learned from the study. As an instance of the ALI supporting academic research, it deserves praise. As a quasi-regulatory exercise, or a prelude to such an exercise, it is more problematic. As noted, the project's claim to have been necessitated by a pressing policy problem quickly proved unfounded. Yet the project was at least as much about academic agendas as it was about "need," which is why it was rigged from the outset—rigged intellectually,

---

[111] *Id.*

[112] *Id.* at 4.

[113] *Id.* at 6.

[114] *Id.* at 24–27. However, corrective justice is deemed "less resonant" in a system in which damages are often paid out through liability insurance. *Id.* at 25.

[115] *Id.* at 34, 50.

[116] *Id.* at 35, 51.

[117] *Id.* at 51–52.

[118] *See* Abraham & White, *supra* note 1.

[119] Harold Demsetz, *Information and Efficiency: Another Viewpoint*, 12 J.L. & ECON. 1, 1 (1969) (criticizing the "nirvana approach" to policy analysis).

not politically. In keeping with the nearly uniform view held by the best and the brightest in the elite U.S. legal academy from roughly 1970 to 1990, the Reporters approached tort law from within an exclusively "public law" mindset. This explains why the project exclusively aims to evaluate tort law, in the domain of accidents, as a species of regulatory law. Apart from offering a cursory reference to "corrective justice" (miscast as a "function" of tort law), it never considers the possibility that tort law has a core deontological justification—that tort law is provided in fulfillment of a duty owed by government to polity members to identify and proscribe various forms of interpersonal mistreatment, and to give victims of such mistreatment an ability to respond to those who have mistreated them. On this completely traditional understanding of tort, several of its putative bugs turn out to be features.[120]

V. Conclusion

The foregoing, admittedly impressionistic analysis suggests that, when attending to tort law, the ALI has done best when acting in the manner of an appellate court rather than a law reform commission or a think tank. Assuming this has been the case, it is likely to continue to be so. Indeed, in our acrimoniously partisan times, efforts by the ALI to stamp its preferred policy solutions on problems—even thoughtful efforts—will almost certainly be greeted with, and will engender, skepticism. In private law, no less than constitutional law, partisan lines have been drawn. For example, there are signs that lawyers and courts, no doubt in some cases opportunistically serving the interests of their clients, have taken up Justice Scalia's damaging offhand suggestion that the same lawyers who disparage "living constitutionalism" should view the ALI's Restatements with a jaundiced eye.[121] In this climate, it seems likely that the ALI's best hope for another century of stellar contributions to American tort law is to pursue the sort of incremental, architecturally sensitive reconstruction that has always characterized the work of our best courts.

---

[120] *See, e.g.,* John C.P. Goldberg, *What Are We Reforming?: Tort Theory's Place in Debates over Malpractice Reform,* 59 VAND. L. REV. 1075 (2006); Benjamin C. Zipursky, *Coming Down to Earth: Why Rights-Based Theories of Tort Can and Must Address Cost-Based Proposals for Damages Reform,* 55 DEPAUL L. REV. 469 (2006).

[121] *See supra* note 4; *see, e.g.,* 39 OH. REV. CODE § 3901.82 (2018) ("The 'Restatement of the Law, Liability Insurance' that was approved at the 2018 annual meeting of the American Law Institute does not constitute the public policy of this state and is not an appropriate subject of notice."); Dakter v. Cavallino, 866 N.W.2d 656, 678 (Wis. 2015) (Ziegler, J., concurring) (questioning the majority's reliance on treatises, including the Restatement (Second) of Torts, as reliable guides to Wisconsin law).

9

The Restatement of Property

The Curse of Incompleteness

Thomas W. Merrill

I. Introduction

The most striking feature of the many iterations of the Restatement of Property is that the effort remains incomplete. No doubt there are gaps in other Restatements. But the Restatement of Property is in a class by itself in terms of what is missing. A partial list of subjects that have never been addressed, notwithstanding seventeen volumes produced over ninety-plus years, includes: adverse possession, accession, bailments, eminent domain, fixtures, recording acts, riparian rights, warranties of title, waste, and zoning.

The incompleteness of the property enterprise is most starkly revealed in the Restatement (First) of Property, published in five volumes between 1936 and 1944. The First Restatement was almost entirely about interests in land; personal property was not covered at all. Even within the limitation to land, a large number of important topics were not addressed, including adverse possession, eminent domain, leases, mortgages, warranties of title, and land use regulation. The basic strategy for attempting to fill the gaps, pursued in Second and Third Restatements, was to assign new Reporters to oversee volumes devoted to topics not covered in the initial effort. This generated two significant gap-fillers: volumes on Landlord and Tenant published in 1977 and Mortgages published in 1997. But the piecemeal strategy still left major holes in coverage, including all of personal property law. And the use of multiple Reporters, who inevitably have had different ideas, introduced a larger problem of incoherence in basic approach. Almost comically, the law professors who served as Reporters during the first three series of the Restatement of Property produced three different, and mutually inconsistent, versions of the Rule Against Perpetuities.

The incompleteness of the Restatement of Property has had several important consequences. It has undoubtedly diminished its influence. If a Restatement has nothing to say about a topic, obviously it will have no influence on the development of the law in that area. And even if it does have something to say, lawyers and judges are less likely to consult the Restatement if they are not confident that they will find something relevant there. The incompleteness of the Restatement effort also had the effect of removing certain topics one would expect to find in a Restatement of Property—such as trespass to land and nuisance and certain "natural rights of property" like riparian rights—to the Restatement of Torts. So the incompleteness of the Restatement of Property also resulted in a fragmentation of issues of central relevance to the institution of property among entirely different restatement projects.

Thomas W. Merrill, *The Restatement of Property* In: *The American Law Institute*. Edited by: Andrew S. Gold and Robert W. Gordon, Oxford University Press. © Oxford University Press 2023. DOI: 10.1093/oso/9780197685341.003.0010

A major effort is now underway to rectify the problem of incompleteness in the form of a new Restatement (Fourth) of Property, designed to produce, when finished, a relatively complete Restatement of both real and personal property, comparable to the coverage one finds in the Restatement of Contracts and the Restatement of Torts. The project is being overseen by Professor Henry Smith of Harvard, assisted by a large team of Associate Reporters (including the author). The general strategy is to produce a comprehensive Restatement that reflects a general unity of approach and style, and fills most of the gaps in the existing Restatement efforts. After some initial delays, perhaps inevitable in such a large undertaking, the project has picked up speed and is now churning out content at a high rate. At this point, the main impediment to eventual completion of the Fourth Restatement is the need to secure spots on the crowded agendas of the American Law Institute (ALI) Council and Membership in order to gain approval of the segments of the Fourth Restatement as they emerge.

II. The First, Second, and Third Restatements of Property

If the First Restatement of Property produced a badly truncated version of property law, this did not correspond to the initial vision.[1] Planning for a Restatement of Property began in 1926, when the ALI Executive Committee asked Harry A. Bigelow of the University of Chicago to prepare a report dealing with "the Scope and Classification of the Subject of Property."[2] Bigelow responded with a seventy-page memo setting forth a blueprint for the anticipated project. The memo began with a discussion of the meaning of property, which Bigelow defined in very broad terms. Property, he stipulated, refers to the rights of persons with respect to "things," both tangible and intangible, which other persons have a duty to respect. As defined, "property" potentially included not just rights to land and chattels but also security interests, choses in action, enforceable contracts, intellectual goods, and even reputations. The potential domain of property, he concluded, is very broad.

Bigelow then proceeded to exclude from this broad universe various topics that by convention were regarded as discrete fields of study. Thus, although the definition was broad enough to encompass contracts, Bigelow acknowledged that contracts would be subject to a separate projected Restatement of Contracts. Similarly, although his definition included intangible rights like reputation, Bigelow acknowledged that this should be covered in the Restatement of Torts. Although Bigelow regarded trusts as being more comfortably nested within the field of property, he also recommended that trusts be the subject of a separate Restatement, given that trusts were studied by scholars who specialized in that subject and were not generalists in the field of property. (George Bogert, a trusts specialist and one of Bigelow's colleagues at Chicago,

---

[1] This portion of the chapter draws on material in Thomas W. Merrill & Henry E. Smith, *Why Restate the Bundle?: The Disintegration of the Restatement of Property*, 79 BROOK. L. REV. 681 (2014).

[2] HARRY A. BIGELOW, PRELIMINARY REPORT TO THE COUNCIL ON SCOPE AND CLASSIFICATION OF THE SUBJECT "PROPERTY" 2 (1926) [hereinafter Bigelow Memo] (reproducing resolution).

assisted Bigelow in preparing the memo.[3]) Equity presented a particular puzzle, and Bigelow devoted considerable space to considering whether topics like specific performance of land sale contracts should be included in a Restatement of Property or in a Restatement of Equity, a task complicated by uncertainty over whether there would be a Restatement of Equity. (No such Restatement was ever produced, although the ALI did sponsor a pathbreaking Restatement of Restitution.[4])

Viewed from a distance, Bigelow's memo laid claim to a very capacious undertaking. The Council tacitly endorsed Bigelow's effort and appointed him Reporter for the Restatement of Property. The strategy was also to have decisive effects on the future shape of the Restatement project. It explains, for example, why wills and intestate succession are included under the umbrella of the Restatement of Property, whereas trusts are subject to a separate Restatement, even though, from the perspective of modern legal practice and law school curricula, it would make more sense to cover both topics in a single Restatement, for example, "Trusts and Estates." Both wills and trusts fell within Bigelow's broad definition of "property," but trusts were specifically hived off, whereas wills and estates were not.

Bigelow's memo was equally fateful in his discussion of the order in which topics within the field of property should be taken up by the projected Restatement. He argued that the first thing to tackle was estates in land and future interests. Only later would the project turn to the legal incidents of ownership, servitudes, personal property, and intellectual property. This ordering of priorities goes a long way toward explaining the incompleteness of the Restatement of Property, and especially the heavy emphasis on land at the expense of personal and intangible rights. Estates in land came first, and the ALI never got around to restating much of what Bigelow slated for coverage at a later time.

Bigelow's priorities were undoubtedly influenced by the law school curriculum of the 1920s, which made the estate system derived from English feudalism the centerpiece of the study of property.[5] Interestingly, however, Bigelow sought to justify his ordering of topics in a very modern way, by generating an empirical study of the relative frequency with which different topics in property law appear in reported judicial decisions. The empirical study, he suggested, supported his recommendation to tackle real property and the estate system first.[6] Yet an examination of his data, reproduced in an appendix to the memo, casts doubt on this. Even in the 1920s, mortgages and liens generated more litigation than estates; for that matter, so did personal property disputes (even after excluding cases involving sales) and landlord-tenant law. Today, of course, the topic Bigelow put at the forefront has declined greatly in significance, and the ones he put off to the future have emerged as having even greater importance

---

[3] Id. at 2 (noting Bogert's participation). Bogert later served on the Advisory Committee for the First Restatement of Trusts, see Restatement (First) of Trusts iii (1935), and, of course, has his name on a prominent treatise devoted to trusts.

[4] Restatement (First) of Restitution: Quasi Contracts and Constructive Trusts (1937).

[5] See, e.g., Richard R. Powell, Cases and Materials on the Law of Possessory Estates (1933). This five-volume set, designed for use at Columbia Law School, included an introductory volume on "Possessory Estates," two volumes on "Trusts and Estates," a volume on "Vendor and Purchaser," and a volume on "Landlord and Tenant." Id. at v–vii. All five volumes dealt almost exclusively with real property. Id.

[6] Bigelow Memo, supra note 2, at 14.

than they had in his day. Rigorous adherence to empiricism would have produced a sequencing of topics for the projected Restatement much more consistent with future trends.

Perhaps most significantly, Bigelow's ambitious agenda sowed the seeds of incompleteness. The projected scope of the project was so broad that it would take a herculean effort to bring it to conclusion. Perhaps Bigelow was Hercules, but we will never know, for he resigned his position as Reporter after being appointed Dean of the University of Chicago Law School in 1929.[7] His replacement was Richard R. Powell, of Columbia Law School, who had also advised on the planning memo and was a member of the original Advisory Committee on Property.

Powell was a natural choice to take over as Reporter. He was deeply learned and widely respected in his field. His labors as Reporter eventually lead to the publication of a treatise on the Law of Property, which still bears his name.[8] Nevertheless, Powell did not have the temperament needed to execute Bigelow's ambitious program. Powell's scholarship was characterized by an insistence on "meticulous accuracy."[9] He was also fascinated by details rooted in English history, reflecting a tradition that regarded property law as having started with *Coke upon Littleton* (1628). Biographical sketches of his years at Columbia feature his mastery of the Socratic teaching method, including an exchange in which he asked a student to explain "[w]hat effect did the Statute of Quia Emptores have upon the creation of tenancies in frankalmoign?"[10] Powell's announced intention, upon taking over as Reporter, was to avoid misleading generalities and "particularize extensively," although he admitted that this "has the disadvantage of restricting the immediate aid rendered by the Institute to quite narrow fields in the Law of Property."[11] Powell was neither a theorist nor a reformer by temperament. He recognized that the law evolved, but did so slowly, and his central conviction was that in order to understand the law one had to start with history. Although it would be inaccurate to characterize Powell as a legal formalist of the sort associated with Christopher Columbus Langdell, he unquestionably regarded the Restatement enterprise as one in which the task is to uncover the superior "rule" implicit in existing legal sources.

This rule-based and historically grounded orientation is highly visible in the first four volumes of the Restatement produced under Powell's supervision. Perhaps the most telling example is Chapter 5, for which Powell was solely responsible, which spends 127 pages explicating "Fees Tail and Related Estates."[12] The fee tail had been abolished in virtually every state for over 100 years when the Restatement was prepared. The chapter is therefore devoted to explicating the estates into which attempts to create a fee tail will be converted under different statutes in different states, and the

---

[7] RESTATEMENT (FIRST) OF PROPERTY, vol. I, intro. x (1936).

[8] RICHARD R. POWELL, POWELL ON REAL PROPERTY (1st ed. 1949). The current edition, a loose-leaf treatise published in seventeen volumes, is *Powell on Real Property* (Michael Allen Wolf, general ed., 2013).

[9] John Ritchie III, *Book Review*, 63 HARV. L. REV. 732, 734 (1950) (reviewing RICHARD R. POWELL, I THE LAW OF REAL PROPERTY (1st ed. 1949)).

[10] JULIUS GOEBEL JR., A HISTORY OF THE SCHOOL OF LAW COLUMBIA UNIVERSITY 268 (1955); *see also Text of the Resolution of the Columbia University Faculty of Law in Honor of Richard Roy Belden Powell on the Occasion of his Retirement*, 60 COLUM. L. REV. 105 (1960).

[11] Richard R. Powell, *Restatement of the Law of Property*, 16 A.B.A. J. 197, 198 (1930).

[12] RESTATEMENT (FIRST) OF PROPERTY §§ 59–106 (1936).

case law interpreting these statutes. The result was definitive. But given the obscurity of the topic, its fundamental irrelevance, and the impossibility of stating a single rule for all jurisdictions, this was surely a misplaced commitment of resources for a Restatement, especially given all the other items waiting on Bigelow's agenda.

Whether it was due to the change in leadership, or to Powell's insistence on a meticulous elaboration of the old estate system, the Restatement of Property soon lagged badly behind other Restatement efforts. The first two volumes did not appear in print until 1936, well after Agency, Contracts, Torts, and other efforts had made their initial debut.[13] At some point in the mid-1930s, William Draper Lewis, the Executive Director of the ALI, became alarmed. As Deborah DeMott describes in her chapter in this volume, Lewis was under increasing pressure from Andrew Carnegie, the principal donor at the time, to wrap things up. In 1935, the decision was made to transfer a group of property specialists working on the legal incidents of ownership, under the leadership of Everett Fraser of the University of Minnesota Law School, from the Restatement of Property to the Restatement of Torts.[14] This explains why a collection of topics denominated "natural rights in land"—including nuisance, lateral and subjacent support, and riparian water rights—appears in Volume IV of the Restatement of Torts rather than in the Restatement of Property.

By the time Powell delivered the first two volumes of the Restatement of Property in 1936, a further decision was made to subdivide the property working group. Powell would continue to lead "Group 1," explicating the constructional principles that govern estates in land and future interests and the Rule Against Perpetuities. A new "Group 2," under the leadership of Oliver Rundell of the University of Wisconsin Law School, would tackle servitudes.[15] Powell delivered his third volume, on constructional principles, in 1940, and a fourth and final volume, on the Rule Against Perpetuities and related restrictions on the creation of property interests, in 1944. Rundell also completed the work on servitudes in 1944.[16]

After that, World War II ended the original Restatement project. Although Torts and Contracts were relatively complete efforts, the Restatement of Property covered only estates in land and servitudes. If one looked into the Restatement of Torts, one could find significant additional material relevant to property, including a fairly complete treatment of the right to exclude and privileges overriding the right to exclude and the incidents of ownership covered by Fraser's ad hoc group transferred from Property to Torts. But the balance of Bigelow's ambitious agenda, including all of personal property, leases, mortgages and liens, and intellectual property, went untouched.

I do not mean to demean Powell's work on the Restatement of Property. It was of the highest quality and was quickly recognized as being canonical—with respect to

---

[13] Volumes 1 and 2 of the RESTATEMENT (FIRST) OF CONTRACTS appeared in 1932; volumes 1 and 2 of the RESTATEMENT (FIRST) OF AGENCY appeared in 1933; volumes 1 and 2 of the RESTATEMENT (FIRST) OF TORTS appeared in 1934; the RESTATEMENT (FIRST) OF CONFLICTS OF LAW appeared in 1934; and volumes 1 and 2 of the RESTATEMENT (FIRST) OF TRUSTS appeared in 1935.

[14] RESTATEMENT (FIRST) OF TORTS vii, intro. (1939).

[15] RESTATEMENT (FIRST) OF PROPERTY, vol. 1, intro. xiii (1936).

[16] RESTATEMENT (FIRST) OF PROPERTY: FUTURE INTERESTS CONTINUED AND CONCLUDED (1940); RESTATEMENT (FIRST) OF PROPERTY: SOCIAL RESTRICTIONS IMPOSED ON THE CREATION OF PROPERTY INTERESTS (1944); RESTATEMENT (FIRST) OF PROPERTY: SERVITUDES (1944).

the narrow band of issues covered. The problem is that too few topics were covered, and those that were covered looked backward to the world of Jane Austin, where rural estates in land were the principal source of wealth and family prestige. Estates in land and future interests, constructional rules like the Doctrine of Worthier Title and the Rule in Shelley's case, and the mysteries of the Rule Against Perpetuities were of declining importance in the age of the automobile and the radio. They have become even more marginal in the years since then.

When the ALI decided to revive the Restatement of Property project in 1970, an aging Powell was again appointed to the Advisory Committee, but the position of Reporter went to A. James Casner of Harvard Law School.[17] Casner was a protegee of Powell's, having obtained a J.S.D. degree from Columbia under Powell's supervision while a young scholar on leave from Maryland Law School. Powell was sufficiently impressed by his student that he had Casner appointed to the Advisory Committee for the First Restatement, where he worked on Chapter 7, which dealt with class gifts (the topic of his dissertation), and prepared the index for volumes one and two. Casner made important contacts as the junior member of the Advisory Committee, especially in developing a friendship with Barton Leach of Harvard Law School. Leach later secured Casner a visiting professorship at Harvard, which turned into an offer of tenure. After serving as an intelligence officer in World War II, Casner returned to Harvard. He and Powell briefly discussed collaborating on a property treatise, but Powell decided to develop a treatise on his own. Casner then put together another team of authors to produce the *American Law of Property*, which was effectively a competing treatise to Powell's.[18] Casner and Leach also collaborated on a popular property casebook.[19] Casner maintained close ties with the ALI during this period, serving as Reporter for a Restatement of Estate and Gift Taxation before also being appointed the new Reporter for Property.

Casner lacked Bigelow's philosophical bent and did not share Powell's scholarly fascination with historically derived rules. He was, by temperament, a reformer. Casner had stirred up the tax bar with his proposal for a one-time generation-skipping tax based on life expectancies as part of his work on estate and gift taxes. When asked for his advice about how to proceed with a new Restatement of Property, Casner argued that the first task should be landlord-tenant law. He reasoned, sensibly enough, that the First Restatement had said nothing about this area of property law. But he was also motivated by the awareness that landlord-tenant law was a hot topic at the time among those agitating for legal reform to assist the poor, and he saw the Restatement as a means for lending support to these efforts.

Casner eventually produced two volumes entitled *Landlord and Tenant*.[20] Like Powell's work on estates land and future interests, the quality is impressive. Leases

[17] The information on Casner and his tenure as Reporter of the RESTATEMENT (SECOND) OF PROPERTY has been gleaned from an historical video interview with Casner produced by the ALI in 1990. *ALI Audiovisual History—A James Casner* (1990), *available at* http://www.youtube.com/watch?v=QTH1 q5B_1nk&dist=PLlC004D53890D3AA1.

[18] AMERICAN LAW OF PROPERTY: A TREATISE ON THE LAW OF PROPERTY IN THE UNITED STATES (A. James Casner ed., 1952).

[19] A. JAMES CASNER & W. BARTON LEACH, CASES AND TEXT ON PROPERTY (1st ed. 1950).

[20] 1 & 2 RESTATEMENT (SECOND) OF PROPERTY: LANDLORD AND TENANT (1977).

are used much more widely than life estates and remainders, and consequently they have attracted much more legislative interest. Casner's work on topics like the application of the Statute of Frauds to leases and the allocation of the duty to repair between lessors and lessees were informed by numerous fifty-state surveys of legislative provisions as well as decisional law. The work was also conceptually creative in a constructive way. For example, Casner offered an interesting reconceptualization of the venerable doctrine of constructive eviction in terms of the lessor's interference with one or more permissible uses of property by the lessee.[21]

Unfortunately, Casner's efforts to use the Restatement as a vehicle to advance landlord-tenant reform proved to be too controversial to pass smoothly through the ALI approval process. The Advisory Committee included a number of practicing lawyers who specialized in negotiating commercial leases;[22] they were skeptical about the need for an implied warranty of habitability and rules mandating that landlords mitigate damages when tenants abandon leaseholds. Casner also had to contend with Charles J. Meyers, of Stanford Law School, who argued, following the tenets of the nascent law and economics movement, that mandatory tenant rights would diminish the supply of rental units and increase prices.[23]

After seven years of wrangling, two volumes on landlord-tenant law emerged in 1977. The final product reflected a compromise between Casner and the reformers, on the one hand, and the traditionalists on the other. For example, the Restatement endorsed the implied warranty of habitability in residential leases, but said it could be waived by the landlord in return for consideration, provided such a waiver was not "unconscionable or significantly against public policy."[24] The Restatement also rejected a duty on the part of landlords to mitigate damages when tenants default, offering the rather dubious rationale that this would encourage tenants to abandon property. As a result, the Restatement's landlord-tenant volumes did not satisfy either the reformers or the traditionalists.

The timing of the release of the volumes was not auspicious for these sorts of attempts at compromise. The reform movement had the wind in its sails in the late 1970s, and the Restatement volumes were greeted with derision by those who thought it failed to grasp the inevitable path of the future. They were right up to a point. In the years after the release of the Restatement volumes, virtually every state adopted the implied warranty of habitability for residential leases, with a majority making it nonwaivable. And a majority of states adopted a duty to mitigate damages for residential tenancies. Significantly, these reforms mostly proceeded through legislative enactments rather than common law revision. So it is unclear whether the Restatement would have had a greater impact if it had followed Casner's lead and had fully embraced the position of the reformers. The largest number of states (twenty-one to date) embraced the reforms by adopting the Uniform Residential Landlord and Tenant

---

[21] *Id.* § 6.1 ("Landlord's Conduct Interferes With Permissible Use").

[22] In contrast to the FIRST RESTATEMENT, which was dominated by academics, Casner was the only academic on the landlord-tenant volumes. RESTATEMENT (SECOND) OF PROPERTY: LANDLORD AND TENANT intro. at ix (1977). The other committee members were either practitioners or judges. *Id.*

[23] Charles J. Meyers, *The Covenant of Habitability and the American Law Institute*, 27 STAN. L. REV. 879, 893 (1975).

[24] RESTATEMENT (SECOND) OF PROPERTY: LANDLORD AND TENANT § 5.6 (1977).

Act of 1972, drafted by the National Conference of Commissioners on Uniform State Laws, rather than by judicial revision of the common law.

After the landlord-tenant project was done, Casner convinced the ALI to undertake a series of volumes on Donative Transfers—essentially wills and intestate succession.[25] Again, there was logic to this, since Bigelow's original blueprint had hived off trusts but implicitly left wills and intestate succession within the domain of property. It was no coincidence, however, that estate planning had become the central concern of Casner's own scholarly efforts, while his interest in basic property law had waned. Casner never revised the *American Law of Property* after it was published in 1952–1954, and no supplement was produced after 1977. Instead, he devoted his scholarly energies largely to a multivolume treatise on estate planning.[26] Once again, Casner's reforming impulse informed the agenda. This time, his initial target was the venerable Rule Against Perpetuities.

The First Restatement had considered the Rule Against Perpetuities in Volume IV, where Powell had produced a typically thorough Restatement of the conventional understanding of the Rule, derived from John Chipman Gray's treatise on the subject.[27] The traditional rule, as explicated by Powell and before him Gray, was complex and a potential trap for those not advised by the best lawyers. But it had the virtue of allowing the validity of future interests to be determined as soon as a conveyance took effect, because the rule was applied by considering all possible future contingencies ("what might happen"). Casner, prodded by his colleague Barton Leach, was a proponent of changing the rule by considering what actually did happen ("wait and see").[28] This reform had the virtue of eliminating some very low-probability scenarios easily overlooked by lawyers (fertile octogenarians, unborn widows, and the like), but at the price of creating long periods of uncertainty, which could impair the alienability of property.

Casner's advocacy of "wait and see" triggered an emphatic rebuke by his former mentor Powell, in a dramatic confrontation at the ALI Annual Meeting in 1978.[29] The gist of the Powell critique was that wait and see "leaves the location of who owns what unascertainable for the entire period of the rule."[30] Others pointed out that wait and see had been adopted by only a small number of jurisdictions, and that no intervening change in circumstances had occurred since 1944 that would justify eliminating the traditional rule. Casner nevertheless eventually prevailed, and "wait and see" was officially endorsed by the ALI with the publication of the Restatement (Second) of Property: Donative Transfers in 1983. The reform was eventually adopted by a

---

[25] See ALI Audiovisual History, supra note 17, at 57:25–59:13.

[26] A. JAMES CASNER, ESTATE PLANNING: CASES, STATUTES, TEXT, AND OTHER MATERIALS (1st ed. 1953). As Deborah DeMott emphasizes in her chapter, the scholarly or treatise-writing interests of early Restatement Reporters heavily influenced the coverage of their volumes.

[27] JOHN CHIPMAN GRAY, THE RULE AGAINST PERPETUITIES (1st ed. 1886).

[28] Leach had long been a critic of the traditional rule, largely on the ground that it generated unfair surprises. See, e.g., Barton Leach, Perpetuities in Perspective: Ending the Rule's Reign of Terror, 65 HARV. L. REV. 721, 730 (1952).

[29] Casner foreshadowed his endorsement of wait and see by urging its use as a constructional principle in comments to the Landlord and Tenant Volume. RESTATEMENT (SECOND) OF PROPERTY: LANDLORD AND TENANT § 1.8 cmt. b (1977).

[30] A.L.I., 55TH ANNUAL MEETING: PROCEEDINGS 1978, at 250–56, 285–86 (1979).

significant number of states, although (again) primarily through adoption by state legislatures of the Uniform Statutory Rule Against Perpetuities, rather than through judicial decisions relying on the Restatement.[31] In fact, some important courts like New York rejected "wait and see" on the ground that such a reform was the province of the legislature, not the courts.[32]

Casner soldiered on as Reporter for another decade, producing successive volumes on estate planning, namely, powers of appointment (1986), class gifts (Casner's dissertation topic) (1988), and gifts (1992).[33] Yet he made no move to fill the other gaps that remained under Bigelow's original plan.

The Casner era marked a decisive turn away from the conception of the Restatement as a distillation of the law as it is, to a view of the Restatement as a vehicle for laying down the law as it should be. The distinction is not between "descriptive" and "normative" approaches to the law. Anyone who has worked on a Restatement project is aware that this inevitably entails normative judgments. Often, a given legal issue will have generated divergent positions among the states (e.g., the "Maine rule" and the "Connecticut rule"), and the Restatement will have to make a judgment about which is the better view. Or, the doctrine in a given area may be poorly articulated or confused, in which case a proper Restatement will attempt to offer a clearer exposition of the underlying principle or rule. These sorts of normative judgments, which can be called interstitial or "internal" to the existing state of the law, are not only permissible but desirable. Indeed, these kinds of judgments can be said to constitute the very rationale for undertaking to restate the law.

A very different type of normative posture is to approach the existing state of the law in the manner of a law reform commission or legislative body, seeking to transform the law into something different. Obviously, this is a permissible posture for a legislature, which is accountable to the public through periodic elections. Perhaps the same can be said of an administrative body exercising delegated authority from the legislature, and subject to appointment and removal by elected officials. It is more controversial when judges undertake to reform the law in this manner, although one can cite numerous examples of this happening. When the ALI endorses wholesale legal reform, however, it would seem that the proper vehicle is a proposed uniform statute, which individual legislatures can accept or reject as they think proper. Advocating reform using the vehicle of a Restatement, when the position being pushed is not in some sense present or at least implicit in the current state of law, is to transgress the legitimate function of a Restatement, and would seem to have no claim on the allegiance of courts.

Casner seems to have crossed the line between normative analysis internal to the existing state of the law and naked advocacy of reform, if not in the Landlord and Tenant volumes, most certainly in his endorsement of the "wait and see" reform of

---

[31] HELENE SHAPO ET AL., THE LAW OF TRUSTS AND TRUSTEES § 214, at n.28 (2011). The Pennsylvania legislature adopted the "wait and see" reform as early as 1947.

[32] Symphony Space, Inc. v. Pergola Props., Inc., 669 N.E.2d 799, 808 (N.Y. 1996).

[33] RESTATEMENT (SECOND) OF PROPERTY: DONATIVE TRANSFERS, div. II, pt. V (1986) (Powers of Appointment); RESTATEMENT (SECOND) OF PROPERTY: DONATIVE TRANSFERS, div. II, pt. VI (1988) (Class Gifts); RESTATEMENT (SECOND) OF PROPERTY: DONATIVE TRANSFERS, div. III (1992) (Requirements for Effectuating a Donative Transfer).

the Rule Against Perpetuities. Something similar happened in other Restatements at about the same time, for example Prosser's Restatement (Second) of Torts, with its advocacy of strict products liability.[34] In an interview conducted near the end of his life, Casner forthrightly defended the conception of a Restatement as an instrument of legal reform.[35] He acknowledged that it was difficult to draw the line between Restatement-style reform, which implicitly invites the judiciary to change the law by adopting the "better view" of existing alternatives, and reform produced by promulgating uniform laws, which targets the legislature as the appropriate instrument of legal change. But Casner betrayed no doubt about the propriety of asking committees of lawyers, headed by law professors, to agitate for legal reform under the guise of "restating" the law. Epistemological modesty was not part of his makeup.

When the ALI decided to launch a third series of property Restatements, it abandoned the practice of appointing a single Reporter to oversee the effort. Instead, the ALI decided that it would appoint different Reporters to head up different topics within the field of property. This approach could have been used as a kind of "plug the gap" strategy—and to some extent it was. Of the three projects undertaken as part of the third series, one—the Restatement of Mortgages[36]—clearly filled a major gap left open by the First and Second Restatements. Unlike security interests in personal property, which are subject to Article 9 of the Uniform Commercial Code (adopted by every state except Louisiana), security interests in real property—mortgages—are largely governed by common law. It was thus a strong candidate for a Restatement, and much overdue. The project was ably executed by Reporters Grant Nelson and Dale Whitman, and has been widely praised and cited.

The other two projects undertaken as part of the Third Restatement, however, essentially revisited topics previously covered by the earlier Restatements. Moreover, the appointment of specialists to oversee particular topics may have accentuated the trend toward using the Restatements as platforms for pushing reform. Specialists are likely to have strong views about the right and wrong ways to approach a topic and to see their position of leadership as an occasion to advance those views.

The first of the revisitations was the Restatement (Third) of Property: Servitudes, published in two volumes in 2000. The ALI had already restated servitudes, in Volume V of the First Restatement, under Reporter Oliver Rundell.[37] The First Restatement version was a quintessential effort to rationalize the law as it is, with all its quirks and curlicues. The Reporter for the new servitudes project, Susan French, and her colleagues were eager to further streamline the law. Since most servitudes—whether they are easements, covenants, licenses, or profits—originate in some contractual undertaking, the new Restatement advocated the adoption of a very contract-like conception of servitudes, centered on the intent of the original contracting parties and subject to standard contractual defenses like restraint of trade, unconscionability, and violation of public policy.[38] Old requirements, like privity of estate and touch and

[34] RESTATEMENT (SECOND) OF TORTS § 402A (1965).
[35] ALI Audiovisual History, supra note 17, at 1:08:38–1:11:20.
[36] RESTATEMENT (THIRD) OF PROPERTY: MORTGAGES (1997).
[37] RESTATEMENT (FIRST) OF PROPERTY: SERVITUDES (1944).
[38] RESTATEMENT (THIRD) OF PROPERTY: SERVITUDES §§ 2.2, 3.1, 3.6, 3.7 (2000).

concern, designed to limit the promises that could be imposed on nonconsenting future owners, were eliminated.[39] Whatever the merits of this reconceptualization as a proposal for legislative reform, it proved to be too great a leap for the courts. To date, the courts have largely ignored the contractual approach of the Third Restatement, and have instead continued to apply the "outmoded" common law in determining when servitudes run with the land.[40]

The other reformist effort appeared under the title Restatement (Third) of Property: Wills and Other Donative Transfers, which appeared in volumes released between 1999 and 2011 under the leadership of Reporter Lawrence Waggoner and Associate Reporter John Langbein.[41] The reader will recall that Casner produced four volumes under a similar title as part of the Second Restatement, the last volume of which was released in 1992. The best explanation for the new series of volumes is simply that the new Reporters disagreed with the previous Reporter on a number of fronts and were eager to advance their own preferred positions. Perhaps most strikingly, the Third Restatement repudiated Casner's "wait and see" reform of the Rule Against Perpetuities, offering up yet another version of the Rule Against Perpetuities.[42] Under the Waggoner-Langbein proposed reform, the rule would prohibit any conditional gift for the benefit of persons born more than two generations after the transferor. Ironically, by the time the Third Restatement repudiated "wait and see," that approach had become the majority rule in the states, although again largely through the adoption of legislation.[43] No state, however, had ever adopted the Waggoner-Langbein two-generation proposal. It was offered up as a pure reform, with no pretense of restating the law at all.[44]

None of this is to suggest that the ALI's perambulation about the Rule Against Perpetuities was significantly responsible for the widespread demise of the Rule.

---

[39] *Id.* at ch. V, introductory note; § 3.2. As the Executive Director observed when the volumes were released, "[t]he large ideas in this Restatement are very different from those that governed its predecessor." *Id.* at ix.

[40] Note, *Touch and Concern, the Restatement (Third) of Property: Servitudes, and a Proposal*, 122 HARV. L. REV. 938, 944–45 (2009).

[41] 1 RESTATEMENT (THIRD) OF PROPERTY: WILLS AND OTHER DONATIVE TRANSFERS (1999); 2 RESTATEMENT (THIRD) OF PROPERTY: WILLS AND OTHER DONATIVE TRANSFERS (2003); 3 RESTATEMENT (THIRD) OF PROPERTY: WILLS AND OTHER DONATIVE TRANSFERS (2011).

[42] RESTATEMENT (THIRD) OF PROPERTY: WILLS AND OTHER DONATIVE TRANSFERS, ch. 27, introductory note (2010). Reporter Waggoner had previously been supportive of the "wait and see" approach, but had urged the adoption of a fixed number of years as the waiting period rather than the traditional lives in being plus twenty-one years. *See* Lawrence W. Waggoner, *Perpetuities: A Perspective on Wait-and-See*, 85 COLUM. L. REV. 1714, 1714 (1985).

[43] The Uniform Rule imposes a fixed maximum duration of ninety years for uncertainty about the vesting of a future interest. *See* UNIFORM STATUTORY RULE AGAINST PERPETUITIES (1986). As suggested by comments from David Seipp, the organized bar may have played a role in this legislative reform movement, given that wait and see significantly reduced the potential for malpractice liability on the part of lawyers who muff the traditional rule.

[44] Reporter Waggoner acknowledged that the new position on perpetuities was "aspirational." Lawrence W. Waggoner, *What's in the Third and Final Volume of the New Restatement of Property that Estate Planners Should Know About*, 38 ACTEC L.J. 23, 42 (2012). He justified this on the ground that perpetuities law is "now statutory," so "[i]f the Restatement is to be successful in shaping the law, it will have to be through legislation." *Id.* at 42–43. This ignored that perpetuities law, even if embodied in legislation, draws on common law concepts, which in turn require judicial interpretation. In any event, it was an acknowledgment that the Restatement had taken on a role indistinguishable from an editorial supporting law reform.

As scholars have documented, the Rule has been the victim of a kind of "race to the bottom" as states have competed for trust business, dangling the allure of perpetual trusts before the credulous rich as an inducement to locate trust assets in the state.[45] Waggoner and Langbein were correct that some form of the Rule Against Perpetuities is desirable, and they had sound reasons for rejecting Casner's "wait and see" reform. But with the ALI now on record as endorsing three different versions of the Rule, it is hard to argue that the common-law version of the Rule (Powell's version) is entitled to continued respect, if only because of the embedded wisdom of tradition. At this point, the idea that yet another reform of the rule endorsed by the ALI will stanch its evisceration by special interest legislation is fanciful. By the time the ALI has restated itself three times, any credibility it can claim for the value of the Rule based on expert knowledge has evaporated.

This brief overview suggests that the incompleteness of the Restatement of Property can largely be laid to the proclivities of individual Reporters. Bigelow's scoping of the project in extremely broad terms, his resignation as Reporter before significant progress had been made, Powell's slow and meticulous leadership animated by his fascination with historical obscurities, Casner's dogged pursuit of particular reforms, the fragmentation of authority among multiple Reporters for the third round, and the overtly reformist rather than "restatist" aspirations of two of the topics covered in the third round—all of these factors contributed to the production of seventeen volumes that somehow have failed to cover anything approaching the full scope of the law of property. This has reduced the attention it has received from lawyers and scholars and has diminished its influence with the courts.[46]

III. The Concept of Property

Is the incompleteness of the initial three series of the Restatement of Property attributable to the concept of property adopted by the Reporters and their Advisers? As previously mentioned, Bigelow adopted an extremely broad definition of property in his scoping memo. Property, he stipulated, refers to the rights of persons with respect to "things," whether tangible or intangible, which other persons have a duty to respect.[47] This was almost certainly too broad. If one defines "things" to include enforceable promises, then the definition includes all of the law of contracts. If "things" include bodily security, the value of exchangeable rights, and reputations, then the definition includes all of the law of torts. But the immediate question is why the first three series of the Restatement of Property covered too little. It seems difficult to attribute this to a scoping memo that covered too much.

In previous writing, Smith and I have described how Bigelow, and the initial Executive Director of the ALI, William Draper Lewis, were enamored of the typology

---

[45] Robert Sitkoff & Max Schanzenbach, *Jurisdictional Competition for Trust Funds: An Empirical Analysis of Perpetuities and Taxes*, 115 YALE L.J. 356 (2005).

[46] *See* Merrill & Smith, *supra* note 1 at 682, citing internal data from the ALI indicating that "[t]he *Restatement of Property* generates only one-quarter the royalties [from Westlaw] generated by the *Restatement of Contracts*, and merely 15% of the royalties of the *Restatement of Torts.*"

[47] Note 2 *supra*.

of legal concepts introduced by Wesley Newcomb Hohfeld, then a young professor at Yale.[48] Hohfeld engaged in what today would be called conceptual analysis. His most famous contribution was to break apart the concept of legal right into four distinct ideas—right, privilege, power, and immunity—each having its own "correlate" and "opposite."[49] He also criticized the distinction between in personam and in rem rights, arguing that all legal rights pertain to relations among persons, rather than relations of persons to things.[50]

In the aforementioned article, Smith and I hypothesized that Hohfeld's conceptual scheme was an important source of the Legal Realists' depiction of property as a formless "bundle of rights," and that this picture of property militates against any serious effort to identify a unifying theme or themes in property law. As a matter of intellectual history, this seems correct: Hohfeld was a major source of inspiration for the Realists and for the popularity of the bundle of rights metaphor (although there is no evidence that Hohfeld ever used this metaphor). Moreover, Bigelow was a devoted fan of Hohfeld, and the initial definitional provisions of the First Restatement, for which Bigelow was responsible, are a pure distillation of Hohfeld.[51] And Lewis, the Executive Director of the ALI, tried to convince the initial round of Reporters for other Restatement projects to adopt Hohfeld's terminology in their respective undertakings.[52]

It not clear, however, that either Hohfeld's conceptual scheme or the bundle of rights metaphor can be regarded as the root cause of the incompleteness of the first three series of the Restatement of Property. After all, even if one imagines that property consists of a bundle of rights, one could still strive to restate all the sticks in the bundle. More to the point, the efforts of Bigelow and Lewis to impose Hohfeld's scheme on the various Restatement projects utterly failed. With respect to the Restatement of Property in particular, Richard Powell, who succeeded Bigelow after two years, had no interest in Hohfeld or any other theory of property. Nor did Casner, or the various Reporters responsible for the volumes in the third series of the Restatement.

One could argue that the heavy emphasis on Hohfeld in the initial scoping of the project had a more subtle influence. Scholars like Bigelow many have thought that once legal concepts were broken down into their constituent elements having more precise meanings, there was no further need to develop any substantive theory of property. In other words, Hoheldian precision would obviate the need for any understanding of the core attributes of property as an institution. There may be something to this, at least insofar as Bigelow and Lewis are concerned. But again, Bigelow quickly dropped out of the picture, and Lewis gave up on his initial efforts to cajole the Reporters to embrace Hohfeldian terminology. Powell, Casner, and their successors were doctrinalists, not legal philosophers.

---

[48] Merrill & Smith, supra note 1.

[49] Wesley Newcomb Hohfeld, Some Fundamental Legal Conceptions as Applied in Judicial Reasoning, 23 YALE L.J. 16, 28–59 (1913).

[50] Wesley Newcomb Hohfeld, Fundamental Legal Conceptions as Applied in Judicial Reasoning, 26 YALE L.J. 710, 718–33 (1917).

[51] RESTATEMENT (FIRST) OF PROPERTY ch. 1 (1936). For details, see Merrill & Smith, supra note 1 at 699–707.

[52] Merrill & Smith, supra note 1 at 697–99.

In the end, it is hard to attribute the incompleteness of the initial Restatement efforts to any substantive concept of property or lack thereof. Judged by what they produced, the various Reporters in the first three series of the Restatement of Property thought that property is limited to land. Powell never ventured beyond rights to land. Casner's volumes on Landlord and Tenant were expressly limited to leases of land, even though personal property leases were already beginning their explosive growth when these volumes were produced.[53] And the volumes on Mortgages and Servitudes were limited to rights in land. The only exception were the volumes on Donative Transfers produced by Casner and then by Waggoner and Langbein, although by excluding trusts (which are the primary vehicle for intergenerational transfers of stocks and bonds and other intangible rights) they had little to say about personal property as such. Still, it is utterly implausible to think that the various Reporters who produced these volumes imagined that property is limited to land. The treatises authored by Powell and Casner make clear that they understood property includes movables and even some intangible rights. They confined themselves to land because that is what interested them, or, given the limits of time and human endurance, that is all they got around to covering.

IV. The Fourth Restatement

The Fourth iteration of the Restatement of Property was launched in late 2014. The central objective was to produce a comprehensive Restatement of property, something that had eluded the first three efforts—to the considerable detriment of the value and influence of the Restatement of Property as a whole. Other objectives, at least implicitly, were to try to achieve a certain unity of intellectual approach and style, and to focus on questions relevant to the contemporary practice of law, rather than engaging in fusty antiquarianism.

In an effort to achieve these objectives, the ALI, under a new Executive Director, Richard Revesz, adopted an innovative organizational model for the project. The Fourth Restatement will be led by a single Reporter, Henry Smith of Harvard Law School. But he will be assisted by a small troop of Associate Reporters, initially six and currently eight in number. The use of a single Reporter is designed to assure consistency among the individual sections, a uniform style, and coherence in terms of general intellectual orientation. The bevy of Associate Reporters is designed to create economies of scale that could not be achieved using a single Reporter. As the process has evolved, Smith has often paired two Associate Reporters or a small subcommittee of Associate Reporters to tackle specific topics. As usual, the work product will be subject to oversight by an Advisory Committee, the ALI Council, and the Membership at large.

Smith was an inspired choice as Reporter. He was still relatively young (in his fifties), but had already established a reputation as a prolific scholar. He has both a Ph.D. (in linguistics) and a law degree from Yale and was versed in interdisciplinary scholarship (including law and economics and systems theory). Some of his early work

---

[53] See Thomas W. Merrill, *The Economics of Leasing*, 12 J. LEGAL ANAL. 221 (2020) (recounting the dramatic growth in personal property leasing after World War II).

revealed a willingness to engage closely with historical sources.[54] He has taught property and contracts at Northwestern University School of Law, and property at Yale and Harvard, and is the co-author of a newish casebook on property.[55] He is not closely identified with any subfield of property but has an eclectic interest in almost everything. Perhaps most importantly, he is on record as being skeptical about the first three efforts to produce a comprehensive Restatement of Property,[56] and thus is well aware of the pitfalls that could undermine the effort.

Those named as Associate Reporters tend to be on the junior side (although not exclusively) and were deliberately chosen for their different backgrounds and areas of expertise. To cite some examples, John Goldberg, a torts scholar, has taken the laboring oar in drafting provisions dealing with the torts of trespass to land and nuisance; Christopher Newman, who has written about intellectual property licenses, has been assigned to provide initial drafts on the law of bailments and licenses; Sara Bronin, a land use expert (and zoning commissioner in Hartford, Connecticut), has taken primary responsibility for preparing the material on zoning; Wilson Feyermuth, an expert on real estate transactions and title security, has been given the lead on drafting provisions dealing with the Statute of Frauds and warranties of title.

In one critical respect, the Fourth Restatement has followed the lead of Bigelow's scoping memo. The Reporters would presumably not disagree with Bigelow's very broad conception of property, as the rights of persons to things that others have a duty to respect (although they might add further qualifications). But, unlike Bigelow, they have postponed any attempt to offer a definition of "property," preferring to wait until more topics are developed that may bear on the articulation of a general definition. The Reporters have also explicitly embraced Bigelow's general strategy of carving out discrete topics that have been or are in the process of being covered by other Restatements. Thus, no effort will be made to restate contracts or trusts or intellectual property (the ALI is currently developing a Restatement of Copyright).

In other respects, however, the Reporters have sought to avoid the mistakes that undermined the efforts of the first three Restatements. Most importantly, no attempt has been made to prescribe a sequencing of production, with property in land first, personal property to come later, and so forth. Personal property will get equal attention with real property, and public rights like zoning and eminent domain will be covered as well as private rights.[57] The organizational structure, consisting of a single supervising Reporter and a bevy of Associate Reporters, permits the simultaneous production of multiple topics across the board. Thus, estates in land and future interests are being restated while at the same time work is proceeding on personal property topics like bailments and fixtures and material on zoning is being finalized. Meanwhile, the property torts like trespass and nuisance, which are critical to an understanding of property, and "natural rights" like riparian rights, have been returned from their exile in the Restatement of Torts. This is with the understanding that the

---

[54] *E.g.*, Henry E. Smith, *Semi-common Property Rights and Scattering in the Open Fields*, 29 J. LEGAL STD. 131 (2000).

[55] THOMAS W. MERRILL & HENRY E. SMITH, PROPERTY: PRINCIPLES AND POLICIES (2007). A second edition appeared in 2012, a third in 2017, and a fourth in 2022 (adding Maureen Brady as an additional editor).

[56] Merrill & Smith, *supra* note 1.

[57] The Fourth Restatement will probably cover aspects of eminent domain, but not regulatory takings.

relevant sections of the Restatement of Torts will be revised to assure that the provisions in the two Restatements are identical.

Another mistake being avoided is to eschew any attempt, analogous to Bigelow's and Lewis's attempt to impose Hohfeldian analysis on the different part of the Restatement of Property, to adopt any particular academic discourse or mode of analysis on the various parts of the Restatement. Smith has been labeled a proponent of an "essentialist" theory of property,[58] but no attempt has been made to posit an essentialist definition of property, with the expectation that every discrete subject must conform to such a conception. No Reporter or Associate Reporter will be allowed to pursue particular hobby horses, or revise the treatment of particular issues in past Restatements based on personal disagreement. Overt attempts to achieve legislative-style reform will be strongly discouraged. But of course, normative judgments are inevitable, and the Reporters will occasionally endorse minority positions that seem more sensible and will even offer new ways of conceptualizing old problems, if this makes existing doctrines seem more readily explicable.

While hoping to avoid the mistakes of earlier efforts that have conspired to leave the Restatement of Property incomplete, there is no desire to deviate from the first three Restatements without good cause. Accordingly, large chunks of the previous Restatement efforts—for example, material on estates in land and future interests, major portions of the volumes on servitudes, and significant portions of landlord and tenant law (now called Leases)—will be incorporated into the Fourth Restatement, as updated and integrated into the new volumes. Given its unfortunate desuetude, and to avoid further embarrassment, no effort will be made to offer a fourth version of the Rule Against Perpetuities.

V. Conclusion

Over the course of nearly a century, the ALI has devoted enormous resources of time and energy into developing a Restatement of Property. Much of that work is first-rate, but it has suffered from a central failing of being incomplete. There are multiple explanations for this, mostly related to the foibles of the individual Reporters assigned to the task over the years. A Fourth Restatement is now underway, having as its central mandate the production of a comprehensive Restatement of Property, which can take its place alongside of the Restatements of Torts and Contracts as one of the central pillars of the American common law. Operating under a novel organizational structure comprised of a single Reporter and multiple Associate Reporters, there is reason for cautious optimism that this objective will finally be achieved. Whether or not this prediction proves to be correct, the long struggle associated with the various iterations of the Restatement of Property provides important lessons about the promise and pitfalls of any effort to provide a comprehensive Restatement in an important area of the law.

---

[58] Katrina Wyman, *The New Essentialism in Property*, 9 J. LEGAL ANAL. 183 (2017).

10

The International Law Profile of the ALI

George A. Bermann[*]

I. Introduction

International law today occupies a prominent place on the American Law Institute (ALI) research agenda. This chapter documents the wide range of subjects and forms that the ALI's engagement with international law has entailed over the years. However, international law did not always figure importantly in the work of the ALI and was in fact relatively slow in coming. This is for several reasons. International law did not correspond particularly well with the ALI's initial priority subjects, which were common law fields governed at the state level.[1] As a constitutional matter, U.S. states do not conduct foreign relations as such, and any acts taken at the state level that might incidentally impact U.S. foreign relations more likely take legislative and regulatory rather than common law form. But, more generally, international law cases for a long time occupied a modest place on the dockets of U.S. courts, in the practice of law firms, and even in law school curricula.

An important exception was the ALI's 1945 Statement of Essential Human Rights,[2] produced against the background of human rights atrocities in the years

---

[*] Gellhorn Professor of Law, Jean Monnet Professor of EU Law, and Director of Center for International Commercial and Investment Arbitration, Columbia Law School.

[1] Michael Traynor, *The First Restatements and the Vision of the American Law Institute: Then and Now*, 32 S. ILL. U. L.J. 145, 146 (2007).

[2] https://www.ali.org/news/articles/statement-essential-human-rights/#:~:text=Its%20goal%20was%20to%20define,documents%20relating%20to%20individual%20rights (last visited Dec. 26, 2020). The Statement presented the following as essential human rights:

    Article 1. Freedom of Religion
    Article 2. Freedom of Opinion
    Article 3. Freedom of Speech
    Article 4. Freedom of Assembly
    Article 5. Freedom to Form Association
    Article 6. Freedom from Wrongful Interference
    Article 7. Fair Trial
    Article 8. Freedom from Arbitrary Detention
    Article 9. Retroactive Laws
    Article 10. Property Rights
    Article 11. Education
    Article 12. Work
    Article 13. Conditions of Work
    Article 14. Food and Housing
    Article 15. Social Security
    Article 16. Participation in Government
    Article 17. Equal Protection
    Article 18. Limitations on Exercise of Rights

George A. Bermann, *The International Law Profile of the ALI* In: *The American Law Institute*. Edited by: Andrew S. Gold and Robert W. Gordon, Oxford University Press. © Oxford University Press 2023. DOI: 10.1093/oso/9780197685341.003.0011

leading up to World War II and during the war itself. The idea originated with Professor Warren A. Seavey of Harvard Law School, who in 1941, well before the war's end, successfully urged ALI Director William Draper Lewis to launch a project to "ascertain[] and formulat[e] basic principles of Justice which should exist in every civilized state."[3] Seavey argued, and Lewis agreed, that the ALI was perfectly positioned to carry out the task, by virtue of its capacity to harness collective efforts on the part of the country's leading legal minds and the high prestige that the ALI had garnered.[4]

In 1942, with the support of the Carnegie Endowment for International Peace and the American Philosophical Society, the ALI convened a Committee consisting of representatives of Canada, China, France, pre-Nazi Germany, Italy, India, Poland, the Soviet Union, Spain, Syria, the United Kingdom and a number of Latin American countries, and presided by ALI Director Lewis. The Committee was charged with helping establish a statement of principle on human rights for the international community in the postwar world or, as the ALI put it, "defin[ing] the indispensable human rights in terms that would be acceptable to men of good will in all nations."[5] Although the statement produced by the Committee was never formally adopted by the ALI,[6] it was submitted to the UN Secretariat for consideration as background material for the 1948 Universal Declaration of Human Rights.[7] The principal drafter of the Declaration, John P. Humphrey, later wrote that "the best of the texts from which I worked was the one prepared by the American Law Institute, and I borrowed freely from it."[8]

Today, international law is anything but absent from the ALI agenda.[9] Through the efforts, particularly of recent ALI Directors, Geoffrey C. Hazard Jr., Lance Liebman and Richard Revesz, it has become genuinely mainstreamed in the ALI's work, principally, but not exclusively, in two distinct varieties: Restatements and Principles.

---

[3] Warren Seavey, Laying the Foundations for a New World Order (A Project for the American Law Institute), at 1 (July 15, 1941). Seavey was concerned that the war, together with technological developments, would "affect what we now believe to be our basic individual rights [in ways that could not] be foretold." *Id.* at 3.

[4] *Id.* at 4.

[5] https://www.ali.org/news/articles/statement-essential-human-rights/#:~:text=Its%20goal%20was%20 to%20define,documents%20relating%20to%20individual%20rights (last visited Dec. 26, 2020).

[6] The Statement and the work leading up to it was discussed by Mary Robinson, in the Annual Dinner Address at the American Law Institute's 80th Annual Meeting, 80 A.L.I. PROC. 232, 233–34 (2003).

[7] U.N. General Assembly Resolution 217 A (III) (Dec. 10, 1948), reprinted at https://www.refworld.org/ docid/3ae6b3712c.html (last visited Dec. 29, 2020).

[8] JOHN P. HUMPHREY, HUMAN RIGHTS AND THE UNITED NATIONS: A GREAT ADVENTURE (1984).

[9] Michael Traynor wrote in 2007:

The international implications of the law of the United States are growing, whether that law is federal or state, common law or statute, or regulatory law of the many administrative agencies, federal, state, and local, that have been created since the Institute was founded in 1923.

Traynor, *supra* note 1 at 146. *See also* George A. Bermann, *The American Law Institute Goes Global*, 16 WILLAMETTE J. INT'L L. 3000 (2008).

II. Restatements of the Law in the International Law Field

International law first made an appearance in ALI Restatements, albeit inconspic-uously, through the 1934 Restatement (First) of Conflict of Laws,[10] inasmuch as that instrument was in principle as applicable to international as to domestic cases. Reporters of Conflicts Restatements over time have become increasingly conscious of the field's international dimension, beginning with the 1971 Restatement (Second) of Conflict of Laws.[11] Still, reflecting back on the Second Restatement in 2007, Michael Traynor, former ALI President, saw the need to adopt a decidedly more comparative and international law outlook on conflicts of law, urging that U.S. work on the subject:

> [t]ake into appropriate account the growing and relevant international efforts such as those to achieve harmonization of the law; international cooperation and coordi-nation mechanisms as in international insolvency law, and international intellectual property law; the articulation of international principles as in UNIDROIT's Principles of International Commercial Contracts, which are akin to the Restatements; and the emergence of a *lex mercatoria*. It is not a coincidence that in contrast to our aggres-sive term, "the conflict of laws," other countries use the more peaceful term, "private international law."[12]

Those working on the current Restatement (Third) of Conflict of Laws[13] are in fact more conscious than their predecessors of the international dimension of conflict of laws. Two members of the ALI, one of them himself a Reporter on the Restatement, have convincingly written of "the importance of international law, and of comparative law, for conflict of laws in general and the new Restatement in particular."[14]

The ALI's first foray into international law proper by means of a Restatement was the 1965 Restatement (Second) of the Foreign Relations Law of the United States, so named because it was produced in what the ALI considered its second

---

[10] Reporter for the *First Conflict of Laws Restatement* was Joseph Beale. On the First Restatement, *see* Lorenzen & Heilman, *The Restatement of the Conflict of Laws*, 83 U. PA. L. REV. 555 (1935); William Richman & David Riley, *The First Restatement of Conflict of Laws on the Twenty-Fifth Anniversary of Its Successor: Contemporary Practice in Traditional Courts*, 56 MD. L. REV. 1196 (1997).

[11] Reporter for the *Second Conflict of Laws Restatement* was Willis L.M. Reese. On the Second Restatement, *see* Traynor, *supra* note 1 at 149–59; Willis L.M. Reese, *Conflict of Laws* and the *Restatement Second*, 28 LAW & CONTEMP. PROB. 679 (1963); Alan D. Weinberger, *Party Autonomy and Choice-of-Law: The Restatement (Second), Interest Analysis, and the Search for a Methodological Synthesis*, 4 HOFSTRA L. REV. 605 (1976); Patrick Borchers, *Courts and the Second Conflicts Restatement: Some Observations and an Empirical Note*, 56 MD. L. REV. 1232 (1997).

[12] Traynor, *supra* note 1, at 157–58.

[13] As of the time of this writing the Restatement (Third) of Conflict of Laws is in progress. Its Reporters are Kermit Roosevelt III, Laura Little, and Christopher Whytock. On the Third Restatement, *see* Lea Brilmayer & Daniel Listwa, *Continuity and Change Is the Draft Restatement (Third) of Conflict of Laws: One Step Forward and Two Steps Back*, to which Reporter Kermit Roosevelt III and Bethan Jones responded, *Yale L.J. Forum* (Oct. 22, 2018); Carlos Vazquez, *Introduction to Symposium on Third Restatement of Conflict of Laws*, 110 AM. J. INT'L L. UNBOUND 137 (2016).

On the Conflict of Laws Restatement, in this volume.

[14] Ralf Michaels & Christopher Whytock, *Internationalizing the New Conflict of Laws Restatement*, 27 DUKE L.J. 349 (2016–2017).

generation of Restatements.[15] Given its unprecedented scope, the Restatement required a large Reporter team, consisting of Adrian Fisher, Noyes Leech, Covey Oliver, Cecil Olmstead, Robert E. Stein, and Joseph Sweeney. Writing about the Restatement, Professor Harold Meier observed that "it was not at all clear that there even was such a field as foreign relations law, and much of the work . . . went into determining which legal areas should be treated and which should not in that undertaking."[16]

Soon enough there could be no doubt that foreign relations *was* a field of law, and 1987 brought the far more comprehensive and systematized Restatement (Third) of the Foreign Relations Law of the United States, a product that excited great interest, and some controversy, in the international law community. Critics in academia,[17] among international law practitioners,[18] and within the ALI itself[19] viewed the Restatement as unduly internationalist in outlook and too quick to embrace customary international law as enforceable federal law. The U.S. State Department was especially alarmed at the Restatement (Third), its interventions triggering what one of the Restatement (Fourth) Reporters has described as an "acrimonious" relationship with the Reporters,[20] as evidenced by the fact that when the Restatement (Third) had been completed, the State Department reportedly pressed the ALI to postpone its publication.

The Restatement came in for particularly severe criticism by Supreme Court Justice Antonin Scalia in the case of *United States v. Stuart*, in which he objected to reliance in treaty interpretation on preratification materials, observing that the Restatement (Third)'s willingness to consult such materials for purposes of treaty interpretation "must be regarded as a proposal for change, rather than a restatement of existing doctrine, since the commentary refers to not a single case, of this or any other United States court, that has employed the practice."[21]

---

[15] On the Second Restatement of Foreign Relations Law, *see* Daniel Wilkes, *Book Review, Restatement (Second), Foreign Relations Law of the United States*, 18 WESTERN RES. L. REV. 355 (1966).

[16] Harold G. Maier, The Restatement of Foreign Relations Law of the United States, Revised: How Were the Controversies Resolved?, 1981 Proceedings of the Annual Meeting of the American Society of International Law 180 (1987).

[17] Paul B. Stephan, *Courts, the Constitution, and Customary International Law: The Intellectual Origins of the Restatement (Third) of the Foreign Relations Law of the United States*, 44 VA. L. REV. 33 (2003). John B. Houck, *Restatement of the Foreign Relations Law of the United States (Revised): Issues and Resolution*, 1986 INT'L LAWYER 1361 (1986); Rudolf Bernhardt et al.,, *Review, Restatement of the Law Third: The Foreign Relations Law of the United States*, 86 AM. J. INT'L L. 608 (1992).

[18] John B. Houck, *Restatement of the Foreign Relations Law of the United States (Revised): Issues and Resolution*, 1986 INT'L LAWYER 1361 (1986).

[19] *See* Michael Traynor, *The Future of Foreign Relations Law of the United States*, 18 SW. J. INT'L L. 5, 6 (2011).

[20] For a description of the tensions associated with the Restatement (Third), *see* Paul B. Stephan, *Courts, the Constitution and Customary International Law: The Intellectual Origins of the Restatement (Third) of the Foreign Relations Law of the United States*, 44 VA. J. INT'L L. 33 (2003).

[21] 489 U.S. 353, 375 (1989). Of particular concern to Justice Scalia was Restatement Third's § 314, Comment *d* (1987) and § 325, Reporter's Note 5. According to the former, if no statement of understanding accompanies the ratification of a treaty, an understanding can be inferred from "report[s] of the Senate Foreign Relations Committee or . . . Senate debates." According to the latter, relevant to determining the meaning of a treaty are "[c]ommittee reports, debates, . . . [t]he history of the negotiations, . . . [and] internal official correspondence and position papers prepared for use of the United States delegation in the negotiation."

There followed in turn the very recent Restatement (Fourth) of the Foreign Relations Law of the United States, which, appearing in 2018, was the first Restatement (Fourth) to be completed. The production of three successive Foreign Relations Restatements in a relatively short period of time naturally signifies the growing salience of international law cases in the courts of the United States, and in U.S. law more generally, as well as foreign relations law's rapidly evolving character. But it also signifies the ALI's alertness to significant developments in the law, an alertness demonstrated as well across other chapters in this volume. According to the Reporters, the participation of the State Department was considerably more supportive than had been the case with the Restatement (Third). This may be because the drafters of the Restatement (Fourth) were, by the account of one of them, less "aspirational" than their predecessors had been, because State Department personnel participated as advisory committee members on all parts of the Restatement, and because six of the eight Reporters were not only law school professors but also former staffers at the State Department themselves. This is not to say that there were no differences of view. For example, the Reporters thought the department took a distinctively expansive view of executive authority in foreign affairs. Still, by all accounts, the department's role was a decidedly constructive one.

Within a year of the Restatement (Fourth)'s appearance, the ALI approved a first Restatement of the U.S. Law of International Commercial and Investor-State Arbitration. The State Department contributed importantly to this Restatement as well, but—unsurprisingly in light of the subject—with scarcely any ideological overtones.

In content, the foreign relations and international arbitration law Restatements obviously deal with international subject matter. Even so, their focus is decidedly on the treatment of those subjects in U.S. law and, more particularly, in U.S. courts. In that respect, they are no different from any of the ALI's other Restatements. By contrast, as will be seen, the ALI's Principles of Law go well beyond restating U.S. law.

Still, the foreign relations and international arbitration Restatements are distinctive from many other Restatements in certain ways. They treat matters of federal law and, to one degree or another, are statute- and treaty-based. This is clearest in the case of international arbitration, where the Federal Arbitration Act (FAA) (including its Chapters Two and Three, implementing the New York and Panama Conventions, respectively)[22] stands center stage, even if not field-preemptive of state law.[23] The statutory and treaty elements of foreign relations law are, by comparison, more fragmented, but they too are nevertheless prominent, as exemplified by the Foreign Sovereign Immunities Act[24] and the Hague Service[25] and Evidence[26] Conventions.

---

[22] 9 U.S.C. §§ 9ff.

[23] Kindred Nursing Centers Ltd. Partnership v. Clark, 510 U.S. ___, 137 S. Ct. 1421, 1426 (May 15, 2017). The FAA is conflict-preemptive only. "The FAA thus preempts any state rule discriminating on its face against arbitration [and] displaces any rule that covertly accomplishes the same objective by disfavoring contracts that ... have the defining features of arbitration agreements."

[24] 28 U.S.C. §§ 1330ff.

[25] 20 U.S.T. 361, 658 U.N.T.S. 163 (1965).

[26] 23 U.S.T. 2555, T.I.A.S. 7444, 847 U.N.T.S. 231.

And yet, foreign relations and international arbitration law as fields exhibit the single most important characteristic justifying Restatements of the Law, namely, a sprawling case law in need of substantially greater clarity and coherence. For this reason, the drafting of these Restatements, despite their distinctiveness, followed basically the same goal and methodology that, over the decades and across fields of law, the ALI had perfected.

The following sections examine these two Restatement more closely, with attention to some of their distinctive features and challenges.

A. The Restatements of Foreign Relations Law of the United States

The several foreign relations law Restatements referred to above represent the paradigm of an international law subject as applied and enforced in U.S. courts. As described in the Restatement (Third) of the Foreign Relations Law of the U.S., the Restatement consists of "(a) international law as it applies to the United States; and (b) domestic law that has substantial significance for the foreign relations of the United States or has other substantial international consequences."[27] The Restatement (Third), for which Louis Henkin and Andreas Lowenfeld served as Reporters, was especially broad and far-reaching in coverage, treating in separate parts (I) the relation between international law and U.S. law, (II) persons in international law, (III) treaties and other international agreements, (IV) jurisdiction and judgments, (V) the law of the sea, (VI) the law of the environment, (VII) protection of natural and juridical persons, (VIII) international economic relations, and (IX) remedies for violation of international law. It is best known, and controversially so, particularly for its treatment of the extraterritorial application of U.S. law and its embrace of international comity more generally.[28] The ALI's interest in extraterritoriality has continued, as evidenced by its 2011 conference on the extraterritorial application of the U.S securities law.[29]

With the burgeoning of international law in U.S. courts, the ALI chose, when the time came for a Restatement (Fourth) of Foreign Relations Law of the U.S., to limit the Restatement provisionally to three main topics: jurisdiction, the domestic effect of treaties, and sovereign immunity. Even as limited, due to the explosion of law in the field, this was a massive enterprise, and conducted by the most elaborately structured constellation of Reporters in ALI history: Sarah Cleveland and Paul Stephan as Coordinating Reporters,[30] and Reporters William Dodge and Anthea Roberts (jurisdiction), David Stewart, and Ingrid Wuerth (sovereign immunity), and Curtis Bradley and Edward Swaine (treaties). The 2018 Restatement (Fourth) has drawn

---

[27] RESTATEMENT (THIRD) FOREIGN RELATIONS LAW § 1 (1987).

[28] *See, e.g.*, Austen L. Parrish, *Reclaiming International Law from Extraterritoriality*, 93 MINN. L. REV. 815 (2009); Kathleen Hixson, *Extraterritorial Jurisdiction Under the Third Restatement of Foreign Relations Law of the United States*, 12 FORDHAM INT'L L.J. 127 (1988).

[29] *See generally* Genevieve Beyea, *Transnational Securities Fraud and the Extraterritorial Application of U.S. Securities Laws: Challenges and Opportunities*, 1 GLOBAL BUS. L. REV. 139 (2010).

[30] *See* THE RESTATEMENT AND BEYOND: THE PAST, PRESENT AND FUTURE OF FOREIGN RELATIONS LAW (Sarah Cleveland & Paul Stephan eds., 2020);

considerable interest, reflecting not only a growing consciousness of the field's importance but also the centrality of the Restatement within it.[31]

Unsurprisingly, the features and challenges that make the Restatements of Foreign Relations and International Arbitration Law distinctive are largely traceable to their international pedigree.

1. Distinctive Features of the Foreign Relations Law Restatement

Perhaps the most distinctive feature of the Foreign Relations Law Restatement is the necessity to take into consideration the work of judicial bodies outside the United States. Ignoring the authority of international courts and tribunals in a project on foreign relations law is simply not an option. Nor is it possible, or desirable, to ignore the products of international law-building entities like the International Law Commission, established by the UN General Assembly, or the law and practice in national jurisdictions outside the United States. These bodies set standards, impose constraints or create expectations that inevitably affect, if only indirectly, the margin of maneuver of international law decision makers in the United States.

More generally, the Restatement of Foreign Relations Law stands to have greater implications for foreign governments and persons than any other ALI Restatement. The Reporters of the Restatement (Fourth) needed constantly to determine whether and to what extent those implications should factor into their deliberations and determinations. At the very least, they thought it important to convene on more than one occasion a group of foreign advisers whose insights and experiences could potentially be instructive.

Given the uniqueness of the federal government's interest in U.S. foreign relations, the Foreign Relations Restatement also elicited within the federal government an unprecedented level of interest in, and contribution to, the project. That interest and contribution was heavily concentrated in the single body, the Department of State, chiefly responsible for the conduct of U.S. foreign relations. While the tenor of the Restatement is certainly not to be dictated by the State Department, neither are the department's views to be ignored.

2. Distinctive Challenges of the Foreign Relations Law Restatement

Both of the features just mentioned presented the Reporters of the Foreign Relations Restatement with challenges, but they are not alone in doing so. All fields of law addressed by a Restatement are subject to change, but they are particularly so in the international environment and under circumstances considerably beyond our control. Similarly, while the law in all fields has a political dimension, in foreign relations law that dimension is particularly salient. Among the most divisive issues in foreign relations law in a period of political polarization, is the extent to which the United States should "go its own way" vis-à-vis other nations,[32] with all that that implies.

---

[31] *See generally* Leila Nadya Sadat, *The Proposed Restatement (Fourth) of the Foreign Relations Law of the United States: Treaties—Some Serious Procedural and Substantive Concerns*, 2015 B.Y.U. L. Rev. 1673 (2015); William S. Dodge, *Jurisdiction, State Immunity, and Judgments in the Restatement (Fourth) of US Foreign Relations*, 19 Chinese J. Int'l L. 101 (2020); N.L. Dobson, *Reflections on "Reasonableness" in the Restatement (Fourth) of US Foreign Relations Law*, 62 Q.I.L. 19 (2019).

[32] *See generally* Hilde Eliassen Restad, *Old Paradigms in History Die Hard in Political Science: US Foreign Policy and American Exceptionalism*, 1 A. Pol. Thought 53 (2012); Joseph Lepgold & Timothy McKeown,

Differences in international "outlook" within the United States are especially pro-nounced at the present time. It is exceptionally difficult for Restaters to strike the right balance and, in doing so, avoid the arousal of political passions and escape political attack. As best it could, and in consultation with the Reporters of the Restatement (Fourth), the ALI populated the project's advisory committee with individuals having diverse perspectives. On some issues, the positions taken could be controversial inter-nationally as well.

Reporters on the Foreign Relations Restatement, having participated as Advisers on other projects, report that they found the field especially challenging also due to a combination of three attributes of the project: (1) the multiplicity of sources of law bearing upon U.S. foreign relations, (2) the widely disparate and fragmented issues of which foreign relations law is composed, and (3) the absence of core organizing prin-ciples around which other fields of law are built and from which other Restatements benefit.

In all these respects, the Restatement of the Foreign Relations Law of the U.S. broke new ground.

B. The Restatement of U.S. Law of International Commercial and Investor-State Arbitration

In 2019, there appeared, close on the heels of the Restatement (Fourth) of Foreign Relations Law, a new international law product, the Restatement of the U.S. Law of International Commercial and Investor-State Arbitration,[33] with George Bermann as Reporter and Jack Coe, Christopher Drahozal and Catherine Rogers as Associate Reporters. Unlike the Foreign Relations Restatement, and as its name indicates, the International Arbitration Restatement focused on a specific and well-defined subfield of international law, chosen on account of its rapidly growing prominence and the judiciary's relative lack of experience in the field, but above all the lack of clarity and consistency in the law, the existence of the FAA notwithstanding. This Restatement concerns itself with all situations in which arbitration agreements, arbitral proceed-ings, and arbitral awards come before U.S. courts. It thus covers principally (1) the enforcement or denial of enforcement of agreements to arbitrate, (2) the courts' in-volvement in ongoing arbitral proceedings (as in the grant of interim relief or orders for the production of documents), and (3) post-award proceedings (most promi-nently actions to confirm or vacate awards made in the United States and actions to recognize or enforce awards made outside the United States).

---

110 POL. SCI. Q. 369 (1995); K.J.J. Holsti, *Exceptionalism in American Foreign Policy: Is It Exceptional?*, 17 EUR. J. INT'L REL. 381 (2011).

[33] On the International Arbitration Restatement generally, *see* George Bermann et al., *Restating the U.S. Law of International Commercial Arbitration*, 113 PENN ST. L. REV. 1333 (2009); Tiffany Ng, *Choice of Procedural Law in International Commercial Arbitration: Providing "Proper Notice" to a Foreign Party to Ensure That the Arbitral Award Can Be Enforced*, 10 HASTINGS BUS. L.J. 491 (2014); Peter B. Rutledge, *The Constitutional Law of International Commercial Arbitration*, 38 GA. J. INT'L & COMP. L. 1 (2009).

1. Distinctive Features of the International Arbitration Restatement

A truly distinctive feature of the Restatement of U.S. Law of International Commercial and Investor-State Arbitration is its concern, not with private behavior or the behavior of U.S. government departments and officials but with an adjudicatory system independent of the United States. U.S. courts are called upon to give effect to agreements that vest adjudicatory authority in privately constituted tribunals, to intervene in one fashion or another in those tribunals' proceedings, and above all, to enforce the international arbitral awards they render. U.S. courts thus powerfully affect the efficacy of an international adjudicatory order lying outside the U.S. judicial system. In this respect, the United States is no different from other jurisdictions, but it nonetheless places U.S. courts in an unusual posture.

The delicacy of the task is only heightened by the fact that prominent among the reasons why parties resort to arbitration over litigation is their determination to avoid judicial jurisdiction over their disputes.[34] Striking a sound balance between the authority of arbitral tribunals and national courts is a perennial preoccupation of all who operate in or near the international arbitral arena. Not a year goes by without a case implicating that balance making its way to the U.S. Supreme Court.[35]

2. Distinctive Challenges of the International Arbitration Restatement

All that precedes represent challenges to any effort to restate U.S. international arbitration law. But there are other challenges as well. Those who practice in the international arbitration field constitute a powerful and highly cohesive community that both prizes its high degree of autonomy and acknowledges its accountability, impulses that are constantly in potential tension. Work on the Restatement repeatedly raised the navigational challenge of ensuring, at the same time, both the efficacy and the legitimacy of the international arbitration system. Illustrative are the debates surrounding the question of arbitrators' immunity from civil liability.

A second and not unrelated challenge arises from the fact that the United States operates in a highly competitive environment for the attraction of international arbitration activity. The degree to which a jurisdiction attracts international arbitration business depends in large part on the degree to which it is viewed as "arbitration-friendly."[36] The friendliness of a jurisdiction to arbitration depends in turn on its arbitration legislation and the practice of its courts. A Restatement may play a major part in affecting foreign perceptions in this regard.

---

[34] Daniel M. Kolkey, *Reflections on the U.S. Statutory Framework for International Commercial Arbitration: Its Scope, Its Shortcomings, and the Advantages of U.S. Adoption of the UNCITRAL Model Law*, 1 AM. REV. INT'L ARB. 491 (1990); Dalma R. Demeter & Kayleigh M. Smith, *The Implications of International Commercial Courts on Arbitration*, 33 J. INT'L ARB. 441 (2016).

[35] *See* Suzette Parmley, *How the "Predilection" for Arbitration Is Shaping Supreme Court Case Law*, N.J. L.J., Sept. 24, 2020, https://www.law.com/njlawjournal/2020/09/24/how-the-predilection-for-arbitration-is-shaping-supreme-court-case-law/ (last visited Dec. 29, 2020); Richard Deutsch, Clare Cavaliero Pincoski, & Ian S. Wahrenbrock, *Important Issues Fill International Supreme Court Arbitration Docket*, PILLSBURY ALERT, https://www.pillsburylaw.com/en/news-and-insights/international-arbitration-scotus.html (last visited Dec. 29, 2020).

[36] *See* George A. Bermann, *What Does It Mean to Be Pro-Arbitration?*, 34 ARB. INT'L 341 (2018); Lance Roskens, *Pro-Arbitration Policy: Is This What the Parties Really Intended?*, 2005 J. DISP. RESOL. 1 (2005).

Further complicating the work of the Restatement was the need to deal in a single work with both international commercial arbitration and investor-state arbitration, the former arising out of contract and the latter arising chiefly out of international treaty, as well as allowing for the fundamental differences for U.S. courts between investor-state awards rendered under the auspices of the International Centre for the Settlement of Investments Disputes, on the one hand, and under the auspices of other arbitral institutions or on an ad hoc basis, on the other.

Just as in the case of the Foreign Relations Restatement, both the distinctiveness and the challenges associated with the International Arbitration Restatement reflect the fact that the law being restated is law operating in an international environment.

III. Principles of the Law in the International Law Fields

International law figures at least as prominently in a second important category of ALI products—Principles of the Law—as it does in Restatements of the Law. Like Restatements, Principles unquestionably help render the law clearer and more coherent than it would otherwise be. But they have other emphases and objectives as well.

Some sets of ALI Principles in the international law field deal exclusively with the law produced not by the United States, or any other country for that matter, but rather by international organizations.[37] The ALI takes an interest in such bodies of law if only because international law forms part of U.S. law and is binding upon it.[38]

Other sets of Principles address neither the law as applied in U.S. courts nor the law produced by international organizations. Rather, they deal with *relations* between and among national legal systems, including but not limited to the United States. For want of a better term, projects falling within this second category may best, for reasons explained later, be viewed as projects of a "transnational" nature.

Both set of Principles, as well as other ALI activities associated with them, are examined in the following.

A. Principles of the Law of International Organizations

International law is made in significant part by international organizations in whose creation nation-States participate. Not all international organizations have lawmaking authority. For example, their importance notwithstanding, neither Interpol nor the World Health Organization has lawmaking authority as such. But other international organizations, among them the World Trade Organization (WTO), most certainly do.

---

[37] *See generally* JOSE E. ALVAREZ, INTERNATIONAL ORGANIZATIONS AS LAW-MAKERS (2005).

[38] Ware v. Hylton, 3 U.S. (3 Dall.) 199, 281 (1796) ("When the United States declared their independence, they were bound to receive the law of nations, in its modern state of purity and refinement."); Chisholm v. Georgia, 2 U.S. (2 Dall.) 419, 474 (1793) ("[T]he United States had, by taking a place among the nations of the earth, become amenable to the law of nations.").

The ALI ventured energetically into the law made by international organization in 2001 through its project on *Principles of World Trade Law: The World Trade Organization*, the ultimate goal of which was not only to explicate the somewhat arcane, but important, case law of the WTO, and its predecessor the General Agreement on Tariffs and Trade (GATT) produced between 1948 and 2010, but also to subject that case law to scrutiny. This ambitious project was decidedly interdisciplinary, bringing together five economists (Kyle Bagwell of Columbia and now Stanford, Gene Grossman of Princeton, Henrik Horn of Stockholm, Doug Irwin of Dartmouth, and Robert Staiger of Stanford and now Dartmouth) and two lawyers (Petros C. Mavroidis of Columbia and Alan O. Sykes of Chicago and now Stanford). The project set out first to identify the purposes of the framers of the GATT and WTO, then determine the extent to which WTO case law, both of WTO panels and the Appellate Body, have been faithful to those purposes, and finally, to the extent it was not, explain the deviation and explore correctives. The project yielded a set of annual volumes, edited by Henrik Horn and Petros Mavroidis and published by Cambridge University Press, evaluating the case law of WTO panels and the Appellate Body for the period between 2001 and 2009, with a view to determining whether their rulings "made sense" from both an economic and legal point of view.[39] Among the recommendations to emerge was introduction into the WTO of institutional arrangements for collaboration between lawyers and economists. The work culminated in a 2013 book on *Legal and Economic Principles of World Trade Law*, again edited by Horn and Mavroidis, and published by Cambridge University Press.[40]

B. Principles of Transnational Law

While the ALI is demonstrably interested in the law that emanates from international organizations, it is also interested in law that addresses relations *between and among* nation-states, the United States of course included. The ALI has come to address the study of legal relations *across* jurisdictions—that is, "transnational" as distinct from international law[41]—through two quite different approaches.

A first approach, reflected in a growing number of ALI projects, is premised on the interdependence of national legal systems, in recognition of the fact that, in this age, no legal system can effectively function entirely on its own. In short, understanding how legal systems interact and may improve their interactions is no less important than understanding the law that individual legal systems, such as the United States, produce. The ALI has devoted considerable resources to the problems and prospects for what may be described as "inter-jurisdictional cooperation."

---

[39] https://www.cambridge.org/core/series/american-law-institute-reporters-studies-on-wto-law/4217D 8E1681E117423FB0970E3AC9A28 (last visited Dec. 29, 2020).

[40] https://www.cambridge.org/core/books/legal-and-economic-principles-of-world-trade-law/10E3D A38FA9C71437110B4AED70918F1 (last visited Dec. 29, 2020).

[41] The term "transnational" is variously defined as "going beyond national boundaries." *See* https://www.dictionary.com/browse/transnational; https://www.merriam-webster.com/dictionary/transnational; https://www.lexico.com/en/definition/transnational (last visited Dec. 29, 2020).

Second, states (and their courts) around the world are increasingly facing the same or similar problems and have a distinct interest in addressing them collectively and arriving, to the extent circumstances allow, at common solutions. The ALI has entered onto this terrain as well, devising projects that, in a word, pursue what may be called "common solutions to shared problems."

These two approaches represent distinctly different ways by which the ALI can contribute to the development of transnational law, as I have defined it here, and are best examined separately.

1. The Law of Interjurisdictional Cooperation

National legal systems, and national courts in particular, interact in a number of important ways. States can show restraint in exercising jurisdiction over non-nationals and nonresidents. They can render assistance to one another in the conduct of domestic litigation, for example, in obtaining evidence located abroad. They can limit the extraterritorial application of their own laws and otherwise take other countries' interests into account in their policymaking. They can agree to enforce in their courts the laws of another country and the judgments of another country's courts. They can of course also come into conflict, as through the issuance of anti-suit injunctions seeking to bar parties from pursuing litigation in a foreign court. All these matters of course arose in the three sets of Restatements treated earlier: the Restatements of Conflict of Laws, the Restatements of the Foreign Relations Law of the U.S., and the Restatement of the U.S. Law of international Commercial and Investor-State Arbitration.

However, the ALI has come to address some of these issues more frontally in the form of Principles of the Law, the exemplar of which is the product entitled Intellectual Property: Principles Governing Jurisdiction, Choice of Law, and Judgments in Transnational Disputes (2008), for which Jane Ginsburg and Rochelle Dreyfus served as Reporters.[42] In the ALI's own words:

> This is a set of Principles on jurisdiction, recognition of judgments, and applicable law in transnational intellectual property civil disputes, drafted in a manner that endeavors to balance civil-law and common-law approaches. The digital networked environment is increasingly making multiterritorial simultaneous communication of works of authorship, trade symbols, and other intellectual property a common phenomenon, and large-scale piracy ever easier to accomplish.... Without a mechanism for consolidating global claims and recognizing foreign judgments, effective enforcement of intellectual property rights, and by the same token, effective defenses to those claims, may be illusory for all but the most wealthy litigants.[43]

---

[42] On these Principles, see generally Marketa Trimble, Advancing National Intellectual Property Policies in a Transnational Context, 74 MD. L. REV. 203 (2015); Andrew F. Christie, Private International Law Principles for Ubiquitous Intellectual Property Infringement—A Solution in Search of a Problem, 13 J. PRIV. INT'L L. 152 (2017); Rochelle Dreyfuss, The ALI Principles on Transnational Intellectual Property Disputes: Why Invite Conflicts?, 30 BROOK. J. INT'L L. 819 (2005); Francois Dessemontet, A European Point of View on the ALI Principles—Intellectual Property: Principles Governing Jurisdiction, Choice of Law, and Judgments in Transnational Disputes, 30 BROOK. J. INT'L L. 849 (2005).

[43] https://www.wipo.int/edocs/lexdocs/laws/en/us/us218en-part1.pdf (last visited Dec. 29, 2020).

The ALI approached the same general topic through a very different vehicle in its project on Recognition and Enforcement of Foreign Judgments: Analysis and Proposed Federal Statute,[44] produced by Andreas Lowenfeld and Linda Silberman. Although the project's initial impetus was the drafting of a federal statute to implement a potential Hague Jurisdiction and Judgments Convention, it was clear by the time the project got underway that no Convention was forthcoming. Even so, the ALI authorized continuing work on a federal statute on recognition and enforcement of foreign country judgments in light of the desirability of having a uniform federal regime in this area of the law. (The existing law varies from state to state, notwithstanding the existence of a Uniform Act on the subject.) On the agenda were also international *lis pendens* and provisional measures in aid of foreign proceedings.

This project culminated in a draft federal statute designed to implement the then contemplated Hague Convention on the Recognition and Enforcement of Foreign Judgments. Although that treaty did not come to be and implementation was thus not needed, the draft legislation has influenced the literature and practice of international civil procedure. In fact, the enactment of federal legislation on the subject should not be contingent on the United States' entry into a treaty, and Congress has shown at least some interest in enacting such a statute, even in the absence of a treaty and any need for implementing legislation. In 2011, a House of Representatives committee heard testimony from Reporter Linda Silberman urging congressional consideration of the ALI proposed federal statute, or something along the same lines, on the ground that "it will provide a Federal uniform standard for recognition and enforcement in foreign judgments in the United States and [have] the potential to enhance recognition and enforcement of U.S. judgments in other countries."[45] In 2019, a new Hague Convention on the subject of judgment recognition and enforcement was signed,[46] and the possibility that the ALI will return to the project of drafting federal implementing legislation cannot be excluded.[47]

2. Law as Common Solutions to Shared Problems
A second set of the ALI's "transnational" projects studies the prospects for coordination among national legal systems in addressing legal problems they have in common, with a view to law reform and/or legal harmonization across jurisdictions. Perhaps the earliest and best known are the Principles of Transnational Civil Procedure, headed by Geoffrey Hazard, former Director of the ALI, and Michele Taruffo, produced in 2006 in partnership with the International Institute for the Unification of

---

[44] On the project, *see generally* Linda J. Silberman & Andreas F. Lowenfeld, *A Different Challenge for the ALI: Herein of Foreign Country Judgments, an International Treaty, and an American Statute,* 75 IND. L.J. 635 (2000); Yuliya Zeynalova, *The Law on Recognition and Enforcement of Foreign Judgments: Is It Broken and How Do We Fix It?,* 31 BERKELEY J. INT'L L. 150 (2013).

[45] Hearing before the Subcommittee on Courts, Commercial and Administrative Law of the Committee on the Judiciary, House of Representative, 112th Cong, 1str Sess. (Nov, 15, 2011), *available at* https://www.govinfo.gov/content/pkg/CHRG-112hhrg71239/html/CHRG-112hhrg71239.htm (last visited Dec. 30, 2020).

[46] Hague Convention on the Recognition and Enforcement of Foreign Judgments in Civil or Commercial Matter (July 2, 2019), *available at* https://www.hcch.net/en/instruments/conventions/full-text/?cid=137 (last visited Dec. 30, 2020).

[47] 9 U.S.C. §§ 9ff.

Private Law (UNIDROIT).[48] The intent was to establish principles for the conduct of transnational litigation, bridging the common law/civil law divide, that could become an international standard incorporated in the procedural law of jurisdictions worldwide, as well as in the practice of international arbitration. The ALI conceived of the work as "reduc[ing] uncertainty for parties litigating in unfamiliar surroundings and promot[ing] fairness in judicial proceedings."[49] The ALI later built on that achievement by taking part in a recent project on transnational civil procedure presented at the 2019 General Assembly of the European Law Institute (about which more later) in Vienna.[50] That enterprise, which as of this writing is ongoing, contemplates adoption of European Rules of Civil Procedure, with an initial focus on case management, pleadings, evidence, collective redress, and appeals.

The ALI pursued much the same purpose in connection with more particular substantive and procedural issues. The single substantive law issue receiving greatest attention was international insolvency, a project that, like the WTO Principles, proceeded in stages.[51] Initially, Jay Westbrook examined the conduct of cross-border bankruptcy proceedings among the then NAFTA countries, with a view to establishing common ground and shared principles among the three countries. The initiative resulted in the ALI's publication of *Transnational Insolvency Cooperation among the NAFTA Countries* (2003).

Thereafter, jointly with the International Insolvency Institute (III), the ALI went on to produce *Global Principles for Cooperation in International Insolvency Cases* (2012),[52] on which Ian Fletcher, Bob Wessels, and Jay Westbrook took the lead, with the purpose of expanding the learning and recommendations of the NAFTA project to relations with and among other countries around the world. The principles have since been endorsed by the National Conference of Bankruptcy Judges, the National Bankruptcy Conference, and the Canadian Judicial Council.[53]

Without doubt, the single most important procedural issue of international dimensions receiving the ALI's attention was aggregate litigation. Under the leadership of Reporter Sam Issacharoff and Associate Reporters Robert Klonoff, Richard Nagareda, and Charles Silver, the ALI identified common solutions to common problems in the conduct of aggregate litigation, both the advantages and complexities of which

---

[48] *See* Geoffrey C. Hazard Jr. & Michele Taruffo, *Transnational Rules of Civil Procedure Rules and Commentary*, 30 CORNELL INT'L L.J. 493 (1997); *See also* Rolf Stürner, *The Principles of Transnational Civil Procedure: An Introduction to Their Basic Conceptions*, 69 RABEL J. COMP. & INT'L PRIVATE L. 201 (2005); H. Patrick Glenn, *The ALI/UNIDROIT Principles of Transnational Civil Procedure as Global Standards for Adjudication?*, 9 UNIF. L. REV. 829 (2004).

[49] *See* https://www.ali.org/publications/show/transnational-civil-procedure/.

[50] *See* https://www.europeanlawinstitute.eu/projects-publications/completed-projects/completed-proje cts-sync/civil-procedure (last visited Dec. 30, 2022).

[51] The NAFTA Cooperation project formed part of the ALI's Transnational Insolvency project, co-sponsored by the International Insolvency Institute.

[52] The Global Principles for Cooperation in International Insolvency Cases formed part of the ALI's Transnational Insolvency project, co-sponsored by the International Insolvency Institute. On the *Global Principles, see* Bob Wessels, *English and American Courts Apply Global Principles for Cooperation in International Cases*, LEIDENLAWBLOG (Oct. 28, 2013), *available at* https://leidenlawblog.nl/articles/engl ish-and-american-courts-apply-global-principles-for-cooperation-in-inte (last visited Dec. 30, 2020); Ian F. Fletcher & Bob Wessels, *A Final Step in Shaping Rules for Cooperation in International Insolvency Cases*, 9 INT'L CORP. RESCUE 283 (2012).

[53] https://www.ali.org/publications/show/transnational-insolvency/.

Note : Photos courtesy of the American Law Institute archives except where noted.

Plate I The American Law Institute's first annual banquet (1923)

Plate II William Draper Lewis (ALI Director 1923–1947)

Plate III Benjamin N. Cardozo (ALI Vice President 1923–1932)

Plate IV Samuel Williston (Restatement of the Law, Contracts Reporter) with draft manuscript and notes for his treatise on contracts. Reproduced with the permission of the Harvard Law School Library, Historical & Special Collections.

Plate V Joseph H. Beale (Reporter, Restatement of the Law, Conflict of Laws)

Plate VI Restatement of the Law, Security Committee outside of the home of
William Draper Lewis (1937)

Plate VII William Lloyd Prosser (Reporter, Restatement of the Law Second, Torts)

Plate VIII Karl Llewellyn (Chief Reporter, Uniform Commercial Code)

Plate IX Soia Mentschikoff (Assistant Reporter, Uniform Commercial Code)

Plate X Herbert Wechsler (ALI Director 1962–1984)

Plate XI E. Allan Farnsworth (Reporter, Restatement of the Law Second, Contracts)

Plate XII Chief Justice of the United States John G. Roberts Jr. presents the Henry J. Friendly medal to Associate Justice Ruth Bader Ginsburg (2018 ALI Annual Meeting)

Plate XIII The American Law Institute's 75th Annual Meeting (1989)

Plate XIV Former ALI Deputy Director Stephanie A. Middleton with Restatement of the Law, The U.S. Law of International Commercial and Investor-State Arbitration Reporter George A. Bermann and Associate Reporters Jack J. Coe, Catherine A. Rogers, and Christopher R. Drahozal (project meeting 2016)

Plate XV Principles of the Law, Policing Adviser J. Scott Thomson (project meeting 2016)

Plate XVI Principles of the Law, Policing Reporter Barry Friedman and Associate Reporter Tracey L. Meares (project meeting 2017)

Plate XVII ALI Council Member Ketanji Brown Jackson (2018 ALI Council Meeting)

Plate XVIII Deborah A. DeMott (Reporter, Restatement of the Law Third, Agency)

Plate XIX   ALI President David F. Levi (2018 ALI Council Meeting)

Plate XX   Restatement of the Law, The Law of American Indians Reporter Matthew L.M. Fletcher, Wenona T. Singel, and Kaighn Smith Jr. (2018 ALI Annual Meeting)

Plate XXI Restatement of the Law, The Law of American Indians Adviser Leondra Krueger (project meeting 2018)

Plate XXII Stephanie A. Middleton, Kenneth C. Frazier, Guy Miller Struve, and Roberta Cooper Ramo (Restatement of the Law, Corporate Governance project meeting 2019)

Plate XXIII ALI Past President Roberta Cooper Ramo (2019 Annual Meeting)

Plate XXIV ALI Council Member Wallace B. Jefferson with Restatement of the Law, Copyright Reporter Christopher Jon Sprigman and Associate Reporter R. Anthony Reese (ALI Council Meeting 2019)

Plate XXV ALI Director Richard L. Revesz, Council Member Troy A. McKenzie, and Restatement of the Law, Children and the Law Reporter Elizabeth S. Scott and Associate Reporters Emily Buss, Solangel Maldonado, and David D. Meyer (ALI Council Meeting 2019)

Plate XXVI ALI Council Member Conrad K. Harper (2017 ALI Annual Meeting)

Plate XXVII ALI Council Member Carol F. Lee accepts the Distinguished Service Award (2019 Annual Meeting)

were of growing interest worldwide. The result was the ALI's Principles of Aggregate Litigation.[54] The Reporters defined the term "aggregate litigation" broadly to encompass not only class actions but a wide range of other modes in which cases may be bundled together for trial and/or settlement, with a view to identifying the kind of cases to which the various modes best lend themselves. The Principles, which are addressed to judges, legislators, and counsel in making sound aggregation decisions and in effectively managing cases in which aggregation occurs, not only excited great interest but stimulated further discussion and debate on a grand scale.[55]

Just as the ALI amplified its work on principles of international civil procedure by commissioning the drafting of a federal statute on the recognition and enforcement of foreign judgments, so too did it amplify its work on international cooperation and harmonization of law through means other than production of a set of principles. In this case, that other means was activity on the international law conference circuit. At a 2016 conference on Doing Business Across Asia: Legal Convergence in an Asian Century, which launched the Asian Business Law Institute,[56] former ALI President Michael Traynor addressed the question, "How Could a Set of Uniform Asian Rules Take Shape? Would the UNIDROIT Principles Be Useful?"

IV. The International Influence of the ALI

Besides greatly enriching its portfolio of activity, the ALI's turn to international law subjects has inured to its and the international legal community's benefit in other important, if collateral, ways.[57]

The membership of the ALI has always, understandably, been comprised of U.S.-based judges, academics, and practitioners. However, the numbers of non-U.S.-based members in all three categories have grown of late, as has their active participation in specific ALI projects, mostly those of international dimension. They represent a growing ALI asset, particularly in the development of Principles of Law that are of interest outside as well as within the United States. Less obvious would seem to be the contribution of foreign jurists to the ALI Restatements of U.S. Law. But their activity in connection with Restatements is also observable, whether as members' consultative group participants, advisory committee members and even, albeit on rare occasions, Reporter.

---

[54] *See generally* Sam Issacharoff et al., *The ALI's New Principles of Aggregate Litigation*, 8 J.L. ECON. & POL'Y 183 (2011); Samuel Issacharoff, *The Governance Problem in Aggregate Litigation*, 81 FORD. L. REV. FORDHAM L. REV. 3165 (2013).

   On the Principles of Aggregate Litigation, in this volume.

[55] Roger H. Trangsrud, *Aggregate Litigation Reconsidered*, 79 GEO. WASH. L. REV. 293 (2011) (collecting fifteen articles analyzing and evaluating different aspects of the project, and charting further evolution on the subject); Nancy J. Moore, *The Absence of Legal Ethics in the ALI's Principles of Aggregate Litigation: A Missed Opportunity—And More*, 79 GEO. WASH. L. REV. 717 (2010).

[56] *See* https://law.asia/event/doing-business-across-asia-legal-convergence-in-an-asian-century/ (last visited Dec. 30, 2020); http://www.mylegaladvisor.in/conference-on-legal-convergence-in-asia/ (last visited Dec. 30, 2020).

[57] *See generally* Michael Traynor, *The First Restatements and the Vision of the American Law Institute, Then and Now*, 32 S. ILL. U. L.J. 145, 146 (2007).

Independent of the growth in non-U.S. members, the ALI's international law work stands to bring comparative law as well into the equation. This was very much the hope of Michael Traynor, who wrote some twenty years ago in connection with the Restatements of Conflict of Laws:

> The U.S. law of conflict of laws has not been marked by serious, sustained, and wide-spread attention to comparative law. The international implications of our law, however, are growing rapidly. We have much to learn from foreign countries. When the principles are substantially the same or in harmony, that fact alone can reinforce a sense that the domestic principle is an acceptable one. When the principles are different, that fact can prompt a reexamination of the domestic principle. That reexamination may lead to a reinforcement of the domestic principle or a modification of it in light of the teaching of comparative law.[58]

***

> ... The international implications of commercial transactions, intellectual property, employment by multijurisdictional entities, torts, privacy, and various subjects are increasing. We can no longer afford to resolve such issues with approaches based on precepts that are rooted in old problems such as guest statutes (giving nonpaying guests the right to sue a negligent driver) or statutes limiting the contractual rights of married women or on parochial perspectives limited to the United States or particular states in the United States. We need to educate each other on comparative law principles and pull together to find the best principles and approaches that offer the promise of commanding wide acceptance.[59]

Reporters have developed a corresponding urge to bring a comparative law dimension to the Restatements, if only in the Reporters' Notes. This is not a new idea. Michael Traynor advocated this very move as well:

> [T]he ALI is making an effort to enhance its comparative law analysis in traditional projects. In particular, we are asking our Reporters to consider pertinent laws and approaches in other countries and to cite them in the Reporters' Notes. Even in such largely domestic subjects as restitution and unjust enrichment, agency, and property, the analysis will be enriched by such efforts. The ALI's work products may also become even more useful to practitioners, courts and scholars in the United States as well as in foreign countries. Moreover, in developing subjects such as employment law, privacy, international intellectual property, and torts that implicate more than one country, it has become increasingly relevant and important to know more about the law of other countries. This development will also lead to greater involvement of

---

[58] Michael Traynor, *Conflict of Laws, Comparative Law, and the American Law Institute*, 49 AM. J. COMP. L. 391, 395 (2001).
[59] *Id.* at 403.

foreign judges, scholars, and practitioners in ALI's work and corresponding enrichment of the final product.[60]

The work of Reporters is of course onerous, and taking this path would heighten the burden considerably. But there are ways in which the burden may be shared by overseas ALI members who would almost certainly welcome the opportunity to contribute in this effort, and in the process strengthen their connection with the ALI. The more the ALI ventures into comparative law, as well as international law, the greater the exposure and prominence it will enjoy among foreign audiences, whether judicial, academic, or practitioner.

At the same time, the ALI's international law activities have fostered fuller engagement by the U.S. government in the activities of the ALI. The Foreign Relations and International Arbitration Restatements in particular have engaged the Department of State in the work of the ALI as never before, with ALI members, notably Jeffrey Kovar, Mary Catherine Malin, and Michael Mattler taking leading parts in the recent Restatement (Fourth) of the Foreign Relations Law of the U.S. and the Restatement of the U.S. Law of International Commercial and Investor-State Arbitration. The State Department's involvement was naturally aided by the presence of current and past Legal Advisers in the ALI Council, among them John Bellinger, Conrad Harper, and Harold Koh, and by the presence in ALI membership and among Reporters of current and past International Law Counselors at the Department. ALI member and frequent Adviser on Restatement projects, Peter Trooboff, has at the same time generated important ties with the American Society of International Law.

As the discussion of projects earlier in this chapter documents, inclusion of international law subjects on the ALI agenda has also opened up substantial possibilities for cooperation with foreign and international legal institutions,[61] of which UNIDROIT is only one example. It is doubtful that the prospering of international partnerships with overseas entities into which the ALI has entered would have been achieved had the ALI not itself moved as it has into international law domains.

Especially worthy of mention is the ALI's working relationship with the European Law Institute (ELI), based in Vienna, Austria. Establishment of the ELI was inspired and facilitated in large measure by the ALI example, and ALI members, including Lance Liebman and George Bermann, were active in the ELI's founding. As of this writing, a joint ALI-ELI project on Principles for a Data Economy is well underway, with Neil Cohen and Christiane Wendehorst as Reporters for the ALI and ELI, respectively. As the ELI has written, "[w]ith the rise of an economy in which data is a tradeable asset globally, more certainty is needed with regard to the legal rules that are applicable to the transactions in which data is an asset." In its pursuit of greater clarity and certainty in the law, the project corresponds perfectly to the ALI's fundamental and time-honored objectives. At the same time, the project exemplifies the ALI's commitment to the search for common solutions to shared problems, recognized earlier in this chapter.

---

[60] *Id.* at 402–03.
[61] Traynor, *supra* note 19, at 6–7.

Restatements and Principles do not exhaust the means by which the ALI can tackle international law subjects. Reference has already been made to the ALI's 1945 Statement of Essential Human Rights,[62] its Proposed Federal Statute on Recognition and Enforcement of Foreign Judgments,[63] its participation in the ELI project on European Rules of Civil Procedure,[64] its conferences on Doing Business Across Asia: Legal Convergence in an Asian Century[65] and its work on the extraterritorial application of the U.S. securities laws.[66] Going forward, further expansion in the modes of the ALI's engagement with international law is to be expected.

Given the ever greater consciousness of U.S. law's connectedness to other parts of the world, there can be little doubt that the ALI's engagement with international law in its many manifestations will continue to grow apace.[67] International law is firmly and solidly part of the ALI profile.

---

[62] *See supra* notes 2–6, and accompanying text.
[63] *See supra* note 46, and accompanying text.
[64] *See supra* note 52, and accompanying text.
[65] *See supra* note 58, and accompanying text.
[66] *See supra* note 30, and accompanying text.
[67] *Id.* at 8–9.

11

Constructing a Legal Field

The Restatement of the Law Governing Lawyers

W. Bradley Wendel[*]

I. Introduction

I begin my student textbook on Professional Responsibility with an epigram from Isaiah Berlin: "Everything is what it is, and not another thing."[1] But what is this thing called the law governing lawyers, and how is it different from other things? The development of an area of law governing lawyers is a story of the gradual coalescing of a body of positive law, with characteristic legal problems and principles, and a sufficiently coherent relationship among them to constitute a unified field. Cornell Law School Professor Charles Wolfram, the Reporter for the American Law Institute's (ALI's) Restatement of the Law Governing Lawyers, published a paper during the preliminary stages of the project in which he wondered out loud whether there was any deep relationship among the diverse strands of law bearing on the conduct of lawyers:

> [I]t is questionable whether the task may be defined so that the restatement avoids surveying unrelated legal precepts linked only by virtue of the appearance of lawyers as incidental actors. Or is there a logical way in which the regulation of lawyers can be said to cohere?[2]

In addition to the problem of a hodgepodge of legal principles, there was the perennial issue of the relationship between positive law and ethics in the regulation of the conduct of lawyers. To further complicate matters, the word "ethics" itself was historically

[*] Edwin H. Woodruff Professor of Law, Cornell Law School. I gratefully acknowledge the research funding provided by the Judge Albert Conway Memorial Fund for Legal Research, established by the William C. and Joyce C. O'Neil Charitable Trust. Considerable thanks are owed to Bob Gordon and Andrew Gold for their organizing and editorial work and to the participants in the conference on draft chapters for their very helpful suggestions.

[1] Isaiah Berlin, *Two Concepts of Liberty, in* THE PROPER STUDY OF MANKIND 191, 197 (Henry Hardy ed., 1997) (alluding to the Preface to JOSEPH BUTLER, FIFTEEN SERMONS PREACHED AT THE ROLLS CHAPEL (1765)).

[2] Charles W. Wolfram, *The Concept of a Restatement of the Law Governing Lawyers*, 1 GEO. J. LEGAL ETHICS 195, 197–98 (1987). Other prominent legal ethics scholars shared Wolfram's concern. Ted Schneyer, for example, doubted that the law governing lawyers was any more intellectually coherent than the law governing securities brokers. *See* Ted Schneyer, *The ALI's Restatement and the ABA's Model Rules: Rivals or Complements*, 46 OKLA. L. REV. 25, 25 (1993). *See also* Geoffrey C. Hazard Jr., *Rules of Legal Ethics: The Drafting Task*, 36 REC. ASS'N B. CITY N.Y. 77, 79–80 (1981) (observing that, in the early history of the regulation of lawyers, the three principal problems of forensic misconduct, intraprofessional competition, and preserving client confidence, were "widely separated, both analytically and functionally").

W. Bradley Wendel, *Constructing a Legal Field* In: *The American Law Institute*. Edited by: Andrew S. Gold and Robert W. Gordon, Oxford University Press. © Oxford University Press 2023. DOI: 10.1093/oso/9780197685341.003.0012

associated with professional self-regulation by the organized bar, statements of aspiration or ideals sometimes embodied in codes of conduct for lawyers, and concepts from moral philosophy as applied to the practice of law. Unsurprisingly, coherence among these competing sources of authority can be elusive.

The Restatement was pivotal in establishing the law governing lawyers as the thing that it is, and not another thing. It clarified that the most important principles of ethics in the field often known as legal ethics are immanent within the positive law regulating the legal profession, not proclaimed by bar leaders on ceremonial occasions or offered by moral philosophers as a critique of the lawyer's role. It distanced itself from the self-regulatory aspect of professional codes of conduct, which sought to establish normative primacy for the organized bar. More controversially, the Restatement pushed back, if only very gently, on a conception of the lawyer's role as oriented primarily around the interests of clients, not the public interest or respect for law. Again quoting Professor Wolfram, beginning in the late nineteenth century, "lawyers apparently shifted their official explanation of their role from one of law guardian to that of client guardian."[3] While the Restatement did not decisively re-establish the "law guardian" ideal, it took sides in a debate centered on the duties of lawyers whose clients used their services to engage in criminal or fraudulent activity.[4]

My contention is that the Restatement's position on this and other issues makes progress in harmonizing the "law guardian" and "client guardian" ideals by showing how the fiduciary principle of loyal, competent, and diligent representation of clients is compatible with an overarching obligation of fidelity to law. There remains some tension, however, between the profession's own self-conception and the expectation that the wider political community have for lawyers. In the history of the professional regulation project, the Watergate scandal is regarded as a turning point. Important legal principles regarding the response by lawyers to evidence of client wrongdoing were developed in the wake of the early 2000s' financial accounting scandals involving companies like Enron. More recently, the involvement of some lawyers in the efforts to interfere with the peaceful transition of authority to President Joe Biden serves as a focal point for public criticism of lawyers and for debate over the extent to which lawyers should see themselves as having robust "law guardian" duties.

Appreciating the Restatement project and its normative commitments requires situating it within the history of regulation of the legal profession in the United States. Much of this history involves the evolution of standards of conduct prepared by the American Bar Association (ABA), which has long dominated lawyer regulation. While it is true that the ALI is a latecomer to lawyer regulation, however, the Restatement now occupies a position on a par with the ABA Model Rules of Professional Conduct in the field of legal ethics and professional responsibility. Because of the importance of the ABA in early lawyer-regulatory efforts, section II describes how the ABA's sought to accommodate the distinct domains of ethics and law in the emerging field. This problem recurred in the Restatement drafting process, as described in section

---

[3] Charles W. Wolfram, *Toward a History of the Legalization of American Legal Ethics—II: The Modern Era*, 15 GEO. J. LEGAL ETHICS 205, 208 (2002).

[4] *See, e.g.*, Fred C. Zacharias, *Fact and Fiction in the Restatement of the Law Governing Lawyers: Should the Confidentiality Provisions Restate the Law*, 6 GEO. J. LEGAL ETHICS 903 (1993).

III. The sometimes constructive tension between law and ethics was resolved by the Restatement drafters decisively in favor of viewing the regulation of lawyers as a task to be committed to positive law, comprised of common law doctrines, court rules, statutes, and regulations—a far cry from its beginning as a subject for reflection, inspiration, and occasional fraternal enforcement. However, as explained in section IV, the result is not a document detached from ethics but one animated by a characteristic ethical stance. The question for the Restatement and the regulation of lawyers going forward is whether that ethical stance will respond sufficiently to the demands placed by the public on the legal profession. One response, considered briefly in section V, is that positive law, as represented by the Restatement, does not exhaust the field of norms governing lawyers, and that what might be called "ethics beyond the law" remains an essential part of the normative landscape of lawyering.

II. The American Bar Association and the Evolution of the Regulation of Lawyers

For much of the history of the American legal profession, lawyers were regulated only episodically after being admitted to practice, mostly with respect to their fees, solicitation of clients, and occasional gross misconduct before a tribunal.[5] There were no formal codes of conduct or "ethics" rules in effect until 1908.[6] However, in 1905, President Theodore Roosevelt gave a commencement address at Harvard University in which he criticized the "most influential and most highly remunerated members" of the legal profession for providing assistance to clients to enable them to "evade the laws which are made to regulate in the interest of the public the use of great wealth."[7] The ABA, a relatively recently formed social club of elite lawyers,[8] reacted with alarm to Roosevelt's speech. Concerned that the president's progressive regulatory agenda might encompass the legal profession, the ABA resolved to promulgate a code of conduct suitable to the vocation of lawyers as "high priests at the shrine of justice."[9] The resulting Canons of Ethics were intended to guide the education and professional socialization of lawyers, with the ultimate aim of resisting the forces of commercialization that threatened to "reduce our high calling to the level of a trade, to a mere means of livelihood or of personal aggrandizement."[10] The content of the Canons borrowed heavily from an 1817 book on "professional deportment" by David Hoffman, a Baltimore law professor, and lectures given in 1854 by George Sharswood,

---

[5] *See* Charles W. Wolfram, *Toward a History of the Legalization of American Legal Ethics—I. Origins*, 8 U. Chi. L. Sch. Roundtable 469 (2001); Hazard, *supra* note 3, at 78–79.

[6] *See* James M. Altman, *Considering the A.B.A.'s 1908 Canons of Ethics*, 71 Fordham L. Rev. 2395, 2399 (2003).

[7] Theodore Roosevelt, *The Harvard Spirit* (June 28, 1905), *in* IV Presidential Addresses and State Papers 407, 419–20 (1910), *quoted in* Charles M. Yablon, *The Lawyer as Accomplice: Cannabis, Uber, Airbnb, and the Ethics of Advising "Disruptive" Businesses*, 104 Minn. L. Rev. 309, 325 n.77 (2019).

[8] Altman, *supra* note 7, at 2402.

[9] *Id.* at 2412 (*quoting* Lucien Hugh Alexander, *Some Admissions Requirements Considered Apart From Educational Standards*, 28 A.B.A. Rep. 619 (1905)).

[10] *Id.*

a Pennsylvania judge.[11] Hoffman and Sharswood relied on exhortation and repeated catechetical reading to influence behavior,[12] largely because there was in the nineteenth century no effective institutional apparatus for policing the conduct of lawyers.[13] In this regulatory vacuum, the ABA hoped to create a normative world that could function as a kind of law, independent from the law of the state,[14] and thereby to preserve the autonomy of the profession from external regulation and enhance the social prestige and economic returns of lawyers.[15]

By themselves, the Canons were backed by no regulatory authority.[16] The ABA was, and remains, nothing more than a private association pursuing the interests, economic and otherwise, of its members. For this reason, ABA-promulgated rules have frequently been criticized as self-interested,[17] possibly in contrast with Restatement provisions adopted by the more impartial ALI. Nevertheless, courts occasionally made reference to the Canons in the course of exercising the inherent authority they have always possessed to regulate admission to practice and the conduct of lawyers appearing before tribunals.[18] Although it would take decades (not until the 1960s and 70s) for this development to fully ripen,[19] the use of the Canons to illuminate standards of care owed by lawyers under independently existing common law doctrines foreshadowed the increase in importance, relative to disciplinary enforcement, of malpractice litigation and motions to disqualify counsel for conflicts of interest. As the law of lawyering was slowly developing in the courts, the ABA came around to a new approach to codes of conduct. No longer would the role of the ABA's official statements be solely to inspire lawyers to live up to the highest aspirations of their professional calling. Instead, they would be proposed as legally binding disciplinary standards, to be adopted and enforced by state courts. The paradigm shift from hortatory precepts to authoritative standards for professional discipline occurred in the transition from the Canons to the ABA's 1969 Model Code of Professional Responsibility.[20]

The distinctive feature of the Model Code reflected the contested nature of the regulation of lawyer conduct by both law and ethics. The Code was divided into three types of norms: first ethical precepts stated at a high level of generality, retaining the name "Canons"; then somewhat more specific formulations of ethical ideals, called Ethical Considerations (ECs); and finally, Disciplinary Rules (DRs) stating mandatory duties, the violation of which would subject a lawyer to professional discipline.[21]

---

[11] See, e.g., Michael S. Ariens, American Legal Ethics in an Age of Anxiety, 40 St. Mary's L.J. 343, 349–51 (2008); Russell G. Pearce, Rediscovering the Republican Origins of the Legal Ethics Codes, 6 Geo. J. Legal Ethics 241 (1992); Stephen E. Kalish, David Hoffman's Essay on Professional Deportment and the Current Legal Ethics Debate, 61 Neb. L. Rev. 54 (1982).

[12] As David Luban and Michael Millemann point out, the term "canon" alludes to the distinction between sacred texts included in the Bible and extracanonical or apocryphal texts. See David Luban & Michael Millemann, Good Judgment: Ethics Teaching in Dark Times, 9 Geo. J. Legal Ethics 31, 45 (1995).

[13] Kalish, supra note 12, at 63.

[14] See Susan P. Koniak, The Law Between the Bar and the State, 70 N.C. L. Rev. 1392, 1402–04 (1992).

[15] Deborah L. Rhode, Why the ABA Bothers: A Functional Perspective on Ethics Codes, 59 Tex. L. Rev. 689, 690–94 (1981).

[16] Wolfram, supra note 6, at 484–85.

[17] Richard L. Abel, Why Does the ABA Promulgate Ethical Rules?, 59 Tex. L. Rev. 639, 653–67 (1981).

[18] Geoffrey C. Hazard Jr., The Future of Legal Ethics, 100 Yale L.J. 1239, 1254 & n.77 (1991).

[19] Wolfram, supra note 4, at 214–16.

[20] Hazard, supra note 19, at 1251–52.

[21] Hazard, supra note 3, at 81–82; Luban & Millemann, supra note 13, at 44.

The structure and content of the Model Code was intended to respond to the reasons why lawyers and professional regulators might care about the distinction between law and ethics. The incorporation of ECs and DRs in the same document seemed like a way to have the best of both normative worlds.[22] Yet it did not take long before the Model Code was widely perceived as a failed experiment. The EC/DR dichotomy was not as neat in practice as it was in theory. Disciplinary agencies and state bar ethics committees differed in their interpretive approaches, with some using the language of ECs to interpret, or even expand, the mandatory duties stated in the DRs.[23] Numerous gaps in the coverage of the Model Code encouraged interpreters to see the ECs and even the higher-level Canons as the starting point for crafting new duties. More importantly, public dissatisfaction was also building about the organized profession's failure to do much about lawyer misconduct.[24]

The Watergate scandal featured the direct participation of numerous lawyers, including John Dean, John Ehrlichman, and Egil "Bud" Krogh, in the wrongdoing and subsequent cover-up.[25] The public not unreasonably drew the conclusion that there was something wrong with the ethics of lawyers. Otherwise, why did they fail to appreciate the ethical implications of assisting Richard Nixon's cover-up? Dean and Krogh both noted the lack of any serious law school course on legal ethics. Krogh said, "In law school, I took this curious course on ethics. But there was nothing about conflicts or the role of lawyers. We were in completely unknown territory. I was completely unprepared."[26] Dean similarly observed the absence of guidance: "In 1972, legal ethics boiled down to 'don't lie, don't cheat, don't steal and don't advertise.' When I took the elective course in ethics at law school, it was one-quarter of a credit. Legal ethics and professionalism played almost no role in any lawyer's mind, including mine. Watergate changed that — for me and every other lawyer."[27] The response by the ABA was to add a requirement that accredited law schools teach a mandatory course on legal ethics.[28]

The connection between legal ethics and Watergate is firmly established as a part of the folklore of the American profession, but one should be skeptical of the claim that knowing about *ethics* would have made any difference to the conduct of Nixon's lawyers. John Dean told the story of his gradually dawning realization that a number of White House lawyers were exposed to criminal liability; but his concern they could all end up in prison was prompted by a review of federal criminal statutes, not any laws or ethical standards pertaining specifically to lawyers.[29] He was correct, of course, that

---

[22] Abel, *supra* note 18, at 642 n.14.

[23] *See* Hazard, *supra* note 3, at 85–90; Theodore J. Schneyer, *The Model Rules and Problems of Code Interpretation and Enforcement*, 1980 AM. B. FOUND. RES. J. 939 (1980).

[24] Abel, *supra* note 18, at 648–49; Murray L. Schwartz, *The Death and Regeneration of Ethics*, 1980 AM. B. FOUND. RES. J. 953, 958 (1980).

[25] *See* Mark Curriden, *The Lawyers of Watergate: How a "3rd-Rate Burglary" Provoked New Standards for Lawyer Ethics*, A.B.A. J. (June 1, 2012).

[26] *Id.*

[27] *Id.*

[28] *See* Mark Hansen, *1965–1974: Watergate and the Rise of Legal Ethics*, A.B.A. J. (Jan. 1, 2015). For the current version of the requirement, *see* Am. B. Ass'n, Standards and Rules of Procedure for Approval of Law Schools, Standard 303(a)(1).

[29] *Id.*

lawyers are subject to criminal liability to the same extent as non-lawyers for conduct amounting to obstruction or conspiracy.[30] But one hardly requires an ethics course to learn not to commit crimes.[31] Dean also said that it was unclear at the time that his client was the institution of the presidency, not the individual occupying the office, Richard Nixon.[32] That principle actually developed or became much clearer after Watergate, so one can hardly fault Dean for not being aware of it at the time. But it was perfectly clear at the time that a lawyer is not permitted to counsel or assist a client in conduct the lawyer knows is criminal,[33] regardless of whether the client is an individual or an institution. Nevertheless, Watergate is conventionally cited as an important factor, if not the turning point, in the transformation of legal ethics into the law of lawyering.[34] But there is little evidence that the scandal was the proximate cause of what is undeniably the pivotal moment in the transformation—the ABA's adoption of the Model Rules of Professional Conduct.[35] The Model Rules were a response to a number of developments which were independent of each other, and had nothing to do with Nixon and his bumbling crew of "plumbers."

In 1980, the ABA Commission on Evaluation of Professional Standards, generally known as the Kutak Commission after its chair, Robert J. Kutak, published the draft of what became the Model Rules.[36] At the time of the adoption of the Model Rules, many scholars lamented the "de-moralization" of legal ethics.[37] But it was becoming clear that the law governing lawyers was developing all on its own, as a subject apart from the *ethics* of practicing law. The expansion of tort liability beginning in the late 1950s had not left lawyers untouched, and they now faced more significant exposure to liability for malpractice.[38] Judges were considerably more assertive in supervising the conduct of lawyers appearing in their courts, which included monitoring law firm conflicts for their effect on the adversarial process.[39] Rules of conduct intended

---

[30] *See, e.g.*, United States v. Cintolo, 818 F.2d 980 (1st Cir. 1987).

[31] Less cynically, Kathleen Clark argues that a law school course on legal ethics might at least have given future Deans and Kroghs the opportunity to "develop the practical skills to deal with difficult professional situations where their client or supervisor wanted their assistance in illegal activity." Kathleen Clark, *The Legacy of Watergate for Legal Ethics Instruction*, 51 HASTINGS L.J. 673, 674 (2000). As to Krogh, at least, Clark observes that he was inexperienced, overawed by the power and prestige of the presidency, and persuaded that his actions were justified by considerations of national security. *Id.* at 674–75 (quoting *In re* Krogh, 536 P.2d 578 (Wash. 1975)).

[32] Curriden, *supra* note 26.

[33] AM. B. ASS'N MODEL CODE OF PROF'L RESP., DR 7-102(A)(7).

[34] *See, e.g.*, Wolfram, *supra* note 4, at 209.

[35] *See* Ted Schneyer, *Professionalism as Bar Politics*, 14 LAW & SOC. INQUIRY 677 (1989); Hazard, *supra* note 3.

[36] *See* Hazard, *supra* note 3, at 77. The Model Rules were subsequently revised comprehensively by the Ethics 2000 Commission. *See* Margaret Colgate Love, *The Revised ABA Model Rules of Professional Conduct: Summary of the Work of Ethics 2000*, 15 GEO. J. LEGAL ETHICS 441 (2002). The Commission on Ethics 20/20 then tinkered with the rules in a few, relatively inconsequential ways. *See* James E. Moliterno, *Ethics 20/20 Successfully Achieved Its Mission: It Protected, Preserved, and Maintained*, 47 AKRON L. REV. 149 (2014); Bruce A. Green, *ABA Ethics Reform from MDP to 20/20: Some Cautionary Reflections*, 2009 J. PROF. LAW. 1 (2009).

[37] *See* Luban & Millemann, *supra* note 13, at 45; *see also* Schwartz, *supra* note 25; William H. Simon, *The Trouble with Legal Ethics*, 41 J. LEGAL EDUC. 65, 66 (1991); Stephen Gillers, *What We Talked About When We Talked About Ethics: A Critical View of the Model Rules*, 46 OHIO ST. L.J. 243, 246 (1985).

[38] *See* Wolfram, *supra* note 4, at 214–16.

[39] For an interesting history of the development of the law on disqualification for conflicts of interest, *see* Daniel J. Bussel, *No Conflict*, 25 GEO. J. LEGAL ETHICS 207 (2012)

to be enforced through a disciplinary process were frequently used as evidence of the standard of care in malpractice cases, the basis for disqualifying a law firm from representation due to a conflict of interest, a ground for voiding a lawyer-client fee agreement, and other legal penalties imposed on lawyers outside the disciplinary process.[40] A more activist Supreme Court was scrutinizing and striking down protectionist practices embodied in codes of professional ethics, such as minimum fee schedules[41] and restrictions on advertising by lawyers.[42] Finally, the late 1970s witnessed the early stirrings of the regulatory response of the Securities and Exchange Commission (SEC) to the involvement by lawyers in the fraudulent transactions of their clients.[43] The scope and limits of the SEC's enforcement authority over the legal profession would become a hugely controversial issue around the time of the drafting of the Restatement.[44]

Geoffrey Hazard, the Reporter to the Kutak Commission, believed that the Model Rules were expressing a justifying narrative structured around loyalty to clients, partisan advocacy, indifference to harms to third parties or the public interest, and a generally libertarian assumption that safeguarding the autonomy of private parties is a morally worthy end.[45] The legal profession was still believed to serve the public interest, but would do so indirectly, through the adversarial representation of clients.[46] Partisan advocacy and representation of private clients in the course of transactional and counseling engagements should be tempered by the inherent limitation in any principal-agent relationship, under which the agent is permitted (or required) to perform any lawful act directed by the principal, but not to perform unlawful acts.[47] A couple of the controversies arising under the ABA Model Rules would come back to haunt the Restatement drafting process, however, in ways that highlight the structural tension between the client guardian and law guardian conceptions of the lawyer's role that continue to structure both the law of lawyering and the field of normative legal ethics.

---

[40] Schneyer, *supra* note 3, at 32–33.
[41] *See* Goldfarb v. Virginia State Bar, 421 U.S. 773 (1975).
[42] *See* Baird v. State Bar of Arizona, 407 U.S. 1 (1971).
[43] *See* SEC v. National Student Mktg. Corp., 457 F. Supp. 682 (D.D.C. 1978).
[44] *See, e.g.,* Susan P. Koniak, *When the Hurlyburly's Done: The Bar's Struggle with the SEC*, 103 COLUM. L. REV. 1236 (2003).
[45] *See* Hazard, *supra* note 19, at 1242–46.
[46] Hazard, *supra* note 3, at 93–94.
[47] *See generally* Deborah A. DeMott, *The Lawyer as Agent*, 67 FORDHAM L. REV. 301 (1998). Lawyers often acknowledge the limitation on the scope of permissible representation by referring to the rule of professional conduct prohibiting assistance in client conduct the lawyer knows to be criminal or fraudulent. *See* AM. B. ASS'N, MODEL RULES OF PROF'L CONDUCT, Rule 1.2(d) [hereinafter MODEL RULE xx]. That is not the end of the matter, however, because in addition to the express prohibition of Rule 1.2(d), there is an internal limitation as a result of the generally applicable law of agency, which renders a lawyer powerless to do something on behalf of the client that the client is not lawfully permitted to do, regardless of whether the client's conduct would be deemed a crime or fraud. *See* W. Bradley Wendel, *Lawyers' Constrained Fiduciary Duties: A Comment on Paul R. Tremblay, at Your Service: Lawyer Discretion to Assist Clients in Unlawful Conduct*, 70 FLA. L. REV. FORUM 7 (2018).

III. The ALI Restatement of the Law Governing Lawyers

The genesis of the ALI's Restatement was a proposal by Geoffrey Hazard, the drafter of the Model Rules who was also serving at the time as Director of the ALI, for a "mini-Restatement" of lawyer confidentiality, including the attorney-client privilege, the work product doctrine, and duties of confidentiality recognized by the common law of agency and the lawyer disciplinary codes.[48] Charles Wolfram responded with a much more ambitious proposal, which included the formation and termination of the lawyer-client relationship, the agency structure of the relationship and the division of decision-making authority between lawyers and clients; the regulation of lawyer-client fee arrangements, including standards of excessiveness, specific rules governing contingent fees, and prohibitions on sharing fees with non-lawyers; the duty of competent representation and the standards governing civil liability for negligence and breach of fiduciary duty; forensic misconduct, including the introduction of perjured testimony and false evidence; concurrent and successive conflicts of interest for private and government lawyers, imputation of conflicts, and remedies, including disqualification; and the confidentiality doctrines that were in Hazard's original mini-Restatement proposal.[49] The Council approved the project with the broader scope outline by Wolfram, now designed as the Chief Reporter, appointed Professors John Leubsdorf and Thomas Morgan as Associate Reporters, and gave the project the title of *Restatement of the Law Governing Lawyers*.[50]

Regarding the significance of ethical norms, Wolfram aligned the Restatement project with the approach of the ABA Model Rules, aiming to state enforceable rules for lawyer conduct, remaining agnostic on matters of ethics, either in the sense of the profession's normative self-understanding or universal norms of morality:

> Because this is a Restatement of the Law, the black letter and Comment do not discuss other important subjects, such as matters of sound professional practice or personal or professional morality or ethics. Such other non-legal considerations may be referred to in the Reporter's Notes, but those discussions do not, as is traditional, constitute the position of the Institute.[51]

---

[48] *See* Wolfram, *supra* note 3, at 199–200; *see also* Lawrence J. Latto, *The Restatement of the Law Governing Lawyers: A View from the Trenches*, 26 HOFSTRA L. REV. 697, 701–02 (1998).

[49] RESTATEMENT OF THE LAW GOVERNING LAWYERS, PRELIMINARY DRAFT NO. 1 (Jan. 20, 1986), at 10–22.

[50] Wolfram, *supra* note 3, at 200 n.6; *see also* 8 A.L.I. REP. No. 4 (July 1986), at 6. To the endless bafflement of my students, this project was approved at a time when the third series of Restatements on other subjects (Torts, Property, Agency, etc.) were being developed. However, this was the ALI's first effort at restating the law governing lawyers. The Summer 2000 *ALI Reporter* states simply, seemingly unaware of how strange it sounds to the uninitiated: "The long-awaited official text of the Institute's *first* Restatement of the Law Governing Lawyers has now been published as part of Restatement *Third*." 22 A.L.I. REP. No. 4 (Summer 2000), at 12 (emphasis added).

[51] Charles W. Wolfram, *Legal Ethics and the Restatement Process—The Sometimes-Uncomfortable Fit*, 46 OKLA. L. REV. 13, 15 (1993) (quoting the "boilerplate warning" attached to all drafts of the Restatement, beginning with Tentative Draft No. 4).

Wolfram also committed the Restatement project to a position of independence from the organized bar, either the ABA or any group such as the American Trial Lawyers' Association, which represented plaintiffs' personal injury practitioners.[52] This independence would be bolstered by reliance on "traditional legal materials—judicial decisions, statutes, court rules, and scholarly writing."[53] The black-letter rules would be "strongly grounded in existing decisions of courts,"[54] and would presumably follow the traditional ALI practice of deferring to a significant majority position among courts even if the minority view seemed wiser to the Reporters, unless there is a detectable trend in the direction of the minority position and it appears to be better reasoned.[55]

The Restatement required more than ten years before the ALI gave its final approval in 1998,[56] apparently setting a record for time required for completion.[57] Along the way there was a kerfuffle caused by ALI members with ties to the insurance industry attempting to covertly influence the development of the section governing the representation of clients whose defense was being paid for—and possibly directed—by liability insurers.[58] In the main, however, the debates were substantive and aboveboard, although there was spirited controversy regarding some of the departures from existing law. Much of the contentiousness of the process was likely related to the unique nature of a Restatement of the Law Governing Lawyers, as opposed to other subject-specific Restatements. As lawyers, ALI members were all interested in the subject and had strong views about the matters it addressed.[59] These controversies, and the response of the ALI to them, throw light on the normative vision that was developing at the time in the law governing lawyers.

---

[52] See Reporter's Memorandum at 2–3, in PRELIMINARY DRAFT NO. 1., supra note 50.

[53] Id. at 3.

[54] Id. at 6. This should not be confused with question of whether norms of conduct expressed in court-adopted rules of professional conduct may be used as evidence of the standard of care in civil lawsuit against a lawyer. For a comprehensive overview of this long-running, and often frustrating debate, see Latto, supra note 49, at 722–31. The position taken by the final version of the Restatement is the sensible one: Proof of violation of a rule may be considered by a trier of fact as an aid to understanding the duty of care, but it does not create a cause of action, nor is violation of a rule negligence per se in the sense of establishing a conclusive presumption that may not be rebutted by evidence to the contrary. See RESTATEMENT (THIRD) OF THE LAW GOVERNING LAWYERS § 52(2) (2000) [hereinafter RESTATEMENT § xx].

[55] See Latto, supra note 49, at 712–17 (describing the unofficial but well-settled "Rule Respecting Restatements"). The rule has since been codified in the ALI Style Manual. See Richard L. Revesz, Clarifying the Nature of the ALI's Work, A.L.I. Q. NEWSLETTER, July 21, 2015.

[56] 20 A.L.I. REP. No. 4 (Summer 1998), at 1.

[57] See Latto, supra note 49, at 697.

[58] See Charles W. Wolfram, Bismarck's Sausages and the ALI's Restatements, 26 HOFSTRA L. REV. 817 (1998). Larry Fox used a fictionalized version of the story to criticize the conduct of the lawyers involved. See Lawrence J. Fox, Leave Your Clients at the Door, 26 HOFSTRA L. REV. 595 (1998). ALI President Charles Alan Wright used his President's Column to remind ALI members of the expectation that they "leave client interests at the door," citing a norm stated an aspirational principle that would have been familiar as an Ethical Consideration in the ABA Model Code: "Members should speak and vote on the basis of their personal and professional convictions and experience without regard to client interests or self-interest." 19 A.L.I. REP. No. 2 (Winter 1997), at 2–3.

[59] I owe this observation to Linda Mullenix.

A. Disclosure to Prevent Client Frauds

One controversial issue that repeatedly confronted the ABA, which was also a point of contention in the Restatement drafting process, concerned the duty or permission of a lawyer to disclose confidential information to prevent, rectify, or mitigate a client's financial crime or fraud, in furtherance of which the lawyer's services were used. The Ethics 2000 Commission, which comprehensively revised the Model Rules, recommended an amendment to Model Rule 1.6(b) permitting, but not requiring, such disclosure.[60] The full ABA House of Delegates rejected this proposal, however, leaving a lawyer with only the option of making a "noisy withdrawal" from the representation—that is, disavowing any transactional documents, opinion letters, and the like that the lawyer had previously prepared.[61] This was on February 2, 2002,[62] not long after a little company called Enron filed for bankruptcy protection. Public outrage led to consideration by Congress of legislation that became the Sarbanes-Oxley Act, and one provision, Section 307, empowered the SEC to draft rules for the conduct of securities lawyers who discovered that their client has committed fraud with their (presumably unwitting) assistance.[63] In what can be understood as a rearguard action to preserve a semblance of self-regulation, and in response to pressure from the ABA's own Task Force on Corporate Responsibility, the ABA House of Delegates adopted the proposal that had originally been considered by the Ethics 2000 Commission, amending Rule 1.6(b) to permit disclosure of confidential information to the extent reasonably necessary to prevent, rectify, or mitigate substantial financial injury to another that is the result of a crime or fraud in furtherance of which the client has used the lawyer's services.[64]

Exceptions to the duty of confidentiality tend to get a lot of attention in legal ethics scholarship as well as coverage in the legal press, because as much as any legal issue this highlights the tension between duties of loyal client service and obligations to

---

[60] *See* Love, *supra* note 37, at 450.

[61] The noisy withdrawal option was included in a comment to Rule 1.6, not in the black-letter text, so its authority was already undermined by its placement. *See* Geoffrey C. Hazard Jr., *Lawyers and Client Fraud: They Still Don't Get It*, 6 GEO. J. LEGAL ETHICS 701, 720–26 (1993); Am. B. Ass'n, Standing Comm. on Prof'l Resp., Formal Opinion 92-366 (1992) (explaining the noisy withdrawal option). The ABA Ethics Committee recognized that "[s]uch a 'noisy' withdrawal is, of course, likely to have the collateral consequence of disclosing, inferentially, information relating to the representation that is otherwise protected as a client confidence under Rule 1.6." *Id.*; *see also id.* at 7 n.9 ("It must be recognized, therefore, that a 'noisy' withdrawal may result in a disclosure of 'information relating to representation' that is generally prohibited by Rule 1.6."). The comment to Rule 1.6 thus functions like Magritte's caption on a picture of a pipe, "*Ceci n'est pas une pipe*." The noisy withdrawal solution was not solution at all—just a kludge employed by the ABA to avoid the problem created by the collision of the ABA's prohibition on disclosure with the tort principles under which lawyers who did not effectively put a stop to a client fraud in which their services had been employed could be held secondarily liable for the fraud. *See* Hazard, *Client Fraud*, *supra*, at 728–36.

[62] *See* Love, *supra* note 37. at 443–44.

[63] *See* Koniak, *supra* note 45, at 1238; Roger C. Cramton, *Enron and the Corporate Lawyer: A Primer on Legal and Ethical Issues*, 58 BUS. LAW. 143, 156 (2002).

[64] *See* Roger C. Cramton, George M. Cohen, & Susan P. Koniak, *Legal and Ethical Duties of Lawyers After Sarbanes-Oxley*, 49 VILL. L. REV. 725, 729–33 (2004). The new rules are currently codified at Model Rules 1.6(b)(2), (b)(3). The ABA also amended Rule 1.13 on the representation of organizational clients to permit, in Section (c), disclosure of confidential information which the lawyer reasonably believes necessary to prevent a violation by an organizational constituent of a legal duty owed to the organization that is reasonably certain to result in substantial injury *to the organization* (as opposed to a third party).

third parties or the public interest.[65] As Charles Wolfram has argued, the comprehensive legal regulation of lawyers was a response to a shift in the organized bar's own governing ideology, from serving as guardians of the law to purely private guardians of client interests.[66] The bar hung on tenaciously to the purely private conception of ethical lawyering as private guardianship, but in the end blinked in the face of the public pressure created by the scandals at Enron and other companies. As is always the case with large-scale financial frauds, lawyers were in the thick of things, and were faulted in hindsight for failing to take effective steps to put a stop to their clients' wrongdoing. The financial accounting scandals of the early 2000s can be seen as the high-water mark of the client guardian conception of ethical lawyering.

The Restatement took a position on confidentiality exceptions in line with the Ethics 2000 Commission draft that was rejected by the House of Delegates. Despite the prohibition on disclosure in Model Rule 1.6, the Restatement gave lawyers discretion to disclose confidential information when the lawyer reasonably believes disclosure is necessary to prevent a future crime or fraud that threatens substantial financial loss, or to rectify or mitigate a past loss, in cases in which the lawyer's services are used in the matter.[67] For a time corporate lawyers were in a kind of limbo, because lawyers remained subject to discipline under their admitting state's version of Model Rule 1.6 (most, but not all, prohibiting disclosure in these circumstances). The substantive position of the ALI was vindicated in the end, however, by the amendments to Rule 1.6(b) and the regulations enacted by the SEC under the Sarbanes-Oxley Act. The current state of the law does not put lawyers in the position of guarantors or regulators of the soundness of transactions or in the role of deputy SEC enforcement counsel, but it does provide them the necessary tools to disassociate themselves from fraudulent transactions and, ideally, to persuade clients to comply with legal requirements.

B. Screening, Conflicts of Interest, and Lawyer Mobility

The Restatement also took a position out ahead of the ABA's view on screening to cure imputed conflicts of interest.[68] The screening issue arises out of lateral mobility by lawyers. When a lawyer moves from Old Firm to New Firm, it is possible that the moving lawyer may have confidential information pertaining to a specific client of Old Firm. Indeed, there is a presumption that lawyers practicing together in a firm have access to all the confidential information of all the clients of the firm;

---

[65] In addition to sources already cited, *see, e.g.*, Thomas G. Bost, *Corporate Lawyers After the Big Quake: The Conceptual Fault Line in the Professional Duty of Confidentiality*, 19 GEO. J. LEGAL ETHICS 1089 (2006); Keith R. Fisher, *The Higher Calling: Regulation of Lawyers Post-Enron*, 37 U. MICH. J.L. REFORM 1017 (2004); Geoffrey C. Hazard Jr., *Rectification of Client Fraud: Death and Revival of a Professional Norm*, 33 EMORY L.J. 271 (1984).

[66] Wolfram, *supra* note 4, at 208.

[67] *See* RESTATEMENT § 67.

[68] Susan R. Martyn, *Conflict about Conflicts: The Controversy Concerning Law Firm Screens*, 46 OKLA. L. REV. 53 (1993). Professor Martyn joined a minority report written by Lawrence J. Fox, submitted to the ABA's Ethics 2000 Commission regarding screening. *See* MINORITY REPORT CONCURRING IN GREAT PART; RESPECTFULLY DISSENTING ON A FEW IMPORTANT MATTERS, *available at* https://www.americanbar.org/groups/professional_responsibility/policy/ethics_2000_commission/e2k_dissent/.

this presumption underwrites the imputation of conflicts of interest to all lawyers in the same firm.[69] An exception long recognized at common law—the *Silver Chrysler* rule—allowed a moving lawyer to rebut the presumption of shared confidences acquired while working at Old Firm.[70] But what if a moving lawyer could not rebut this presumption? There was a serious risk that New Firm could be disqualified from the representation of a client whose interests were materially adverse to those of a client of Old Firm.[71] Courts consistently permitted a firm to bring in a lawyer from government service, provided the incoming lawyer was subject to a screening mechanism designed to prevent inadvertent disclosure of confidential information pertaining to the government.[72] Although the Model Rules recognized screening in this context,[73] there was considerable resistance within the ABA to allowing the use of nonconsensual screens to protect a hiring law firm against the risk of disqualification after hiring a lawyer who had previously worked at a private law firm.[74] The Ethics 2000 Commission had proposed a screening provision for moving private lawyers, but it was rejected by the House of Delegates.[75] The Restatement went the other way. The final version of the Restatement permits New Firm to remain in the representation after hiring a lawyer from Old Firm, provided that an adequate screen is erected in a timely fashion, the moving lawyer was not exposed at Old Firm to confidential information that is likely to be significant to the client of New Firm, and notice is given to the affected client of Old Firm.[76]

Like the scope of confidentiality exceptions, the permissibility of screening to cure imputed conflicts brings the tension between law, ethics, and the economic interests of lawyers into relief. From an ethical point of view, a moving lawyer can be characterized as having betrayed a duty of loyalty to the former client, and when the former client looks to New Firm for protection, all the firm will say is "trust us."[77] Traditionalists objected to screens as retreating from the highly fiduciary premise of the lawyer-client relationship, from which it follows that a client should not have monitor the lawyer to ensure compliance with duties of loyalty and confidentiality. Critics of screening characterized the Restatement position as a repudiation of the ideal of law as a profession in favor of a frank admission that the legal services industry is a business—one

---

[69] MODEL RULE 1.10(a); RESTATEMENT § 123.

[70] *See* Silver Chrysler Plymouth, Inc. v. Chrysler Motors Corp., 370 F. Supp. 581 (E.D.N.Y. 1973), *aff'd*, 518 F.2d 751 (2d Cwr. 1975).

[71] MODEL RULE 1.9(b).

[72] *See, e.g.*, Armstrong v. McAlpin, 625 F.2d 433 (2d Cir. 1980) (en banc), *vacated for lack of jurisdiction*, 449 U.S. 1106 (1981).

[73] *See* MODEL RULE 1.11(b). The 1983 version of the rule, before modifications by the Ethics 2000 Commission, is available at https://www.americanbar.org/groups/professional_responsibility/policy/eth ics_2000_commission/e2k_redline/.

[74] The qualification "non-consensual" is important, because the former client of Old Firm could give informed consent to the moving lawyer working on the adverse matter at New Firm. *See* MODEL RULE 1.9(b). Any conflict that would have been imputed to New Firm under Rule 1.10(a) was waived by the client. The screening issue only has bite where the former client refuses to consent and thus the adverse representation, with the screening of the moving lawyer, is "crammed down" on the former client.

[75] *See* Robert A. Creamer, *Lateral Screening after Ethics 2000*, PROF. LAW. 85 (2006).

[76] *See* RESTATEMENT § 124(2). The ABA came into line with the Restatement position in 2009, with amendments to Rule 1.10(a). *See, e.g.*, Edward A. Adams, *ABA House OKs Lateral Lawyer Ethics Rule Change*, A.B.A. J. (Feb. 16, 2009).

[77] *See* MINORITY REPORT, *supra* note 69; Martyn, *supra* note 69, at 56–57.

in which lawyers stand to benefit economically if there is less risk to hiring law firms of being disqualified for a conflict of interest. However, courts were becoming more accepting of screening in cases where lawyers moved from one private law firm to another, in part as a response to the tactical use of disqualification motions.[78] Among practicing lawyers there was a wide range of views on screening, with the majority position seeming to be a kind of resigned pragmatism[79]—lawyers are going to move around, law firms are going to grow, and there is no solid evidence that screens do not work, so why not give legal recognition to screening as a way of removing the imputation of conflicts?

IV. The Restatement and Fiduciary Ethics

The Restatement as a whole should not be seen as a concession to the caricatured view that lawyers have abandoned professional ideals to become nothing more than participants in a money-grubbing trade.[80] One of the most important contributions made by the ALI project is its construction of a legal field organized around a coherent and attractive normative core. In seeking to treat the entire field of the law governing lawyers, the Restatement drew the attention of lawyers to not just the possibility of professional discipline but of the role of standards of professional conduct in civil lawsuits seeking money damages, litigation sanctions (including disqualification for conflicts of interest), and other nondisciplinary remedies.[81] The Restatement aspires to be a unification not only of disparate areas of doctrine, however, but also to a distinctive ethical conception of lawyering.

Borrowing from Wolfram's observation that the official ideology of the profession shifted from guardianship of the law to guardianship of clients, I understand the Restatement as having established an interesting hybrid ideal. It does not envision lawyers as having robust, freestanding duties as guardians of the law, justice, morality, or the public interest. However, the obligation of competent, diligent representation of clients is internally limited by a recognition that the law establishes boundaries on what lawyers permissibly may do in the course of representing clients.[82]

---

[78] *See, e.g.,* Robert A. Creamer, *Expanding Screening Further,* 20 PROF. LAW. 3 (2010). Ted Schneyer disputes whether there was in fact a trend in the courts in the direction of recognizing screening for moving private lawyers. *See* Schneyer, *supra* note 3, at 40 n.67. In my judgment, the Reporters made the right call in applying the "Rule Respecting Restatements," *see supra* note 56, to favor screening.

[79] *See* Susan P. Shapiro, *If It Ain't Broke ... An Empirical Perspective on Ethics 2000, Screening, and the Conflict-of-Interest Rules,* 2003 U. ILL. L. REV. 1299, 1309–15 (2003) (pointing out the reliance on anecdotes and the absence of rigorous empirical evidence showing the effectiveness of screens to protect the interests of former clients).

[80] *See, e.g.,* Shapero v. Kentucky Bar Ass'n, 486 U.S. 466, 490 (1988) (O'Connor, J., dissenting) ("Restrictions on advertising and solicitation by lawyers ... act as a concrete, day-to-day reminder to the practicing attorney of why it is improper for any member of this profession to regard it as a trade or occupation like any other.").

[81] *See* Nancy J. Moore, *Restating the Law of Lawyer Conflicts,* 10 GEO. J. LEGAL ETHICS 541, 544–46 (1997).

[82] Here I agree substantially with Andrew Gold. *See* Andrew S. Gold, *The Internal Limits on Fiduciary Loyalty,* 65 AM. J. JURIS. 65 (2020).

The normative pivot of the entire Restatement is found in the section defining the lawyer's duties to the client:

> To the extent consistent with the lawyer's other legal duties... a lawyer must, within the scope of the representation ... proceed in a manner reasonably calculated to advance a client's lawful objectives, as defined by the client after consultation.[83]

This paragraph neatly encapsulates the fiduciary relationship between lawyer and client, the obligation of an agent to follow the instructions of the principal, the tort duty of reasonable care, the agency duty of communication, the anti-paternalist ideal that the objectives of the representation are for the client to determine autonomously, and the internal limits on these duties provided by the client's legal entitlements (the client's "*lawful* objectives").[84] A few Restatement sections retreat explicitly from the model of client guardianship. As noted earlier, it permits the disclosure of confidential information when a lawyer reasonably believes that disclosure is necessary to prevent, rectify, or mitigate a substantial financial loss caused by a client crime or fraud in which the lawyer's services had been employed.[85] The Restatement follows the position of the Model Rules, adopted by the Kutak Commission after extensive debate, prohibiting lawyers from introducing testimony or other evidence known by the lawyer to be false.[86] It also recognizes the developing law establishing tort and other duties to nonclients,[87] for example in the context of providing opinion letters to third parties with the expectation that the third party will rely on the lawyer's use of reasonable care.[88]

The more important point, however, is holistic. By situating the law governing lawyers within existing bodies of agency, tort, evidence, and procedural law, the Restatement repudiated the traditional view that only the organized bar was

---

[83] RESTATEMENT § 16(1).

[84] *See* Deborah DeMott, *The Fiduciary Character of Agency and the Interpretation of Instructions, in* PHILOSOPHICAL FOUNDATIONS OF FIDUCIARY LAW 321 (Andrew S. Gold & Paul B. Miller eds., 2014) (the Reporter of the Restatement (Third) of Agency observing that a basic feature of a fiduciary agency relationship is the obligation on the part of the agent to follow the instructions of the principal, interpreted reasonably in light of the principal's wishes as the agent understands them); Stephen Ellmann, *Lawyers and Clients,* 34 UCLA L. REV. 717 (1987) (emphasizing client autonomy in the allocation of decision-making authority); David Luban, *Paternalism and the Legal Profession,* 1981 WIS. L. REV. 454 (1981) (noting that professions have historically had a tendency to lose sight of the interests of patients or clients in decision-making models that foreground other ideals or commitments). Matters get much more complicated when clients lack the capacity to participate in the decision-making process in a meaningful way. For an exploration of the Restatement's approach to these cases, and a critique of a Supreme Court case on decision-making in the criminal defense context, *see* W. Bradley Wendel, *Autonomy Isn't Everything: Some Cautionary Notes on* McCoy v. Louisiana, 9 ST. MARY'S J. ON LEGAL MALPRACTICE AND ETHICS 92 (2018).

[85] RESTATEMENT § 67.

[86] RESTATEMENT § 120. For a history of the controversy over client perjury, by one of the central participants in the debate, *see* Monroe H. Freedman, *Getting Honest About Client Perjury,* 21 GEO. J. LEGAL ETHICS 133 (2008).

[87] RESTATEMENT § 51. The landmark case discarding the traditional limitation of liability to those with whom the lawyer was in privity of contract is *Lucas v. Hamm,* 364 P.2d 685 (Cal. 1961). *Lucas* became notorious for its secondary holding, that the Rule Against Perpetuities is a "trap for the unwary" and thus failing to account for it when drafting a trust instrument is not a violation of the professional standard of care. *Id.* at 690. This part of *Lucas* has been distinguished away, but it continues to amuse law students.

[88] *See, e.g.,* Greycas, Inc. v. Proud, 826 F.2d 1560 (7th Cir. 1987).

competent to regulate the provision of legal services. As Wolfram observed around the time the Restatement was finalized: "It stretches the point only slightly to say that the practice of law in America is now, as with many other contemporary areas of corporate or personal economic endeavor, a regulated industry."[89] Returning to the example of confidentiality exceptions, the ABA's opposition to permitting disclosure to prevent client frauds eventually yielded to the pressure of tort liability for aiding and abetting, which was perfectly indifferent to whether the legal profession thought it should somehow be exempt from generally applicable law. Similarly, the ABA's position on the duties of a lawyer who received confidential information inadvertently sent by opposing counsel is much less important in practice than the principles, recognized by the Restatement, governing inadvertent waiver of the attorney-client privilege.[90] Taken as a whole, the Restatement stands for the proposition that lawyers who want to understand their legal rights and duties much look much farther afield than at the ABA's latest code of professional responsibility, or their own admitting state's disciplinary rules.

Given the origins of this field of law in hortatory statements of ethical ideals, one may be tempted to write off the Restatement as a kind of lowest-common-denominator ethics, aimed at practitioners who are interested only in doing the bare minimum that will keep them out of trouble with courts and disciplinary agencies.[91] I believe, however, that there is considerable ethical value in a fiduciary relationship of trust, confidence, and loyalty, oriented toward sustaining an institutional resolution of what would otherwise be deep and intractable social conflict.[92] The role of lawyers is to promote not the bare interests of clients, but their *lawful* objectives. This obligation does not license abusive litigation, loophole-seeking, evasion, playing the "audit lottery," or other sadly familiar tactics. It does not see the law as the enemy but as the source of the client entitlements that it is the lawyer's duty to promote.[93] Nor does it require or even permit lawyers to act directly on a sense of justice or responsibility to the public interest. Instead it reflects a decision made by our political community to entrust the resolution of disagreement about matters of justice and the public interest to official institutions and procedures. This is not amoralism but a political-ethical stance, reflecting the values underlying the ideal of the rule of law.[94] It is not a full return to the nineteenth-century vision of lawyers as guardians of the law, but it also rejects the ethic of unrestrained zeal on behalf of clients. The Restatement should therefore be understood not as replacing ethics with law but as establishing an ethic among lawyers of respect for law.

---

[89] Wolfram, *supra* note 4, at 207.

[90] *Cf.* MODEL RULE 4.4(b) (lawyer receiving inadvertently sent information should notify opposing counsel); RESTATEMENT § 79, cmt. h (adopting contextual standard of reasonableness to assess waiver of privilege).

[91] *See, e.g.*, Schwartz, *supra* note 25, at 959; Luban & Millemann, *supra* note 13, at 47–51.

[92] *See* W. BRADLEY WENDEL, LAWYERS AND FIDELITY TO LAW (2010); W. Bradley Wendel, *Understanding the Complex Loyalty of Lawyers: Dual-Commission, Governance Mandate, and Intrinsic-Limit Analyses, in* II OXFORD STUDIES IN PRIVATE LAW THEORY (John Oberdiek & Paul B. Miller eds., 2023) (forthcoming).

[93] *See* Robert W. Gordon, *A New Role for Lawyers? The Corporate Counselor After Enron*, 35 CONN. L. REV. 1185, 1191 (2003).

[94] *See, e.g.*, Jeremy Waldron, *The Concept and the Rule of Law*, 43 GA. L. REV. 1 (2008). David Luban, *Natural Law as Professional Ethics: A Reading of Fuller, in* LEGAL ETHICS AND HUMAN DIGNITY (2007).

V. Conclusion: What Remains of Ethics Beyond the Law?

The analytic separation between law and morals (to allude to a famous article by H.L.A. Hart)[95] serves to remind lawyers that the law and ethics are distinct domains. Hart's point was that, from the bare fact of something's being "law," little else follows, including no obligation to obey this norm.[96] It is important to keep in mind that even if the law governing lawyers says a lawyer must do X as a matter of law (e.g., maintain the confidences of a deceased client even where disclosure would avoid the wrongful conviction of another), as a matter of ethics a very different conclusion may be called for.[97] In addition, many problems faced by lawyers in their practice present difficult, subtle normative questions calling for the exercise of judgment.[98] Bright-line rules stating minimal duties obscure or interfere with the necessary process of exercising judgment. There is long-standing concern among many legal ethics scholars about a positive-law approach to regulating lawyers resulting in a "technocratic" approach to ethical problems in which the self-interest of the lawyer and the client is the only relevant value.[99] Understanding lawyers' duties in terms of ethics, not law, may imply that they should be complied with for their own sake, with none of the Holmesian bad man stance or loophole-seeking shenanigans that sometimes characterize lawyers' advice to clients concerning compliance with law.[100]

The events surrounding the 2020 presidential election, including the attempted armed insurrection at the U.S. Capitol on January 6, 2021, have again focused public attention on whether lawyers have any duties beyond simply pursuing client interests.[101] Among the astonishing revelations that have come out as a result of the work of the House select committee investigating the January 6 riot, it was reported that one of Donald Trump's lawyers, John Eastman, urged the filing of an action before the Supreme Court to challenge the election results in Wisconsin.[102] Eastman admitted that the lawsuit had no legal merit, but said he understood there was a heated fight underway on the Court and that four justices might have the "spines" to take up the lawsuit. Eastman also wrote a memo in which he proposed a plan by which Vice

---

[95] H.L.A. Hart, *Positivism and the Separation of Law and Morals*, 71 HARV. L. REV. 593 (1958).

[96] *Id.* at 618.

[97] *See, e.g.*, Wolfram, *supra* note 52, at 18–20 (discussing *State v. Macumber*, 544 P.2d 1084 (Ariz. 1976), and observing that although it is consistent with well-settled legal principles, "the result stinks!").

[98] Luban & Millemann, *supra* note 13, at 39; Simon, *supra* note 38, at 66.

[99] *See* Heidi Li Feldman, *Codes and Virtues: Can Good Lawyers Be Good Ethical Deliberators?*, 69 S. CAL. L. REV. 885 (1996); *see also* Erwin Chemerinsky, *Pedagogy Without Purpose: An Essay on Professional Responsibility Courses and Casebooks*, 1985 AM. B. FOUND. RES. J. 189 (arguing that post-Watergate developments, including the mandatory law school professional responsibility course and the Multistate Professional Responsibility Examination, have entrenched a simplistic belief that memorizing a few rules and demonstrating knowledge on a multiple-choice test are sufficient to be an ethical lawyer).

[100] *See* W. Bradley Wendel, *The Rule of Law and Legal-Process Reasons in Attorney Advising*, 99 B.U. L. REV. 107 (2019).

[101] I am grateful to several conference participants, but particularly Roberta Ramo, for pressing me to consider this aspect of legal ethics and its relationship with the Restatement.

[102] *See* Luke Broadwater & Maggie Haberman, *Trump Lawyer Cited "Heated Fight" Among Justices Over Election Suits*, N.Y. TIMES, June 15, 2022.

President Mike Pence would refuse to count the electoral votes from seven states, resulting in an electoral college victory for Trump.[103] Eastman met with Trump, Pence, and the Vice President's counsel and chief of staff on January 4 and 5; in these meetings, Pence and his advisers pressed Eastman into conceding that his plan would violate the Electoral Count Act and likely be rejected by a unanimous Supreme Court.[104] Not only did the Vice President's lawyer push back on these efforts, but the Acting Attorney General, Jeffrey Rosen, succeeded (possibly only barely) in thwarting a plan to replace him with a lower-ranking Justice Department official who would then lead an effort to ask states not to certify their election results.[105]

As I see it, ethical lawyering at its foundation is a matter of loyal client service, competent and diligent representation, while acting in ways that manifest respect for the legal system and the political value of the rule of law. The last weeks of the Trump administration provided an opportunity for lawyers to show either that they were committed to working within the rule of law or would be willing to burn it all down to remain in power. The ethic of respect for the law, as reflected in the Restatement, proved surprisingly resilient in the face of the efforts of Trump and his supporters to overturn the election. Lawyers like John Eastman, along with Rudy Giuliani, Sidney Powell, Lin Wood, and other hard-core election denialists, were resisted successfully by lawyers and judges who took seriously their obligation to refuse to assist clients in conduct that was not authorized by applicable law. This happy result is likely the product more of professional socialization or character than the content of the law governing lawyers. But the overlap between the behavior of the "good" lawyers in the wake of the 2020 election shows that the ethical vision recognized in the Restatement of the Law Governing Lawyers is a mainstream, not critical or countercultural position. The consilience between the law and ethics of lawyering is evidence in the mature field of the law governing lawyers, which the ALI Restatement had a significant role in bringing about.

---

[103] *See* Eastman v. Thompson, ___ F. Supp. 3d ___, 2022 WL 894256 (C.D. Cal. Mar. 28, 2022) (order on attorney-client privilege claims asserted by Eastman in response to subpoena from House Jan. 6 committee; finding crime-fraud exception applied to these communications).

[104] *Id.* at *4.

[105] *See* Michael Kranish, *New Details Emerge of Oval Office Confrontation Three Days Before Jan. 6*, WASH. POST, June 14, 2022; Nicholas Wu & Kyle Cheney, *Why Scott Perry Stands Out in the FBI's Investigations of Trump Allies*, POLITICO, Aug. 10, 2022 (stating that "Trump came within an eyelash of dismissing DOJ's leadership and installing Clark in the days before Jan. 6, relenting only when senior leaders in the White House and Justice Department threatened to resign en masse").

12

A Short History of the Restatement of Restitution and Unjust Enrichment

Emily Sherwin

I. Introduction

There has been much debate over time about whether the American Law Institute (ALI), and in particular its Restatement projects, should aim at collecting, describing, and rationalizing predominant rules of law within a field, or should aim instead at social reform though law.[1] The first of these is a doctrinal and analytical effort; the second is a moral or political effort. The choice of approach depends on the aspirations of those working on the project.

From its inception, however, the series of Restatements leading to the Restatement (Third) of Restitution and Unjust Enrichment has been different. Rather than fine-tuning prevailing doctrine or reshaping it to meet social needs, the aim of these projects, through three incarnations, has been to study a seemingly disparate set of legal claims and draw out their common rationale: the principle that one person should not be unjustly enriched at another's expense. In other words, the primary role of the restitution Restatements has not been to clarify legal doctrine or to support legal, social, or political change, but to make and defend a theoretical insight into the nature and functions of the common law.

The first Restatement in the restitution series was published in 1937.[2] It combined the work of Reporter Warren Seavey on Quasi-Contract with the work of Reporter Austin Scott on Constructive Trusts and related equitable remedies. The great legal advance made in this Restatement was the insight that these two substantively and procedurally disparate sets of claims rested on the much broader ground of relief against forms of unjust enrichment. A second Restatement of the subject, partially compiled in the 1980s by Reporter William Young, was abandoned in favor of a broader project on remedies that ultimately proved too complex. That might have been the end of the line for restitution as a Restatement topic, if not for a contested decision to revive the subject in the 1990s.

The product of that decision is the Restatement (Third) of Restitution and Unjust Enrichment, assembled by Reporter Andrew Kull and published in 2011.[3] The third

---

[1] A symposium on this much-discussed topic appears at 32 S. ILL. U. L.J. 32 (2007). Andrew Kull, Reporter for the Restatement (Third) of Restitution and Unjust Enrichment, wrote an entry in which he defended the restitution Restatements as an instance of "radical reconception" of an area of law rather than what is ordinarily thought of as law reform. Andrew Kull, *Restitution and Reform*, 32 S. ILL. U. L.J. 83, 86 (2007).

[2] RESTATEMENT OF THE LAW OF RESTITUTION: QUASI CONTRACTS AND CONSTRUCTIVE TRUSTS (1937).

[3] RESTATEMENT OF THE LAW (THIRD): RESTITUTION AND UNJUST ENRICHMENT (2011).

Emily Sherwin, *A Short History of the Restatement of Restitution and Unjust Enrichment* In: *The American Law Institute*. Edited by: Andrew S. Gold and Robert W. Gordon, Oxford University Press. © Oxford University Press 2023.
DOI: 10.1093/oso/9780197685341.003.0013

Restatement is an ambitious two-volume set designed to clarify, expand, and update the central insight of the first Restatement of Restitution, that prevention of unjust enrichment is in fact a cornerstone of American law. It offers a comprehensive description of the role that unjust enrichment plays in private law, explained in modern terminology that is readily understandable by lawyers and judges.

II. 1937: Restatement of the Law of Restitution: Quasi Contracts and Constructive Trusts

As of 1930, the ALI was planning separate Restatement volumes on the topics of Trusts and Quasi-Contracts, with Quasi-Contracts to be managed by Warren Seavey and Trusts by Austin Scott (both Seavey and Scott were members of the faculty at Harvard). In 1933, the ALI announced rather suddenly that it had decided instead to commence work on a volume covering "two closely related subjects, Quasi-Contracts and Constructive Trusts which together cover 'Restitution and Unjust Enrichment.' "[4] At the time, the combination of these topics was surprising and the proposed title was mysterious. Quasi-contracts were a procedural device developed in English law to give relief against various forms of wrongdoing, including both failure to honor informal promises and wrongful takings of money or other property. Constructive trusts were a conceptual device developed by equity courts to allow recovery of products and proceeds of wrongdoing. Initially the constructive trust remedy was used against defaulting fiduciaries; later it was used against any person shown to be in possession of money or property that ought to belong to someone else.

The great insight reflected in the ALI's newly announced Restatement project was that these two quite different legal devices were linked by a common objective, to prevent one person from profiting unjustly at another person's expense.[5] In other words, the project aimed to construct from relatively obscure materials a new foundation for legal claims between parties, which did not depend on the presence of a legally binding contract or act of legally wrongful harm. Restitution—meaning, roughly, a legal obligation to yield up value that ought to belong to someone else—was presented as an independent basis for legal claims, comparable to agreed exchange or tortious

---

[4] 11 A.L.I. Proc. 335 (1934). Professor Kull reports that certain stenographic minutes of Advisers' meetings, which might have shed light on the decision to combine Quasi-Contracts and Constructive Trusts in a Restitution volume, appear to have gone missing from the Harvard Law Library during a renovation. Andrew Kull, *Three Restatements of Restitution*, 68 Wash. & Lee L. Rev. 867, 869 n.6 (2011).

[5] Topic 1 of the first Restatement was titled "Underlying Principles." In a note introducing the section, the Reporters explained that "[t]he rules stated in the Restatement of this subject depend for their validity upon certain basic assumptions in regard to what is required by justice in the various situation. In this [introductory section], they are stated in the form of principles since either they are too indefinite to be of value in a specific case, or, for historical or other reasons, they are not universally applied." Restatement of Restitution ch. 1, Topic 1.

The first principle read as follows:

§1. Unjust Enrichment.
A person who has been unjustly enriched at the expense of another is required to make restitution to the other.

The comment then explained, rather unhelpfully, that "[a] person is unjustly enriched if the retention of the benefit would be unjust." *Id.* §1 cmt. a.

conduct but grounded instead in the conceptually independent principle of unjust enrichment. Although the legal category of restitution, and the unjust enrichment principle that supported it, were inferred from existing remedial patterns, the claim that restitution constituted an independent ground for legal relief was a major change in traditional understandings of the rights and duties that make up private law.[6]

Seavey and Scott understood the jurisprudential significance of what they were doing. In an article published immediately after the publication of the first Restatement, they wrote that "because of the way in which the English law developed, a group of situations having distinct unity has never been dealt with as a unit and because of this has never received adequate treatment."[7] This proposition almost immediately gained support among lawyers, judges, and academics in the United States (although it was ignored in England for another generation).

Sometime in the later stages of preparation of the first Restatement addressing restitution and unjust enrichment, the Reporters made what was probably a mistake: they dropped the term "Unjust Enrichment" from the original title, retaining only "Restitution," "a word which to the best of our knowledge is not used as a title in any law digest or treatise."[8] They explained this choice on the ground that "Restitution" connotes "the right to recover back something which one once had."[9] Restitution, however, had no settled meaning in legal vocabulary and was not a ground for legal relief in the manner that "tort" and "contract" are grounds for relief. Nor was it fully descriptive of the contents of the Restatement: unjust enrichment remained the motivating principle and the scope of the claims described in the body of the Restatement was significantly broader than recovery of particular assets.[10] A fuller title might have headed off later confusion about the scope and importance of the volume.

Title problems notwithstanding, the Restatement of Restitution was a pathbreaking addition to American legal literature. The insight that unjust enrichment plays a fundamental role in law, however, did not originate with Seavey and Scott. Its origins go back as far as Roman law, which incorporated a limited idea of relief based on unjust

---

[6] *See, e.g.,* Douglas Laycock, *The Scope and Significance of Restitution,* 67 TEX. L. REV. 1277, 1277–78 (1989).

[7] Warren A. Seavey & Austin W. Scott, *Restitution,* 54 L.Q. REV. 29, 29 (1938). This statement probably was technically correct, but it is somewhat misleading. "Restitution" had been used in the first Restatement of Contracts to describe an alternative remedy for breach involving restoration of value conferred. *See* RESTATEMENT OF CONTRACTS § 247 cmt. a (1932) ("Restitution is a remedy that is available in many kinds of cases, breach of contract being only one of these. In some cases it may be the only available remedy.... In some cases it is an alternative remedy, as in the case of a tort whereby the defendant has been enriched at the plaintiff's expense"). The term "restitution" also appeared in the famous 1936 article by Lon Fuller and William Perdue on the "reliance" interest in contract law. Fuller and Perdue described three interests protected by contract law, one of which was the "restitution" interest, which Fuller described as based on the principle of unjust enrichment. L. L. Fuller & William R. Perdue Jr., *The Reliance Interest in Contract Damages,* 46 YALE L.J. 52, 53–54 (1936). It is at least debatable, however, whether the term "restitution," as used in the setting of alternative remedies for breach of contract, described a form of relief based on unjust enrichment or simply an alternative remedy for breach. For the view that restitution as a remedy for breach should not be viewed as an instance of relief against unjust enrichment, *see* RESTATEMENT (THIRD) OF RESTITUTION AND UNJUST ENRICHMENT, *supra* note 3, ch. 4, Topic 2, Reporter's Note to Introductory Note.

[8] *Id.*

[9] *Id.*

[10] *See* Andrew Kull, *Restitution and Unjust Enrichment, in* RESEARCH HANDBOOK ON UNJUST ENRICHMENT AND RESTITUTION, ch. 4, at 62–77 (Elise Brant, Kit Barker, & Simone Degeling eds., 2020) (lamenting the title change).

enrichment. From Rome, the idea of unjust enrichment made its way into European civil law in Germany and elsewhere, again in a relatively limited way.[11] In eighteenth-century England, Lord Mansfield recognized something like a principle of unjust enrichment when he held that an advantage-taker was required by "the ties of natural justice" to refund money recovered on technical grounds in a contract action.[12]

English courts did not follow up, but as time went on American judges were more receptive to claims of unfair gain.[13] By the end of the nineteenth century, American academics had begun to focus on the possibility of legal claims based on unjust enrichment, independent of tort or contract. Andrew Kull traces early academic interest in unjust enrichment as a ground for legal relief to James Barr Ames, a legal historian and one of five members of the Harvard Law School faculty.[14] Ames taught and wrote in the 1880s, fifty years before the ALI began work on the Restatement of Restitution. During that period, he published several articles linking equitable remedies such as constructive trusts, as well as quasi-contract remedies given by law courts, to the underlying principle that one person should not be unjustly enriched at the expense of another.[15]

It seems, then, the notion of unjust enrichment as a ground for relief, and the specific connection between unjust enrichment and the forms of legal relief later considered by Seavey and Scott in the first Restatement of Restitution, had been circulating for some time among American scholars and, as Kull suggests, was known to American lawyers and judges.[16] The role played by Seavey and Scott was, first, to collect and

---

[11] *See* JOHN P. DAWSON, UNJUST ENRICHMENT: A COMPARATIVE ANALYSIS (A SERIES OF LECTURES DELIVERED UNDER THE AUSPICES OF THE JULIUS ROSENTHAL FOUNDATION AT NORTHWESTERN UNIVERSITY SCHOOL OF LAW IN APRIL 1950), at 119–27 (1951).

[12] Moses v. Macferlan, 97 Eng. Rep. 676, 681 (K.B. 1760).

[13] *See* Andrew Kull, *James Barr Ames and the Early Modern History of Unjust Enrichment*, 25 OXFORD J. LEGAL STUD. 297, 311–316 (2005). In an impressively researched edition of Developments in the Law, editors of the *Harvard Law Review* trace the history of restitution in the United States, beginning with nineteenth-century American courts' reliance principle of unjust enrichment. *Developments in the Law: Unjust Enrichment*, 133 HARV. L. REV. 2061, 2084–2100 (2020).

[14] *See* Kull, *supra* note 13, at 303.

[15] *See* James Barr Ames, *Purchase for Value Without Notice*, 1 HARV. L. REV. 1, 3 (1887), and James Barr Ames, *The History of Assumpsit*, 2 HARV. L. REV. 53, 64 (1888), both described in Kull, *supra* note 13, at 302–05. Soon after Ames made the connection between quasi-contract and unjust enrichment, William Keener, a junior colleague of Ames, made a similar observation in a discussion of quasi-contract remedies. William A. Keener, *Recovery of Money Paid Under Mistake of Fact*, 1 HARV. L. REV. 211, 211 (1887), *cited in* Kull, *supra*, at 305–07. Ames was likely familiar with both Roman and civil law doctrines referring to unjust enrichment, although his focus was on English and American doctrinal developments. On Roman and Civilian parallels, *see generally* Helen Scott, *Comparative Taxonomy: An Introduction, in* RESEARCH HANDBOOK ON UNJUST ENRICHMENT AND RESTITUTION, *supra* note 10, at 145, 147–60. Ames's role, and also the significant role of Ames's colleague William Keener, is also discussed in *Developments in the Law: Unjust Enrichment*, *supra* note 13, at 2086–88. In the same era, Learned Hand also published an article referring to unjust enrichment and its relation to restitutionary remedies. Learned Hand, *Restitution or Unjust Enrichment*, 11 HARV. L. REV. 209, 209 (1896).

[16] *See* Kull, *supra* note 13, at 307–09 (citing journals, treatises, and cases). Interestingly, Seavey, in a short biography that combines reminiscences by Seavey with commentary by a former student at Harvard, indicates that in 1932, ALI Director William Draper Lewis gave Seavey a choice of subject matter for a new Restatement project. In response, Seavey suggested a Restatement "dealing with the question of payment for the value of a benefit.... There had been two ways of dealing with this, one in the law courts and one in the courts of chancery." Seavey then "invited Scott, a colleague and reporter of Trusts, to work on the equity

formalize the various forms of relief for unjust enrichment found in American law, lay them out, and give them a name ("Restitution"). More importantly, by collaborating to include these forms of relief in a single Restatement, they formalized Ames's insight and demonstrated that unjust enrichment stands alongside tort and contract as a foundational category in American private law.

As presented by Ames and later in the Restatement, restitution based on unjust enrichment was an invented class of legal claims, assembled from a variety of fictions that previously had enabled courts to give relief but were difficult to explain on reasoned grounds. From the outset, however, the underlying idea of legal relief against unjust enrichment was not problem-free. Seavey and Scott demonstrated that unjust enrichment stood apart from tort and contract as an independent ground of relief, but the restitution claims they described also provided an alternative to compensatory damages for wrongdoing or breach. Thus, while the Restatement provided significant new insights into the range of legal rights arising from private interaction, it also raised new questions about when and to what extent unjust enrichment gives rise to a claim. Some recoverable enrichments are products of mistake rather than unfairness, some unjust distributions do not and probably should not support legal remedies between parties.

On the remedial side, the concept of restitution based on unjust enrichment provided a rationale for quasi-contract claims and tracing remedies such as constructive trusts and subrogation, but it left important details to be determined. In simple cases, the plaintiff's loss is equivalent to the defendant's gain, so the restitution remedy is not puzzling. In other situations, the defendant's gain may exceed plaintiff's loss, or the plaintiff may have suffered no loss at all, or the defendant may not have realized a gain; in these instances the ideas of restitution and unjust enrichment pull apart and courts must make reasoned choices about how to allocate the assets at stake.[17]

III. Interim: Rise and Fall, and the Second Restatement of Restitution

The first Restatement of Restitution was published in 1937, less than four years after the project was launched. It was mainly well received, both by the American legal academy and by courts and lawyers. Citations were common, and courses in the new subject of Restitution were added to the curriculum in many law schools.

---

part.... There was no name for the combination but we finally christened it 'Restitution' ..." WARREN A. SEAVEY & DONALD B. KING, WARREN A. SEAVEY'S LIFE AND THE WORLD OF LEGAL EDUCATION 67 (2005). ALI records indicate that quasi-contract was subject of interest as early as 1930. *See* 8 A.L.I. PROC. 50–51 (1930).

[17] *See* Kull, *supra* note 10, at 63–64 (noting these inconsistencies and suggesting that they were exacerbated by the decision to drop "unjust enrichment" from the title of the first Restatement); Doug Rendleman, *Measurement of Restitution: Coordinating Restitution with Compensatory Damages and Punitive Damages*, 68 WASH. & LEE L. REV. 973, 981–90 (2011) (discussing "giving up" and "giving back" and other puzzles affecting measurement of restitution).

Leading scholars specialized in the topic, most prominently John Dawson and George Palmer.[18]

The eloquent Professor Dawson, one of the few voices urging caution, described restitution based on unjust enrichment as an idea that was both attractive and dangerous if untamed:

> To the person who has suffered loss, the loss alone is a grievance. But if this loss can be located and identified in the gain received by another, the anguish caused by the loss will be felt as more than doubled. One can see this, for example, in the system developed by Karl Marx, who tapped an inexhaustible supply of resentment ... When we come to the narrower issues arising in disputes between individuals, we often find it possible to trace more directly the connection between losses incurred and gains received ... [A] similar response can be expected, without any overtones whatever of social or economic reformism ...[19]

At the same time, Dawson held out hope that the principle set out by the Restatement could be kept under control if approached with care:

> We have done much and can do more to fortify ourselves. If we know the forest is enchanted we have not too much to fear.[20]

Despite early enthusiasm, the Restatement fell on hard times in the United States during the second half of the twentieth century.[21] One difficulty was that the volume itself did not stray far from the models of quasi-contract and constructive trust. It began with a broad statement of the principle of unjust enrichment,[22] and the Reporters' preface stated that "the principles by which a person is entitled to restitution are the same whether the proceeding is one at law or in equity."[23] Yet the body of the work remained divided, presenting first the various grounds of recovery available through the fictitious procedures of quasi-contract and, second, the tracing remedies available in equity. Even at the time this was difficult material, not familiar to all lawyers, and it became less familiar as assumpsit fell out of regular use and courts of equity were merged procedurally with courts of law. Few modern lawyers are familiar with either the "common counts" or the fictions surrounding the Chancellors' remedial powers.

---

[18] *See, e.g.*, JOHN P. DAWSON & GEORGE E. PALMER, THE LAW OF RESTITUTION (1978); John P. Dawson, Restitution Without Enrichment, 61 B.U. L. REV. 563 (1981); Laycock, *supra* note 6. *See generally* Kull, *supra* note 4, at 869.

[19] Dawson, *supra* note 11, at 5–6.

[20] *Id*. at 152.

[21] The decline of restitution and unjust enrichment in the United States in the later twentieth century was recently noted by the editors of the *Harvard Law Review*, although they also observe some resurgence in recent years. And, of course, their own interest in the subject is very encouraging to those of us who view unjust enrichment as an important and feature of the private law. *See Developments in the Law: Unjust Enrichment, supra* note 13, at 94–98.

[22] Section 1, at 12.

[23] Introductory Note, at 4.

Meanwhile, general changes were underway in American attitudes toward law and legal doctrine, beginning in academic circles. American Legal Realism was already a significant force in the 1920s and 1930s when the ALI embarked on its initial Restatement projects. Realism took a number of forms, not all compatible, but several themes stand out.[24] Realists were opposed to what they called "mechanical jurisprudence" and suspicious of rules and other verbal formulae employed by courts. Most took the view that legal doctrine is rationally and causally indeterminate: rules of law neither justify nor explain judicial decisions. Instead, judges respond primarily to facts before them and facts about the world, whether or not those facts are picked out as relevant by applicable legal rules.[25]

Initially, many prominent Realists took a dim view of the ALI and its Restatement projects.[26] For example, Leon Green referred to the project to restate tort law as "hopeless,"[27] and Charles Clark described the contracts project as "rigid."[28] Edward Robinson accused the ALI of thinking "that it can help simple-minded lawyers by giving an artificial and arbitrary picture of the principle in terms of which human disputes are supposed to be settled."[29]

As time went on, antipathy between Realists and the ALI subsided. Prominent Realists became associated with ALI,[30] and later Restatements reflected the influence of Realism on American law and legal scholarship. Realists continued to maintain that the traditional legal decision-making bore no relation to social and economic conditions in the world it purported to govern, but at least some Realists, such as Herman Oliphant, suggested that doctrine could be useful if amended in ways that invited judges to respond to relevant facts.[31] An example of this idea put into practice is the prominent role played by "unconscionability" in the Restatement (Second) of Contracts,[32] which followed the lead of Karl Llewellyn's Uniform Commercial Code.[33] For better or worse, unconscionability is an invitation to judges to engage in fact-specific judgment as they resolve disputes. Through mechanisms of this kind, the

---

[24] An excellent source on this subject is Brian Leiter, *American Legal Realism, in* THE BLACKWELL GUIDE TO THE PHILOSOPHY OF LAW AND LEGAL THEORY 50 (Martin P. Golding & William A. Edmundson eds., 2005). In his contribution to this volume, Robert Gordon discusses in detail the complex relationship between Realism, on the one hand, and the ALI and its Restatements, on the other. *See* Robert W. Gordon, *Restatements and Realists*, in this volume.

[25] Leiter refers to this as the "sociological" branch of American Legal Realism. *Id.* at 54, 55–56. *See, e.g.,* Herman Oliphant, *A Return to Stare Decisis*, 14 A.B.A. J. 107 (1928) (suggesting that decisions are responsive to social forces operating on judges).

[26] *See generally* Brian Leiter, *Legal Realism & Legal Doctrine*, 163 U. PA. L. REV. 1975, 1976 (2015).

[27] Leon Green, *The Duty Problem in Negligence Cases*, 28 COLUM. L. REV. 1014, 1014 (1928).

[28] Charles E. Clark, *The Restatement of the Law of Contracts*, 42 YALE L.J. 643, 650 (1933).

[29] Edward S. Robinson, *Law—An Unscientific Science*, 44 YALE L.J. 235, 260–61 (1934).

[30] A notable example is Charles Alan Wright, ALI President from 1993 to 2000 and an avowed Realist. *See* Leiter, *supra* note 26, at 1975–76. At least one of the Advisers to the first Restatement of Restitution, Edwin W. Patterson, appears to have been open to some of the Realists' ideas. *See* Harry W. Jones, *Edwin Wilhite Patterson: Man and Ideas*, 57 COLUM. L. REV. 607, 612–16 (1957) (suggesting, not too persuasively, that Patterson embraced a form of "moderate Realism").

[31] Oliphant, *supra* note 25, at 75; *see* Leiter, *supra* note 26, at 1977.

[32] RESTATEMENT (SECOND) OF CONTRACTS § 153 (unilateral mistake), § 208 (unconscionable contract or term) (1981).

[33] *See* UCC § 2-302.

project of restating the law was able, at least by the second round of Restatements, to coexist with moderate forms of Realism and related approaches to legal doctrine.

The Restatement of Restitution was an innovative project, but it was not a Realist project. Its insight was an insight about the content of legal doctrine and, based on that content, about the objectives of private law. It introduced the term "Restitution," and it relied on the very broad idea of unjust enrichment to describe a ground for legal relief between parties that did not depend on contract or tort. The content of unjust enrichment, however, was explained in terms of legal claims—specifically, ancient legal (and equitable) claims that relied heavily on procedural fictions. It was unlikely to appeal to Realists, and even less likely to appeal to partisans of later theoretical developments such as Legal Process, Critical Legal Studies, and Law and Economics. This left the brave Restatement of Restitution without a jurisprudential home in later twentieth-century America.

Another difficulty for the first Restatement was that various post-Realist academic and scholarly trends resulted in a general turn toward public law and away from private law. Theorists drawn to Critical Legal Studies not only lacked interest in the private side of law, they questioned whether private rights can exist independently of collective politics.[34] Those drawn to Law and Economics were intensely interested in legal rules governing private transactions, but more for their effects on markets and maximization of societal wealth than for their effects on the individuals involved.[35] Against this background, interest in a previously unrecognized legal justification for private claims waned, particularly when working examples relied on bygone procedural mechanisms.[36] As the twentieth century proceeded, courses in Restitution were dropped from law school curricula, writing on restitution subsided, and law students were likely to graduate without encountering basic restitution concepts: "subrogation," for example, might be a mystery unless they had chanced upon it in an insurance contract.[37]

The fate of restitution in other common law countries was quite different, although acceptance took some time.[38] About three decades after the ALI published the first Restatement of Restitution, English scholars, judges, and lawyers embraced the new category of law, and their enthusiasm has never diminished.[39] Robert Goff and Gareth

[34] Leiter, *supra* note 24, at 65. Leiter describes, skeptically, the Critical claim that because the government has authorized private activity, there can be no limits on government intervention in private activity. *Id.*

[35] *See, e.g.*, Saul Levmore, *Explaining Restitution*, 71 Va. L. Rev. 65 (1985) (analyzing restitution in terms of its economic effects).

[36] In commentary published in 1998, John Langbein attributed the decline of restitution in the United States, in characteristically strong terms, to "the marginalization of private law" in the wake of Legal Realism and kindred trends. John H. Langbein, The Later History of Restitution, in Restitution: Past, Present, and Future: Essays in Honour of Gareth Jones 57, 61–62 (W.R. Cornish et al. eds., 1998).

[37] This is less likely in the few states, such as California, in which remedies, including multiple forms of restitution, are still tested on the bar exam. *See* https://www.calbar.ca.gov/Admissions/Examinations/California-Bar-Examination/California-Bar-Examination-Scope.

[38] For discussion of the differing modern attitudes toward restitution in the United States and England, *see* Chaim Saiman, *Restitution in America: Why the U.S. Refuses to Join the Global Restitution Party*, 28 Oxford J.L. Stud. 99 (2008).

[39] For a concise analysis of how and why the topic of restitution and unjust enrichment succeeded so well in England and the Commonwealth, along with suggestions about why interest may have waned in the United States, *see* Andrew Burrows, Unjust Enrichment & Restitution, in The Oxford Handbook of the New Private Law 293, 294–301 (Andrew S. Gold et al. eds., 2021).

Jones published the first edition of their treatise on Restitution in 1966 (citing the ALI Restatement in the first footnote); eight more editions followed, the latest in 2016.[40] Peter Birks, a leading English scholar of restitution, followed in the 1980s with a series of books and articles applying intense scrutiny to the analytical structure of restitution and unjust enrichment.[41] Scholars in other parts of the commonwealth have written voluminously on the subject and continue to follow restitution claims in the courts with great interest.[42]

Against the background of tepid interest in restitution in the United States and keen interest elsewhere, questions arose at the ALI in the 1970s about a possible Second Restatement of Restitution.[43] Updates in other subjects had been underway during the 1960s and 1970s, and some of these, particularly in the areas of contracts and torts, overlapped with problems in restitution. The Director at the time, Herbert Wechsler, acknowledged the need but initially postponed the project for budgetary reasons; then in 1980 he commissioned Columbia professor William Young to begin work and appointed a number of eminent Advisers, including John Dawson and Dan Dobbs, both prominent scholars in the fields of remedies and restitution.

From this point onward, however, things went downhill. Young labored diligently, but problems, including the need to reconcile the new volume with modern procedural developments, changes in personnel at the ALI, a recalcitrant Adviser, and unruly meetings, slowed the project. In 1984, the project was suspended, and effectively ended, by the new Director Geoffrey Hazard.[44]

Suspension of the second Restatement almost spelled the end of restitution as a continuing Restatement topic. In 1987, Hazard commissioned a report on the possibility of a new restitution project from the eminent remedies scholar Douglas Laycock; Laycock strongly supported the idea.[45] Hazard, however, requested an additional opinion from Dale Oesterle, who had written critically about established restitutionary tracing rules. Oesterle recommended replacing the restitution project with a new Restatement of Remedies, and for a time Hazard appeared ready to follow this plan and give up the prospect for a new volume on the topic of restitution.[46]

---

[40] ROBERT GOFF & GARETH JONES, THE LAW OF RESTITUTION (1966). Six of the further editions are titled The Law of Restitution; the final two are titled The Law of Unjust Enrichment.

[41] See, e.g., PETER BIRKS, AN INTRODUCTION TO THE LAW OF RESTITUTION (1985). Birks, and to a lesser extent other English scholars, focused attention on the precise relation between restitution and unjust enrichment. American scholars in the field of restitution have been content to view restitution as an invented term for a body of law and unjust enrichment as the central value at work within that body of law.

[42] A prominent example is the recently published Research Handbook on Unjust Enrichment, which includes commentary from scholars from Australia, Canada, England, Hong Kong, Israel, Singapore, South Africa, and the United States. See RESEARCH HANDBOOK ON UNJUST ENRICHMENT AND RESTITUTION, supra note 10. Other notable volumes (there are many) include ROBERT CHALMERS, CHARLES MITCHELL, & JAMES PENNER, PHILOSOPHICAL FOUNDATIONS OF THE LAW OF UNJUST ENRICHMENT (2009); and HANOCH DAGAN, THE LAW AND ETHICS OF RESTITUTION (2004. A conference on "Rethinking Restitution: History, Sociology, Doctrine, and Theory" is planned for this September "in" Australia, with participants from around the world.

[43] The story of the Second Restitution Restatement, as presented here, is based primarily on Kull's thorough description in Kull, supra note 4, at 871–79.

[44] Despite his discouraging experience with the ALI in the 1980s, Young later served as an Adviser to the Third Restatement. Kull, the Reporter, describes Young as a knowledgeable and hard-working Adviser who contributed greatly to the success of the project. Id. at 874.

[45] See id. at 876–77.

[46] Id. at 877–78.

Apparently, Laycock considered taking on the Remedies project but eventually concluded that it would be unmanageable, given the overlap with other topics.[47] In any event, Hazard eventually reversed course, endorsed a Restitution project in 1996, and recruited Andrew Kull as Reporter. Preliminary work commenced in 1997.[48]

IV. 2011: The Restatement (Third) of Restitution and Unjust Enrichment

Fourteen years later, the ALI released the Restatement of the Law (Third) of Restitution and Unjust Enrichment. The aim of the third Restatement was to preserve but modernize the insight of the first Restatement, that legal claims between parties are not limited to claims based on wrongdoing (tort) or breach of a legally valid agreement (contract) but also include claims based on unjust enrichment alone. The revision was massive. Fiction-based forms of action were relegated to notes, historically equitable claims were no longer isolated from historically legal claims, and remedies were treated independently from grounds for relief.

The addition of Unjust Enrichment to the title of the volume was no accident: the Reporter had long believed that the last-minute deletion of "Unjust Enrichment" from the title of the first Restatement had been a mistake.[49] Restitution originally had no legal meaning, and in the United States it had come to mean the category of claims described in the first Restatement. Unjust enrichment was more descriptive and provided a more promising basis for further development of the field, because it identified the basis for restitution claims. So the two were combined. The relation was loose because recovery in restitution does not always depend on an unjust enrichment, and does not always require a corresponding loss, but together the terms were sufficiently descriptive of what was covered and why.[50]

The new title also reflected a distinctly American approach to the subject matter. In the decades following publication of the first Restatement, most, though not all, commentators in England and the British Commonwealth had come to believe that the law of restitution and unjust enrichment should be tamed and rationalized by imposing a strict taxonomic order on the doctrinal rules it comprises. The term "restitution" describes a remedy, while the term "unjust enrichment" describes a ground for relief, and the conceptual line between the two should not be blurred or crossed. In the words of Peter Birks: "the word 'restitution' cannot stand in the same series as the words 'contract' and 'tort.' These words denote events which trigger legal responses while 'restitution' denotes a response triggered."[51] Further, in the interest of

---

[47] *Id.* at 878–79.

[48] *Id.* at 880.

[49] *See* Kull, *supra* note 10.

[50] Edwin Patterson, an Adviser to the first Restatement, explained the compatibility of restitution and unjust enrichment this way: "that the two concepts do not exactly coincide will be relatively unimportant unless those who use the volume attempt to give them exact meaning and apply them deductively." Edwin W. Patterson, *Book Review: Restatement of the Law, Restitution,* 47 YALE L.J. 1420, 1421 (1938).

[51] PETER BIRKS, AN INTRODUCTION TO THE LAW OF RESTITUTION 16 (1985). At the time, Birks viewed restitution and unjust enrichment as coextensive, although analytically different in kind. In later work, he

doctrinal symmetry, restitution must not overlap with other legal categories, particularly the category of contract law. From these premises, it followed that a Restatement of "Restitution and Unjust Enrichment," with no clear conceptual line drawn between the two, must be a confused jumble of substantive grounds for relief and remedial rules that do not always match.[52] In fact, Birks was sufficiently convinced of the logical divide between restitution and unjust enrichment that, part way through the project, he expressed his dim view of the third Restatement in a "Letter to America" published on the internet. Birks's letter informed America and the world that the nascent third Restatement project failed to take account of the internal logic of restitution law, and as a result was analytically unsound.[53]

Fortunately for the vitality of the subject, the Reporter did not succumb to Birks's pressure. The first Restatement had expressed, and the third Restatement now fully embraced, what has been called "the American big tent" view of restitution and unjust enrichment.[54] Restitution is a somewhat unruly assortment of legal claims, based on but not always perfectly aligned with the motivating principle of unjust enrichment. It encompasses a wide array of claims that operate independently of tort and contract law but also sweeps in gain-based relief in the context of tortious wrongs and contractual disputes. Given this deliberately vague definition of the field of restitution, the new Restatement proceeded to enumerate with precision and care the various doctrinal applications of the unjust enrichment principle that state and federal courts had developed in the decades between the original and the sequel.

Throughout, the third Restatement remained faithful to the "big tent" approach. At first glance, the separate treatment of remedies in Part III of the third Restatement might suggest a distinction between unjust enrichment as a ground for relief and restitution as a method of enforcement, consistent with the dominant English approach to the subject. Analytically, however, the third Restatement did not sharply distinguish between the "restitution" and "unjust enrichment" elements of the material covered. Instead, it continued to treat "restitution" as the name given to a field of law and

---

revised to some extent his structural analysis of restitution and unjust enrichment, taking the view that restitution (the remedial side) was narrower in scope than unjust enrichment (the remedial principle). *See* PETER BIRKS, UNJUST ENRICHMENT 3, 11 (2003).

[52] The English view that Restitution and Unjust Enrichment are separate legal concepts appears to be the motivation for an alternative *Restatement of the English Law of Unjust Enrichment*, published by Andrew Burrows (now a justice of the English Supreme Court) closely on the heels of the ALI's Restatement (Third) of Restitution and Unjust Enrichment. Burrow's restatement, also composed with the assistance of a panel of academics, judges, and lawyers, states at the outset that:

(1) A claimant has a right to restitution against a defendant who is unjustly enriched
(2) A right to restitution is a right to the reversal of the defendant's enrichment ...

ANDREW BURROWS (ASSISTED BY AN ADVISORY GROUP OF ACADEMICS, JUDGES, AND PRACTITIONERS), A RESTATEMENT OF THE ENGLISH LAW OF UNJUST ENRICHMENT (2012).

[53] *See* Peter B.H. Birks, *A Letter to America: The New Restatement of Restitution*, 3(3) GLOBAL JURIST FRONTIERS vol. 2 (2003), https://www.degruyter.com/document/doi/10.2202/1535-1653.1096/html.

Bravely (or possibly mischievously), Reporter Kull includes a citation to Birks's letter in the Reporter's Notes to Section 1 of the Restatement. RESTATEMENT (THIRD) OF RESTITUTION AND UNJUST ENRICHMENT, *supra* note 3, at 12, note a.

[54] Elise Bant, Kit Barker, & Simone Degeling, *The Evolution of Unjust Enrichment Law: Theory and Practice, in* RESEARCH HANDBOOK ON UNJUST ENRICHMENT AND RESTITUTION, *supra* note 10, at 2.

"unjust enrichment" as the principle that motivates most if not all of that field.[55] To the extent of this small rebellion against excessive doctrinal precision, the effects of American Legal Realism may be at work even in a not-very-Realist work such as the Restatement (Third) of Restitution and Unjust Enrichment.[56]

For the most part, however, the third Restatement is not a Realist document. True to its heritage, it takes the body of law that lies behind restitution and unjust enrichment very seriously. It invites courts to decide restitution claims according to the patterns established in prior cases, rather than by intuitive conclusions about what is unjust in particular factual situations. This is evident in the Reporter's extended commentary on the meaning of unjust enrichment in the introductory section of Volume I. The Reporter states:

> A significant tradition in English and American law refers to unjust enrichment as if it were something identifiable *a priori*, by the exercise of a moral judgment anterior to legal rules. This equitable conception of the law of restitution is crystalized by Lord Mansfield's famous statement in Moses v. Macferlan ... : 'the gist of this kind of action is, that the defendant, upon the circumstances of the case, is obliged by the ties of natural justice and equity to refund the money.'"

In the Reporter's view, however:

> The concern of restitution is not, in fact, with unjust enrichment in such a broad sense, but with a narrower set of circumstances giving rise to what might more appropriately be called *unjustified* enrichment. Compared to the open-ended implications of the term 'unjust enrichment,' instances of unjustified enrichment are both predictable and objectively determined, because the justification in question is not moral but legal. Unjustified enrichment is enrichment that lacks an adequate legal basis: it results from a transaction that the law treats as ineffective to work a conclusive alteration in ownership reinterpreted by courts in particular situations as they arise; it is a legal concept to be applied consistently with the expectations generated by the pattern of its applications over time, and the Restatement that maps it is a Restatement of *law*.

Returning to Professor Dawsons' advice: "If we know the forest is enchanted we have not too much to fear."[57]

---

[55] The first note to Section 1 states:

The identification of unjust enrichment as an independent basis of liability in common-law legal systems—comparable in this respect to a liability in contract or tort—was the central achievement of the 1937 Restatement of Restitution ... The use of the word "restitution" to describe the cause of action as well as the remedy is likewise inherited from the original Restatement, despite the problems this usage creates.

RESTATEMENT (THIRD) OF RESTITUTION AND UNJUST ENRICHMENT § 1 cmt. a, at 3.

[56] But *cf.* Lionel Smith, *Legal Epistemology in the Restatement (Third) of Restitution and Unjust Enrichment*, 92 B.U. L. REV. 899, 908–09 (2012) (suggesting that both the first and the third Restatements revealed Realist tendencies by suggesting that constructive trusts are simply remedial devices).

[57] Dawson, *supra* note 20.

The lengthy and detailed description of the specific subject matter of restitution and unjust enrichment in the third Restatement is too extensive and varied to comment on usefully in this short history. The Restatement took fourteen years to complete and fills two volumes. It is true throughout to the insight of Ames, Seavey, and Scott that there is a law of restitution, based on unjust enrichment, which occupies a position in private law analogous to that of the law of tort and the law of contract. It continues cover restitution in the setting of tortious wrongdoing and contractual exchange as well as restitution based solely on unjust enrichment. Much of the specific substantive material, however, is new. Extensive Reporter's Notes appear throughout, tracking judicial decisions over the nearly 75 years that passed between the publication of the first Restatement and the publication of the third.[58] Altogether, the third Restatement was a remarkable achievement, especially for a sole Reporter.

Among the seventy sections included in the Third Restatement, there are a few flashes of Realism, although not many. An example is Section 28, governing claims by cohabitants following a break up. The section provides that if one cohabitant "owns a specific asset to which the other had made substantial, uncompensated contributions in the form of property or services," the other may claim restitution "as necessary to prevent unjust enrichment."[59] Not surprisingly, this provision provoked lively debate in meetings of the Advisory Council: its effect is to delegate to judges the power to decide what is just and unjust in a particular fraught situation. Debates ensued, and judicial discretion ultimately prevailed.[60] For the most part, however, the third Restatement opts for guidance rather than discretion, and backs up its guidance with concrete examples from decided cases.

A major difference between the third Restatement and the original Restatement prepared by Seavey and Scott is that the third Restatement is written for modern readers. Quasi-contract and the writ of assumpsit appear only in explanatory historical notes.[61] Equity plays a role, but equity procedures are barely touched upon except as needed to describe the special judicial powers, inherited from separate courts of equity, that make tracing particularly effective as a means of capturing unjust enrichment.[62] On the other hand, the range of legal settings in which restitution provides a ground for relief is much greater than the range identified in the first Restatement,

---

[58] Interestingly, Professor Seavey reports in his autobiography that by the time the first Restatement was completed, he had amassed a great number of relevant cases, but the ALI rules in force at the time prevented him from citing them in the volume, "since the theory was that the Restatement was to be authoritative and that citing cases would make it an ordinary text book." Seavey & King, *supra* note 16, at 67. Seavey objected to this limitation and persuaded the ALI Council to allow him to place a selection of cases in a pamphlet inserted in a slot inside the back cover. *Id.* at 68. Apparently, this is the origin of the Reporter's Notes that now appear in Restatement texts. True to the tradition, the third Restatement displays an enormous number of reported cases, painstakingly assembled by Reporter Kull. On the initial rule against case citation and its evolution, *see* Deborah A. DeMott, *Restating the Law in the Shadow of Codes: The ALI in Its Formative Era*, in this volume.

[59] RESTATEMENT (THIRD) OF RESTITUTION § 28.

[60] For commentary on this section and the controversy surrounding it at the time of its drafting, *see, e.g.*, Doug Rendleman, *Restating Restitution: The Restatement Process and Its Critics*, 65 WASH. & LEE L. REV. 933 (2008); Chaim Saimon & Emily Sherwin, *Love, Money, and Justice: Restitution Between Cohabitants*, 77 U. COLO. L. REV. 711 (2006).

[61] RESTATEMENT (THIRD) OF RESTITUTION AND UNJUST ENRICHMENT § 4 cmts. a, b, e, § 70 cmts. b, c, e.

[62] *Id.* § 4 cmt. b.

and coverage is updated to reflect the modern transactional world. For example, in addition to rights between former cohabitants, the third Restatement addresses restitution claims in the context of class actions and common funds, restitution claims based on appropriation of intellectual property, and restitution claims in the vicinity of a murder.[63] At the same time, the Reporter was careful throughout not to get too far ahead of the law: all of the illustrations (which number over a thousand) track real, decided cases.[64]

Was this a contentious Restatement project? The most strenuous objections came from English observers such as Birks who felt the project was overlooking important logical truths about the law of restitution and unjust enrichment.[65] Internally, there were bound to be some turf wars, particularly in the neighborhood of contract law. Consistently, however, the polite but steady determination of the Reporter, the tactical ingenuity of veterans like Douglas Laycock, and the very significant diplomatic skills of Director Lance Liebman headed off any significant difficulty.

It remains to be seen whether restitution will recover as a field of study and a subject of scholarly commentary in the wake of the third Restatement. The utility of restitution as an element of private law is unquestionable, and the third Restatement provides an invaluable roadmap. Nevertheless, American law schools continue to emphasize the public side of law and to give less attention than they once did to legal encounters between individuals. One hopeful sign is a new casebook on Restitution and Unjust Enrichment, published in 2018 by Andrew Kull and Ward Farnsworth, which is now in use at a number of schools.[66] Another is a "Developments in the Law" project on Unjust Enrichment, conceived and carried out by the editors of the *Harvard Law Review*, which examines both the intellectual history of restitution and unjust enrichment and a variety of modern applications.[67]

V. Conclusion

The Restatement of Restitution and Unjust Enrichment, as it has evolved over time, is a model Restatement project. The 1937 volume presented and defended the insight that unjust enrichment of one person by another provides a third basic ground of recovery in American law, in addition to tort and contact. Though clearly present in the law, this type of claim had gone unremarked for centuries as an independent basis for relief. The achievement was remarkable, and it generated a worldwide response from courts and commentators that continues in full force today.

---

[63] *See id.* §§ 28 (cohabitants); 29 (common funds); 42 (intellectual property), 45 (homicide).

[64] One possible exception to the remark in the text, that the third Restatement never gets too far ahead of the law, is a section governing opportunistic breach of a contract. The gist of the section is that in certain situations involving a deliberate and profitable breach and a damage remedy that is unlikely to provide adequate relief, the claimant may recover profits the defendant realized as a result of the breach in place of damages for loss. *Id.* § 39.

[65] Gareth Jones, of Cambridge, was quite the opposite—an exemplary participant who made many useful contributions.

[66] ANDREW KULL & WARD FARNSWORTH, RESTITUTION AND UNJUST ENRICHMENT: CASES AND NOTES (2018).

[67] *Developments in the Law: Unjust Enrichment, supra* note 13.

The next important achievement of the Restatement of Restitution and Unjust enrichment, occurring in its third round, was to save the great insight of the first round from fading into obscurity. The third Restatement accomplished this by gathering an enormous amount of evidence to confirm that restitution is in fact an independent basis of legal liability and by translating the insight of the first Restatement into modern language with modern illustrations. By and large, it did so without either minimizing the role of doctrine in the manner of American Legal Realism or losing sight of the basic significance of the field in an effort to achieve perfect doctrinal symmetry among its various components.

Restitution is a project in which the ALI should take great pride. Not every restatement of law is likely to produce a major insight into the nature of private law, but this one did. Meanwhile, we should make an effort to teach the next generation of lawyers how to understand and use the rules of restitution and unjust enrichment that are laid out so carefully in the third Restatement.

PART III
CODES

13

The Uniform Commercial Code and the Ongoing Quest for an Efficient and Fair Commercial Law

Robert E. Scott[*]

I. Introduction

The commercial law that we have today is the product of a number of different and often competing institutions.[1] At one time or another over the past two hundred years, common law courts, state and federal legislatures, and private legislative groups such as the American Law Institute (ALI) and the Uniform Law Commission (ULC) have all struggled to take the lead in generating commercial law rules that are efficient as between the transacting parties and fair in their treatment of affected third parties. And yet each of these institutions has failed to deliver on that normative goal in important respects. The story of American commercial law, then, is a story of an as yet unachieved quest by succeeding institutions to produce better commercial law rules than the institutions that preceded it. The Uniform Commercial Code (UCC) project sits at the center of this story, and its successes and failures exemplify the challenge of creating commercial law in an environment of continuing technological change and uncertainty.

For around seven hundred years, from 1200 to 1900, only one institution—common law courts—produced commercial law in England and America.[2] For much of that time, commercial law as we know it today was nonexistent; commercial parties primarily relied on the practice of exchanging penal bonds in order to trade goods and services.[3] Modern commercial law developed after the industrial revolution as common law courts began to resolve contract disputes in ways that over time evolved into widely acceptable default rules. The courts functioned unaided for many years because intrinsic to common law adjudication is a mechanism for generating

[*] Alfred McCormack Professor of Law, Emeritus and Director, Center for Contract and Economic Organization, Columbia Law School. I am grateful for helpful comments from Andrew Gold, John Goldberg, Robert Gordon, Carol Lee, Elizabeth Scott, and David Seipp.

[1] This introduction draws on Alan Schwartz & Robert E. Scott, *Obsolescence: The Intractable Production Problem in Contract Law*, 121 COLUM. L. REV. 1659, 1661–70 (2021).

[2] *See generally* A.W.B. Simpson, *Innovation in Nineteenth Century Contract Law*, 91 L.Q. REV. 247 (1975) (describing the role of early common law courts). This situation changed in England in 1898 with the Sale of Goods Act and changed in America in 1898 with the Negotiable Instruments Law and again in 1906 with the Uniform Sales Act. These statutes, however, largely replicated the common law.

[3] Alan Schwartz & Robert E. Scott, *The Common Law of Contract and the Default Rule Project*, 102 VA. L. REV. 1523, 1533–37 (2016).

Robert E. Scott, *The Uniform Commercial Code and the Ongoing Quest for an Efficient and Fair Commercial Law* In: *The American Law Institute*. Edited by: Andrew S. Gold and Robert W. Gordon, Oxford University Press. © Oxford University Press 2023. DOI: 10.1093/oso/9780197685341.003.0014

a particular subset of efficient commercial law rules. The mechanism starts when a contract lacks a term to resolve a dispute between litigating parties and the court must step in to fill the gap in their agreement. The court's decision then becomes a rule when future parties facing the same dispute determine to leave a similar gap in their contract rather than draft an express term that regulates the dispute in a different way. If subsequent contracting parties do leave a gap, the first case becomes a precedent in the sense that the court will resolve the later dispute with the rule that it used to resolve the initial dispute. Rules of decision in earlier cases thus become default terms in contracts that are written thereafter unless those parties contract out.[4] And while courts cannot calculate the magnitude of any third-party effects from a proposed rule, courts do commonly consider both fairness and public policy concerns when creating these default rules.

This common law adjudication mechanism creates "transcontextual" commercial law rules: the rule solves a contracting problem for parties functioning in diverse contexts. If the rule in the first case failed to apply broadly to different parties in different circumstances, future parties in other areas would have realized that the rule did not work for them and, rather than leaving a contract gap, they would have explicitly contracted about the problem for themselves. Note as well that a common law default rule roughly tracks changing commercial patterns. When commerce materially changes, parties do different deals under new contracts. If the future parties' contracts nevertheless also leave a gap when a solution to the problem could be found, the rule in the first case continues to function as a precedent: The rule has thus been "updated." If parties facing new commercial situations instead create contracts that expressly govern the issue, the rule in the first case becomes vestigial. But then, the common law mechanism, triggered by current disputes, will create new rules.[5]

The updating feature of the common law mechanism has an inherent limitation, however. Parties in different commercial contexts often require solutions that are specific to their circumstances, and generalist courts are ill-equipped to supply specific solutions to particular industries. Facing the inherent limitations of the common law process, the American legal establishment came to understand that a modern economy would benefit from a set of laws that applied to discrete bodies of commercial law. Moreover, American lawyers were unsatisfied with the common law mechanism. The main source of their impatience was that default rules are slow to form. Litigation must proceed over time in different contexts before a default rule is fully established. Consequently, most of the common law default rules were developed over the course of the nineteenth century, and the process of commercial law rule development slowed considerably thereafter.[6] In addition, these commercial lawyers observed

---

[4] For a complete description of how the common law functions, *see* Schwartz & Scott, *id.* at 1546–51.

[5] This explanation for how commercial contract law is made complements the standard narrative. In that narrative, great judges—Mansfield, Cardozo, Hand—created rules that last. The mechanism explanation is consistent with this view: The more commercially sophisticated and competent the judge is in the first case, the more likely the judge is to solve the parties' contracting problem efficiently. And then later parties are more likely to leave a gap into which the first court's rule can fit. But the mechanism explanation does not rely on unusual judicial creativity. Rather, an efficient commercial law rule is the joint product of a plausible judicial solution to a contracting problem *together with* the uncoordinated decisions of heterogeneous contracting parties to accept that solution.

[6] *See* Schwartz & Scott, *supra* note 3, at 1534–37.

from experience that courts are poor regulators of a modern economy. Courts cannot find facts, apart from case records, and so cannot form accurate views of the context in which a possible rule will function and the effects of current rules. Compounding the problem is the fact that judges are generalist lawyers. The typical judge has little commercial expertise and cannot effectively resolve the economic issues that a possible rule may pose. Given the several deficiencies of common law courts, a consensus emerged: another rule generating mechanism was required.

The widespread dissatisfaction with the common law process produced two major statutory interventions in the twentieth century that sought to change commercial law itself. The first effort at a codification of commercial law occurred at the turn of the twentieth century when the National Conference of Commissioners on Uniform State Laws, now known as the Uniform Law Commission,[7] produced the Negotiable Instruments Law, followed shortly thereafter by the Uniform Sales Act.[8] Ultimately, seven Uniform Acts were enacted between 1896 and 1933 governing various aspects of a commercial transaction. This early codification effort soon proved obsolete, however. The various uniform acts were far from uniform, especially in the case of personal property security interests: state rules governing trust receipts and conditional sales varied widely. Grant Gilmore famously remarked that "pre-code personal security law closely resembled that obscure wood in which Dante discovered the gates of hell."[9] Even more troubling was the fact that these early codifications basically reified the past; they had little relevance for the dramatic changes in commercial law that occurred after their enactment. As just one example, the Sales Act failed to treat the host of issues raised by the emergence of long-term supply and distribution contracts and the complex contractual relationships that they stimulated. As a consequence, only the courts were able to keep sales law current with these changing commercial practices throughout the interwar period.[10]

Obsolescence coupled with the lack of uniformity thus led in the mid-twentieth century to a second effort by the ALI and the ULC to codify much of commercial law under the umbrella of the UCC. The UCC was promulgated and drafted during the 1940s by a distinguished group of scholars and practitioners, headed by Professor Karl Llewellyn, under the joint auspices of the ALI and the ULC. The UCC was intended to be a unified, integrated, and comprehensive statutory treatment of commercial transactions as a "single subject of the law, notwithstanding its many facets."[11] The drafters viewed this new code as a "single uniform law that would deal with all the phases which may ordinarily arise in the handling of a commercial transaction, from start to finish."[12] True to the drafters' ambition, the UCC was ultimately adopted in every state

---

[7] To avoid confusion I will use the contemporary designation ULC throughout this chapter.

[8] The Negotiable Instruments Law was enacted in 1896; the Uniform Sales Act was promulgated in 1906 and ultimately adopted in thirty-four states

[9] Grant Gilmore, *The Good Faith Purchaser Idea and the Uniform Commercial Code: Confessions of a Repentant Draftsman*, 15 GA. L. REV. 605, 620 (1981).

[10] As a further example, the holder in due course doctrine in the NIL assumed a world (long since passed) in which commercial paper passed between multiple parties. But by the 1930's most disputes concerned the check collection process and banks as holders of paper, issues on which the statute had nothing to offer. Grant Gilmore, *On Statutory Obsolescence*, 7 U. COLO. L. REV. 461, 469–71 (1966–1967).

[11] General Comment of the National Conference of Commissioners on Uniform State Laws and the American Law Institute (1962).

[12] *Id.*

(except for portions of Article 2 in Louisiana) and in the District of Columbia and all U.S. territories.

The drafters' faith in the benefits of a publicly supplied collection of commercial law default rules was justified: private parties cannot solve every contracting problem that they face. Contracting parties seldom can internalize the full gain from creating a useful solution to a common commercial problem—others can copy their innovation—but nonetheless they bear the full cost.[13] When the cost exceeds the share of the gain to contracting parties, the problem will not be solved efficiently without outside help. Responding to this dilemma, the drafters promised to address these common problems and supply commercial parties with apt solutions in the form of UCC provisions. And, in many respects, as I discuss more fully later, the UCC delivered on that promise.

But the seventy-plus year history with the UCC reveals a deeper institutional problem. A public program of supplying commercial law rules must satisfy two conditions: the rules must first solve commercial problems as the parties would have solved them, and the rules must update promptly as economic conditions change. The source of the difficulties that plague the commercial law production process is the problem of obsolescence. An efficient commercial law rule must not only solve a commercial problem in the current state of the world, but it also should solve the problem in future states of the world that are "relevantly similar" to the current state. Yet if the commercial problem takes a different form in a future state, the efficient solution to the problem can change as well. In that case, the legal rule becomes obsolete: the rule no longer solves the commercial problem in its current form.[14]

Obsolescence is a significant concern because the commercial world of today is dissimilar in significant ways from the world that existed when the UCC was promulgated.[15] Article 2 on sales took its current form by 1952 and has not been materially

---

[13] Charles J. Goetz & Robert E. Scott, *The Limits of Expanded Choice: An Analysis of the Interaction Between Express and Implied Contract Terms*, 73 CAL. L. REV. 261, 292–93 (1985).

[14] The UCC Article 2 warranty provisions illustrate the obsolescence problem. Article 2 primarily regulates quality issues with the implied warranty of merchantability: Goods must be "fit for the ordinary purposes for which they are used" or "pass without objection in the trade." UCC § 2–314(2) (AM. L. INST. & UNIF. L. COMM'N 1952). This regulation was once efficient when sellers traded homogenous standard goods to large numbers of similarly situated buyers. However, the warranty is commonly disclaimed today because many sellers trade heterogenous—that is, customized—goods to buyers with particular needs. The UCC solution thus is no longer apt. Because the UCC is a statute, however, it necessarily continues to supply the original solution until it is amended. Though the UCC solution does not solve very many parties' contracting problem of how best to allocate between them the risk that the goods will be nonconforming, parties still face these quality issues and the need for a term to regulate them.

[15] *See, e.g.,* LISA BERNSTEIN & BRAD PETERSON, MANAGERIAL CONTRACTING: A PRELIMINARY STUDY 2–3 (2020) (unpublished manuscript) (on file with author) (footnotes omitted).

> Over the past four decades a number of technological and other changes have strongly affected American manufacturing—among them: firms outsourcing all but core competencies, shorter product cycle times, the increased pace of technological change, the widespread adoption of just-in-time inventory methods, the outsourcing of design and innovation not just production, and the need to meet a variety of competitive challenges including those created by the introduction of high quality Japanese products in the early 1980s. These changes, in turn, have led to new problems that procurement contracts have to solve and have fundamentally changed the nature of contractual relationships in manufacturing.

amended since then.[16] Somewhat perversely, the obsolescence problem also negatively affects those areas of commercial law in the UCC that have been updated, including Article 9 on secured credit, and Articles 3 and 4 on commercial paper and banking.[17] Here, focused interest group pressures stimulated reform proposals that have led to regular updating.[18] But this focused response to the risk of obsolescence raises yet another concern: while interest group pressure did produce new commercial law rules, the public interest was not represented in the revision process.[19]

This chapter proceeds as follows. Section II briefly describes the drafting history of the UCC project and explores the political economy of its promulgation and enactment. In section III, I discuss the benefits of this experiment in codification: important innovations in sales law and the rules regulating personal property security illustrate how the drafters of the Code were able find new ways to facilitate efficient commercial exchange. Section IV turns to the ongoing costs of codification. The pressure to update commercial law rules produces one of two suboptimal results: either competition between interest groups deters meaningful revision or a dominant interest group overcomes barriers to revision while capturing rents from third parties in the process.

The persistent and significant costs of obsolescence demand a critical reexamination of the institutional features of the commercial law production process. I conclude that the disregard for the public interest justifies skeptics asking whether there is a role for institutions other than the private lawmakers who created the UCC in developing commercial rules that take broader social interests into account.[20] Until that question is resolved, the search for a better commercial law remains elusive.

---

[16] An institution called "The Permanent Editorial Board" is supposed to keep the UCC current, but the Board's recommendations must be approved by the ALI and ULC before being recommended to the states for adoption. The Board has made few significant recommendations and fewer have been adopted. *See Permanent Editorial Board for Uniform Commercial Code*, ULC, https://www.uniformlaws.org/committees/community-home?CommunityKey=ffaa1a04-3d69-40f5-95bd-7adac186ef28 (last visited Oct. 10, 2020) (documenting the activities of the Permanent Editorial Board). I discuss the failed efforts to revise Article 2 in *infra* section IV.A.

[17] *See, e.g.*, UCC art. 9 (AM. L. INST. & UNIF. L. COMM'N amended 2010); *id.* arts. 3, 4 (AM. L. INST. & UNIF. L. COMM'N amended 2002).

[18] Article 9 regulating secured credit has been updated twice—in 1972 and again in 1999. It was subsequently amended in 2010. Article 3 on negotiable instruments and Article 4 regulating bank deposits and collections were revised in 1990 and amended in 2002. For discussion of the interest group pressures that stimulate updating of specialized commercial fields, *see generally* Alan Schwartz & Robert E. Scott, *The Political Economy of Private Legislatures*, 143 U. PA. L. REV. 595 (1995).

[19] Article 9 of the UCC is an apt example of the potential divergence between private and public interests. Article 9 rationalized numerous pre-Code statutes governing the priority of secured creditors' claims and in the process simplified and reduced the costs of issuing secured debt. But critics have long argued that the priority given to secured creditors in Article 9 functions to redistribute wealth away from unsophisticated creditors, particularly tort claimants, employees and small suppliers. *See, e.g.*, Lynn M. LoPucki, *The Unsecured Creditors' Bargain*, 80 VA. L. REV. 1887, 1941–47 (1994). I discuss the political economy of the recent revisions to Article 9 in *infra* Part IVB.

[20] The supplementary role of contract law as the backstop to specific statutory regulation is made explicit, for example, in UCC § 1–103(b) (AM. L. INST. & UNIF. L. COMM'N 2001) ("Unless displaced by the particular provisions of the UCC, the principles of law and equity, including the law merchant and the law relative to capacity in contract, principal and agent, estoppel, fraud, misrepresentation, duress, coercion, mistake, bankruptcy and other validating or invalidating cause supplement its provisions.").

II. The Political Economy of the UCC Project

The story of the UCC project and Karl Llewellyn's unique role in the drafting and process of initial enactment has been told many times already.[21] The following synopsis suffices to illuminate the inherent tensions in the codification process.[22] The rise of the modern industrial state in the late nineteenth century exposed the significant diversity that existed in the commercial law of various states. The resulting uncertainty led to proposals for the enactment of a federal commercial code to govern interstate commercial transactions.[23] These proposals, in turn, stimulated the formation of the ULC in 1892. Rather than accept federal intrusions on traditional state authority, the ULC proposed to formulate and seek adoption by states of various uniform laws governing different aspects of commercial law. One of those uniform statutes was the Uniform Sales Act, drafted by Samuel Williston and adopted by the ULC in 1906. The Sales Act, in turn, was modeled on the English Sale of Goods Act of 1893.

As the years went by, many scholars noted problems with the Sales Act, and, in fact, a number of states declined to enact the statute. One of those critics was Llewellyn, then teaching at the Columbia Law School. Llewellyn had two principal objections to the Sales Act. First, he objected to those default rules that were based on artificial doctrinal conceptions, such as the location of "title" in the goods. These defaults were "inefficient" in the sense that they did not reflect the terms of agreement that most parties in the relevant trade would have made for themselves. Second, the Sales Act default rules applied in the main to all transactions equally and thus were insufficiently tailored to the circumstances of particular trades and industries. The deficiencies of the Sales Act led to reform initiatives. In 1940, the Federal Sales Act was introduced in Congress.[24] The Commissioners in the ULC reacted to the threat of federalization by lobbying against federal enactment and beginning to draft a revised Uniform Sales Act. Perhaps most significantly, they recruited Llewellyn, one of the strongest advocates for the federalization of sales law, to their project.[25]

By 1945, the ULC had formed a collaboration with the ALI and, working in tandem, they expanded the revised sales act project to include the drafting of a comprehensive commercial code.[26] Llewellyn and the other proponents of the project sought to avoid previous difficulties in achieving uniformity by creating a "code" in the true sense—a

---

[21] See, e.g., Alan R. Kamp, Downtown Code: A History of the Uniform Commercial Code, 1949–1954, 49 BUFF. L. REV. 359 (2001); Alan R. Kamp, Uptown Act: A History of the Uniform Commercial Coe 1940–49, 51 SMU L. REV. 275 (1998); Ingrid M. Hillinger, The Article 2 Merchant Rules: Karl Llewellyn's Attempt to Achieve the Good, the True, the Beautiful in Commercial Law, 873 GEO. L.J. 1141 (1985); Zipporah B. Wiseman, The Limits of Vision: Karl Llewellyn and the Merchant Rules, 100 HARV. L. REV. 465 (1987); Dennis M. Patterson, Good Faith, Lender Liability, and Discretionary Acceleration: Of Llewellyn, Wittgenstein, and the Uniform Commercial Code, 68 TEX. L. REV. 169 (1989); Kathleen Patchel, Interest Group Politics, Federalism, and the Uniform Law Process Some Lessons from the Uniform Commercial Code, 78 MINN. L. REV. 83 (1993).

[22] This part draws on Robert E. Scott, The Rise and Fall of Article 2, 62 LA. L. REV. 1011, 1032–41 (2002).

[23] See Committee on Commercial Law, Report, 10 A.B.A. REP. 332–44 (1887).

[24] See Karl Llewellyn, The Needed Federal Sales Act, 26 VA. L. REV. 558 (1940).

[25] WILLIAM TWINING, KARL LLEWELLYN AND THE REALIST MOVEMENT 270–301 (1973).

[26] The marriage between the ALI and the ULC was proposed and arranged in the 1940s by William Schnader, a prominent attorney who was a Vice President of the ALI and also served as President of the ULC. See Patchel, supra note 22, at 98.

systematic, preemptive, and comprehensive enactment of a whole field of law. Many observers noted, however, the striking differences in the rule form between Article 2 and the other substantive articles of the Code. Article 2 contains a large number of broad standards, vague admonitions, and "muddy" rules. Many sections are little more than statements of principle that delegate broad discretion to courts to apply them to specific circumstances.

The decision to produce a code was primarily instrumental. The ALI and ULC believed that this consolidation of commercial law into a single statutory scheme would enable them to sell the entire project to the states on a "take it or leave it" basis thus avoiding the selective enactment that had occurred with earlier uniform acts.[27]

While Llewellyn worked on the UCC project for more than ten years, responsibility for drafting key provisions dealing with credit instruments, bank collections, and secured transactions—Articles 3, 4, and 9—was assigned to others. William Prosser was the principal Reporter for Article 3, Fairfax Leary followed by Walter Malcolm were the Reporters for Article 4, and Allison Dunham and Grant Gilmore were the Reporters for Article 9. In short order, the drafting process of these articles came to be dominated by representatives of banking and commercial financing interests.[28] In particular, financial institutions and those sympathetic to their needs played a significant role in the drafting and ratification of Article 9. When the UCC project had just gotten underway after World War II, Homer Kripke, then associated with CIT Financial Corp., served as a key Adviser to the Reporter, Grant Gilmore, and to the other drafters of what eventually became Article 9. In addition, Kripke then served as one of the two principal drafters for what became the 1972 revision of Article 9. Articles 3, 4, and 9 were, in the main, characterized by detailed, precise rules that allocated commercial risks in ways favorable to the commercial interests that participated so actively in the drafting process. No doubt the clarity of the new rules governing secured financing, credit instruments, and payment systems reduced transactions costs in the relevant credit markets. But, equally clearly, the rules favored the interests of sophisticated repeat players in those markets over those of occasional participants in financing transactions.[29]

The Article 2 project, on the other hand, proceeded without the active participation of external interest groups. The project was dominated by Llewellyn and his band of academic reformers.[30] The revisions that the academic reformers agreed to during the drafting process were those that they felt were necessary to secure the approval of the far more conservative lawyers and other legal professionals that dominated the two sponsoring private legislative bodies. Once Article 2 passed the twin hurdles of approval by the ALI and the ULC, it was essentially carried along by widespread industry support for the credit and financing articles. Although Pennsylvania adopted the Code in 1952, it was not until the comprehensive lobbying following the New York

---

[27] William D. Hawkland, *The Uniform Commercial Code and the Civil Codes*, 56 LA. L. REV. 233–36 (1995).

[28] Kamp, *supra* note 22, at 382–88; Gilmore, *supra* note 9, at 619–26; Schwartz & Scott, *supra* note 18, at 638–45.

[29] Robert E. Scott, *The Politics of Article 9*, 80 VA. L. REV. 1783, 1815–45 (1994); Schwartz & Scott, *supra* note 18, at 643–48.

[30] TWINING, *supra* note 25 at 280–90.

Law Revision Commission analysis of the Code in 1956 that the professional community joined forces to ensure the enactment of the Code in New York and thereafter within a decade in every other American state except Louisiana.[31]

III. The Many Innovations of the UCC

Since the academic focus in recent years has turned to the deficiencies of the UCC, especially as scholars confront the effects of obsolescence, it is too easy to neglect the singular contributions the UCC introduced. In this section, I highlight the two most important innovations the Code brought to commercial law: Llewellyn's contributions to contract theory in Article 2, and Gilmore and Kripke's elegant harmonization of personal property security interests in Article 9.

A. Llewellyn's Contribution to Contract Theory: The Default Rules of Article 2

As noted earlier, Karl Llewellyn had two principal objections to Willistonian formalism, as embodied in the Uniform Sales Act.[32] First, he objected to those default rules that were based on artificial doctrinal conceptions, such as the location of "title" in the goods.[33] Second, the Sales Act default rules were insufficiently tailored to the circumstances of particular trades and industries.[34] Llewellyn's effort to solve the first problem by substituting more efficient defaults was, in general, a conspicuous success. His attempt to solve the second problem by creating a mechanism for the recognition and incorporation of tailored, industry-specific defaults was, in the end, a noble failure.

1. Regulating Contractual Breakdown: Efficient Allocation of Commercial Risks
The singular contribution to commercial law in Article 2 was a series of default terms for salvaging broken contracts that reduced contracting costs for many (if not most) parties to sales transactions. Under the Sales Act, most risk allocation questions were resolved by determining who had the title to the contract goods. The problem was, that while everyone knew that the party who had the title assumed the relevant risk, no one knew who had the title.[35] The resulting uncertainty increased transactions

---

[31] By 1975, Louisiana had enacted Articles 1, 3, 4, and 5. Subsequently, Article 9 and portions of Article 2 were enacted as well

[32] This part draws on Scott, *supra* note 21, at 1032–41.

[33] Karl Llewellyn, *Through Title to Contract and a Little Bit Beyond*, 15 N.Y.U. L. REV. 159, 168–70 (1938); Karl Llewellyn, INTRODUCTION TO CASES AND MATERIALS ON SALES, at iv (1929) ("title is a wholly unnecessary major premise").

[34] Karl Llewellyn, *On Our Case Law of Offer and Acceptance I*, 48 YALE L.J. 1, 12, 28 (1938) (a meaningful rule is one that is defined by "operative fact"; such rules are "understandable and clear about what the action is which is to be guided and ... must state clearly how to deal with the raw facts as they arise ...").

[35] As Llewellyn observed, under the Sales Act, title governed questions of "risk of loss, action for the price, the applicable law in an interstate transaction, the place and time for measuring damages, and the power to defeat the other party's interest, or to replevy, or to reject." Karl Llewellyn, *Through Title to Contract and a Bit Beyond*, 15 N.Y.U. L. REV. 159 (1938). He went on to say that "this would be an admirable way to go at it if

costs and complicated efforts to contract out of the legal default. Llewellyn's risk of loss rules illustrate his commitment to legal defaults that reduce transactions costs for contracting parties. Rather than using artificial conceptions of title, Article 2 assigns the risk of loss in general to the party in control of the goods, on the (generally sound) intuition that the party in control can best take precautions to reduce endogenous risk and/or insure against exogenous risks.[36] A similar approach is reflected in the "salvage" rules of Article 2—rejection, cure, acceptance, and revocation of acceptance.[37] These rules were also drafted with the purpose of reducing contracting costs by encouraging ex post adjustments by the party with the comparative advantage in mitigating the costs of broken contracts.[38]

Llewellyn was particularly sensitive to the costs of strategic behavior in the performance of sales contracts. He initially proposed to substitute a substantial performance standard in place of the traditional perfect tender rule as the more efficient default rule for sales contracts in which the seller's investment in the transaction exposed it to the risk of opportunism by the buyer.[39] Llewellyn understood, however, that a substantial performance rule operated as a double-edged sword. Requiring a buyer to accept goods that "substantially conformed" to the contract reduces the risk of strategic rejections by the buyer, but, in turn, it exposes the buyer to an opportunistic tender by the seller of substandard goods. His solution to this dilemma reflects his understanding that legal defaults that impose flexible adjustment on one party become opportunities for exploitation by the other. In the end, Llewellyn returned to the perfect tender rule, but, by incorporating a cure provision, he was able to create a structure for mutual adjustment that accomplishes many of the same purposes as a substantial performance rule.[40]

The remedial scheme introduced in Article 2 is a final example of efficient defaults for resolving broken contracts. Llewellyn began by focusing on a central question: Which party is responsible for salvaging the broken contract? This question,

---

the Title concept had been tailored to fit the normal course of a going or suspended situation during its flux or suspension. But Title was not thus conceived, nor has its environment of buyers and sellers had material effect upon it." *Id. See* Jody S. Kraus, *Decoupling Sales Law from the Acceptance-Rejection Fulcrum,* 104 YALE L.J. 129, 130–32 (1994).

[36] UCC § 2-509. Comment 1 to 2-509 states: "The underlying theory of these sections on risk of loss is the adoption of the contractual approach rather than an arbitrary shifting of the risk with the 'property in the goods.'" Comment 3 explains why a merchant seller bears the risk of loss until actual receipt by a buyer: "The underlying theory of this rule is that a merchant who is to make physical delivery at his own place continues meanwhile to control the goods and can be expected to insure his interest in them. The buyer, on the other hand has no control of the goods and it is extremely unlikely that he will carry insurance of goods not yet in his possession."

[37] *See* UCC §§ 2-601–2-608.

[38] ALAN SCHWARTZ & ROBERT E. SCOTT, SALES LAW AND THE CONTRACTING PROCESS 230–311 (2d ed. 1991); Kraus, *supra* note 35 at 135–60.

[39] 11-A of the 1941 Revised Uniform Sales Act proposed to substitute the standard of mercantile performance for the traditional sales law standard of perfect tender. *See* Report and Second Draft, THE REVISED UNIFORM SALES ACT (1941), *reprinted in* 1 UNIFORM COMMERCIAL CODE DRAFTS 269, 378–81 (Elizabeth S. Kelly ed., 1984). Under this test the buyer was required to accept performance where the risks and burdens on the buyer were not materially increased and the goods met the "operating or marketing requirements of the buyer in the course of his business."

[40] *See* UCC § 2-508.

in turn, requires an answer to a deeper one: Given the default rule of expectation damages, why would anyone ever breach (except inadvertently)? And yet, we observe advertent breach. There are two possible explanations for a promisor's decision to breach in the face of an expectation damages rule. The first is benign: the decision to breach is a "cry for help"—a request that the contracting partner adjust to the broken contract by covering (or reselling) on the market and submitting a "damages" bill to the promisor. The alternative explanation is strategic: breach is motivated by the imperfections in the judicial system that systematically deny the promisee its contractual expectancy. Promisors who breach, under this conception, are able to exploit these imperfections to secure a favorable settlement of the disputed transaction. The challenge for contract theory is to predict when the benign scenario is more likely than the malign one (and vice versa).

Under the Article 2 scheme, the nature of the market for substitute goods determines which of these explanations is more likely in any particular case.[41] Where the market is thin, the implicit assumption is that breach is more likely to be strategic and the promisee can trump the "cry for help" by demanding either specific performance or the contract price (as the case may be).[42] However, where there is an available market for the contract goods, the promisee is limited to market damages. This motivates the promisee to adjust efficiently to the circumstances by salvaging the broken contract on the market, either by resale or by cover (or, in the alternative, relying on proof of what such an action on the market would have yielded).

The success of Article 2 in substituting legal defaults that encourage cost minimizing efforts to salvage broken contracts should not be underestimated. While the people for whom Llewellyn was drafting were not sophisticated theorists, they were sophisticated commercial lawyers who were well aware of the inefficiencies embedded in the Sales Act. In drafting these provisions of the Code, as well as a set of defaults that reduced contract formation costs, Llewellyn relied upon his long career as a commercial lawyer. Tearing down the "wall" of title and drafting sophisticated schemes to facilitate the salvaging of disputed contracts was seen then, as it is now, as a major improvement in the legal regime, one that would likely ensure the support of the ALI and ULC members whose approval was necessary for the Code project to succeed.

---

[41] The UCC's remedial scheme implicitly adopts an initial presumption that breach is a cry for help. Thus, specific performance (or an action for the price) is an extraordinary remedy. (See §§ 2-703, 2-711). The promisee buyer has an option of either covering on the market (§ 2-712) or establishing what a cover contract would have cost (§ 2-713). But, in either case, as long as there is a market for the goods, the buyer is presumed to have the comparative advantage in salvaging the broken contract and must act on the market and subsequently submit a damage claim to the seller. The same presumption holds for the promisee seller, who must initially choose between resale (§ 2-706) or proof of what a resale would have yielded on the market (§ 2-708(1)). In either case, only when the promisee can show that the market for substitutes is thin does the Code presumption shift toward the malign story. In such a case, the promisee buyer can secure specific performance (§ 2-716 cmt. 2: "inability to cover is 'other proper circumstances' "), and the promisee seller can recover the price (§ 2-709(1)b: "unable after reasonable effort to resell").

[42] §§ 2-716, 2-709(1)(b). The argument is that in a thin market a promisee is unlikely to enjoy a comparative advantage over the promisor in covering on the market while, at the same time, the promisee is more vulnerable to strategic claims that the cover contract was unreasonable since market prices are more difficult to prove. ROBERT E. SCOTT & JODY S. KRAUS, CONTRACT LAW AND THEORY 113–15 (5th ed. 2013).

2. Regulating Ongoing Contractual Relationships

Llewellyn's solution for regulating ongoing contractual relationships was even more ambitious than his scheme for regulating broken contracts. Here, Llewellyn relied on an intuitive sense (derived from his years as a commercial lawyer) that ongoing contractual relationships were not efficiently regulated by binary default rules that allocated risks on an "all or nothing" basis. What Llewellyn saw was similar to the findings of Stewart Macaulay a generation later.[43] Parties adjusted voluntarily to changed circumstances during the life of the contract. If an exogenous shock delayed the delivery of goods in a particular industry, the buyer would accept the late delivery and look for a price discount on a subsequent transaction. Not only were these patterns of flexible adjustment ubiquitous, but Llewellyn saw as well that the parties coped with moral hazard problems in much the same way: strong social norms in the form of trade practice or even contract-specific patterns of interaction developed to police opportunism on both sides of the transaction.

The solution to the dilemma of relational contracting seemed straightforward. Rather than impose abstract and general rules to regulate ongoing relationships, the law should simply identify and incorporate the "working rules" already being used successfully by the parties themselves. These working rules (or "bylaws" as Llewellyn also called them) needed the imprimatur of the state: the "jurisdiction" of the working rules was uncertain because they arose from custom and practice. Legal incorporation was necessary, therefore, in order to resolve "trouble" cases where the relevant norms were in dispute.

Llewellyn addressed the incorporation objective by reversing the common law presumption that the parties' writings and the legal default rules (the law of contract) are the definitive elements of the agreement. Rather, Article 2 explicitly invites incorporation by defining the content of an agreement to include trade usage, prior dealings and the parties' experiences in forming the contract. The parol evidence rule under the Code admits inferences from trade usage even if the express terms of the contract seem perfectly clear and are apparently "integrated."[44] The invitation to contextualize the contract in this manner is explicitly embodied in the Code's definition of agreement,[45] and it was amplified in Section 1-205 (now 1-303), which specified that course of dealing and usages of trade give particular meaning to, and qualify the terms of, an agreement.[46]

---

[43] Stewart Macaulay, *Non-Contractual Relations in Business*, 28 AM. SOC. REV. 555 (1963).

[44] UCC § 2-202 cmts. 1, 2 (1995) ("This section definitely rejects ... the requirement that a condition precedent to the admissibility of [evidence of course of dealing, usage of trade or course of performance] is an original determination by the court that the language used is ambiguous. [Section 2-202] makes admissible evidence of course of dealing,, usage of trade and course of performance to explain or supplement the terms of any writing stating the agreement of the parties in order that the true understanding of the parties ... may be reached.").

[45] UCC § 1-201(3) defines "agreement" as "the bargain of the parties in fact as found in their language or by implication from other circumstances including course of dealing or usage of trade or course of performance as provided in this Act."

[46] UCC § 1-205(3) (1995). Comment 1 to § 1-205 provided that: "the meaning of the agreement is to be determined by the language used by them and by their action, read and interpreted in the light of commercial practices and other surrounding circumstances. The measure and background for interpretation are set by the commercial context, which may explain and supplement even the language of a formal or final writing."

Since Llewellyn's purpose was to incorporate flexible and tailored defaults, he needed a mechanism by which these local norms could be identified by courts. That mechanism was the merchant tribunal—a panel of experts that would find specific facts—such as whether the behavior of a contracting party was "commercially reasonable." To avoid questions of constitutionality, Llewellyn proposed to retain the lay jury as the final arbiter of the facts, informed by the merchant tribunal's judgment about the relevant commercial working rules that applied to the particular dispute.[47] Unfortunately, the idea of the merchant tribunal was entirely too radical for the commercial lawyers in the ALI who dominated the drafting process. By 1944, Llewellyn had abandoned this key device for discovering the relevant social norms, while still retaining the architecture of incorporation, including the injunction that parties conform their behaviors to the supereminent norm of commercial reasonableness. Viewed in retrospect, eliminating the merchant jury while retaining the hopelessly vague notion of commercial reasonableness was a drafting disaster.[48]

B. Grant Gilmore and Homer Kripke's Article 9

Grant Gilmore and Homer Kripke (Gilmore's principal Adviser and the drafter of the 1972 revisions) believed that secured debt was a good thing.[49] Thus, they wanted more of it. Not surprisingly, therefore, Article 9 was enthusiastically received by secured lenders. Indeed, that enthusiasm explains the rapid success enjoyed by state legislators in securing adoption of the UCC in the 1960s. But the enthusiasm that secured lenders showed for Article 9 begs the question of why they found it so attractive.

Two partial explanations emerge. First, Article 9 imposed certainty and uniformity onto a field previously characterized by quirky, indeterminate, and widely varying

---

[47] REVISED UNIFORM SALES ACT, 1941 DRAFT § 59-D(1): "the special finding of the merchant experts shall be received in evidence, and shall be sufficient to sustain the evidence." In addition to the issue of substantial performance, the merchants tribunal was competent to opine on the effect of any mercantile usage on the terms of a contract, the mercantile reasonableness of any action by either party and "any other issue which requires for its competent determination special merchants knowledge rather than general knowledge." See REVISED UNIFORM SALES ACT, § 59(1), (C)(D).

[48] Jim Whitman has noted that the abandonment of the merchants tribunal was not accompanied by a similar jettisoning of the many issues that the tribunal was to decide:

> But when the commissioners abandoned Section 59, they did not abandon a host of provisions that assumed the institutional framework of Section 59. Llewellyn's Code retained its deference to "custom", the "law merchant", good faith" and "reasonableness". In Llewellyn's romantic vocabulary, however, "custom" the "law merchant", "good faith" and "reasonableness" were not terms of substantive law, but were procedural directives, indications to a court that it should refer its decision to lay specialists with a feel for commercial law.

James Whitman, *Commercial Law and the American Volk: A Note on Llewellyn's German Sources for the Uniform Commercial Code*, 97 YALE L.J. 156, 174 (1987). Thus, while the idea behind the provisions on commercial reasonableness was that the merchant juries would, over time, develop default rules defining "reasonable" behavior in particular contexts, the absence of these juries has caused courts to rely on intuition. As a result, the norm of reasonableness has become a major source of non-uniformity in the application of the Code. *Id.* at 175.

[49] Homer Kripke, *Law and Economics: Measuring the Economic Efficiency of Commercial Law on a Vacuum of Fact*, 133 U. PA. L. REV. 929, 931 n.14 (1985). Kripke wrote: "I confess to a prejudice on favor of secured chattel financing going beyond that of most conventional teachers of commercial law. I have a vested intellectual interest...." *Id.* at 933 n.21.

rules that recall Gilmore's earlier reference to the gates of hell. The Article 9 scheme of clear, bright-line rules for regulating asset-based financing caused both prospective creditors and debtors to believe that the new system provided laws superior not only to the quagmire of regulations that previously governed the field but to other entirely different methods of financing as well. There is undoubtedly some truth to this explanation. The preexisting regime of pigeonholed classifications, each with its own filing system and special set of rules, created unnecessary costs as well as traps for the unwary, and left—under virtually any rationale—odd holes in coverage and scope.

But there is a second explanation as well. It is undoubtedly true that the enthusiasm of secured creditors for the new system derives in part from the fact that Article 9 unabashedly promoted the institutionalization of secured credit; it vastly expanded on pre-Code laws both in explicit coverage and in the dramatic lowering of costs. Perhaps the most notable feature of the new law was the institutionalization of the "floating lien" that protected future advances financing.[50] A series of provisions were adopted that collectively enabled a single creditor to acquire first-in-line priority and use it to control the financing of a debtor's entire production process from acquisition of raw materials to fabrication of finished products to sales and subsequent realization of account receivables. Both the floating lien and to a lesser extent the purchase money security interest exempt certain secured creditors from important features of Article 9's general "first-in-time" priority rule, giving such creditors a favored status compared to other secured and unsecured creditors.[51] Moreover, both classes of creditors were afforded relatively lenient filing requirements for preserving their priority claims to the debtor's assets.[52]

Thus, when one views Article 9's primary innovations—the dual characteristics of certainty in results and partiality toward some secured creditors, the reason for the enthusiasm of financial institutions for Article 9 and thus for the UCC as an entity becomes clear. The new scheme provided secured creditors a regulatory system that not only reduced uncertainty in general but settled many of the long-standing doubts in their favor.[53]

---

[50] The term "floating lien" is a short hand reference to a series of original Article 9 provisions including UCC § 9-201 (concerning the general validity of security interests); UCC § 9-204(3) (authorizing future advances financing); UCC § 9-205 (use or disposition of collateral without accounting); UCC § 9-306 (concerning secured creditors rights on disposition of collateral), and UCC § 9-312(7) (giving future advances priority as of the date of original filing).

[51] The floating lien permitted a creditor to take a blanket security interest in all of the debtor's collateral, whether presently held or after-acquired, to serve as security for both present as well as future uncommitted advances. Thus the floating lien essentially gave the secured creditor the opportunity to gain exclusive control over all of the debtor's financing opportunities; the creditor was exempted from Article 9's basic "first-in-time" priority system. The PMSI provisions functioned in a similar manner. These rules guaranteed that purchase money lenders would generally receive favored treatment in relation to all other creditors, secured or unsecured, during insolvency proceedings. See, e.g., 11 U.S.C. § 547(c)(3). PMSI creditors did not need to submit to the limitations of the general first-in-time rule. UCC § 9-112.

[52] The financing statement that the creditor filed to insulate this blanket security from third parties needed to contain only a bare description of the collateral. UCC §§ 9-110, 9-402.

[53] The history of the floating lien illustrates this point well. Courts in the nineteenth century substantially resisted granting priority in advance of the debtor's ownership of particular collateral, reasoning that was justified in part by the notion that certain parts of a business, notably inventory and receivables, should be left available for general creditors. See, e.g., Zartman v. First National Bank, 82 N.E. 127, 128 (NY 1978). This approach was ratified by Benedict v. Ratner, 268 U.S. 353, 360 (1925), where Justice Brandeis ruled that security interests in after-acquired property were void as fraudulent conveyances. Ultimately, the drafters

The evidence of this enthusiasm is clear from a glance at the contemporary market for credit. Secured financing has undergone an enormous transformation since the enactment of Article 9. Perhaps the most vivid illustration of this is the dramatic increase in the number and size of firms that rely on secured debt as their principal means of financing both ongoing operations and growth opportunities. With the rise of securitization, secured debt has become the linchpin of private financing, prompting even large firms to employ leveraged buyouts as a means of fleeing public equity markets for the safe harbors of Article 9. When viewed in these terms, it is unsurprising that most practitioners and commentators regard Article 9 as a blazing success. As I discuss in section IV, however, this intertwining of innovative and efficient rules with the special interests of the dominant interest group affected by Article 9's rules has remained throughout the various revisions to Article 9 and, as a consequence, has clouded ultimate judgments about the success of the Code in the twenty-first century.

IV. The Political Economy of the UCC Revision Process

In recent years, the UCC has undergone a complete revision. The principal impetus for the revision project has been the need to adapt the statute to technological change. This process resulted initially in the revisions of Articles 3 (Commercial Paper) and 4 (Bank Collections) (as well as the promulgation of Article 4A on Electronic Transfers), the recommended repeal of Article 6 (Bulk Sales), and the addition of Article 2A (Leases). Subsequently, revisions to Articles 5 (Letters of Credit) and 8 (Investment Securities) were completed. The two substantive revisions that then remained were especially important events in commercial law: Article 9, regulating secured lending, had last been rethought in 1972 and Article 2, regulating sales, had never been revised. Both revisions generated substantial controversy. The Article 9 revision was completed in 2002 and adopted in all fifty states. But much of the scholarly literature of the past several decades asks whether the revision promotes the normative purposes of the Code or whether it reflects the political economy of the revision process itself.[54] The outcome in the case of Article 2 was quite different: all attempts to revise the article failed after twenty years of effort. Some scholars have argued that these different outcomes were predictable. Where the legal regime regulates the interests of relatively cohesive industries, the UCC lawmaking process is likely to function much differently than where the regulatory effects are diffused. Thus, the normative implications of the revision of Article 9 are substantially different from the implications of the failure to revise Article 2.

---

of Article 9 overturned the Brandeis holding. 1 GRANT GILMORE, SECURITY INTERESTS IN PERSONAL PROPERTY 355 (1965).

[54] See, e.g., Scott, supra note 29; Lucian Bebchuck & Jesse Fried, The Uneasy Case for the Priority of Secured Claims in Bankruptcy, 105 YALE L.J. 857 (1996); Lynn M. Lopucki, The Unsecured Creditor's Bargain, 80 VA. L. REV. b1887 (1994); James J. White, Reforming Article 9 Priorities In Light of Old Ignorance and New Filing Rules, 79 MINN. L. REV. 853 (1995); Robert E. Scott, The Truth About Secured Financing, 82 CORNELL L. REV. 1436 (1997).

A. The Article 2 Revision Process:
The Institutionalization of Obsolescence

The Article 2 revision process has had a tortured history. In 1987, the Permanent Editorial Board for the UCC set out, under the auspices of a study committee, to consider modernizing the statute. Four years later, the study committee issued its report and recommendations, and the ALI and ULC appointed a drafting committee to begin work on a comprehensive revision of Article 2.[55] An important goal of this effort was a proposed Article 2B designed to address the unique characteristics of software licensing transactions. The first public indication that the project was beginning to unravel surfaced when the ALI declined to approve the proposed Article 2B for computer information contracts on the ground that the drafting process, dominated by the software and information industry, had produced a "seller-friendly" statute.[56] The ULC decided, however, to go forward with the project on its own, reissuing the statute as the Uniform Computer Information Transactions Act (UCITA).[57]

The split between the ALI and ULC broke into the open in 1999, when Revised Article 2 was brought forward for final approval. The revised article was approved by the ALI, but two months later the leadership of the ULC withdrew the draft from its members' consideration after encountering severe opposition from industry interests. In an attempt to patch the tattered alliance together, ALI and ULC agreed on a newly reconstituted drafting committee which was directed to focus only on "non-controversial," technical amendments to the existing statute.[58] Yet, in August 2001, ULC members voted overwhelmingly to reject the Proposed Amendments to Article 2 that had just been approved the preceding May by the ALI. This vote followed a last-minute effort by the Article 2 drafting committee to amend the scope provisions of Article 2 in response to continuing criticism from representatives of the software and information industries. In the months that followed, the Article 2 drafting committee approved a new version that did not amend the basic scope section of Article 2, but did amend the definition of "goods" to exclude "information." The amendments, as revised, were then approved by the ULC in August 2002 and subsequently by the ALI in May 2003.

But multiple efforts to secure adoption of the 2003 amendments failed. The amendments generated considerable controversy and faced interest group opposition in the various state legislatures. Over the next eight years, not a single state adopted the amendments to Article 2. Recognizing the inevitable, the ALI withdrew the proposed amendments in May 2011, and so the story of the attempts to revise Article 2 ended not with a bang but with a whimper.

---

[55] In the interest of full disclosure, I was appointed as one of the initial members of the drafting committee for Article 2, but resigned shortly after my appointment.

[56] Scott, *supra* note 21, at 1049.

[57] The controversy over UCITA centered on the provisions of the statute that endorsed market practices in which consumers signify advance acceptance of subsequently disclosed terms. UCITA was adopted in Virginia and Maryland but has continued to encounter stiff opposition from consumer interests in other jurisdictions. *Id.* at 1049–50.

[58] *See* Richard E. Speidel, *Revising UCC Article 2: A View from the Trenches*, 52 HASTINGS L. REV. 607, 615–17 (2001).

The open split between the ALI and ULC and the subsequent failure to secure adoption of even "technical" amendments reflects the intense interest group competition that emerged during the Article 2 revision process. Retail manufacturing interests, opposed to provisions that extended warranty liability for economic loss to remote sellers, were successful in blocking the adoption of the initial revisions to Article 2. In turn, consumer interests (including large-firm licensees), opposed to the "seller-friendly" provisions in the proposed Article 2B, were able to separate the computer information article from the rest of the UCC project. From there the battleground moved to rival efforts to either secure or block the further enactment of UCITA.[59] Thus, even in the subsequent effort to bring forward the seemingly uncontroversial amendments to Article 2, each side was able to block approval of the other's proposals but was unable to secure approval of its own.

It is unlikely that Article 2 will ever be revised to deal directly with the unique contracting problems presented by new contracting practices. Despite the dramatic changes in contracting practices brought on by the information revolution, Article 2 remains today essentially as it was drafted by Llewellyn seventy years ago. Whatever happens in the future, therefore, common law courts will be called upon to resolve the increasingly intense normative debate over the domain of free contract in computer information transactions, as well as to fill gaps in commercial disputes arising from the new technology. Ultimately, the law will be updated by the common law mechanism that creates commercial law rules, but there will be few rules and they will develop slowly.

B. The Perverse Effects of the Successful Revisions to UCC's Specialized Statutes

The UCC ushered in a new moment for uniform specialized statutory rules, ranging from commercial paper and bank deposits, to letters of credit, to documents of title, and to secured credit.[60] Unlike the failure to revise sales law, every one of these specialized commercial statues has been revised, some more than once. But just as the concern about private interests supplanting the public interest led scholars to doubt the fairness of the original statutes, the history of the revisions to the UCC's specialized commercial statutes reveals a similar pattern and a similar skepticism. I first take up Article 9, the exemplar of this problem.

As I noted in section III, there was extensive interest group participation, largely by asset-based financers and banks, in the original drafting of Article 9. Grant Gilmore

---

[59] In the meantime, the ALI began a project to draft *Principles for the Law of Software Contracts*. The *Principles* were published by the ALI in 2010 and are now offered to courts to aid them in resolving disputes over computer information transactions. For more discussion on the *Principles, see generally* Robert A. Hillman & Maureen A. O'Rouke, *Principles of the Law of Software Contract: Some Highlights,* 84 Tu. L. Rev. 1519 (2010); Juliet M. Moringiello & William L. Reynolds, *What's Software Got to Do With It? The ALI Principles of the Law of Software Contracts,* 84 Tu. L. Rev. 1541 (2010).

[60] These specialized statutes, each of which has been recently revised, are found in UCC Articles 3 and 4, 5, 7, and 9, respectively. Article 6 covering Bulk Sales proved to be an impediment to current commerce and the 1989 revision recommended repeal. *See* Article 6 prefatory note.

documented the accommodations that led banks and finance companies to support the UCC project that they had earlier rejected as a radical reform.[61] This support developed after Homer Kripke, then a legal counsel to CIT Financial Corp., became one of the key Advisers to Gilmore and the other drafters.[62] Kripke subsequently described how, during their drafting deliberations, banking interests blocked proposed clauses that would have imposed on them the costs of various consumer-protection provisions.[63] He reported that avoiding arousing the opposition of banks and finance companies was necessary in order to ensure passage of the UCC project.[64] Thus, it is undeniable that the original Article 9 was the creation of an interest-group-dominated process.

The business lawyers who served on the Article 9 study group revising Article 9 in the 1990s had similar preferences concerning the regulation of commercial practice.[65] The study group was comprised of two academic reporters and sixteen members— three legal academics and thirteen practicing lawyers, the largest number of whom were in-house counsel for banks and finance companies or private attorneys representing secured financing interests.[66] The Study Group revising Article 9 defined its mission as resolving "technical" problems that were susceptible to legal expertise, rather than undertaking possibly controversial reforms.[67] The privileged status of hands-on working knowledge of Article 9 rules thus gave the in-house counsel and the private commercial lawyers the power to determine the course of the revision. Efforts by the academic members to place significant reform proposals on the agenda were uniformly unsuccessful.[68] Buoyed by these successful efforts to draft revisions

---

[61] *See* GRANT GILMORE, THE AGES OF AMERICAN LAW 86 (1967).

[62] *See* Grant Gilmore, *Dedication to Professor Homer Kripke*, 56 N.Y.U. L. REV. 1, 9, 11 (1981).

[63] *See* Homer Kripke, *The Principles Underlying the Drafting of the Uniform Commercial Code*, 1962 U. ILL. L. F. 321, 323–24 (1962) (describing how pushback from finance companies ultimately lead to "one of the weakest compromises in the Code").

[64] *See id.* at 322, 326–27.

> The determined opposition of well-knit groups tends to induce the legislature to do nothing, which is a victory for the opposition. The Code would have been a sitting duck target for any determined special interest or combination of special interests who chose to attack one or more features of the bill persistently. Thus, it was important not to arouse the opposition of banks or finance companies....

[65] Donald Rapson, then Vice President and Assistant General Counsel of the CIT Group, Inc., and a participant in the Article 9 revision process, provides further evidence of the role of interest groups at the level of the study group. In describing the general UCC revision process, he says:

> The question, however, is whether the "environment" of the drafting committee process inhibits drafting fair and efficient statutory rules that advance the public interest.... I fear that the process makes that very difficult to do.... Although the individual members of the drafting committee are supposed ... to vote their own consciences independently of their personal affiliations, the fact remains that their statements and votes are publicly made in the glare of the interest groups. Drafting committee members whose practice, employment, or academic consulting is for or on behalf of an interest group may be hard pressed to take an action contrary to that group.

Donald J. Rapson, *Who Is Looking Out for the Public Interest? Thoughts About the UCC Revision Process in the Light (And Shadows) of Professor Rubin's Observations*, 28 LOY. LA. L. REV. 249, 260–61 (1994).

[66] *See* Scott, *supra* note 29, at 1807–08. In the interest of full disclosure, I served as one of the academic members of the Article 9 study group.

[67] *See id.* at 1805–09.

[68] *Id.* at 1807–09.

reflecting only the interests of secured creditors, the 1999 revisions to Article 9 were ultimately adopted in all fifty states.

The many successful revisions to the specialized commercial statutes in the UCC demonstrate that particular industries have been effective in creating, and preserving, law when the costs fall on diffuse groups. Indeed, the same influences that affected first the creation and then subsequent revision of Article 9 affected Articles 3 and 4 as well. These articles affect banks—but no other cohesive interest group—and bank lawyers played a large role in the original drafting process. These lawyers' preferences also were close to those of the business lawyers in the ULC and the ALI. Because the political situation had not changed since the original UCC, it is unsurprising that the revised Articles 3 and 4 would resemble the original rules in relevant respects. The consensus view of participants in the revisions to Articles 3 and 4 was that the successful efforts to revise Articles 3 and 4 had produced "bankers' legislation."

These reports from participants in the Article 3 and 4 revision process are consistent with the observation that these study groups were industry dominated.[69] Both revisions passed the ALI and ULC, and both have been enacted into law in every state except New York. The new proposals are compatible with industry interests, but whether they serve the interests of other constituencies is hard to determine a priori. It is clear that Articles 3 and 4 are widely thought to be industry products, but that does not answer the question of whether the revisions are also in the public interest. There are, however, good reasons to believe that they are not.[70]

In sum, banks and asset-backed lenders were initially successful in securing the adoption of UCC Articles 3, 4, and 9. Unsurprisingly, these agents have secured updates that create gains for them and have prevented amendments that would reduce those gains. To the extent that there is a public interest independent of the financers' interest, it has not been represented in the creation of these current statutes.

V. Conclusion

Viewed from the vantage point of the end of the first quarter of the twenty-first century, the legacy of the Uniform Commercial Code is decidedly mixed. Article 2, the most ambitious and widely cited of the various articles of the Code, is hopelessly obsolete with little prospect of a revision that might address the very different contracting problems that commercial parties face today. To be sure, Articles 3, 4, and 9 have been revised frequently and remain relevant in their specialized spheres: they continue to provide the foundational rules governing the regulation of the markets in secured credit and commercial paper. But the evidence that these revisions were promoted and successfully promulgated by the very parties most affected by the regulation

---

[69] This history is described in Edward L. Rubin, *Thinking Like a Lawyer, Acting Like a Lobbyist: Some Notes on the Process of Revising Articles 3 and 4*, 26 Loy. LA. L. Rev. 743, 744–48 (1993), and in Kathleen Patchel, *Interest Group Politics, Federalism, and the Uniform Law Process: Some Lessons from the Uniform Commercial Code*, 78 Minn. L. Rev. 83, 101–10 (1993).

[70] *See* Rubin, *supra* note 69, at 746, 788 (detailing industry influence during the deliberations of the ABA committee reviewing the revisions to Articles 3 and 4).

raises the continuing specter of distributional unfairness toward the third-party interests that are also subject to these commercial laws.

And yet, it is undeniable that the UCC has had a profound influence on the development of commercial law over the past seventy years. The innovations introduced by Llewellyn's Article 2 were broadly adopted in the Second Restatement of Contracts and subsequently by common law courts. As a consequence, long-term supply and distribution contracts throughout the world, whether or not they are specifically covered by the UCC, operate under the umbrella of the Code's default rules governing open terms, the battle of the forms, contract interpretation, excuse, and the incorporation of customary practices. Similarly, the incredible growth in the worldwide volume of personal property security transactions stands as a testament to the confidence that market actors have in the scheme of priority rules for Article 9 first introduced by Grant Gilmore and Homer Kripke. In the end, however, the question we must pose today *is the same question* the American bar posed at the beginning of the twentieth century: Can the state create institutions that are better than the common law courts at producing both efficient and fair commercial law rules? The answer, so far, is not clear.[71]

[71] One of the remaining open issues that affects a final judgment on the success of the Code's statutory interventions concerns the impact of modern arbitration practice on the continued growth and vitality of common law decision-making. While common-law commercial litigation remains vibrant in particular areas beyond sales law, including corporate transactions and bankruptcy, it is undeniable that much of commercial litigation today occurs behind the veil of arbitral awards thus robbing the common law of valuable opportunities for growth.

14

From Restatement to Model Penal Code

The Progress and Perils of Criminal Law Reform

*Kimberly Kessler Ferzan**

I. Introduction

On February 24, 1923, in a room of the Red Cross Building in Washington, D.C., the Council of the American Law Institute (ALI) held its first meeting.[1] This meeting structured the business to come: officers were elected, term limits were determined by lot, and an Executive Committee was formed.[2] One week later, on Saturday, March 3, 1923, the Executive Committee gathered, and among the most pressing orders of business was the need to obtain financial support.[3] To that end, the group agreed to draft a report for the Carnegie Corporation.[4]

The March 17, 1923, Statement by the Council of the ALI to the Carnegie Corporation set forth what it had done, how the ALI had formed, what the ALI desired to do, and what financial assistance was needed.[5] This statement raised significant worries about the state of the law *writ large* as of "grave concern."[6] As the Council noted, "[T]here exists defects in the administration of justice, that whole topics of the law and parts of nearly all topics are unnecessarily uncertain, [and] that better adjustment of the law to the needs of life is an end to be desired."[7] For the most part, the answer was Restatements: "The idea of the restatement of the law a year ago was more or less vague. It is now clear. The work can be done, and it is worth doing."[8] Whereas conflict of laws, business organizations, and torts were planned to be undertaken first,[9] criminal law was another matter.

From the very beginning, criminal law reform was expected to be difficult. As the Council expressed, "The doubt … is whether existing defects in the administration

* I thank Ed Cooper, Andrew Gold, and David Seipp, as well as the participants attending the conference on the ALI Centennial papers held at Penn Carey Law for their helpful feedback. Penn librarian Genevieve Tung, as well as Penn students Andrew Lief and Lauren Yagoda, provided excellent research assistance, and Penn librarian Evan Silverstein provided excellent citation assistance.

1 1 A.L.I. PROC. [i] (1923).
2 *Id.* at 4–6.
3 *Id.* at 10–11.
4 *Id.* at 11.
5 *Id.* at 49–50.
6 *Id.* at 54.
7 *Id.* at 59.
8 *Id.*
9 *Id.* at 60.

Kimberly Kessler Ferzan, *From Restatement to Model Penal Code* In: *The American Law Institute*. Edited by: Andrew S. Gold and Robert W. Gordon, Oxford University Press. © Oxford University Press 2023. DOI: 10.1093/oso/9780197685341.003.0015

of criminal justice are of a character to be remedied by the restatement that it is the object of the Institute to produce."[10] Instead, the Council proposed a report on the existing defects in criminal law and procedure in order to determine what a Restatement could provide.[11]

And so, with funding in hand, the ALI got down to business, appointing Reporters for various Restatements. Criminal law, in contrast, got a committee.[12] That committee, comprised of Herbert Hadley as Chair, William Mikell, and John Milburn,[13] came to a clear conclusion in 1924: "All of the members of the Committee unite in recommending 'that The American Law Institute undertake a restatement of the substantive law of crimes.'"[14]

But almost forty years would go by before the Model Penal Code (MPC) would be approved by the ALI membership. Change to the criminal law was to be greeted with committee after committee, reports and reports about other reports, and financial woes. Beyond the inner workings of the ALI, progress was delayed by the Great Depression and World War II.

The problem with criminal law was that it had too many problems. Criminal law appeared so flawed that although every committee that studied it argued for immediate intervention, the task seemed insurmountable and the likely impact of ALI work insubstantial. These worries proved unfounded. As Gerard Lynch would observe in 2003, the MPC was not only "one of the great intellectual accomplishments of American legal scholarship of the mid-twentieth century" but also "one of the most successful law reform projects in American history."[15]

This chapter proceeds in four sections. It begins with the pre-MPC committees and reports. Here, we see how the chaotic state of the criminal law called for reform and how the need for direction transformed the project from Restatement to model code. The chapter then turns to the MPC, discussing how it innovated American criminal law and briefly surveying its substantial impact on law reform. It then sets forth the arguments for updating the MPC, including the recent projects that revised both sentencing and sexual assault. Finally, it evaluates the MPC. If we look at what motivated the Hadley committee and what MPC Reporter Herbert Wechsler's key aspirations were, the success of the MPC is mixed. Some key provisions were sparsely adopted, and some were later undermined. And the Code never offered the kind of uniformity that the Hadley committee sought. But it is a mistake to ask whether any state's adoption of the code in whole or in part defines it success. Rather, the MPC's success lies in the fact that it is a theoretical and conceptual lodestar for past and future reformers.

---

[10] *Id.* at 70.
[11] *Id.* at 70–71.
[12] *Id.* at 28, 29, 35–36, 41.
[13] *Id.* at 47.
[14] *Minutes of the Seventh Meeting of the Council—Dec. 5, 6, and 7, 1924*, 2 A.L.I. PROC. 233, 252 (1924).
[15] Gerard E. Lynch, *Revising the Model Penal Code: Keeping It Real*, 1 OHIO ST. J. CRIM. L. 219, 220 (2003).

II. The Problems with Criminal Law and the Need for a Model Penal Code

Whether one uses the terms "chaotic," "unprincipled," "sorry state,"[16] or "disastrous,"[17] each and every one of these descriptions applies to the criminal law that existed at the ALI's founding. In 1925, Hadley's committee reported on this state of the criminal law. Codified statutes had varying relationships with crimes that were indictable at common law.[18] The English common law's influence ranged from reception statutes that simply made acts punishable at common law punishable in the state; to those that left definitions to courts, which in turn relied on the common law for interpretation; to those that used the common law's definition.[19] No state had a comprehensive criminal code.[20] Haphazard codification created uncertainty. It was not clear, for example, whether a crime indictable at common law still existed if other crimes had been codified, nor were there general interpretive principles for the statutes on the books.[21] Bottom line: it was extremely difficult to ascertain what the criminal law actually required.

Indeed, each state presented substantial problems. For a glimpse at the underlying terrain, consider Pennsylvania. Mikell was involved in a proposed code for Pennsylvania, having been appointed to a commission on July 23, 1917, by the governor of Pennsylvania. He observed:

> Sixty years have passed since the Code of 1860 went into effect. During that time many hundreds of penal acts have been passed by the Legislature. Acts creating new offenses; acts repealing in whole or in part existing offenses; acts amending acts creating offenses; acts amending acts amending acts creating offenses, etc.
>
> A large number of these acts were drawn without any reference to previously existing acts, with the result that the body of the penal law as it exists today is a jumble of inconsistencies. Many sections are badly drawn; many are inconsistent; many are in conflict; there is much over-lapping due to different acts covering in part the same subject matter; many are obsolete. In addition, the penalties provided for the various offenses under the existing law are inconsistent with each other. For crimes of the same character very different penalties are prescribed; some genial offenses are punishable more severely than serious ones; the mere attempt to commit a crime is even in some cases punished more severely than the completed crime itself.
>
> [T]here is an utter lack of principle in the grading of crimes as felonies and misdemeanors, either according to the moral gravity of the offense or the severity of the penalty annexed.... [After noting inconsistencies with embezzlement, attempts,

---

[16] Paul H. Robinson & Markus D. Dubber, *The American Model Penal Code: A Brief Overview*, 10 New Crim. L. Rev. 319, 322 (2007).

[17] Joshua Dressler, *The Model Penal Code: Is It Like a Classic Movie in Need of a Remake?*, 1 Ohio St. J. Crim. L. 157, 157 (2003).

[18] Herbert S. Hadley, Wm. E. Mikell, & John G. Milburn, Report to the Council by the Committee on a Survey and Statement of the Defects in Criminal Justice—Apr. 1, 1925, 3 A.L.I. Proc. 439, 474–75 (1925) (hereinafter Hadley report).

[19] *Id.* at 475.

[20] "No state has ever attempted to codify the whole body of the law applicable to crimes." *Id.*

[21] *Id.* at 475–76.

rape, counterfeiting, Mikell concluded:] Purposely and of malice aforethought cutting out a person's tongue, eye or hand is a misdemeanor only; but giving away a toy on which is painted by way of advertisement a flag of the United States, is a felony.[22]

Criminal law was not just a challenge within any state but also across states. There were widespread disparities. The 1925 Hadley report questioned what happens if A owes B a dollar but accidentally hands B five? If B does not originally realize the mistake, but later, realizing it, spends the money, has B committed larceny? Yes, in Oregon, but no, in Alabama, the committee lamented.[23] Jurisdictions disagreed over whether "mere words" were sufficient for provocation.[24] As for defenses, states varied in terms of whether retreat was required before the defendant resorted to self-defense or whether there was a volitional prong to the insanity test.[25]

There were problems beyond the substance. One was that there was too much unpunished crime. Although the committee had difficulty getting any statistics about crime prevalence,[26] they reached the following empirical conclusions: too many crimes, too few criminals apprehended, too many cases not tried, too many defendants acquitted, and too many defendants avoided punishment for other reasons.[27]

Americans also did not seem to take criminal law seriously.[28] In the committee's eyes, no one was exempt from blame for the United States' predicament. First, "we are a nation of many different races and the individualistic independent attitude of the pioneer American and the mistaken conceptions of what liberty means on the part of our alien population have both worked to prevent an effective enforcement of law."[29] The committee found fault in everything from the Framing, for its "strong individualistic" ethic, to railroads and labor unions.[30] "It is a notable fact that while public opinion in this country is more stern in demanding severe penalties for the graver crimes in the enactment of criminal laws than in England, the standard of public opinion as to the observance and enforcement of law after the law is enacted is much higher in England than in the United States."[31] Additionally, the committee reported that in terms of convictions, "[w]hile reasonably satisfactory results have been secured in the prosecution of offenses committed by those without money or influence, it is often possible for a defendant with money and influence to delay the trial of a criminal charge, and justice delayed in criminal as in civil cases is often justice defeated."[32]

The committee had many specific concerns that went beyond the need for a substantive Restatement of law. First, the committee found that police were not well

---

[22] The Proposed Criminal Code of Pennsylvania, in the William Mikell papers, Manuscripts Collection, MSS.019, Biddle Law Library, University of Pennsylvania Law School, Philadelphia, PA (footnotes omitted).
[23] Hadley report, *supra* note 18, at 484.
[24] *Id.* at 485.
[25] *Id.* at 485–87.
[26] *Id.* at 444.
[27] *Id.* at 445–48. As David Seipp pointed out to me, this perception of lawlessness was undoubtedly influenced by Prohibition.
[28] *Id.* at 451.
[29] *Id.* at 452.
[30] *Id.* at 452–53.
[31] *Id.* at 453.
[32] *Id.* at 472.

chosen, well trained, or well led.[33] Second, criminal procedure was a mess.[34] Although in the committee's opinion, criminal procedure doctrines may have been justifiably tilted toward the accused, the committee found no rationale for various technicalities.[35] Third, there were too many variations from state to state from double jeopardy to burdens of proof to defenses.[36] "[With respect to the insanity test,] ... the result ... is either that, in one or the other group of states, some persons escape just punishment for a crime who should be convicted, or that some insane persons are punished for their acts."[37] Finally, the committee far preferred the efficiency of English courts: "[T]he predominant factor is the difference between the power of the English and the American judge in the trial of a case."[38] This "right of the trial judge" in England was "constantly exercised" and was "a material aid in the administration of justice."[39] Because of this power, English trials lacked "the browbeating and the attempts to confuse honest witnesses, the making of pointless objections to testimony, the efforts to work error into the record through offers of doubtfully legal evidence or subtly-worded requests to charge, and the efforts to distract the minds of the jury from the point in issue, so much in evidence in criminal trials in American courts."[40]

At the end of the day, the committee did not think all the ills of the criminal justice system were within the expertise of lawyers.[41] It did recommend a Restatement of the substantive law of crimes, arguing that it was the "same picture of uncertainty and inconsistency presented by other topics of the law, such as contracts, agency and torts."[42] Moreover, it thought that a Restatement of criminal law as "even more advisable" than other fields because the "foremost legal writers of this country with few exceptions have not been attracted to the criminal law[, and as] a consequence the law of crimes has not been subjected to the scientific and careful written exposition that has been lavished on the law of contract, agency, tort and other branches of the civil law, and therefore there is a greater need of an authoritative statement of its principles."[43] In sum, it recommended a Restatement forthwith.

Yet, early on, the reformers realized that a Restatement might not fully scratch the itch. In 1928, both Dean Justin Miller of USC Law School, as then Chair of the American Bar Association's Criminal Justice section,[44] and in response, Mikell, wrote letters to William Draper Lewis, urging the ALI take on recommendations for change, not a mere substantive Restatement.[45]

---

[33] *Id.* at 454.
[34] *Id.* at 459.
[35] *Id.* at 459–64.
[36] *Id.* at 469–71.
[37] *Id.* at 470.
[38] *Id.* at 471.
[39] *Id.* at 472.
[40] *Id.* at 472–73.
[41] *Id.* at 488.
[42] *Id.* at 489.
[43] *Id.*
[44] American Bar Association, *Criminal Justice Section Leadership 2021–2022*, https://www.americanbar.org/content/dam/aba/administrative/criminal_justice/leadership2021.pdf (last visited Sept. 29, 2021).
[45] On September 22, 1928, Miller wrote to William Draper Lewis, September 22, 1928 Letter from Justin Miller to William Mikell, in the William Mikell papers, Manuscripts Collection, MSS.019, Biddle Law Library, University of Pennsylvania Law School, Philadelphia, PA (suggesting a Restatement should follow the same lines as other Restatements, but noted there were "a number of points on which [he] would like

The idea of a model code slowly began to take root. The American Bar Association, the Association of American Law Schools, and the ALI formed a joint committee, writing a report in 1931 with a twofold recommendation: that the ALI undertake both a Restatement and a model code.[46] William Draper Lewis analyzed the report at the request of the ALI Council in 1932, but the general financial conditions of the United States, and the significant amount of work required on the pending Restatements made undertaking another project infeasible.[47] However, by February 10, 1934, conditions had improved and the ALI began again, aiming for an advisory committee to begin on the project.[48] And, in May 1934, President Franklin D. Roosevelt wrote a letter to the ALI urging it to focus on criminal law: "There is urgent need for intelligent, painstaking and patriotic work in this field.... I need not point out to you that the adaptation of our criminal law and its administration to meet the needs of a modern, complex civilization is one of our major problems."[49]

At last, in 1935, the new advisory committee issued its report, examining the earlier joint committee's report.[50] As the advisory committee noted, the joint committee recommended both a Restatement and a model code: "The Restatement will be a statement of what the law is; the Code of what it should be."[51] The advisory committee's recommendation was to focus more on a new code of criminal law, including not just the substantive criminal law but also court organization and administration, policing, probation, prisons, parole, and pardons.[52] The committee recognized that substantive criminal law reform needed to be done in harmony with criminal procedure and sentencing administration.[53] For the Restatement, the advisory committee recommended that it be "limited to carefully prepared memoranda wherever necessary for the formulation of code sections."[54] Reconciling the myriad state criminal laws would be "futile" but "the clear definition of the common law of crimes is a matter of first importance."[55]

Not only did the general approach of a model code begin to take root but so did some of its central themes. First, the advisory committee saw the key purpose of the criminal law as "the protection of society."[56] Second, the idea clearly surfaced that "criminal intent" should have a meaning that applies across crimes.[57] Third, despite the

to see some substantial changes made in substantive criminal law"); October 12, 1928 Letter from William Mikell to William Draper Lewis in the William Mikell papers, Manuscripts Collection, MSS.019, Biddle Law Library, University of Pennsylvania Law School, Philadelphia, PA (noting "I think, therefore, that it would be valuable in the Restatement, after stating the law as it is, to put in the form of notes recommendations for changes").

[46] *Report of the Advisory Committee on Criminal Justice to the Council—Jan. 30, 1935*, 12 A.L.I. PROC. 369, 372 (1935).
[47] *Id.* at 373.
[48] *Id.*
[49] *Id.* at 375.
[50] *Id.* at 377.
[51] *Id.* at 379.
[52] *Id.* at 381.
[53] *Id.* at 385.
[54] *Id.* at 382.
[55] *Id.* at 382.
[56] *Id.* at 383.
[57] *Id.* at 391.

fact that inconsistency among states was a major concern for the Hadley committee, this committee abandoned an ambition of uniformity: "[I]t cannot be expected that the whole Code will be adopted throughout the United States."[58] Recognizing that sometimes localities might have good reason to do things differently, it suggested that "it may be that alternate provisions will be recommended."[59]

And, then, more time passed. A code of criminal procedure had been accomplished.[60] But for the substantive criminal law, funding was needed.[61] A decade later, no progress had been made, and there was still no funding, though 1946 brought a resolution that the ALI should write a model code.[62]

In 1951, the ALI wrote a proposal for a MPC.[63] In that proposal, the ALI noted that "[f]or almost twenty years the Institute's agenda of unfinished business has included a proposal to prepare a model penal code." But the Rockefeller Foundation, which the ALI implored to fund the drafting, had expressed hesitation about the project.[64] Specifically, the Foundation had worried about whether the solution to crime was criminal law or instead the behavioral sciences and whether the problem was with substantive law or procedure.[65] The Foundation made a grant to explore the project— a "pondering committee."[66]

In response, in the 1951 proposal, yet another committee wholeheartedly supported a model code. Perhaps most significantly, the committee highlighted the centrality of criminal justice to society and the potential impacts on all citizens:

> Whatever views are held about the penal law, no one will question its importance to society. This is the law on which men place their ultimate reliance for protection against all the deepest injuries that human conduct can inflict on individuals and institutions. By the same token, penal law governs the strongest force that we permit official agencies to bring to bear on individuals. Its promise as an instrument of safety is matched only by its power to destroy. If penal law is weak or ineffective, basic human interests are in jeopardy. If it is harsh or arbitrary in its impact, it works a gross injustice on those caught within its toils. The law that carries such responsibilities should surely be as rational and just as law can be. Nowhere in the entire legal field is more at stake for the community or the individual.[67]

The committee also noted that criminal law needed serious academics,[68] that the substance remained flawed and that the case law may be "accidental or fortuitous"

---

[58] *Id.* at 404.

[59] *Id.*

[60] *Report of the Executive Committee to the Council on the Future on the Institute*, 12 A.L.I. Proc. 409, 421 (1935).

[61] *Id.*

[62] American Law Institute, Criminal Law, Report of the Special Committee on Future Programs (1946).

[63] Model Penal Code (1951) (The Proposal to Prepare a Model Penal Code).

[64] *Id.* at 1.

[65] *Id.* at 1–2.

[66] *Id.* at 2.

[67] *Id.* at 2–3.

[68] *Id.* at 3.

subject to "the mood that dominated a tribunal" or "a flurry or public excitement,"[69] with no substantive law that operated as a constraint on discretion.[70] The committee ended with a plea that would resonate with today's reformers: "The challenge is, in substance, that the penal law is ineffective, inhumane and thoroughly unscientific."[71] The ineffectiveness was located in recidivism;[72] the inhumaneness, embodied in punishment practices and the death penalty, was located in vengeance under the guise of retributivism instead of rehabilitation;[73] and the lack of science was embodied in the failure to see crime as "a symptom of deviation" amenable to diagnosis and therapy.[74]

Again, an ALI committee concluded that the remedy was a model code. Not only would it be a tool for substance but a model for drafting in an area in which "legislative drafting on the whole is at its lowest level and where the drafting difficulties are immense."[75] Even where there would likely be substantive disagreement, the committee thought a model code could offer answers: "There will be need, in any case, for such use of alternatives since many legislative choices may so largely turn on matter of opinion that the Institute will not be ready to endorse a single answer to the question raised. Where that is so, the commentary will provide a full discussion of the reasons for this mode of presentation, marshaling the relevant considerations on the issue that the draft does not resolve."[76] Still, the committee thought there were many points of generality (mens rea, justifications, and insanity) that would not vary significantly from state to state.[77]

III. Finally—The Model Penal Code

At long last, in 1952 with funds in hand, the MPC was undertaken.[78] Columbia Law Professor Herbert Wechsler was the Reporter, and there was an advisory committee of esteemed state and federal judges, prosecutors and defense lawyers, directors of prisons, criminologists, psychologists, and code reformers.[79] Wechsler remarked that this committee did not provide "summary approval" but rather "cynical acid."[80]

It is difficult to overstate how substantial this undertaking was. Although committee after committee reported the woes of the extant criminal law, there were no models for this kind of wholesale criminal law reform. Before the MPC, "[w]hat passed for major 'reform' in that period was the federal criminal code in 1948 putting the offenses in alphabetical order."[81] As Wechsler himself remarked, "Even the

---

[69] *Id.* at 6.

[70] *Id.* at 7.

[71] *Id.*

[72] *Id.*

[73] *Id.* at 8.

[74] *Id.* at 8–9.

[75] *Id.* at 11.

[76] *Id.* at 13.

[77] *Id.* at 13–14.

[78] Herbert Wechsler, *The Challenge of a Model Penal Code*, 65 HARV. L. REV. 1097, 1097 (1952).

[79] Herbert Wechsler, *The American Law Institute: Some Observations on Its Model Penal Code*, 42 A.B.A. J. 322 (1956).

[80] *Id.*

[81] Robinson & Dubber, *supra* note 16, at 323, 330. Indeed, as Paul Robinson and Marcus Dubber note, "the Model Penal Code drafters had virtually no existing American criminal codes to which to turn, with

problem of determining what method of classification of crimes ought to be employed is a very difficult problem."[82] As Gerard Lynch describes the Herculean task:

> Surveying hundreds of years of common-law evolution in the criminal law, identifying underlying principles, and formulating rules that represented the best of the thinking of judges who had grappled over that period with the violent and destructive results of the unruly passions of humankind, the drafters of the code, marshaled by the incredible energy, formidable intelligence, and sheer will of the great Herbert Wechsler, developed an intellectually coherent approach to this mass of material, and created a body of rules not only doctrinally consistent, but drafted for easy adoption by legislative bodies.[83]

Wechsler had central substantive ambitions. The MPC was to have four parts: general provisions, specific offenses, provisions for treatment and correction, and administrative organization of correction.[84] Among the key innovations that Wechsler was quick to highlight were the approach to culpability, the rejection of strict liability, the treatment of insanity, and the rethinking of punitive practices.[85] Specifically, he sought to remedy how "chaotic" culpability had been, as it was difficult to determine what terms meant and to which elements they applied.[86] The drafters were "against strict liability": "Philanthropic or not, we are against [strict liability]—both in the regulatory area, and a fortiori, insofar as it has spread to some of the offenses that we view less lightly, as in bigamy and rape. Such liabilities not only are unjust but they dilute the moral force of the whole penal law."[87] For insanity, the common law M'Naghten test was to be broadened, including a re-engineered irresistible impulse test, while a total impairment requirement was to be rejected.[88] With respect to incarceration, prison terms were to be rationalized, with indeterminate sentences, extended terms when necessary, and the use of presentence reports and parole boards.[89]

Wechsler had a clear view of his task. He recognized that he was offering a model but not striving for uniformity.[90] His goal was to aid legislatures and to provide a treatise-like treatment for courts.[91] Wechsler did view his task as perplexing. As he remarked in a session, "Now, I don't know. I said yesterday we are drawing a line here between formulating the Code that would only be of use in heaven where they don't

---

the possible exception of the recently reformed criminal code of Louisiana which was of "only limited significance ... because of the unique history and nature of Louisiana law ... which alone ... was rooted in ... codified European civil law."

[82] *Friday Morning Session—May 22, 1953*, 30 A.L.I. Proc. 143, 144 (1953).
[83] Lynch, *supra* note 15, at 219.
[84] Wechsler, *supra* note 79, at 322.
[85] *Id.* at 323–94.
[86] *Id.* at 323–23.
[87] *Id.* at 324.
[88] *Id.* at 392.
[89] *Id.* at 393–94.
[90] *Id.* at 321.
[91] *Id.* at 321; *see also Friday Morning Session—May 22, 1953*, 30 A.L.I. Proc. 143, 145 (1953).

need law, of course ... , and formulating one that would win immediate adoption. I don't quite know how to draw a line between what is practical and what is ideal."[92]

Commentators have attributed the MPC's success to Wechsler's pragmatism and focus. Robinson and Dubber remark, "It cannot be said that the Model Penal Code systematically worked out the implications of any particular theory of punishment (or treatment). Adopting an approach that has been characterized as 'principled pragmatism,' the code drafters never lost sight of the code's ultimate goal, the reform of American criminal law. Instead of rewriting criminal law in strict consequentialist terms, the code drafters took care to ground the code firmly in existing law and frequently sacrificed theoretical consistency for pragmatic expediency."[93] "The Model Penal Code thus arose from a painstaking critique of positive law, rather than from a systematic theory of criminal liability. Wechsler was no theoretician. As a major figure in the American legal process school, Wechsler saw the problems of substantive criminal law as problems of police."[94] Sandy Kadish observed of the Code, "[i]t sought to be critical and reformist, but more Fabian than radical, and it was drafted with acute awareness that it was to serve as a model for American legislatures in the late twentieth century, not as a visionary code for Erewhon."[95]

Pragmatic or not, the ingenuity of the code is breathtaking. The MPC ultimately offered a wide range of key innovations for the general conceptualization of the criminal law as well as for the substantive elements of crimes and defenses. First, the code separates a general part—the building blocks for crimes—from the special part, the particular substantive crimes.[96] Hence, voluntary acts, mental states, causation, complicity, and the like are defined. Mental states themselves are limited to four defined terms: purpose, knowledge, recklessness, and negligence, and interpretive rules are provided so that it can be ascertained what mental state applies to what element. Recklessness is created as an explicit default rule, thought to roughly approximate the unspoken default of general intent under the common law.

The general part transforms how one approaches a criminal statute. Consider a hypothetical statute that reads: "No person shall destroy the property of another.... When the property is valued at more than $1,000, the offense shall be a felony." What if the defendant was sleepwalking when she trampled her neighbor's roses? Not a voluntary act, as defined in the general part. What if the defendant thought the property was her own? No mens rea, as defined in the general part, which specifies that the default mental state is recklessness and defines recklessness as a conscious disregard of a substantial and unjustifiable risk. What if the property was only destroyed because

---

[92] *Thursday Morning Session—May 20, 1954*, 31 A.L.I. Proc. 71 (1954).

[93] Robinson & Dubber, *supra* note 16, at 325.

[94] *Id.* at 334.

[95] Sanford H. Kadish, *Fifty Years of Criminal Law: An Opinionated Review*, 87 Cal. L. Rev. 943, 949 (1999).

[96] Though Robinson and Dubber take the general part to be "hardly revolutionary" compared to European codes (Robinson & Dubber, *supra* note 16, at 330), Wechsler characterized his approach as more thorough and exhaustive: "The effort here was to exhaust the possibilities of useful generalization about the use of penal sanctions, going far beyond the fragmentary formulations found in penal codes drafted in the Anglo-American tradition and even beyond the more extensive statements of the newer European codes." Herbert Wechsler, *Codification of Criminal Law in the United States: The Model Penal Code*, 68 Colum. L. Rev. 1425, 1428–29 (1968).

of a freak gust of wind combining with the defendant's conduct? No causation, as defined in the general part. That is, all of the depth of reasoning that one would need to understand what the statute means is provided by a rigorous, coherent, and complete set of rules.

Wechsler was not averse to rethinking substantive crimes. Premeditation, and degrees of murder generally, are eliminated. Voluntary manslaughter is far more excuse-like, focusing on the extreme mental or emotional disturbance of the defendant and abandoning the need for a provoking act from the victim. Felony murder is abandoned. Theft is harmonized. And, at times, the MPC was daring. Despite the Council originally overruling the Reporters' decision not to criminalize consensual sodomy,[97] the ALI ultimately approved the Reporters' recommendation to exclude the crime from the code.[98] Following the United Kingdom's Wolfenden Report, the MPC sided with individual liberty in matters of "private morality."[99] This stand was unprecedented in the United States, and many states soon followed suit.[100]

The MPC's defenses are generous, both procedurally and substantively. With few exceptions, the state is required to disprove the existence of the defense. For instance, unreasonable mistakes in the law of self-defense are clearly identified as warranting punishment at the level of negligence, not purpose. Duress and necessity are broadened, and critically, the MPC expands on the M'Naghten insanity test.

Wechsler's focus on dangerousness, as the central justification for criminalization and punishment, is not only apparent in the sentencing principles but also in key substantive provisions. Attempts are punished as much as completed crimes, and rather than waiting for an attempt to reach "dangerous proximity,"[101] the taking of a substantial step suffices. Conspiracies can be unilateral, that is, made with an undercover police officer, and one can be complicit in a crime that one unsuccessfully tries to aid.

Despite its preventive goals, the Code reads as quite consistent with a retributive, liberal perspective. It aims at conduct that constitutes harm to others, not the enforcement of private morality, reflecting a liberal perspective on criminalization. And, its emphasis on the guilty mind, both in ruling out strict liability and in defaulting to a subjective appreciation of risk (as opposed to mere negligence), are more consistent with a desert-based view than one that aims to incapacitate the dangerous. After all, dangerous actors may lack guilty minds but still impose risks. Indeed, a code that took prevention and rehabilitation as its sole goals would cease to be a criminal law at all. It would simply be a regime of state intervention and treatment.

Promulgated in 1962, the Code became widely influential. "Essentially every criminal law coursebook in widespread use in American law schools reprints the MPC, rather than any state's actual code, as the one example of an integrated criminal code students are exposed to in substantial completeness."[102] The MPC "prompted a wave

---

[97] WILLIAM N. ESKRIDGE JR., DISHONORABLE PASSIONS: SODOMY LAWS IN AMERICA 1861–2003, at 123 (2008). Associate Reporter Louis Schwartz was the central figure in forcefully advocating for the removal of consensual sodomy from the criminal law. *Id.* at 121–24.

[98] MODEL PENAL CODE, Commentary to § 213.2, at 372 (1980).

[99] *Id.*

[100] *Id.* at 372–73.

[101] *See, e.g.,* People v. Rizzo, 158 N.E. 888 (N.Y. 1927).

[102] Lynch, *supra* note 15, at 220.

of state code reforms in the 1960s and 1970s, each influenced by the Model Penal Code."[103] As Robinson and Dubber report, thirty-four states recodified their criminal laws, which were influenced by the MPC.[104] "Thousands of court opinions have cited the Model Penal Code as persuasive authority for the interpretation of an existing statute or in the exercise of a court's occasional power to formulate a criminal law doctrine."[105] The official commentaries also serve as an influential interpretive guide.[106] The MPC innovation of four mental states "may be the code's most important contribution to American criminal law reform."[107]

Although the substantive provisions were extraordinarily successful, the MPC sentencing provisions were less influential because they were based on a treatment theory of punishment in which defendants should be rehabilitated before entering society; under such an approach, broad indeterminate sentences made sense.[108] However, the treatment theory was discredited, and simultaneously, discretionary schemes were subject to criticism for bias, unpredictability, and shifting discretion/lawmaking from the legislature to the judiciary.[109]

As a footnote to the arduous process of reforming the criminal law, it is worth noting the "strange hybrid" of the code's commentaries, not all of which were written when the MPC's substantive provisions were considered.[110] Though some areas of the Code were accompanied by detailed commentaries, other original commentaries were "much thinner."[111] With Wechsler taking on the role of Executive Director of the ALI, the task of completing the commentaries fell to Peter Low, as Reporter, along with John Jeffries, Marvina Halberstam, Sanford Fox, and Kent Greenawalt.[112] The commentaries are ultimately a mixture of the detailed thought process of Wechsler at the time or the attempt to "give reasoned support to decisions made two decades earlier."[113] Even the latter, however, was ultimately blessed by Wechsler.[114]

---

[103] Robinson & Dubber, *supra* note 16, at 320.

[104] *Id.* at 326:

> The two decades following the 1962 promulgation saw a host of state recodifications. New codes were enacted in Illinois, effective in 1962; Minnesota and New Mexico in 1963; New York in 1967; Georgia in 1969; Kansas in 1970; Connecticut in 1971; Colorado and Oregon in 1972; Delaware, Hawaii, New Hampshire, Pennsylvania, and Utah in 1973; Montana, Ohio, and Texas in 1974; Florida, Kentucky, North Dakota, and Virginia in 1975; Arkansas, Maine, and Washington in 1976; South Dakota and Indiana in 1977; Arizona and Iowa in 1978; Missouri, Nebraska, and New Jersey in 1979; Alabama and Alaska in 1980; and Wyoming in 1983. All of these thirty-four enactments were influenced in some part by the Model Penal Code. Draft criminal codes produced in other states, such as California, Massachusetts, Michigan, Oklahoma, Rhode Island, Tennessee, Vermont, and West Virginia, did not pass legislative review and may yet be revived.

[105] *Id.* at 327.

[106] *Id.*

[107] *Id.* at 335.

[108] *Id.* at 328.

[109] *Id.*

[110] Kent Greenawalt, *A Few Reflections on the Model Penal Code Commentaries*, 1 Ohio St. J. Crim. L. 241, 243 (2003).

[111] *Id.* at 241.

[112] *Id.* at 242.

[113] *Id.* at 243.

[114] *Id.* at 242.

IV. Revising the Model Penal Code

If criminal law could rightly feel neglected by the delay in the first code, it might also question why Restatement projects are often on second and third iterations, while the MPC stays largely stagnant. It has been a continual question whether a revision is necessary and what the appropriate aims of such a revision should be.

For instance, in its first issue, the *Ohio State Journal of Criminal Law* featured a symposium on whether there ought to be a Model Penal Code (Second). The answers varied from rethinking aspects of the mens rea provisions,[115] to undertaking smaller projects or focusing on current criminalization problems like drug offenses.[116] Notably, even if the MPC itself is "evergreen," its adoption is not. As Paul Robinson and Michael Cahill noted, "[C]urrent American criminal codes are in serious trouble."[117] Robinson and Cahill blamed code degradation on both "designer offenses," specialized crimes overlapping with general offenses created in response to special interest group lobbying and "crime de jure" offenses created in response to news stories.[118] They note that when Illinois adds "defacing delivery containers" to a code that already covers destruction of property, these ad hoc and ill-thought amendments may disrupt offense definitions (by introducing new terms) or grading schemes (by punish one type of conduct more severely than other graver offenses).[119] As a result, whatever the MPC once brought order and structure to has been eviscerated: "We think the best analogy may be barnacles collecting on the hull of a ship. The cumulative effect is a distortion of the original hull shape such that is can no longer perform its function. At this point, one might justifiably say that the barnacles have dwarfed the ship."[120]

Doug Berman likewise issued a clarion call. In particular, he worried that the teaching of the MPC lulls students into believing the law is "quite enlightened and orderly" when our actual practices "have become quite grim and messy."[121] Though he admitted that his concerns were more with criminal law pedagogy and procedure than with the original MPC itself, he noted that it now appears "increasingly academic and almost naively optimistic."[122] And so, in 2003, Berman pled for rescue: "[B]ecause I view the modern criminal law landscape to be as unruly today as when the original

---

[115] Kenneth W. Simons, *Should the Model Penal Code's Mens Rea Provisions Be Amended?*, 1 Ohio St. J. Crim. L. 179 (2003).

[116] Dressler, *supra* note 17, at 160; Lynch, *supra* note 15, at 231–33 ("a Model Controlled Substances Act would potentially be a major contribution to the debate that could stand a significant chance of passage in jurisdictions that are considering reform in this area"); *see also* Robinson & Dubber, *supra* note 16, at 329 ("In 1962 the Model Penal Code included no drug offenses. In an appendix to the code's Special Part, the drafters merely remarked that 'a State enacting a new Penal Code may insert additional Articles dealing with special topics such as narcotics, alcoholic beverages, gambling and offenses against tax and trade laws.'").

[117] Paul H. Robinson & Michael T. Cahill, *Can a Model Penal Code Second Save the States from Themselves?*, 1 Ohio St. J. Crim. L. 169, 169 (2003).

[118] *Id.* at 170–71.

[119] *Id.*

[120] *Id.* at 172.

[121] Douglas A. Berman, *The Model Penal Code Second: Might "Film Schools" Be in Need of a Remake?*, 1 Ohio St. J. Crim. L. 163, 165–66 (2003).

[122] *Id.* at 166.

MPC was first developed, I now hope the ALI might, like the proverbial Western hero in a white hat, ride into town with a MPC Second to bring renewed order."[123]

Still, one wonders whether broad reform is even possible. As Lynch notes, "Our post-modern era values diversity and fragmentation in the intellectual life more than it values consensus and middle-of-the-road 'common sense.' The skeptic wonders not only whether it is worthwhile to commission a new compendium of the current conventional wisdom on criminal law, but even whether it would be possible to create such a document."[124] Robinson and Cahill think that the politics of criminal code reform leave the ALI in a particularly ideal situation for reform. Prosecutors and defense attorneys are too busy.[125] Judges and legislators don't want to undermine hard-fought reasoning and wins.[126] They think "if a group like the American Law Institute . . . —respected, independent, and balanced—produces a code, that code gives the local groups a benchmark against which they can test their local recodification proposals."[127]

Crucially, the ALI revisited two significant substantive areas: sentencing, including the death penalty, and sexual assault. The ALI undertook sentencing reform in 1998, with the final draft of the MPC: Sentencing project being approved in May 2017.[128] Chief Reporter Kevin Reitz notes, "If there is a single explanation for the failure of the original Model Penal Code's punishment provisions to gain and hold influence over American legislatures, it can be found in the Code's offender-based sentencing theory."[129] The drafters had an "insufficiently critical optimism" about rehabilitation and an "unworkable supposition" that retributivism was irrelevant.[130]

The revision, aimed both at jurisdictions that had adopted the MPC and those that had not,[131] envisions "utilitarianism within limits of proportionality."[132] The sentencing revision was governed by "limited retributivism, under which considerations of desert establish upper and lower limits of penalties in specific cases, and utilitarian rationales may then be consulted to select the types of severities of sanctions within the allowable range."[133] This was a significant shift from the rehabilitative and incapacitative ambitions of the original MPC.[134]

To illustrate the profound shift in ideology, consider the reorientation of sentencing structure.[135] The original code gave very little power to judges. A provision that set the sentence between one to three years minimum and ten years maximum *only*

---

123 *Id.* at 167.

124 Lynch, *supra* note 15, at 223.

125 Robinson & Cahill, *supra* note 117, at 173–74.

126 *Id.* at 174–75.

127 *Id.* at 175

128 Model Penal Code: Sentencing, Proposed Final Draft (Approved May 2017), Robina Institute of Criminal Law and Criminal Justice (June 5, 2017), https://robinainstitute.umn.edu/publications/model-penal-code-sentencing-proposed-final-draft-approved-may-2017.

129 Kevin R. Reitz, *American Law Institute, Model Penal Code: Sentencing, Plan for Revision*, 6 BUFF. CRIM. L. REV. 549, 555 (2002).

130 *Id.*

131 *Id.* at 538.

132 Model Penal Code: Sentencing (Proposed Final Draft, 2017), at 370.

133 Reitz, *supra* note 129, at 528.

134 *Id.* at 529.

135 *Id.* at 539.

gave judges the power to set the minimum term. Correction officials would then assess the defendant's rehabilitative progress, determining ultimately whether to hold the defendant beyond his minimum term, with the ability to hold him to the maximum allotted by statute.[136] In light of the significant worries about our incapacitative and rehabilitative assessments vested in back-end decision makers, the new code focuses far more on front-end sentencing guidelines that are far more cabined by desert. Ultimately, the revision offers guidance on the "general purposes of the sentencing system; rules governing severity... the elimination of mandatory minimum penalties; mechanisms for combating racial and ethnic disparities in punishment; instruments of prison population control; victims' rights in the sentencing process; the creation of judicial powers to review many collateral consequences of conviction; sentencing commissions, sentencing guidelines, and more."[137]

In the course of reexamining the MPC's sentencing provisions, the death penalty was revisited. Originally, the ALI took no position on whether capital punishment should be retained or abolished but set forth parameters for a sentence of death.[138] As the sentencing project began, Director Lance Liebman suggested that the death penalty could be on the table, but ought not to be the first order of business for the nascent project.[139] At the Annual Meeting in 2007, two members moved for the ALI to oppose capital punishment, leading to the creation of an ad hoc committee to study the death penalty.[140] Ultimately, in May 2009, the ALI withdrew the MPC's death penalty administration provision "in light of the intractable institutional and structural obstacles to ensuring a minimally adequate system for administering capital punishment."[141] This retraction was in lieu of substantial study or a political position, as the ALI ultimately believed that the moral and political question was not something upon which the ALI could gain consensus and make a substantial contribution.[142] Attendees at the 2009 Annual Meeting praise the respectful tenor and the rigorous argumentation that led to that result.[143]

The sexual assault provisions were also problematic. Indeed, they were, in the words of one commentator, "notoriously obsolete and culturally unenlightened."[144] From the marital rape exemption and the discounting of offenses against "voluntary social companions," to outdated evidentiary and procedural bars in the absence of corroboration and prompt complaint, the MPC did not stand the test of time with respect to rape.[145] Urging reform, Deborah Denno suggested that it would not be "too

---

[136] *Id.* at 540–44.
[137] *Id.*
[138] AMERICAN LAW INSTITUTE, MODEL PENAL CODE (1985), explanatory note to Article 210, at 216.
[139] *Wednesday Morning Session—May 14, 2003*, 80 A.L.I. PROC. 242, 243 (2003).
[140] 29 A.L.I. REP. 1, 6 (2007).
[141] 32 A.L.I. REP. 1, 2 (2009).
[142] REPORT OF THE COUNCIL TO THE MEMBERSHIP OF THE ALI 1, 5 (Apr. 15, 2009) ("Introduction" and "Proposed Motion").
[143] *See* Roberta Cooper Ramo, *The American Law Institute at 100: A Three-Decade Personal Reflection*, in this volume.
[144] Robert Weisberg, *Sexual Offenses*, in REFORMING CRIMINAL JUSTICE VOLUME 1: INTRODUCTION AND CRIMINALIZATION 139, 141 (Erik Luna ed., 2017), *available at* https://law.asu.edu/sites/default/files/pdf/academy_for_justice/Reforming-Criminal-Justice_Vol_1.pdf.
[145] *See generally* Deborah W. Denno, *Why the Model Penal Code's Sexual Offense Provisions Should Be Pulled and Replaced*, 1 OHIO ST. J. CRIM. L. 207 (2003).

difficult to reach consensus," "reforms can remain 'real' not radical," and "[h]ard jobs can get done."[146]

The hard job did get done, with the membership approving the revision in May 2022, but it was difficult. As Robert Weisberg describes the project, "the MPC is trying to leap 50-plus years forward over the many incremental changes that evolved in states" and its draft revisions "brought unprecedented public attention to the ... ALI."[147] There were "many iterations" of the definition of consent in light of the "roiling controversy among this elite group of lawyers."[148]

Debates ranged from the definitions of consent and penetration, to the role of existing law and approaches in crafting the model code, to critical questions of mens rea.[149] The definition of consent proved challenging from the beginning of the project to the very end. After the Council approved one definition of consent that had a communicative aspect, dueling motions were filed—one to make consent an internal choice or "willingness" and another to make communication more affirmative.[150] This led to a prolonged discussion on the floor of the Annual Meeting,[151] with the "willingness" conception receiving the membership's approval. Yet, before final project approval, the U.S. Department of Justice urged revision to the formulation, and the Reporters and Council revisited some language, specifically including the evidentiary usage of lack of resistance. Some scholars continued to worry even on the eve of the draft's final approval that it was regressive with respect to consent.[152]

Stephen Schulhofer, the Reporter on the project, suggested he hit three types of resistance: pushback from "the misogynists, the low-information opponents, and the well-informed, very thoughtful opponents."[153] While misogynists aimed to keep the existing hierarchy and low-information opponents believed what they saw on television, thereby prompting overemphasis on college campus behavior,[154] the thoughtful opponents pressed the difficulties that come from issues with the criminal justice system. Specifically, these theorists worried about expanding a criminal law in which there are "abuses of prosecutorial discretion; shocking racial disparities; intense leverage deployed to coerce guilty pleas, especially when the evidence is the weakest; overly punitive sentencing; mass incarceration; and by no means least, our overly rigid, vastly over-inclusive system of sex-offender registration."[155] The problem for the project was that "both pictures have a lot of disturbing truth."[156] Time will tell whether states adopt these revisions or look to them as a new interpretive authority.

---

[146] *Id.* at 218 (citations omitted).
[147] Weisberg, *supra* note 144, at 150; *see, e.g.,* Judith Shulevitz, *Opinion: Regulating Sex,* N.Y. Times, June 28, 2015, https://www.nytimes.com/2015/06/28/opinion/sunday/judith-shulevitz-regulating-sex.html.
[148] Weisberg, *supra* note 144, at 157.
[149] *Id.* at 157–64.
[150] *Text of Proposed Amendments and Changes Submitted at 2016 Annual Meeting,* 93 A.L.I. Proc. 401, 408–409 (2016) (setting forth Stith/Love motion and Anderson motion).
[151] *See generally Tuesday Morning Session—May 17, 2016,* 93 A.L.I. Proc. 110 (2016).
[152] Michelle J. Anderson & Deborah Tuerkheimer, *The Thinking About Consent Has Evolved Drastically. This Code May Turn the Clock Back,* N.Y. Times, May 16, 2022, https://www.nytimes.com/2022/05/16/opinion/metoo-sexual-assault-consent.html.
[153] Stephen J. Schulhofer, *Reforming the Law of Rape,* 35 Law & Ineq. 335, 348 (2017).
[154] *Id.* at 348–49.
[155] *Id.* at 350.
[156] *Id.* at 351.

V. Assessing the Model Penal Code

Whether the MPC succeeded requires us to determine whom we are asking and what their metrics are. Let's start with the aspirations of the Hadley committee and Wechsler. Consider four principal issues identified by Hadley Committee. They were (1) the uncertain role of the common law; (2) the differing approaches of various states (surrounding, for instance, retreat, provocation, and insanity); (3) the problems with administration of justice including under enforcement, policing, and courtroom theatrics; (4) greater scholarly guidance.

In some respects, the Hadley complaints still exist. Centrally, states continue to differ in crime definitions and defenses, and retreat, provocation, and insanity are all areas that present vast disagreement. Moreover, the MPC is not the leading authority on any of these particular issues. The question of retreat is largely dictated by stand your ground laws.[157] The MPC's reconceptualization of legally adequate provocation was not widely adopted; it is also subject to debate as feminists argue that it offers mitigation to aggressive male violence, while other theorists point to the likely positive distributive impact of mitigating doctrines.[158] Though I will turn to insanity more specifically when discussing Wechsler's ambitions, for now, it suffices to note that jurisdictions offer a patchwork of different tests.[159] Moreover, to the extent that we have replaced under policing and under enforcement with over policing and over enforcement,[160] it is hard to see this as a success on that criterion.

The MPC did triumph along two criteria. First, it clarified criminal statutes and their relationship to common law. To be sure, some jurisdictions still rely on common law definitions, others have common law crimes, and most have allowed courts to interpret the statutes in various ways.[161] Still, today's theorists may have difficulty imagining how completely disordered earlier codes were. Recall putting crimes in alphabetical order was a systemizing achievement. Second, the influence of the MPC and its commentaries in the understanding and interpretation of the criminal law cannot be disputed.[162] Other ALI projects look to the MPC.[163] The federal criminal law did not adopt the MPC, and yet, even the Supreme Court's opinions are influenced by its interpretive clarity.[164]

---

[157] Cynthia Ward, *"Stand Your Ground" and Self-Defense*, 42 AM. J. CRIM. L. 89 (2015).

[158] Victoria Nourse, *Passion's Progress: Modern Law Reform and the Provocation Defense*, 106 YALE L.J. 1331 (1997); Aya Gruber, *A Provocative Defense*, 103 CAL. L. REV. 273 (2015).

[159] *See* Clark v. Arizona, 548 U.S. 735, 749 (2006) (surveying the myriad state approaches).

[160] According to Professor Douglas A. Berman, "mass incarceration and extreme prison punishments are the most pressing modern sentencing problems in the United States." Berman, *supra* note 121, at 166.

[161] Anders Walker, *The New Common Law: Courts, Culture and the Localization of the Model Penal Code*, 62 HASTINGS L.J. 1633 (2011); Carissa Byrne Hessick, *The Myth of Common Law Crimes*, 105 VA. L. REV. 965 (2019).

[162] Kadish, *supra* note 93, at 946 (noting the "maturation of American criminal law scholarship" as among the MPC's chief contributions).

[163] RESTATEMENT OF THE LAW THIRD, TORTS: INTENTIONAL TORTS TO PERSONS (TENTATIVE DRAFT NO. 1) § 101 cmt. g (Apr. 8, 2015) (explaining how element analysis of the Model Penal Code would clarify tort doctrine).

[164] *See, e.g.*, Elonis v. United States, 575 U.S. 723 (2015) (Alito, J., concurring) (suggesting the Court ought to specify the mens rea under the statute and using a combination of Model Penal Code and common law reasoning to arrive at recklessness); Borden v. United States, 141 S. Ct. 1817 (2021), slip opinion available

Success, in light of Wechslerian goals, is also mixed. Recall that Wechsler emphasized the approach to culpability, the rejection of strict liability, the treatment of insanity, and the rethinking of punitive practices. In some respects, existing law substantially departs from Wechslerian ambitions. First, as noted earlier, the ALI itself rethought the sentencing provisions. Second, "[s]trict liability pervades U.S. criminal law."[165]

Perhaps the clearest rejection of the MPC is the treatment of insanity throughout the United States. For insanity, "the tale is one of the rise and fall of the ... Model Penal Code test...."[166] Nowhere else was the MPC so widely embraced and so quickly abandoned. It is also a lesson in how popular opinion and political influence can undermine even the most conscientiously examined criminal provisions. In consultation with mental health professionals, the MPC made substantial innovations to insanity. It broadened the M'Naghten rule by requiring appreciation, not mere knowledge, of wrongfulness; it offered a choice between lacking appreciation of legal or moral wrongfulness; and it appended a volitional prong.[167] It received a "warm reception,"[168] being adopted by approximately half of state legislatures, some state courts on their own initiative, and all but one federal circuit.[169]

Then, John W. Hinkley tried to assassinate Ronald Reagan, and he was acquitted by reason of insanity.[170] The public found the result unjust. States rewrote their codes, and M'Naghten became the majority rule.[171] The American Psychiatric Association and the American Bar Association defected.[172] The Justice Department and the U.S. Attorney General originally aimed for abolition of the defense, and Congress ultimately adopted a rule, with procedural provisions that eliminated the control prong, required severe disorders, and placed the burden of persuasion on the defendant by clear and convincing evidence.[173] "When the dust cleared, the sun of the Model Penal Code test had set."[174]

Notably, in significant respects, the narrative about the MPC has lost a thread of the story. While scholars today question how we teach and write about the criminal law, and as the MPC is cast as an outdated relic, and worse—a Disney version of *Law and Order*, it may be worth asking whether scholars ever faithfully teach the Code. Wechsler's pragmatism made the MPC attractive to theorists of all stripes, and retributivists have found it to be as much of a model and an ideal as those who favor

at https://www.supremecourt.gov/opinions/20pdf/19-5410_8nj9.pdf (explicitly relying on Model Penal Code culpability terms and hierarchy).

[165] Michael Serota, *Strict Liability Abolition* 97 N.Y.U. L. REV. 1429 (2022), *available at* https://ssrn.com/abstract=4047185.

[166] Stephen J. Morse, *Before and After Hinckley: Legal Insanity in the United States*, *in* THE INSANITY DEFENCE: INTERNATIONAL AND COMPARATIVE PERSPECTIVES (Ronnie Mackay & Warren Brookbanks eds., 2022), *available at* https://ssrn.com/abstract=3784179.

[167] Kadish, *supra* note 95, at 959; Morse, *supra* note 166, at 2.

[168] Kadish, *supra* note 95, at 959.

[169] *Id.*; Morse, *supra* note 166, at 2.

[170] Morse, *supra* note 166, at 2.

[171] Kadish, *supra* note 95, at 959.

[172] *Id.*

[173] Federal Insanity Defense Reform Act, 18 U.S.C. § 17 (1984).

[174] Kadish, *supra* note 95, at 959.

incapacitation, deterrence, or rehabilitation.[175] Indeed, though some criticize the Code for prioritizing preventive goals,[176] other retributivists find the MPC's conclusions completely hospitable to their more desert-based theories.[177] What is perhaps lost in the substantive course on criminal law is the relationship between substantive rules and sentencing that sets the robust Wechslerian vision so radically apart from today's practices. That is, the substantive course teaches a rule for early intervention for attempts, and it couples that with equal punishment for attempts and completed crimes. That's what first-year law students learn. But missing in the first-year course is that that punishment was indeterminate in ways that allowed for early release of those who were no longer dangerous and further detention of those who were. It was dangerousness all the way down. Because the Code is so hospitable to opposing views, that vision of the criminal law has been obscured.

But beyond the missing stories and the failed attempts, in other ways, the MPC was a monumental success. What the MPC achieved is so ingrained into the fabric of criminal law that we take much of what it did for granted. It is hard to overstate the importance of the conceptual innovations. The MPC drafters did more than put the code in A to Z order. They reconceptualized crimes into a coherent structure, and they imposed order with element analysis and mens rea definitions. As Kadish remarked, "This is all old hat now, the standard stuff of the first-year criminal law class. But it was a breakthrough to articulate so lucidly and powerfully a conception of culpability requirements comprehending all crime definitions, and it has been transforming in its impact on the law and on legal education and scholarship."[178] Dressler is in accord: "For me, the MPC drafters' work on mental state categories is their greatest gift to the American criminal law."[179]

Today, criminal law certainly needs to be reformed. But it does not need to be rethought. Rather, more than ever, we need the public will to return to the central questions the reformers asked years ago, and to reimpose order on the chaotic and haphazard criminalization of our recent past. Even as we seek to limit the breadth and depth of our criminal laws, we want reflective principles for how to write the criminal law we again wish to have. More than ever, we must return to our Model Penal Code.

[175] Lynch, *supra* note 15, at 222 (noting the MPC "is quite consistent with Kantian notions of fairness and desert").

[176] Paul H. Robinson, *Punishing Dangerousness: Cloaking Preventive Detention as Criminal Justice*, 114 HARV. L. REV. 1429 (2001).

[177] Kimberly Kessler Ferzan, *Holistic Culpability*, 28 CARDOZO L. REV. 2523 (2007).

[178] Kadish, *supra* note 95, at 953.

[179] Dressler, *supra* note 17, at 157.

PART IV
PRINCIPLES

15

Special Interests at the Gate

The ALI Corporate Governance Project, 1978–1992

*William W. Bratton**

I. Introduction

Corporate law and corporate governance are not the same thing. They overlap at some points but not at others. Their relationship is complicated and evolves dynamically. No one-line statement can summarize it.

Corporate law is the cases and statutes pursuant to which all corporations are formed and operated. Corporate governance, which tends to matter only in larger corporations, starts with the cases and statutes and adds best practices enunciated by policy entrepreneurs and endorsed by constituent communities. Corporate law sets out a framework within which private actors can create and operate their own producing organizations. Corporate governance is a field of action on which managers, employees, financial interest holders, and other constituents allocate power in large producing corporations. Corporate law facilitates the imposition of management accountability when it sets out rights and duties pursuant to which litigants can hold those in charge of corporations responsible for their defalcations. Corporate governance imposes accountability as investors and managers go back and forth in the on-going allocation of control. Where corporate law facilitates productive investment of capital, corporate governance wrestles with dollars and cents investment outcomes. Although some experts specialize in one or the other, many do both. Indeed, there is significant overlap not only as regards the cast of characters but the terms and dynamics of regulation. Within the area of overlap, however, lawyers and business people tend to emphasize different things. Where lawyers tend to connect governance to accountability, with an emphasis on legal accountability, business people associate it with productive efficiency, seeing no necessary tie to legal accountability.

So close are corporate law and corporate governance that a novice observer could be forgiven the assumption that the two have always travelled together as natural and inevitable concomitants of production in large firms. But such is not the case. Where corporate law has always been there, corporate governance appeared as a concept only in recent history. The concept coalesced during the early 1970s[1] in reaction to a perceived deficit in management performance.

* Nicholas F. Gallicchio Professor of Law Emeritus, University of Pennsylvania Carey Law School; de la Cruz/Mentschikoff Chair in Law & Economics and Senior Lecturer, University of Miami School of Law; Research Associate, European Corporate Governance Institute.

[1] The phrase "corporate governance" had its first published appearance only in 1972. *See* Mariana Pargendler, *The Corporate Governance Obsession*, 13(42) J. CORP. L. 359, 373 (2016).

William W. Bratton, *Special Interests at the Gate* In: *The American Law Institute.* Edited by: Andrew S. Gold and Robert W. Gordon, Oxford University Press. © Oxford University Press 2023. DOI: 10.1093/oso/9780197685341.003.0016

Corporate governance quickly became a topic of general concern during those early years, even as its more particular contents were heavily contested. There was a politics. To the left stood progressives who saw corporate governance as an institutional vehicle with a potential to facilitate social reform. To the right stood corporate managers themselves, ever ready to suborn the new construct, rendering it innocuous and leaving intact their own privileges and prerogatives. The space between the left and the right was occupied by moderate voices looking for enhanced management accountability within the inherited institutional context.

In 1978, the American Law Institute (ALI) launched a Corporate Governance Project (the Project) intended to yield a focal point statement of the meaning and content of corporate governance, taking a middle ground perspective. The idea was to articulate extralegal governance principles along with restatements or revisions of the parts of corporate law that bear most directly on governance, integrating the two toward the end of enhanced management accountability. Unfortunately, a moderate perspective did not assure a moderate response as the Project went forward. Far from providing a focal point for general agreement respecting the content of corporate governance, the Project became a platform for the rearticulation of points of dispute, especially on the question whether legal accountability entailed a sacrifice of productive efficiency.

The goal of an enduring focal point statement would have proved elusive even in a more harmonious context, for the meaning and content of corporate governance has evolved dynamically. The 822-page *Principles of Corporate Governance: Analysis and Recommendations* (the Principles), finally approved by the ALI's members in 1992,[2] very much reflects the political economic dispensation that prevailed at the time of the Project's origin. Things look very different today. That said, the Project's progenitors by no means wasted their time as they inched their way through a hostile environment to complete their task. The Principles stood (and continue to stand) head and shoulders above the rest of the literature as the best treatise ever produced on corporate law.[3] The Principles also stood (and continue to stand) as the formal source of the monitoring model of the corporate board of directors, the model that continues to dominate thinking both in corporate law and corporate governance.

This chapter recounts the Project's origins and evolution.

---

[2] Publication would take a further two years. *See* 1 AMERICAN LAW INSTITUTE: PRINCIPLES OF CORPORATE GOVERNANCE: ANALYSIS AND RECOMMENDATIONS (1994) [hereafter cited as 1 *ALI Principles*], and 2 AMERICAN LAW INSTITUTE: PRINCIPLES OF CORPORATE GOVERNANCE: ANALYSIS AND RECOMMENDATIONS (1994) [hereafter cited as 2 *ALI Principles*]. The *Principles'* Chief Reporter noted that this was not a record-breaking period of gestation: the Restatement (Second) of Contracts took nineteen years, the Restatement (Second) of Conflict of Laws also took nineteen years, and the Restatement (Second) of Torts took twenty-one years. Melvin Aron Eisenberg, *An Overview of the* Principles of Corporate Governance, 48 BUS. LAW. 1271 (1992).

[3] The term "treatise" is used loosely. For an illuminating discussion of interplay between Restatement projects and their Reporters' paralleling treatises during the ALI's early history, *see* Deborah A. DeMott, *Restating the Law in the Shadow of Codes: The ALI in Its Formative Era*, in this volume.

II. Motivation

Although corporate governance was a new topic of concern at the time of the Project's initiation in 1978, management accountability was not. Adolf Berle and Gardiner Means famously had problematized it in *The Modern Corporation and Private Property*,[4] published in 1932. Berle and Means described a separation of ownership and control—the shareholders owned but could not control, due to dispersed holdings and resulting collective action problems. Managers accordingly wielded considerable power in the economy and the polity without the accountability that befalls a conventional property owner operating in a traditional product market.[5]

Berle and Means's structural account would endure. But policy concerns about management accountability would ease, a least for a while. As economic expansion succeeded depression and war, corporate managers came to enjoy great prestige. They were seen as the successful planners behind the postwar boom.[6] Their considerable power was thought to follow ineluctably from organizational expertise. Moreover, even as structural impediments had foreclosed the possibility of effective market control,[7] the post–New Deal regulatory state was seen to have made up the deficit, adequately controlling the managers' behavior and keeping them responsive to constituent demands.[8] Berle, writing during the postwar period, came to see managers, constrained by the threat of regulation, as quasi-civil servants.[9]

All of this caused corporate law to fall back from the policy margin. Indeed, it came to be viewed as a backwater. In 1962, Bayless Manning, one of the era's prominent corporate law academics, pronounced corporate law dead as a field of intellectual effort, a dry-as-dust doctrinal inheritance lacking in policy salience.[10]

The managerialist era ended during the 1970s. The first blow came with the demise of the once great Penn Central railroad in 1970. The company's passive and inattentive board of directors figured prominently in the causal postmortem.[11] The bad news compounded when the economic bill for the Vietnam War came due in 1972 and 1973. The economy went into a severe recession aggravated by the Mideast oil crisis even as inflation increased.[12] The stock market collapsed with the economy and spent a long time in recovery—there would be no money to be made investing long term in equities for a decade. The appearance of international competition in manufactured goods added to the stock of chronic problems.[13] The malaise undermined the economic assumptions of the managerialist era.[14]

---

[4] ADOLF A. BERLE JR. & GARDINER C. MEANS, THE MODERN CORPORATION AND PRIVATE PROPERTY 1 (1933).

[5] *Id.* at 1–2, 4, 13–35.

[6] ADOLPH A. BERLE, THE AMERICAN ECONOMIC REPUBLIC 82, 91 (1963).

[7] *See* William W. Bratton, *The "Nexus of Contracts" Corporation: A Critical Appraisal*, 74 CORNELL L. REV. 407, 413 (1989).

[8] BERLE, *supra* note 6, at 99, 169.

[9] *Id.* at 88.

[10] Bayless Manning, *The Shareholder's Appraisal Remedy: An Essay for Frank Coker*, 72 YALE L.J. 223, 245 n. 37 (1962).

[11] *See* JOSEPH R. DAUGHEN & PETER BINZEN, THE WRECK OF THE PENN CENTRAL 290, 303 336 (1971).

[12] GERALD F. DAVIS, THE VANISHING AMERICAN CORPORATION: NAVIGATING THE HAZARDS OF A NEW ECONOMY 47 (2016).

[13] *Id.* at 55–56.

[14] *Id.* at 55.

The public service gloss also faded. The New Deal political coalition that created and maintained the strong regulatory state fell apart. Managers, formerly cooperative in the face of overwhelming state power, defected. No longer afraid of noncompliance, they skirted regulatory boundaries and played a hostile game against regulatory initiatives. Accountability concerns crystallized when corporate "questionable payments" were uncovered in the Watergate investigation. At company after company secret slush funds had been channeled into domestic political contributions and bribes of foreign officials.[15] CEOs and board members consistently denied any knowledge. A governance gap needed to be filled accordingly. Legal compliance came to be seen as a part of top management's job, right up there with business planning. And the job was not being done.[16]

The conceptual framework surrounding large corporations underwent a substantial change. The happy story of managers as capable technocrats who enhanced social welfare under the watchful eye of the big stick state no longer resonated. It had become difficult to associate management power with either productive efficiency or responsiveness to constituent needs. The separation of ownership and control came back to the forefront as a problem in need of solution.

Corporate governance was invented to tackle the job. The role of the board of directors, long seen as a moribund institution,[17] was reconsidered. We should, it was thought, give the board a more focused job description, assigning it the task of monitoring management performance. If boards could be induced to monitor successfully, corporate performance would improve.[18] The monitoring function in turn required independent directors and a committee structure keyed to monitoring functions.[19] The approach, fully developed in Melvin Eisenberg's *The Structure of the Corporation*,[20] which appeared in 1976, caught on quickly.

The burning question concerned implementation. Progressives backed a preemptive federal incorporation scheme, variously suggesting minimum standards of conduct and stepped-up liability,[21] a universal and mandatory director independence requirement, and an expanded shareholder franchise.[22] Bills were introduced in Congress and hearings held.[23]

The progressives had become manifestly frustrated—they were dissatisfied with the level of new regulation and outraged by corporate noncooperation even as they

---

[15] Joel Seligman, *A Sheep in Wolf's Clothing: The American Law Institute Principles of Corporate Governance Project*, 55 GEO. WASH. L. REV. 325, 333–35 (1987).

[16] Bayless Manning, *Principles of Corporate Governance: One Viewer's Perspective on the ALI Project*, 48 BUS. LAW. 1319, 1319–20 (1992).

[17] MILES MACE, DIRECTORS: MYTH AND REALITY 2–3, 41, 43 (1971).

[18] MELVIN ARON EISENBERG, THE STRUCTURE OF THE CORPORATION: A LEGAL ANALYSIS 156–57 (1976).

[19] *See id.*

[20] EISENBERG, *supra* note 18.

[21] William L. Cary, *Federalism and Corporate Law: Reflections Upon Delaware*, 83 YALE L.J. 663, 700–03 (1974); Harvey Goldschmid, *Symposium, The Greening of the Board Room: Reflections on corporate Responsibility*, 10 COLUM. J. L. & SOC. PROBS. 15, 17–28 (1973)

[22] RALPH NADER, MARK GREEN, & JOEL SELIGMAN, TAMING THE GIANT CORPORATION 118–31 (1976).

[23] Seligman, *supra* note 15, at 337–38.

despaired of marshaling political backing for new initiatives.[24] Policy entrepreneurs looked to governance institutions for reform platforms. For them, director "independence" meant putting like-minded types onto corporate boards with socially responsible results.[25] Federal incorporation was a wedge intended to open up this possibility.[26]

The corporate establishment went on the defensive. It conceded the need for monitoring boards populated by independent directors, even as it vigorously opposed new federal governance mandates. Managers and their lawyers cleaned house.[27] To assist them, the corporate committee of the American Bar Association (ABA) put out a guidebook for effective board monitoring.[28] Even the Business Roundtable (BRT), the club comprised of the CEOs of the two hundred (or so) largest companies, pronounced in favor of independence and monitoring.[29] By the time the New York Stock Exchange, pressured by the Securities and Exchange Commission (SEC), in 1977 amended its rules to require an independent audit committee, 90 percent of public companies already had made the change.[30] The ALI Project, approved by the Council in May 1978, was viewed as part of this defensive response—a private legal organization would pursue a private solution to the governance problem, thereby defusing the threat of new regulation.[31]

The Project's eventual Chief Reporter, Melvin A. (Mel) Eisenberg of Berkeley Law, and its chief public defender, the ALI's President from 1980 to 1993, Roswell B. (Rod) Perkins, would later insist that the Project was indistinguishable from any other ALI undertaking. The ALI no longer limited itself to common law subjects, having successfully taken up securities and tax. Corporate law had long been one of the topics on its back burner.[32] The Project, they said, should be seen as having risen to the top of the ALI's agenda in the ordinary course.[33] But the conventional wisdom was otherwise, closely linking the Project with the politics of the day.[34]

---

[24] Elliott J. Weiss, *Social Regulation of Business Activity, Reforming the Corporate Governance System to Resolve an Institutional Impasse*, 28 UCLA L. REV. 343, 347–48 (1981).

[25] Victor Brudney, *The Independent Director-Heavenly City or Potemkin Village?*, 95 HARV. L. REV. 597, 603–04 (1982).

[26] Weiss, *supra* note 24, at 426–32 (suggesting that corporations be required to nominate directors from a centrally qualified list).

[27] See Seligman, *supra* note 15, at 335.

[28] American Bar Association Committee on Corp Laws, Section of Corporate, Banking and Business Law, *The Corporate Director's Guidebook*, 32 BUS. LAW. 1595 (1978).

[29] Business Roundtable, *The Role and Composition of the Board of Directors of the Large Publicly Owned Corporation*, 33 BUS. LAW. 2083 (1978).

[30] Seligman, *supra* note 15, at 338.

[31] Approval followed a series of conferences jointly sponsored with the ABA. Roswell B. Perkins, The Genesis and Goals of the ALI Corporate Governance Project, at 9–12 (paper presented at Inaugural Conference of The Samuel and Ronnie Heyman Program on Corporate Governance, of Benjamin N. Cardozo School of Law, Sept. 12, 1986).

[32] An uncompleted Corporate Law Restatement had been undertaken between 1926 and 1932.

[33] Eisenberg, *supra* note 2, at 1271; Perkins, *supra* note 31 at 9–12.

[34] *See, e.g.,* Manning, *supra* note 16, at 1331. But *cf.* Jonathan R. Macey, *The Transformation of the American Law Institute*, 61 GEO. WASH. L. REV. 1212, 1214–16 (1993) (mentioning institutional turf jealousies).

As it happened, federal incorporation stalled and faded on Capitol Hill, the Congress limiting itself to the insertion of a monitoring mandate within the Foreign Corrupt Practices Act of 1977.[35] The Project proceeded nonetheless, with Ray Garrett Jr., a prominent Chicago lawyer and former SEC chairman, as Chief Reporter and Harvey Goldschmid of the Columbia Law faculty as Deputy Chief Reporter. John C. (Jack) Coffee Jr., of Columbia Law, and Mel Eisenberg would join as Reporters.[36] Upon Garrett's death in 1980, Stanley A. Kaplan of the Chicago Law faculty, a senior and much-revered member of the business law professoriate, succeeded as Chief Reporter. There also were forty-four Advisers, of which ten with particular expertise in the subject matter[37] were to take a leading role as "consultants." A three-year time-table was projected.

III. Initiation and Collateral Attack

The Reporters went forward, their output denominated "Principles of Corporate Governance and Structure: Restatement and Recommendations." The pace was slower than anticipated. Tentative Draft No. 1[38] (TD No. 1) appeared in advance of the ALI's 1982 Annual Meeting. Its sections were drafted in the mode of model legislation and tended to begin with a pronouncement that "corporate law should provide," signaling mandates as the outcome in view.

TD No. 1's recommended mandates included, inter alia, the following:

(1) A capacious yet cogent statement of the corporation's objective and structure, encompassing both enterprise and shareholder value and, following the cases, recognizing the pertinence of ethical considerations and allowing for corporate eleemosynary support (in reasonable amounts).[39]

(2) Structural recommendations that encapsulated the monitoring model, including a majority independent board,[40] and audit[41] and nominating[42] committees made up entirely of independent directors, plus a majority independent compensation committee.[43]

(3) The first formal and integrated statement of the duty of care and the business judgment rule in the history of corporate law, a statement that broke new theoretical ground in distinguishing between the standard of conduct (the duty)

---

[35] Pub. L No. 95-213, 91 Stat. 1494.

[36] Ernest L. Folk, of the Virginia Law faculty, also joined as a Reporter but withdrew in 1981.

[37] The consultants included four prominent lawyers in private practice (Lloyd Cutler, Joseph Hinsey IV, Milton Kroll, and Bernard Weisberg), one general counsel (George W. Coombe Jr.), four academics (Louis Loss, Bayless Manning, Robert Mundheim, and Donald Schwartz), and a former CEO (Irving S. Shapiro).

[38] ALI, PRINCIPLES OF CORPORATE GOVERNANCE AND STRUCTURE: RESTATEMENT AND RECOMMENDATIONS, TENTATIVE DRAFT No. 1 (Apr. 1, 1982) [hereinafter cited as TD No. 1].

[39] Id. § 2.01, at 17.

[40] Id. § 3.03, at 72.

[41] Id. § 3.05, at 82–84.

[42] Id. § 3.06, at 97–98.

[43] Id. § 3.07, at 106–08.

and the standard of review (the business judgment overlay).[44] The formulation of management duties contained three features that fairly could have been described as aggressive: first, a "rational basis" requirement within the business judgment rule; second, a duty to make "reasonable inquiry" before entering a transaction; and, third, a duty to attend to the effectiveness of internal compliance systems.[45]

(4) The first installment of a rationalized set of parameters for shareholder derivative actions, including an innovative (and tight) damages cap applicable to violations of the duty of care.[46] The provisions took a firm position on the great procedural issue of the day: whether a board of directors' decision to dismiss a properly qualified and pleaded derivative complaint was entitled to the protection of the business judgment shield on subsequent judicial review. One line of authority had answered the question answered in the affirmative,[47] while a second line held out a possibility of substantive judicial second-guessing.[48] The Project's drafters chose the latter approach and filled in some detail—the board's business judgment was to be weighed against (i) the potential benefit to the corporation of a litigation recovery and (ii) public policy concerns.[49]

TD No. 1 promptly became the most controversial document in the history of American corporate law. The controversy had started even before TD No. 1 was published. In January 1982, Andrew Sigler, the CEO of Champion International and chair of the BRT's corporate governance task force, circulated a letter to BRT members encouraging them to oppose the ALI's proposals[50] with the objective of stopping the Project. The stated justification was political. The Project stemmed from the 1970s effort to deflect federal incorporation proposals. Since any such threat had dissipated, new tactics were called for. Cooperation should cease: the BRT should shelve its own previous pronouncements on the composition and structure of boards; the pronouncements were no longer needed and always could be pulled down and dusted off in case of a resurgence of anti-managerial activism.[51] Sigler followed up the letter with a choice quote in a *New York Times* piece run in the wake of that year's ALI Annual Meeting. The Project, he said, was "a ludicrous imposition of an unworkable method by a bunch of people who don't know anything about it."[52] Walter Wriston, the CEO of Citibank, also had a zinger ready: "We don't require four law professors to tell us how to run our business. They aren't restating the law, they're trying to change the way corporations operate. It's not a Restatement, it's a 'prestatement' of what they think the law should be, and it shows a complete misunderstanding of how the process operates."[53]

---

[44] *Id.* § 4.01 at 140–41.

[45] *Id.* §§ 4.01(b), 4.01(d)(3), at 141.

[46] *Id.* § 7.06, at 378–82.

[47] Auerbach v. Bennett, 47 N.Y. 2d 619, 393 N.E.2d 994, 419 N.Y.S. 2d 920 (1979).

[48] Zapata Corp. v. Maldonado, 430 A. 2d 779 (Del. 1981).

[49] TD No. 1, *supra* note 38, § 7.03(c), at 299.

[50] Victor Brudney, *The Role of the Board of Directors: The ALI and Its Critics*, 37 U. MIAMI L. REV. 223, 228 (1983).

[51] *Id.*

[52] Tamar Lewin, *The Corporate-Reform Furor*, N.Y. TIMES, June 10, 1982, at D1, col. 3.

[53] *Id.*

The BRT, having thus stated its ultimate objective in advance of TD No. 1, targeted TD No. 1 more specifically in a bill of particulars in February 1983.[54] This was a seventy-page takedown prepared by a team at the law firm of Weil, Gotshal & Manges under the leadership of the firm's crack litigator, Dennis Block, and its high-level adviser to boards of directors, Ira M. Milstein.[55] The Weil team, following the BRT line, went for the jugular and recommended that the Project be abandoned in its present form.[56] Its BRT Statement was otherwise a kitchen sink document. But some leading themes were clear enough:

(1) The Project was a legal initiative and as such intrinsically inappropriate. Its Reporters, as lawyers and law professors, inevitably tended to mandate and prohibit. This was the wrong approach for corporate governance, a field that needed to be kept clear for innovation and freedom of action. As a new field, corporate governance should be allowed to evolve at the level of practice without having a particular structural model locked down in a rule.[57]

(2) The Reporters, as lawyers, did not know what they were doing. No one with any experience in running a company could possibly have had a hand in TD No. 1's preparation, which in any event completely lacked input from management scientists and economists.[58]

(3) The Project failed to respect the distinction between restatement and reform. TD No. 1 passed off controversial structural innovations and resolutions of long-standing doctrinal conflicts as black-letter law,[59] burying the critical qualifications in the comments.

(4) The Project inappropriately and naively looked to litigation as a source of positive governance inputs.[60]

(5) The Project, in particular the structural recommendations, lacked adequate empirical backing. There was no proof that the system needed reform. The burden of persuasion accordingly fell on the Reporters, who had failed to meet it.[61]

(6) TD No. 1, and in particular its stepped-up duty of care and pared-back business judgment rule, would (i) increase deadweight costs, (ii) decrease productivity, (iii) depress risk-taking, and (iv) make it difficult to recruit qualified individuals to serve as directors.[62]

The preceding points and variations thereon would be repeated over and over by a range of opponents for the remainder of the Project's gestation.

---

[54] THE BUSINESS ROUNDTABLE, STATEMENT OF THE BUSINESS ROUNDTABLE ON THE AMERICAN LAW INSTITUTE'S PROPOSED "PRINCIPLES OF CORPORATE GOVERNANCE AND STRUCTURE: RESTATEMENT AND RECOMMENDATIONS" (1983).

[55] Kenneth R. Andrews, *Corporate Governance Eludes the Legal Mind*, 37 U. MIAMI L. REV. 213, 214 n.3 (1983).

[56] Business Roundtable, *supra* note 54, at 67.

[57] *Id.* at 5, 32

[58] *Id.* at 2, 4, 19–24.

[59] *Id.* at 2–3, 12.

[60] *Id.* at 3, 37.

[61] *Id.* at 26–32.

[62] *Id.* at 6.

The BRT, in sum, did a *volte face* on corporate governance. This move, while sudden and audacious, could hardly have been thought surprising. The CEOs were only doing from the right what progressives already had been doing from the left with federal incorporation initiatives—trying to capture this new thing called corporate governance. (Indeed, from management's point of view, the progressive federal incorporation push had been aimed at wresting away lawmaking territory—the drafting and enactment of state corporate codes—captured by management long before.[63]) Once the progressives exited the policy stage after 1980, the managers had no further interest in cooperating with policy entrepreneurs interested in structural adjustments that constrained the managers' freedom of action. Independent directors and audit, nominating, and compensation committees were here to stay. But so long as "independence" was loosely and congenially defined and numerical mandates were avoided, "independent" boards could be populated with fellow CEOs and other sympathetic types, denuding any threat to management autonomy.[64] The Project, as embodied in TD No. 1, manifestly sought to rouse corporate law to foreclose this tactic, mandating the structural standards devised during the 1970s to make boards independent in fact. Such an initiative threatened management's control not only of board composition but of corporate lawmaking, a double-sided loss. The Project accordingly needed to be put down or, failing that, neutralized.

The BRT, as it went into opposition, followed the same take-no-prisoners strategic path its members' companies had been taking when faced with new regulatory initiatives. And, just as they did with new regulation, the CEOs used corporate lawyers as their agents of opposition. Corporate lawyers who also happened to be ALI members were persons of particular interest. There were meetings, lobbying campaigns, and get-out-the-vote drives. Attendance grew at the ALI's Annual Meeting, as did the number of corporate types on the membership roster. It was later even rumored that corporate clients were retaining ALI members to represent their views within the ALI, while law firms that supported the Project were losing corporate clients.[65] Rod Perkins, speaking at the 1991 Annual Meeting, urged the members to leave their clients at the door so as to "preserve our integrity as an organization."[66]

IV. Defensive Adjustments

The ALI had initiated the Project on the assumption that corporate governance, like contract and tort law, was, as Rod Perkins put it, "a field in which rational and dispassionate analysis and clarification ... could fruitfully be brought to bear by the ALI."[67] Now the BRT and its agents were mooting just the opposite. To its credit, the ALI stuck

---

[63] *Cf.* Melvin Aron Eisenberg, *The Modernization of Corporate Law: An Essay for Bill Cary*, 37 U. MIAMI L. R. 187, 188–91 (1984) (describing in structural terms the nonneutral evolution of corporate codes).

[64] *See* Brudney, *supra* note 25, at 610–12.

[65] Macey, *supra* note 34, at 1229.

[66] Tuesday Morning Session, May 14, 1991, *in* 68 ALI PROC. 225. For an account of interest group influence on the drafting and subsequent evolution of the Uniform Commercial Code, *see* Robert E. Scott, *The Uniform Commercial Code and the Ongoing Quest for an Efficient and Fair Commercial Law*, in this volume.

[67] Roswell B. Perkins, *Thanks, Myth, and Reality*, 48 BUS. LAW. 1313, 1314 (1992).

to its guns and proceeded with the Project. Its resolve was signaled when Perkins took the lead in rebutting the BRT's charges. He reached out to his fellow business law-yers, asking them to endorse the subject matter's suitability and thereby confirm the Project's legitimacy.[68] The initiative eventually proved successful—the Project came to enjoy widespread support among the members. Perkins would not, however, manage to tamp down interest group jockeying and insulate the Project in a cocoon of reason and probity—the BRT's neutralization campaign would continue to the end. But he did manage to steer the ship in that direction and finally guide it to port in 1992.[69]

High tension prevailed during the period 1982 to 1984, as those responsible for the Project retreated on substantive points and regrouped their forces. No vote was taken on TD No. 1 at the 1982 meeting and the Project was omitted entirely from the 1983 Annual Meeting agenda, reappearing with extensive revisions the following year. Final approval was (optimistically) set back to 1987, with Perkins assuring his cor-porate law constituents that all points were contingent until final votes were taken.[70] Meanwhile, a special subgroup of the Project's Advisers who also held seats on the ALI Council was designated to work with the Reporters to "help shape issues for the consideration of the Council."[71] The subgroup's membership imported an establish-ment imprimatur at the highest level—it included Judges Henry Friendly and Charles Breitel, Lloyd Cutler (a Dean of the Washington bar), two other partners from large law firms, and a former chair of the ABA's business law section. Interestingly, this con-cessionary process refinement never really left the drawing board—the special sub-group never met with the Reporters.[72]

Meanwhile, no corresponding concessions were made regarding the composition of the Project's Advisers. That group would remain substantially the same from the Project's inception to its conclusion. Not so with the Reporters. Kaplan stepped down as Chief Reporter in 1984 to be replaced by Mel Eisenberg. The post of Deputy Chief reporter was phased out even as Harvey Goldschmid stayed on as a Reporter. Two new Reporters were added, Marshall Small, who was just ending a term as the chair of Morrison & Foerster, joined in 1982, and Ronald (Ron) Gilson of the Stanford Law faculty joined in 1984.

These process concessions did not placate the Project's opponents. They wanted more, for it was turning out that the ALI was an uncongenial territory for collateral attack. The opponents complained that there was no opportunity early in the drafting and approval process for intervenors to impose binding directives on or otherwise corner the Reporters.[73] Opponents could of course make motions at the Annual Meeting. But that was proving to be too late in the game. Time constraints at the meeting limited room for maneuver. And, in any event, the membership tended to be

---

[68] *See* Roswell B. Perkins, *Remarks at Meeting of Section on Corporation., Banking and Business Law of the American Bar Association* (Oct. 29, 1984) [hereafter cited as *Perkins 1984*]; Roswell B. Perkins, *Remarks at a Forum of the Association of the Bar of the City of New York: Background and Status of the ALI Corporate Governance Project* (Mar. 14, 1983) [hereafter cited as *Perkins 1983*].

[69] *See* Manning, *supra* note 16, at 1326. In contrast, Geoffrey Hazard, who succeeded Herbert Wechsler as the ALI's Director in mid-1984, is not remembered as a supporter of either the Project or its Reporters.

[70] *Perkins 1984*, *supra* note 68, at 4–5.

[71] *Perkins 1983*, *supra* note 68, at 9.

[72] Melvin Eisenberg, Memorandum to Author 3–4 (July 21, 2021) (copy on file with author).

[73] Perkins, *supra* note 31, at 9.

supportive of the Project,[74] a membership the overwhelming majority of which knew little or nothing about corporate law.[75]

The opponents had a point, but not much of one, for a special input channel for the business bar already had been conceded, albeit a tightly institutionalized one. The council of the business law section of the ABA designated an Ad Hoc Committee on the ALI Corporate Governance Project, called CORPRO. CORPRO was granted access to the Reporters and the Council for the purpose of registering comments and criticisms.[76] CORPRO's members put the grant to use, commenting on every draft and in the end exerting a stronger influence on the Project's terms than did the Advisers and Consultants.[77] They assigned themselves the role of ameliorating the expertise deficit identified by the BRT, for, unlike most of the Reporters, they were experienced business lawyers privy to the inner workings of "real life" corporations.[78]

CORPRO's participation had a double-gestured aspect. On the one hand, it operated as an opposition party with an agenda. As such, its members did not bring their experience and skills to the Project in the spirit of dispassionate analysis and clarification. They instead pursued an agenda grounded in existing cases and statutes, protesting every departure therefrom. They wanted the Principles to be shorter, simpler, and as closely tracking the Model Business Corporation Act (MBCA) as possible.[79] They would eventually claim responsibility for a list of modifications in the Principles' terms.[80] But they would never be satisfied, and at the final bell would formally register "disappointment" regarding the remaining distance between the Principles and the MBCA.[81] On the other hand, CORPRO's members, particularly those who also were ALI members, acted as a loyal opposition. As such, they engaged constructively with the Reporters, working out drafting compromises as a way of settling points of dispute.[82] The more it worked in this mode, the more CORPRO brought the corporate bar inside the Project's tent, enhancing the Project's legitimacy.

The two years of retrenchment ended with the appearance of Tentative Draft No. 2 in April 1984 (TD No. 2). It contained revisions of TD No. 1's provisions on corporate purpose, board structure, and the duty of care. The section on corporate purpose

---

[74] Professor Eisenberg recalls only a single time when the membership rejected a section proposed by the Reporters. The opposition had come from CORPRO, which thereafter worked together with the Reporters to draft a mutually satisfactory substitute. Eisenberg, *supra* note 72, at 9.

[75] Manning, *supra* note 16, at 1326–27.

[76] *Perkins 1984, supra* note 68, at 7–8.

[77] Elliott Goldstein, *CORPRO: A Committee That Became an Institution*, 48 Bus. Law. 1333, 1335 (1992).

[78] *Id.*

[79] E. Norman Veasey, *The Emergence of Corporate Governance as a New Legal Discipline*, 48 Bus. Law. 1267, 1268 (1992).

[80] Goldstein, *supra* note 77, at 1336 ("a revision of section 2.01, the separating of all of the 'grey letter' aspirational provisions dealing with the composition of the board of directors and its committees into a new Part III-A; a revision of section 4.01, limiting the board's monitoring function, and strengthening the statement of the business judgment rule; suggesting the change of the title of Chapter V to 'Duty of Fair Dealing,' and recommending changes in section 5.02 to bring it more closely in line with safe harbor statutes of the states and the Model Act; participating in a revision and rearrangement of Part VI dealing with transactions in control; recommending a universal demand requirement for derivative actions; and urging changes in section 7.04 to allow derivative actions pleaded with insufficient particularity to be dismissed before the commencement of discovery.").

[81] Veasey, *supra* note 79, at 1269.

[82] Eisenberg, *supra* note 72, at 8–9.

emerged more or less unscathed. Elsewhere there were high-profile concessions. The first of these appeared on the cover page, where the title of the Project had been changed to negate the claim to status as a statement of positive law. What had been a "Restatement and Recommendations" was downgraded a notch to an "Analysis and Recommendations."[83] Downgrading continued in the sections on governance structure. The description of the board's duties[84] and the audit committee requirement[85] now more closely tracked the terms of existing corporate codes and the stock exchange rules.[86] Moreover, the majority disinterested board was no longer something the law "should" provide. It was instead recommended as a matter of good corporate practice in a section no longer printed in the boldface type that signified a black-letter pronouncement.[87]

The statements of the duty of care and business judgment rule also underwent modification. Where TD No. 1 had required that a director "make reasonable inquiry when acting upon corporate transactions" and "be reasonably concerned with the existence and effectiveness of monitoring programs, including law compliance programs," TD No. 2 substituted a more vaguely phrased duty that the director be "informed with respect to the subject of the business judgment to the extent he reasonably believed to be appropriate under the circumstances."[88] The board's duty to monitor legal compliance—the great governance result of the questionable payments scandals—was consigned to the comments. The rational basis requirement remained, but only for a year. Tentative Draft No. 4 would substitute a more conditional and slightly subjective requirement that the director "rationally believes that his business judgment is in the best interests of the corporation."[89] Thus phrased, the statement of the business judgment rule was approved at the 1985 Annual Meeting.

The concessions did not silence the Project's opponents. But they did contain them. The Reporters, by stepping back from their preferred formulations and yielding to widely expressed concerns, concretely demonstrated openness and responsiveness to outside inputs. The Project's legitimacy was thereby reconfirmed and the BRT accordingly frustrated in the achievement of its primary objective.

V. The Duty of Loyalty

The 1984 Annual Meeting also occasioned the first appearance of the Principles' provisions on the duty of loyalty, contained in Tentative Draft No. 3 (TD No. 3). These sections took hold of three sets of components: (1) the processes attending internal corporate approval—disinterested director approval, shareholder approval, and ex

---

[83] ALI, PRINCIPLES OF CORPORATE GOVERNANCE AND STRUCTURE: ANALYSIS AND RECOMMENDATIONS, TENTATIVE DRAFT NO. 2 (Apr. 13, 1984).

[84] *Id.* § 3.02, at 66–67.

[85] *Id.* § 3.03, at 76.

[86] The nominating committee suffered a similar downgrade. *Id.* § 3.06, at 96–97.

[87] *Id.* § 3.04, at 84.

[88] *Id.* § 4.01, at 6.

[89] ALI, PRINCIPLES OF CORPORATE GOVERNANCE AND STRUCTURE: ANALYSIS AND RECOMMENDATIONS, TENTATIVE DRAFT NO. 4, § 4.01 at 7 (Apr. 12, 1985).

post ratification, (2) litigation burdens of pleading and proof, and (3) three variant standards of judicial review—business judgment, fairness, and waste. The sections combined the components into a complete and integrated sequence of instructions for adjudication of loyalty issues. Each of the field's core fact patterns got a separate, tailored treatment—director and officer self-dealing transactions,[90] transactions between corporations with interlocking boards,[91] compensation grants,[92] use of corporate position, property and information,[93] corporate opportunities,[94] and competition with the corporation.[95]

The assembled instructions were, simply, a tour de force. No one before had thought these matters through in this thoroughgoing way. Now, the sections did not restate the law. They could not have done so given a set of complete instructions as the end in view, for the law charitably could have been described as sketchy and more accurately would have to have been described as confused.[96] The Reporters, faced with a doctrine in disarray, took up the building blocks and did the job themselves, making explicit what was inchoate in the cases and statutes.

Nor would the sections become the law, putting aside the adoption of the corporate opportunity section by the Supreme Courts of Oregon[97] and Maine.[98] But that should not interfere with our appreciation of the Reporters' accomplishment. Even if one did not concur with a particular result or treatment, the whole stood forth as invaluable resource—a compendium of the doctrinal choices and policy possibilities attending any and all cases in the field. This was ALI work product at its best. The duty of loyalty now had a conceptual framework and could never be the same again.

The core provision covered self-dealing transactions. It contained a trio of innovative terms:

(1) There was an absolute requirement of full disclosure by the interested fiduciary.[99] An incompletely disclosed but substantively fair transaction could not be rehabilitated on the basis of hindsight by a reviewing court. In effect, the monitoring model here confronted the doctrinal inheritance to signal change. If internal approval was going to afford transactional insulation, and CORPRO would be demanding just that, then the attending process requirements could not stop at disinterest on the part of the approving directors. All material facts needed to be on the table as well.

(2) There was a distinct standard of judicial review to be applied in the wake of fully informed disinterested director approval. It was quasi business judgment: the

---

[90] ALI, PRINCIPLES OF CORPORATE GOVERNANCE AND STRUCTURE: ANALYSIS AND RECOMMENDATIONS, TENTATIVE DRAFT NO. 3, § 5.08, at 107–09 (Apr. 13, 1984) [hereinafter cited as TD No. 3].

[91] *Id.* § 5.10, at 151.

[92] *Id.* § 5.09, at 141–43.

[93] *Id.* § 5.11, at 155–57.

[94] *Id.* § 5.12, at 194–97.

[95] *Id.* § 5.13, at 218–20.

[96] *See* William W. Bratton, *Reconsidering the Evolutionary Erosion Account of Corporate Fiduciary Law*, 76 BUS. LAW. 1157, 1180–85 (2021).

[97] Klinicki v. Lundgren, 298 Or. 662, 695 P.2d 906 (1985).

[98] Northeast Harbor Golf Club, Inc. v. Harris, 661 A.2d 1146 (1995).

[99] TD No. 3, *supra* note 90, § 5.08(a)(1), at 107.

transaction was vulnerable only if the approving directors "could not reasonably have believed the transaction to be fair to the corporation."[100] The notion was that the difficult case concerned a self-dealing transaction in a noncommodified good or service as to which no exact comparable was available as a fairness yard-stick. The available not-quite-comparable transactions would be spread across a pricing range. So long as the self-dealing price was within the range, the dir-ectors' belief was reasonable.[101] Mel Eisenberg described the test as "interme-diate"—even with disinterested director approval, the reviewing court should be left free to apply a "smell test."[102]

(3) Disinterested director approval ex ante and disinterested director ratification ex post received different treatments. Only ex ante approval got the quasi-business judgment review just described. After the fact ratification meant full-blown fair-ness review, subject to a damages cut off in the event ratification preceded the outcome of a litigation challenge.[103]

Features (1) and (2) would survive into the Principles' final version.[104] Feature (3) would be watered down, extending the quasi business judgment standard to ex post ratification on the condition the failure to obtain ex ante approval was excusable and had not resulted in injury to the corporation, and the corporation furthermore had had a representative on its side of the contract.[105] The sections' original title also would be modified. TD No. 3 termed the sections "the Duty of Loyalty," which was of course perfectly accurate. The title was later downgraded to the "Duty of Fair Dealing" at the behest of CORPRO.[106] In this case, it was the Reporters who stood on the side of the law and the ABA factotums who stood on the side of radical change. In 1984, even as the Reporters were rationalizing the terms of the duty of loyalty for the first time, the drafters of the MBCA were removing the term "fiduciary" from their code and commentary[107] on the ground that it unjustifiably heightened expectations about the character of management duties and encouraged plaintiffs.

One can see how the Reporters and the Council could be amenable to accepting this change, for innovation was what the Project was all about. One wishes they had resisted. Although only a change of denomination, it was not just rhetorical. It cut off today's bundle of management duties from their historical antecedents, removing the notion of a selfless trustee from the conceptual baseline and substituting the standard

---

[100] *Id.* § 5.08(a)(2)(A), at 107.

[101] *See* Marshall L. Small, *Conflicts of Interest and the ALI Corporate Governance Project—A Reporter's Perspective*, 48 Bus. Law. 1377, 1383 (1992).

[102] Eisenberg, *supra* note 2, at 1287. Compare Small, *supra* note 101 at 1383 (describing the standard as business judgment); John F. Johnston & Frederick H. Alexander, *The Effect of Disinterested Director Approval of Conflict Transactions under the ALI Corporate Governance Project—A Practitioner's Perspective*, 48 Bus. Law. 1393, 1394 (1992) (objecting to a business judgment characterization).

[103] TD No. 3, *supra* note 90, § 5.08(c), at 108–09. For discussion, *see* Small, *supra* note 101, at 1388–89.

[104] *1 ALI Principles*, *supra* note 2, § 5.02, at 209–210.

[105] *Id.* § 5.02(a)(2)(C), at 210. It was a last-minute conforming change. *See* Small, *supra* note 101, at 1389.

[106] Thursday Morning Session, May 15, 1986, *in* 63 A.L.I. Proc. 187, 227.

[107] *See* Norwood P. Jr. Beveridge, *The Corporate Director's Fiduciary Duty of Loyalty: Understanding the Self-Interested Director Transaction*, 41 DePaul L. Rev. 655, 656 (1992), *citing* MBCA, § 8.30(a) cmt. at 222 (1984). Reference also can be made to MBCA, subchapter F, introductory cmt. (2012) (avoiding use of the term fiduciary except to describe historical antecedents).

of conduct appropriate for a self-interested contracting party. There comes a point where such a shift makes a difference.

In the event, the drafters of the MBCA went back to their own statute five years later[108] to make it crystal clear that disinterested director approval results in business judgment as the standard of review for a self-dealing transaction.[109] One wonders whether the earlier appearance of a stricter ALI treatment had causative role.

VI. An Academic Challenge

The sections on the duty of loyalty (by then termed the duty of fair dealing) came up for extended discussion at the 1986 Annual Meeting. Judge Frank Easterbrook took the floor to moot a conceptual expansion of Section 5.09. The section extended the standards of review applied to director and shareholder approval to advance directives in charters and bylaws that sanctioned self-dealing arrangements. The question, said Easterbrook, was this: "[T]o what extent is a corporation fundamentally a contract among a large number of sophisticated and commercial venturers, and to what extent is it a form imposed by external law."[110] Section 5.09 gave weight to the latter answer, for it allowed for modification of fiduciary duties by contract but not complete elimination. Easterbrook wanted to open a much wider door for modification in initial charter provisions and charter amendments inserted prior to initial public offerings.[111]

With this intervention the Project directly encountered the nexus of contracts corporation, the deregulatory project of corporate law's law and economics movement, and with it a different form of challenge. Easterbrook and his Chicago Law colleague Daniel R. Fischel had a corporate governance project of their own, a theoretical project grounded in Jensen and Meckling's famous microeconomic model of corporate organization.[112] In the Jensen and Meckling model, private contracting and stock market pricing combined effectively to control management agency costs, but did so only given strict, unrealistic assumptions. Easterbrook and Fischel expanded the model to accommodate the real-world corporate governance framework. The field of private contracting grew accordingly, encompassing not only the face-to-face bargaining but also corporate law itself and internal corporate legislation enacted over time.[113] Easterbrook and Fischel also expanded the set of market controls of agency costs. In addition to stock market pricing as employed in the model, they relied on the market for corporate control, the product markets, and executive labor markets.

---

[108] See Douglas M. Branson, *Recent Changes to the Model Business Corporation Act: Death Knells for Main Street Corporation Law*, 72 NEB. L. REV. 258, 267–70 (1993).

[109] See MBCA §§ 8.61(b), 8.62.

[110] Friday Afternoon Session, May 16, 1986, *in* 63 A.L.I. PROC. 395, 411.

[111] *Id.* at 413–14.

[112] Michael Jensen & William Meckling, *Theory of the Firm: Managerial Behavior, Agency Costs and Ownership Structure*, 3 J. FIN. ECON. 305 (1976).

[113] Frank H. Easterbrook & Daniel R. Fischel, *The Corporate Contract*, 89 COLUM. L. REV. 1416, 1429–31 (1989).

In the emerging "contractarian" picture, the four markets operate together to assure agency cost minimization on a multiperiod basis.[114]

Two claims about corporate law followed. First, there should be a presumption against having any more of it than already exists. Because rational actors arrange governance in contracts and markets price the contract terms, legal mandates are justifiable only in the unlikely event that "the terms chosen by firms are both unpriced and systematically perverse from investors' standpoints."[115] Second, the inherited corporate law regime is economically rational,[116] justifying a strong normative presumption in its favor. The two claims, taken together, ratified corporate law's status quo, a natural result in a framework asserting the evolutionary dominance of maximizing arrangements.

A fundamental critique of the Project followed. Easterbrook (accurately) described it as an attempt finally to solve the problem of separated ownership and control described by Berle and Means by transferring power from unaccountable managers to better incented actors such as independent directors and judges.[117] But, in Easterbrook's view, Berle and Means had diagnosed incorrectly in the first place—there was no structural problem of misaligned incentives. Managers operated under competitive constraints and were accordingly accountable to the market; investors bought their interests at prices discounted for residual agency costs.[118] Fischel added a retrospective look at the formative events of the 1970s. Since when, he asked, did a handful of bankruptcies and a slush fund scandal imply a productive crisis for corporate capitalism? Bankruptcies just meant that markets were working properly and the payments, while questionable from a public policy point of view, had been made for the benefit of the shareholders.[119] Another law and economics scholar, Judge Ralph Winter, suggested that charter competition assured consonance between investor interests and the terms of corporate law.[120] He added that the Project was behind the times, academically speaking. It represented a single academic viewpoint, a viewpoint that had come in for serious challenge.[121] Others opined similarly.[122]

An alliance of convenience[123] emerged between the BRT and its agents and the contractarian academics, with the academics fleshing out the BRT's points about the unsuitability of legal analysis,[124] costs and benefits,[125] and the need for empirical

---

[114] FRANK H. EASTERBROOK & DANIEL R. FISCHEL, THE ECONOMIC STRUCTURE OF CORPORATE LAW 4, 18–21, 91, 93, 96–97 (1991).

[115] Id. at 21.

[116] Id. at 315.

[117] Frank H. Easterbrook, Managers' Discretion and Investors' Welfare: Theories and Evidence, 9 DEL. J. CORP. L. 540, 541–42 (1984).

[118] Id. at 542.

[119] Daniel R. Fischel, The Corporate Governance Movement, 35 VAND. L. REV. 1259, 1265–68 (1982).

[120] Ralph K. Winter Jr., The Development of the Law of Corporate Governance, 9 DEL. J. CORP. L. 524, 527 (1984).

[121] Id. at 528–29.

[122] Barry D. Baysinger & Henry N. Butler, Revolution Versus Evolution in Corporate Law: The ALI's Project and the Independent Director, 52 GEO. WASH. L. REV. 557 (1984); William J. Carney, The ALI's Corporate Governance Project: The Death of Property Rights?, 61 GEO. WASH. L. REV. 898 (1993); Macey, supra note 34.

[123] But cf. id. at 1213 (describing a "holy alliance").

[124] Id. at 1212–13.

[125] Fischel, supra note 119, at 1282.

support.[126] There were differences in motivation, of course. Where the CEOs criticized the Project as part of a multifront fight to preserve their own insulation, the professors saw the Project as an ancillary front in the fight for paradigmatic dominance within the academy.

The contractarians did score academic successes, precipitating fundamental changes in the way academics view corporate law. Henceforth, policy discussions would proceed in a microeconomic framework importing a healthy skepticism about potential perverse effects from new regulation (if not a blanket presumption disfavoring new regulatory initiatives to control management). There also would be an openness to considering private contracting and market correction as solutions to governance problems (if not a blanket presumption favoring private contracting and market control). But things worked out differently for contractarianism as regarded the Project's more particular concerns. Management accountability continued to take primary place as corporate law's central policy concern. Furthermore, the blanket characterization of everything in corporate governance as contract would be deemed insufficiently robust to justify turning corporate law into a thoroughgoing default regime. In the consensus view, fiduciary duties would have to remain mandatory because proxy voting did not offer a process context suited to effective noncompetitive transacting.[127]

VII. Takeovers

The takeover wars of the 1980s raged in the background while the Project went through the drafting and approval process. They impacted corporate law and governance in novel and fundamental ways. The takeover boom denuded management of insulation from market pressure, demonstrating the power and transformative potential of capital market inputs for the first time since the early twentieth century. The takeovers also brought forward the shareholders as the primary corporate constituents, ushering in a new era of solicitude of their interests, an era that continues today.

Perhaps in recognition of the background turmoil, the Principles' section on corporate control transactions, introduced in 1990 in Tentative Draft No. 10,[128] adjusted the drafting mode. The Council[129] and the Reporter, Ron Gilson, opted for principles over rules, erring on the side of general statement and eschewing sequences of precise instructions. The general statements, in turn, were minimal:

---

[126] Baysinger & Butler, *supra* note 122, at 580–81.

[127] Two of the leading exponents of the consensus were Project Reporters. *See* John C. Coffee Jr., *No Exit?: Opting Out, the Contractual Theory of the Corporation, and the Special Case of Remedies*, 53 BROOK. L. REV. 919 (1988); John C. Coffee Jr., *The Mandatory/Enabling Balance in Corporate Law: An Essay on the Judicial Role*, 89 COLUM. L. REV. 1618 (1989); Melvin A. Eisenberg, *The Structure of Corporation Law*, 89 COLUM. L. REV. 1461 (1989).

[128] ALI, PRINCIPLES OF CORPORATE GOVERNANCE AND STRUCTURE: ANALYSIS AND RECOMMENDATIONS, TENTATIVE DRAFT No. 10 (Apr. 16, 1990).

[129] *See* Wednesday Afternoon Session, May 16, 1990, *in* 67 A.L.I. PROC. 135, 148 [hereafter *1990 Session*].

(1) The decision whether or not to sell control lies within the board's business judgment.[130]
(2) When the corporation does sell itself, shareholder approval is required.[131]
(3) Actions of a board resisting a hostile tender offer must be reasonable responses to the offer.[132] A corollary accompanied this principle: a resisting board could take nonshareholder interests into account if "to do so would not significantly disfavor the long-term interests of shareholders."[133]

Some thought the corollary recognizing other constituent interests out of step with the law on the books, but that was arguable. More pointed opposition came from the management interest and the mergers and acquisitions bar, which variously worried about fine points of state law conformity, questioned how the sections impacted on practitioners advising parties to control transactions, or argued for language parroting that of the Delaware cases.[134] There was also a question whether the subject matter should be omitted entirely as unripe.[135] The sections were sent back to the Reporters, who presented them again in substantially the same form in 1991.[136] Approval followed in the ordinary course.[137]

Why were takeovers relatively easy in comparison with the Project's other topics? The principles-based drafting certainly helped. But one suspects that the interest group alignment also mattered. The alliance of convenience between the managers and the contractarians dissolved on this topic. Where the managers wanted hostile takeovers shut down, the contractarians saw a robust control market as an essential constraint in lowering agency costs. Business interests fragmented as well. Capital favored takeovers because it liked the premium payoffs they entailed. Only the managers opposed reasonableness review. But the law on the books no longer favored that position. Moreover, the Reporters' concession regarding nonshareholder interests left the managers considerable running room.

VIII. At the Finish

The ALI saved the thorniest bit—the sections on shareholder derivative actions—for last. These implicated the day-to-day practices of more than a few of the ALI's members, which included plaintiffs' lawyers in addition to inside and outside corporate counsel. The sections also traversed one of the fault lines on which progressives and conservatives invariably differ—the use of litigation as a regulatory tool.

---

[130] *1 ALI Principles, supra* note 2, § 6.01(a), at 389.

[131] *Id.* § 6.01(b), at 389.

[132] *Id.* § 6.02(a), at 405.

[133] *Id.* § 6.02(b)(2), at 405.

[134] *See Motions Submitted in Advance of 1990 Annual Meeting Relating to T.D. 10,* at 7–58 (May 8, 1990).

[135] *See 1990 Session, supra* note 129, at 168; Eisenberg, *supra* note 72, at 11.

[136] ALI, PRINCIPLES OF CORPORATE GOVERNANCE AND STRUCTURE: ANALYSIS AND RECOMMENDATIONS, TENTATIVE DRAFT NO. 11 (Apr. 25, 1991).

[137] Tuesday Morning Session, May 14, 1991, *in* 68 A.L.I. PROC. 207, 254.

The Reporters had put their broad view of the matter on the table in TD No. 1: private enforcement and judicial review were essential parts of an effective duty of loyalty regime. They never wavered on the point. They also held to their view, expressed in section 7.03 in TD No. 1,[138] that dismissal of well-pleaded derivative actions by special committees of independent directors should be subject to substantive judicial review. The successor section maintained this position, doing a more nuanced job of drawing a line between business judgment constraint and direct review: if the action concerned a duty of care violation, the business judgment shield covered it; if the duty of loyalty or takeover defense were implicated, dismissal could be sustained only on a finding that the board "reasonably determined that dismissal was in the best interests of the corporation, based on grounds that the court deems to warrant reliance."[139]

This bifurcated approach was repeated on the other great issue of the day—the treatment of the "demand requirement." This had originated as a sensible means of assuring that the board had notice and an opportunity to take over what was in the end the corporation's cause of action. It had evolved into a backdoor (and jerrybuilt) way to slip board-level enforcement decisions concerning duty of loyalty defalcations into the business judgment zone.[140] Under the Project's approach, the board's refusal of the plaintiff's demand ripens into a case for dismissal of the complaint only when the underlying transaction or conduct already lay in business judgment territory. With a complaint alleging a breach of the duty of loyalty, the board's refusal of the demand is reviewed under the same intermediate standard applied to the board's approval of the action or transaction in question.[141] As it happened, the final version of the section in question was a compromise initiated by CORPRO with the cooperation of the Reporters.[142]

One final blast from the BRT would follow,[143] once again drafted at the Weil Gotshal firm.[144] It objected to comments on the section added after the approving meeting by the Reporter, Jack Coffee, on the ground that they undercut the Black Letter. Those involved supported the Reporter[145] and the shot went wide. One wonders why it was taken.

---

[138] *See supra* text accompanying notes 46–49.

[139] *2 ALI Principles, supra* note 2, § 7.10(a)(2), at 130.

[140] *See, e.g.,* Eisenberg, *supra* note 2, at 1291–92.

[141] *2 ALI Principles, supra* note 2, § 7.04(b), at 70.

[142] Wednesday Morning Session, May 13, 1992, *in* 69 A.L.I. Proc. 67, 68–70.

[143] *Memorandum, Principles of Corporate Governance: Analysis and Recommendations—Proposed Comment to Section 7.04(a)* (Nov. 23, 1992).

[144] *See* Dennis J. Block, Stephen A. Radin, & Michael J. Maimone, *Derivative Litigation: Current Law Versus the American Law Institute,* 48 Bus. Law. 1443, 1443 n *, 1470–73 (1992). *See also* Michael P. Dooley & E. Norman Veasey, *The Role of the Board in Derivative Litigation: Delaware Law and the Current ALI Proposals Compared,* 44 Bus. Law. 503 (1989).

[145] John C. Coffee Jr., *New Myths and Old Realities: The American Law Institute Faces the Derivative Action,* 48 Bus. Law. 1407, 1421–22 (1992).

IX. Afterward

Commentaries published at the time of the Project's completion described failures. The pattern of attack and response was presented as evidence of a misstep: the ALI had strayed from its historical doctrinal role to enter the politicized world of public policymaking, a place where rational and dispassionate analysis and clarification are not the usual mode of proceeding. Unseemly interest group machinations came with the territory, so it was no good bemoaning their presence.[146] At the same time, the Project's critics were said to have made fair points about methodological and process limitations.[147] Corporate governance was about efficient production as well as legal accountability. The Project had been short on expertise respecting the former and excessively weighted toward the latter.[148]

These points were fair. They ring hollow today even so. The ALI, far from retreating to safe places, continues to enter politicized precincts, dealing with interest group inputs in the ordinary course. There is an inevitable sacrifice of authoritativeness,[149] but no apparent loss of legitimacy. The fact that such a project lacks the gravitas of a traditional restatement surprises no one, least of all its Reporters. Furthermore, in a world saturated with interest group machinations it matters more than ever to have an institution that provides protected space for rational and dispassionate analysis by accomplished members of the legal profession. The ALI may not be perfect when viewed through a public choice lens, but it still comes forth as the best we have in an imperfect world. Rod Perkins and the Reporters were right to stay the course, doing things the way they are done at the ALI.

The Principles, viewed with the benefit of hindsight, got a lot of things right. The duty of care, as enunciated by the Delaware courts, now has an emphatic and mandatory compliance component.[150] The distinction between standards of conduct and standards of review introduced in the Principles' articulation of the duty of care and the business judgment rule also has entered the law. The Principles' corporate purpose statement remains cogent even in light of a recent burst of scholarly commentary on the topic. For this author, no one yet has offered anything better. Finally, and most importantly, the monitoring model has triumphed, becoming mandatory early in this century through stock exchange rules backed up by provisions of the Securities Exchange Act of 1934.

But that very triumph also requires us to situate the Principles in their own time. Monitoring has won on the ground in part due to the appearance of investment institutions as empowered actors in corporate governance. They are nowhere to be seen in the Principles because they all followed a passive strategy at the time of the Project's

---

[146]   Macey, *supra* note 34, at 1225.

[147]   *Id.* at 1218; Manning, *supra* note 16, at 1326.

[148]   *Id.* at 1323. *Cf.* Michael P. Dooley, *Two Models of Corporate Governance*, 47 Bus. Law. 461 (1992) (providing a close textual criticism of the sections on fiduciary duty and derivative actions).

[149]   *Cf.* John C.P. Goldberg, *Torts in the American Law Institute*, in this volume (concluding that the ALI best work on torts has come in the mode of an appellate court rather than in the mode of an expert agency).

[150]   *In re* Caremark International Inc. Derivative Litigation, 698 A.2d 959 (Del. Ch. 1996); Stone v. Ritter, 911 A.2d 362 (Del. 2006).

inception and had only recently become active at the time of its completion.[151] The Reporters accordingly did not "miss" investment institutions, leaving a "gap" in the Project. It was just that they worked against a dynamic background which was changing materially even as they put down their pens.

The subsequent developments cast new light on the interest group machinations and policy conflicts surrounding the Project. There turn out to be winners and losers. On the loss side we find management. The BRT has lost its fight to preserve its own prerogatives, a loss that came at the hands of activist institutional shareholders rather than lawyers. The burden of persuasion at the policy table is now on the BRT. If it wants to retrieve the lost ground, it must show that insulation enhances long-term value, something it has not done. On the winning side we find the Reporters themselves. The Principles would look even better today had the Reporters' original vision been respected and the round of concessions in TD No. 2 never been made. Ironically, the contractarians join them on the winning side, for it now is clear that market constraints substantially can reduce agency costs. Moreover, shareholders now pay so much attention to governance as to import tractability to the idea of universal opting out. This does not, however, mean that the contractarians were right at the time of the 1986 Annual Meeting. It would take a couple of decades before the institutional conditions necessary for shareholder intervention in business planning finally coalesced.

But coalesce they did. No sensible observer models shareholders as helpless anymore. Negative implications follow as regards representative litigation's role in corporate governance. Not that anyone suggests that derivative litigation be abolished. It is just that few view the continued accretion of procedural barriers as a mighty policy problem.

One last change should be noted: the emergence of Delaware as a source of quality corporate law and of Delaware jurists as central figures in corporate governance discussions. Of course, Delaware played the same leading role as corporate charterer and fiduciary adjudicator back in 1978 that it plays today. But, back in 1978, Delaware also widely was viewed as having been captured by management. The progressives, with their federal incorporation drive, recently had sought (unsuccessfully) to put it out of business as a corporate lawgiver. Thus did Delaware present a problem for the Project, a problem the Reporters elided as they hewed to the middle of the road. Certainly, the Principles would privilege neither Delaware case law nor the Delaware code. But, at the same time, any structural attack on Delaware was avoided—the Reporters enunciated corporate law principles without focusing on the background of charter competition. At the same time, actors from Delaware got no special place at the Project's process table. There was only one Delaware jurist[152] and no Delaware lawyer among the Project's Advisers.[153]

If the Project had been initiated in 1992 rather than in 1978, this quiet exclusion of Delaware would have been inconceivable. By then Delaware's Chancellor William

---

[151] *See* Ronald J. Gilson & Reinier Kraakman, *Reinventing the Outside Director: An Agenda for Institutional Investors*, 43 STAN. L. REV. 863 (1991).

[152] William T. Quillen, then a member of the Delaware Supreme Court.

[153] Ernest L. Folk, of the Virginia law faculty, the drafter of the 1967 revision of the Delaware corporate code, had been an initial Project Reporter. But he did not last long, leaving the Project in its early days, in 1981, well before the appearance of TD No. 1. An inference of incompatibility can be drawn.

T. Allen had emerged as the country's leading corporate law judge. During the 1980s, he and his brethren had reinvented the Delaware fiduciary law applicable to mergers and hostile takeovers, taking it in a direction that balanced management and capital interests. The Delaware jurists simultaneously reached out and joined the national governance discussion, taking leading roles. Their successors continue the enterprise, keeping their own fiduciary law closely attuned to the interests and views of both management and capital.

They have at the same time taken it further and further away from the exhaustively articulated template in the Principles, accepting business judgment review of disinterested director approval[154] and moving to broad standards and case-by-case scrutiny on all the facts.[155] So far their experiment seems to be succeeding. No negative implications for the Principles follow, however. Recent innovations in Delaware case law presuppose a governance framework grounded in director independence and inclusive of active shareholders. They accordingly could not have been undertaken before the second decade of this century.

We shall see how these developments influence the Restatement of Law, Corporate Governance, a new ALI project which recently produced its first Tentative Draft.[156] The titular change is noteworthy. What was seen as practice four decades ago, triggering controversy respecting appropriateness as ALI subject matter, now has the status of law.

---

[154] Benihana of Tokyo, Inc. v. Benihana, Inc., 891 A.2d 150 (Del. Ch. 2005).

[155] Bratton, *supra* note 96, at 1209–10.

[156] ALI, RESTATEMENT OF THE LAW OF CORPORATE GOVERNANCE, TENTATIVE DRAFT NO. 1 (Apr. 2022). Critical commentary already is on the table. *Compare* Stephen M. Bainbridge, *A Critique of the American Law Institute's Draft Restatement of the Corporate Objective*, UCLA School of Law & Economics Working Paper 22-07 (2022) *available at* https://ssrn.com/abstract=4181921, *with* Eric W. Orts, *The ALI's Restatement of the Corporate Objective Is Flawed*, THE CLS BLUE SKY BLOG (June 6, 2022), *available at* https://clsbluesky. law.columbia.edu/2022/06/06/the-alis-restatement-of-the-corporate-objective-is-seriously-flawed. *See also* Stephen M. Bainbridge, *Do We Need a Restatement of the Law of Corporate Governance?*, UCLA School of Law & Economics Working Paper 22-06 (2022), *available at* https://ssrn.com/abstract=4156924.

16

The ALI Principles of the
Law of Family Dissolution

Addressing Family Inequality Through
Functional Regulation

*Linda C. McClain** and Douglas NeJaime***

I. Introduction

This chapter reflects on the American Law Institute (ALI) *Principles of the Law of Family Dissolution* (Principles), a project completed in 2000.[1] Upon approval, President Charles Alan Wright expressed an expectation that the Principles "will be extremely influential in American law and a product of which this Institute can be very proud."[2] In the last two decades, with few exceptions, state lawmakers have not enacted, and courts have not expressly adopted, the Principles' recommendations.[3] Accordingly, some scholars have dismissed the Principles as a "failed" project.[4] In this

* Robert Kent Professor of Law, Boston University School of Law.
** Anne Urowksy Professor of Law, Yale Law School. We owe a special debt to Chief Reporter Ira Ellman, and Reporters Kate Bartlett and Grace Blumberg, for speaking with us about their work on the Principles and for reacting to an earlier draft of this Chapter. For helpful comments, we also thank Susan Appleton, Cynthia Grant Bowman, Naomi Cahn, John Goldberg, Kim Ferzan, Bob Gordon, Courtney Joslin, and David Seipp, as well as participants in the Third Annual Nonmarriage Roundtable at Washington University School of Law, the Boston University School of Law Faculty Workshop, and the ALI at 100 Workshop at the University of Pennsylvania Carey Law School. For excellent research assistance, we thank Grace Choi, Sam Davis, Madison Harris-Parks, and Brittany Swift. We are grateful to Sara Oswald at the Biddle Law Library at the University of Pennsylvania Carey School of Law for her archival work.

[1] *See* AMERICAN LAW INSTITUTE, PRINCIPLES OF THE LAW OF FAMILY DISSOLUTION: ANALYSIS AND RECOMMENDATIONS (2002) (hereinafter Principles). The Principles were adopted on May 16, 2000, at the ALI Annual Meeting in Washington, D.C. In addition to Wright's leadership, ALI Director Geoffrey Hazard initiated and led the Principles project until 1999, when Lance Leibman became Director. *Id.* at xv.

[2] Tuesday Morning Session—May 16, 2000, A.L.I. PROC. 106, 144 (2000).

[3] *See* Michael R. Clisham & Robin Fretwell Wilson, *American Law Institute's Principles of the Law of Family Dissolution, Eight Years After Adoption: Guiding Principles or Obligatory Footnote?*, 42 FAM. L.Q. 573 (2008); Margaret F. Brinig, *Feminism and Child Custody Under Chapter Two of the American Law Institute's Principles of the Law of Family Dissolution*, 8 DUKE J. GENDER L. & POL'Y 301, 301 (2001) ("Chapter Two holds the distinction of being the only portion to have been adopted by a state legislature."). For a critique of Clisham and Wilson's analysis, *see* Katharine T. Bartlett, *Prioritizing Past Caretaking in Child-Custody Decisionmaking*, 77 L. & CONTEMP. PROBS. 29 (2014).

[4] *See* David Westfall, *Unprincipled Family Dissolution: The American Law Institute's Recommendations for Spousal Support and Division of Property*, 27 HARV. J.L. & PUB. POL'Y 917, 960 (2004) ("The *Principles* are a failed effort at family law reform and may not even enjoy the support of most of the members of the ALI."). *See also* Clisham & Wilson, *supra* note 3, at 576 ("[T]he *Principles* have not had the influence the ALI hoped for with legislators or courts . . .").

Linda C. McClain and Douglas NeJaime, *The ALI Principles of the Law of Family Dissolution* In: *The American Law Institute*. Edited by: Andrew S. Gold and Robert W. Gordon, Oxford University Press. © Oxford University Press 2023.
DOI: 10.1093/oso/9780197685341.003.0017

chapter, we offer a different perspective, viewing the Principles as an important authority that, operating in dialogue with courts, legislatures, advocates, and scholars, has contributed to and advanced a progressive agenda in family law.[5]

Because family law in the 1990s was "less settled"—indeed, "in flux"[6]—it was a prime candidate for the greater "flexibility" afforded by a "Principles" project than a "Restatement."[7] When first introducing a draft of the family dissolution project to the ALI membership, President Wright observed that the Principles "did not purport to be a Restatement," but, instead, "to state what the Institute believes are the principles that enlightened jurisdictions should follow," for example, by adopting legislation.[8] As esteemed ALI Council member Bennett Boskey later explained the virtues of Principles projects: "[B]y concentrating on the cutting edge of the law the Institute can contribute recommendations for sound and useful development in what is often a fast-paced arena."[9] Consistent with this aim, Katharine Bartlett, Reporter on the family dissolution Principles, explained the Reporters' effort "to find 'best practices' without necessarily being constrained by existing law."[10] In this chapter, we show how the Principles' Reporters, themselves influential scholars who had been developing their own approaches to legal regulation of the family, intervened in cutting-edge

---

[5] *See* Douglas NeJaime, *The Constitution of Parenthood*, 72 STAN. L. REV. 261, 324 (2020). *Cf.* Jill Elaine Hasday, *The Canon of Family Law*, 57 STAN. L. REV. 825, 829–30 (2004) (explaining how legal scholars influence family law in direct and indirect ways).

[6] *See* Principles, *supra* note 1, at xv ("Director's Foreword" by Lance Liebman).

[7] *See* Bennett Boskey, *The American Law Institute: A Glimpse at Its Future*, 12 GREEN BAG 2d 255, 261 (Spr. 2009). One important question— beyond the scope of this chapter—is why the ALI did not undertake a family law reform project before the 1990s, given the significant ferment in family law in the second half of the twentieth century (e.g., state adoption of no-fault divorce, the dismantling of coverture marriage and gender-based family laws, and emerging issues about cohabitation and nonmarital children). Family law, a mix of common law and statutory law, would have seemed an apt topic, given the ALI's aim of being a "progressive institution" in the sense of improving the state of American common law (*see* Kenneth S. Abraham & G. Edward White, *The Work of the American Law Institute in Historical Context*, in this volume) and its willingness to undertake projects involving statutory reform, such as its influential Model Penal Code—which had implications for family law (*see* Kimberly Kessler Ferzan, *From Restatement to Model Penal Code: The Progress and Perils of Criminal Law Reform*, in this volume). In 1965, the Minutes of the ALI Council referenced "possible work by the Institute in family law and divorce law." The ALI, Minutes of the One Hundred and Twenty Sixth Meeting of the Council (Dec. 13, 16, & 18, 1965) [hereinafter ALI Council Minutes]. Not until 1985 does "Family Law" reappear in the minutes—as one of several subjects under consideration by a Special Committee on Institute Program (chaired by Judge Patricia Wald) as future ALI projects "in the next several years." ALI Council Minutes (May 14, 1985). This appears to be the genesis of the Principles project, which commenced in 1990 after delays due to securing necessary funding (obtained from the State Justice Institute). ALI Council Minutes (Dec. 12, 1987; May 12, 1991).

[8] Tuesday Afternoon Session—May 16, 1995, 72 A.L.I. PROC. 45, 73 (1995).

[9] Boskey, *supra* note 6, at 261. Well after completion of the family dissolution Principles, an ALI Reporters handbook clarified the distinction between Restatements and Principles: "Restatements are primarily addressed to courts. They aim at clear formulations of common law and its statutory elements or variations and reflect the law as it presently stands or might appropriately be stated by a court." AMERICAN LAW INSTITUTE, CAPTURING THE VOICE OF THE AMERICAN LAW INSTITUTE: A HANDBOOK FOR ALI REPORTERS AND THOSE WHO REVIEW THEIR WORK 3 (2015 ed.). "Principles," in contrast, "are primarily addressed to legislatures, administrative agencies, or private actors. They can, however, be addressed to courts when an area is so new that there is little established law." *Id.* at 4. For further discussion, *see* Abraham & White, *supra* note 7.

[10] *See, e.g.,* Katharine T. Bartlett, *U.S. Custody Law and Trends in the Context of the Law of Family Dissolution*, 10 VA. J. SOC. POL'Y & L. 5, 6 (2002) (noting that "Principles" strive to find "best practices" rather than "restate" the prevailing law and also recognizing role of empirical and normative questions in crafting custody rules).

issues in ways that staked out and elaborated a progressive family law agenda that would gain traction in the decades after the Principles' publication.

For the Reporters, a progressive family law agenda should reflect the ways that individuals form and live out relationships, rather than marshal the power of law to impose a narrow vision of the family and leave unprotected those who fail to conform. The need to meet families where they are yielded a legal framework that vindicates critical equality commitments and adopts a functional, rather than formal, approach to legal regulation. A functional approach accommodates the family relationships that individuals form, values the work of care that individuals contribute to their families, and recognizes that relationships give rise to rights and responsibilities. We link the Principles' concern with *family inequality* to its *functional* approach to recognition and regulation. Relations *within families*—particularly gender-differentiated roles in different-sex couples—and distinctions *between families*—particularly marital-status distinctions that also implicated sexual orientation discrimination—concerned the ALI's Reporters.[11] Rather than distinguish family relations based on gender, sexual orientation, or marital status, the Reporters articulated generally applicable principles that sought to mitigate inequalities by reflecting, and accommodating, families' lived experiences. Drawing on archival materials, interviews, and other sources, this chapter demonstrates how concerns with inequality shaped the Principles' functional approach to both adult and parent-child relationships.

The Reporters recognized the decline of rigid gender roles in family law and in society. Still, given the persistent gendered realities of family life, they worried about the harms that purportedly neutral legal rules inflicted on women. This concern with inequality led the Reporters to be skeptical of contract models premised on equal bargaining power of spouses or nonmarital partners. Contract models were "too formalistic" in ignoring the reality of how people live: relationships, over time, give rise to duties.[12] Accordingly, the Reporters sought to reward nonmonetary investments in family relationships and to provide financially for spouses and partners (disproportionately, women) who sacrificed economic opportunities in the interest of the family unit. This perspective is reflected in the ALI's approach to alimony ("compensatory spousal payments") and property distribution for divorcing couples, as well as in its application of that approach to unmarried "domestic partners."

The treatment of unmarried couples also reflected the Reporters' concerns with inequality based on marital status and sexual orientation. When the project began, no state permitted same-sex couples to marry. Although various municipalities had domestic partnership laws, no state did. By the time the Reporters finished, the federal government and many states had "defense of marriage laws" limiting marriage to one man and one woman and even, in some instances, prohibiting alternative formal statuses. Vermont had enacted a civil union regime for same-sex couples, and California

---

[11] On these two dimensions of equality, *see* LINDA C. MCCLAIN, THE PLACE OF FAMILIES: FOSTERING CAPACITY, EQUALITY, AND RESPONSIBILITY 5–7, 117–219 (2006). On the relationship between equality principles and the functional turn in family law, *see* Susan Frelich Appleton, *Gender and Parentage: Family Law's Equality Project for Our Empirical Age, in* WHAT IS PARENTHOOD? CONTEMPORARY DEBATES ABOUT THE FAMILY 237–56 (Linda C. McClain & Daniel Cere eds., 2013); NeJaime, *supra* note 5, at 334–40.

[12] Interview with Ira Ellman, Apr. 7, 2021 ("Ellman Interview").

had adopted a domestic partnership law. Against that backdrop, the Principles proposed to treat as "domestic partners" two persons—whatever their gender—who shared life as a couple, and to bring them under the protective umbrella of marriage law for purposes of property distribution and alimony. In the ALI's perspective, same-sex couples whose relationships "closely resemble marriages *in function*"[13] should not be forced to live outside of family dissolution rules.

Similar equality concerns animated the Principles' approach to parenthood. The Reporters sought to protect parent-child relationships formed outside of marital families, which necessarily included families formed by same-sex couples. Unlike the paradigmatic different-sex couple, same-sex couples with children typically include a nongenetic parent. Accordingly, commitments to equality based on marital status and sexual orientation, as well as concerns with children's welfare, led the Reporters to elaborate an increasingly capacious functional approach to parental recognition. The law should recognize actual parent-child relationships, regardless of biological connection. To implement this approach, the Principles adopted two concepts—de facto parent and parent by estoppel—that, while rooted in common law and equitable doctrines, represented important advances.

The Principles tackled critical issues that have preoccupied family law in the years since, but there were limits to their approach. The Principles addressed inequality only partially and stopped short of fully elaborating a functional approach to family recognition. Given the project's law reform ambitions, political and practical considerations constrained the Reporters, leading them to accept key dimensions of the "traditional" family. They explicitly disavowed any intention to encourage nonmarriage over marriage and, to the contrary, predicted that the Principles would reduce the "incentive to avoid marriage" to escape responsibilities to a partner.[14] Yet combatants in the culture wars opposed the Principles for weakening—or "de-privileging"—marriage by assimilating nonmarital relationships to the model of marriage.[15] Similarly, the functional approach to parental recognition did not reach its logical conclusion of parity between biological and nonbiological parent-child relationships. Even so, conservative critics assailed the functional categories that included LGBTQ parents and other nonbiological parents for "fragmenting parenthood" by reducing the role of biology as its basis.[16]

Nonetheless, in identifying and advancing a functional approach to family recognition in part as a means to address persistent inequality in both law and society, the ALI supplied an emergent family law agenda with credibility. Since the Principles' publication, the functional approach, in important respects, has grown dramatically, justified in part on equality grounds. The law of parental recognition has embraced functional criteria as part of a broader agenda to protect children's relationships with their primary caregivers and to vindicate commitments to equality based on gender, sexual

---

[13] Principles, *supra* note 1, at 915 (emphasis added).

[14] *Id.* at 916.

[15] *See, e.g.,* INSTITUTE FOR AMERICAN VALUES ET AL., THE MARRIAGE MOVEMENT: A STATEMENT OF PRINCIPLES 22 (2000); INSTITUTE FOR AMERICAN VALUES ET AL., THE FUTURE OF FAMILY LAW 5, 16–18 (2005).

[16] *See, e.g.,* THE FUTURE OF FAMILY LAW, *supra* note 15, at 16, 37.

orientation, and marital status.[17] While the ALI's status-based approach to nonmarital adult relationships remains less dominant than the contract model it criticized, its position is a vital reference point and model in ongoing debates over legal remedies for unmarried partners. Given declining marriage rates and rising rates of nonmarital cohabitation, the need for such legal remedies arguably persists even though marriage for same-sex couples eliminated a significant source of inequality evident to the Principles' Reporters.[18] In other areas, such as premarital and marital agreements, the Principles' insistence on tempering freedom of contract has provided an important source of authority for influential law reform projects.[19]

To be clear, we are not arguing that the Principles caused any particular changes in the law or had some measurable effect. Rather, the Principles participated in larger shifts in family law by identifying and working out a progressive family law agenda. Some scholars and judges, including those involved in the Principles project, had already begun to elaborate functional principles. The ALI provided an important institutional site from which to more comprehensively develop a functional family law approach that would tackle troubling forms of inequality.[20] For us, the question is not whether courts and legislatures adopted the Principles' proposals. Instead, the question is whether the ALI—in keeping with the aims of a "principles" project—identified and elaborated concepts that have become central to critical debates in family law and that have been treated as significant authorities as the law has moved in new directions.[21]

II. Adult Relationships

An image from the tech world, path determination, seems apt to describe the impact that the selection of Ira Ellman as (initially) Reporter and then Chief Reporter and Grace Blumberg as Reporter had on the chapters of the Principles relating to adult-adult relationships.[22] Blumberg and Ellman shared a skepticism about contract as an

---

[17] On the pervasiveness of functional approaches to parental recognition, *see* Courtney G. Joslin & Douglas NeJaime, *How Parenthood Functions*, COLUM. L. REV. (forthcoming 2023) (manuscript at *25) (map showing functional parent doctrines in thirty states and the District of Columbia).

[18] On the growing prevalence of and reasons for nonmarital cohabitation in the United States, *see* Deirdre Bloome & Sharon Ang, *Marriage and Union Formation in the United States: Recent Trends Across Racial Groups and Economic Backgrounds*, 57 DEMOGRAPHY 1753 (Sept. 10, 2020); Nikki Graft, *Key Findings on Marriage and Cohabitation in the U.S.*, Pew Research Center (Nov. 6, 2019), https://www.pewresearch.org/fact-tank/2019/11/06/key-findings-on-marriage-and-cohabitation-in-the-u-s/.

[19] *See, e.g.*, Barbara A. Atwood & Brian H. Bix, *A New Uniform Law for Premarital and Marital Agreements*, 46 FAM. L.Q. 313, 314–15, 329–30 (2012) (noting the Principles' "sharp criticism" of the Uniform Premarital Agreements Act and contrasting approach as among factors making "timing seem right" for promulgating the new Uniform Premarital and Marital Agreements Act).

[20] Moreover, we are focused only on particular sections of the Principles. We do not, and cannot in a chapter of this length, address each major section.

[21] *See* NeJaime, *supra* note 5, at 324 (situating the ALI Principles in family law's functional turn); Interview with Katharine Bartlett, Jan. 19, 2021 ("Bartlett Interview") (observing that the Reporters promoted a "functional approach" to thinking about the issues that "had influence beyond the actual language of the provisions proposed").

[22] In his "Director's Foreword" to the Principles, Lance Liebman observed that "finding the right Reporters proved difficult," but that after "valiant early contributions" by several professors, "the team of Ira

adequate model for adult relationships because it failed to recognize that relationships themselves could give rise to duties. Instead, they favored a status-based approach in which law would acknowledge and address the realities of family life, including inequalities between men and women (as spouses and cohabitants), marital and nonmarital families, and different-sex and same-sex couples.

The Principles' functional approach reached both marital and nonmarital relationships and justified assimilating some unmarried couples to the law of marriage. This ambitious and controversial approach emerged over time.[23] At the 1995 ALI Annual Meeting, Ellman stated that a "project on Family Dissolution ... largely means divorce," although there was a "contemplated" chapter on "the dissolution of nonmarital relationships" and chapters on custody and child support would address both marital and nonmarital children. In that sense, the project was "on the dissolution of both formal and informal families." However, Ellman introduced draft chapters on property (Chapter 4) and compensatory payments (Chapter 5) as "really exclusively divorce topics."[24] The completed Principles, however, made most of Chapters 4 and 5 applicable to some nonmarital couples on the rationale that relationships meeting the criteria of "domestic partners" (Chapter 6) "closely resemble marriages in function, and their termination therefore poses the same social and legal issues as does the dissolution of a marriage." Similarly, Chapter 7 (Agreements) specified rules for how both spouses *and domestic partners* could make agreements to alter or confirm the "legal rights and obligations" they would otherwise have to each other under the Principles or "other law governing marital dissolution."[25]

The Reporters' approach to spousal support and domestic partners shows how concerns with inequality based on gender, marital status, and sexual orientation shaped a functional approach to intimate relationships. The Principles' approach to spousal support aimed to address the economic inequality arising in marriage due to the persistence of the gendered pattern of a wife's investment in homemaking and caretaking and a husband's investment in market labor. The Principles reflected and extended Ellman's scholarly approach, seeking to compensate spouses for economic losses arising from sharing behavior in marriage.[26] The Principles' status-based approach to unmarried cohabitants aimed to address gendered patterns of care and work in nonmarital families. The Principles adapted Blumberg's proposal to "assimilate cohabitants to married persons" for purposes of property division and spousal support.[27]

Ellman, Chief Reporter, and Kate Bartlett and Grace Blumberg, Reporters took over and led the work to its happy conclusion." Principles, *supra* note 2, at xv.

[23] For examples of critiques, *see* RECONCEIVING THE FAMILY: CRITIQUE ON THE AMERICAN LAW INSTITUTE'S PRINCIPLES OF FAMILY DISSOLUTION (Robin Fretwell Wilson ed., 2006).

[24] Tuesday Afternoon Session—May 16, 1995, 72 A.L.I. PROC. 45, 66 (1995).

[25] Principles, *supra* note 1, at 915, 945–46.

[26] Ira Mark Ellman, *The Theory of Alimony*, 77 CAL. L. REV. 3 (1989).

[27] Grace Ganz Blumberg, *Cohabitation without Marriage: A Different Perspective*, 28 UCLA REV. 1125, 1166 (1981).

A. Spousal Support

1. Ellman's Call to Focus on (Gendered) "Economic and Social Realities"

In a 1989 article, *The Theory of Alimony*, Ellman contended that neither contract theory nor partnership concepts provided an adequate model for marriage or alimony awards. Ellman noted the stark disconnect between modern alimony law's formal gender neutrality and the "economic and social realities that usually make the wife economically dependent rather than the husband." Those "realities" included wives' greater "domestic burden" from shouldering primary responsibility for "domestic needs"—particularly childcare—even as the majority of wives worked outside the home. Contract would not remedy a wife's loss from such marital investment at divorce.[28]

Ellman painted a vividly gendered picture of why marriage—without an "enforceable long-term contract"—is a "risky investment." The "traditional wife" invests in a marriage early by having and raising children and providing her husband "with the supportive domestic environment that furthered his market success," expecting to later share "in the fruits" of that success. A wife may give her husband "the best years of her life" without a return on her investment; a husband exits the marriage able to take "much of the gain realized" (such as increased earning capacity) into a new marriage. While such "specialization" "makes sense" if couples they view their marriage as a "sharing enterprise," a "disproportionate loss" is suffered by the spouse who specialized in domestic labor if the commitment to share breaks down.[29]

Ellman did not argue that family law should discourage gendered role specialization and sharing behavior or encourage more egalitarian marriages. Rather, given how spouses actually conduct their lives, alimony law should reward, not punish, sharing behavior and sacrifices. Ellman proposed to reconceptualize alimony as one spouse's obligation to compensate the other for "residual" loss (i.e., loss surviving the marriage) in the latter's earning capacity arising from engaging in domestic labor during marriage. He proposed several principles for redefining alimony as "compensable marital investment."[30]

2. Chapter 5: Status (and the Passage of Time) Give Rise to Duties

Chapter 5 incorporates Ellman's critique of contract and partnership models and his proposed theoretical framing around compensation for financial losses. Its objective is "to allocate financial losses that arise at the dissolution of a marriage according to equitable principles that are consistent and predictable in application." This shift from spousal need to compensation for losses "arising from the marriage and its failure" transforms a spouse's petition "from a plea for help to a claim of entitlement."[31]

The commentary emphasizes *status*—being in a relationship—and the relationship's *duration* as giving rise to duties that survive a marriage's end: "[A]s marriages lengthen,

---

[28] Ellman, *supra* note 26, at 4 n.2, 13, 40.

[29] *Id.* at 42–44, 48.

[30] *Id.* at 49, 53–73. Ellman argued that any loss in an "egalitarian marriage" would fall on both spouses, but they might still be in unequal positions after divorce since husbands usually have greater earnings than wives. *Id.* at 45–46.

[31] Principles, *supra* note 1, at 787, 790.

continuing obligations between former spouses depend less on explicit agreement and promise than on their relationship itself, molded by them jointly, with consequences for them and their children." How spouses conduct their joint lives grounds such duties. Section 5.03 specifies different awards based on several categories of compensable loss, approximating "the fact patterns that typically support alimony claims in existing law." One category mirrors Ellman's article: earning-capacity loss incurred during marriage and continuing after dissolution due to "one spouse's disproportionate share, during marriage, of the care of the marital children...." Chapter 5 also recognizes loss arising from other forms of caretaking when one or both spouses have a moral obligation to engage in it.[32]

Chapter 5 also went beyond Ellman's article by recognizing compensable loss in a marriage of "significant duration" without inquiring into sharing behavior. Section 5.03(2)(a) deems a "compensable loss" the "loss of living standard experienced at dissolution by the spouse who has less wealth or earning capacity." Time itself is a proxy for changes in a marital relationship. Equitable principles require accounting for "losses that arise from the changes in life opportunities and expectations caused by the adjustments individuals ordinarily make over the course of a long marital relationship."[33]

The significance of time in entwining lives and engendering obligations is also evident in Chapter 4 (on dividing property). Section 4.12 provides that, in sufficiently long-term marriages, a portion of each spouse's separate property should be (gradually) recharacterized at dissolution as marital property, with the percentage increasing with the length of the marriage. In support, the Reporters appealed to how spouses think about their property as a marriage lengthens and drew a parallel to Chapter 5's increase in the amount of compensatory payments based on a marriage's length.[34]

In defending the controversial recharacterization provision at an ALI meeting, Ellman argued that equity becomes more important than ownership in a long marriage: "people should not leave a marriage of 25 or 30 years' standing with significant differences in financial status." Dean Herma Hill Kay called the provision a "brilliant stroke" that "corresponds" to the expectations of "most people" in long marriages who "feel that the sharp distinctions that the law imposes on separate and community property [that is, who formally has title to property] really are not very meaningful in their lives."[35]

3. Gender Dynamics and Feminist Criticisms of Chapter 5

Chapter 5's illustrations of compensable losses—intended to represent typical cases[36]—reveal the gender dynamics not evident from the gender-neutral language of its principles. The reasoning behind using feminine pronouns ("she"/"her") for the "long-time homemaker" was that "in understanding the nature of the obligation

---

[32] *Id.* at 793, 798 (§ 5.03(2)(b)), 801.

[33] *Id.* at 787, 798 (§§ 5.02(2)(a), (3)(b)).

[34] *Id.* at 769 (§ 4.12).

[35] Wednesday Morning Session, May 17, 1995, 72 A.L.I. Proc. 91, 130, 140 (1995). By a vote of 95 to 101, a motion to recommit Section 4.18 (what became Section 4.12) to the Reporters for reconsideration failed. *Id.* at 142.

[36] Ellman Interview, *supra* note 12.

that arises in the long-term marriage, it is useful to think first about the traditional homemaker wife, as perhaps the clearest case"—the most "persuasive application" of compensation for loss. However, the same approach applies when husbands are "financially dependent upon their wives." Further, because the Principles make persons who qualify as "domestic partners" under Chapter 6 subject to most of Chapters 4 and 5 (absent an express opt-out), Chapter 5's principles would apply to same-sex partners who were not (then) able to marry. Chapter 5's reasoning would equally apply to long-term cohabitation (whatever the partners' gender): "As a marriage lengthens, the parties assume roles and functions with respect to one another. In sharing a life together, they mold one another."[37]

Although the Principles sought to address gender inequality, they did not go as far as some feminist critics of alimony law urged. At one Annual Meeting, family law scholar Carol Bruch moved (unsuccessfully) to resubmit—rather than approve— Chapter 5 "in light of [the] large body of thoughtful scholarship" elaborating "what horrible injustices have occurred to women under our spousal support laws" and attempting to "right the wrongs of unequal living standards after divorce."[38] Bruch argued that, as a "Principles," rather than a "Restatement," the draft should be "an improvement" of the current law, not "an apology" or "rationale" for it.[39]

B. Unmarried Cohabitants as "Domestic Partners"

1. Blumberg's Argument for a Status-Based Approach to Cohabitation
In a generative 1981 article, *Cohabitation without Marriage: A Different Perspective,* Blumberg noted the American "romance with freedom of contract" despite its obvious limits as applied to intimate relationships. She contended that "publicly created status is a much more sustainable vehicle for handling support and property claims of unmarried and married cohabitants." Contract theory produced "unjust results" given cohabitants' unequal bargaining power. Further, this dynamic was gendered: inequality in economic power between men and women produced unequal bargaining power in marriage and cohabitation since "self-interest would lead the man to give up as little [wealth] as possible." Cohabitants often followed marriage-like gendered patterns, investing in "the male" due to "pervasive sexual segregation in the labor force, gender-based pay differentials, higher female unemployment rates, and a tradition of male primacy." Challenging a view that nonmarital cohabitation freed women from "traditional roles," Blumberg contended that sociological studies and case law revealed that "the woman wanted to marry and was economically powerless," while

---

[37] Principles, *supra* note 1, at 809, 811.

[38] Wednesday Morning Session, May 15, 1996, 73 A.L.I. Proc. 109, 110, 117 (1996) (mentioning Professors Krauskopf, Brinig, Czapanskiy, and herself). Bruch drew on her experience as "a housewife of seven years" to criticize the "demeaning" tone of parts of the draft toward "women who have devoted their efforts to a joint enterprise" and to insist on the aptness of an equal partnership model. *Id.* at 121 (1995).

[39] *Id.* at 110. Additionally, Chapter 5 did not require "income equalization at the dissolution of long marriages." *See* Principles, *supra* note 1, at 825–831 (noting "considerable feminist literature" urging post-divorce income sharing, while arguing Chapter 5's approach, though "less ambitious," would still yield "larger awards than those currently granted in many alimony cases").

the man was "domineering and economically powerful"; the cohabitation relationship was "long and traditional in terms of sex stereotyped role assumption."[40]

Such factors demonstrated the inadequacy of a contract model focused on the "intent of the [cohabiting] parties." Cohabiting women engaged in "marriage-like," wifely traditional roles, yet lacked marital remedies like equitable distribution and rehabilitative alimony. Blumberg proposed a "simple solution": "assimilate cohabitants to married persons for purposes of maintenance, property division, and elective share statutes." Instead of *Marvin v. Marvin*'s model of looking to express or implied contract or to equitable remedies,[41] directly imposing "divorce remedies" would be fairer than "pretending concern for cohabitants' 'intent,'" given that most cohabitants do not make express agreements.[42]

Blumberg's status model, treating "a cohabitation of two or more years' duration or a cohabitation of any duration in which there is a child born to the parties ... as though it were a lawful marriage," foreshadowed Chapter 6's approach. In effect, marriage and such cohabitation were functional equivalents. Blumberg countered arguments that treating cohabitants "as though they were married" was unfair with studies showing that cohabitants think that "there is no difference between marriage and cohabitation" and expect "to be treated as though they were married"—although postseparation, men, particularly, tended to reevaluate "marriage-like cohabitation" as "non-marriage-like."[43]

2. Chapter 6's Status-Based Model and Inclusion of Same-Sex Couples

By the late 1990s, when Blumberg and Ellman drafted Chapter 6, they could look to status-based models abroad and in the United States—most prominently Washington State's application of its community-property laws to stable, marriage-like relationships.[44] Further, recognition of the needs of same-sex couples expanded the earlier focus on the gendered dynamics of "heterosexual cohabitation."[45] For Blumberg and Ellman, any chapter on nonmarital cohabitants must include same-sex couples.[46] (At UCLA, Blumberg was involved in efforts to extend family benefits to employees' same-sex partners.[47]) Chapter 6 observes: "[T]here are domestic partners who are not allowed to marry each other under state law because they are of the same sex,

---

[40] Blumberg, *supra* note 27, at 1133, 1163, 1168.

[41] Marvin v. Marvin, 557 P.2d 106 (Cal. 1976).

[42] Blumberg, *supra* note 27, at 1166, 1168.

[43] *Id.*

[44] *See* Ira Mark Ellman, *Contract Thinking was* Marvin's *Fatal Flaw*, 76 NOTRE DAME L. REV. 1365, 1366 (2001) (explaining that the Washington Supreme Court and, subsequently, the ALI Principles chose the approach rejected by *Marvin*, "assimilating unmarried cohabitants into the legal regime of marriage"). In Washington, a community property state, if nonmarital partners are in a "committed intimate relationship" (established through a multifactor test), there is a rebuttable presumption that property they acquire during cohabitation is common property, subject to equitable distribution when the relationship ends. *See* Olver v. Fowler, 168 P.3d 348 (Wash. 2007). In presenting Chapter 6 at the May 2000 Annual Meeting, Blumberg noted the influence of Canada and Australia and, domestically, Washington's case law. *See* Monday Morning Session—May 15, 2000, 77 A.L.I. PROC. 3, 29–30 (2000).

[45] Principles, *supra* note 1, at 933, 1128.

[46] Interview with Grace Blumberg, Mar. 11, 2011 ("Blumberg Interview").

[47] Grace Ganz Blumberg, *The Regularization of Nonmarital Cohabitation: Rights and Responsibilities in the American Welfare State*, 76 NOTRE DAME L. REV. 1265, 1287 (2001).

although they are otherwise eligible to marry and would marry one another if the law allowed them to do so."[48] While the basis for Chapter 6 was contract's inadequacy for dealing with intimate adult relationships, one justification for it was same-sex couples' exclusion from marriage.[49]

Aptly, Chapter 6's Illustrations featured different-sex and same-sex couples. Many illustrations featuring different-sex couples included gendered role specialization, reflecting persistent social realities and fact patterns common in case law.[50] Some examples featuring same-sex partners included economic disparity and role specialization; others featured more egalitarian arrangements.[51]

3. Assimilating Cohabitation to Marriage: A "Unitary System"

When the Principles project commenced, it was not evident that it would take the status-based approach to nonmarital cohabitation championed by Blumberg in 1981. The "Background Paper" for the January 25–26, 1990, meeting, convened to "inform and shape the American Law Institute project to draft Principles of Law Governing Family Dissolution," lists "the dissolution of informal intimate relationships" as among the major issues.[52] Further, it notes a shift in attitudes about such relationships "to tolerance, if not approval," and "increased openness and public tolerance of same gender intimate relationships," reflected in "a body of legislation and developing case law."[53] But the "very preliminary draft" shared with participants states that, while the parts on child support and child custody "shall apply to children of both formal and informal relationships," the parts on property division and spousal support "shall apply only to divorce, i.e., the dissolution of a formal marriage."[54]

Through the mid-1990s, this distinction between marriage and cohabitation continued. In November 1993, when Ellman shared partial drafts of three chapters—Division of Property, Alimony (renamed "Compensatory Payments"), and Child Support—he stressed their "inherent interdependence"; he did not indicate the first two would apply to nonmarital relationships.[55] No work, he reported, had been done on two additional planned chapters, Dissolution of Nonmarital Cohabiting Relationships and Premarital and Separation Agreements.[56] By 1994, it was not clear that the Reporters would reach either additional chapter.[57]

---

[48] Principles, *supra* note 1, at 914.

[49] Blumberg Interview, *supra* note 46.

[50] *Id.*; Ellman Interview, *supra* note 12. See Principles, *supra* note 1, at 921–22 (illus. 3 through 6).

[51] *See* Principles, *supra* note 1, at 923–25 (illus. 7 & 11).

[52] Memo from Marygold S. Melli to Participants in Conference eon the Law and Public Policy of Family Dissolution, Jan. 4, 1990 (attaching Background Paper: Conference on the Law and Public Policy of Family Dissolution).

[53] *Id.* at 2. To be fair, after noting that courts "generally enforce" contracts between cohabitants and flagging questions about such contracts, the Background Paper raises the status question: "Should cohabitation give rise to economic rights or obligations founded otherwise than in contract?" *Id.* at 16.

[54] "Principles of the Law Governing Family Dissolution" ("Very Preliminary Draft"), attached to Background Paper.

[55] Memorandum from Reporter Ira Ellman to the Council, "An Overview of Existing Law and the Project's Current Status," Nov. 11, 1993.

[56] *Id.* at 1.

[57] Memorandum from Reporter Ira Mark Ellman to Council, Nov. 11, 1994, at 1, 23–24.

In October 1998, however, Ellman shared with the Council a preliminary draft of a chapter called "Domestic Unions," addressing "long-term, marriage like, nonmarital relationships."[58] Authored by Blumberg and Ellman, the chapter had the basic elements of the final version of Chapter 6. The initial draft referred to "de facto spouses" and "de facto marriage"[59]—terms that made vividly clear the Reporters' functional approach. The Advisers favored "domestic partners," but Blumberg and Ellman worried about its "inappropriate connotation of a business relationship."[60] By 1999, however, Chapter 6 was renamed "Domestic Partners."[61]

At the May 2000 Annual meeting, when the ALI membership first saw drafts of Chapters 6 and 7, President Wright and Blumberg presented nonmarital cohabitation as "not part of our original agenda." Blumberg explained how Chapter 6 originated in part from judges' practical need for guidance: "[S]ome of our Advisers, particularly the judges, thought that [nonmarital cohabitation] needed rethinking and reformulation [and] that some of their most troubling cases involve the dissolution of nonmarital families and that existing law was often unsatisfactory." The existing law's focus on contract, in the eyes of the Reporters, was part of the problem. Thus, Ellman identified the "difficult problem" posed by Chapters 6 and 7: "how to acknowledge the importance of contract without forgetting that the contract rubric can never provide a complete description of family relations."[62]

By focusing on the lived reality of families, the Reporters developed a functional approach that led them to craft "a unitary system," under which "the same rules apply to all sorts of couples."[63] Thus, Chapter 6's "foundation" was "the equitable concerns" expressed in Chapters 4 and 5, which "define and rationalize the claims that one spouse has upon another at the termination of a marriage" unless they explicitly agree—pursuant to Chapter 7—not to be "subject to these equitable rules." Since Chapter 6 sought to reach "marriage-like cohabitation," the Reporters attempted to draft "rules that would distinguish relationships that are marriage-like from those that are not."[64] The duration of a relationship for a "significant period" would trigger a presumption that the couple were domestic partners, rebuttable by evidence that the parties "did not share life together as a couple."[65] The Principles propose a shorter period if the couple maintains a "common household" with "their common child." If a couple does not meet the state-determined time threshold, Section 6.03(6) allows one party—using a multifactor test—to try to establish that they shared a primary residence and a

---

[58] Chapter 6, Domestic Unions, attached to Memo from Chief Reporter Ira Mark Ellman to Council of the American Law Institute, on submission for October Council Meeting, Sept. 27, 1998.

[59] Memo from Chief Reporter Ira Mark Ellman to Council of the American Law Institute, on submission for October Council Meeting, Sept. 27, 1998.

[60] Id.

[61] Memo on Chapter 6 from Grace Blumberg to Advisers and Members Consultative group, Sept. 24, 1999.

[62] Monday Morning Session—May 15, 2000, 77 A.L.I. PROC. 3, 29–30 (2000).

[63] Monday Afternoon Session—May 15, 2000, 77 A.L.I. PROC. 47, 93 (2000). Blumberg commented that the Reporters, at Wright's urging, considered "foreign" as well as "American law." Some foreign jurisdictions took a functional—rather than contractual—approach to nonmarital cohabitation. Monday Morning Session, *supra* note 62, at 32.

[64] Monday Morning Session, *supra* note 62, at 31.

[65] Principles, *supra* note 1, at 916–17.

life together as a couple for a "significant" period of time.[66] Ultimately, the Principles sought to switch the default rule that unmarried cohabitants have no economic obligations to each other arising from their shared life—absent an agreement to engage in such sharing—to a rule that they do, absent an express agreement otherwise.

4. Competing Assessments of the Functional Approach: Weakening Marriage or Fostering Equality and Diversity?

At the 2000 Annual Meeting, the ongoing culture wars over marriage seeped into the debate over domestic partners. Some members objected that Chapter 6 gave legitimacy to same-sex relationships. Conservative family law scholar Lynn Wardle asserted: "[W]hat you are proposing is same-sex domestic partnership, which overwhelmingly is, I think, a bad idea." Concerns about the ALI giving its imprimatur to nonmarital relationships led to a suggestion to add a proviso of nonendorsement of such relationships. Supporters countered that the issue was not whether nonmarital relationships were "good, bad, [or] moral," but the "reality" that they exist; lawyers, judges, and others needed "rational guidance" about how to address them when they end.[67]

Blumberg's response was pro-marriage but also attentive to the "social fact" of "informal unions."[68] She reminded critics that the Principles' commentary took a position preferring marriage as "more orderly" and "regular," while attempting to deal with the increasing rate of cohabitation. The Reporters were not "endorsing" nonmarital relationships. To the contrary: "All three of us are happily married, and ... I don't know about my Co-Reporters, but I have never cohabited (*laughter*) and I would urge my daughter not to also." Because marriage is "an umbrella of benefits flowing from third parties, the state, and between the parties," Blumberg would tell her daughter that "she is much better protected by the institution of marriage." Chapter 6 simply aims to "deal with the dissolution" of nonmarital relationships, reflecting the stated need of judges for guidance. Signaling support for greater equality among families, Blumberg explained that the Reporters did not add stronger language favoring marriage because, in an environment in which same-sex couples have "no right to marry," but have access to an "equivalent institution" (like the civil union in Vermont), "we would certainly not want to take a position against that equivalent institution."[69]

On one view, the ALI's scheme of bringing domestic partnership under the umbrella of marriage law—with respect to economic consequences at dissolution—may appear moderate. Rather than creating a range of new relationship statuses, the Principles solidified marriage's primacy by expressing a preference for marriage while extending divorce rules to nonmarital cohabitation. The Reporters also distinguished the debate over same-sex marriage in Hawaii and Vermont from the "quite modest" focus of the remedies in Chapter 6, which did not address "the relationship between the couple as a unit and third parties and the state."[70]

---

[66] *Id.*
[67] *Id.* at 36, 43–45.
[68] Monday Afternoon Session, *supra* note 63, at 51.
[69] Monday Morning Session, *supra* note 62, at 44, 46.
[70] *Id.* at 37 (Ellman).

Chapter 6's insistence on a status rather than contract paradigm, however, could also appear progressive, given the legal and political landscape of the late 1990s. Under *Marvin*, a contract-based remedy would not entitle a cohabitant to divorce remedies or assimilate nonmarital dissolution to marital dissolution. Both Blumberg and Ellman had criticized *Marvin*;[71] Blumberg reiterated that criticism when presenting Chapter 6 at the 2000 ALI meeting: applying "the rubric of contract rather than family law, to the rights and obligations of nonmarital cohabitants" for the last twenty-five years had "provoked considerable dissatisfaction."[72] The Principles' proposed status-based approach pressed a new direction for family law—one focused on the reality of intimate relationships.

Given the climate with respect to same-sex marriage, the Principles' choice to treat different-sex and same-sex cohabiting couples the same with respect to their entitlement to marriage-like remedies recognized and accommodated LGBTQ family formation. Significantly, the Principles assumed a functional equivalence not only between same-sex and different-sex cohabitants but also between same-sex cohabitants and different-sex spouses. This point was not lost on the ALI's supporters or its critics.

Of the various chapters addressing adult relationships, Chapter 6 received the most attention in commentary published in the immediate wake of approval of the Principles.[73] In convening a symposium on the Principles at Brigham Young University, Lynn Wardle charged the Reporters with going "far beyond existing law" in recommending "official recognition of homosexual and extramarital concubine-like domestic partnerships, on an economic par with marriage."[74] Other participants predicted that the Principles would threaten and erode the institution of marriage[75] and undermine the traditional, gender-differentiated, heterosexual family.[76]

A different view emerged from a symposium in the *Duke Journal of Gender Law and Policy*. Dean Herma Hill Kay (an Adviser to the Principles project) commended the Reporters for endeavoring to "complete the divorce law reforms begun in the 1960s," including addressing "unresolved" gender issues that remained "embedded in the law and practice of family dissolution."[77] Some contributors praised the Principles for opening up "a range of possibilities" for "gay and lesbian couples in particular."[78] Even those who faulted the ALI for "retaining the status of marriage as normatively

---

[71] Blumberg, *supra* note 27; Ellman, *supra* note 39.

[72] Monday Morning Session, *supra* note 62, at 31.

[73] *See, e.g.*, Lynn Wardle, *Introduction to the Symposium on the American Law Institute's Principles of the Law of Family Dissolution*, 2001 BYU L. REV. i (2001) (observing that "the bulk of the presentations at the BYU Symposium" focused on Chapters 2 and 6).

[74] *Id.* at ii.

[75] William C. Duncan, *Domestic Partnership Laws in the United States: A Review and Critique*, 2001 BYU L. REV. 961 (2001).

[76] F. Carolyn Graglia, *A Nonfeminist's Perspective on Mothers and Homemakers Under Chapter 2 of the ALI's Principles of the Law of Family Dissolution*, 2001 BYU L. REV. 993 (2001). A few contributors offered qualified praise for Chapter 6. *See* Terry S. Kogan, *Competing Approaches to Same-Sex Versus Opposite Sex, Unmarried Couples in Domestic Partnership Laws and Ordinances*, 2001 BYU L. REV. 1023 (2001); Mark Strasser, *A Small Step Forward: The ALI Domestic Partners Recommendation*, 2001 BYU L. REV. 1135 (2001).

[77] Herma Hill Kay, *Foreword*, 8 DUKE J. GENDER L. & POL'Y ii, ii–iii (2001). *See, e.g.*, Tonya L. Brito, *Spousal Support Takes on the Mommy Track: Why the ALI Proposal Is Good for Working Mothers*, 8 DUKE J. GENDER L. & POL'Y 151 (2001).

[78] Mary Coombs, *Insiders and Outsiders: What the American Law Institute Has Done for Gay and Lesbian Families*, 8 DUKE J. GENDER L. & POL'Y 87 (2001).

superior to domestic partnerships" recognized that, if widely adopted, the Principles could promote equality among families by nudging the law toward "recognizing a wider range of relationships."[79]

While Wardle contended that the Principles went far *beyond* existing law, Kay noted that several contributors to the Duke symposium faulted the Principles for being too much like a "Restatement"—*adhering* to current law on property division, instead of taking the opportunity to correct state law, for example, by treating human capital as property.[80]

* * *

More than twenty years after Blumberg's observations about "dissatisfaction" over the limits of contract for addressing economic obligations between cohabitants, that "dissatisfaction" is unabated.[81] Critics highlight that cohabitants seldom recover for engaging in the very sharing behavior that Blumberg and Ellman identified, pointing particularly to women in different-sex relationships who invest in the household and childcare.[82]

Meanwhile, a primary constituency for the ALI's approach to nonmarital cohabitation—same-sex couples—has gained access to a status-based framework— marriage. Blumberg predicted that same-sex couples' quest for marriage could "shed useful light on the social and welfare functions of the family, whether marital or nonmarital."[83] Arguments for marriage equality did highlight the enormous number of governmental benefits and obligations tied to marriage—and withheld from unmarried couples.[84] Marriage equality has also made same-sex couples' efforts to reform the treatment of nonmarital relationships less urgent.

Nonetheless, disagreements that aired upon publication of the Principles over how family law should address unmarried couples continue. The ALI's position may not be the dominant approach, but it remains an influential alternative that many strongly support. Scholars, judges, lawmakers, and lawyers diverge over whether cohabitation and marriage *are* functional equivalents warranting the same economic rules at dissolution and over whether a status-based approach disregards or respects autonomy and choice.[85] An illustrative example is the Uniform Law Commission's recently approved

---

[79] Martha M. Ertman, *The ALI Principles' Approach to Domestic Partnership*, 8 DUKE J. GENDER L. & POL'Y 107 (2001).

[80] Kay, *supra* note 78, at iv (citing Marsha Garrison, *The Economic Consequences of Divorce: Would Adoption of the ALI Principles Improve Current Outcomes?*, 8 DUKE J. GENDER L. & POL'Y 124 (2001); Allan M. Parkman, *The ALI Principles and Marital Quality*, 8 DUKE J. GENDER L. & POL'Y 162 (2001); Penelope Eileen Bryan, *Vacant Promises? The ALI Principles of the Law of Family Dissolution and the Post-Divorce Financial Circumstances of Women*, 8 DUKE J. GENDER L. & POL'Y 177 (2001)).

[81] *See, e.g.*, Albertina Antognini, *Nonmarital Coverture*, 99 B.U. L. R. 2139 (2019); Albertina Antognini, *Nonmarital Contracts*, 73 STAN. L. REV. (2021).

[82] *See* Antognini, *Nonmarital Coverture, supra* note 81.

[83] Blumberg, *supra* note 47, at 1309–1310.

[84] *See, e.g.*, Obergefell v. Hodges, 576 U.S. 644 (2015).

[85] *See, e.g.*, Kaiponanea T. Matsumura, *Beyond Property: The Other Legal Consequences of Informal Relationships*, 51 ARIZ. ST. L.J. 1325, 1322–33 (2019) (summarizing some of the literature). *Compare* June Carbone & Naomi R. Cahn, *Nonmarriage*, 76 MD. L. REV. 55 (2016) (raising autonomy arguments against status-based remedies for nonmarital partners), *with* Courtney G. Joslin, *Autonomy in the Family*, 66 UCLA L. REV. 912, 972–73 (2019) (challenging autonomy arguments against status-based remedies and

Uniform Cohabitants' Economic Remedies Act (UCERA). The leaders of that project adhered to a largely contract-based approach, even rejecting the ALI's view as "radical."[86] Their critics pressed for status-based provisions, appealing to the Principles as a superior model.[87]

III. Parent-Child Relationships

Just as with the ALI's approach to adult relationships, its approach to parent-child relationships carried forward the academic arguments of a key Reporter. By the time Katharine Bartlett joined as a Reporter, she had become one of the nation's leading legal scholars on parenthood. In an influential article, Bartlett critiqued the traditional assumptions that animated the Supreme Court's decisions on the rights of unmarried fathers and argued for a legal framework that prioritized parent-child relationships that exist in fact, regardless of marital status, gender, or biological connection. Bartlett even suggested that a child may have more than two parents.[88]

The Principles tackled parent-child relationships at a critical moment. The Court had repudiated distinctions based on "illegitimacy,"[89] but marital status still mattered. When a married woman gave birth, her husband was treated as a father by virtue of the marriage.[90] When an unmarried woman gave birth, the father could claim parentage based on biology. What should happen to children raised by an unmarried mother and a man who was not the biological father?

The Reporters viewed marital status as a problem in its own right. But marital status implicated another equality concern—sexual orientation.[91] Excluded from marriage, same-sex couples raising children were doing so outside marriage. Tackling sexual orientation inequality meant tackling the role of biology in parenthood. While the paradigmatic unmarried different-sex couple was raising their biological child, the paradigmatic same-sex couple included a nonbiological parent.[92] Premising nonmarital parentage on biological connection harmed LGBTQ parents. Absent a co-parent adoption, which only a few jurisdictions authorized, only the biological parent would be treated as a legal parent. The nonbiological parent lacked standing to seek custody upon dissolution.[93]

---

arguing that conventional approach fails to further "choice" in family forms). *See also* Marsha Garrison, *Is Consent Necessary?: An Evaluation of the Emerging Law of Cohabitant Obligation*, 52 UCLA L. Rev. 815, 817–19 (2005) (calling ALI approach a "conscriptive model" that imposes obligations on couples who have chosen to avoid marriage).

[86] *See* Uniform Law Commission, Uniform Cohabitants' Economic Remedies Act 32 (draft for approval, July 9–15, 2021) ("Prefatory Note").

[87] *See infra* Conclusion.

[88] *See* Katharine T. Bartlett, *Rethinking Parenthood as an Exclusive Status: The Need for Legal Alternatives when the Premise of the Nuclear Family Has Failed*, 70 Va. L. Rev. 879 (1984).

[89] *See* Serena Mayeri, *Marital Supremacy and the Constitution of the Nonmarital Family*, 103 Cal. L. Rev. 1277 (2015).

[90] *See* Douglas NeJaime, *The Nature of Parenthood*, 126 Yale L.J. 2260, 2272 (2017).

[91] Bartlett Interview, *supra* note 21.

[92] *See* NeJaime, *supra* note 90, at 2297.

[93] *See* Douglas NeJaime, *The Story of* Brooke S.B. v. Elizabeth A.C.C.: *Parental Recognition in the Age of LGBT Equality, in* Reproductive Rights and Justice Stories 245 (Melissa Murray et al. eds., 2019).

Given these concerns with inequality, parental recognition—and therefore who has standing to seek custody—became an important feature of the ALI's work on custody. In what follows, we show how the Principles' definition of "parent" evolved over time in ways that grew to include nonmarital, nonbiological parents and to treat them more like legal parents. We then show how the ALI's approach staked out important ground in emergent family law debates and contributed to developments in parentage law at the state level.

A. Toward Functional Parenthood

As the influential work of Joseph Goldstein, Anna Freud, and Albert Solnit had taught in the 1970s, from a child's perspective, a parent-child relationship does not depend on a biological or legal connection.[94] Instead, the child's relationship to her "psychological parent" grew out of the day-to-day interactions between parent and child.[95] This experiential understanding came to animate a functional approach—reflecting the realities of family life, rather than turning on formal markers like marriage or biology.

Such an approach was not prominent in the early stages of the ALI project. At the initial 1990 conference, original Reporter Marygold Melli drew attention to "informal families" and "same gender intimate relationships," but said nothing about nonbiological parents in nonmarital families.[96] When the Reporters eventually addressed "the role of the psychological parent" in an early draft on custody, they focused on stepparents.[97] The 1992 preliminary draft, which provided that a "stepparent . . . may be awarded parental authority and physical custody,"[98] continued to view parent-child relations within the paradigm of the heterosexual marital family.

The addition of Bartlett as a Reporter in 1995 changed the direction—and ambition—of the ALI's approach. Bartlett's functional commitments first emerged in her treatment of custodial responsibility. The preliminary Chapter 2 draft that Bartlett shared in 1995—which represented "a new start" on custody[99]—emphasized past caretaking as the basis for allocating custodial responsibility between parents whose relationship dissolved.[100] Future custodial arrangements should reflect the realities of

---

[94] *See* Joseph Goldstein, Anna Freud, & Albert J. Solnit, Beyond the Best Interests of the Child (1973).

[95] *See id.*

[96] Conference on the Law and Public Policy of Family Dissolution, Background Paper 2–3 (Jan. 4, 1990); Memo to Participants in Conference on the Law and Public Policy of Family Dissolution, from Marygold S. Melli (Jan. 4, 1990).

[97] Preliminary Draft No. 1, § 7.26 (at 11) (1992).

[98] Preliminary Draft No. 3, § 7.26 (at 8) (1992).

[99] Memo to Advisers, Members' Consultative Group, from Kate Bartlett and Ira Ellman 1 (May 8, 1995).

[100] Preliminary Draft No. 5 at 10–11 (1995). *See also* Memo to Advisers, Members Consultative Group, from Kate Bartlett 1 (May 8, 1995). Bartlett was influenced by Elizabeth Scott's foundational article. *See* Elizabeth S. Scott, *Pluralism, Paternal Preference, and Child Custody*, 80 Cal. L. Rev. 615 (1992). The Principles adopted the terms "custodial responsibility" and "decisionmaking responsibility," instead of physical and legal custody. The ALI's draft Restatement of the Law, Children and the Law, also adopts these terms. Restatement of the Law, Children and the Law, Tentative Draft No. 2 § 1.80 (at 3) (Mar. 20, 2019).

the family's pre-dissolution life, aspiring to "continuity and stability in the child's primary parent-child attachment or attachments."[101] But a rule that applied to "parents" required the ALI to answer the question: *Who is a parent?*

1. De Facto Parent

The ALI began from the premise that "parent" meant legal parent. The draft defined the "parent-child relationship" to cover "relationships between child and parent as defined under applicable state law"—at a time when state law definitions largely defined parent in ways that excluded unmarried nonbiological parents. Nonetheless, Bartlett sought to "recognize[] the parenting interests of adults who are not biological or adoptive parents but who have functioned as the child's parents in certain circumstances." Even as the draft defined the "parent-child relationship" to include "functionally-defined parent-child relationships," it treated them formally as "non-parents."[102] The "interests of [these] non-parents," Bartlett affirmed, "ordinarily are subordinate to those of the parents."[103]

The functional perspective, and its blurring of the parent/non-parent distinction, eventually unsettled the Reporters' initial assumption that state law would control the definition of "parent." By 1997, Bartlett had adopted the term "functional parent" alongside "legal parent," and was extending custodial rights to both.[104] By early 1998, the term "de facto parent" had replaced "functional parent"; "a *parent* is either a legal parent or a de facto parent."[105] Ultimately, the Principles defined a de facto parent as "an individual . . . who, for a significant period of time not less than two years, (i) lived with the child and, (ii) for reasons primarily other than financial compensation . . . regularly performed a share of caretaking functions at least as great as that of the parent with whom the child primarily lived."[106]

The inclusion of de facto parent provisions exemplified the functional approach's capacity to mitigate inequality. Nonbiological parents in same-sex couples could qualify as de facto parents.[107] Still, the Principles relegated de facto parents to a lesser status entitled to fewer rights than legal parents.[108]

Treating nonbiological parents in same-sex couples as less than full parents was problematic. The 1990s had witnessed groundbreaking work on parental recognition for LGBTQ parents. Bartlett herself was influenced by Nancy Polikoff's work,[109] particularly a 1990 article making the case for functional parenthood to protect lesbian parents and their children.[110] The Principles had more work to do to vindicate

---

[101] Preliminary Draft No. 5, § 2.02(2)(b) (at 29) (1995).

[102] *Id.* at 21, 41–42, 47.

[103] Memo to Advisers, Members Consultative Group, from Kate Bartlett 1 (May 8, 1995).

[104] Memo to Advisers and Members' Consultative Group, Principles of the Law of Family Dissolution, from Reporter Katharine T. Bartlett xi (June 2, 1997); Preliminary Draft No. 7, § 2.03(a), (b) (1997).

[105] Tentative Draft No. 3, § 2.03 (p. 37) (1998). *See also* Preliminary Draft No. 8, § 2.03 (p. 14) (1998).

[106] Principles, *supra* note 1, § 2.03 Definitions.

[107] Preliminary Draft No. 6, § 2.21 illus. (at 354) (1996) (same-sex couple illustration).

[108] *See, e.g.,* Preliminary Draft No. 7, § 2.21 (at 392–93) (1997); Memo to Members and Advisers, Family Dissolution Project, from Reporter Katharine T. Bartlett 1 (Sept. 17, 1999) ("The rights of de facto parents were inferior in certain respects to those of legal parents.").

[109] Bartlett Interview, *supra* note 21.

[110] *See* Nancy D. Polikoff, *This Child Does Have Two Mothers: Redefining Parenthood to Meet the Needs of Children in Lesbian-Mother and Other Nontraditional Families,* 78 Geo L.J. 459 (1990).

LGBTQ families. Ultimately, many more parents would be captured by a new, and increasingly expansive, functional category—parent by estoppel.

2. Parent by Estoppel

In 1998, Bartlett recognized the temptation to devote more attention to the category of "parent," even as the Reporters were reluctant "to break any new ground."[111] Seemingly in response to feedback from the ALI membership, Bartlett noted that since the child support chapter drew on estoppel principles by preventing individuals from denying support obligations based on their prior conduct, "it may seem unbalanced or even inconsistent not to recognize a comparable principle in Chapter 2."[112] The preliminary draft circulated in 1998 altered the definition of "legal parent" to include an individual "upon whom a child support obligation has [been] imposed under Chapter 3."[113] Bartlett framed the concept as both a logical analogue to the child support chapter and a natural outgrowth of the custody chapter's "functional emphasis."[114]

By the 1998 Council draft a few months later, this new category stood on its own. The notion of "parent" had coalesced around three separate categories: legal parent, parent by estoppel, and de facto parent.[115] The parent by estoppel category included not only a man with a child support obligation but also "a man who acted as the child's father for a significant period of time ... under the reasonable good faith belief that he was the child's biological father."[116] This status reached nonbiological parents in nonmarital families but remained tethered to the heterosexual family. A nonbiological parent in a same-sex couple could not have a reasonable, good-faith belief that she was the child's biological parent.

Bartlett was not done, noting in the 1998 Council draft that she had "reserved [a] section for parent status created by agreement."[117] By 1999, Bartlett presented a section on individuals who functioned as parents under an agreement with the legal parent.[118] Bartlett framed this new pathway in expressly gender-neutral terms— "holding *himself or herself* out as the child's parent"[119]—thus offering a path to parental standing to nonbiological mothers in same-sex couples. The Principles instructed that

[111] Memo to Advisers and Judges and Members Consultative Groups, from Reporter Katharine T. Bartlett 9 (June 9, 1998).

[112] *Id.* Chapter 3, authored by Blumberg and Ellman, reflected the Reporters' concerns with the unequal economic conditions facing children and their custodial parents (primarily, mothers) after divorce. Departing from the prevailing American method, the Principles elaborated a formula that accounted for not only the absolute but also the relative income of parents—aiming to ensure that the residential parent would "not be[] disadvantaged, compared to the child's other parent, by the financial opportunity costs of residential responsibility." Principles, *supra* note 1, § 3.04.

[113] Preliminary Draft No. 8, § 2.03 (at 14) (1998).

[114] Memo to Members and Advisers, *supra* note 108, at 1.

[115] Council Draft No. 5, § 2.03 (1998).

[116] Memo to Members of the Council, The American Law Institute, from Reporter Katharine T. Bartlett xvi (Sept. 25, 1998); Council Draft No. 5, § 2.03 (at 123–24) (1998). In the final version, the "significant period" become "at least two years." § 2.03 Definitions.

[117] Council Draft No. 5, § 2.03 (at 124) (1998).

[118] Council Draft No. 6, § 2.03 (1999). *See also* Memo to Members and Advisers, *supra* note 108, at 1.

[119] Memo to Members and Advisers, *supra* note 114, at 1–2 (emphasis added).

determinations "should not turn upon whether the parties are of the same sex or different sexes."[120]

In the final Principles, a "parent by estoppel" included an individual who

> lived with the child since the child's birth ... or ... lived with the child for at least two years, holding out and accepting full and permanent responsibilities as a parent, pursuant to an agreement with the child's parent (or, if there are two legal parents, both parents), when the court finds that recognition of the individual as a parent is in the child's best interests.[121]

This new pathway offered a way for both parents in a same-sex couple to stand in legal parity, given that "[t]he rights and privileges of a legal parent and a parent by estoppel are the same, and superior in some respects to those of a de facto parent."[122] Like de facto parent protections, it also offered the possibility for multi-parent recognition.[123]

Ultimately, the 2000 draft presented to the ALI membership included the three categories of parent—legal parent, parent by estoppel, and de facto parent[124]—with parent by estoppel in its new, expansive form. Progressives cheered the ALI's functional parent provisions,[125] pointing to how they vindicated LGBTQ families.[126] But conservatives objected.[127] "[W]ith validation of same-sex domestic partnerships and of homosexual parenting," one critic charged, the ALI had become a leader in "the feminist march to complete androgyny."[128]

3. Assigning Custodial Responsibility

Once it was clear who qualified as a parent, how should a court determine custody? This was the original work of Chapter 2. To operationalize the best interest of the child standard, which had long been criticized as indeterminate, the Principles adopted a more concrete approach.[129] Articulated in the first draft that Bartlett circulated, the

---

[120] Principles, *supra* note 1, § 2.03(b) Definitions.

[121] *Id.*

[122] Memo to Council of the American Law Institute, from Reporter Katharine T. Bartlett 1 (Nov. 12, 1999).

[123] On the long-standing nature of multiparent recognition under functional parent doctrines, *see* Courtney G. Joslin & Douglas NeJaime, *Multi-Parent Families, Real and Imagined*, 90 FORDHAM L. REV. 2561, 2575–88 (2022).

[124] Principles, *supra* note 1, § 2.03 Definitions.

[125] *See, e.g.*, David D. Meyer, *What Constitutional Law Can Learn from the ALI Principles of Family Dissolution*, 2001 BYU L. REV. 1075, 1103 ("The boldness of chapter 2's custody provisions lies chiefly in the provisions' expansion of the concept of parenthood and the accompanying erosion of the privileged status traditionally reserved for biological and adoptive parents.").

[126] *See, e.g.*, Nancy D. Polikoff, *Breaking the Link Between Biology and Parental Rights in Planned Lesbian Families: When Semen Donors Are Not Fathers*, 2 GEO. J. GENDER & L. 57, 90 (2000) (noting that the "ALI Principles ... rejected linking parental rights inevitably and exclusively to biology" and thereby "rises to the challenge posed by [planned lesbian and gay] families").

[127] *See, e.g.*, David M. Wagner, *Balancing "Parents Are" and "Parents Do" in the Supreme Court's Constitutionalized Family Law: Some Implications for the ALI Proposals on De Facto Parenthood*, 2001 BYU L. REV. 1175, 1186 (2001) (objecting to the de facto parent category, arguing that "what children really need are ... one or preferably two natural or adoptive parents").

[128] *See, e.g.*, F. Carolyn Graglia, *A Nonfeminist's Perspectives of Mothers and Homemakers Under Chapter 2 of the ALI Principles of the Law of Family Dissolution*, 2001 BYU L. REV. 993, 1012 (2001).

[129] Preliminary Draft No. 5, Introductory Discussion at 4–5 (1995).

"past allocation of care" standard made it to the final version. Reflecting the child-centered concerns centered by a functional approach, the standard uses the facts of past caretaking as the basis for future custodial arrangements.[130]

Preferring a joint custody framework, some men criticized the Reporters' approach for failing to protect fathers' rights.[131] The Reporters, for their part, sought to vindicate gender equality by adopting a functional standard that, while formally gender-neutral, recognized the disproportionate caretaking work done by women in different-sex couples.[132] Moreover, by adopting a clear rule rather than an abstract standard, their approach would reduce the need for women to bargain away financial rights in exchange for custodial rights.[133]

Despite the standard's functional commitments, courts were instructed to depart from the "past allocation of care" in disputes involving de facto parents. A court "should not allocate the majority of custodial responsibility to a de facto parent over the objection of a legal parent or a parent by estoppel," and a de facto parent may be denied parenting time altogether "if, in light of the number of other individuals to be allocated responsibility, the allocation would be impractical."[134]

Ultimately, the treatment of de facto parents exhibited both the promise and limits of a functional approach at the start of the twenty-first century. As Bartlett explained, "greater recognition of individuals who are not legal parents but who have lived with the child and functioned in a parental role" was "consistent with the emphasis on past caretaking patterns."[135] Yet, even as the Principles' approach to custodial responsibility used past caretaking as the relevant measure, it minimized this factor when assigning custody to de facto parents.[136]

B. The Rise of Functional Parenthood

The following discussion situates the ALI's functional approach to parenthood within family law developments over the past quarter century.

State courts responded to the Principles in different ways. Nearing the end of the ALI drafting process, the Massachusetts Supreme Judicial Court adopted the ALI's approach to recognize de facto parents—doing so in a dispute involving a same-sex couple.[137] Other states, though, did not expressly adopt the ALI's approach. Nonetheless, the Principles served as authority to support functional parenthood,

---

[130] Principles, *supra* note 1, § 2.02(e) ("the continuity of existing parent-child attachments after the break-up of a family unit is a factor critical to the child's well-being").

[131] Bartlett Interview, *supra* note 21.

[132] *Id.*

[133] *See* Robert H. Mnookin & Lewis Kornhauser, *Bargaining in the Shadow of the Law: The Case of Divorce*, 88 YALE L.J. 950 (1979).

[134] Principles, *supra* note 1, § 2.18.

[135] Memo to Members of the Council, The American Law Institute, from Reporter Katharine T. Bartlett 1–2 (Sept. 24, 1997).

[136] *See, e.g.,* Julie Shapiro, *De Facto Parents and the Unfulfilled Promise of the New ALI Principles*, 35 WILLAMETTE L. REV. 769, 782 (1999) (observing that "the Principles are a step forward for nonlegal parents," but "this step, as are perhaps most steps in the law, is a small step").

[137] *See* E.N.O. v. L.M.M., 711 N.E.2d 886, 891 (Mass. 1999).

even when the standards articulated by the court broke from the specifics of the ALI. For example, in a pathbreaking decision adopting a de facto parent doctrine in 2000, the Rhode Island Supreme Court noted that "our position here is in harmony with the principles recently adopted by the American Law Institute," which "has recognized that individuals who have been significantly involved in caring for and supporting children and for whom they have acted as parents may obtain legal recognition of their parental rights to visitation and custody."[138]

When courts resisted the functional turn, the ALI appeared as authority in dissents advocating functional doctrines.[139] In some jurisdictions, those dissenting positions eventually became the governing rule. When the Maryland high court rejected de facto parentage in a 2008 decision involving an unmarried same-sex couple, the dissent quoted the ALI's parent by estoppel provisions to support its view that the court should "hold that a *de facto* parent stands in legal parity with a legal parent."[140] In overruling that decision in 2016 in another same-sex couple case, the Maryland high court explained that the ALI "recommended expanding the definition of parenthood to include *de facto* parent as one of the parties with standing to bring an action for the determination of custody."[141]

The ALI's influence may have been compromised by its choice of terminology— itself a sign of the time at which the Principles were drafted. As Bartlett crafted the functional parent concepts, a leading authority on de facto parent status was the Wisconsin Supreme Court's 1995 decision in *In re H.S.H.-K.*[142] Chief Justice Shirley Abramson, who wrote that opinion, was an Adviser to the Principles and consulted with Bartlett.[143] In *H.S.H.-K.*, which featured a same-sex couple, the court ruled that the nonbiological mother could seek visitation as a de facto parent. This landmark decision for LGBTQ rights nonetheless refused to treat a de facto parent as a legal parent.

Accordingly, at the time of Bartlett's ALI work, de facto parent status was not understood as the equivalent of legal parenthood. When the Massachusetts court adopted de facto parenthood a few years later, it relied directly on the ALI in articulating a status entitling the person only to standing to seek visitation.[144] Chief Justice Marshall, who served on the ALI Council, joined that opinion.[145]

The dialogue between courts and the ALI contributed to a particular view of de facto parenthood—one that protected nonbiological parents but offered less than full parental status. Over time, this doctrine would come to appear insufficient and

---

[138] Rubano v. DiCenzo, 759 A.2d 959, 974–75 (R.I. 2000). *See also* Stitham v. Henderson, 768 A.2d 598, 605–06 (Me. 2001).

[139] *See, e.g.,* Moreau v. Sylvester, 95 A.3d 416, 438 n.22 (Vt. 2014) (Robinson, J., dissenting) ("The American Law Institute has likewise recognized that parental rights can arise from intentions and conduct, rather than biology or legal ties."); Chaterjee v. Chaterjee, 253 P.3D 915, 934 (N.M. App. 2011) (Vigil, J. dissenting) (drawing support from the ALI's protection of a "child's relationship with an adult who has functioned as a parent").

[140] *See* Janice M. v. Margaret K., 948 A.2d 73, 101 n.5 (Md. 2008) (Raker, J., dissenting).

[141] *See* Conover v. Conover, 146 A.3d 433, 439 n.6, 449, 451 (Md. 2016).

[142] *See In re* Custody of H.S.H.-K., 533 N.W.2d 419, 447 (Wis. 1995).

[143] *See id.*; Bartlett Interview, *supra* note 21.

[144] *See* E.N.O. v. L.M.M., 711 N.E.2d 886, 891 (Mass. 1999).

[145] *See id.* at 886; Bartlett Interview, *supra* note 21. In an earlier opinion, Marshall endorsed de facto parentage, specifically adopting the term "proposed by the Reporters on the ALI Principles of the Law of Family Dissolution." Youmans v. Ramos, 711 N.E.2d 165, 167 n.3 (Mass. 1999).

discriminatory. Today, a growing number of jurisdictions treat functional parents as legal parents through de facto parent doctrines.[146] This has emerged through judicial decisions and statutory enactments.[147]

Counting jurisdictions that have de facto parent doctrines may reveal less about the role of the ALI's de facto parent provisions and more about the ALI's parent by estoppel provisions, which treated functional parents as equivalent to legal parents. In this sense, parent by estoppel in the Principles is more analogous to what many courts and legislatures today call de facto parent.[148] Indeed, the Washington Supreme Court noted the similarity between the comprehensive de facto parent doctrine it adopted in 2005 and the ALI's parent by estoppel category.[149]

Parent by estoppel covered an individual who, pursuant to a co-parenting agreement with the legal parent, *held out* the child as their child. Such language sounded in registers familiar to presumptions of parentage long part of state family law. The 1973 Uniform Parentage Act treats a man as a father if he lives with the child and "openly *holds out* the child as his natural child."[150] This presumption at first envisioned unmarried *biological* fathers. But by 2002, the California Supreme Court ruled that the lack of a biological connection did not necessarily rebut the presumption.[151] A man, or woman, who was not the biological parent could attain parentage based simply on the conduct of "holding out."[152] Still, at the time of the ALI's work, it was unclear whether the "holding out" presumption would meaningfully move in a nonbiological direction.

Ultimately, parent by estoppel as a term gained little traction.[153] Had the Reporters called it "holding out" parentage, perhaps the continuity between the Principles and subsequent developments would be more clearly appreciated. Adoption of the nonbiological, gender-neutral "holding out" presumption has accelerated in recent years. State courts have increasingly applied existing "holding out" presumptions to reach nonbiological mothers and fathers in nonmarital families.[154] Some states, following

---

[146] *See* Joslin & NeJaime, *supra* note 17, at *21.

[147] *See, e.g., In re* Parentage of L.B., 122 P.3d 161, 177 (Wash. 2005); CONN. PUB. ACT. 21-15, § 38 (2021). The ALI's ongoing Restatement project on Children and the Law includes a de facto parent section that acknowledges the Principles' influence but assimilates recent developments. RESTATEMENT OF THE LAW, CHILDREN AND THE LAW, TENTATIVE DRAFT No. 2 § 1.82 (at 63) (Mar. 20, 2019). The Restatement provides that "a court may award a de facto parent primary custodial responsibility if it is in the child's best interests." *Id.* § 1.82 (at 67). Still, unlike the UPA (2017), the draft Restatement characterizes de facto parents as "third parties," not legal parents. *Id.* § 1.82 (at 63, 65).

[148] Memo to Members of The American Law Institute, from Reporter Katharine T. Bartlett xxxviii (Feb. 25, 2000) ("The rights and privileges of a parent by estoppel are the same as those of a legal parent.").

[149] *See In re* Parentage of L.B., 122 P.3d 161, 176 n.24 (Wash. 2005). De facto parent doctrines in many states, as well as under the UPA (2017), include a requirement that the ALI Reporters included in the parent-by-estoppel provisions—that the person "accept[] full and permanent responsibilities as [a] parent." § 2.03(1)(b)(3). *See* UNIF. PARENTAGE ACT § 609(d)(3) (UNIF. LAW COMM'N 2017) (requiring that a de facto parent "undertook full and permanent responsibilities of a parent"); CONN. GEN. STAT. ANN. § 46b-490a(3) (same).

[150] UNIF. PARENTAGE ACT § 4(a)(4) (Unif. Law Comm'n 1973) (emphasis added).

[151] *In re* Nicholas H., 46 P.3d 932, 936 (Cal. 2002).

[152] *See, e.g., In re* Karen C., 124 Cal. Rptr. 2d 677 (Ct. App. 2002).

[153] New York and Pennsylvania maintain analogous estoppel doctrines. *See, e.g.,* Shondel J. v. Mark D., 7 N.Y.3d 320, 327 (N.Y. 2006) (equitable estoppel in paternity actions); K.E.M. v. P.C.S., 38 A.3d 798, 807 n.6 (Pa. 2012) (citing the Principles in discussion of state's paternity by estoppel doctrine).

[154] *See* Chatterjee v. King, 280 P.3d 283 (N.M. 2012).

the 2017 Uniform Parentage Act (UPA), have enacted a nonbiological, gender-neutral holding out presumption.[155]

The Principles made a compelling case for functional criteria but emerged at a time when a functional family law project that extended equality to nonmarital and LGBTQ parents could venture only so far. Massachusetts provides a useful illustration of how the Principles advanced an equality-inflected functional agenda and yet ultimately proved insufficient. Early on, Massachusetts adopted the ALI's approach to de facto parenthood, with some modification. At the time, this constituted a landmark development for functional parenthood and LGBTQ equality. Yet this approach to de facto parenthood has been criticized for failing to provide parental rights and responsibilities to an individual, including a nonbiological parent in a same-sex couple, who has functioned as the child's parent.[156]

What once appeared progressive and child-protective eventually seemed inadequate. In a 2016 parentage decision, the Massachusetts Supreme Judicial Court cited the inferior treatment of de facto parents, under both Massachusetts law and the ALI Principles, as a basis for finding that de facto parenthood was not a sufficient remedy for a nonbiological co-parent in a same-sex couple. Instead, the court concluded, the nonbiological mother could establish parentage under the state's "holding out" presumption, which the court interpreted to authorize nonbiological parentage.[157] Without saying so, the court shifted from the weaker de facto parent concept of the ALI to the more robust parent by estoppel concept—though the development occurred under the rubric of the "holding out" presumption.

One could read the court's decision as rejecting the ALI's approach: de facto parent status failed to provide sufficient protection to functional parents. But one could also read it as vindicating the ALI's approach: a more comprehensive functional parent doctrine, operationalized through the concept of "holding out," was necessary. Either reading shows the complicated ways that the Principles have participated in the development of a more inclusive and functional family law regime.[158]

IV. Conclusion

The Principles intervened in important and evolving family law debates and advanced reform agendas for both adult-adult and parent-child relationships. But the Principles' power has been uneven. The degree to which the ALI shaped, or even predicted, the direction of the law has varied across these two domains.

The law's treatment of parent-child relationships has moved in a decidedly functional direction. Courts in many states have recognized nonmarital, nonbiological, nonadoptive parents under equitable and common law theories or based on statutory

---

[155] See, e.g., R.I. GEN. LAWS § 15-8.1-401 (2020); VT. STAT. ANN. tit. 15C, § 401 (2020); WASH. REV. CODE § 26.26A.115 (2020); UNIF. PARENTAGE ACT § 204 (UNIF. LAW COMM'N 2017).

[156] See Courtney G. Joslin, Leaving No (Nonmarital) Child Behind, 48 FAM. L.Q. 495, 499–501 (2014).

[157] See Partanen v. Gallagher, 59 N.E.3d 1133, 1141 n.17 (Mass. 2016).

[158] As Bartlett observed in 2014, "the Principles captured trends that had already begun when the Principles were drafted, and have continued since then." Bartlett, supra note 3, at 34.

presumptions.[159] Some states, including those that have adopted the 2017 UPA, have codified de facto parentage and a nonbiological "holding out" presumption.[160]

In contrast, functional regulation of adult relationships has encountered more powerful resistance.[161] With respect to unmarried couples, contract-based frameworks continue to dominate, and ascriptive recognition has lagged.[162] Consider UCERA. The drafting committee recognized that, nearly a half century after *Marvin*, there is "no predictable result when cohabitants dissolve their relationship or one cohabitant dies" and that courts are reluctant to award relief, and, particularly, may fail to recognize "domestic services" performed by one partner as a basis for recovery.[163] Nonetheless, the committee essentially codified *Marvin*. After initially including a bracketed status-based provision on "presumptive equitable partnership,"[164] it declined to include a status-based remedy, describing as "perhaps radical" the ALI's approach of extending "marital remedies" of alimony and equitable distribution to cohabitants.[165] Scholars and advocates who urged the Committee to include a "status-based option" drew on the ALI's approach; they worried about inferring "intent" from the decision not to marry and (echoing Blumberg) about wealth-based power differentials between unmarried cohabitants.[166]

The theoretical, normative, and practical arguments that animate the functional approach apply in important ways to both the adult-adult and parent-child settings, and

---

[159] *See* Joslin & NeJaime, *supra* note 17, at *11–25; NeJaime, *supra* note 5, at 328–34; NeJaime, *supra* note 90, at 2370–72.

[160] *See supra* note 155.

[161] Changes to alimony law in some states reflect the Principles' approach—compensating for losses arising from the changes that marriage and its end bring and adopting a formula that increases both the amount and duration of alimony based on the duration of a marriage. *See, e.g.,* Memorandum in Support of A06728 (New York) (referring, in section on "Justification" for proposed alimony bill, to the ALI Principles' recognition of "economic losses that spouses suffer at the end of marriage" and its suggestion to share those losses "through a formula for determining post-marital spousal support that takes into account the income of the parties and the length of the marriage"). While the memo supporting the legislation that eventually passed in 2015 does not repeat this reference to the Principles, the legislation includes various formula for determining the amount and duration of spousal support. *See* N.Y. Dom. Rel. § 236 (2022). The legislation, however, also includes an income cap on how much of a payor's income will be subject to the alimony guidelines. Of course, other powerful factors also drive changes to alimony law, including lobbying efforts by payors and growing hostility to "permanent" alimony

[162] A few states have developed opt-in formal statuses for adult relationships, such as Colorado's Designated Beneficiary Agreement. Colo. Rev. Stat. Ann. § 15-22.106.1. More recently, municipalities have begun to enact domestic partnership ordinances open to more than two partners. *See, e.g.,* Cambridge Municipal Code, Chap. 2.119020D (enacted in March 2021).

[163] *See* Uniform Law Commission, Uniform Cohabitants' Economic Remedies Act 3–4 (draft for approval, July 9–15, 2021) ("Prefatory Note"). All cited materials about UCERA may be found at the ULC's website: https://www.uniformlaws.org/.

[164] *See* Economic Rights of Unmarried Cohabitants Act 12–14 (Nov. 13, 2019 draft) (including in brackets Art. 4. Presumptive Equitable Partnership) (noting Province of Alberta, Adult Interdependent Relationships Act (2002) as influence).

[165] *See* Uniform Law Commission, Uniform Cohabitants' Economic Remedies Act 32 (draft for approval, July 9–15, 2021) ("Prefatory Note").

[166] *See* Memo from Cathy Sakimura, National Center for Lesbian Rights & Professor Courtney Joslin, UC Davis, to ULC Economic Rights of Unmarried Cohabitants Act Committee, Dec. 3, 2019; Proposed alternative text of Article 4 based on the ALI's Principles of the Law of Family Dissolution (draft of Article 4); *see also* Memo from Patricia A. Cain, Professor of Law, Santa Clara University to ULC Economic Rights of Unmarried Cohabitants Act Committee, Dec. 4. 2019 (urging that "recognition based on status" is "the most important aspect of your project").

yet legal regulation has diverged to a significant extent. Today, scholars point to the parent-child context to justify functional reforms in the adult-adult setting; scholars who resist a functional framework point to the regulation of adult relationships as a model for parental recognition.[167] Conflict over whether and how regulation in these two contexts should converge carries forward a debate that was forged in significant part by the Principles and the critiques it attracted. Today's participants continue to look to the Principles as a touchstone.[168]

Yet today's debate differs importantly from the debate at the time of the Principles. Proponents of the Principles' functional approach sought to meet families where they were, accommodating the realities of family life and tackling inequalities within and between families. While some critics shared these goals, others sought to channel family life into traditional structures and vindicate conventional gender roles.[169] On this view, some inequalities were justified. The Reporters repudiated this motivation to standardize families and channel family life into traditional structures.[170] On this point, their position now enjoys widespread support in the academy and in law reform work. Today, for most family law scholars, the question is no longer *whether* but *how* to construct legal doctrines that track family life and mitigate inequality.[171]

The debate now appears less focused on normative disagreement than on empirical questions. Scholars draw on research addressing some of the key empirical questions that Bartlett identified as important but unanswered at the time of the ALI's work on the Principles.[172] For example, debate rages over the accuracy of a key empirical premise of the Principles' treatment of "domestic partners"—the functional equivalence between spouses and some unmarried cohabitants. Influential studies show that marrying a current partner is not an attractive option for many low- and moderate-income Americans, even if they share children in common.[173] Family law scholars differ on the implications of this work for family law reform.[174] While race and class did not feature prominently in the Principles' analysis of cohabitation, more recent work highlights the role of racial and economic inequality in the decline of marriage among some groups.[175] The emergence of marriage as a marker of privilege

---

[167] *Compare* Joslin, *supra* note 85 (arguing that "capacious parentage rules that recognize, value, and respect chosen family relationships . . . should [also] apply to the horizontal adult-adult relationships"), *with* Carbone & Cahn, *supra* note 85, at 108 (2016) (after examining tensions between the law of nonmarital parentage and the law of nonmarital coupling, arguing for convergence in the direction of the approach of coupling).

[168] *See, e.g.,* Joslin, *supra* note 85, at 984; Carbone & Cahn, *supra* note 85, at 66.

[169] *See* Graglia, *supra* note 76, at 993; Lynn D. Wardle, *Deconstructing Family: A Critique of the American Law Institute's "Domestic Partners" Proposal,* 2001 BYU L. REV. 1189, 1232.

[170] *See* Katharine T. Bartlett, *Saving the Family from the Reformers,* 31 U.C. DAVIS L. REV. 809, 846 (1998) ("the principles offer determinacy in decisionmaking without presupposing, or attempting to promote, a standard family scenario").

[171] *Compare* Carbone & Cahn, *supra* note 85, at 120–21, *with* Joslin, *supra* note 85, at 986–87.

[172] *See* Bartlett, *supra* note 10, at 51–52.

[173] *See, e.g.,* KATHRYN EDIN & MARIA KEFALAS, PROMISES I CAN KEEP: WHY POOR WOMEN PUT MOTHERHOOD BEFORE MARRIAGE (2007); KATHRYN EDIN & TIMOTHY NELSON, DOING THE BEST I CAN: FATHERHOOD IN THE INNER CITY (2013).

[174] *See* Joslin, *supra* note 85, at 972–73 (2019). On reasons for not marrying, *see, e.g.,* Kathryn Edin & Joanna M. Reed, *Why Don't They Just Get Married? Barriers to Marriage Among the Disadvantaged,* 15 FUTURE OF CHILDREN 117 (Fall 2005).

[175] *See* Bloome & Ang, *supra* note 18. *See also* Pew, *The Decline of Marriage and Rise of New Families,* PEW RESEARCH CENTER (Nov. 18, 2010), https://www.pewresearch.org/social-trends/2010/11/18/the-decl

and an engine of inequality bolsters the case for a regulatory system that reaches dependency relationships outside of marriage.[176] But whether that requires the assimilation of cohabitation to marriage remains the subject of fierce debate. The values and goals that animated the Principles' Reporters—equality, autonomy, fairness, and predictability—are now widely shared. But they lead scholars and policymakers to different conclusions about the shape that the law should take.

ine-of-marriage-and-rise-of-new-families/; JUNE CARBONE & NAOMI R. CAHN, MARRIAGE MARKETS: HOW INEQUALITY IS REMAKING THE AMERICAN FAMILY (2014).

[176] See, e.g., Joslin, supra note 85, at 946.

17

Aggregationists at the Barricades

Assessing the Impact of the Principles of the Law of Aggregate Litigation

Linda S. Mullenix[*]

I. Introduction

More than a decade after publication of the American Law Institute's (ALI's) *Principles of the Law of Aggregate Litigation*,[1] distance provides an opportunity to reflect on the Principles' contributions to the legal community and the improvement of civil justice.

ALI Restatements address legal uncertainty through a restatement of basic legal concepts that tell judges and lawyers what the law is. Restatements are intended to clarify legal uncertainties, simplify unnecessary complexities, and promote changes that will better adapt the law to life. Although Restatements largely are based on statutes and judicial decisions, Restatements also consider situations that courts or legislatures may not yet have considered or addressed.[2]

Unlike Restatements, ALI Principles "are primarily addressed to legislatures, administrative agencies, or private actors. They can, however, be addressed to courts when an area is so new that there is little established law. Principles may suggest best practices for these institutions."[3]

This chapter assesses the *Principles of the Law of Aggregate Litigation* in two respects. First, has the Principles induced legislative bodies to enact provisions, based on those Principles, to govern aggregate litigation? Second, has the Principles assisted judges in their management of aggregate litigation through the project's best practices suggestions? To what extent have judges embraced or eschewed the Principles?

The Principles built upon a long-standing ALI concern with the burgeoning and rapidly changing judicial crisis relating to the resolution of complex litigation. Apart from questions whether the Principles fulfilled its stated purpose, the project also

[*] Morris & Rita Atlas Chair in Advocacy, the University of Texas School of Law.

[1] AMERICAN LAW INSTITUTE, PRINCIPLES OF THE LAW OF AGGREGATE LITIGATION (2010) (hereinafter Principles).

[2] Frequently Asked Questions, https://www.ali.org/publications/frequently-asked-questions/ (last visited June 14, 2021). This statement that appeared in the Frequently Asked Questions as of 2021 no longer appears in the FAQs as of August 2022.

[3] *Id.* Frequently Asked Questions. *See also* AMERICAN LAW INSTITUTE, CAPTURING THE VOICE OF THE AMERICAN LAW INSTITUTE: HANDBOOK FOR ALI REPORTERS AND THOSE WHO REVIEW THEIR WORK, at 4–11 (2005).

Linda S. Mullenix, *Aggregationists at the Barricades* In: *The American Law Institute*. Edited by: Andrew S. Gold and Robert W. Gordon, Oxford University Press. © Oxford University Press 2023. DOI: 10.1093/oso/9780197685341.003.0018

raised fundamental questions about the ALI's role in moving the law in certain directions based on the agendas of non-neutral actors.

On one interpretation, the Principles represented a well-intended effort to provide judges with guidance "where there was little established law." On another, perhaps more problematic view, the Principles represented the desires of actors who, frustrated by some judicial resistance to aggregate litigation, used ALI auspices to change the law in a desired direction.

These questions go to the heart of the ALI's role in guiding attorneys, judges, and rulemaking bodies in furtherance of civil justice. At what point do the scholarly, impartial traditions of ALI undertakings shade into something more problematic and questionable? Whether the liberalization of aggregate procedure is a desirable goal is a normative question that the ALI Principles project assumed but did not address.

This chapter concludes that while the Principles project has left its mark, courts and legislative bodies still have not addressed or resolved many issues the Principles identified. Since publication in 2010, most judges seem comfortable with prevailing jurisprudence and not especially interested in rewriting procedural doctrine governing complex litigation. Although the Principles recommended substantial changes in judicial case management, the Reporters and Advisers intended a more robust embrace of liberalized aggregative procedures. The legal system has only partially moved in this direction. The Principles has not resulted in a root-and-branch revision of aggregate procedure. Rather, implementation of the Principles suggests that a more incremental approach to legal reform has prevailed, and the efforts of the avid aggregationists must await another day.

The fundamental questions concerning aggregate procedure that the ALI undertook in its Principles project may be viewed as even more compelling in 2023 than when the project began. The concerns then that led the ALI to authorize the Principles project in 2005 may be greater today, with the significant shift of aggregate litigation into multidistrict litigation (MDL) auspices during the last decade. More than half the federal docket is now comprised of MDL litigation. Academic commentators have noted, with some concern, the evolution of largely judge-made MDL practices that have no direct basis in the MDL statute or federal rules.

II. Paradigm Shifts: From Individual Autonomy to Aggregate Litigation

The history of complex litigation over the past fifty years reflects paradigm shifts from models of individual litigant autonomy to aggregate procedure. The ALI has played a significant role in identifying issues relating to aggregate litigation and recommending doctrinal and statutory proposals for reform. To appreciate the Principles, it is important to understand the historical context in which the ALI initiated the Principles project.

In undertaking the Principles project in 2004, the ALI was not writing on a clean slate. The ALI previously grappled with problems relating to the resolution of complex litigation in the late 1980s, culminating in the 1994 publication of the Complex Litigation: Statutory Recommendations and Analysis.[4] In a sense, the 2010 Principles

---

[4] AMERICAN LAW INSTITUTE, COMPLEX LITIGATION: STATUTORY RECOMMENDATIONS AND ANALYSIS (1994).

was a successor to the Complex Litigation project. The push for another ALI effort suggested that the earlier effort had not sufficiently addressed the issues that complex litigation raised, or that the complex litigation paradigm had shifted sufficiently since 1994 to merit new attention.

The modern era of aggregate litigation substantially began with the 1966 amendment of the class action Rule 23 of the Federal Rules of Civil Procedure.[5] After the Rule 23 amendment, the first decade of class litigation centered on civil rights actions. A new paradigm of public law and institutional reform litigation seeking injunctive relief dominated the litigation landscape.[6] Cases contesting school desegregation, challenging conditions of confinement in prisons and mental health facilities, and confronting other discriminatory conduct exemplified aggregate litigation in this era.[7]

This period of harnessing the class action to resolve social justice problems engendered judicial and political backlash,[8] and by the late 1970s, the civil rights class litigation of the 1960s had somewhat receded. The late 1970s marked a shift to a new form of complex litigation: mass tort litigation.[9] This first-generation of mass tort litigation included the well-known cases of Agent Orange, the Dalkon Shield, DES, and Bendectin.[10] This paradigm shift, and the problems generated by mass tort litigation, garnered the attention of institutional reform organizations including the ALI.

A. The Origins of the Aggregate Litigation Movement, 1986–1996

Mass toxic substances, defective medical devices, and pharmaceutical cases shared novel litigation issues unlike the 1960s institutional reform cases. Foremost was the sheer volume of mass tort cases filed in federal and state courts. Problems of geographic dispersion, latent injury, indeterminate plaintiffs and defendants, and complex issues of causation and scientific proof characterized this litigation.[11] By the mid-1980s some federal and state judges, confronted with dockets congested with mass tort cases, were seized with a crisis mentality.

---

[5] Fed. R. Civ. P. 23. See CHARLES ALAN WRIGHT, ARTHUR R. MILLER, & MARY KAY KANE, 7A FEDERAL PRACTICE at § 1753 (1986) (1966 revision of Rule 23). See generally Linda S. Mullenix, Reflections of a Recovering Aggregationist, 15 U. NEV. L. REV. 1455 (Winter 2015) (portions adapted of this discussion).

[6] See Abram Chayes, The Role of the Judge in Public Law Litigation, 89 HARV. L. REV. 1281 (1976).

[7] See, e.g., Hart v. Cmty. Sch. Bd. of Educ., 383 F. Supp. 769 (E.D.N.Y. 1974, aff'd, 512 F.2d 37 (2d Cir. 1975) (ordering a integration plan for the Mark Twain Middle School in Coney Island, Brooklyn); Soc'y for the Good Will to Retarded Children, Inc. v. Cuomo, 572 F. Supp. 1300 (E.D.N.Y. 1983) (ordering corrective measures at state institution for mentally handicapped children in violation of constitutional rights), vacated, 737 F.2d 1239 (2d Cir. 1984).

[8] Eisen v. Carlisle and Jacquelin, 417 U.S. 156 (1974) (allocating costs of sending notice to class members on plaintiffs); Zahn v. Int'l Paper Co., 414 U.S. 291 (1973) (requiring that all class members in diversity class actions individually satisfy the jurisdictional amount in controversy requirement).

[9] See e.g., PAUL BRODEUR, OUTRAGEOUS MISCONDUCT: THE ASBESTOS INDUSTRY ON TRIAL (1986); MICHAEL D. GREEN, BENDECTIN AND BIRTH DEFECTS: THE CHALLENGES OF MASS TOXIC SUBSTANCES LITIGATION (1996); MORTON MINTZ, AT ANY COST: CORPORATE GREED, WOMEN, AND THE DALKON SHIELD (1985); PETER H. SCHUCK, AGENT ORANGE ON TRIAL: MASS TOXIC DISASTERS IN THE COURTS (1986); JACK B. WEINSTEIN, INDIVIDUAL JUSTICE IN MASS TORT LITIGATION (1995).

[10] Id.

[11] See AMERICAN LAW INSTITUTE, REPORTER'S STUDY ON ENTERPRISE RESPONSIBILITY FOR PERSONAL INJURY VOL. II, at 389–91 (1991) (defining the salient characteristics of a mass tort action).

B. The ALI Complex Litigation Project (1989–1994)

As judges struggled to manage the mass tort litigation on their dockets, many institutional reform organizations initiated research projects to study the phenomenon and propose recommendations to address the burgeoning problems mass tort cases presented.[12] These efforts typically resulted in modest recommendations marginally suited to assist judges grappling with their mass tort dockets. In addition, Congress declined to address mass tort problems with legislation.

In the face of legislative inaction and limited reform proposals, several federal judges seized the initiative to create management techniques to deal with mass tort litigation. For these aggregationist judges, the prospect of individual relitigation of essentially the same claims became untenable. Several reasons motivated these judges: the need to consolidate similar cases into one aggregate unit, the need to foreclose repetitive relitigation of essentially the same case, and the need to alleviate docket congestion and expedite delivery of relief.

Although a cohort of aggregationist judges emerged, many other federal judges resisted certifying mass tort class actions based on their understanding of class action jurisprudence.[13] By the mid-1980s, aggregationist judges with considerable mass tort dockets became frustrated with judicial and legislative inertia in the face of the growing problems of these cases. Thus, a small coterie of federal district court judges handling substantial mass tort dockets became the first generation of aggregationist judges.

These included Judge Jack Weinstein of the Eastern District of New York, handling the *Agent Orange* litigation; Judge Robert Parker of the Eastern District of Texas, handling personal injury asbestos litigation; Judges Lowell A. Reed and James McGirr Kelly of the Eastern District of Pennsylvania, handling the school asbestos litigation; Judge Carl Rubin of the Southern District of Ohio, handling the *Bendectin* litigation; Judge Sam Pointer of the Southern District of Alabama, handling breast implant cases; Judge Mehrige of the Eastern District of Virginia, handling the *Dalkon Shield*

---

[12] There was a flurry of efforts from the mid-1980s through the early 1990s. *See generally* COMPLEX LITIGATION: STATUTORY RECOMMENDATIONS AND ANALYSIS, *supra* note 4 (studying mass tort phenomenon and recommending changes to the multidistrict litigation statute and a federalized choice-of-law regime); REPORTERS' STUDY ON ENTERPRISE RESPONSIBILITY FOR PERSONAL INJURY, *supra* note 12; AM. BAR ASS'N, REVISED REPORT OF THE ABA COMMISSION ON MASS TORTS (1990), 58 U.S.L.W 2747, 2477 (1990) (studying mass tort litigation and making recommendations concerning handling of litigation arising out of single event disasters or negligent product design); REPORT OF THE FEDERAL COURTS STUDY COMMITTEE (Apr. 2, 1990) (part of the 1988 Judicial Improvements Act; containing three recommendations relating to complex litigation); REPORT OF THE AD HOC COMMITTEE ON ASBESTOS LITIGATION (the Reavley Committee Report March 1991) (recommending that Congress consider a national legislative scheme for resolution of asbestos personal injury claims or new statutory authority for consolidation and collective trials of asbestos cases; also recommending that Advisory Committee on Civil Rules study amendments to Rule 23 to accommodate requirements of mass tort cases); MARK A. PETERSON & MOLLY SELVIN, RESOLUTION OF MASS TORTS: TOWARD A FRAMEWORK FOR EVALUATION OF AGGREGATIVE PROCEDURES vii, at 31–37 (1988).

[13] *See, e.g., In re* Bendectin Prods. Liab. Litig., 749 F.2d 300 (6th Cir. 1984) (repudiating class certification of Bendectin claimants); *In re* N. Dist. of Cal. Dalkon Shield Prod. Liab. Litig., 693 F.2d 847 (9th Cir. 1982) (rejecting class certification of nationwide punitive damage class for Dalkon Shield claimants); Yandle v. PPG Indus., Inc., 65 F.R.D. 566 (E.D. Tex. 1974) (rejection of proposed class of asbestos claimants for failure to satisfy Rule 23(b) predominance and superiority requirements).

litigation; and Judge John Grady of the Northern District of Illinois, handling the tainted blood products cases. In addition, in 1989 Judge William W. Schwarzer of the Northern District of California, another leading judicial aggregationist, became the director of the Federal Judicial Center, where he used his position to exercise considerable influence in promoting and advancing the aggregationist agenda.[14]

The aggregationist judges responded to the mass tort crisis with innovative approaches that centered on expansive use of the class action rule. In 1986 and 1987, the efforts of the aggregationist district court judges were vindicated when the Second, Third, and Fifth Circuits upheld class certification in the *Agent Orange* and asbestos mass tort cases.[15] The procedural advances of 1986–1987 inspired a decade of judicial activism in the class action arena.

Judges experimented with novel multiphase class action trial plans,[16] limited issue classes,[17] statistical damage sampling,[18] and settlement classes.[19] The aggregationist judges also introduced novel roles for judicial surrogates such as magistrates and special masters, greatly expanding their roles.[20] Judges appointed special masters to devise multiphase trial plans,[21] to assess the existence of a limited fund,[22] to assist with

[14] *See* William W Schwarzer, *Structuring Multiclaim Litigation: Should Rule 23 Be Revised?*, 94 MICH. L. REV. 1250 (1996); William W Schwarzer et al., *Judicial Federalism in Action: Coordination of Litigation in State and Federal Courts*, 78 VA. L. REV. 1689 (1992).

[15] *See In re* Agent Orange Prod. Liab. Litig., 818 F.2d 145 (2d Cir. 1987); *In re* Sch. Asbestos Litig., 789 F.2d 996 (3d Cir. 1986); Jenkins v. Raymark Indust., 782 F.2d 486 (5th Cir. 1986).

[16] *See, e.g., In re* Bendectin Prods. Liab. Litig., 857 F.2d 290 (6th Cir. 1988) (trifurcated trial of causation and liability); Jenkins v. Raymark Industries, Inc., 109 F.R.D. 269 (E.D. Tex. 1985), *aff'd*, 782 F.2d 468 (5th Cir. 1986) (reversed bifurcated trial); *In re* Beverly Hills Fire Litig., 695 F.2d 207 (6th Cir. 1982) (bifurcated trial of causation and liability).

[17] *See, e.g.,* Castano v. Am. Tobacco Co., 160 F.R.D. 544 (E.D. La. 1995), *rev'd*, 84 F.3d 734 (5th Cir. 1996) (certification of Rule 23(b)(3) limited issue class in nicotine addiction litigation; certification limited to core liability issues); *Jenkins*, 109 F.R.D. at 269 (limited issue trial of state-of-the-art defense and liability for punitive damages); *Agent Orange*, 818 F.2d at 166–67 (limited issues certification for defense of defendant's status as a government contractor); Payton v. Abbott Labs, 83 F.R.D. 382 (D. Mass 1979), *vacated*, 100 F.R.D. 336 (D. Mass 1983) (limited issues trial in DES litigation). *See generally* MANUAL FOR COMPLEX LITIGATION (FOURTH) at § 22.75 (2004) (Issues Classes).

[18] *See* Hilao v. Estate of Marcos, 103 F.3d 767, 782–87 (9th Cir. 1996) (sampling for discovery and aggregated trial of damages); *In re* Shell Oil Refinery, 136 F.R.D. 588 (E.D. La. 1991), *aff'd sub nom.* Watson v. Shell Oil Co., 979 F.2d 1014 (5th Cir. 1992), *reh'g granted*, 990 F.2d 805 (5th Cir. 1993), *other reh'g*, 53 F3d 663 (5th Cir. 1994) (damage sampling approved; case settled before rehearing); Cimino v. Raymark Indus., Inc., 1989 WL 253889 (E.D. Tex. 1989) (approving three-phase trial with damage sampling), *rev'd*, 151 F.3d 297 (5th Cir. 297 (1998).

[19] *See* Georgine v. Amchem Prods., Inc., 83 F.3d 610 (3d Cir. 1996), *rev'd*, Amchem Prods. Inc. v. Windsor, 521 U.S. 591 (1997) (upholding asbestos settlement class); *In re* Asbestos Litig., 90 F.3d 963 (5th Cir. 1997), *vacated*, 117 S. Ct. 2503 (1997) (upholding asbestos settlement class); *In re* General Motors Corp. Pick-Up Truck Fuel Tank Prods. Liab. Litig., 55 F.3d 768 (3d Cir. 1995) (generally approving concept of settlement class but disapproving application to class claimants for lack of adequate settlement); *In re* A.H. Robins Co., 880 F.2d 709 (4th Cir. 1989) (upholding settlement class in Dalkon Shield litigation).

[20] *See* Fed. R. Civ. P. 53 (special masters).

[21] *See* Jack Ratliff, *Special Master's Report in Cimino v. Raymark Industries, Inc.,* 10 REV. LITIG. 521 (1991) (describing appointment as special master by Judge Robert Parker of the Eastern District of Texas, to create a multiphase trial plan for the resolution of asbestos cases).

[22] *See In re* Joint Eastern and Southern Dist. Asbestos Litig., *In re* Keene Corp., 14 F.3d 726 (2d Cir. 1993) (appointment by Judge Jack Weinstein of special master Marvin E. Frankel to assess the financial assets of the Keene Corporation for the purpose of determining the existence of a limited fund to certify a Rule 23(b)(1)(B) class action).

the *Agent Orange* settlement,[23] to create data bases of claimants' alleged injuries and damages,[24] to supervise all pretrial matters and motions,[25] and to conduct discovery and hearings.[26]

By the mid-1980s, the academic community embraced the aggregationist movement. The evolving mass tort landscape inspired scholarship commenting on, approving of, and suggesting innovative techniques for use of the class action rule.[27] A synergetic relationship developed between the judiciary and the academy, with scholars offering support for innovative initiatives such as statistical damage sampling.[28] Some professors became committed aggregationists when they undertook roles as special masters, expert witnesses,[29] or counsel involved in litigation.[30] Critical reaction to the aggregationist movement largely was muted.[31]

Nonetheless, some federal judges began to question the efforts of their aggregationist colleagues. In 1995–1996, three significant appellate decisions restricted district judges' ability to continue to certify mass tort cases.[32] These decisions set the aggregationist judges in tension with more conventional views on the legitimacy of group litigation. By the mid-1990s, critics began to question whether Rule 23 permitted the aggregationist judges' activism.[33] Some suggested that the judges'

[23] *See In re* Joint E. & S. Dist. Asbestos Litig., 1 29 F.R.D. 434 (E.D. & S.D.N.Y. 1990 (appointment of special master Kenneth Feinberg to assist with settlement negotiations); *see also In re* DES Cases, 142 F.R.D. 58 (S.D.N.Y. 1992) (appointment of special master Kenneth Feinberg to assist with settlement negotiations of DES cases).

[24] *See generally* Francis E. McGovern, *Resolving Mature Mass Tort Litigation*, 69 B.U. L. REV. 659 (1989) (describing role as special master in collecting data in the *Jenkins* asbestos litigation in the Eastern District of Texas); Francis E. McGovern, *Toward a Functional Approach for Managing Complex Litigation*, 53 U. CHI. L. REV. 440 (1986) (describing role as special master for Judge Lambros in Ohio, in conducting data collection for resolution of asbestos claims).

[25] *See* Prudential Ins. Co. of America v. United Gypsum Co., 991 F.2d 1080 (3d Cir. 1993) (upholding appointment of special master Dean Henry G. Manne in asbestos abatement litigation).

[26] *See* Hilao v. Estate of Marcos, 103 F.3d 767 (9th Cir. 1996) (describing the role of special master Sol Schreiber in conducting discovery and holding damages regarding determining damages of claimants in the *Marcos* human rights litigation).

[27] The favorable academic commentary on judicial developments in mass tort litigation between 1986 and 1996 is substantial. *See e.g.*, David Rosenberg, *Class Actions for Mass Torts: Doing Individual Justice by Collective Means*, 62 IND. L.J. 561 (1987); David Rosenberg, *The Casual Connection in Mass Tort Exposure Cases: A "Public Law" Vision of the Tort System*, 97 HARV. L. REV. 849 (1984).

[28] *See, e.g.*, Michael J. Saks & Peter David Blanck, *Justice Improved: The Unrecognized Benefits of Aggregation and Sampling in the Trial of Mass Torts*, 44 STAN. L. REV. 815 (1992), *cited with approval in In re* Chevron U.S.A., Inc., 109 F.3d 1016, 1020 (5th Cir. 1997); *In re* Estate of Ferdinand E. Marcos Hum. Rights Litig., 910 F. Supp. 1460, 1467–68 (D. Haw. 1995) ("The Court finds persuasive the analysis of Professors Saks and Blanck in their discussion that aggregate trials do not violate due process") (footnote omitted).

[29] *See, e.g.*, Professor McGovern, *supra* note 24.

[30] Professor Arthur R. Miller, then a Harvard law professor, argued in favor (on appeal) of class certification of the *School Asbestos* litigation in the Eastern District of Pennsylvania in 1986, and the *Castano* tobacco class litigation in the Eastern District of Louisiana in 1996.

[31] *See, e.g.*, Jay Tidmarsh, *Unattainable Justice: The Form of Complex Litigation and the Limits of Judicial Power*, 60 GEO. WASH. U. L. REV. 1683 (1992); Roger H. Trangsrud, *Mass Trials in Mass Tort Cases, A Dissent*, 1989 U. ILL. L. REV. 69 (1989).

[32] *See* Castano v. The Am. Tobacco Co., 84 F. 3d 734 (5th Cir. 1996) (rejection of class certification in tobacco litigation); *In re* Am. Med. Sys., Inc., 75 F.3d 1069 (6th Cir. 1996) (rejection of class certification in penile implant litigation); *In re* Rhone-Poulenc Rorer, Inc., 51 F.3d 1293 (7th Cir. 1995) (rejection of class certification in tainted blood products litigation).

[33] *See generally* Richard L. Marcus, *They Can't Do That, Can They? Tort Reform Via Rule 23*, 80 CORNELL L. REV. 858 (1995).

initiatives tested the limits of judicial authority under the Rules Enabling Act.[34] The judicial activism inspired the Advisory Committee on Civil Rules to place a reconsideration of Rule 23 on its agenda,[35] although the Advisory Committee held this in abeyance pending the Supreme Court's decisions in two asbestos settlement classes.[36]

By the end of the decade, the Supreme Court substantially limited innovative uses of Rule 23 with repudiation of two comprehensive asbestos settlement classes in *Amchem* and *Ortiz*, chiefly based on issues relating to the lack of adequate representation.[37] In these decisions, the Court held that settlement classes were legitimate but needed to satisfy all the same class certification requirements as litigation classes, except that the proponents need not show that a settlement class was manageable because the action would not be tried. The Court admonished that settlement classes were subject to heightened scrutiny at the time of judicial approval. The Court further indicated that in class actions where claimants had differing interests, adequacy of representation required that the settlement proposal incorporate structural assurances of due process protections to all class members. Finally, Justice David Souter took especial pains in *Ortiz* to admonish federal courts judges against any further "adventurous" use of the class action rule.[38]

C. Federalizing Class Litigation Through the Class Action Fairness Act (2005)

Mass tort class litigation did not become moribund because of the Court's settlement class rulings or the appellate decisions limiting certification of mass tort cases. Instead, class counsel made a strategic choice to abandon federal courts and retreat to more hospitable state courts, which ushered in a decade of burgeoning state class litigation. Plaintiffs' counsel forum-shopped for favorable state venues, which resulted in the emergence of what defense counsel haled into plaintiff-friendly state courts called "judicial hell-holes."[39]

Corporate defendants subjected to disadvantageous state class litigation lobbied Congress to enact the Class Action Fairness Act of 2005 (CAFA).[40] CAFA provided

---

[34] 28 U.S.C. §§ 2071–72.

[35] *See* WORKING PAPERS OF THE ADVISORY COMMITTEE ON CIVIL RULES ON PROPOSED AMENDMENTS TO CIVIL RULE 23, 1, 1–4 (1997); Proposed Rules, 167 F.R.D. 523, 539 (1996) (presenting a proposed addition of new Rule 23(b)(4)); Richard Marcus, *Shoes That Did Not Drop*, 46 U. MICH. J.L. REFORM 637, 642–43 (2013) (noting withdrawal of the proposed Rule 23(b)(4) settlement class proposal and massive negative reaction to proposal).

[36] *See* Ortiz v. Fibreboard Corp., 527 U.S. 815 (1999); Amchem Prods. Inc. v. Windsor, 512 U.S. 591 (1997); *see also* Linda S. Mullenix, *Professor Ed Cooper: Zen Minimalist*, 46 MICH. J. OF L. REF. 661 (Winter 2013) (discussing the Rule 23 proposed amendments in this period and the failure of the Advisory Committee to take any action).

[37] *See supra* note 36.

[38] *Ortiz*, 527 U.S. at 845 ("Finally, if we needed further counsel against adventurous application of Rule 23(b)(1)(B), the Rules Enabling Act and the general doctrine of constitutional avoidance would jointly sound a warning of the serious constitutional concerns that come with any attempt to aggregate individual tort claims on a limited fund rationale.").

[39] So labeled because of the propensity of certain state courts to provide quick and easy class certification, often based on the pleadings alone.

[40] Class Action Fairness Act of 2005, Pub. L. No. 109-2, § 5, 119 Stat. 4 (2005).

defendants with a removal provision to federal court, where defendants could rely on more restrictive federal jurisprudence to defeat class certification.[41] CAFA's enactment substantially succeeded in shifting class litigation back to federal court, federalizing class litigation.

When CAFA diverted state class actions to federal court, plaintiffs' attorneys encountered class action jurisprudence that was increasingly restrictive and exacting.[42] It became increasingly difficult for plaintiffs to plead class actions,[43] obtain class certification,[44] or accomplish settlement classes after *Amchem* and *Ortiz*.[45]

By 2005, then, class action attorneys embraced two driving concepts: a need for reform of Rule 23 and class action jurisprudence, along with an emerging appreciation for non-class techniques for resolving complex disputes. A new generation of reform aggregationists emerged that included the older aggregationists of the 1980s, a new cohort of federal judges, and a younger generation of academics eager to embrace innovative ideas for resolving massive, complex cases both within and without the class action rule.

D. The Transformation of the Aggregate Litigation Movement in the Twenty-First Century (2005–)

Although attorneys continued to pursue traditional class litigation, in the post-CAFA era the resolution of complex litigation shifted to innovative use of the federal multidistrict litigation statute.[46] Congress enacted the MDL statute in 1968 to assist federal judges dealing with that era's electronic products antitrust litigation.[47] MDL procedure had, nonetheless, remained a statutory backwater for much of its history. Throughout the 1980s and 1990s the Judicial Panel on Multidistrict Litigation substantially declined to create mass tort MDLs.[48] This resistance abated in 1991 when the panel finally relented and authorized an asbestos MDL.[49]

---

[41] 28 U.S.C. § 1453 (2012) (CAFA removal provision). CAFA's legislative history clearly suggests that the legislative purpose in enacting CAFA was to provide corporate defendants with an alternative forum to—and some relief from—state court venues that unfairly favored class action plaintiffs.

[42] *In re* Hydrogen Peroxide Antitrust Litig., 552 F.3d 305 (2008) (heightened standards for satisfaction of "rigorous analysis" standard for class certification motions).

[43] Bell Atlantic Corp. v. Twombly, 550 U.S. 544 (2007) (plausible pleading standard for antitrust class actions).

[44] Wal-Mart Stores, Inc. v. Dukes, 131 S. Ct. 2541 (2011).

[45] *See supra* note 36.

[46] 28 U.S.C. § 1407.

[47] *See* Wilson Herndon, *Section 1407 and Antitrust Multidistrict Litigation—The First Decade*, 47 ANTITRUST L.J. 1161 (1979); Stanley J. Levy, *Complex Multidistrict Litigation and the Federal Courts*, 40 FORDHAM L. REV. 41 (1971); John T. McDermott, *The Judicial Panel on Multidistrict Litigation*, 57 F.R.D. 215 (1973).

[48] *In re* A.H. Robins Co., "Dalkon Shield" IUD Products Liab. Litig. (No. II), 610 F. Supp. 1099 (J.P.M.L. 1985); *In re* School Asbestos Prods. Liab. Litig., 606 F. Supp. 713 (J.P.M.L. 1985) (declining to create MDL for school asbestos litigation); *In re* Ortho Pharmaceutical "Lippes Loop" Prods. Liab. Litig., 447 F. Supp. 1073 (J.P.M.L. 1978) (declining to create Lippes Loop MDL); *In re* Asbestos and Asbestos Insulation Material Prods. Liab. Litig., 431 F. Supp. 906 (J.P.M.L. 1977) (declining to create an asbestos MDL).

[49] *In re* Asbestos Prods. Liab. Litig. (No. VI), 771 F. Supp. 415 (J.P.M.L. 1991) (approving creation of an asbestos MDL in the Eastern District of Pennsylvania).

By 2005, plaintiffs' attorneys and defense counsel began to align in interest in supporting a new paradigm for resolving complex litigation. Counsel on both sides of the docket realized that they profitably could use the underutilized MDL statute as a mutually advantageous umbrella to resolve large scale litigation for class and non-class claims resolution. This paradigm gave primacy to settlement negotiation, skipping the problematic processes of class certification at the front end.

Plaintiffs' attorneys and defense counsel had good reasons to endorse a shift to the MDL umbrella for resolving complex litigation. For plaintiffs, accomplishing a class or non-class settlement under MDL auspices meant that plaintiffs might no longer be subjected at the outset of litigation to the heightened, restrictive class certification jurisprudence courts developed in the 1990s. Plaintiffs would not have to hazard expensive class certification proceedings that might result in denial, effectively ending their litigation. By postponing or circumventing class certification until the back end of litigation, plaintiffs could proceed with negotiations, settlement, and their attorney fees.

The use of the MDL umbrella similarly allowed defendants to bypass Rule 23 at the outset of litigation, sparing the considerable expense of class certification proceedings that might place the defendant in a disadvantageous negotiation posture if the court certified a class at the front end of litigation. Defense attorneys appreciated the shift to MDL auspices because it gave them freer rein in negotiating settlements where class agreements would be subject to judicial scrutiny only on the back end, with the concurrence of class counsel with whom they were then aligned in interest. If negotiated on a non-class basis, such agreements and fee arrangements would not be subject to the judicial scrutiny Rule 23(e) required, at all.

The modern era of expansive use of MDL auspices began with the *Vioxx* pharmaceutical litigation, which the Judicial Panel on Multidistrict Litigation approved as an MDL in 2005.[50] The *Vioxx* litigation provided a prototype of the twenty-first century MDL aggregate dispute resolution paradigm.[51] After creation of the *Vioxx* MDL, the attorneys crafted a complex settlement agreement that derived its legitimacy based

---

[50] *In Re* Vioxx Prod. Liab. Litig., 360 F. Supp. 2d 1352 (J.P.M.L. 2005) (148 total actions pending in 41 federal district courts sought to recover from a drug company for damages because of alleged increased health risks caused by taking a certain anti-inflammatory drug. The panel found that "centralization under Section 1407 in the Eastern District of Louisiana will serve the convenience of the parties and witnesses and promote the just and efficient conduct of the litigation." *Id.* at 1353–54. The panel also noted that consolidation was "necessary in order to eliminate duplicative discovery, avoid inconsistent pretrial rulings, and conserve the resources of the parties, their counsel and the judiciary." *Id.* at 1354).

[51] *See* Richard A. Nagareda, *Embedded Aggregation in Civil Litigation*, 95 CORNELL L. REV. 1105, 1111 (2010) ("The Vioxx settlement took the form not of a class action settlement but of a contract between the defendant-manufacturer Merck & Company, Inc. and the small number of law firms within the plaintiffs' bar with large inventories of Vioxx clients. The contract described a grid-like compensation framework for the ultimate cashing out of Vioxx claims, but Vioxx claimants themselves literally were nonparties to that contract. The enforcement mechanism for the deal consisted not of preclusion but of contractual terms whereby each signatory law firm obligated itself to do two things: to recommend the deal to each of its Vioxx clients and—" to the extent permitted by" applicable ethical strictures—to disengage from the representation of any client who might decline the firm's advice to take the deal. Absent a signatory law firm's commitment of its entire Vioxx client inventory to the deal, Merck would have the discretion to reject the firm's enrollment such that none of the firm's clients would be eligible to participate.") (footnotes omitted). Other scholars noted the trend towards aggregate settlements even before the Vioxx settlement. *See generally* Howard M. Erichson, *Informal Aggregation: Procedural and Ethical Implications of Coordination Among Counsel in Related Lawsuits*, 50 DUKE L.J. 381, 386 (2000) (citing prominent examples of aggregate settlements).

on contract principles rather than Rule 23 class action due process requirements.[52] Notwithstanding an outpouring of critical commentary,[53] the *Vioxx* agreement provided a blueprint for subsequent large scale non-class aggregate settlements, including the *Zyprexa* MDL litigation.[54]

The *Vioxx* and *Zyprexa* settlements also inspired the concept of the quasi-class action, intended to ameliorate problems engendered by the lack of judicial oversight of fee arrangements in MDL settlements.[55] Judge Jack Weinstein articulated the concept of the quasi-class action in the context of MDL litigation, where settlements are not subject to Rule 23 judicial approval. Judge Weinstein contended that settlements accomplished under an MDL umbrella had the attributes of a Rule 23 class action, hence these settlements constituted quasi-class actions that conferred authority on the supervising judge to oversee and modify attorney fees.

E. The ALI Principles of the Law of Aggregate Litigation (2004–2010)

The ALI's return to problem of complex litigation in 2004 may be understood as its effort to rethink the problem in the context of the paradigm shift evident at the beginning of the twenty-first century. Several consequences flowed from the federalization of class litigation post-CAFA and the *Vioxx* and *Zyprexa* MDL litigation. MDL proceedings began to proliferate after 2005.[56] If the 1980s and 1990s represented the high point of class litigation and experimentation, then MDL proceedings became the dominant paradigm for complex litigation procedure. The Judicial Panel on Multidistrict Litigation now rapidly authorized MDL designation whenever some product defect, pharmaceutical adverse event, antitrust, securities, or small claims consumer harm resulted in large-scale litigation.

By 2004 when the Principles project got underway, the new generation of aggregationists had a goal to reform class and non-class resolution of complex litigation. The twenty-first century aggregationists focused on Rule 23 amendment and judicial revision of Rule 23 jurisprudence. For twenty-first century aggregationists,

---

[52] *Nagareda, id.*

[53] *See, e.g.,* Sybil L. Dunlop & Steven D. Maloney, *Justice Is Hard, Let's Go Shopping! Trading Justice for Efficiency Under the New Aggregate Settlement Regime,* 83 St. John's L. Rev. 521, 522–527, 54–42 (2009); Howard M. Erichson & Benjamin C. Zipursky, *Consent Versus Closure,* 96 Cornell L. Rev. 265 (2011); Frank M. McClellan, *The Vioxx Litigation: A Critical Look at Trial Tactics, The Tort System, and the Roles of Lawyers in Mass Tort Litigation,* 57 DePaul L. Rev. 509 (Winter 2008). The commentary centered on the role of the attorneys in brokering the settlement and subsequent attorney fee issues.

[54] *See, e.g.,* Samuel Issacharoff, *Private Claims, Aggregate Rights,* 2008 Sup. Ct. Rev. 183; Samuel Issacharoff & Robert H. Klonoff, *The Public Value of Settlement,* 78 Fordham L. Rev. 1177 (2009); David Marcus, *Some Realism About Mass Torts,* 75 U. Chi. L. Rev. 1949 (2008); Charles Silver, *Merging Roles: Mass Tort Lawyers as Agents and Trustees,* 31 Pepp. L. Rev. 301 (2004);

[55] *See generally* Jeremy Hays, *The Quasi-Class Action Model for Limiting Attorneys' Fees in Multidistrict Litigation,* 67 N.Y.U. Ann. Surv. Am. L. 589 (2012); Linda S. Mullenix, *Dubious Doctrines: The Quasi-Class Action,* 80 U. Cin. L. Rev. 389 (2011).

[56] Thomas E. Willging & Emery G. Lee III, *From Class Actions to Multidistrict Consolidations: Aggregate Mass-Tort Litigation After Ortiz,* 58 U. Kan. L. Rev. 775 (2010) (reporting data on the increase in use of MDLs).

Rule 23 and its prevailing restrictive class action jurisprudence were the problems.[57] In their view, the Supreme Court and unsympathetic judges stood in the way of attorneys desiring to resolve their complex cases.[58] More radically, these aggregationists endorsed the developing novel concept of non-class settlements. The aggregationists desired a more flexible, fluid, liberal approach to the resolution of aggregate litigation.

III. The Alignment of Interests in the Principles Project

A. The ALI Voice and the Ethos of Objective Neutrality

The ALI prides itself on speaking with a unique voice that encourages neutral expressions of Restatements and Principles.[59] The ALI Reporter's handbook instructs writers to craft provisions that maintain a neutral perspective: "An ALI document represents the product of a collaborative drafting process and is intended ultimately to reflect the voice of The American Law Institute. It should be drafted objectively, in the third person, and not as if it were a personal essay. Its aim is to describe and analyze the law and its processes in a detached and neutral fashion."[60]

The academic Reporters chosen to draft the Principles as well as several of the project's Advisers were committed to the goal of advancing and improving aggregative procedure.[61] Many had with personal experience litigating complex litigation as consultants or counsel,[62] or in their academic scholarship supporting and advocating on behalf of aggregationist innovations.[63] Moreover, the Reporters collaborated with one another in private sector litigation,[64] as well with attorneys conducting complex

---

[57] *See generally The American Law Institute's New Principles of Aggregate Litigation*, 8(2) J.L., ECON. & POL'Y 183 (2011) (panel discussion of problems the Principles' project intended to address and remedy).

[58] *Id.*

[59] HANDBOOK FOR REPORTERS, *supra* note 2, at 1–2.

[60] *Id.*

[61] Professor Sam Issacharoff, New York University School of Law (Chief Reporter), Professors Robert H. Klonoff, Lewis and Clark Law School, Richard A. Nagareda, Vanderbilt University Law School, and Charles Silver, University of Texas School of Law (Associate Reporters). Professor Klonoff joined as an Adviser in 2005, one year after the launch of the Principles project. Chief Justice John G. Roberts appointed Professor Klonoff to the United States Judicial Conference Advisory Committee on Civil Rules in 2011. Professor Klonoff was appointed for a second three-year term ending in 2017. During his service, Professor Klonoff lobbied for adoption of recommendations of the Principles project.

[62] A critic noted:

> [U]nlike most ALI reporters, Prof. Issacharoff has rather more irons in the fire than the average law professor. He very well-respected, evidently quite in demand, and has quite often represented litigants in court. We can only go on what the computerized searches tell us—but what they tell us is that, for the last five years or so, Prof. Issacharoff seemed to have limited his practice to representing plaintiffs in class actions ... These representations include products liability class actions. They extend to various class actions of other sorts.

See Bexis, *31 (or More) Reasons to Watch ALI's Principles of the Law of Aggregate Litigation*, DRUG & DEVICE LAW (Feb. 8, 2007) (citation to cases omitted).

[63] For the substantial scholarly publications of Professors Issacharoff, Klonoff, Nagareda, and Silver advancing aggregationist views, *see* their SSRN authors' pages. Professor Richard Nagareda died in October 2010.

[64] Professors Issacharoff, Silver, and Klonoff collaborated in mass tort and other class litigation. Professors Issacharoff and Silver, former colleagues at the University of Texas School of Law, primarily worked with plaintiffs' counsel. Professor Silver developed a specialty justifying attorneys' fees. While in private practice

litigation who were members of the ALI Council or Advisers to the Principles.[65] Of the thirty-six Advisers, the overwhelming majority were judges involved in complex litigation who might fairly be described as aggregationists,[66] attorneys repeatedly involved in resolving complex litigation and seeking a more liberalized aggregation model,[67] or law professors who endorsed aggregationist views.[68] Notably absent were critics of evolving aggregationist procedure.[69]

In the same fashion that the ALI prides itself on neutrality, the ALI also prides itself on its processes that encourage expression of competing views. The ALI's draft and comment procedures enable plaintiff and defense counsel, judges, and scholars to express opposing perspectives which theoretically result in balanced statements of law or principles. A fair reading of the Principles, however, suggests that the ALI's vetting procedures only partially tempered the views of its dominant aggregationists, but on many issues and through successive drafts, dissenting views were advocated and duly noted.

as a partner at Jones, Day, Professor Klonoff defended corporate clients in class litigation. After entering academic life, Professor Klonoff switched his allegiances to the plaintiffs' side of the docket. His experience as a defense attorney may well have educated Klonoff to the virtues of aggregate litigation for both plaintiffs and defendants.

[65] Professor Issacharoff frequently was retained by plaintiff's attorney Elizabeth Cabraser and continued to collaborate with her during the entire period of drafting the Principles.

[66] The judicial Advisers who might fairly be described as aggregationists included: Judge Lee H. Rosenthal (S.D. Tex), Chief Judge Anthony J. Scirica (3d Cir.), Shira A. Scheindlin (S.D.N.Y), Judge Jack B. Weinstein (E.D.N.Y.), Judge Diane P. Wood (7th Cir.), and two retired judges: Judge Marina Corodemus (N.J. state court) and Judge Sam C. Pointer, Jr. (N.D. Ala.).

[67] The practicing attorneys who might fairly be described as aggregationists included plaintiffs' attorneys Elizabeth J. Cabraser, Dianne Nast, Joseph F. Rice, and Stephen D. Susman. Practicing attorneys involved in aggregate litigation on behalf of defendants included John H. Beisner, Sheila A. Birnbaum, Sheila Carmody, and Jeffrey E. Stone. Adviser Kenneth Feinberg served as the Special Master for administration of the World Trade Center Victims' Compensation Fund and many other such funds and might be fairly characterized as favoring models of aggregate claims resolution. A number of the project's advisers were, or came to be, involved in the federal rulemaking process.

[68] Professor Deborah R. Hensler, Stanford Law School, May Kay Kane, University of California, Hastings College of Law, Professor David F. Levi, Duke University School of Law, Arthur R. Miller, New York University School of Law, Geoffrey P. Miller, New York University School of Law, Judith Resnik, Yale Law School and William B. Rubenstein, Harvard Law School. Professor Arthur Miller and Mary Kay Kane were Reporters on the 1994 ALI *Complex Litigation* project.

[69] *E.g.*, Professor Martin H. Redish, Northwestern Pritzker School of Law. Professor Redish's considerable scholarship critical of aggregate litigation includes: WHOLESALE JUSTICE: CONSTITUTIONAL DEMOCRACY AND THE PROBLEM OF THE MODERN CLASS ACTION (2009); *Rethinking the Theory of the Class Action: The Risks and Rewards of Capitalistic Socialism in the Litigation Process*, 64 EMORY L.J. 451 (2014); *Cy Pres Relief and the Pathologies of the Modern Class Action: A Normative and Empirical Analysis*, 62 FLA. L. REV. 617 (2010); *The Class Action as Political Theory*, 85 WASH. & LEE U. L. REV. 753 (2007); *Class Actions, Litigant Autonomy, and the Foundations of Procedural Due Process*, 95 CAL. L. REV. 1573(2007); *Settlement Class Actions, the Case-or-Controversy Requirement, and the Nature of the Adjudicatory Process*, 73 U. CHI. L. REV. 545 (2006); *Class Actions and the Democratic Difficulty: Rethinking the Intersection of Private Litigation and Public Goals*, 2003 U. CHIC. LEGAL FORUM 71 (2003). A sometime critic of aggregate procedure who served as an Adviser to the Principles was Professor Howard M. Erichson Fordham University School of Law. *See supra* notes 51 and 53.

B. Understanding the Alignment of Party Interests in Complex Litigation

A contextual understanding of the relative posture of litigants involved in complex litigation assists in appreciating the Principles and the controversies it engendered. Litigants may pursue complex litigation through class or non-class procedure, which may unfold in different modalities that affect attorney decisions. The divergent strategic postures of adversarial parties illuminate motivations for several of the Principles' proposals.

First, if litigants pursued an aggregate resolution of their dispute, they might accomplish this through a litigated class or a settlement class. If class counsel sought a litigation class, then defense counsel would vigorously contest certification of the proposed action. By 2004, plaintiffs' attorneys chafed at and sought relief from restrictive Rule 23 class action jurisprudence that hampered their ability to obtain class certification. Plaintiffs' lawyers and academic critics viewed Rule 23 constraints as an impediment to aggregate litigation. They sought relief from Rule 23 requirements for adequacy, predominance of common questions, superiority, limited issues classes, and choice of law. They desired relief from judicial rejection of mass tort class actions under Rule 23(b)(2) or (b)(3).

Defense counsel, on the contrary, had little interest in liberalizing Rule 23 or modifying prevailing jurisprudence which favored defense objections to class certification. If, however, a court certified a class action, defense interests then reverted to a settlement posture, in which defense interests aligned with plaintiffs' in negotiating a settlement and obtaining judicial support for a negotiated agreement.

Second, if litigants pursued resolution through a settlement class, this frequently postponed the certification decision until after the parties reached agreement. At this point plaintiff and defense counsel were aligned in interest in obtaining judicial approval of their deal. By 2004, plaintiffs' attorneys and defense attorneys were aligned in interest in supporting a more relaxed application of Rule 23 requirements needed to certify a class at the back end of the litigation.

Third, if litigants pursued resolution through a non-class settlement under an MDL umbrella, plaintiffs and defense counsel were aligned in interest in accomplishing a non-class settlement free from judicial management, oversight, and doctrinal constraints. By 2004, with the emergence of MDLs as a growing forum for resolution of complex litigation, plaintiff and defense counsel recognized their common interests in creating a model to accommodate these goals.

By 2004, the Reporters, judges, and attorneys involved in aggregate litigation were aligned in interest, centered on two broad concepts: (1) liberalizing class action procedure to enable more facile settlement negotiation and judicial approval, and (2) lessening judicial case management while increasing attorney control over complex settlements. Thus, where litigation adversaries in the ordinary course might counterbalance the most extreme tendencies in each other, to an unusual extent the Reporters' and Advisers' aggregationist goals instead encouraged collaboration in support of a certain model of aggregate procedure.

The Reporters' desire to accomplish a wholesale root-and-branch revision of class and non-class aggregate litigation was manifested in Chief Reporter Samuel

Issacharoff's first memorandum to the Advisory group in August 2004, when he announced that the project would introduce "the discomfort of all the Reporters (Professors Nagareda and Silver, in addition to me) with the current inquiry into predominance and superiority found in the current Federal Rules of Civil Procedure."[70] After several contentious early drafts, critics noted that there appeared to be only one guiding principle to the Principles, which was "to change the law in numerous ways to facilitate the creation of ever more class actions and other forms of mass litigation."[71] This included "consciously breaking with the prevailing terminology found in almost all class action jurisprudence, dispensing with predominance and superiority and the rest of the analytical framework used by courts."[72]

While the multilayered ALI vetting process tempered some of the Reporters' initial aggregationist goals, the final Principles represented an impressive example of nimble crafting to nudge the law in a more favorable direction. While acknowledging disputes in current jurisprudence, the Reporters often showed a marked preference for rules supporting aggregation. Where existing law relied on formalism, the Reporters rejected recognized categories and instead articulated a more "functional" approach to achieve aggregation. The Principles most inventive contribution, however, was creation of new terminology to provide broad leeway to assist in aggregationist ends.

C. Overview of the Final Principles Work Product

By 2004, the aggregationists had distilled their reform efforts to a universe of a dozen prime targets, which became the focus of the Principles project. These included: (1) endorsement of liberalized, expansive judicial consideration of adequacy requirements, (2) restriction or reversal of the Supreme Court holdings in *Amchem* and *Ortiz*, (3) restriction or reversal of the Second Circuit's post-judgment collateral attack holdings in *Stephenson v. Dow Chemical*, (4) endorsement of restrictive intersystem preclusion of duplicative class litigation, (5) endorsement of liberalized, expansive judicial application of predominance requirements, including expansive views of choice-of-law issues, (6) endorsement of liberalized, expansive use of the limited issue class, (7) endorsement of a presumption of settlement fairness, (8) endorsement of unified criteria to assess settlement fairness, (9) endorsement of appropriate use of cy pres relief, (10) endorsement of contractual non-class settlement agreements, (11) endorsement of alternatives to the aggregate settlement rule, and (12) endorsement of limited judicial review for non-class aggregate settlements.

The Principles set forth thirty-five sections. The introductory provisions broadly defined aggregate litigation and general principles. Subsequent sections addressed granular topics such as the handling of common issues, substantive law, and preclusion as constraints on aggregation, judicial case management, and class and non-class settlements. Much like Restatements, each section set forth black-letter principles citing

[70] Reporter's Memorandum at 1 (Aug. 9, 2004).
[71] Bexis, *supra* note 62.
[72] *Id.*

judicial authority and illustrative examples. Each section concluded with Reporters' Notes that assessed of the effect of proposed modifications on current law.[73]

IV. Implementation of the Principles Through Rulemaking

The Reporters' Notes indicated whether the Principles might be implemented through legislative or rulemaking initiatives, judicial interpretations, or without change to existing law. Consistent with an intended reform of existing law, many of the Principles embodied a pro-aggregation approach that favored plaintiffs in class litigation practice, and plaintiffs and defense counsel in settlement settings. As will be seen, the Advisory Committee on Civil Rules adopted some of the Principles recommendations chiefly regarding class settlements, but very few courts embraced the Principles' core proposals. In addition, some of the proposals most likely would have been adopted without encouragement from the project.

The Principles' chief impact has been through Rule 23 amendments. In 2018, the Advisory Committee on Civil Rules adopted several recommendations regarding class action settlements and notice. Legislative bodies, however, have not adopted other proposed statutory or rulemaking recommendations.

A. 2018 Amendment of Rule 23: Principles Adopted

1. Protecting Claimants' Due Process Rights Through Notice and Opportunity to Be Excluded from the Aggregate Proceeding

An emerging issue in class action procedure centered on the extent to which claimants in a class action might be bound by the preclusive effect of any determination made on an aggregate basis. The Principles addressed this issue by providing claimants an opportunity to avoid preclusive effects by excluding themselves from an aggregate proceeding.[74] To accomplish this goal, the Principles noted that implementation of this due process protection would require an amendment to Rule 23(c)(2)(B) to add language requiring "appropriate notice."[75]

In 2018, the Advisory Committee on Civil Rules amended Rule 23(c)(2)(B) to add language requiring "appropriate notice."[76]

---

[73] Principles §§ 1.01–1.05 contain no discussion of the effect on current law (definitions and general principles). The Reporters noted that courts would not necessarily be required to make changes to existing rule language to implement certain sections. *See* Principles § 2.03 (relationship of liability and remedy issue); § 2.12 (adjudication plan for aggregation); § 3.09 (court-designated special officers, special masters, experts, and other adjuncts, except to the extent that a particular jurisdiction does not authorize the types of court-appointed adjuncts described); § 3.15 (recognition that class and non-class settlements distinct as to warrant different treatment); and § 3.16 (definition of non-class aggregate settlement).

[74] Principles § 2.07(a)(3).

[75] Principles § 2.07 Reporters' Notes ("The reference to 'appropriate notice' in subsection (a)(3), however, would require amendment of the existing Rule 23(c)(2)(B), insofar as it categorically requires 'individual notice to all members who can be identified through reasonable notice.'").

[76] Fed. R. Civ. P. 23(c)(2)(B).

2. Judicial Approval of Pre-Certification Class Settlements

A contested area of class action jurisprudence concerned judicial approval of class settlements prior to class certification. The Principles proposed that judges be given limited oversight to scrutinize pre-certification settlements.[77] The Reporters noted that such a requirement of judicial approval of precertification settlements with class representatives would require a change in federal law.[78]

In 2018, the Advisory Committee on Civil Rules amended Rule 23(e) to add language to indicate that the Rule 23(e) requirements extended to pre-certification classes proposed to be certified for settlement.[79] The rule was amended to require that parties must provide the court with information sufficient to enable the court to determine whether to give notice of the proposal to the class.[80]

3. Judicial Review of Fairness of a Class Settlement

The Principles noted that federal courts applied a wide array of factors for evaluating a settlement, but rarely indicated the significance that judges should give to each factor. To bring order to judicial review of settlements the Principles in Section 3.05 recommended four factors to guide this evaluation.[81] The Principles set out a black-letter rule that in reviewing a proposed settlement, a court should not apply any presumption that the settlement is fair and reasonable.[82] The Reporters indicated that a rule change would be necessary to implement these recommendations.[83]

In 2018, the Advisory Committee on Civil Rules amended Rule 23(e) to incorporate the four factors that the Principles recommended.[84] The Advisory Committee did not adopt the Principles' settlement recommendations wholesale, however. The Advisory Committee did not adopt the principle that the failure to satisfy any of the criteria rendered a settlement unfair, the rule against the presumption of settlement fairness, or judicial authority to withhold approval until the parties amended a settlement in a manner the court specified.

A few courts have cited Section 3.05 for the settlement factors courts should consider when evaluating the fairness of a settlement.[85]

---

[77] Principles § 3.02(b).

[78] Principles § 3.02 Reporters' Notes. The Reporters pointed to Rule 23(e)(1)(A) as the rule provision concerning approval, dismissal, or compromise of class actions.

[79] Fed. R. Civ. P. 23(e) (introductory paragraph). The introductory paragraph was amended "to make explicit that its procedural requirements apply in instances in which the court has not certified a class at the time a proposed settlement is presented to the court." Advisory Committee's Note to 2018 Amendment.

[80] Fed. R. Civ. P. 23(e)(1)(A).

[81] Principles §3.05 cmt. b.

[82] Principles §3.05(b). The Reporters noted that some courts have adopted a presumption that a settlement is fair and reasonable under some circumstances but indicated that such a presumption may not be warranted in all cases. Principles §3.05 cmt. c.

[83] Principles §3.05 Reporters' Notes, Effect on current law.

[84] Fed. R. Civ. P. 23(e)(2).

[85] Halley v. Honeywell Int'l, Inc., 861 F.3d 481, 489 n.8 (3d Cir. 2017) (citing § 3.05); Hill v. State Street Corp., 794 F.3d 227, 229 (1st Cir. 2015) (citing § 3.05 cmt. a); In re Trans Union Corp. Privacy Litig., 741 F.3d 811, 813 (7th Cir. 2014) (citing § 3.05 9a) & cmt. b); Reyes v. Bakery and Confectionery Union and Indus. Int'l Pension Fund, 281 F. Supp. 3d 833, 848 (N.D. Cal. 2017) (citing § 3.05 cmt a); In re Heartland Payment Sys., Inc. Customer Data Security Breach Litig., 851 F. Supp. 2d 1040, 1063 (S.D. Tex. 2012) (citing § 3.05 cmt. b); In re New Motor Vehicles Canadian Export Antitrust Litig., 800 F. Supp. 2d 328, 332 (D. Maine 2011) (citing § 3.05(c)).

4. Interlocutory Appeal of Orders Rejecting Settlements

Rule 23(f) provides litigants with an interlocutory appeal of orders certifying or denying class certification. Rule 23(f) did not address the availability of interlocutory appeals of orders rejecting settlements on fairness grounds. To remedy this situation, the Principles authorized a discretionary interlocutory appeal from orders definitively and finally rejecting a class action settlement.[86] The Reporters suggested that no new statute was necessary to implement this type of appellate review.[87] In 2018, the Advisory Committee on Civil Rules amended Rule 23(f) to clarify that approval of a settlement class before final judicial approval did not entitle litigants to an interlocutory appeal at that time; such appeal must await the court's final decision to certify the class at the time of settlement approval.[88]

B. Statutory or Rule Recommendations Not Enacted

1. Interlocutory Review of Merits Determination of Common Issue in a Class Action

The Principles endorsed a more relaxed embrace of certification of limited issue classes. To accomplish this, the Principles noted that legislation would be required to offer litigants an opportunity to pursue an interlocutory appeal when a court made a merits determination of a common or limited issue in a class action.[89] This appeal would be in addition to the existing interlocutory appeal provision in Rule 23(f). The Advisory Committee has not amended Rule 23 to add such a provision to Rule 23(f).

2. Vocabulary of Indivisible v. Divisible Remedies

The Reporters' Notes to Section 2.04 suggested that it might be helpful to achieve more liberalized certification of Rule 23(b)(1)(A) and (b)(2) classes by amending the text of Rule 23 to incorporate the vocabulary of divisible and indivisible remedies.[90] The Advisory Committee has not amended Rule 23 to adopt the language of divisible and indivisible remedies to characterize Rule 23(b)(1)(A) and (b)(2) class categories.

3. Authorization for an Opt-In Class

Section 2.10 of the Principles provided judicial authority to create opt-in mechanisms for voluntary claim aggregation by affirmative claimant assent.[91] Existing class action jurisprudence authorized only opt-out class actions and does not approve of opt-in classes. The Reporters rejected the Second Circuit's decision in *Kern v. Siemens Corp.*,[92] in which the court repudiated certification of a Rule 23 opt-in class that

---

[86] Principles § 3.12 cmt. a.

[87] Principles § 3.12 Reporters' Notes, Effect on current law.

[88] Fed. R. Civ. P. 23(f), Advisory Committee Note to 2018 Amendments. The reference in amended Rule 23(f) to "an order under Rule 23(e)(1)" embraces the whole notice determination, which in (e)(1)(B)(ii) reflects a determination whether the court will likely be able to certify the class.

[89] Reporter's Notes § 2.02, Effect on current Law. *See also* Principles § 2.09.

[90] Reporters' Notes § 2.04, Effect on current Law (but noting that but that amendment of Rule 23 was not necessary for courts to implement the approach of Section 2.04).

[91] Principles § 2.10.

[92] 393 F.3d 120 (2d Cir. 2004).

included foreign claimants of a ski train accident in Kaprun, Austria.[93] The Reporters noted that Section 2.10 was based on the expectation that aggregation by consent would remain exceptional.[94] Section 2.10 reflects the Reporters' preference for an expansive reach of aggregate litigation that would permit litigation embracing foreign claimants that would not otherwise be suitable for certification under existing Rule 23 jurisprudence.

The Reporters noted that if the Second Circuit was correct in repudiating an opt-in class under Rule 23, then a rule amendment might be necessary to effectuate authorization of an opt-in class.[95] The Advisory Committee on Civil Rules has not amended Rule 23 to provide for an opt-in right.

4. Preliminary Approval Proposed Settlements and Notice Requirements

The Principles eschewed decisions giving rise to a presumption that a settlement is fair, adequate, and reasonable if the court gives preliminary approval of a settlement prior to a final hearing.[96] Instead, the Principles endorsed use of preliminary approval to identify and address problems relating to notice or substantive defects in a proposed settlement.[97] The *Reporters* indicated this would require a change in existing law where courts require preliminary approval before notice to class members.[98] The Principles also required that judges make findings of fact and conclusions of law on the record in approving or rejecting a settlement.[99] The Reporters noted this proposal goes beyond current cases and would require a change to existing practice.[100] The Advisory Committee on Civil Rules did not amend Rule 23 to provide guidance for preliminary approval of settlements based on Principles' recommendations.

The Principles provided judges leeway not to order individual notice in cases where likely recovery to class members was too small to justify the costs of providing notice.[101] The Principles stated: "Individual notice should be presumptively viewed by a court as less important when the claims are likely too small to be pursued individually in the absence of a class action."[102] This provision rejected the *Eisen* requirement of individual notice, even in small-claims cases.[103] Instead, the Reporters suggested that under the Due Process Clause, it was more important to balance the benefit of notice against the cost of providing notice.[104] The Reporters indicated this would require a change in procedural rules where a jurisdiction's rules mandated individual notice regardless of the size of individual class members' claims.[105]

---

[93] *In re* Ski Train Fire in Kaprun, Austria on Nov. 11, 2000, 220 F.R.D. 195 (S.D.N.Y. 2003).

[94] Principles § 2.10 cmt. a.

[95] Reporters' Notes § 2.10, Effect on current law. ("On the assumption that the Kern court properly read the current Rule 23, rule amendment would suffice for this purpose.").

[96] Principles § 3.03 cmt. a. *See* Hochstadt v. Boston Scientific Corp., 708 F. Supp. 2d 95, 97 (D. Mass. 2010) (citing § 3.03 cmt. a. and replacing the term "approval" with "review").

[97] Principles § 2.10.

[98] Principles § 3.02 Reporters' Notes, Effect on current law.

[99] Principles § 3.03(b).

[100] Principles § 3.03 Reporters' Notes, Effect on current law.

[101] Principles § 3.04(b).

[102] *Id.*

[103] Principles § 3.04 cmt. a (citing *Eisen, supra* note 8, at 173).

[104] Principles § 3.04 cmt. a.

[105] Principles § 3.04 Reporters' Notes, Effect on current law.

The relaxation of notice requirements for small-claims class actions embodied a pro-aggregationist position, encouraging small claims litigation free from potential constraints of onerous notice costs for plaintiffs or defendants. The Advisory Committee on Civil Rules has not relaxed the notice requirement for small-claims class actions.

5. Standard for Approval of a Settlement Class

During the 1990s a major controversy centered on the standard for judicial approval of a Rule 23(b)(3) settlement class.[106] The Supreme Court resolved this controversy in its 1997 *Amchem* decision, holding that (b)(3) settlement classes needed to satisfy all the same criteria for certification as litigation classes, except for the manageability requirement.[107] Additionally, the Court held that intraclass conflicts of interest among class members defeated the Rule 23(a) requirement for adequacy. The *Amchem* and *Ortiz* holdings concerning the adequacy requirement provided the basis for the Second Circuit decision that permitted a collateral attack of the *Agent Orange* settlement in *Stephenson v. Dow Chemical Co.*[108]

The aggregationists believed the courts had wrongly decided *Amchem*, *Ortiz*, and *Stephenson*. Repudiation of these decisions became a prime target for reform because the aggregationists believed these decisions hampered the liberal approval of settlement classes. To this end, the Principles set forth a provision that permitted approval of a Rule 23(b)(3) settlement classes based on three criteria: (1) an ascertainable class, (2) simple commonality, and (3) numerosity.[109] The Principles eliminated the predominance requirement.[110] The Reporters noted that a move away from *Amchem*'s interpretation of Rule 23 would potentially require a rule change.[111]

The Advisory Committee on Civil Rules in 2018 did not adopt the recommendations for a more liberalized standard for judicial approval of settlement classes. The Reporters' Notes pointed out that the Advisory Committee had considered creation of relaxed standards for approval of a settlement class after *Amchem* but had rejected this approach.[112]

6. Cy Pres Relief

By 2004, courts disagreed on the legitimacy of cy pres relief where monetary distribution to class members was not viable on an individual basis. Among courts that permitted cy pres relief, jurisdictions disagreed concerning the circumstances in which cy pres was appropriate. Thus, some courts held that cy pres relief was permissible only when class members were too difficult to identify, funds were too small to distribute economically, or unclaimed funds existed.[113] In Section 3.07 the Reporters

---

[106] *Amchem, supra* note 36.

[107] *Id.*

[108] 273 F.3d 249, 259–61 (citing *Amchem* and Ortiz, *supra* note 36).

[109] Principles § 3.06(b).

[110] *Id.* ("The court need not conclude that common issues predominate over individual issues."). The Principles added a provision that required settlement proponents demonstrate that a mandatory settlement class embrace claimants with indivisible remedies. Principles § 3.06(c), and that statements by settlement proponents not be used subsequently against them if a court did not approve a settlement. § 3.06(d).

[111] Principles § 3.06 Reporters' Notes, Effect on current law.

[112] Principles § 3.06 Reporters' Notes cmt. a.

[113] Principles § 3.07 Reporters' Notes cmt. b.

approved cy pres relief and set forth criteria to assist courts in determining when cy pres relief was appropriate.[114] The Reporters noted that in some jurisdictions a rule change might be necessary to establish the precise circumstances in which cy pres awards might be allowed.[115] Much to the Reporters' surprise, Section 3.07 became the most cited section of the Principles,[116] with many courts ratifying the Principles' approach to cy pres relief in certain circumstances.[117] The Advisory Committee on Civil Rules in amending Rule 23 did not adopt a provision concerning cy pres relief.

7. Second Opt-Out

The Principles provided class members a second opportunity to opt-out of a settlement where the settlement terms had not been revealed until after the initial period for opting out. This provision also mandated that a court make an on-the-record finding of its reasons if the court declined to allow a second opt-out.[118] The Reporters indicated that this provision would require adoption of a new procedural rule creating a presumption in favor of a second opt-out and requiring on-the-record findings where a second opt-out was not provided to class members.[119] Although Rule 23 has provided for a second-opt out since 2003,[120] the current rule creates no presumption in favor of a second opt-out nor does it require on-the-record findings if a judge declines to order a second opt-out.

V. Implementation of the Principles Through Judicial Decisions

In many instances the Reporters suggested that courts could implement the Principles through judicial interpretation without the need for legislative enactment. Since the first Preliminary Draft in August 2004[121] through July 2021 courts have cited the Principles sixty times. This includes eight citations before the 2010 publication,[122] thirty-eight federal appellate and district court citations after the 2010 publication,[123] eight unreported federal district opinions,[124] and six state court

---

[114] Principles § 3.07(a)–(c).
[115] Principles § 3.07 Reporters Notes, Effect on current law.
[116] See The American Law Institute's New Principles of Aggregate Litigation, supra note 57, at 199–202.
[117] See infra notes 142–162 and accompanying text.
[118] Principles § 3.11.
[119] Principles § 3.11 Reporters' Notes, Effect on current law.
[120] Fed. R. Civ. P. 23(e)(4).
[121] Principles, Preliminary Draft No. 1 (Aug. 2004).
[122] See infra notes 127–133 and accompanying text.
[123] Id.
[124] Thomas v. Byrd, 2017 WL 945770, *2 (E.D. Ark. March 10, 2017) (approving §3.07 cy pres provision); In re Domestic Drywall Antitrust Litig., 2017 WL 370099, *17 (E.D. Pa. Aug. 24, 2017) (citing §§ 2.02–05 criteria for certifying limited issue class, applying factors and declining to certify); In re TRS Recovery Services Inc. and Telecheck Services Inc., Fair Debt Collection Practices Act (FDCA) Litig., 2016 WL 543137, *5 n.13 (D. Maine Feb. 10, 2015) (noting First Circuit's approval of presumption of settlement fairness following adequate discovery and arm's length negotiation; criticizing presumption citing to ALI discussion in § 3.05(c) and cmt. (c)); Parker v. Asbestos Processing, LLC, 2015 WL 127930, *10, 11, n.9 (D.S.C. Jan. 8, 2015) (discussing §§ 2.02–05 discussing competing views of issue class certification on circuits with regard to predominance, noting test adopted by Third Circuit based on ALI principles); In re Profgraf Antitrust Litig., 2014 WL 4745954, *2 (D. Mass. June 10, 2014) (§§ 2.02–05, canvassing circuit

cases.[125] If the unreported and state decisions are removed from this survey, federal appellate and district courts have cited the Principles forty-six times.

A. Pre-Publication Citation to Draft Principles

Judicial pre-publication citation to Principles drafts provides insight into the sections that would gain judicial attention after final approval. This small cohort of cases cited with approval the Principles' endorsement of a liberalized view of the predominance requirement,[126] the Principles' articulation of factors to govern certification of a limited issue class,[127] and the Principles' recommendation for a second opt-out provision where settlement terms changed after a first opt-out period.[128] In three cases courts agreed with the Principles' approach to the use of cy pres remedies[129]—the single principle that subsequently garnered the most judicial attention after final publication.[130] One court cited the Principles in a footnote for the proposition that a denial of class certification should give rise to a rebuttable presumption against the same aggregate treatment in other courts as a matter of comity.[131]

Perhaps the most interesting citation to the Principles occurred early in the drafting process. Judge Jack Weinstein, a Principles' Adviser, used his supervision of the *Zyprexa* litigation in 2006 to express dissatisfaction with the Second Circuit's

---

court views on limited issues classes and predominance requirement, noting Third Circuit reliance on ALI principles); Scovil v. FedEx Ground Package Sys., Inc., 2014 WL 1057079, *1 n.1 (citing with disapproval of § 3.05 presumption of settlement fairness); *In re* Checking Account Overdraft Litig. MDL No. 2036, 2014 WL 12557836, *4 (S.D. Fla. Apr. 1, 2014) (citing § 3.07 for ALI approach to cy pres); Wallace v. Powell, 2013 WL 2042369, *11 (M.D. Pa. May 14, 2013) (citing §§ 2.02–05 on limited issue class and Third Circuit approval of ALI approach; certifying limited issue class).

[125] Karton v. ARI Design & Constr., Inc., 61 Cal. App.5th 734, 744, 276 Cal. Rptr. 46, 54 (Ct. App. 2021) (citing § 3.13 cmt. b for proposition that percentage fee is superior approach to attorney fees); Lafitte v. Robert Half Int'l Inc., 1 Cal. 5th 480, 376 P.3d 672 (Cal. 2016) (same); *In re* Complaint as to the Conduct of Daniel J. Gatti, 356 Or. 32, 48, 49, 333 Pac. Rptr. 994, 1003, 1004 (Or. S. Ct. 2014) (citing § 3.16, adopting ALI definition of aggregate settlement definition and applying to find aggregate settlement); Highland Homes Ltd. v. Texas, 448 S.W.3d 403, 407 (Tex. 2014) (citing § 3.07 cmt. b (2010) for ALI principles relating to cy pres relief but noting that Texas has not had occasion to address the issue; no cy pres issue raised in the case); Pearson v. Philip Morris, Inc., 257 Or. App. 106, 167, 306 P.3d 665, 700 (Or. Ct. App. 2013) (citing § 2.02 on purpose of predominance requirement); Tilzer v. David, Bethune & Jones, 204 P.3d 617, 628–29 (Kan. 2009) (citing § 3.16 definition of aggregate settlement and applying definition to find aggregate settlement).

[126] D.S. v. New York City Dept. of Educ., 255 F.R.D. 59, 73 (E.D.N.Y 2008) (opinion by Judge Jack Weinstein, Principles Adviser).

[127] Hohider v. United Parcel Serv., Inc., 574 F.3d 169, 201–202 (3d Cir. 2009) (opinion by Chief Judge Anthony Scirica, Principles Adviser).

[128] Tardiff v. Knox County, 247 F.R.D. 225, 230 n.6 (D. Me 2008).

[129] *In re* Pharmaceutical Indus. Average Wholesale Price Litig., 582 F.3d 24, 35 (1st Cir. 2009) (citing draft § 3.7, located as final § 3.08); Masters v. Wilhelmina, 473 F.3d 423, 436 (2d Cir. 2007) (citing draft § 3.7, located as final § 3.08 and approving use of cy pres where distribution of benefits not economically feasible); and *In re* Tyco Int'l, Ltd., 535 F. Supp. 2d 249, 262 (D.N.H. 2007) (citing draft § 3.7, located as final § 3.08).

[130] *See infra* notes 142–162 and accompanying text.

[131] *In re* New Motor Vehicles Canadian Export Antitrust Litig., 609 F. Supp. 2d 104, 106 n.5 (citing § 2.11(a), but noting that there was no decision in the case whether the class was certifiable, and the First Circuit left the question open).

Stephenson decision permitting collateral attack on a prior settlement.[132] His citation to the Principles supports the thesis that limiting or overturning the *Stephenson* decision was a major target of the aggregationists' agenda.

B. Preclusive Effect of Intersystem Class Certification

Litigants can pursue class litigation in federal and state court arising out of the same claims. A preclusion problem arises where a litigant might defeat class certification in federal court but be subject to class certification for the same claims in state court. The Reporters rejected the Seventh Circuit's view that issue preclusion applies to a prior denial of class certification[133] and stated that the Seventh Circuit's conclusion represented a minority view among federal circuits.[134]

To avoid intersystem preclusion, the Reporters in Section 2.11 set forth a principle that a court's denial of class certification should raise a rebuttable presumption against the same aggregate treatment in another court as a matter of comity (and not strict preclusion rules).[135] The Reporters indicated that this approach could be implemented by judicial interpretation without the need for a rule change.[136]

By couching the rebuttable presumption based on comity rather than the strict issue preclusion rules, the Reporters skewed their preference for plaintiffs' class litigation to proceed in subsequent forums free from the formal preclusive constraint of a prior denial of class certification elsewhere.

In 2011, the Supreme Court cited Section 2.11 in a footnote to its decision in *Smith v. Bayer*,[137] for the proposition that a denial of class certification in one jurisdiction could not bind proposed class members in another jurisdiction.[138] In 2015, the Ninth Circuit adopted Section 2.11, holding that where a district court faced an earlier denial of class certification in a different district court, the second court should adopt a rebuttable presumption of the correctness of the earlier decision based on comity principles.[139] A New Mexico district court cited Section 2.11 in a footnote for the proposition that res judicata does not apply to a denial of class certification.[140]

---

[132] *In re* Zyprexa, 467 F. Supp. 2d at 269 (citing § 3.14).

[133] *In re* Bridgestone/Firestone, Inc. Tires Prods. Liab. Litig., 333 F.3d 763 (7th Cir. 2003).

[134] Principles § 2.11. cmt b.

[135] Principles § 2.11.

[136] Reporters' Notes § 2.11, Effect on current law.

[137] 564 U.S. 227, 317 n.11, 131 S. Ct. 2368, 2381 n.11 (2011). The Court noted that the RESTATEMENT (SECOND) OF JUDGMENTS § 41(1), at 393 (198) and 18A Wright & Miller, FEDERAL PRACTICE AND PROCEDURE § 445, at 457–58 supported this same proposition.

[138] *Id.*

[139] Baker v. Microsoft Corp., 797 F.3d 607, 616–17, 621 (9th Cir. 2015); *see also* Baker v. Microsoft Corp., 851 F. Supp. 2d 1274, 1279 (W.D. Wash. 2012) (citing § 2.11 and deferring to prior certification denial).

[140] Anderson v. WPX Energy Production, LLC, 297 F.R.D. 632 n.3 (D.N.M. 2014) (also citing Smith v. Bayer Corp.).

C. Cy Pres Relief

To the Reporters' surprise, the Principles' proposal for cy pres relief in Section 3.07 generated the most judicial attention and partial endorsement.[141] Seventeen of the forty-six cases citing the Principles engaged with the Section 3.07 provision for cy pres relief. Section 3.07 embodied a policy choice favoring cy pres relief but would presume further distributions to participating class members unless subsequent distribution to individual class members involved small amounts that would render distribution infeasible, or if "other specific reasons exist that would make such further distributions impossible or unfair."[142]

For a court to order and approve a cy pres remedy, the parties recommending cy pres relief carried the burden to demonstrate by convincing evidence that the parties had no prior "significant meaningful relationship" or affiliations with the intended cy pres recipients. Section 3.07 addressed the question of cy pres recipients and set forth a "reasonable approximation" standard.[143] Thus, recipients of cy pres funds should be those "whose interests reasonably approximate those being pursued by the class," who "can be identified after thorough investigation and analysis."[144] If there were no such recipients, then a court might approve a recipient who did not reasonably approximate class interests.[145]

The First, Third, Seventh, and Eighth Circuits approved several Section 3.07 provisions for cy pres relief, although with some qualifications.[146] Not all federal judges have been enamored of the Reporters' preferences for cy pres relief or the way it should be implemented. Thus, Third Circuit Judge Joseph F. Weis dissented from cy pres relief in preference for further distributions to class members. In contrast to the Section 3.07 provisions, Judge Weis indicated that he would redistribute any remaining funds to class members where possible or have funds escheat to the government.[147]

Fifth Circuit Judge Patrick Higginbotham held that a district court abused its discretion in ordering unused funds to be distributed to charities instead of distributing them to a subclass of individuals who had suffered injuries.[148] He indicated that

---

[141] *See supra* note 117.

[142] Principles § 3.07(b) and § 3.07 cmt. b. *Cf. In re* Lupron Marketing and Sales Prac. Litig., 677 F.3d 21, 32 (1st Cir. 2012) (rejecting presumption in favor of cy pres relief in all cases.)

[143] Principles § 3.07(c), cmt. c.

[144] *Id.*

[145] *Id.*

[146] *In re* Lupron Marketing, *supra; In Re* Baby Products Antitrust Litig., 708 F.3d 163, 172–73, 179–181 (3d Cir. 2013); Holtzman v. Turza, 728 F.3d 682, 689–90 (7th Cir. 2013); Marshall v. National Football League, 787 F.3d 502, 509, 521–22 (8th Cir. 2015) (noting that class action settlement did not involve a cy pres distribution); *In re* BankAmerica Corp. Securities Litig., 775 F.3d 1060, 1063–1066 (8th Cir. 2015) (citing § 3.07 extensively with approval, but disapproving cy pres award in case because chosen recipient not "next best recipient to receive unclaimed funds"); *In Re* Google Referrer Header Privacy Litig., 869 F.3d 737, 744, 747 (9th Cir. 2017) (noting that the Ninth Circuit had not yet adopted § 3.07; further noting that no circuit had yet adopted § 3.07 cmt. b's "significant prior relationship" reference); Nachshin v. AOL LLC, 663 F.3d 1034, 1039 n.2 (9th Cir. 2011) (noting § 3.07(c) recommendation to choose cy pres recipient with reasonably approximate interest to class members).

[147] *In re* Pet Food Prods. Liab. Litig., 629 F.3d 333, 359, 363 n.4 (3d Cir. 2010) (dissenting from § 3.07).

[148] Klier v. Elf Atochem North America, Inc., 658 F.3d 468, 474, 479 n.32 (5th Cir. 2011) (citing § 3.07 and concluding that "[w] the terms of a settlement are sufficiently clear, or, more accurately insufficient to overcome the presumption that the settlement provides for further distribution to class members, there is no occasion for charitable gifts, and cy pres must remain offstage.")

settlement fund proceeds generated by the value of class members' claims belonged solely to class members.[149] And Fifth Circuit Judge Carolyn Dineen King rejected cy pres relief in the *Katrina Canal Breach* litigation, where notice to class members failed to apprise them of the possibility that they might not receive any direct benefit from the settlement.[150]

Eighth Circuit Judge Diana E. Murphy dissented from her court's rejection of a cy pres award where the majority determined the district court abused its discretion in selecting a charity that was not the "next best recipient" under Section 3.07 standards. Judge Murphy contended that the court had not yet adopted Section 3.07 and the litigants had not argued it in the district court.[151] Acknowledging that the First, Third, and Fifth Circuits had endorsed Section 3.07, Judge Murphy concluded that the district court had not abused its discretion in choosing the cy pres recipient.[152]

Ninth Circuit Judge M. Margaret McKeown noted that although the circuit had yet to adopt Section 3.07, it joined the Eighth Circuit in embracing a preference for direct distribution to class members of excess funds in lieu of cy pres relief.[153] In addressing the Section 3.07 "significant prior relationship" test for determining a cy pres recipient, the court noted that this suggestion was unsupported by any illustration, case law, or other authority.[154] Judge John Clifford Wallace, concurring and dissenting in part, recommended that the Ninth Circuit adopt Section 3.07 with the burden on class counsel through sworn testimony to show that prior affiliations played no role in the selection of a cy pres recipient.[155]

Several district courts also have cited Section 3.07 provisions with approval.[156] However, some district courts have flagged potential problems with the ALI's approach, especially where cy pres is the exclusive remedy and class members will receive no relief at all.[157] The court's identification of the problem of a "cy pres only" class was prescient, and the Supreme Court has signaled its willingness to address this issue.[158]

---

[149] *Id.* 658 F.3d at 470 n.32 (citing Principles § 3.07(b)).

[150] *In re* Katrina Canal Breaches Litig., 628 F.3d 185, 198 (5th Cir. 2010) (citing Principles § 3.07 cmt. b.).

[151] *In re* BankAmerica Corp. Securities Litig., 775 F.3d at 1068.

[152] *Id.* 775 F.3d at 1071–72.

[153] *In re* Google Referrer Header Privacy Litig., 869 F.3d at 744 n.5 (but holding that district court did not abuse its discretion in approving the cy pres recipients; *see* 869 F.3d at 747).

[154] *Id.* 869 F.3d at 744 n.4 (referencing § 307 cmt b). The court carefully noted that it was not suggesting that a party's prior relationship with a cy pres recipient could not be a stumbling block to a settlement approval. *See* 869 F.3d at 747).

[155] *Id.* 869 F.3d at 749.

[156] *See In re* Polyurethane Foam Antitrust Litig., 178 F. Supp. 3d 621, 623–24 (N.D. Ohio 2016) (citing § 3.07 cmt b); *In re* Polyurethane Foam Antitrust Litig., 168 F. Supp. 3d 985, 1005 (N.D. Ohio 2016) (same); *In re* Heartland Payment Sys., 851 F. Supp. 2d at 1067 n.18 (S.D. Tex. 2012) (citing § 3.07 and approving cy pres provision in settlement); *In re* Checking Account Overdraft Litig., 830 F. Supp. 2d 1330, 1355–56 (S.D. Fla. 2011) (citing § 3.07 cmt. b and approving cy pres provision); Securities and Exchange Commission v. Bear Stearns & Co., Inc., 626 F. Supp. 2d 402, 416 (S.D.N.Y. 2009) (citing Draft No. 2 of the PRINCIPLES OF THE LAW OF AGGREGATE LITIGATION § 3.07 and approving the cy pres distribution).

[157] Graff v. United Collection Bureau, Inc., 132 F. Supp. 3d 470, 484–85 (E.D.N.Y. 2016).

[158] *See* Frank v. Goas, 586 U.S. ___, 139 S. Ct. 1041, 203 L. Ed. 2d 404 (2019) (per curiam; not deciding cy pres issue but remanding case for further proceedings to determine litigant standing).

D. Attorney Fees

Courts determine class counsel fees based on one of three methodologies: (1) a percentage of the common benefit fund, (2) a lodestar approach, or (3) a combined methodology of a percentage with a lodestar cross-check. The common benefit approach awards the plaintiffs' attorneys a percentage of the common benefit fund they have accomplished for the class in the settlement. The lodestar approach tasks the judge with reviewing the attorneys' hourly billing rate and hours expended, to determine a fee lodestar. The lodestar is then adjusted upward by a multiplier. In jurisdictions applying a hybrid approach, the court first determines a common fund percentage fee, but cross-checks that percentage by analyzing the fees under a lodestar approach.

In Section 3.13 the Principles rejected cases preferring the lodestar approach solely or that allowed a court to choose between the lodestar or percentage methods.[159] Instead, the Principles endorsed an attorney fee regime based on the percentage approach, but permitted judges to use a lodestar cross-check under certain circumstances.[160] The Principles also required that attorney fees be based on the actual value of the judgment or settlement to class claimants[161] and rejected cases that awarded attorney fees based on the total fund without regard to the actual value of the judgment or settlement.[162]

Only two district courts have referred to Section 3.13's discussion of methodologies for determining attorney fees.[163]

E. Applicable Law in Certifying Class Litigation

An impediment to certifying diversity class actions arises from the presence of multiple laws that would defeat the predominance requirement for class certification under Rule 23(b)(3). The Principles recognized five basic approaches to evaluating choice-of-law problems in relation to class certification, endorsed three, and rejected two.[164] The Reporters indicated that its proposals for assessing choice-of-law problems could be accomplished through judicial decision, with no need for a national choice-of-law statute.[165]

---

[159] Principles § 3.13 Reporters' Notes, Effect on current law.

[160] Principles § 3.13(a), (b); cmt. b. *Cf.* Fed. R. Civ. P. 23(h) (attorney fees) (no preference for percentage or lodestar approach).

[161] Principles § 3.13(a).

[162] Principles § 3.13, Reporters' Notes, Effect on current law. Other provisions relating to the timing of setting attorney fees and submission of accounting records are within judicial discretion and would require not change in existing law. *See* Principles § 3.13(d) and (e); Reporters' Notes § 3.13, Effect on current law.

[163] *In re* Heartland Payment Sys., 851 F. Supp. at 1073 n.25 (extensive quotation of § 3.13; adopting percentage method with lodestar cross check); Schulte v. Fifth Third Bank, 805 F. Supp. 2d 560, 599 (N.D. Ill. 2011) (citing § 3.13).

[164] Principles §2.05 cmt. b.

[165] Reporter's Notes § 2.05 cmt. b, noting that the proposal of a national choice-of-law statute was accomplished in the ALI's COMPLEX LITIGATION: STATUTORY RECOMMENDATIONS AND ANALYSIS §§ 6.01–6.08.

The Principles approach in Section 2.05 provided more judicial latitude in certifying classes with applicable law issues.[166] Thus, the Principles eschewed traditional doctrinal analysis in favor of a more open-ended methodology. The traditional, doctrinal approach to the applicable law problem in relation to the predominance requirement asked the judge to assess whether the differences among state laws created so many individual issues so as to defeat the predominance of common questions. Typically, in most class actions where state law differed (for example, state tort law principles), the presence of these differences would defeat the predominance requirement as well as certification of a Rule 23(b)(3) damage class action.

The Principles Reporters found the traditional approach to the applicable law problem in relation to satisfaction of the predominance issue to be too constricting and too often used to defeat class certification. Instead, the Reporters suggested that in litigation involving multiple bodies of law, "[t]he real question for the court is not a formal one (whether multiple bodies of law apply to the claims for which aggregate treatment is sought) but, rather, a *functional* one (whether bodies of law are relevantly the same in functional content)."[167]

In providing a framework for analysis of choice-of-law issues based not on formal law but rather on an opaque concept of functionality, the Principles endorsed an aggregationist solution that favored plaintiffs. Thus, Section 2.05 potentially relieved plaintiffs from the strict doctrinal approaches most federal courts used when confronted with applicable law issues and provided leeway for certifying such class litigation.

One district court, in a proposed multistate class action, cited Section 2.05 to support creation of subclasses to address variations in state law.[168]

VI. Implementation of Principles Requiring No Change to Existing Law

In many sections the Reporters suggested that courts might accomplish their recommendations with no change to existing law because prevailing jurisprudence already encompassed their proposals. In some instances, the Reporters shaded their views in favor of aggregationist outcomes. Consistent with the view that existing law already embraced some of the project's recommendations, a few courts have cited the Principles for such unremarkable propositions as the need for adequate class representatives and their fiduciary duties.[169] Because courts already employ various

---

[166] Reporter's Notes § 2.05, Effect on current law ("The approach of this Section is designed to be quite modest in its description of broadly recognized situations in which choice-of-law analysis does not counsel against aggregate treatment of common issues.").

[167] Principles § 2.05 cmt. b.

[168] *In re* Checking Account Overdraft Litig., 307 F.R.D. 630, 646, 652 (S.D. Fla. 2015) (citing § 2.05(b)); *In re* Checking Account Overdraft Litig., 286 F.R.D. 645, 656 (S.D. Fla. 2012) (same); *In re* Checking Account Overdraft Litig., 281 F.R.D. 667, 681 (S.D. Fla. 2012) (same).

[169] Monk v. Wilkie, 30 Vet. App. Rptr. 167, 196 (Ct. App. Vet. Claims 2018) (citing § 1.04 cmt. a and § 1.05 cmt. c); LaRocque v. TRS Recovery Services, Inc., 285 F.R.D. 139, 152 n.28 (D. Me. 2012) (citing § 1.05 cmt. 1).

judicial adjuncts, courts have not cited the Principles' uncontroversial provision relating to the use of adjuncts.[170]

A. Certification of Limited Issues Classes

By the early twenty-first century, federal courts disagreed concerning the proper certification of limited issues classes under Rule 23(c)(4)(a). The core issue concerned whether courts could certify limited issues classes that did not independently satisfy the Rule 23(b)(3) predominance requirement. For example, plaintiffs' attorneys could propose a class limited to determination of the liability issue, leaving apart any consideration of damage issues (where individual damages of class claimants would defeat predominance). Because the attorneys so narrowly proposed a class certification limited to one or more issues in the litigation, this approach avoided the problem that other issues such as damages would defeat the predominance requirement. Some appellate courts, most notably the Fifth Circuit, rejected the view that limited issue classes could be certified without meeting the predominance requirement, arguing that proposed limited issue classes could not accomplish an end run around the Rule 23 predominance requirement.[171]

In Section 2.02, the Reporters canvassed competing jurisprudence and embraced the trend to permit certification without a predominance requirement. The Principles incorporated language from decisions that set forth multiple conditions to certify a limited issue class. The Principles permitted certification where it would "materially advance the resolution of multiple civil claims by addressing the core of the dispute in a manner superior to other realistic procedural alternatives, so as to generate significant judicial efficiencies."[172]

The Reporters' Notes stated that the approach in Section 2.02 was "designed to lend precision to the inquiry presently undertaken by the courts within the vocabulary of existing procedural law."[173] In so doing, the Principles eschewed the competing view that required proposed limited issues classes to satisfy the Rule 23(b)(3) predominance requirement. While Section 2.02 gave aggregationists a victory that allowed for a more liberalized certification of limited issues classes, the Reporters' Notes also recognized that courts generally had not certified issues classes in products liability and personal injury classes.[174]

A few courts have referred to Section 2.02 and its standards in certifying or refusing to certify limited issues classes,[175] but the Principles recasting of the criteria for

---

[170] Principles § 3.09. The Principles set forth an array of court-designated special officers, masters, experts, and other adjuncts that courts might utilize in managing complex litigation, which the Reporters generally endorsed.

[171] *Castano*, 84 F.3d at note 21 ("A district court cannot manufacture predominance through the nimble use of subdivision (c)(4).").

[172] Principles § 2.02(a).

[173] Reporter's Notes § 2.02, Effect on current law.

[174] Reporter's Notes § 2.03, Effect on current law. *See* Gates v. Rohm and Haas Company, 655 F.3d 255, 269 (3rd Cir. 2011) (citing § 2.04 Reporters' Notes cmt. b; declining to certify plaintiffs' proposed common evidence and trial plan in proving medical necessity on aggregate basis).

[175] *Gates*, at 273 (citing §§ 2.02–05 factors courts should consider when evaluating whether to certify a limited issue class); *cf.* Martin V. Behr Dayton Thermal Prods. LLC, 896 F.3d 405, 412 (6th Cir. 2018) (noting

approving limited issues classes has not, to date, gained widespread traction among federal courts.

B. Certification of Hybrid Rule 23(b)(1)(A), (B), and (b)(2) Class Actions

By 2004, most federal courts resisted certifying certain proposed class actions under Rule 23(b)(1)(A), Rule 23(b)(1)(B), and (b)(2), commonly understood as mandatory, non-opt-out classes. Typically, these proposed actions sought injunctive relief based in equity. Where a proposed (b)(2) injunctive class also entailed damages, such as in some employment discrimination litigation, courts typically refused to certify the class, except in narrow instances where damages could be shown to be incidental to the injunctive relief. In addition, many courts refused to certify proposed mass tort medical monitoring classes under Rule 23(b)(1)(A) or (b)(2) because medical monitoring classes could not be used to obtain damages as an end run around the Rule 23(b)(3) predominance requirements, or where the class members lacked "cohesiveness."[176]

The Reporters' solution to the impediments to certifying Rule 23(b)(1)(A) and (b)(2) classes was simply to define the problem away in Section 2.04. Thus, eschewing the classic distinctions between law and equity-based class actions, the Reporters instead created a new vocabulary of divisible and indivisible remedies to guide analysis.[177] In addition, the Reporters changed existing law to afford litigants a right to exit the class where the action entailed a damages remedy.[178]

The Reporters suggested that "[t]he vocabulary of this Section—focused on the functional distinction between divisible and indivisible relief rather than on the formal categories of law and equity—was designed to explicate with greater precision the approach taken in recent years by courts under the auspices of Rules 23(b)(1)(A) and (b)(2)."[179] The Principles then substituted its rhetorical preference to liberalize certification of Rule 23(b)(1)(A) and (b)(2) class actions, replacing existing doctrinal jurisprudence and eroding doctrinal distinctions among existing class categories.

Finally, the Reporters noted that it might be helpful to achieve this end by amending Rule 23 to incorporate the vocabulary of divisible and indivisible remedies, but that amendment of Rule 23 was not necessary for courts to implement the approach of Section 2.04.[180]

Third Circuit's endorsement of Principles' functional approach to analyzing limited issue class certification); Smith-Brown v. ULTA Beauty, Inc., 335 F.R.D. 521, 535 (N.D. Ill. 2020) (citing § 2.02(a)(1) and declining to certify plaintiffs' proposed limited issue class); *In re* Suboxone Antitrust Litig., 421 F. Supp. 3d 12, 71 (E.D. Pa. 2019) (citing § 2.02(e) and *Gates*); Clark v. The Prudential Ins. Co. of America, 940 F. Supp. 2d 186, 191–92 n.2) (D.N.J. 2013) (same); *In re* Heartland Payment Sys., 851 F. at 1052 (citing § 2.02 cmt. a).

[176] *See* Barnes v. The American Tobacco Co., 161 F.3d 127 (3d Cir. 1998).
[177] Principles § 2.04.
[178] Principles § 2.04(c).
[179] Reporter's Note § 2.04, Effect on current law.
[180] *Id. See supra* note 91. The Advisory Committee on Civil Rules in 2018 did not adopt this terminology.

Since 2010, courts have not engaged with Section 2.04 or its proposal for courts to reconsider class certification of proposed (b)(1)(A) and (b)(2) classes using a functional approach. Instead, the only reference to Section 2.04 has been in support of refusal to certify a medical monitoring class because of the presence of individualized issues, relying on established jurisprudence.[181]

C. Preclusive Effect of Class Certification Decisions and Collateral Attack for Lack of Adequacy

A major target of the aggregationists was the Second Circuit's decision in *Stephenson v. Dow Chemical*[182] and the application of the Rule 23(a) adequacy requirement for class certification. In *Stephenson*, the court upheld a collateral attack by Vietnam veterans challenging the preclusive effect of a prior *Agent Orange* settlement because of a lack of adequate representation at class certification. The court permitted the collateral attack because of conflicts of interest between currently injured and future claimants.

The Reporters contended that *Stephenson* was wrongly decided because the court relied on conflicts engendered by the settlement agreement and not on class conflicts present at the time of certification.[183] The Reporters disapproved of *Stephenson* because it undermined the finality of class settlements, rendering agreements vulnerable to collateral attack on adequacy grounds years after settlement approval.[184] Section 2.07 called for a limitation of *Stephenson* by redefining adequacy to narrowly embrace a duty of loyalty of attorneys and claimants to avoid "structural conflicts of interest" at class certification.[185]

Although the Reporters' root-and-branch attempt to repudiate the *Stephenson* decision recast class preclusion doctrine, the Reporters nonetheless characterized their provisions as merely describing "the emerging understanding of due process in the context of aggregate litigation."[186] In attacking *Stephenson*, the Reporters stated that the *Stephenson* decision had not "garnered much following in subsequent case law."[187] The Reporters utilized *Stephenson* to more broadly criticize existing judicial decisions construing the Rule 23(a) adequacy requirement.[188]

---

[181] *Gates*, at 269 (citing § 2.04 Reporters' Notes cmt. b).

[182] 273 F.3d 249 (2d Cir. 2001), *aff'd by equally divided Court*, 539 U.S. 111 (2003).

[183] Reporters' Notes § 2.07 cmt. d.

[184] The Reporters were candid in their rejection of the *Stephenson* decision: "The treatment of loyalty as a precondition to aggregate treatment in subsection (a)(1) disapproves of the analysis of class representation in Stephenson v. Dow Chemical ..." Reporters Notes Reporters' Note § 2.07 cmt. d.

[185] Principles §2.07(a); Reporters' Notes § 2.07 cmt. e. *See also* Principles § 3.14(a)(2), (b) (disallowing collateral post-judgment challenges to settlement, except in limited defined circumstances governed by § 2.07); Principles § 3.14 Reporters' Notes, Effect on current law.

[186] Reporters' Notes § 2.07, Effect on current Law.

[187] Reporters' Notes § 2.07 cmt. d.

[188] *Id.* stating that "... case law on class actions in recent years increasingly reflects that the concept of adequate representation increasingly reflects that the concept of adequate representation has been overloaded with multiple, varying meanings, not all of which carry the same significance for post-judgment challenges to a class judgment."

Since 2010, no court has cited Section 2.07 concerning intersystem preclusion and collateral attack of prior class decisions.

D. Settlement of Future Claims

The problem of settlement of future claimants in mass tort litigation was a focal point in the Supreme Court's *Amchem* and *Ortiz* decisions.[189] The Court repudiated two nationwide global settlements of asbestos claims because of findings that the class representatives had not adequately represented future claimants in the litigation and settlement negotiations.[190] The Court's analysis centered on the intraclass conflict between presently injured and future claimants who had not manifested injury at the time of settlement. The Court indicated that intraclass conflicts should be addressed by structural assurances of due process[191] but did not specify what structural assurances would satisfy this requirement.

The aggregationists criticized the Court's treatment of the future claimant problem in *Amchem* and *Ortiz* as "overly formalistic,"[192] noting that many settlements were denied approval because of the parties' failure to create subclasses of litigants with differing interests. The aggregationists complained that the requirement to create subclasses frequently increased cost of litigation and magnified difficulties of accomplishing settlement in the presence of numerous represented parties. The aggregationists favored a more liberalized approach to the approval of settlement classes, centering analysis on a settlement's avoidance of "structural conflicts of interest" among class members.[193] In Section 3.10, the Reporters suggested that their proposal was consistent with "emerging trends in mass-harm settlement," but was nonetheless "inconsistent with some of the more formalistic readings of *Amchem* and *Ortiz*."[194] Again, the Reporters skewed their views of an emerging trend to comport with their goal of nudging courts towards a more relaxed acceptance of settlement classes with differing claimant interests.

Since 2010, no courts have cited Section 3.10.

E. Rejection of Proposed Settlements and the Role of Objectors

The Principles endorsed existing class action jurisprudence that provided objectors with compensation when their objections materially improved a settlement.[195] The Reporters noted that this provision reflected existing authority and would not require a rule change.[196] However, a gap in the law existed regarding objector compensation

---

[189] *See supra* note 37.
[190] *Id.*
[191] *Amchem*, 521 U.S. at 627; *Ortiz*, 527 at 852–56.
[192] Principles § 3.10 Reporters' Notes, Effect on current law.
[193] Principles § 3.10(b) and (c).
[194] Principles § 3.10 Reporters' Notes, Effect on current law.
[195] Principles § 3.08(a).
[196] Principles § 3.08 Reporters' Notes, Effect on current law.

when objectors successfully convinced a court to reject a settlement in its entirety. In Section 3.08, the Principles provided a mechanism for awarding objectors fees in this circumstance.[197] The Reporters suggested that this provision arguably would not require a rule change.[198]

The Reporters also set forth provisions to sanction class counsel and defense attorneys who misrepresented the benefits of settlements, or objectors pressing insubstantial objections that were not reasonably advanced for the purpose of improving or rejecting a settlement.[199] The Reporters indicated that these sanctioning provisions might require a rule change in jurisdictions whose rules did not cover these situations.

A court has cited Section 3.08 once, declining to sanction an objector for filing an alleged frivolous appeal.[200]

VII. Radical Reform: Non-Class Aggregate Settlements

The Principles most controversial provisions centered on proposals to govern non-class aggregate settlements.[201] When the Principles project began in 2004, courts had scant experience with non-class aggregate settlements accomplished under an MDL umbrella. By 2010, the use of MDL procedure for aggregating claims was burgeoning along with non-class aggregate settlements.[202] The Reporters favored development of non-class settlements grounded in contractual principles rather than the due process representational principles undergirding traditional class litigation. The new non-class aggregate settlement paradigm invested substantial power in the attorneys litigating these cases, and substantially less judicial authority in judges overseeing MDL litigation. The Reporters therefore attempted to set forth liberal principles that endorsed and supported this procedural development.

The *Principles* defined non-class aggregate settlements in terms of the interdependency of claimants with a potential for conflict of interests among individual claimants. Unlike class litigation where class claimants are represented by class counsel who have a fiduciary duty to all class claimants, claimants in a non-class aggregate settlement are represented individually by many attorneys. The claimants may have claims that vary in liability theories or damages or other remedies. In such an aggregate settlement situation, all claimants must be informed of potential or actual conflicts and consent to the aggregate settlement. The Principles therefore identified the central

---

[197] Principles § 3.08(b).

[198] Principles § 3.08 Reporters' Notes, Effect on current law. In 2018, the Advisory Committee amended Rule 23(e) to require judicial approval of any payment or other consideration for forgoing or withdrawing an objection or appeal. *See* Fed. R. Civ. P. 23(e)(5)(B).

[199] Principles § 3.08(c) and (d).

[200] Hill v. State Street Corp., 794 F.3d 227, 231 (1st Cir. 2015) (citing Principles § 3.08 cmt. c).

[201] Principles §§ 3.15–3.18. Section 3.14 recognizes that the difference between class and non-class treatment of settlement classes is sufficiently distinct as to warrant different treatment. *See* § 3.14 Reporters' Notes, Effect on current law.

[202] More than half the federal civil docket cases are now consolidated in MDLs. *See* United States Panel on Multidistrict Litigation, Calendar Year Statistics, https://www.jpml.uscourts.gov (collecting data) (last visited on July 19, 2021).

problem of non-class settlements as an ethical problem in the context of the aggregate settlement rule.[203]

The Principles' most controversial proposals set forth alternative circumstances in which non-class aggregate settlements could bind individual claimants, entailing different concepts of consent. Thus, claimants would be bound if each were permitted to review the settlements of all others subject to the agreement, or to the formula by which proceeds would be divided among claimants.[204] In addition, claimants would be bound if each participating claimant entered into a written agreement to be bound to a substantial-majority vote of all claimants concerning an aggregate settlement proposal.[205] Finally, claimants to a non-class aggregate settlement were provided with only limited avenues for judicial review.[206]

Legislative or rulemaking bodies would need to set forth the criteria for settlements that could be resolved by substantial majority vote of claimants.[207] The Reporters acknowledged that their proposals departed from existing rules of professional responsibility in all jurisdictions.[208] The Reporters included a proposed model rule for how the provisions for non-class aggregate settlements might be codified.[209]

The Principles' provisions for non-class aggregate settlements were interesting for what the Reporters did not address. They did not address issues relating to judicial management over non-class settlements conducted under MDL auspices, including judicial authority to make interim rulings or orders. The Reporters did not address issues relating to attorney fee arrangements in non-class aggregate settlements or judicial authority over non-class aggregate fee arrangements. Nor did they address issues relating to appointment of counsel in non-class aggregate settings, or judicial authority to approve or disapprove a non-class aggregate settlement.

Since 2010, the use of MDL procedure to aggregate cases has increased dramatically.[210] It is difficult to assess non-class aggregate settlements because such settlements typically do not result in published records. In a relatively small number of instances non-class settlements have garnered attention when there are disputes relating to attorney fees.[211] Thus, it is difficult to assess the extent to which the Principles' proposals for non-class aggregate litigation have gained traction in federal or state courts. To date, only one court has cited these provisions.[212] This does not mean, however, that actors in arena are not conducting their aggregate litigation in conformity with and reliance on the Principles.

---

[203] Principles § 3.15 cmt. a; *see also* Sullivan v. DB Investments, Inc., 667 F.3d 273, 340 n.11 (3d Cir. 2011) (citing § 3.13cmt a; cmt e); Principles § 3.16 cmt. a (noting all jurisdictions have adopted the aggregate settlement rule as requiring the consent of all clients to an aggregate settlement).

[204] Principles § 3.17(a). The Reporters suggested that this proposal comported with the ethical codes of all states, with the modification of how informed consent would be obtained. Principles § 3.17(a) Reporters' Notes, Effect on current law.

[205] Principles § 3.17(b)–(e). The Reporters note that the proposed vote of a substantial majority rule would require a change to the professional responsibility rules of all jurisdictions.

[206] Principles § 3.18. This proposal was subject to enactment of the proposals in § 3.17(b)–(e).

[207] Principles § 3.17(c); § 3.17 Reporters' Notes, Effect on current law.

[208] Principles § 3.17 Reporters' Notes, Effect on current law

[209] Principles §3.18 Reporters' Notes, Effect on current law.

[210] *See supra* note 205.

[211] *See, e.g., Zyprexa, supra* note 133.

[212] Sullivan v. DB Investments, Inc., 667 F.3d 273, 340 n.11 (3d Cir. 2011) (J. Scirica concurring).

VIII. Conclusion

Ironically, perhaps, the *Principles of the Law of Aggregate Litigation* was outdated when finally published in 2010. In carefully crafting the Principles during the first decade of the twenty-first century, the Reporters were fighting the last complex litigation wars of the 1990s. Thus, the Reporters devoted most of their efforts to recast Rule 23 class action litigation and jurisprudence. The Principles project largely eluded the most significant development in complex litigation after 2010: the MDL domination of the federal civil docket and developing problems with the resolution of aggregate litigation under MDL auspices.

One may understand the Principles' lack of attention to MDL litigation because the earliest MDLs to draw attention emerged after the ALI launched the Principles project in 2004. Moreover, during the five years drafting the Principles, the troubling issues relating to MDL aggregate litigation were nascent and developing slowly. However, aware of this background, parallel universe of MDL litigation, the Reporters envisioned and proposed a non-class aggregate settlement regime and tacked a few novel controversial sections to the end of the Principles.

The impact of the Principles can be judged on its own terms. On the one hand, the project accomplished its greatest success with the 2018 Rule 23 amendments that codified recommendations relating to class action settlement and notice. On the other hand, it took the Advisory Committee on Civil Rules eight years after publication of the Principles to amend Rule 23. Moreover, the 2018 Rule 23 amendments can hardly be characterized as a radical rewriting of the class action rule.

Never known as a radical institution forging revolutionary changes to federal procedure, the Advisory Committee proceeded as it always has done: glacially, deliberately, and conservatively. Thus, consistent with prior practice, the Advisory Committee merely codified what by 2018 had become well-received practice. One might question whether the Advisory Committee independently might have amended Rule 23 in the same fashion, without the nudge from the Principles' project. Notably, the Advisory Committee did not amend Rule 23 to effectuate the Principles' more radical suggestions, including recasting the terminology of class action procedure or changing existing class categories. The Advisory Committee did not create an opt-in class, and again declined to add a Rule 23 provision for certification of settlement classes by applying liberalized standards.

Regarding the Principles' judicial impact, the Reporters' efforts to inspire reinterpretation of class principles through judicial interpretation have had scant impact. Compared to Restatement projects, it might fairly be said that the Principles has garnered meager judicial attention over the nineteen years since publication of the first draft in 2004. Generally, judges have not been buying what the Principles had to sell. The Reporters' recommendations for changing established jurisprudence largely have failed to gain judicial traction.

The Principles' star citation in a 2011 Supreme Court decision concerning intersystem preclusion merited a footnote reference. The Court has not cited any other provisions. More than one-third of reported federal citations reference the Principles' recommendations for cy pres relief. However, although a few courts have embraced the cy pres recommendations wholesale, other courts have qualified their endorsements. No other section of the Principles has garnered as much attention as the cy pres provision. Instead, courts have made scattered references to various principles, in many instances providing footnote fodder or additional support to existing jurisprudence in the *Manual for Complex Litigation (Fourth)* or the Wright and Miller treatise on federal procedure. Some courts have cited the Principles for unremarkable statements of law relating to the adequacy and fiduciary duties of class representatives.

Moreover, a citation survey of the Principles is notable not so much for what judges have endorsed but for what they have not endorsed. Judges have not adopted the terminology of divisible and indivisible remedies. Judges have not recast the conventional understanding of mandatory classes under Rules 23(b)(1)(A) and (b)(2). Judges have not embraced the suggestions that class certification problems be considered through a functional lens. The Principles has not succeeded in changing prevailing applications of the predominance requirement for class certification. While some judges have looked to the Principles for guidance on certifying limited issues classes, most continue to rely on existing jurisprudence to determine that certification decision. Judges have not embraced the concept of an opt-in class. Judges have not eviscerated the *Amchem* and *Ortiz* holdings. While a few courts have cited the Principles' views on preclusion, judges have not wholesale overruled the *Stephenson* decision. Finally, courts have not relied on the Principles' recommendations concerning non-class aggregate settlements.

For committed aggregationists, the legislative and judicial impact of the Principles might be characterized as underwhelming, if not disappointing. The impact has the quality of the proverbial tree falling in a forest with no one there. Who now remembers, let alone cites, the predecessor ALI Complex Litigation Project? Will the *Principles of the Law of Aggregate Litigation* likewise slip into relative footnote obscurity? It also might be noted that the Reporters and Advisers spent some time advocating their product to international audiences. At this time, it is difficult to assess what impact the Principles may have made abroad among other legal systems considering aggregate litigation initiatives, apart from explaining American aggregation approaches to foreign readers. This impact must await further study. Nonetheless, for critics skeptical of trends in aggregate litigation, the Principles' meager domestic impact probably provides a source of some relief: in the end, the most extreme aggregationists failed to breach the barricades of federal procedure.

The experience of drafting, finalizing, and publishing the Principles suggests that the ALI processes worked just as they should. The ALI deliberative drafting and comment procedures served to temper the excesses of the Reporters' initial goals. Defense reactions and contributions served to counterbalance the plaintiffs' program to liberate class action procedure from restrictive jurisprudence. Everyone could reasonably rely on the Advisory Committee on Civil Rules to do nothing revolutionary. The Reporters' intellectually rich linguist formalism and opaque jargon may have served as a prophylactic protecting against judicial experimentation. Predictably, judges comfortable with the law have continued to turn to received jurisprudence when managing class litigation. Thus, the next revolution in aggregate procedure will have to wait for another day.

PART V
RESTATEMENTS AND
LEGAL THEORY

18

Restatements and Realists

*Robert W. Gordon**

I. Introduction

In hindsight, it seems obvious that the aims of the American Law Institute's (ALI's) founders and drafters of its first Restatements and those of the movement of iconoclastic legal intellectuals who were called Legal Realists were bound to collide. Indeed the clash between Restaters and Realists has often been portrayed as an epic final battle between an expiring old order of legal "Formalism" and "conceptualism" or—most unkindly—between "transcendental nonsense" and a brash new jurisprudence variously labeled "sociological" or "functional" jurisprudence.

That picture is not entirely wrong but needs qualification and nuance. Exactly what Formalism was and what was arguably wrong with it, and whether the Restatements' drafters and their sponsors actually were Formalists, are much disputed. And although it's evident that many Realists severely criticized both the ALI's general aims and their concrete realization in the first Restatements, it's useful to try to recapture what the specific critiques were and to assess their validity. Finally, it's worth asking whether there were any ways in which the ALI might have responded constructively to the Realist assault.

Take "Formalism" first, sometimes called "classical" legal thought. The conventional view that today's lawyers have of late-nineteenth- to early-twentieth-century legal thought is very much the view bequeathed to us by its Progressive and Realist critics. For some of these critics, "Formalism" meant something like Max Weber's logical-formal-rationality, the idea that all of law could be organized into a harmonious system of consistent principles, with all the rules and subrules of the system deducible from the principles: a gapless and complete system in which right answers to all legal questions could be arrived at through correct reasoning from abstract premises. For some, it meant conceptualism, the notion that all or almost all of private law doctrines could be explained as deriving from basic norms such as protection of the individual will ("will theory"). The task of conceptualist legal science was to extrude the principles from the cases and then organize the cases under the principles. The task of judges was not to make law but to declare or discover the preexisting law. Formalists assumed (their critics said) that private-law reasoning was, and ought to be, an autonomous science, entirely distinct from political, economic, or moral reasoning. Policy considerations, consequentialist accounting of social harms

* Thanks to Elias Banks Schultz for expert research assistance, and to Barbara Fried, Andrew Gold, Jack Schlegel, David Seipp, and participants in an ALI conference for contributors to this volume in June 2022, for helpful comments.

Robert W. Gordon, *Restatements and Realists* In: *The American Law Institute*. Edited by: Andrew S. Gold and Robert W. Gordon, Oxford University Press. © Oxford University Press 2023. DOI: 10.1093/oso/9780197685341.003.0019

or benefits of particular legal outcomes, were for legislatures to consider in modifying the common law—which however they should do as little as possible.

Sometimes however "Formalism" meant something a lot less elaborate, simply that legal decisions were best expressed (in court decisions, in codes, in scholarly literature expounding them) as narrow, bright-line rules, requiring few facts to be proved and little discretion in their application, and that written instruments such as constitutions, statutes, wills, and contracts should be interpreted in accord with their apparent plain textual meanings, without supplementary inquiry into contexts.[1]

Once the Progressive and Realist critics had described Formalism in these ways, the basic lines of critique were clear. The supposed gapless complete system of logically related principles, the supposed determinate relation of principles to rules, and of rules to results in particular cases, the supposed autonomy and neutrality of the classical system were all sham and delusion. Common law judges made law all the time, could not help but make law, whenever they applied rules to new fact-situations. If they denied their discretion to make law, they were likely unthinkingly to freeze the law in traditional ways and fail to adapt it to changing needs. In constitutional cases especially, the law they made was anything but apolitical: in fact, it enacted the premises and program of an outworn set of natural-law principles, or an outworn classical political economy ("the Fourteenth Amendment does not enact Mr. Herbert Spencer's Social Statics"[2]). (Criticisms of the narrower view of Formalism as strict rule-following or textualism were the same as they have always been, that the approach fails, sometimes seriously and indefensibly, to do substantive justice in individual cases.)

The Progressive-Realist critics—beginning, in the standard story, with Holmes— sought to liberate legal reasoning from both conceptualism and mechanical rule-following. In their view law was not a "Heaven of Legal Concepts," to quote the German legal theorist Rudolf von Jhering's satiric view of his formalist contemporaries' vision of law,[3] but a social product demanded by and serving social "interests," and properly directed to the service of valued social ends, and therefore to be executed and evaluated by how effectively it served those ends. This "social jurisprudence," as it was called in Europe, or "sociological jurisprudence," to use Roscoe Pound's term, acknowledged that judges needed to take account of interests and purposes served by legal rules, and that jurists, or legal scientists, needed to study the "law in action," the rules' actual social effects.[4]

The Progressive-Realist critique summarized in the preceding has been, for most of the last century, the generally received account of the dominant modes of legal thought from around 1870 to around 1920. The founding of the ALI has sometimes

---

[1] Roscoe Pound, one of the earliest and most influential critics, combined the critiques into a single charge that Formalist judges believed in results reached by strict rule-bound reasoning from a priori conceptions. Roscoe Pound, *Mechanical Jurisprudence*, 8 COLUM. L. REV. 605 (1908).

[2] Lochner v. New York, 198 U.S. 45, at 75 (Holmes, J. dissenting).

[3] *See* Rudolf von Jhering, *In the Heaven for Legal Concepts: A Fantasy*, C. L. Levy (trans.), 58 TEMPLE L.Q. 799, at 808–09 (1985), from Jhering's SCHERZ UND ERNST IN DER JURISPRUDENZ: EINE WEIHNACHTSGABE FÜR DAS JURISTISCHE PUBLIKUM (1884).

[4] On "social jurisprudence," *see* FRANZ WIEACKER, HISTORY OF PRIVATE LAW IN EUROPE WITH SPECIAL REFERENCE TO GERMANY 431–41 (1995), and, especially, Duncan Kennedy, *Three Globalizations of Law and Legal Thought*, in DAVID TRUBEK & ALVARO SANTOS (EDS.), THE NEW LAW AND ECONOMIC DEVELOPMENT: A CRITICAL APPRAISAL, at 19, 37–62 (2006).

been conveniently slotted into this account as the last gasp of establishment Formalism before it was besieged, and eventually overrun, by its Progressive-Realist adversaries.

But there are serious problems with this account. It turns out not to be easy to find judges of the period who believed in, or engaged in, strict top-down reasoning from a priori principles, and very easy indeed to find judges who candidly acknowledged that common law judges made law, that the effective service of valued social purposes was the ultimate aim of law, and that hard cases or novel cases required discretionary choice among available principles and precedents.[5] The view of classical judges as mechanical slot machines, spitting out hard-and-fast rule-based answers as soon as facts were fed to them, has proved equally frangible—although legal historians acknowledge that under the pressure of caseloads, much judicial decision-making of the late nineteenth century had indeed become more formal in the sense of conforming to bureaucratic routine.[6]

The two figures whose work was most commonly identified with Formalism were C.C. Langdell and Joseph Henry Beale, both practitioners of analytic jurisprudence and the case method of teaching, both affiliated with Harvard—Langdell, of course, as its pioneering Dean and Beale as a professor who later brought the Harvard system to Chicago as a missionary Dean. Langdell had famously been labeled by Holmes as a "legal theologian" who believed law was based on "logic" rather than "experience," and as a result became most of the Realists' practice target for Formalism, and remains so to this day. The Realist Jerome Frank chose the label "Bealism" to stand in for his (highly colored and caricatured) version of Formalism, which he called "legal fundamentalism." Heroic ingenious effort has gone recently into rehabilitating both thinkers, especially Langdell, who has been revealed to be an accomplished practitioner, a practical-minded educational innovator, and a surprisingly flexible and undogmatic legal theorist.[7] Langdell died well before the founding of the ALI, but Beale was an influential agent in its founding, and of course served as the Reporter for the first Restatement of Conflicts.[8] Another ALI figure who was a frequent target of Realist critique was Samuel Williston, the great Contracts scholar and Reporter for the first Restatement of Contracts.

But was it right to tag the ALI and its Restatements as a reactionary Formalist project? At the outset in 1923, it would seem not. As N.E.H. Hull has been at pains to demonstrate, the ALI was the brainchild of the legal profession's moderate reform wing, best classified as legal Progressives: they included, among many other such worthies, Judges Benjamin Cardozo, Learned Hand, and Julian Mack; former and

[5] For many examples and abundant quotations, see BRIAN TAMANAHA, BEYOND THE FORMALIST-REALIST DIVIDE (2010), Harry N. Scheiber, *Instrumentalism and Property Rights: A Reconsideration of Styles of Judicial Reasoning in the 19th Century*, WIS. L. REV. 1 (1975).

[6] See LAWRENCE FRIEDMAN, HISTORY OF AMERICAN LAW 606 (4th ed. 2019).

[7] See, in particular (on Langdell's practice and deanship) WILLIAM LAPIANA, LOGIC AND EXPERIENCE: THE ORIGIN OF MODERN AMERICAN LEGAL EDUCATION (1994), BRUCE A. KIMBALL, THE INCEPTION OF MODERN PROFESSIONAL EDUCATION: C. C. LANGDELL, 1826–1906 (2014), DANIEL COQUILLETTE & BRUCE KIMBALL, ON THE BATTLEFIELD OF MERIT: HARVARD LAW SCHOOL, THE FIRST CENTURY 304–435 (2015); and (on Langdell's and Beale's jurisprudence), ANTHONY J. SEBOK, LEGAL POSITIVISM IN AMERICAN JURISPRUDENCE 83–112 (1998).

[8] On Beale's role in the ALI, *see* Symeon C. Symeonides, *Conflict of Laws in the ALI's First Century*, in this volume.

future Justice Charles Evans Hughes; and Professors William Draper Lewis (the ALI's first Director), Roscoe Pound, Arthur Corbin, Ernst Freund, Edmund Morgan, and John Henry Wigmore. "Progressive" is a relative term of course, and among the ALI's founders were nativists who wanted to protect the elite bar from contamination by night-schooled immigrant lawyers. But in terms of basic jurisprudential divides, the founders were "social" jurists, mostly friendly to social legislation and the growing administrative state and critics of classical-constitutional decisions on "freedom of contract,"[9] and who saw the ALI as a vehicle for modernizing law to adapt it to valued social ends.[10]

Prominent critics of classical formalism were involved in the ALI's projects from the start. Williston chose Arthur Corbin as his chief Associate Reporter for the Contracts Restatement. Grant Gilmore famously cast Williston and Corbin as antagonists, battling over conflicting views of contract obligation, resulting in the "schizophrenia" of the First Restatement, "matter" versus "anti-matter."[11] Corbin, like Pound, was a sort of proto-Realist. Unlike the most extreme Realist skeptics, Corbin did not think cases useless for prediction of decisions in future cases. He believed that the operative facts in the decided cases were a great storehouse of data on customs and mores, that in each new case the judge made a tentative generalization from the facts in that case and in previous cases. Each such generalization "is drawn from a group of related situations and is to be corrected or replaced by other generalizations by other judges and scholars as new situations and new life conditions press on their attention."[12] By such means law evolves along with social change. Williston by contrast favored general abstract statements of legal principles and was much more of a narrow rule-formalist. He was, however, a moderate Progressive both in politics and jurisprudence and, like Pound, a critic of "freedom-of-contract" dogmatism in either private or public law.[13] Despite their differences, Williston and Corbin worked together cooperatively to the end.[14] Francis Bohlen, the Principal Reporter of the first Restatement of Torts, was also a "social" jurist who by the 1920s had "believed that a useful way of thinking about tort law was to identify the 'social interests' whose 'invasion' was reflected in particular tort claims."[15] Among Bohlen's Advisers on the ALI project was Leon Green, famous later as an arch-Realist critic.

For the Contracts project, Williston also chose as an Adviser Herman Oliphant,[16] who in the very year of the ALI's founding (1923) was beginning to lead the young

---

[9] See, e.g., Roscoe Pound, Liberty of Contract, 18 YALE L.J. 454 (1909); Samuel Williston, Freedom of Contract, 6 CORNELL L.Q. 365 (1920–1921).

[10] See N.E.H. Hull, Restatement and Reform: A New Perspective on the Origins of the American Law Institute, in THE AMERICAN LAW INSTITUTE: SEVENTY-FIFTH ANNIVERSARY, 1923–1998 (1998).

[11] GRANT GILMORE, THE DEATH OF CONTRACT 59–65 (1974)

[12] ARTHUR CORBIN, CONTRACTS § 1333 (1962).

[13] See Williston, supra note 10.

[14] An illuminating comparison of Williston and Corbin and account of their collaboration is Daniel J. Klau, What Price Certainty—Corbin, Williston, and the Restatement of Contracts, 70 B.U. L. Rev. 511 (1990).

[15] See G. Edward White, The Emergence and Doctrinal Development of Tort Law, 1870–1930, 11 U. ST. THOMAS L.J. 463, at 490 (2014).

[16] Corbin late in life said that Williston had picked him and Oliphant as Advisers in part because of their familiarity with Wesley N. Hohfeld's classification of concepts, which proved to be a major influence on Realist thinking. Corbin letter to William Twining, in TWINING, KARL LLEWELLYN AND THE REALIST MOVEMENT, 397 n.31 (1973).

rebels of the Columbia Law faculty to reorganize its curriculum along "functional" lines, that is, by effects on different areas of social life (familial, economic, political) and by fields of social science rather than doctrinal fields,[17] and who was to become a prominent Realist. In 1923, Oliphant was an optimist about the ALI's prospects.[18] But his optimism was based on the hope that, in making the choice among conflicting rules or principles, the ALI would investigate the "social structure affected by the body of law being studied" in order to assess the relative utility of the rules proposed.[19] This call for comprehensive law-in-action studies was eventually to become one of the principal enterprises of the Realist movement, albeit one with limited successes.[20] But needless to say the ALI did not take up this challenge, accepting instead Roscoe Pound's advice to stick with arranging cases under familiar doctrinal categories such as "Contract, Tort, Trust."[21]

And, in fact, it did not take long before the Restatements came under fire from the legal theorists beginning to think of themselves as Realists.[22] Myres McDougal in 1937 provided a concise summary of the critiques:

Some reviewers have pointed to naivete in fundamental assumptions—assumptions that certainty is obtainable and obtainable by high abstractions, that certainty is more important than flexibility, that "substantive law" is all-comprehensive and designed to govern human conduct in and out of courts, that the defects of "the law" can be cured by restating it as it is, that a restatement of the law as it is a restatement of it as it ought to be, and so forth; others have deplored the omission of historical, economic, and sociological backgrounds and of studies of comparative experience in other countries, the ignoring of, except by indirection, consideration of what "the law" ought to be, a failure to study the social consequences of institutions and doctrines, the omission of supporting authorities, reasoned discussion, and contrast of conflicting opinion, the use of "doctrinal" rather than "factual" classifications and of the blackletter-comment-illustration formula of expression, and so forth. Yet to all of these criticisms the officials of the American Law Institute have remained impervious.[23]

---

[17] On the Columbia reforms, the canonical source is Brainerd Currie, *The Materials of Law Study*, 3 J. Leg. Educ. 331 (1951).

[18] Herman Oliphant, *The Problems of Logical Methods from the Lawyer's Point of View*, 10 Proc. Acad. Pol. Sci. in the City of New York 17 (1923).

[19] *Id.* at 19.

[20] The most thorough and generous appraisal of this aspect of the Realist enterprise is John Henry Schlegel, American Legal Realism and Empirical Social Science (1995).

[21] Twining, *supra* note 17, at 24.

[22] The opening salvos, which came with tentative attempts to name members of Realist disposition, were Karl Llewellyn's articles in a dispute with Pound: *A Realistic Jurisprudence—The Next Step*, 30 Colum. L. Rev. 431 (1930), and *Some Realism about Realism*, 44 Harv. L. Rev. 1222 (1931). For a comprehensive and illuminating account of the dispute, its background and its consequences, *see* N.E.H. Hull, Roscoe Pound and Karl Llewellyn, Searching for an American Jurisprudence 173–222 (1997). In 1930 there also appeared the polemic most often, though also rather misleadingly, thought to exemplify Realism, Jerome Frank's Law and the Modern Mind.

[23] Myres McDougal, *Book Review [of the Restatement of Property]*, 32 Ill. L. Rev. 509, at 511 (1937).

Let's break down this broadside critique, which was expressed both in reviews of specific Restatement projects and of the ALI's approach as a whole, into its different components.

II. Critiques of Form

The early Restatements were unadorned statements of black-letter rules, each followed by brief "Comments" and a few "Illustrations," examples of concrete applications. No cases were cited. The choice of form was deliberate. The aim after all was to drastically lighten the burden of practitioners trying to assimilate a wild proliferation of case law, by simplifying and rationalizing the law of each doctrinal field, while also engaging in the modest reform project of modernizing the rules in accord with professional opinion on best practices. The form was chosen to mimic that of a code, while avoiding state legislatures and the supposed inflexibility of codes: it was hoped that the product of leading scholars, reviewed and approved by the cream of bench, bar, and academy, would furnish its own sufficient authority. The ALI's founders had planned to follow the publication of each Restatement with a treatise providing further discussion of the rules and citation to relevant cases. This plan was relatively easy to fulfill with respect to the Restatements of Contracts and Conflicts, since Williston had already completed his treatise and Beale's was well underway (it appeared in 1935, one year after the Restatement). But the plan to supplement with treatises proved impractical. What remained was the Black Letter.

The "resulting statement" of this set of decisions, wrote Dean Charles Clark of Yale in a scathing review of the Contracts Restatement in 1933, was the actual "law nowhere and in its unreality only deludes and misleads. It is either a generality so obvious as immediately to be accepted, or so vague as not to offend, or of such antiquity as to be unchallenged as a statement of past history."[24]

> From the beginning, the plan seems to have suffered from a vacillation between the two positions that the restatement should announce a more or less binding and final rule of law and that it should be an informed and informing statement of actual legal realities. On the former plane it is subject to the defects of a code with an added question as to the nature of the sovereign authority behind it, but at least it then has the opportunity of boldly forcing reform. On the latter plane it is bound by conditions as they are, but it is realistic and actual. The plan has swung more and more to the former position, but with the important limitation that the now law must be stated. In result this has meant the assumption of the chief defects of each position-the rigidity of a code (with the added unreality that it is a declaration unsupported either by a sovereign or by past precedent) and without the opportunity for reform and advance which a code affords.[25] ...
>
> [T]he black letter itself is, as must be expected, a compromise to cover various views. With one leg it steps forward; with the other it goes backward. It is caught

---

[24] Charles E. Clark, *The Restatement of the Law of Contracts*, 42 YALE L.J. 643, at 654 (1933)
[25] *Id.* at 650.

between stating the law which should be and the law which is and often ends by stating only the law that was....

The necessity of agreement on black letter forces each participant to a choice of position which, when stated as a group result, must inevitably tend towards (a) the ancient historical rather than the modern rule or possible future trend, (b) the conventional safe and unoriginal point of view and (c) a compromise which goes only to the point whereon all are agreed.[26]

Finally Clark—in words that could easily have been written by his colleague Arthur Corbin,[27] but for the fact that Corbin happened to be the Associate Reporter for the project under review—scolded the Restaters for their textual formalism: "[W]ithout interpretation, or background against which meaning can be discovered, the black letter statements are not understandable. The idea that words speak for themselves, without interpretation in the light of the circumstance under which they were composed or arranged, has been too often exploded with reference to wills, contracts and written instruments generally, to be believed again with respect to the restatements."[28]

Clark was one of several reviewers who complained that the Restatements failed to disclose when they were stating dominant views of existing law or proposing its revision.

Edwin Patterson believed this practice concealed a fundamental schizophrenia about the aims of the project. Were the Restatements based on a deductive theory that all the existing rules could be derived from a few natural-law like propositions? Or on an inductive theory that "jurists can observe thousands of cases and formulate laws of judicial behavior"?[29]

The text [of the Restatement of Contracts] is in the form of assertions in the present tense rather than either norms (statements of what ought to be), commands (statements of what shall be) or predictions (statements of what will be). The form is consistent with the implication that this is merely a report of what the law is. Yet clearly the Restatement, if it has any utility for the future, will be taken in one of the other senses above mentioned. In which sense is it to be taken? Aside from the definitions which state that one thing is equivalent to another, the commonest forms of statement are: "is operative," "must be made," "party is bound," "duty is discharged." Do these statements prescribe conduct or predict what courts will do?[30] ... The Restatement purports, in the main, to treat judicial precedents as authoritative support for a set of rational propositions, rather than as the data of statistical inferences.[31] ... Conflicting statutes are mentioned (not cited), thus preserving the theory that the Restatement

---

[26] *Id.* at 656.

[27] Corbin was the leading critic of a strict parol evidence rule (one presuming any writing emerging from contract negotiations to be the complete and final evidence of that agreement, and excluding any supplementary, clarifying, or contradicting evidence outside the "four corners" of the writing). Arthur L. Corbin, *The Parol Evidence Rule*, 53 YALE L.J. 603 (1944).

[28] *Id.* at 655.

[29] Edwin W. Patterson, *The Restatement of the Law of Contracts*, 33 COLUM. L. REV. 397, at 400 (1933).

[30] *Id.* at 403.

[31] *Id.* at 404.

is a summation of law in force, yet conflicting decisions are ignored, thus indicating that it is an analytical system of ideal principles.[32]

Thurman Arnold similarly noted that the desire to expound legal doctrine in formulations familiar to practicing lawyers conflicted sharply with the aim of rational clarification:

> There appears to be a deep seated prejudice throughout the restatement [of Trusts] against stating that any judicially recognized rule or concept has been shown to be useless. It is sometimes done by implication, but never directly. To say that a rule of law is simply a way of talking which conceals the real issue of the case seems to be reserved for law review articles and excluded from the restatement. Such a statement in black letter type would be a real innovation. It appears to be condemned as "destructive criticism" of the "law" instead of "restatement." The result of this attitude is that if all sorts of things have been called "trusts," we are under a positive duty to define trusts so that our definition includes all of them. Hence the broad and inclusive definition with which the restatement begins, and the conventional lines which it follows.[33]

The Reporters' treatises that were part of the ALI's original plan could have explained why older doctrines were sometimes chosen (e.g., because too familiar to practitioners to be abandoned), and sometimes discarded in favor of newer ones (e.g., because in forward-looking jurisdictions doctrine was being modernized to adapt to changed conditions); but the treatise project had been shelved.

Hessel Yntema, looking back at the early Restatements in 1936, thought that ALI had paid too high a price in sacrificing its reformist aims to delivering a product acceptable to the practicing bar.

> This much is certain, that the notion of improving the law by restating it as it is, is unsatisfactory. Nay more, it constitutes an indefensible retreat from the objective of the Institute. The Institute was created to ameliorate, not to perpetuate, the existing difficulties in the legal system.... Where there is diversity in the law, how can it be stated in a single rule? Where there is uniformity, what is the need for restatement? If the law is to be restated as it is, there is no escape from this dilemma. In consequence of this conception, it is convenient to suppress the treatises, since they would demonstrate the insecure basis upon which the supposed law as it is rests. Consequently, too, most of the data to which attention should be given in a responsible formulation of law have to be excluded in the preparation of the Restatement—data as to the practical needs to be met and as to the appropriateness of the means of regulation employed to meet them. The conception of restating the law as it is necessarily cannot admit such considerations, because they might require an improvement and therefore a change in existing law. If, as may well be the case, any such considerations have obtruded themselves into the present Restatement, they have been smuggled.[34]

---

[32] *Id.* at 404 n.22.

[33] Thurman Arnold, *The Restatement of the Law of Trusts*, 31 COLUM. L. REV. 800, at 821 (1931).

[34] Hessel E. Yntema, *What Should the American Law Institute Do?*, 34 MICH. L. REV. 461, 468 (1936).

III. Critiques of Substance—Inadequacy of Legal Rules to Determine Results

It was hardly to be expected that once the Restatements appeared, legal thinkers associated with Realism would find them adequate guides to the realities of either existing or emerging law. The "core claim" of Realism, as Brian Leiter has helpfully put it, is that "judges respond primarily to the stimulus of facts. Put less formally—but also somewhat less accurately—the Core Claim of Realism is that judges reach decisions based on what they think would be fair on the facts of the case, rather than on the basis of the applicable rules of law.... What the descriptive Formalist really claims is that judges are (primarily) responsive to legal reasons, while the Realist claims that judges are (primarily) responsive to nonlegal reasons."[35] The nonlegal reasons vary from Realist to Realist. For some, like Jerome Frank, they are grounded in the experience and psychology of the individual judge,[36] but Frank's view is atypical. For others, like Karl Llewellyn, they are grounded in situation-sense, the judge's educated feel for the result called for by commercial custom, fairness to the parties in the particular case, and sound policy for future similar cases. Realists also disagree on the weight to be given legal versus nonlegal reasons for decisions, ranging from close to nihilism (rules = random noise[37]) to the much more common position of "distrust of the theory that traditional prescriptive rule-formulations are the heavily operative factor in producing court decisions.... It will be noted that 'distrust' in this and the preceding point is not at all equivalent to 'negation in any given instance.'"[38] Obviously the nihilist will find nothing useful in a Restatement, since neither the generalizations from case law in the Restatements nor anything in the cases themselves, but their facts will be reliable guides to results. For the skeptic, the Restatement formulations may have some utility in guiding lawyers to appropriate rhetoric for argument (and judges for decision), but not much for prediction.

IV. Critique of Overabstraction, or "Lumping"

Karl Llewellyn illustrated this type of critique at length in his pioneering casebook on Sales, which contrasts "lump-concept thinking" to "narrow-issue" thinking (the immediate topic is "title" to goods).

---

[35] Brian Leiter, *Rethinking Legal Realism: Toward a Naturalized Jurisprudence*, 7 TEX. L. REV. 267, at 275, 278 (1997).

[36] *See generally* JEROME FRANK, LAW AND THE MODERN MIND (1930).

[37] Felix Cohen sometimes steered close to this extreme when characterizing such doctrinal formulations as "Where is a corporation?": "[T]he traditional language of argument and opinion neither explains nor justifies court decisions. When the vivid fictions and metaphors of traditional jurisprudence are thought of as reasons for decisions, rather than poetical or mnemonic devices for formulating decisions reached on other grounds, then the author, as well as the reader, of the opinion or argument, is apt to forget the social forces which mold the law and the social ideals by which the law is to be judged." Felix Cohen, *Transcendental Nonsense and the Functional Approach*, 35 COLUM. L. REV. 809, at 812 (1935).

[38] Karl N. Llewellyn, *Some Realism About Realism—Responding to Dean Pound*, 44 HARV. L. REV. 1222, at 1237 (1931).

Lump-concept thinking moves in terms of *wide premises*. Decide that on specific facts "title" is in either B or S, and you can then proceed to draw a dozen conclusions, as to risk, price, rules of damages, levy by creditors, etc.; among the dozen will be one deciding the case at hand. And the ruling in one case as to "who had title" is authority for a "like" ruling in another case, though the narrow issues in the two cases are quite different; the emphasis in the deciding and in later use of the holding is on the lump-concept *as a lump....* The advantages of narrow-issue thinking and concepts are obvious.... The meaning of a case is always clearer when one knows and states exactly what issue was decided, *as well as* what ratio decidendi was expressed ... Secondly, the policy aspects of the narrow focus come in for observation and study under narrow-issue thinking ... The narrow issues that arise on questions "of title" are largely questions involving the allocation of a great number of distinct risks: risk of destruction; risk of disposing of the goods (can S have price, or only damages?); risk of being able to cover in the event of non-delivery ... ; risk of B's insolvency ... risk of S's or B's dishonesty or bad faith ... Narrow-issue thinking leads to weighing these differences as a matter of sense, in order to see whether similar differences should follow in law.[39]

Some form of the anti-lumping critique was the most common Realist critique of the Restatements.[40] It emerged frequently in debates within the ALI itself over early Restatements. Perhaps the most famous was Walter Wheeler Cook's repeated

---

[39] Karl N. Llewellyn, Cases and Materials on the Law of Sales 565 (1930). Elsewhere, however, Llewellyn added: "But, of course, once satisfactory narrow categories have been found and tested, the eternal quest returns for wider synthesis—but one that will stand up in use." Jurisprudence 56n (quoted in Twining, *supra* note 17, at 137).

[40] The anti-lumping critique, as G. Edward White noted in his exceptionally perceptive and useful history of the ALI, directly challenged the premise of the ALI's founding documents' diagnosis of "the law's uncertainty and complexity." Among the causes of these ills, the founders surmised, was:

A case is decided. Another case arises not differing in any essential respect, but the court believes that application to it of the principle established in the first case would produce injustice. Confronted with such a situation the court may refuse to follow the prior decision ... [but attempt] to distinguish the two cases on account of some immaterial difference in their respective facts. The result is that we have no clear statement of any legal principle, the law on the subject being left confused and uncertain.

Report of the Committee on the Establishment of Permanent Organization for the Improvement of the Law Proposing the Establishment of an American Law Institute [1923], in The American Law Institute—Seventy-Fifth Anniversary 173, 228–29 (1998). White pointed out:

[A]n alternative reading suggested that the reason some courts had responded to "novel" fact patterns by formulating "illogical distinctions" or "numerous special rules" was that legal principles were inherently dependent on the facts to which they were applied. It therefore made no sense to speak of principles independent of their contextual setting.... The alternative reading of uncertainty radically changed the meaning of a legal "principle," suggesting that it was ... a cluster of contradictory values pointing in different directions depending on the context of its application. The alternative reading of complexity even more radically stripped "principles" of any determinate content, since their meaning not only varied with the context in which they were applied but was the creation of that context.

G. Edward White, *The American Law Institute and the Triumph of Modernist Jurisprudence*, 15 Law & Hist. Rev. 1, at 9 (1997).

attempts to break down the lump-concept of "domicile" in Beale's draft Restatement of Conflicts. Beale wanted one definition of domicile for all purposes.[41] Cook responded:

[A]s I see it any concept such as domicil is a tool which lawyers use, judges use, in determining what ought to be done in a concrete situation. As I see it, the same word is used in dealing with a great variety of situations. The reporter has enumerated some of them: Divorce, taxation, jurisdiction to enter a personal judgment, what to do with a man's personal property when he dies intestate; and other purposes. A judge or court deciding a case always has one of those concrete situations before him. In passing upon the exact scope of the concept as applicable to that case the Judge always has in mind that case and not all the other purposes. I believe that it is extraordinarily unlikely that the court would always draw the line, that it ought always to draw the line delimiting the boundary of the concept at exactly the same place for all these purposes. I do not believe that has happened or ever will happen. I do not believe you can determine the exact scope of any legal concept unless you know what you are trying to do with it ...

The court has a concrete problem to solve. It is trying to decide whether the courts of the state should grant a divorce on constructive service; whether the man is sufficiently connected with the State to make that a reasonable thing to do. It may be reasonable to do that, but not reasonable to apply the same concept in the case involving the validity of the provisions of a will. The court has a will to consider, or a divorce, or the administration of an estate, or whatever it may be, and the exact point at which it draws the line is undoubtedly drawn with the concrete problem that they have before them in mind.[42]

Cook had a similar critique of Williston's approach to Contracts. Reviewing Williston's treatise, he quoted a well-known passage from Williston's own preface to the first edition:

The law of contracts ... after starting with some degree of unity now tends from its very size to fall apart. The simplest applications of fundamental principles of contracts when found in an insurance policy or a contract of suretyship are often considered by writers on those topics as peculiarities of the law of insurance or of suretyship, controlled by no general rules. *It therefore seems desirable to treat the subject of contracts as a whole and to show the wide range of application of its principles.*[43]

Cook comments that given the realism of Williston's premises, the conclusion is especially perverse:

---

[41] 3 A.L.I. Proc. 222 (1925).

[42] *Id.* at 226–28. Cook followed up his critique with an article and then book-length rebuttal to Beale's approach to Conflicts, The Logical and Legal Bases of the Conflict of Laws (1942). On Cook's disagreement with Beale, *see* Symeonides, *supra* note 9.

[43] [emphasis added] 1 Williston on Contracts, at iii (1st ed. 1924), quoted in Cook, *Williston on Contracts*, 33 Ill. L. Rev. 497, at 504 (1939).

Reduced to its lowest terms the assumption is that in so far as the law of contracts "tends to fall apart," the result is one to be deplored, and counteracted if possible by treatises like the present, designed to show the "unity" of contract law. For example, if in dealing with life insurance contracts courts and writers take the type of transaction into account in reaching their decisions, they are thereby failing to apply the "fundamental principles of contracts" and asserting, at least by implication, that the cases before them are "controlled by no general rules." If one asks what justification the author gives for this assumption, the answer is that there is no discussion of it at all: it is merely assumed that the alleged "unity" does or at least should exist. The assumption is, of course, one which many at least of the so-called 'realists' would at once challenge. They would inquire what warrant there is for assuming, for example, that the formation of a life insurance contract must or should necessarily be governed by some "general principle of contracts" equally applicable to all other types of contract. They would inquire, where do such "principles" come from? Are they distilled from the decisions of the courts? If not, what is their source?[44]

Leon Green made essentially the same point about the Restatement of Torts, to which he had served as one of the ALI's Advisers, but which he concluded was unsafe for practitioner use.

[T]the negligence doctrines used in firearms cases, in fire cases, in physician and surgeon cases, in traffic cases and other groups of cases are not identical by any means. In other words, doctrines have little integrity of their own. They take on the color of the transactions in which they are used. There is no general norm which will work in all types of cases; that is only a dream of those who have not examined the cases closely. Any supposedly general norm will be found of value only in the cases from which it was developed. The defense doctrine of "consent" is a good example. It is not the same in fight cases, sex cases, and surgical operation cases, but the Restatement treats it as though it were something constant in all these cases. Of course, in widely different cases, as in traffic and employee cases, where the consent doctrine goes under the name of assumed risk, no such thing would be thought of. But the differences are just as vital, though not so easy to see in cases which are not so widely set off.[45]

Green, famously, organized his casebook on Torts[46] around specific occupations of parties, such as "Occupancy, Ownership, Development of Land," "Manufacturers, Dealers," and "Builders, Contractors, Workmen," "Power, Telephone and Telegraph, Water, and Gas Companies," "Traffic and Transportation," and the like, while omitting altogether, except in the interstices of reprinted opinions, traditional doctrinal categories such as causation.

Herman Oliphant, another renegade ALI Adviser, after giving a few examples of his own of how context and situation determine results (e.g., courts will enforce covenants not to compete against former owners on sale of a business, but not against

---

[44] *Id.* at 504–05.
[45] Leon Green, *The Torts Restatement*, 29 ILL. L. REV. 582, 589 (1935).
[46] LEON GREEN, THE JUDICIAL PROCESS IN TORT CASES (1931).

employees), generalized the Realist distrust of abstraction into—what looks at first like a surprisingly reactionary!—paean to the old common law. That is, the common law before the abolition of the writ system, before the advent of analytic jurisprudence and other endeavors to theorize private law. He praises the fact-bound empiricism of *stare decisis*.

> The political virtues of stare decisis are difficult to exaggerate. It has two active qualities, one affording us the counsel of experience; the other, the latitude of trial and error. The first element of its strength and security is its unalterable refusal to indulge in broad speculation, and its untiring patience to keep attention pinned to the immediate problem in order that a wise solution for it may be found. It stoutly refuses to answer future questions, prudently awaiting the time when they enter the field of immediate vision and become issues of reality in order that to their solution may be brought the illumination which only immediacy affords and the judiciousness which reality alone can induce. It is indifferent to broad generalizations or is made apprehensive by them. It accepts few generalizations, narrow or broad, until they have been transmuted into the wisdom of experience by experimentation. It uses generalizations to suggest and to orient that experimentation but not to replace it. The second element in the strength and security of stare decisis is but another aspect of the constant immediacy of its ends. It leads us forward over untried ground, a step at a time, no step being taken until it is judged wise, and the stages of its advance are so short that the direction of march can be quickly shifted as experience dictates.[47]

But as social life became more complex, the legal system reduced the number of actions, and "abstraction and generalization ran riot," and "absolutes and universals begin to replace mere generalizations. Broad principles begin to spring from few cases. If there be only one case in point and that be in conflict with some implication of our favorite universals, it is wrong—wrong on principle. This search becomes partly one for mere word patterns."[48] Efforts like the ALI's to continually restate the law in the form of broad doctrinal principles are in vain:

> Such further restatements will be made necessary by exceptions and conflicts which appear from time to time. They can be reduced and subtended only by expanding present generalizations into yet larger bubbles of unreality. Nothing new and nothing vital lies in this direction. This path inevitably leads to viewpoints more and more remote from life, more and more obsolescent....
>
> With eyes cleared of the old and broad abstractions which curtain our vision, we come to recognize more and more the eminent good sense in what courts are wont to do about disputes before them. judges are men and men respond to human. situations. When the facts stimulating them to the action taken are studied from a particular and current point of view, which our present classification prevents, we acquire a new faith in stare decisis. From this viewpoint we see that courts are dominantly

---

[47] Herman Oliphant, *A Return to Stare Decisis*, 14 A.B.A. J. 71, 75 (1928). This was Oliphant's presidential address to the Association of American Law Schools in 1927.
[48] *Id.* at 74–75.

coerced, not by the essays of their predecessors but by a surer thing, by an intuition of fitness of solution to problem, and a renewed confidence in judicial government is engendered.[49]

But even though Oliphant is arguing that judges, responding to the stimulus of facts of particular cases, do a better job of fitting solutions to concrete problems than the doctrinal theorists and Restaters do, he is certainly not recommending anything like the abandonment of the scholarly enterprise and return to the good old days of parsing cases. On the contrary: the solution is for *social science* to replace the hit-or-miss empiricism of the old judges with a systematic understanding of how social forces impact the law.

> Law teachers should have and law students should get either before or after they come to the law school a comprehensive knowledge of the whole social structure. This should not consist of theories as to domestic. economic and political life nor of unrelated description of disjoined social phenomena. The whole life which law affects should be viewed comprehensively as an interrelation of processes. This understanding cannot be got today by a hit and miss apprenticeship in life any more than living in our bodies can teach us its structure and functioning. Systematized study, deliberately focused toward getting an adequate knowledge of the entire social structure as a functioning and changing but coherent mechanism, is a basic prerequisite.[50]

Oliphant's ambitious agenda naturally raises the question of whether the Realist critics of the Restatements had anything to propose that the ALI could as a practical matter have undertaken instead. We will return to this question, but for the moment pause to agree with Hanoch Dagan's judgment that the Realists were not generally against rules but wanted to improve rules by stating them in narrower categories, not individual cases, "relying on empirical data, normative conclusions, and situation sense."[51]

A. Law Is Policy, But Where's the Policy Analysis? (Herein Also of Hohfeld)

One of the most consistent strands of critique of both Progressive and Realist critics of Formalist (or classical) legal thought was that Formalist judges' decision of cases on purportedly neutral principles concealed inarticulate policy choices. As Holmes memorably put it in *The Path of the Law*:

> I think that the judges themselves have failed adequately to recognize their duty of weighing considerations of social advantage. The duty is inevitable, and the result of the often proclaimed judicial aversion to deal with such considerations is simply to leave the very ground and foundation of judgments inarticulate, and often

---

[49] *Id.* at 107, 159.
[50] *Id.* at 159.
[51] Hanoch Dagan, *The Realist Conception of Law*, 57 U. TORONTO L.J. 607, 647 (2007).

unconscious, as I have said. When socialism first began to be talked about, the comfortable classes of the community were a good deal frightened. I suspect that this fear has influenced judicial action both here and in England, yet it is certain that it is not a conscious factor in the decisions to which I refer. I think that something similar has led people who no longer hope to control the legislatures to look to the courts as expounders of the Constitutions, and that in some courts new principles have been discovered outside the bodies of those instruments, which may be generalized into acceptance of the economic doctrines which prevailed about fifty years ago, and a wholesale prohibition of what a tribunal of lawyers does not think about right. I cannot but believe that if the training of lawyers led them habitually to consider more definitely and explicitly the social advantage on which the rule they lay down must be justified, they sometimes would hesitate where now they are confident, and see that really they were taking sides upon debatable and often burning questions.[52]

The strong version of the claim was that there were no significant differences between private and public law: all private law doctrines distributed wealth and power; all put the power of the state behind some parties and policy choices rather than others they might have chosen instead. Sometimes the implication of that view was that judges should not take sides on burning public-law issues, but should leave major policy decisions to legislatures: this position generally counseled against invalidating statutes on constitutional grounds. But the implication even for common law decision-making was that judges needed to bring distributional conflicts to the surface and have intelligent grounds for deciding one way or another. Even issues involving the most apparently anodyne and innocuous doctrinal rules, such as those of Offer and Acceptance, made it necessary to ask, "What acts are those which will cause society to come forward with its strong arm?"[53] As Morris Cohen put it: "A contract ... between two or more individuals cannot be said to be generally devoid of all public interest. If it be of no interest, why enforce it? For note that in enforcing contracts, the government does not merely allow two individuals to do what they have found pleasant in their eyes. Enforcement, in fact, puts the machinery of the law in the service of one party against the other. When that is worthwhile and how that should be done are important questions of public policy."[54] Some Realists took this position to its logical limits. The lawyer-economist Robert L. Hale redescribed the legal constitution of the market economy through contract-tort-property rules as delegations of state power to some participants to coerce others.[55] Lon Fuller (a prominent critic of the Realist movement but something of a Realist himself[56]) redescribed all of contract law as founded in tort-like injury to reliance interests.[57]

---

[52] O.W. HOLMES JR., THE PATH OF THE LAW [1897], *reprinted in* 110 HARV. L. REV 991, 999–1000 (1997).

[53] Arthur L. Corbin, *Offer and Acceptance and Some of the Resulting Legal Relations*, 26 YALE L.J. 169, 170 (1916).

[54] Morris Cohen, *The Basis of Contract*, 46 HARV. L. REV. 553, 562 (1933).

[55] *See* Robert L. Hale, *Coercion and Distribution in a Supposedly Non-Coercive State*, 38 POL. SCI. Q. 470 (1923). The definitive study of Hale is BARBARA FRIED, THE PROGRESSIVE ASSAULT ON LAISSEZ-FAIRE: ROBERT HALE AND THE FIRST LAW AND ECONOMICS MOVEMENT (2001).

[56] On Fuller's relationship to Realism, *see* Duncan Kennedy, *From the Will Theory to the Principle of Private Autonomy: Lon Fuller's Consideration and Form*, 100 COLUM. L. REV. 94 (2000).

[57] Lon L. Fuller & William R. Perdue Jr., *The Reliance Interest in Contract Damages*, 46 YALE L.J. 52 (1936) & 46 YALE L.J. 373 (1937). On the protection of reliance in the First Restatement of Contracts, *see* Richard

The first generation of ALI Reporters would probably have subscribed in a very general way to these sentiments, except that they would have considered the great bulk of common law doctrines relatively settled and cases requiring policy argument and decision exceptional and largely limited to anomalous situations and newly arising issues. Fuller wrote a very acute review of *Williston on Contracts*, which captured this disposition. Fuller started off by accepting that all legal decisions involve questions of policy, but that lawyers and judges save time and difficulty in routine cases by resort to formal doctrines, simple rules that obviate the need to reanalyze policy considerations at stake in every case.

> Turning to Professor Williston's legal method, if we ask at what point he gives up the attempt to shape the law by direct reference to social interests, I think the answer will have to be, at the very outset. What may be called the bases of contract liability, notions like consideration, the necessity for offer and acceptance, and the like, are nowhere in his work critically examined in the light of the social interests they serve. These things are accepted on faith. This neglect to refer to underlying social desiderata cannot properly be called "logic". It is simply an acceptance of what is conceived to be received legal tradition. It is, if anything, policy, but policy as it is assumed to be crystallized in certain inherited formulae.... Yet if we ask at what point in Professor Williston's method "policy" becomes relevant, it will be found, I think, that in general he admits "policy" only where "logic" has failed, that is, where a syllogistic marshalling of traditional concepts fails to yield a certain answer, or, occasionally (as in the problem of the offer revoked after the offeree has begun performance of the requested act), where the answer yielded seems too unjust to be acceptable.... Even in this matter of summoning policy as a kind of trouble shooter for logic, I think it can be said that Professor Williston is not, in comparison with his contemporaries, especially inclined to favor policy. He follows a conservative diagnostic practice, and is slow to declare logic in distress.... He is no ardent practitioner of ... the manipulation of legal theory to bring about the result conceived to be socially desirable without making explicit the social interests thus served. He shows none of the eager ingenuity of an Ames, a Cardozo, or a Vance, to perform feats of juristic legerdemain in the interest of justice and the better life.[58]

Contrast to the Williston of Fuller's review, the attitude of Oliphant, in his initially very optimistic vision of the mission of the new ALI. Oliphant notes that the ALI's mission statement excludes from its remit any attempt to restate law in controverted matters of social policy. He assumes the ALI means such matters as

> the rights of the parties in the struggles of labor and capital and the scope of the due-process clause of the Constitution in fixing the limits of social legislation. Just why

---

R.W. Brooks, *Canon and Fireworks: Reliance in the Restatements of Contracts and Reliance on Them*, in this volume.

[58] Lon L. Fuller, *Williston on Contracts*, 18 N.C. L. REV. 1, 9–10 (1939).

are such subjects to be excluded? Is it because they are still controverted? It cannot be that, for two reasons: There is almost no field of law but has large unsettled areas. For example, the law of private corporations has large parts still the subject of debate, but it would not be excluded for that reason. In the second place, a restatement of the law will have little utility unless it covers much debated ground, because where the law is almost wholly undisputed, no restatement is needed. If the work of the Institute is to be limited to undebated matters, then one could argue that there is no greater objection to beginning with the law of industrial relations, of due process, than with other branches of the law. Where any of the questions in these subjects have been answered by the courts and answered with substantial unanimity, the emotional conflict is settled and they might just as well be restated.[59]

He goes on to argue that the ALI was right to exclude such issues, not because they are debated questions, but because they

involve social-policy judgments having a marked emotional content.... [But] [t]he exclusion of such questions does not exclude those debated questions having no marked emotional flavor, and such questions cannot be avoided. The Institute in its work will be constantly meeting opposing views on what the law is or should be. While it may state both views, it will have to name one as the better, and, in so choosing, will be stating new law.[60]

And this is where the need for social science makes itself felt:

Until we study the business or social structure affected by law, we must often guess as to which of the two rules work better. Until that study has been made we can only guess as to whether rules of law differ in utility, reason that a large part of the task ahead of us is merely discover which rules of law have a utility not limited to certainty. This can be learned only by studying the structure affected by the body of law.[61]

Eventually, having failed to convince his Columbia colleagues to convert the law school into a research institute, Oliphant brought Cook and Yntema with him to the short-lived Johns Hopkins Institute of Law.

Of course not all the Realists turned to empirical social science as a source of enlightenment about policy choices.[62] Some, like Corbin and most of the Realist-influenced law teachers who followed, were content to hypothesize policy rationales for, or functional purposes of, legal rules from the facts of decided cases. Others, like Llewellyn, drew upon practical experience of commercial customs. But they were all sure that the answers they sought, the "real reasons for the decision," lay in some part outside the black-letter rules.

---

[59] Oliphant, *supra* note 19, at 17–18.
[60] *Id.* at 18.
[61] *Id.* at 19.
[62] Those few who did, after a half-century of neglect and disparagement, finally received their due in respectful treatment in SCHLEGEL, *supra* note 21.

Since the breach between the First Restaters and the Realists seems in hindsight to have been inevitable, it's reasonable to ask why skeptics about the adequacy of legal rules and principles to predict or explain legal outcomes should ever have welcomed the ALI and its projects. Clearly the sponsorship of the leading lights of Progressive and "sociological" jurisprudence such as Pound and Cardozo helped. One sponsor had exceptional influence on the proto-Realists. This was Wesley Newcomb Hohfeld, briefly on the Yale Law faculty before his early death in 1918. Hohfeld's ideas carried enormous weight with Corbin, Llewellyn, and Cook, among many others, and were treated with reverent respect by the ALI's founders. Reporters for the First Restatements were instructed to apply Hohfeldian categories and analysis.[63] It may seem curious that Hohfeld's taxonomy of "Fundamental Legal Conceptions,"[64] an extraordinarily abstract exercise in analytical jurisprudence, such as might have been predicted to be Formalist blather to Realists-in-waiting, should have so impressed them. But the oddity vanishes when one appreciates what Hohfeld did, which was to disambiguate general notions of "rights" and to reanalyze them as operative legal relations. What did it mean for someone to have a right? In whom, if anyone, did it give rise to a legal duty to respect the right? To whom, if anyone, did it give a remedy for infringement of the right, and what remedy? Hohfeld's acolytes perceived this schema as a powerful tool for identifying latent policy choices underlying legal doctrines. Cook provided an especially telling example of this method by applying Hohfeldian analysis to the U.S. Supreme Court's decision granting an injunction against the United Mine Workers for trying to recruit into their union at-will employees of a mine who had been required to sign yellow dog contracts promising not to join a union.[65] Cook used Hohfeld's categories to ask if the mining company had a right, protectible by an injunction or damages, against the union; or whether the right was merely a privilege, like the privilege to set up a competing business regardless of the injury to a competitor. This was the important policy choice in the case, and it could not be avoided by a conclusory declaration of a "right" in the employer whose correlative was a duty to abstain from interfering with the right.[66]

Yet as the First Restatements gradually appeared, they made only limited and selective use of Hohfeldian terms and categories.[67] In any case, the main use of Hohfeldian

---

[63] Corbin late in life told William Twining, Llewellyn's biographer, that Williston chose Corbin and Oliphant as Advisers, telling them that he "wished every part of the Restatement to be *consistent* with Hohfeld. He singled out Oliphant and me, as being more expert in Hohfeld's analysis than himself, to keep out a constant eye for any inconsistency.... I regarded my function as supplementing Williston in two ways: (1) Analysis of facts and terminology; (2) The modernization of doctrine to accord with the evolutionary process." Williston told Corbin that he accepted Hohfeld's classification of concepts, though not his terminology. WILLIAM TWINING, KARL LLEWELLYN AND THE REALIST MOVEMENT 397 (1973) n.31. Edwin Patterson, reviewing the Contracts Restatement, said he found only three of Hohfeld's eight categories (right, duty, power) in it. Patterson, *supra* note 30, at 403 n.19.

[64] Wesley N. Hohfeld, *Fundamental Legal Conceptions as Applied in Judicial Reasoning*, 26 YALE L.J. 710 (1917).

[65] Hitchman Coal & Coke Co. v. Mitchell, 245 U.S. 229 (1917).

[66] *See* Walter Wheeler Cook, *Privileges of Labor Unions in the Struggle for Life*, 27 YALE L.J. 779 (1917). For the intellectual history of "privileges" to inflict injury in analytical jurisprudence, *see* Joseph William Singer, *The Legal Rights Debate in Analytical Jurisprudence from Bentham to Hohfeld*, WISC. L. REV. 975 (1982).

[67] For a detailed discussion of the limited and selective use the Restatement projects made of Hohfeldian terms and categories, *see* White, *supra* note 41, at 27–35. Thomas W. Merrill & Henry E. Smith, *Why Restate*

analysis was to bring concealed policy choices to the surface. It could not tell you how the policy choices were to be made. That would require a different sort of science, and the lawyers were divided about whether to hand off that set of tasks to another group of specialists, like economists or sociologists or behavioral psychologists, or to try to do it themselves. The ultimate compromise, adopted by most Realist legal scholars in the 1940s and 1950s, was to borrow snippets of concepts and insights from neighboring fields and to add "and Materials" to the "Cases" of the casebooks.[68]

B. Restatements as Symbol and Ritual

One prominent Realist supplied a positive justification for the ALI's projects, albeit in an ironic and backhanded way. This was Thurman Arnold. A colleague of Arnold's at Yale, the psychologist Edward S. Robinson,[69] wrote a book in 1935 analyzing law and lawyering and judicial decision-making from the viewpoint of psychology. Not surprisingly, this analysis revealed myriads of influences on judicial decisions besides those officially stated as reasons, many unconscious or unacknowledged, some consciously suppressed because thought illegitimate or because of confirmation bias or prejudice. Robinson called for an objective science of law that would undertake to study these influences on judicial behavior. As things are now, "legal knowledge and legal education are so organized that students are trained to look at the priests of the law rather than anthropologists seeking an accurate understanding of a tremendous significant type of human behavior."[70] Robinson believed that the ALI's Restatement projects were antithetical to this form of scientific inquiry. The Reporters looked at conflicting cases and presumed to decide *"what the law really is."* They suppressed uncertainty by purported authoritative fiat.

> [T]he undertaking ... is plainly founded upon the belief that too much truth about the law is disastrously confusing and that the remedy may be found in an authoritative suppression of the facts rather than in better education of the public and the bar as to the actual psychological and sociological nature of the law.... There is some reason to believe that it would be easier and more satisfactory to learn law by random sampling of the cases with all their contradictions and complexities than by reading the abstract propositions in the volumes issued by the Institute.[71]

---

the Bundle: *The Disintegration of the Restatement of Property*, 79 BROOK. L. REV. 681 (2014), tell us that the first Restaters of Property, despite their announced aim of faithfully incorporating Hohfeld's terminology, made use of it only fitfully. But, they say, Hohfeld's influence was more powerfully registered in their adoption of his disaggregated "bundle of rights" conception of property.

[68] *See* LAURA KALMAN, LEGAL REALISM AT YALE, 1927–1960, at 145–228 (1986).

[69] Arnold, Robinson and Jerome Frank co-taught a seminar at Yale Law School for many years on "The Judicial Process from the Point of View of Social Psychology," known to students as "The Cave of the Winds."

[70] EDWARD S. ROBINSON, LAW AND THE LAWYERS 71 (1935).

[71] *Id.* at 36.

To Herbert Goodrich, the dean and eventual federal judge who was gradually taking over the ALI's leadership from William Draper Lewis,[72] these were fighting words (all the more so, I imagine, because of their superior and condescending tone). Goodrich protested that a good deal of thought and effort from the best minds in the profession had gone into the Restatements, and that although of course they were fair game for criticism, it was outrageous to attribute dishonesty, and absurd to propose random sampling of cases as a substitute.[73] Thurman Arnold stepped into the fight. He observed that this was a dispute between priests and anthropologists, between those engaged in a practice taking its practitioners' internal point of view and naturalistic observers of the practice from outside.

This spiritual trouble would be avoided if the scholar realized that there is need for both a science of law and a science about law—the one for ceremonial use inside the institution and the other for observation from above. An objective or naturalistic attitude toward human institutions is one that can be taken only by one writing about them from the outside.... An objective history of a church can scarcely be written by its bishop, if he wishes to maintain the church as it is. He may use the understanding which he derives from such an attitude in order to make the operation of the church more effective, but while he is on the public stage he must play his part in accordance with the assumptions underlying the lines which he speaks....

The symbols of the law, both primitive and modern, arise out of a series of contests which dramatize the various conflicting ideals hidden under the term "justice." Out of those contests parables are spun, and maxims derived which reflect the contradictory moral and economic notions of the man on the street. These maxims can never get far from those notions, or the man on the street will complain of the law as unjust or uneconomic. The man on the street is not one character, but a whole cast of characters. His firmly held beliefs contradict each other, and he reconciles them in mysticism, or loses them in elaborate dialectic. The most important institution wherein such conflicts are reconciled, either by ceremony or logic, is the judicial system. It cannot, therefore, be a place where hard, cold truth is sought, yet it must be a place where everyone thinks that truth is searched for....

We dramatize that rule of law in our judicial system and in our constitution. We do not conduct parades as they do both in England and Japan. Our ceremonies are built on the pattern of a feast of pure reason. The spectacle of a hundred or so prominent lawyers and scholars sitting in a great hotel listening to the Restatement discussed section by section is congenial to our protestant way of looking at the symbols of our government.[74]

[72] Goodrich succeeded Lewis as Director in 1947. On his central role in the development and expansion of the ALI, see N.E.H. Hull, Back to the "Future of the Institute": William Draper Lewis's Vision of the ALI's Mission During Its First Twenty-Five Years and Its Implications for the Institute's Seventy-Fifth Anniversary, in THE AMERICAN LAW INSTITUTE—SEVENTY-FIFTH ANNIVERSARY, supra note 105, at 129–58.

[73] Herbert F. Goodrich, Institute Bards and Yale Reviewers, 84 U. PA. L. REV. 449, at 451–52 (1936).

[74] Thurman W. Arnold, Institute Priests and Yale Observers—A Reply to Dean Goodrich, 84 U. PA. L. REV. 811, at 813–14 (1936).

Now Arnold was an inveterate joker, but his satirical style concealed a serious point. Governance, he believed, especially in a time like the 1930s of bitter social division and political controversy, required stabilization and reassurance of the populace through the manipulation of symbols. Both law and economics painted pictures of an ideal but imaginary order of free-market capitalism under the rule of law, administered by benevolent elites. Examples of such symbols are the fiction that giant enterprises are just like competitive small proprietors, the ritual of the criminal trial and the appearance of subjugation of administrative agencies to judicial review.[75] The ALI enterprise was also such a symbol. The actual messiness, the inescapable conflicts, and the distributional stakes of law could be hidden behind a public drama of grave authoritative pronouncement of consensus on best legal practices. Arnold's picture of the symbolic functions of the ALI was actually not all that distant from that of the ALI's own founders, who believed that in a time of great "popular dissatisfaction with the administration of justice"—in the words of Pound's famous speech (1906) that had inaugurated the movement for moderate law reform resulting in the ALI—the public needed the reassurance that only a visible and concerted effort of the great and good could give it, that the defects in the legal system were being corrected, all to the aim of securing more perfect justice.[76]

V. Could the ALI Have Accommodated the Realist Critiques? Ultimately, It (Partially) Did!

The answer at first seems fairly plain. Most of the Realist critics were thinking within a different conceptual frame from the Principal Reporters of the First Restatements, even though, since they were all lawyers who had been trained in much the same way, they had a lot of language in common.

The Restaters could seemingly have accommodated some of the milder critiques, such as that the dogmatic form of the Restatements concealed disagreements about the best rules, and that these conflicts should be openly discussed in comments, along with reasons for adopting the rule chosen. (This was to have been one of the functions performed by the abandoned project of the treatises.) The Restaters could have been more aggressive about law reform, more ruthless in pruning the common law, especially the law of property and trusts, of its archaic or obsolete doctrines— but at the cost of alienating practitioners. They could have been more consistent in incorporating Hohfeldian terms and categories (one of their announced aims)— again however at the cost of trying to impose on practitioners an unfamiliar system and jargon.

---

[75] See generally THURMAN W. ARNOLD, THE SYMBOLS OF GOVERNMENT (1935); THE FOLKLORE OF CAPITALISM (1937). My understanding of Arnold's thought has been greatly improved by Mark Fenster, The Symbols of Government: Thurman Arnold and Post-Realist Legal Theory, 51 BUFF. L. REV. 1053 (2003).

[76] As many historians have noted, there was a definite nativist element in this reform effort, the fear that the legal system was being brought into disrepute by the unethical practices of night-school trained immigrant, especially Jewish, lawyers. See White, supra note 40; JEROLD AUERBACH, UNEQUAL JUSTICE: LAWYERS AND SOCIAL CHANGE IN MODERN AMERICA (1976), William P. LaPiana, A Task of No Common Magnitude: The Founding of the American Law Institute, 11 NOVA L. REV. 1085, 1123–24 (1987).

Could they have done more to meet the core Realist claim that the black-letter rules and principles were too general and abstract, and thus failed to accurately reflect the variations in factual context that led, in the case law, to varied results? That would obviously have been difficult to do without defeating the aim to synthesize out of the existing cases fields of unified legal principles such as Contracts and Torts. Sometimes the Realists seemed to talk as if all decisions were uniquely determined by the facts of individual cases, so that no generalizations were possible. But that position was rare: the Realists certainly thought that decisions were patterned and that the patterns were discoverable by investigation. But the problem for them was that the investigations had not been done, had barely even been started, and their confident proponents—as they were to discover—had massively underestimated the difficulties of conducting them. The mission, after all, was to use sociology to discover the conflicting "interests" at stake in the formulation of a legal rule, psychology to discover the motivations of judges, and ethics and economics to assess the policy aims of the law and the actual consequences of the law in action (which incidentally would also require further research into the army of officials and laymen who applied it). Yet if fields of legal doctrine were really only miscellaneous collections of policies, was there any point into trying to "restate" them?[77] Several of the leading Realists thought not, and that a better way of implementing their view of law as policy was to sign up for the New Deal.[78]

Despite such obstacles as these, the next generation of ALI Reporters partially accommodated their Realist critics and imported their approaches into the Restatements and Uniform Code projects of the postwar era. A scaled-down version of Realist method suggested that the cases themselves often supplied enough data about their factual context to allow scholars to find general factual patterns determining results—and this was the method used by Corbin, Cook, and Llewellyn, among others. In drafting the Uniform Commercial Code's Article 2 on Sales, as is well known, Llewellyn solved the problem—with how much success is much debated among Contracts scholars—of reconciling the need for generality in legal statement, but for particularity in adjudication, by framing the law in terms of broad standards ("reasonable," "good faith," etc.) and relying on merchant custom (and in his original plan for the Code, merchant tribunals) to fill in the particulars.[79] Another bold simplifying move, which Williston would surely have approved would have been for the Restaters to assert that their rules, whether or not they accurately expressed the state of the existing law, or the emerging law, were definite enough, if treated as codes, to guide the bench and bar and the bar's clients to certain and predictable results.[80]

In many other ways the Second (and later) Restatements managed to take a moderate Realism on board without being swamped by it. They are much more candid and

---

[77] This question is asked by Merrill and Smith, *supra* note 68.

[78] These included Frank, Oliphant, Arnold, Clark, Felix Cohen, William O. Douglas, and Walton Hamilton. *See* Roy Kreitner, *Biographing Realist Jurisprudence*, 35 LAW & SOC. INQUIRY 765 (2010).

[79] *See* Robert E. Scott, *The Uniform Commercial Code and the Ongoing Quest for an Efficient and Fair Commercial Law*, in this volume.

[80] This move, turning Realism upside down by asserting the functionality of rule-formalism, is that made by the present-day new private-law formalists. *See* Scott, *id.*, and Andrew S. Gold & Henry E. Smith, *Restatements and the Common Law*, in this volume.

explicit at articulating the policy, or "functional," rationales for legal rules, and consequentialist arguments for evaluating them. They accommodate diverse policy objectives and factual variations by resting legal rules as broad standards and multifactor
balancing tests. They do not shrink from confronting highly controversial policy
choices—sometimes at the cost of setting off fierce struggles for contending views
among the ALI's constituencies—and taking sides. They are much more likely than
the First Restatement generation to consult and cite empirical evidence supporting
their views. They don't steer clear of legal fields thickly grown with statutes, and they
direct their recommendations to legislatures and law reformers and members of Rules
Committees as well as to common law courts.

"One phase of legal realism," however, as Edwin Patterson noted in 1933,

> will not lend itself to translation in terms of the Restatement: the so-called psycho-
> analysis (not exclusively Freudian) of judicial decisions. A decision for defendant
> motivated by the judge's prejudice against a Democratic plaintiff or a labor union
> plaintiff can be rationalized by quoting general principles; but the genuine motives
> are incompatible with the use of those principles or rules which are regarded as le-
> gitimate guides in the process of deciding. The legal system, because it is designed to
> exclude such illegitimate motivation, fails to take it into account. The study of illicit
> judicial motivation looks to choice of personnel (by electorate or appointing official,
> by lawyer choosing the venue of trial) rather than to choice of rules, to politics and
> advocacy rather than to law.[81]

This mode of Realism eventually found its disciplinary home in the "judicial behavior" school of Political Science.

To return now to where we started: Careful historians of legal thought know better
than to identify the founding jurists and Reporters of the ALI with "Formalism" as it
was described and caricatured by the legal Realists. Those founders themselves were
legal Progressives, "social" jurists, and law reformers.[82] The choices and compromises
to which they committed themselves, however, in producing the first Restatements,
wedded them to a product that was in form, if not in theory, hard to distinguish from
a Formalist code. A view of law that limits the relevant universe of study to the rules
announced in appellate cases and carefully excludes from its purview all other fields,
may not be classical Formalism, but is certainly intellectually parochial.

The Realist Felix Cohen, in his well-known polemic against the "Transcendental
Nonsense" that he believed characterized the First Restatements, ended it with a
prophecy:

> The age of the classical jurists is over, I think. The "Restatement of the Law" by the
> American Law Institute is the last long-drawn-out gasp of a dying tradition. The more

[81] Patterson, *supra* note 30, at 426–27.

[82] William Draper Lewis, the first Director of the ALI, for example, was very receptive to bringing the
social sciences into legal education, although he thought they would be best imported by legal scholars
who incorporated relevant insights from other disciplines into their writing and teaching. William Draper
Lewis, *The Social Sciences as the Basis of Legal Education*, 61 U. PA. L. REV. 531 (1913).

intelligent of our younger law teachers and students are not interested in "restating" the dogmas of legal theology. There will, of course, be imitators and followers of the classical jurists, in the years ahead. But I think that the really creative legal thinkers of the future will not devote themselves, in the manner of Williston, Wigmore, and their fellow masters, to the taxonomy of legal concepts and to the systematic explication of principles of "justice" and "reason," buttressed by "correct" cases. Creative legal thought will more and more look behind the pretty array of "correct" cases to the actual facts of judicial behavior, will make increasing use of statistical methods in the scientific description and prediction of judicial behavior, will more and more seek to map the hidden springs of judicial decision and to weigh the social forces which are represented on the bench. And on the critical side, I think that creative legal thought will more and more look behind the traditionally accepted principles of "justice" and "reason" to appraise in ethical terms the social values at stake in any choice between two precedents. "Social policy" will be comprehended not as an emergency factor in legal argument but rather as the gravitational field that gives weight to any rule or precedent, whether it be in constitutional law, in the law of trade-marks, or in the most technical details of legal procedure.[83]

A reasonably accurate prophecy, except in one respect. All these currents of thought are represented in current scholarship and thinking about law. Yet the work of doc-trinal rationalization, and of Restatement, continues.

---

[83] Cohen, *supra* note 38, at 833–34.

19

The Restatements as Law

*Frederick Schauer**

I. Introduction

What is the relationship between the Restatements and "the law"? Under one view, a Restatement is a descriptive summary of the law, and as such stands outside of the law as an external describer and observer.[1] Another view would focus on *Restatements* as importantly different from "statements," and thus, again from an external point of view, as a series of prescriptions about what the law ought to be or how the law ought to change.[2]

There is, however, a third and less well-recognized view—that the Restatements *are* the law, or at least that they are part of the law, or at least that parts of them can be part of the law. Under this view, the Restatements are not external to the law and do not merely describe the law from the outside or prescribe, also from the outside, what the law ought to be. Rather, Restatements can be—and sometimes are—themselves a component of the *corpus juris* and are thus internal to the law or, simply, law. Or at least that some of them (or some of the provisions of some of them) are. Or at least

* David and Mary Harrison Distinguished Professor of Law, University of Virginia. I have benefited greatly from comments by Andrew Gold, John Goldberg, and Carol Lee on an earlier draft and from suggestions about cases and doctrines from my colleagues Ken Abraham, George Cohen, George Geis, Jason Johnston, Gregg Strauss, and Ted White. Questions and comments at a faculty seminar at the Arizona State University College of Law and at an authors' meeting for this volume have also been of great assistance.

[1] Thus, one view sees the Restatements as, at least in part, "recapitulations" of the existing law. Mark J. Roe, *Legal Origins, Politics, and Modern Stock Markets*, 120 HARV. L. REV. 460, 478 (2006). Slightly more ambiguous is the view, from the very first Restatement, that the Restatements are and should be treated by courts "as prima facie a correct statement of what may be termed the general common law of the United States." 1 RESTATEMENT OF CONTRACTS xiv (1932), as quoted in CALEB NELSON, STATUTORY INTERPRETATION 623 n.2 (2011). So too with the view that a Restatement is a "widely accepted distillation of the common law . . . ," as the Supreme Court described the Restatement (Second) of Torts in *Field v. Mans*, 516 U.S. 59, 70 (1995).

[2] As discussed at greater length later, this prescriptive function is close to one of the ALI's own perceptions of the goal of the Restatements, albeit tempered by the ALI's view that the Restatements' prescriptions are typically interstitial. As the first Director put it, "[i]f a situation on which at present there is no law is a situation that is likely to arise, the restatement will deal with it, and dealing with it will make new law." Comments of William Draper Lewis, as quoted in Ricky Revesz, *Director's Letter*, A.L.I. REP. (Fall 2020). But although under this view the Restatements engage in prescription only when the existing law is silent or when the sources of existing law go in different and conflicting directions, there remains room, even as the ALI sees it, for occasional prescription when even the weight of the law seems out of touch with public opinion (as Lewis put it) or current expert views about what the law ought to be. *Id.* Thus, the ALI's own view bears some affinity with Ronald Dworkin's characterization of legal decision-making as involving some (unspecified or underspecified) reconciliation of the goals of fit (with existing law) and (normative) justification. RONALD DWORKIN, LAW'S EMPIRE (1986), somewhat modifying RONALD DWORKIN, TAKING RIGHTS SERIOUSLY (1977). For valuable commentary on Dworkin's distinction, *see* James E. Fleming, *Fit, Justification, and Fidelity in Constitutional Interpretation*, 93 B.U.L. REV. 1283 (2013); Lawrence B. Solum, *The Unity of Interpretation*, 90 B.U.L. REV. 551 (2010).

Frederick Schauer, *The Restatements as Law* In: *The American Law Institute*. Edited by: Andrew S. Gold and Robert W. Gordon, Oxford University Press. © Oxford University Press 2023. DOI: 10.1093/oso/9780197685341.003.0020

that they can be. The goal of this chapter is to situate the Restatements within some of the main strands of modern analytic jurisprudence, and in doing so to defend the third of the alternatives just suggested—that Restatements do not stand outside of the law and thus do not from an outsider perspective describe what the law is or prescribe what the law ought to be. Rather, Restatements are inside the law and thus are, or at least can be, part of the law themselves.

II. Just Enough Jurisprudence

Among the enduring contributions of H.L.A. Hart was his development of the idea of a *rule of recognition*.[3] One of three varieties of what Hart called *secondary rules*—rules about rules[4]—a rule of recognition is a rule that tells legal subjects and legal officials which rules are valid *legal* rules and, conversely, which rules are not. Parts of the Administrative Procedure Act,[5] for example, serve this validating or recognizing function, telling participants in the legal system whether some directive emanating from some agency or official is actually the law—or not. And in determining—recognizing—which rules are valid legal rules, a rule of recognition also, and necessarily, determines which rules, norms, principles, standards, and so on are *not* part of the law. Thus, although it is a morally and socially good idea to write thank-you notes upon receiving a gift, no court is going to allow a cause of action by an insulted gift-giver against a rude gift-receiver who has failed to comply with the social rule about thank-you notes. The thank-you-note rule is indeed a rule, both of etiquette and arguably of morality, but it is not a legal rule because no rule of recognition validates it as such.

Although any mature legal system contains multiple rules of recognition of the kind just described, the question inevitably arises as to what makes *those* rules valid. The Administrative Procedure Act is a rule of recognition, but what makes that act a legally valid determinant of which regulations count as law and which do not? The answer to that question is that a further rule of recognition—here Article I of the U.S. Constitution—tells us which purported acts of Congress are actually to count as law.[6] And because the Administrative Procedure Act was indeed enacted according to and consistent with the provisions of the Constitution, the Constitution as itself

---

[3] H.L.A. HART, THE CONCEPT OF LAW (Penelope A. Bulloch, Joseph Raz, & Leslie Green eds., 3d ed. 2012) (1961). Among the more useful analyses are Larry Alexander, *Connecting the Rule of Recognition and Intentionalist Interpretation: An Essay in Honor of Richard Kay*, 52 CONN. L. REV. 1513 (2021); Richard S. Kay, *Preconstitutional Rules*, 42 OHIO ST. L.J. 187 (1981); Grant Lamond, *The Rule of Recognition and the Foundations of a Legal System, in* READING HLA HART'S *THE CONCEPT OF LAW* 97 (Luís Duarte d'Almeida, James Edwards, & Andrea Dolcetti eds., 2013); Andrei Marmor, *Legal Conventionalism, in* HART'S POSTSCRIPT: ESSAYS ON THE POSTSCRIPT TO THE *CONCEPT OF LAW* 193 (Jules Coleman ed., 2001).

[4] Hart's additional two secondary rules (and there could be still others), not directly relevant here, are rules of adjudication and rules of change. Rules about rules, it is worth noting, can be understood as a subset of the even larger category of decisions about decisions or decision-making about decision-making. *See* Cass R. Sunstein & Edna Ullmann Margalit, *Second-Order Decisions*, 110 ETHICS 5 (1999).

[5] 5 U.S.C. §§ 551–59 (2018).

[6] *See* Kent Greenawalt, *The Rule of Recognition and the Constitution, in* THE RULE OF RECOGNITION AND THE U.S. CONSTITUTION 1 (Matthew D. Adler & Kenneth Einar Himma eds., 2009).

a rule of recognition enables us to determine, and in this case to conclude, that the Administrative Procedure Act is valid law and thus itself a valid rule of recognition.

At this point, of course, the natural question is what makes the Constitution itself valid. The Administrative Procedure Act can validate an administrative rule as law, and the Constitution can validate the Administrative Procedure Act as law, but what validates the Constitution? At this stage of the progression, however, the Hartian argument is that no other rule validates a constitution. Rather, a constitution as a master rule of recognition becomes law—becomes valid, although Hart himself resisted using that word in this context[7]—simply by virtue of it being accepted as authoritative by legal officials.[8] This empirical fact of acceptance is what Hart labeled the *ultimate rule of recognition*—the contingent social recognition of what, in the final analysis, was to count as law and what was not.[9]

As should be apparent from the foregoing, it is a mistake to label the Constitution, or any equivalent master rule of recognition, as the ultimate rule of recognition.[10] Rather, the ultimate rule of recognition is what recognizes the Constitution as the final positive law source of legal validity in the first place. And, importantly, the ultimate rule of recognition can also recognize various other documents and sources as well. The English constitution, for example, is an amalgam of documents—*Magna Carta* and the Bill of Rights of 1689, among others—and less canonically written understandings—for example, the role of the queen, the principle of freedom of speech, and those principles of procedural justice typically described as principles of "natural justice."[11] But these multiple sources are parts of the highest law in England because, and only because, a complex ultimate rule of recognition recognizes them as such.[12] Thus, a hypothetical ultimate rule of recognition in the United States could

---

[7] For Hart, the concept of validity is limited to rule-determined validity. When there is no further rule that renders a rule valid or invalid, the very idea of validity was, for him, simply inapt.

[8] HART, *supra* note 3, at 79–110. *See also* NEIL MACCORMICK, H.L.A. HART 136–41 (2d ed. 2008). For further explanation, analysis, and qualified criticism, *see* Julie Dickson, *Is the Rule of Recognition Really a Conventional Rule?*, 27 OX. J. LEGAL STUD. 373 (2007); Grant Lamond, *Legal Sources, the Rule of Law, and Customary Law*, 59 AM. J. JURIS. 25 (2014).

[9] Jurisprudence *cognoscenti* will recognize the affinity between Hart's conception of an ultimate rule of recognition and Hans Kelsen's idea of the *Grundnorm*, the foundational norm that makes it possible to determine which other (and lesser) norms are validly part of the legal order. HANS KELSEN, INTRODUCTION TO THE PROBLEMS OF LEGAL THEORY (Stanley L. Paulson & Bonnie Litschewski Paulson trans., 1992) (1934); HANS KELSEN, PURE THEORY OF LAW (Max Knight trans., 1967) (1960); Stanley L. Paulson, *Did Walter Jellinek Invent Hans Kelsen's Basic Norm?*, *in* HANS KELSEN'S PURE THEORY OF LAW: CONCEPTIONS AND MISCONCEPTIONS 351 (Matthias Jestaedt, Ralf Poscher, & Jörg Kammerhofer eds., 2020). But Kelsen's *Grundnorm* was the hypothesis, presupposition, fiction, or transcendental understanding that made legal cognition possible. By contrast, and much more relevant to this chapter, Hart's ultimate rule of recognition is not a hypothesis, assumption, presupposition, or anything of that sort, but, rather, a matter of hard empirical fact.

[10] *See* JOHN GARDNER, LAW AS A LEAP OF FAITH 107 (2012); Larry Alexander & Frederick Schauer, *Rules of Recognition, Constitutional Controversies, and the Dizzying Dependence of Law on Acceptance*, *in* THE RULE OF RECOGNITION AND THE U.S. CONSTITUTION, *supra* note 3, at 175; Douglas Edlin, *The Rule of Recognition and the Rule of Law*, 64 AM. J. COMP. L. 371 (2016); Leslie Green, *The Concept of Law Revisited*, 94 MICH. L. REV. 1687, 1706 (1996).

[11] *See generally* O. HOOD PHILLIPS & PAUL JACKSON, O. HOOD PHILLIPS' CONSTITUTIONAL AND ADMINISTRATIVE LAW (6th ed. 1978).

[12] I refer, conventionally, to "English law" and not to the law of Great Britain or the United Kingdom, in order to avoid complex constitutional issues about the constitutional status of the modern entities of which England is but a part. *See* D.C.M. YARDLEY, INTRODUCTION TO BRITISH CONSTITUTIONAL LAW (5th ed. 1978).

recognize the Declaration of Independence as valid law, but at least for now the actual ultimate rule of recognition in the United States does not do so.[13]

The ultimate rule of recognition for any legal system is grounded not on any further rule, but simply on acceptance. Accordingly, the ultimate rule of recognition cannot itself be legally valid or legally invalid, although of course it can be criticized on moral or political or other extralegal grounds. The ultimate rule of recognition just *is*, and its is-ness is a matter of empirical fact.

Hart led us astray by labeling this ultimate determinant of legal validity a *rule*.[14] But the ultimate criterion of legal validity need not have a single canonical formulation, and its contours may change over time, sometimes even imperceptibly. Better than calling this ultimate determinant of legal validity a "rule," a more accurate designation would be a "practice," and the ultimate determinant of legal validity in any legal system is the practice or set of practices by judges and other officials to treat some norms or rules as legally valid and authoritative and others not. I could, for example, write a document, entitle it "The Constitution of the United States of America," and proceed to validate it according to its own terms. But it would still not be law in the United States because, and only because, the practice of American judges and other legal officials is to treat the document sitting behind glass at the National Archives as supreme law and to treat my internally valid purported constitution as nothing other than a stupid joke.[15]

Importantly, the idea of these ultimate practices of recognition as distinguishing between law and not law is not about a formal constitution. It is about determining what things are law and what are not. And although that determination might be understood as constitutional in a small "c" sense, it seems preferable simply to understand the determination of what counts as law and what does not as not necessarily being a constitutional determination in the ordinary sense of what a constitution is and what a constitution does. For example, prior to the 1940s, English judges generally refused to treat "secondary" books and articles about the law as authoritative unless the author were dead.[16] Commentary by living authors of secondary sources was not treated as authoritative at all, and indeed was not even allowed into the realm of permissible legal sources. But starting in the 1940s, English courts began gradually to cite, and thus to treat as authoritative, various commentaries by living authors, perhaps most prominently Arthur Goodhart, who was Hart's predecessor as Professor of Jurisprudence at Oxford. Over time the practice became more entrenched, although

---

[13] *See* Frederick Schauer, *Why the Declaration of Independence Is Not Law—And Why It Could Be*, 89 So. Cal. L. Rev. 619 (2016).

[14] *See* Frederick Schauer, *Is the Rule of Recognition a Rule?*, 3 Transnat'l Legal Theory 1 (2012); Anthony J. Sebok, *Is the Rule of Recognition a Rule?*, 72 Notre Dame L. Rev. 1539 (1997).

[15] *See* Frederick Schauer, *Amending the Presuppositions of a Constitution, in* Responding to Imperfection: The Theory and Practice of Constitutional Amendment 145 (Sanford Levinson ed., 1995).

[16] *See* Alexandra Braun, *Burying the Living? The Citation of Legal Writings in English Courts*, 58 Am. J. Comp. L. 27 (2010); Neil Duxbury, *Better Read than Dead?*, 32 Amicus Curiae 25 (2000). *See also* D.L. Carey Miller, *Legal Writings as a Source in English Law*, 8 Comp. & Int'l L. of Southern Africa 236 (1975); Stephen Waddams, *The Authority of Treatises in English Law (1800-1936), in* Law and Authority in British Legal History 1200-1900, at 274 (Mark Godfrey ed., 2016).

still not as entrenched as it is in the United States, and it is thus fair to say—now—that the ultimate rule of recognition in England, and indeed in the rest of the United Kingdom, recognizes the work of living secondary authors as legitimate legal authority in a way that the 1930s (and earlier) ultimate rule of recognition would not have recognized.[17]

Implicit in the previous paragraph is a conclusion that some, perhaps most prominently John Chipman Gray, would resist—that valid sources of law *are* law, such that there is no defensible or useful distinction between law and a source of law.[18] Nor between a legitimate legal authority and law.[19] If the recognitional practices of the relevant cohort of officials treat some source as law, then it simply *is* law. The central lesson of Hart's analysis of the idea of an ultimate rule of recognition, his mislabeling of it as a "rule" notwithstanding, is that in order to determine what is law in some jurisdiction we are required to look, empirically, at what the relevant officials actually treat as law and what they do not. If in some society the relevant officials were to treat the indications of tea leaves as law and were to use those indications to make and justify their decisions in the name of the law, then in that society those indications would simply be law. More realistically, judges who treat the original public meaning of the constitutional text as authoritative are treating that meaning as law.[20] And although provisions of the West Virginia Constitution and statutes[21] mandate that the common law of the Commonwealth of Virginia as it existed in 1863 is to be treated as the law in West Virginia, the same conclusion would follow even with no explicit constitutional

---

[17] This is as good a place as any to flag a potential distinction between citations to authority in briefs and judicial opinions, on the one hand, and sources that are genuinely authoritative, on the other. A source of law is authoritative if it is taken, on account of its provenance (or "pedigree," as Dworkin, *supra* note 7, puts it), to provide a not necessarily conclusive reason for some decision. Thus, various things that courts might cite (see, for example, the baseball history in *Flood v. Kuhn*, 407 U.S. 258 (1972), or quotations from Shakespeare, as in *Levy v. Louisiana*, 391 U.S. 68, 72 n.6 (1968)) might not be taken as in any way authoritative, and thus could not in any way be law. But the basic Hartian point is that various sources other than statutes, judicial opinions, and constitutional provisions might, contingently, be taken as authoritative in the sense of providing a reason for a decision. In such cases, those sources, whatever they may be, would be law.

[18] Gray, famously, distinguished between law and sources of law, believing that even statutes and decisions of a jurisdictions highest court were not law, but only the sources of law that judges in particular cases would draw upon in making their decisions in particular cases. It was those decisions, and only those decisions, that were, for Gray, really law. JOHN CHIPMAN GRAY, THE NATURE AND SOURCES OF LAW (1909). There is perhaps a place in jurisprudential thought for Gray's peculiar conclusion that even statutes were not themselves law, but Gray's conclusion, one that makes phrases such as "according to the law" and "based on the law" nonsensical, need not detain us here.

[19] *See supra* note 17, and, more extensively, Frederick Schauer, *Authority and Authorities*, 95 VA. L. REV. 1931 (2008).

[20] "[T]he original public meaning of the Constitution is the law." Amy Coney Barrett & John Copeland Nagle, *Congressional Originalism*, 19 U. PA. REV. CONST. L. 1, 3 (2016). *See also* Ian Bartrum, *Two Dogmas of Originalism*, 7 WASH. U. JURIS. REV. 157, 179 (2015).

[21] W. VA. CONST. art. VIII, §13; W. VA. CODE § 2-1-1 (2020). An insightful jurisprudential analysis is James Audley McLaughlin, *The Idea of the Common Law in West Virginia:* Morningstar v. Black & Decker *Revisited*, 103 W. VA. L. REV. 125 (2000). To be clear, therefore, the basic point is that, for example, Virginia law does not (or did not) become West Virginia law because of some formal and explicit legislative or constitutional act. The same thing could have taken place solely by virtue of what West Virginia judges just *did* even absent a statutory or constitutional provision, and even absent a distinct judicial announcement to that effect.

or statutory imprimatur or command, as long as West Virginia judges in practice actually did treat the law of Virginia as West Virginia law.[22]

The upshot of the foregoing is that what counts as law and what does not is entirely a matter of convention and that the conventions actually in force are entirely a matter of empirical fact. At least from a broadly positivist perspective, and *a fortiori* even from the form of antipositivism represented in the work of Ronald Dworkin, the domain of law can, in theory, include just about anything.[23] As David Lyons puts it, "the tests for law in a system are whatever officials make them—and Hart suggests no limits on the possibilities."[24]

III. On the Authority and Legality of Restatements

It should be obvious from the foregoing that there is no reason from a legal positivist perspective, and indeed from some nonpositivist perspectives, that a Restatement could not be part of the law. If what the relevant legal officials treat as legally authoritative is, by definition, law, then a practice by which legal officials treated the Restatements as legally authoritative would be sufficient for those Restatements so treated, or those parts of Restatements so treated, to be themselves part of the law. And this would be so even if that practice were never explicitly formulated in a single canonical or official formulation. Just as the rules (or conventions, if you will) of grammar and etiquette are understood as decision-guiding and thus authoritative even absent a singular canonical formulation, so too with the way in which various sources can become law simply by virtue of widespread accepted use.

---

[22] Much the same can be said about the syllabus of an opinion, which is understood not to be part of the law for the opinions of the Supreme Court of the United States, United States v. Detroit Timber & Lumber Co., 200 U.S. 321 (1906), but which is treated as authoritative in, for example, Ohio and West Virginia. *See* McLaughlin, *supra* note 21, at 163–66. And although it is true that the syllabus for an opinion of the Supreme Court of the United States is not prepared by the Court in the way that the equivalents in Ohio and West Virginia are court-prepared, the basic point, with its foundations in Hart, is that nothing about the idea of law could prevent the syllabus of a U.S. Supreme Court opinion from being treated as authoritative law despite its having been created by the Reporter of Decisions, and nothing about the idea of law could prevent the syllabi of the Ohio and West Virginia supreme court opinions from being systematically rejected as authority despite their having been prepared by the courts themselves.

[23] The account described here is one that is most commonly described these days as "inclusive legal positivism"; *see* Kenneth Einar Himma, *Inclusive Legal Positivism, in* THE OXFORD HANDBOOK OF JURISPRUDENCE AND PHILOSOPHY OF LAW 125 (Jules Coleman, Scott Shapiro, & Kenneth Einar Himma eds., 2002), although it has been labeled as "incorporationism," Jules Coleman, *Incorporationism, Conventionality, and the Practical Difference Thesis,"* 4 LEGAL THEORY 381 (1998), and as "soft positivism" by Hart, who embraced it in the "Postscript" to *The Concept of Law.* HART, *supra* note 3, at 250–54. Indeed, Ronald Dworkin has commented on the compatibility between this form of legal positivism and his own account of law. Ronald Dworkin, *Thirty Years On,* 116 HARV. L. REV. 1655 (2002). The contemporary competitor to inclusive legal positivism, exclusive legal positivism, which is associated most closely with Joseph Raz, *see, e.g.,* JOSEPH RAZ, THE AUTHORITY OF LAW: ESSAYS ON LAW AND MORALITY (1979); Andrei Marmor, *Exclusive Legal Positivism, in* OXFORD HANDBOOK, *id.* at 104, takes issue with inclusive legal positivism largely with respect to the legality *vel non* of decisional inputs that cannot be identified by their source, most obviously morality. With respect to things like Restatements, therefore, there are few differences of importance among inclusive positivism, exclusive positivism, and Ronald Dworkin, all of whom recognize the open-ended conventionality of determining which source-based factors can count as law.

[24] David Lyons, *Principles, Positivism, and Legal Theory,* 87 YALE L.J. 415, 423–24 (1977).

That which is possible, however, need not be that which actually occurs. It would be possible for "God Bless America" to be the national anthem of the United States, but it isn't, and hasn't been, and is unlikely to be in the foreseeable future. Conceptually possible, yes, but actually occurrent, no. So maybe the same might be said about the status of the Restatements. It would be possible, according to the Hartian framework, for the law of North Korea or articles in *People* magazine to count as law in the United States, but they don't. And so perhaps the same holds true for the Restatements.

It turns out, however, that important provisions of the Restatements do have a status that North Korean law and articles in *People* do not have, and that many of the sources that are more traditionally thought of as law do have. Consider, to take one of the more obvious examples, Section 90 of the Restatement of Contracts. That section, setting forth the requirements for so-called promissory estoppel, is a particularly good example because, by allowing a cause of action under some circumstances even absent consideration, it is widely thought to depart from the traditional common law of contract.[25] This departure notwithstanding, courts have not only relied extensively on Section 90,[26] but have also frequently relied solely on Section 90 to support a cause of action that otherwise would have been rejected. In *Ravelo by Ravelo v. County of Hawaii*,[27] for example, the Supreme Court of Hawaii relied on Section 90 of the Restatement (Second) to allow a cause of action that a lower court had rejected, and in doing do cited only the Restatement and on earlier Hawaii case,[28] one that had in turn relied on (and cited) only Section 90 of the Restatement (First). And even more clearly, the Supreme Court of Maine in 2008 described Maine as having "adopted" the principle and definition of promissory estoppel from Section 90,[29] relying for that conclusion on an earlier Maine case announcing that "[p]romissory estoppel is an accepted doctrine in Maine,"[30] the earlier case relying on a still earlier one that "declared" Section 90 as "the law of Maine" and that had also said that "[W]e now adopt as the law of Maine the comprehensive formulation of [promissory estoppel] set forth in the Restatement...."[31]

Similarly clear examples of Restatement provisions having been treated as law, and not just as a summary of existing law, and not just as recommendations about what the law ought to be, come from the Restatements of Torts. Section 402A of the Restatement (Second) of Torts deals with strict products liability and has been cited 2,499 times since its issuance. Among those courts citing this section is the Supreme Court of Nevada, which, citing no other authority, announced in 2009 that "The Restatement (Second) of Torts section 402A governs strict products liability."[32] And

---

[25] *See* Eric Alden, *Rethinking Promissory Estoppel*, 16 NEVADA L.J. 659 (2016); Michael Gibson, *Promissory Estoppel, Article 2 of the U.C.C., and the Restatement (Third) of Contracts*, 73 IOWA L. REV. 659 (1988); Marco J. Jimenez, *The Many Faces of Promissory Estoppel: An Empirical Analysis Under the Restatement (Second) of Contracts*, 57 UCLA L. REV. 669 (2010).

[26] A Westlaw search on August 23, 2021, for example, revealed 1,008 citations to Section 90 in the "all state cases" database.

[27] 658 P.2d 883 (Haw. 1983).

[28] Anthony v. Hilo Electric Light Co., 442 P.2d 64 (Haw. 1968).

[29] Harvey v. Dow, 962 A.2d 322, 325 (Me. 2008).

[30] June Roberts Agency, Inc. v. Venture Properties, Inc., 676 A.2d 46, 49–50 (Me. 1996).

[31] Chapman v. Bomann, 381 A.2d 1123, 1127 (Me. 1978).

[32] Rivera v. Philip Morris, Inc., 209 P.3d 271, 276 (Nev. 2009).

to the same effect, even if in less peremptory form, the Supreme Court of Montana stated that Montana "adopt[ed]" Section 402A as its law.[33]

Indeed, torts provides multiple other examples of the Restatement(s) being treated as an authoritative source of law. One of these is Section 520, on abnormally dangerous activities, which has been cited 371 times and has been treated as establishing the law on many occasions.[34] And so too with the tort of intentional infliction of emotional distress. In Delaware, for example, Section 46 of the Restatement (Second) of Torts is taken not only to describe the law but also to *be* the law, with one court saying that "Delaware courts *apply* § 46 of the Restatement (Second) of Torts in analyzing claims for intentional infliction of emotional distress."[35] And in Wyoming, the Wyoming Supreme Court has said that the state has "adopted" Section 46 as the law.[36]

Even clearer than the various Restatement provisions on contracts and torts that have become the law are the Restatements on Conflict of Laws, which are commonly treated in wholesale manner as the entire approach to choice of law issues in a state. Thus, Kansas and New Mexico courts have said that their state "follows" the Restatement (First) of Conflict of Laws,[37] with judges in Mississippi and Michigan using virtually identical language to assert that their states take the Restatement (Second) as establishing the relevant law.[38] And when it is thus sensible and common to refer to a state as a "First Restatement state" or a "Second Restatement state,"[39] it becomes clear that with respect to issues of choice of law, where in most states the cases are few and far between, the Restatements simply *are* the relevant law. And even more clear, and even more wholesale, is the way in which, in the 1950s, both the Northern Mariana Islands and the United States Virgin Islands adopted the Restatements—"all of them"—as the common law in their jurisdictions.[40]

The examples just given support the conclusion that various Restatement provisions, and sometimes a *Restatement* in toto, are treated as *being* the law, and are thus, by virtue of being so treated, the law. But this conclusion, it must be acknowledged, goes beyond what the American Law Institute (ALI) claims for the status of the Restatements it has produced. Although justifiably proud of the place of the

---

[33] Brandenburger v. Toyota Motor Sales, U.S.A., Inc., 513 P.2d 268, 273 (Mont. 1973).

[34] *See* Cadena v. Chicago Fireworks Mfg. Co., 697 N.E.2d 802, 813 (Ill. App. 1998) (announcing that Illinois had "adopted" Section 520), *overruled on other grounds*, Ries v. City of Chicago, 950 N.E.2d 631 (2011); Pullen v. West, 92 P.3d 584, 591 (Kan. 2004) (asserting that Section 520 had been adopted as the law of Kansas on *Williams v. Amoco Production Co.*, 734 P.2d 1113, 1123 (Kan. 1981)).

[35] Cooper v. Bd. Of Educ. Of Red Clay Consolidated Sch. Dist., 2009 WL 3022129 (Superior Ct. of Delaware, New Castle County, Sept. 16, 2009) (emphasis added), citing Cummings v. Pinder, 574 A.2d 943 (Del. 1990), which treats § 46 as being the law of Delaware on the subject of intentional infliction of emotional distress.

[36] Anderson v. Solvay Minerals, Inc., 3 P.2d 236, 241 (Wyo. 2000).

[37] Layne Christensen Co. v. Zurich Canada, 38 P.3d 757 (Kan. App. 2002); Flemma v. Halliburton Energy Services, Inc., 303 P.3d 814, 819 (N.M. 2013).

[38] Savelle v. Savelle, 650 So. 2d 476, 479 (Miss. 1995) (Prather, J., dissenting); Chrysler Corp. v. Skyline Industrial Service, Inc., 502 N.W.2d 715 (Mich. App. 1993).

[39] And there are likely to be Third Restatement states in the not too distant future.

[40] Richard L. Revesz, *Restatements as Legislative Enactments*, ALI Q. NEWSLETTER, Aug. 7, 2018. Thus, the Virgin Islands Code provides that the rules of the common law as expressed in the Restatements "shall be the rules of decision in the courts of the Virgin Islands in cases to which they apply, in the absence of local laws to the contrary." V.I. CODE ANN. TIT. 1, § 4. Similar language appears in the Code of the Northern Marianas. 7 N. MAR. I. CODE § 3401. For commentary, *see* NELSON, *supra* note 1, at 598.

Restatements in the landscape of American law, this place is typically described by the ALI in prescriptive terms. The Restatements "influence" the law,[41] it is said, or provide "guidance" to judges[42] or "guidance" to legislators.[43] And in doing so, the Restatements, unlike the ALI's model Codes, attempt with few exceptions not to depart from existing majority common law rules.[44] And this modest view of the status of the Restatements is not only the view of the ALI but also of many commentators. Mark Roe, for example, announces that "the Restatements are not themselves law. The uniform codes become law when enacted."[45]

The deflationary view of the ALI about the legal status of its own Restatements may reflect a position that bespeaks more of a substantive constraint on what is to count as valid law than we find in traditional legal positivism, which rejects just this kind of substantive constraint.[46] The Restatements are not, to be sure, the products of an elected legislature, nor of a judiciary whose status is derived from a democratically accepted constitution, nor of any other body with official governmental or constitutional status. And so perhaps the ALI and those who agree with it about the status of the Restatements are of the view that acceptance by officials, especially the courts, is a necessary but not sufficient determinant of what is law "properly so called," to use John Austin's phrase.[47] Under such a view, democratic provenance is among the necessary properties of legality, making democracy, or at least governmental legitimacy, among the necessary conditions for legality. This view differs from the traditional natural lawyer's view that substantive moral correctness, or at least the absence of substantive grave moral error, is a necessary condition for legality. But it still imposes a moral or political constraint, beyond mere acceptance by officials, on what is to count as law. And so perhaps it is this belief in a substantive constraint view that explains the ALI's modesty.

Yet the view that the Restatements have a more robust status is hardly without its influential supporters. Judge (then Professor) Guido Calabresi, purporting to be summarizing not only his own views but also those of the founders of the Restatement movement, is worth quoting at length: "The restatements should have a force of law equivalent to that given a longstanding judicial precedent of the jurisdiction. They should be treated, in other words, with no more or less deference than would be given to a common law rule or set of doctrines."[48] And thus, if it sensible to refer to a

---

[41] Richard L. Revesz, *When Legislatures and Agencies Rely on Restatements of the Law,*" ALI Q. Newsletter, Dec. 9, 2019.

[42] Richard L. Revesz, *Restatements and the Federal Common Law,* ALI Q. Newsletter, Sept. 27, 2016.

[43] Richard L. Revesz, *Restatements and Federal Statutes,* ALI Q. Newsletter, Mar. 10, 2016.

[44] Richard L. Revesz, *Codes and Majority Rules,* ALI Q. Newsletter, Dec. 18, 2017.

[45] Roe, *supra* note 1, at 478 n.53. Roe treats the Restatements and the uniform codes as relevantly similar, a conflation that neither I nor the ALI accept. Rarely would a court treat a uniform code, whose prescriptive stance is more patent, as itself the law absent explicit legislative or judicial adoption, but the same does not appear to hold true of the Restatements. Or at least so I maintain here.

[46] Substantive constraints on what is to count as law are traditionally associated with one or another variety of a natural law view, but there is nevertheless at least some connection between the view that substantive immoral laws are not laws at all and the view that laws lacking a certain kind of democratic provenance are not laws at all.

[47] John Austin, The Province of Jurisprudence Defined (Wilfrid E. Rumble ed., 1995) (1832).

[48] Guido Calabresi, A Common Law for the Age of Statutes 84–85 (1982).

common law rule or set of doctrines as "the law," then it is not only a possibility but also a frequently realized possibility that the same can be said of the Restatements.

IV. On Law, Legal Authorities, Legal Sources, and the Alleged Distinction Between Binding and Persuasive Authority

Of course the ALI's deflationary or modest view of the status of its own product might simply be a shrewd political strategy. If the Restatements are to be considered as law, and thus if the creators of the Restatements are to be understood as lawmakers, then one can imagine a concern in some quarters about the democratic provenance of the Restatements and the process of their creation.[49] We can well understand, therefore, why the ALI might worry that claiming to be a lawmaker would inspire official criticism of the makeup of that body, or, even worse, prompt calls for the ALI to be more officially subject to official oversight, or, even worse yet, to elections.

More likely, however, the view that the Restatements are not law, and cannot become law unless explicitly adopted as such by a court or legislature, is a product of a widespread view about the distinction between so-called binding law and various forms of nonbinding, or "persuasive," authority. It is thus time to examine this venerable distinction closely, using the Restatements as the lens for the examination.

The view to which I refer is broader than John Chipman Gray's.[50] The common modern distinction between binding and persuasive authority[51] does not deny, *contra* Gray, that statutes are law, nor that reported opinions of higher courts are law, nor even that earlier "on point" decisions of the same court are law. The modern view does, however, distinguish between binding authority, which it takes to be law, and the various other sources that courts may use to support or explain their decisions,

---

[49] Indeed, this fear has come close to being realized in the legislative enactments or proposals in at least nine states (see, for example, Arizona House Bill 2272, signed into law on March 30, 2022, Arkansas Code Annotated § 23-60-112, signed into law on April 1, 2019, and Michigan Compiled Laws § 500.3032 signed into law on December 18, 2018) to prohibit their courts from using as authority the Restatement of the Law, Liability Insurance. (With thanks to Ricky Revesz for providing a full recapitulation of the various legislative actions). The very fact of organized resistance to the Restatement on Liability Insurance supports the conclusion that various segments of industry and the bar have little doubt that the Restatements can be law.

[50] *See supra* note 18. Theodore Benditt accurately characterizes Gray's views: "[F]or the same reasons that statutes are not law, neither are prior judicial rulings, even if they are the rulings of the same court and even of the same judge. After all judicial precedents are only words, written in the past by some judge, and it is only as currently interpreted that they have an impact on the community." THEODORE M. BENDITT, LAW AS RULE AND PRINCIPLE 7 (1978). Charitably, Neil MacCormick describes Gray's distinction between law and sources of law, and his denigration of latter as law, as an "unguarded moment." MACCORMICK, *supra* note 8, at 154. And for further criticism, *see* WILLIAM TWINING, KARL LLEWELLYN AND THE REALIST MOVEMENT 20–22, 447–48 (2d ed. 2012).

[51] The distinction is ubiquitous in the courts, *see, e.g.*, Calderon-Ortega v. United States, 753 F.3d 250 (1st Cir. 2014); Nuh Nhloc Loi v. Scribner, 671 F. Supp. 2d 1189, 1202 (S.D. Cal. 2009); United States v. Cisneros, 456 F. Supp. 2d 826, 839 (S.D. Tex. 2006), and has become the subject of much commentary, most of it supportive but some critical. *See* Stephen R. Barnett, *From* Anastasoff *to Hart to West's Federal Appendix: The Ground Shifts Under No-Citation Rules*, 4 J. APP. PRAC. & PROC. 1 (2002); Kevin Bennardo, *The Third Precedent*, 25 GEO. MASON L. REV. 148 (2017); Maggie Gardner, *Dangerous Citations*, 95 N.Y.U. L. REV. 1619 (2020); Amy J. Griffin, *Dethroning the Hierarchy of Authority*, 97 OR. L. REV. 51 (2018); Allison Orr Larsen, *Factual Precedent*, 162 U. PA. L. REV. 59 (2013).

these various other sources often riding under the misleading banner of "persuasive authority."[52]

The phrase "persuasive authority" is potentially misleading because it elides the distinction between authority in a strong sense and the lawyer's weaker use of the word "authorities" as the umbrella label for pretty much everything that gets cited in a brief or law review article. As has been well developed in the jurisprudential and philosophical literatures, authority in the strong sense is "content independent."[53] Something that is genuinely authoritative is a (not necessarily conclusive) reason for action or reason for decision because of its source and not because of its content. When parents, frustrated with a child's resistance to their explanations, reasons, and arguments, say "because I said so!," the parents are relying on their status, position, or power, all independent of the soundness of the reasons or arguments that might also be offered for the same outcome. So too with the orders of sergeants to the privates under their command. And so too with the law. Courts (and citizens) are expected (at least by the law) to follow constitutional provisions they believe unwise or obsolete, statutes they think misguided, and the judicial decisions of higher courts they think mistaken, and that expectation—or obligation—arises independent of the subject's agreement or disagreement with the content of the directive they are expected to follow.[54]

From this perspective, the phrase "persuasive authority" is oxymoronic, precisely because genuine authority, in law or out, is inconsistent with the idea of content-dependent persuasion. To the extent that I follow a directive—or a precedent—because and only because I agree with its conclusion or reasoning, then I am not treating it as authoritative in the strong sense to which I refer here.

Moreover, even authority in the strong sense need not be absolute. Reasons can be genuine reasons and still have less than conclusive weight.[55] And thus genuine legal authorities can provide content-independent reasons for decision while still on occasion being overridden our outweighed by reasons inclining in the opposite direction. A statute may be law in any interesting sense of "law," but still vulnerable to being

---

[52] A very good analysis, at times consistent and at times inconsistent with what I offer here, is Chad Flanders, *Toward a Theory of Persuasive Authority*, 62 OKLA. L. REV. 55 (2009). *See also* FREDERICK SCHAUER, THINKING LIKE A LAWYER: A NEW INTRODUCTION TO LEGAL REASONING 67–76 (2009); H. Patrick Glenn, *Persuasive Authority*, 32 McGILL L.J. 261 (1987).

[53] The original idea comes from H.L.A. HART, ESSAYS ON BENTHAM 254–55 (1982). For subsequent elaboration, explication, application, and criticism, *see*, among many sources, JOSEPH RAZ, THE MORALITY OF FREEDOM 35–37 (1986); Edmund Tweedy Flanigan, *Do We Have Reasons to Obey the Law?*, 17 J. ETHICS & SOC. PHIL. 159 (2020); Noam Gur, *Are Legal Rules Content-Independent?*, 5 PROBLEMA 175 (2011); Heidi M. Hurd, *Challenging Authority*, 100 YALE L.J. 1611 (1991); P. Markwick, *Independent of Content*, 9 LEGAL THEORY 43 (2003); Kevin Toh, *Some Moving Parts of Jurisprudence*, 88 TEX. L. REV. 1283 (2010).

[54] Note that the claim in the text is a claim about what it is to accept authority, and not a claim about whether some agent ought or ought not to accept some authority in some context. Thus, the claim is about, for example, what it is to have an obligation to obey the law, and not about whether citizens or even officials do have such an obligation, the existence of such an obligation being the subject of frequent challenge. *See* M.B.E. Smith, *The Duty to Obey the Law*, in A COMPANION TO PHILOSOPHY OF LAW AND LEGAL THEORY 465 (Dennis Patterson ed., 1999). And *see generally* Margaret Martin, *Raz's The Morality of Freedom: Two Models of Authority*, 1 JURISPRUDENCE 63 (2010).

[55] *See* JOSEPH RAZ, PRACTICAL REASON AND NORMS 27 (2d ed. 1990) (1975); FREDERICK SCHAUER, PLAYING BY THE RULES: A PHILOSOPHICAL EXAMINATION OF RULE-BASED DECISION-MAKING IN LAW AND IN LIFE 5–6, 113–15 (1991); Barry Loewer & Marvin Belzer, *Prima Facie Obligation: Its Deconstruction and Reconstruction*, in JOHN SEARLE AND HIS CRITICS 359 (Ernest Lepore & Robert Van Gulick eds., 1991); Frederick Schauer, *A Comment on the Structure of Rights*, 27 GA. L. REV. 415 (1993).

overridden by a constitutional provision or constitutional decision. And a court decision will again be law but nevertheless not controlling when it conflicts in some particular application with the authority of a validly enacted statute.

The distinction that seems important, therefore, is not the distinction between binding and persuasive authority, because, as it was put even well over 100 years ago: "As a court attaches some weight to any of the matters herein described as of imperative authority or of persuasive authority or of quasi-authority, and as a court has it in its power to disregard even imperative authority, the question naturally arises whether the attempted distinctions between the kinds of authority are not wholly imaginary, or at least unimportant."[56] Among the many important features of Eugene Wambaugh's observation is his entirely correct assertion that courts can disregard what he calls "imperative" authority. And not only can they disregard imperative or allegedly binding authority, but they also actually do so on numerous occasions. Sometimes such disregarding (at least in the sense of not following) is justified by recourse to any number of canons of construction permitting courts to override even a statute or to determine that it is inapplicable for one tortured reason or another. *Riggs v. Palmer*[57] has become iconic,[58] but it is merely one among countless examples in which what appeared under any sensible account to be binding law did not carry the day, the law's bindingness being treated as defeasible in favor of broad considerations of equity or fairness or justice, typically framed in terms of characterization of what some legislative body intended or would have intended for the particular matter at issue.[59] And, a fortiori, the same holds true for what appear to be controlling precedents. Few other than John Chipman Gray would dissent from calling such precedents "law," but the supposition that they are controlling if applicable cannot stand up to close inspection.

But although courts have the power to wiggle out of the constraints of even clear and seemingly clearly applicable statutes or seemingly directly applicable controlling precedents, they usually do not totally ignore such allegedly binding law, and are commonly criticized when they do. Courts can override, distinguish, limit, interpret, or construct, but rarely do they completely disregard. When such sources are applicable, departing from their prescriptions must be explained, and courts typically cannot pretend that they do not exist.

By contrast, there are other authorities that are used in a genuine content-independent authoritative way but whose nonuse would rarely attract claims of

---

[56] Eugene Wambaugh, The Study of Cases: A Course of Instruction in Reading and Stating Reported Cases, Composing Head-Notes and Briefs, Criticizing and Comparing Authorities, and Compiling Digests 109 (1894), as quoted in Flanders, *supra* note 52, at 55.

[57] 22 N.E. 188 (N.Y. 1889).

[58] *Riggs* has become iconic now largely because of its having been featured by Ronald Dworkin both in *Taking Rights Seriously* and in *Law's Empire*, but earlier it was treated as notable by the *Harvard Law Review* shortly after the case was decided, Recent Case, *Wills—Murder of the Testator by Legatee*, 3 Harv. L. Rev. 234 (1889), was discussed at some length by then Judge Cardozo, Benjamin N. Cardozo, The Nature of the Judicial Process 40–41 (1921), and occupies a significant place in the Hart and Sacks Legal Process materials. Henry M. Hart Jr. & Albert M. Sacks, The Legal Process: Basic Problems in the Making and Application of Law 90–92 (William N. Eskridge Jr. & Philip P. Frickey eds., 1994). By far the most thorough dissection of *Riggs* is Nelson, *supra* note 1, at 7–27.

[59] *See* John F. Manning, *The New Purposivism*, 2011 Sup. Ct. Rev. 113.

professional incompetence were they to be totally ignored. The Supreme Court justices who cite to foreign law are ordinarily citing to it as authority, and not merely because they are persuaded by its reasoning or content,[60] but the justice who ignores foreign law is on much firmer ground than the judge who ignores a facially applicable statute or constitutional provision. And if, counterfactually, Judge Gray's dissenting opinion in *Riggs v. Palmer* had been the decision of a unanimous New York Court of Appeals, few would have faulted him for not mentioning the "no man may profit from his own wrong" principle, to say nothing of not mentioning the law of Quebec, the Code of Napoleon, or the author of Rutherforth's *Institutes*, among the many other sources that Judge Earl's actual majority opinion used to support its conclusions.

If the foregoing is correct, then the important distinction is not between the conclusive and the overridable, nor between the binding and the persuasive, but between the mandatory and the optional. Some authorities are not imperative in Wambaugh's sense of being absolute but are nevertheless mandatory in the sense of it being at least presumptively necessary either to follow them or to explain why they are not being followed. But other so-called authorities are entirely optional, in the sense that ignoring them will typically attract little professional disapproval. In this dichotomy, facially applicable statutes, most constitutional provisions, and most on-point and within-jurisdiction decided cases are mandatory, while treatises, law review articles, cases from other jurisdictions, and much more, although often used as authority in the content-independent sense, and thus very much part of the law, are nevertheless optional.

So where in this dichotomy between the mandatory and the optional do we find the Restatements? At the very least, they are optional but respectable. A judge who cites to a Restatement is not open to the kind of criticism that would be directed to the judge who cites to the teachings of astrology or even, although less so these days, to *Wikipedia* or articles in popular magazines.[61] So too with citations to foreign law.[62] And so although there are some authorities whose use would be widely condemned, it is plausible to believe that there are at least some optional but respectable authorities, used as authority in a content-independent way, that still ought to be considered as law.[63] Moreover, and most relevantly here, many optional authorities are less optional,

---

[60] *See* Ernest A. Young, *Foreign Law and the Denominator Problem*, 119 HARV. L. REV. 148 (2005). Young's conclusion that most references to foreign law are source-based and thus authority-based, rather than being content-based and thus persuasive, is a challenge to the conventional view that the typical reference to foreign law is using it as a content-based source of support. *See, e.g.,* Vicki C. Jackson, *Constitutional Comparisons: Convergence, Resistance, Engagement*, 119 HARV. L. REV. 109 (2005); Claire L'Heureux-Dubé, *The Importance of Dialogue: Globalization and the International Impact of the Rehnquist Court*, 34 TULSA L.J. 15 (1998); Anne-Marie Slaughter, *A Global Community of Courts*, 44 HARV. INT'L L.J. 191 (2003). Young's sound critique is that if foreign law were being used in a genuinely persuasive way, the courts using it would discuss why the reasoning of the foreign court is in fact persuasive, as opposed to merely relying on the content-independent, and thus not persuasion-dependent, fact that the foreign court has reached such-and-such a conclusion.

[61] On the internet- and electronic database–fostered proliferation of sources previously thought unthinkable, or at least uncitable, *see* Frederick Schauer & Virginia J. Wise, *Non-Legal Information and the Delegalization of Law*, 29 J. LEGAL STUD. 495 (2000). Indeed, the claims and data in that article are even more true twenty years later.

[62] *See supra* note 60.

[63] As a linguistic matter, there may be a revealing distinction between "law" and "the law." Few would deny that the decisions of the Supreme Court of Wyoming are law, but few would accept that those decisions should be considered as "the law" by a New Jersey court.

such that the failure to mention them at all would at the very least raise eyebrows. The court that allows a cause of action sounding in promissory estoppel without even mentioning Section 90 of the Restatement would produce such raised eyebrows.[64] So too with a court that engaged in an exercise of interest analysis in a choice of law situation without mentioning the Second Restatement of Conflict of Laws or the court that applied (or even the court that did not apply) the law on the tort of invasion of privacy by disclosure of private facts with no mention at all of Section 652 of the Restatement (Second) of Torts.[65]

The argument offered here is consistent with but slightly stronger than the following from Kent Greenawalt: "If many states reach the same conclusion about an issue of common law, and that becomes embodied in some influential document such as the Restatement of Torts, people in another state may reasonably assume that is 'the law' for the whole country."[66] If we remove Greenawalt's scare quotes around "the law," and if we substitute "consider" for "may reasonably assume," we are very close to my claim here. When a conclusion is embodied in a Restatement, it may be considered as the law,[67] subject to the qualification that not everything that is considered as the law will be controlling in a particular case, as Eugene Wambaugh observed long ago, and as is even more true now.

V. Restatements and the Hierarchy of Law

Implicit in all of the foregoing is the conclusion that there is no fundamental difference among a legal authority, a source of law, and law. If courts or other officials treat the U.S. Constitution, the constitution of a particular state, or the previous decisions of courts as authoritative, then those documents become sources of law, and are thus the law. By the same token, therefore, when courts or other officials treat all or some sections of some Restatement as authoritative, then those Restatements or Restatement sections similarly become sources of law and are in the same manner simply the law. The jurisprudential lesson from Hart and others is that whatever courts treat as authoritative is the law, and the lesson from the examples in the previous section is that courts have

---

[64] On Section 90 and promissory estoppel in particular, and on how Section 90 appears to be treated as law, *see* MELVIN ARON EISENBERG, THE NATURE OF THE COMMON LAW 78, 135 (1988). That said, Eisenberg does at times treat the Restatements as little more than summaries of existing law or predictions of what courts would do. *Id.* at 167 n.1.

[65] The ALI typically and appropriately counts the citations to the Restatements as a measure of their influence. *See* Revesz, *supra* note 40. But here again perhaps the ALI is being too modest. An even stronger measure would come from counting of citations to a topic that did *not* cite to the Restatement, and then compare that number to the number of cases that did rely, at least in part, on a Restatement provision. Thus, only roughly a third of all court decisions dealing with promissory estoppel do not mention Restatement Section 90, and much the same applies to the tort of invasion of privacy by disclosure of private facts, where again the influence of Section 652 of the Restatement (Second) of Torts is best demonstrated by the small proportion of cases dealing with that tort that do not mention Section 652 at all.

[66] KENT GREENAWALT, STATUTORY AND COMMON LAW INTERPRETATION 187 (2013).

[67] Thus, my conclusion is different from and stronger than that of Shyamkrishna Balganesh, who maintains, correctly and consistently with what I argue here, that there is a "hierarchy of legal authority," Shyamkrishna Balganesh, *Relying on Restatements*, 123 COLUM. L. REV. ___ (forthcoming 2023), but who would relegate the status of the Restatements to "strongly persuasive secondary sources," *id.*, a status justifiable on neither jurisprudential nor empirical grounds.

often treated the Restatements, or particular Restatement sections, as authoritative, and have thus treated them as the law. And if they are so treated, then they *are* the law.

This is not to say, however, that all sources of law, and thus all parts of the law, are equally authoritative. And a good window into the place of the Restatements in the hierarchy of legal authority, and thus in the hierarchy of law, comes from the *Introduction to Advocacy* long distributed to first year students at the Harvard Law School not only as a guide to appellate advocacy, and not only as a guide to brief-writing, but also as a more general guide to the proper use of legal authorities. And in the version used when this author was just such a first-year law student,[68] Restatements occupied a prominent place in the hierarchy of legitimate authorities, below constitutions, statutes, and reported decisions, to be sure, but above treatises, which were above law review articles, which were above student-written notes and comments in law reviews, and which were above other secondary sources, such as newspaper articles. And a separate section was reserved for discouraged sources, such as the annotations in *Annotated Law Reports* and *Law Reports Annotated*, as to which students were explicitly warned "as a general rule" not to cite to them at all, and legal encyclopedias such as *Corpus Juris Secundum* and *American Jurisprudence*, whose citation was to be "very rare." Thus, by putting Restatements above such sources, and indeed by discouraging the use of the latter while encouraging the use of the former, and by putting the Restatements ahead even of treatise and lawyer- or faculty-written law review articles, the editors of *Introduction to Advocacy* made clear that the Restatements were legitimate sources of legal authority and thus legitimate sources of law.

It is true, of course, that the Restatements are not at the top of the hierarchy of authority. But occupying such a "lesser" position is by no means inconsistent with the status of the Restatements as law. State constitutions, for example, are uncontroversially law, but their prescriptions or mandates may be overridden by the U.S. Constitution or interpretations thereof. And so too with reported cases. The decisions of trial courts and intermediate state courts are law only insofar as they are not overridden by the decisions of state supreme courts, and the decisions of state supreme courts are authoritative only insofar as they are not inconsistent with the Constitution of the United States and U.S. Supreme Court opinions. And so too, therefore with the Restatements. They are treated as law, as the previous section has made clear, but they may still be overridden by sources above them in the hierarchy of authority.

Consider again, for example, Section 90 of the Restatement(s) of Contracts, which, in crystallizing and to some extent creating the idea of promissory estoppel as the basis for contractual liability absent consideration, is as good an example as we have of a Restatement provision establishing and being the law. Nevertheless, just as Section 90 has at times supplanted earlier cases, so too has it at times been supplanted either by cases or statute.[69] And Section 139 of the Restatement (Second) of Contracts, which allows Section 90 recovery under some circumstances when what would otherwise be

---

[68] HARVARD LAW SCHOOL BOARD OF STUDENT ADVISORS, INTRODUCTION TO ADVOCACY: BRIEF WRITING AND ORAL ARGUMENT IN THE AMES COMPETITION (8th ed. 1965).

[69] *See, e.g.*, Congregation Kadimah Toras-Moshe v. DeLeo, 540 N.E. 2d 691 (Mass. 1989) (rejecting the charitable subscription clause in Section 90).

a Statute of Frauds requirement has not been met, has occasionally been explicitly rejected by courts otherwise accepting Section 90.[70]

The two examples in the previous paragraph are examples of the fact that just as the weight of authority is a variable, so too is the status of a source as authority, and thus as law, is a variable. Indeed, rather than thinking about the Restatements s being located at some place in a hierarchy, it might be better to consider them as having, as Ronald Dworkin argued with respect to legal principles in *Taking Rights Seriously*, as having the dimension of weight. Not all of the Restatements will have the same weight, and not all of the provisions of even a single Restatement will have the same weight. But not all legal principles have the same weight, and not even all legal rules have the same weight. In this respect the Restatements are no more the law than most of the other more familiar legal items and legal sources. But nor are they any less.

VI. Conclusion

This chapter on the Restatement is plainly not the place to offer a full account (and theory, if you will) of legal sources, nor, of course, a full account of the nature of law itself. That said, we cannot deny that an account of the status of the Restatements presupposes an account of the nature of sources of law, and an account of the nature of sources of law presupposes, in turn, a potentially contested account of the nature of law itself.

Thus, the loosely positivist account offered here is open to challenge on any number of different levels. Most of those challenges, however, would insist that the conceptions of legal sources and legality presupposed here are too broad and not too narrow. But in a world in which the domain of acceptable legal sources is growing exponentially,[71] albeit not without expressions of concern on normative grounds,[72] the idea of considering the Restatements as other than valid legal sources and even as law themselves is so far from the contemporary boundaries that it would be difficult even to imagine what it would be like to suppose that the Restatements have a status that would disqualify them as sources of law, and thus as law themselves. And this is a consequence of which the American Law Institute should be justly proud.

---

[70] *See* Olympic Holding Co., LLC v. ACE Ltd., 909 N.E. 2d 93 (Ohio 2009).

[71] At the extreme, we find the claim of at least one judge that it is appropriate to do his own Internet factual research on the factual background of particular cases before him, RICHARD A. POSNER, REFLECTIONS ON JUDGING 131–48 (2013), and of another that it is acceptable to engage in extra-record factual research on the history, including litigation history, of a particular institutional party. Parents Involved in Community Schools v. Seattle School Dist., 551 U.S. 701, 803 (2007) (Breyer, J., dissenting).

[72] *See* Frederick Schauer, *The Decline of "The Record": A Comment on Posner*, 51 DUQ. L. REV. 51 (2013); David H. Tennant & Laurie M. Seal, *Judicial Ethics and the Internet: May Judges Search the Internet in Evaluating and Deciding a Case?*, 16 PROF. LAW. 2 (2005).

20

Restatements and the Common Law

Andrew S. Gold[*] and Henry E. Smith[**]

I. Introduction

The common law has always struck some as unruly, sprawling, and mysterious, unlike tidier, more systematic codes. Next to codification, restating the law is a less radical way to tame the common law. And from the beginning of the American Law Institute (ALI), the common law has been the target of the Restatement project, in its many phases. Ambivalence about doctrine and about "system" in the law accompanied the journey of Restatements from a mildly conceptualistic reformism to a half-hearted kind of Realism. In this process, the Restatements have sought to overcome the complexity of the law and to state it more systemically, while at the same time becoming a product of a legal culture that is increasingly skeptical of system in the law.

This is a pity, because a better understanding of system can help us discover how Restatements might draw out the best in the common law without falling into the rigidities to which codes are susceptible. Such an understanding can also help diagnose where Restatements have fallen short—how they have reinforced a tendency to regard the law as a heap of targeted rules and vague standards that fails to benefit from more sophisticated notions of system. The kind of system that is implicit in the common law's hybrid of spontaneous and made order is a looser yet selectively interconnected system whose parts specialize and work in tandem to produce system effects.

Of the many ways that Restatements can achieve "fit" with the law, one is what we term "architectural." A Restatement can differ from the law in some formulations and results and yet still conform to the set of loose interrelationships immanent in the law. These relationships help actors and decision makers track consequences, thereby managing complexity. And such a version of system contributes to the guidance function of law.

This chapter will employ a theory of system in the law to analyze how Restatements fit into the intellectual atmosphere of their times, how they have tackled the common law, and how they could do better. Section II examines the beginnings of the Restatements with a special focus on the jurisprudence of one of the movers of the project, Benjamin Cardozo. Section III then shows how Restatements have struggled with notions of system in the common law, eventually opting for a neo-Realist version of narrow rules and vague standards, at the expense of interconnection. In Section IV, we show how, in terms of complexity and system, Restatements achieve simplicity and

[*] Professor of Law, Brooklyn Law School.
[**] Fessenden Professor of Law, Harvard Law School.

Andrew S. Gold and Henry E. Smith, *Restatements and the Common Law* In: *The American Law Institute.*
Edited by: Andrew S. Gold and Robert W. Gordon, Oxford University Press. © Oxford University Press 2023.
DOI: 10.1093/oso/9780197685341.003.0021

reform, and how Restatements can reflect and contribute to architectural fit. We conclude with some lessons for the future of common law Restatements.

II. Varieties of System in the Restatements

Restatements were originally envisioned as a solution to the uncertainty and complexity caused by unwritten and dispersed common law. The Restatement enterprise was prompted by a sense that the law had become too "complex" and "uncertain," but the remedy of system was applied in a thin sense. This thin sense of system supposedly contrasted with that of an integrated code; perhaps unfairly, codes were associated with "system" in the law. While not meant to supplant the case law, Restatements did substitute for codification, which many opposed and which never got off the ground in the nineteenth century.[1] The substitute, thin, even flat, kind of system can be seen in the earliest Restatements of contracts, torts, property, and restitution. And even this minimal sense of system led to a Realist attack that promoted a move even further from system in subsequent rounds of Restatements.

A. Background and Early Stirrings

As is well known, "complexity" and "uncertainty" in the law were prime concerns cited by the initiators of the ALI and the Restatements.[2] They were not alone: a common lament at the time was that increasing complexity of law and the greater volume of litigation were overwhelming lawyers' and judges' ability to know the law. Laypeople were largely ignored, whether through neglect or by design.[3]

In the Realist era, the focus shifted to the increasing complexity of society, but all of these complaints and concerns shared some basic assumptions. Generally, there was an awareness that certainty and flexibility were in some tension with each other. The formalists who supposedly advocated for deductive legal science—the "Langdellians" of the familiar caricature—were accused of overprizing certainty and ignoring the increasing importance of flexibility in a post-horse-and-buggy era. Taking the most extreme and sometimes caricatured versions of such formalism as a foil, the Realists downplayed certainty in their quest for flexibility to meet new challenges.

Caught in between these poles were early reformist figures like Roscoe Pound and Cardozo, who argued that both certainty and flexibility were important and that different mixes of them were appropriate in different contexts. Pound decried mechanical

---

[1] See, e.g., Lewis A. Grossman, Langdell Upside-Down: The Anticlassical Jurisprudence of Anticodification, 19 YALE J.L. & HUMAN. 145 (2007); Aniceto Masferrer, The Passionate Discussion Among Common Lawyers About Postbellum American Codification: An Approach to Its Legal Argumentation, 40 ARIZ. ST. L.J. 173 (2008).

[2] American Law Institute, Report of the Committee on the Establishment of a Permanent Organization for the Improvement of the Law 71–78 (1923); see also G. Edward White, The American Law Institute and the Triumph of Modernist Jurisprudence, 15 LAW & HIST. REV. 1 (1997).

[3] Presumably laypeople were not dealing directly with the opinions in cases even in an earlier era with a smaller judicial output. For that matter, the discourse around these issues, from the ALI founders all the way through the Realists, was quite focused on elites.

jurisprudence (anticipating Realism),[4] but he saw a role for formalism in commercial contexts where certainty was at a premium.[5] In his jurisprudential writing, including his forays into equity, Pound repeatedly explored the need to combine formalism and contextualism.[6] Pound even saw different areas of the law as potentially specializing and employing various degrees of formalism to achieve specialization.[7] This led to a vehement attack by Felix Cohen, who saw no use for formalism of any kind in any way, accusing Pound of retrograde thinking.[8]

Another prominent pre-Realist is especially important to both the history of legal thought and particularly to the development of Restatements. Like Pound, Cardozo anticipated much of later Legal Realism, but he stopped well short of full-blown Realism. Sometimes, despite his general sympathy, he had rather sharp words for those he termed "neo-realists":

> The neo-realists have suffered at times from this missionary ecstasy. Over-zealous among the faithful,—when I call them over-zealous, I do not mean to disparage their brilliancy and power,—overzealous ones, have not been satisfied to teach that order and certainty and rational coherence are goods to be subordinated on occasion to others more important. There has been a petulant contempt of them as if to dethrone them from the rank of idols was to prove them evil altogether. Not only are principles and rules and concepts shorn of their ancient tyranny. They are degraded altogether, stripped with contumely of every vestige of their bygone power; indeed, the process of humiliation is carried even farther, and there is taken from them the regenerative capacity to reproduce in their own image.[9]

In particular, like Pound, Cardozo saw the need to reconcile the need for certainty and flexibility, taking a moderate stand on formalism. He saw that combining formalism and contextualism was no easy task, and it would require some kind of system to bring them together and to reconcile them as needed. In his theoretical writings and speeches, Cardozo repeatedly stressed this necessity for creatively combining certainty and flexibility and identified this as a theme running throughout the history of law. Invoking fellow moderates Pound and Paul Vinogradoff, Cardozo sets out a general picture:

> "Law must be stable, and yet it cannot stand still." Here is the great antinomy confronting us at every turn. Rest and motion, unrelieved and unchecked, are equally destructive. The law, like human kind, if life is to continue, must find some path of

---

[4] Roscoe Pound, *Mechanical Jurisprudence*, 8 COLUM. L. REV. 605 (1908).

[5] *See, e.g.*, Roscoe Pound, *Jurisprudence*, in THE HISTORY AND PROSPECTS OF THE SOCIAL SCIENCES 444, 472–73 (Harry Elmer Barnes ed., 1925).

[6] *See, e.g.*, Roscoe Pound, *The Call for a Realist Jurisprudence*, 44 HARV. L. REV. 697 (1931); Roscoe Pound, *The Decadence of Equity*, 5 COLUM. L. REV. 20 (1905).

[7] ROSCOE POUND, INTERPRETATIONS OF LEGAL HISTORY 154 (1923); Roscoe Pound, *The Theory of Judicial Decision III: A Theory of Judicial Decision for Today*, 36 HARV. L. REV. 940, 951 (1923).

[8] *See* FELIX S. COHEN, ETHICAL SYSTEMS AND LEGAL IDEALS 1–40 (1933); *see also* JEROME FRANK, LAW AND THE MODERN MIND 227 (1930).

[9] Benjamin Nathan Cardozo, *Jurisprudence*, in SELECTED WRITINGS OF BENJAMIN NATHAN CARDOZO: THE CHOICE OF TYCHO BRAHE 7, 14 (Margaret E. Hall ed., 1980).

compromise. Two distinct tendencies, pulling in different directions, must be harnessed together and made to work in unison. All depends on the wisdom with which the joinder is effected. The subject has a literature that takes us back to Aristotle and earlier. Νόμος is to be supplemented by ἐπιείκεια; the tables by the edict; law by equity; custom by statute; rule by discretion.... Fusion in due proportion is the problem of the ages.[10]

Cardozo was involved at the beginning of the ALI and supported the idea of Restatements.[11] He saw the Restatements themselves as addressing this timeless problem of combining certainty and flexibility. On the occasion of the presentation to the membership of the first Restatement sections, Cardozo saw the playing out of this "problem of the ages":

Now, almost for the first time, at least on any scale so large, a multitude of these rules and principles, gathered from their setting and scientifically arranged, have been stated tersely, accurately, fully, with a definiteness of form approaching the pronouncements of a statute. We are now to see whether our law has found a medium of expression that will solve or help to solve the age-long problem of uniting flexibility to certainty, that will give us the virtues of a code without the blighting pretension to literal inerrancy, a code that instead of repressing the forces and tendencies of growth by the imposition upon the law of a form forever fixed, will stir them to new life by its revelation of a harmony and an order till then unthought of and unseen.

Today we lay before you the first fruits of the harvest.[12]

Even accounting for the occasion and the floweriness, it is of a piece with Cardozo's other writings and indeed his judicial philosophy.[13]

The ALI likewise fell somewhere in the middle of this spectrum of formalism and contextualism, of orientation to certainty versus flexibility. Where and how the ALI fits into the picture is contested.[14] Some see Wesley Hohfeld and the ALI founders as reformers but ones who thought better concepts would lead to reform.[15] It is certainly

---

[10] Benjamin Nathan Cardozo, *The Growth of the Law, in* SELECTED WRITINGS OF BENJAMIN NATHAN CARDOZO: THE CHOICE OF TYCHO BRAHE 186, 186 (Margaret E. Hall ed., 1980) (citations to Pound and Vinogradoff omitted). Later in the same chapter, Cardozo extols the role that past commentators played in building up the common law, mentioning Kent and Story and currently Williston and Wigmore as encouragement for the ALI Restatements. *Id.* at 190. Using a troubling eugenic metaphor of a kind all too common at the time, he goes on to state that "[t]hey have shown what can be done for law by a wise science of eugenics. If all this can be accomplished by individual initiative and endeavor, how much greater will be the authority of one who speaks, not merely in his own name, but in that of an organized profession." *Id.*

[11] ANDREW L. KAUFMAN, CARDOZO 173–75 (1998).

[12] Benjamin Nathan Cardozo, *The American Law Institute, in* SELECTED WRITINGS OF BENJAMIN NATHAN CARDOZO: THE CHOICE OF TYCHO BRAHE 395, 397–98 (Margaret E. Hall ed., 1980) (Address at the Third Annual Meeting, May 1, 1925, of the American Law Institute).

[13] KAUFMAN, *supra* note 11, at 573–77; RICHARD A. POSNER, CARDOZO: A STUDY IN REPUTATION 105–07 (1990).

[14] This is bound up with the reception of Hohfeld, including his work's relation to the bundle of rights picture of property.

[15] N.E.H. Hull, *Restatement and Reform: A New Perspective on the Origins of the American Law Institute,* 8 L. & HIST. REV. 55, 58–59 (1990); *see also* N.E.H. Hull, *Vital Schools of Jurisprudence: Roscoe Pound, Wesley Newcomb Hohfeld, and the Promotion of an Academic Jurisprudential Agenda, 1910–1919,* 45 J. LEGAL EDUC. 235, 270 (1995).

the case that a wide-ranging speech given by Hohfeld in 1914 at the annual meeting of the American Bar Association, in which he stressed reform and clearer conceptualism, was held out as a great inspiration to the founding of the ALI.[16] Others doubt the extent of Hohfeld's interest in reform and the depth of the ALI founders' understanding of his conceptual scheme.[17] Still others join the Realists as seeing the ALI as more of a rearguard action, emphasizing the role of carryover notions of legal science.[18]

At any rate, in most accounts of the early ALI, its initial motivations and the early Restatements are taken as falling uneasily—wherever that is—between two eras. The search for principles looks like older legal science and an example of autonomous conceptualism. On the other hand, the early ALI sought to reform law and was more oriented to cases that in turn reflected changing conditions. Some of the most prominent actors shared with Hohfeld the hope that clarifying terminology would lead to or at least facilitate reform of some kind, an elite-driven one to be sure.

The residual conceptualism and whiff of legal science in this enterprise led to a sharp critical reaction from prominent Legal Realists. Thurman Arnold, Myres McDougal, and other Realists saw the early efforts as not only too backward looking but as inherently hopeless.[19] While Realism was a big tent and Realists differed on many points, we can identify at least one major common theme: to varying degrees, the Realists preferred shallow and narrow concepts, which would allow them to stick closer to the facts and give judges the needed flexibility to implement sound policy and make needed changes to the law.[20]

From the point of view of system in the law, however, the early ALI and the Realists shared more in common than they realized. The previous formalist era may not have been quite as formalist as its opponents made out.[21] In particular, the formalism they opposed presented very little if any obstacle to a rising reductionism in legal

---

[16] Wesley Newcomb Hohfeld, *A Vital School of Jurisprudence and Law: Have American Universities Awakened to the Enlarged Opportunities and Responsibilities of the Present Day?*, in FUNDAMENTAL LEGAL CONCEPTIONS AS APPLIED IN JUDICIAL REASONING AND OTHER LEGAL ESSAYS 332–84 (Walter Wheeler Cook ed., 1923).

[17] White, *supra* note 2, at 30.

[18] *Id.* at 3–4 (noting this strain of scholarship and outlining argument that the ALI founders wanted to be responsive to change and wound up inadvertently discrediting pre-modern legal epistemology).

[19] Thurman Arnold, *Institute Priests and Yale Observers—A Reply to Dean Goodrich*, 84 U. PA. L. REV. 813 (1939); Myres McDougal, *Book Review*, 32 ILL. L. REV. 510 (1937) (reviewing Volumes 1 and 2 of the Restatement of Property); *see also* Leon Green, *The Torts Restatement*, 29 ILL. L. REV. 582 (1935); *see generally* White, *supra* note 2, at 36 ("In review after review of the early Restatements critics demonstrated their disaffinity with the jurisprudential assumptions guiding the project.")

[20] *See* Felix S. Cohen, *Transcendental Nonsense and the Functional Approach*, 35 COLUM. L. REV. 809, 820 (1935) ("In every field of law we should find peculiar concepts which are not defined either in terms of empirical fact or in terms of ethics but which are used to answer empirical and ethical questions alike, and thus bar the way to intelligent investigation of social fact and social policy."); Karl N. Llewellyn, *Some Realism About Realism—Responding to Dean Pound*, 44 HARV. L. REV. 1222, 1223 (1931) ("[Those involved in the new movement] want law to deal, they themselves want to deal, with things, with people, with tangibles, with definite tangibles, and observable relations between definite tangibles—not with words alone; when law deals with words, they want the words to represent tangibles which can be got at beneath the words, and observable relations between those tangibles."); *see also* Arthur L. Corbin, *Jural Relations and Their Classification*, 30 YALE L.J. 226, 226–30 (1921) (expressing preference for operative not abstract concepts).

[21] *Compare* ANTHONY J. SEBOK, LEGAL POSITIVISM IN AMERICAN JURISPRUDENCE 48–112 (1998); BRIAN Z. TAMANAHA, BEYOND THE FORMALIST-REALIST DIVIDE: THE ROLE OF POLITICS IN JUDGING 67–90 (2010), *with* Brian Leiter, *Legal Formalism and Legal Realism: What Is the Issue?*, 16 LEGAL THEORY 111, 117 (2010).

thinking. To the extent that the Restatements employed Hohfeldian conceptualism, this was in practice very reductionist. How much Hohfeld was a reductionist is contested, and he died before he could follow through on the few hints he left about a theory of "aggregate" legal relations.[22] Nonetheless, in the most reductionist aspect of his program—the breaking down of in rem rights into mere collections of individual right-duty relations holding between pairs of actors—Hohfeld seems to have been quite reductionist indeed.[23] Importantly, the ALI, especially its first Director William Draper Lewis, endorsed Hohfeld's approach, at least at the beginning of the Property Restatement.[24] The original Property Reporter, Harry Bigelow, was a Hohfeldian and made clear that he did not even believe that there was such a category as in rem rights.[25]

As has been pointed out at the time and ever since, the ALI did not apply Hohfeld's scheme consistently or even very widely.[26] The early Restatements were a mixed bag in terms of the exact theory they presupposed. Nevertheless, they did partake of the growing reductionism in the law. There is little evidence that any of the Restatements was oriented to developing a deep notion of system or to drawing out interconnections between different aspects of the law or between different areas of the law. Teasing out the motivations of the Reporters is no easy task, but in a sense it is not necessary. The work product speaks to some extent for itself.

Restatements, from the earliest on, were long lists of sections, often quite repetitive. The process for considering sections evolved into a section-by-section discussion before a vote on a group of sections. And the organization of Restatements into Volumes, Divisions, Chapters, and so on was not all that hierarchical. Curiously, Chapter numbering can be continuous even through different higher-level divisions. For example, the Restatement Second of Torts consists of forty-eight continuously numbered Chapters spread over four Volumes and thirteen Divisions. Sections are typically numbered from beginning to end consecutively with no hierarchy other than the aforementioned groupings. The tendency is toward one thing after another.

More substantively, the early Restatements took a "pragmatic" and nonsystematic approach to basic concepts. To take one example, nineteenth-century systematizers had made much of the notion of possession, which features in many parts of property law and beyond.[27] Possession naturally forms the backbone of a system but it can be treated as highly variable with context. Proto-Realists and later Realists heaped scorn on any abstract notion of possession and emphasized how possession

[22] Ted Sichelman, *Very Tight "Bundles of Sticks": Hohfeld's Complex Jural Relations, in* WESLEY HOHFELD A CENTURY LATER: EDITED WORK, SELECT PERSONAL PAPERS, AND ORIGINAL COMMENTARIES 345 (Shyamkrishna Balganesh, Ted Sichelman, & Henry E. Smith eds., 2022).

[23] Wesley Newcomb Hohfeld, *Some Fundamental Legal Conceptions as Applied in Judicial Reasoning*, 26 YALE L.J. 710, 718–33 (1917); Thomas W. Merrill & Henry E. Smith, *Why Restate the Bundle?: The Disintegration of the Restatement of Property*, 79 BROOK. L. REV. 681, 698–99 (2014).

[24] Merrill & Smith, *supra* note 23.

[25] Harry A. Bigelow & Richard R. Powell, *Discussion of Property Tentative Draft No. 1*, 7 A.L.I. PROC. 199, 207–15 (1929).

[26] George R. Farnum, *Terminology and the American Law Institute*, 13 B.U. L. REV. 203 (1933); Merrill & Smith, *supra* note 23, at 696–703.

[27] James Gordley & Ugo Mattei, *Protecting Possession*, 44 AM. J. COMP. L. 293, 294–300 (1996) (discussing nineteenth-century German debate about possession); Richard A. Posner, *Holmes, Savigny, and the Law and Economics of Possession*, 86 VA. L. REV. 535 (2000).

meant something different for acquisition, adverse possession, trespass, etc.[28] In the Restatements themselves, we see fairly conventional definitions, but they are associated with a particular problem (trespass), and new definitions are offered when a new area comes along.[29] Thus there is a separate definition for personal property for purposes of conversion. Indeed, the only general definitions of possession in the first round of Restatements appear in the Restatement of Torts. No Restatement of Property until the Fourth has offered any general definition of possession.[30]

B. The Earliest Restatements

The first round of Restatements met with criticism from the Realists for not going far enough in downplaying conceptualism. A more thoroughgoing reductionism eventually moved the Restatement enterprise further down the path toward thin concepts and the heap-of-rules treatment of the law. In one way or another, this has been a major theme in the history of restating the common law subjects.

Perhaps the most famous such trajectory comes from the law of contracts. The uneasy relationship of Samuel Williston and Arthur Corbin is said to be reflected in the First Restatement of Contracts. In the Whig history of the era, epitomized by Realist Grant Gilmore, Corbin managed to set the stage for an eventual triumph of Realism through the introduction of Section 90's promissory estoppel.[31] Through Section 90, the door was opened to a more free-form policy-oriented approach to contractual liability that undid any formalism about contract enforcement that Williston may have favored. Such trends were carried further still in the Second Restatement.

The conventional story of Section 90 and related issues in the Contracts Restatements are taken as developments of a less formal, more contextual—and less conceptualistic—contract law. Despite some overstatement, there is some truth in this.[32] But there is a less apparent shift away from conceptualism and system in a reductionist direction that is also in play, especially when it comes to promissory estoppel. The Contracts Restatements also came along in the final stages of the fusion of law and equity. As with the equity of the statute and even the rise of administrative law, equity has been mined by the Realists and their successors as a source of reassurance that there is precedent for their innovations.[33] And it is certainly true that innovations

---

[28] Burke Shartel, *Meanings of Possession*, 16 MINN. L. REV. 611 (1932); *see also* Joseph W. Bingham, *The Nature and Importance of Legal Possession*, 13 MICH. L. REV. 535 (1915).

[29] RESTATEMENT OF THE LAW, PROPERTY § 7 (1936) ("Definition of Possession" for land); RESTATEMENT OF THE LAW, PROPERTY § 216 (1936) ("Definition of Possession" for chattels); RESTATEMENT OF THE LAW SECOND, TORTS § 157 (1965) ("Definition of Possession" for land); RESTATEMENT OF THE LAW SECOND, TORTS § 216 (1965) ("Definition of Possession of Chattel").

[30] RESTATEMENT OF THE LAW FOURTH, PROPERTY VOL. 1, § 1.1 (Tentative Draft 2, 2021).

[31] GRANT GILMORE, THE DEATH OF CONTRACT 87–88, 95, 103 (1974).

[32] For a skeptical take, *see* Robert E. Scott, *Hoffman v. Red Owl Stores and the Myth of Precontractual Reliance*, 68 OHIO ST. L.J. 71 (2007). *Compare* Robert E. Scott, *Hoffman v. Red Owl Stores and the Limits of the Legal Method*, 61 HASTINGS L.J. 859, 865 (2010) *with* William C. Whitford & Stewart Macaulay, *Hoffman v. Red Owl Stores: The Rest of the Story*, 61 HASTINGS L.J. 801 (2010).

[33] J.M. Landis, *Statutes and the Sources of Law*, *in* HARVARD LEGAL ESSAYS 213, 215 (1934), 213, *reprinted* in 2 HARV. J. ON LEGIS. 7 (1965); Harlan F. Stone, *The Common Law in the United States*, 50 HARV. L. REV. 4, 13–14 (1936); *see also* Jerome Frank, *Civil Law Influences on the Common Law—Some Reflections on "Comparative" and "Contrastive" Law*, 104 U. PA. L. REV. 887, 890–91 (1956) (discussing views of Landis,

in the common law often have their origins in equity.[34] For example, certain kinds of equitable fraud (e.g., fraud in the inducement) were first dealt with in equity and then when they become more familiar became the subject of common-law rules. Likewise, the loosening of privity rules was often first broached in equity and then led to innovations in the common law.[35]

The Contracts Restatements partook of this mining of equity, and in the process contributed to the flattening of equity itself. The "estoppel" in "promissory estoppel" shows its origins in equity. Precontractual behavior could constitute an abuse of the contacting process and could be said to be in the vicinity of fraud if not fraud itself. Traditional equity gathered much of this opportunistic behavior under the heading of "constructive fraud." Nevertheless, this traditional approach to constructive fraud would look for specific triggers in bad faith and disproportionate hardship and would then apply rules of thumb to alter legal results that were a product of bad bargaining behavior. These problematic signs could arise in the pre-agreement process. Constructive fraud was also the traditional approach to unconscionability—a similar evaluation of the contract and the process by which it came to be.[36] Overall, Contracts Restatements partake in the move toward standards. This is a way for an unarticulated shallow system to handle complexity as best it can.[37]

To all this we can add that the kinds of system implicit in these approaches leave telltale signs. Replacing a more articulated (if looser than advertised) system, the reformers, especially the Realists, flattened law and equity.[38] This required them to solve problems head on, all at the same level, with bespoke (and shallow) concepts. Thus, where equity would use triggers, presumptions, and rules of thumb to address problematic behavior before and during contracting, we now need a mono-level rule or standard to solve the problem. The inherent complexity and uncertainty (of the serious kind discussed in Section III) cannot be solved with a few ex ante rules. For example, the coming to the nuisance defense involves highly interdependent behavior, which has defied attempts to reduce it to a rule or to model the behavior using conventional economic tools. For this reason, coming to the nuisance is usually treated as a standard or higher-order ex post evaluation.[39] Complex ex ante rules not only require

---

Stone, Crawford and Cardozo, and discussing the influence of the civilian tradition); *see generally* Henry E. Smith, *Equity and Administrative Behavior, in* EQUITY AND ADMINISTRATION 326, 345–46 (P.G. Turner, ed., 2016).

[34] WILLIAM W. BILLSON, EQUITY IN ITS RELATIONS TO COMMON LAW 7 (1917) ("Conceptions of right which by the equity jurisprudence had been made familiar to the popular and professional mind, and proven practicable and wholesome, had a constant tendency to find their way by degrees into the common law even unavowedly and illicitly."); Henry E. Smith, *Equity as Meta-Law*, 130 YALE L.J. 1050, 1065–66, 1109 (2021).

[35] Smith, *supra* note 34, at 1108–09.

[36] For an insightful analysis of the equitable nature of unconscionability in an evaluation of the Uniform Commercial Code, *see* Arthur Allen Leff, *Unconscionability and the Code—The Emperor's New Clause*, 115 U. PA. L. REV. 485, 539 (1967).

[37] Alan Schwartz and Robert Scott locate the cause of the preference for standards in the political economy of the private legislature. Alan Schwartz & Robert E. Scott, *The Political Economy of Private Legislatures*, 143 U. PA. L. REV. 595 (1995).

[38] Smith, *supra* note 34, at 1063–64, 1090–91, 1096, 1136–42.

[39] John C.P. Goldberg & Henry E. Smith, *Wrongful Fusion: Equity and Tort, in* EQUITY AND LAW: FUSION AND FISSION 309, 315–18 (John C.P. Goldberg, Henry E. Smith, & P.G. Turner eds., 2019). Goldberg and

too much information; they are likely to be far too inflexible over time—and vulnerable to the very misuse and opportunism by parties that is their target. Restatement Reporters are thus backed into a corner, where hand-waving and ex post (but mono-level) standards are the only trick left in the bag.

The innovations of the Contracts Restatements have left a mixed legacy. They have probably accomplished the purpose of making judges less reluctant to police bargains. On the other hand, they provide little guidance and lead to varying approaches. This leads to some disappointment in how much reform they actually accomplished. Indeed, the traditional equitable approach, while somewhat more focused, may have been more stringent within its domain.[40] However that may be, to the extent that the Restatements partake of an anti-conceptualist version of the fusion of law and equity, their post-fusion analogs for equitable concepts and structures have been a disappointment, especially when it comes to the guidance function of the law.

Torts holds a special place in the Realist approach to law. Grant Gilmore saw contract dissolving into tort.[41] Leon Green saw tort as regulation by other means.[42] Because any problem can be couched as a matter of harm, a tort law unmoored from traditional categories of injury and the conceptual apparatus of duty can be seen as an all-purpose "default" kind of law. And there has indeed been a trend to replace more articulated areas of law with new causes of action in tort.[43] Thus, to the extent that Restatements of torts have expanded in scope, this may reflect the anti-system system of private law increasingly adopted by Restatements. At any rate, the Torts Restatements have moved in the direction of bespoke sections. They have also trended toward standards. Emblematic for this latter trend is the Second Torts Restatement's treatment of nuisance, which turns on a host of undefined factors to be balanced in an equally undefined fashion.[44]

Especially with Property, Realism was in the air, as we have already seen. In the mid-twentieth century, the bundle of rights attained the status of conventional wisdom. In the commentary, the field as a whole became consciously anti-conceptualist.[45] Not only did this intellectual atmosphere work its way into the Restatements, it may also help explain why Property has been so resistant to restatement.[46] So far, unlike contracts and torts, there is no comprehensive Property Restatement in any of the rounds of restating.

Smith argue that these difficulties led to a narrow and uninformative approach to coming to the nuisance in Restatement (Second) of Torts § 840D (1979). *See id.* at 316–17.

[40] Smith, *supra* note 34. *Cf.* Philip A. Hamburger, *More Is Less*, 90 Va. L. Rev. 835 (2004).

[41] Gilmore, *supra* note 31.

[42] Leon Green, *Tort Law Public Law in Disguise*, 38 Tex. L. Rev. 1 (1959).

[43] *See, e.g.*, John C.P. Goldberg & Robert H. Sitkoff, *Torts and Estates: Remedying Wrongful Interference with Inheritance*, 65 Stan. L. Rev. 335 (2013).

[44] Restatement (Second) of Torts §§ 821F, 822, 826 (1979) (nuisance). Reasonableness in nuisance turns on five gravity-of-the-harm factors, id. § 827, and three utility-of-the conduct factors, id. § 828, all of which are open-ended and unstructured.

[45] Thomas W. Merrill & Henry E. Smith, *What Happened to Property in Law and Economics?*, 111 Yale L.J. 357 (2001).

[46] Merrill & Smith, *supra* note 45, at 707; *see also* Thomas W. Merrill, *The Restatement of Property: The Curse of Incompleteness*, in this volume.

Perhaps the most innovative intervention of the ALI in the common law was the Restitution Restatement. The first Restatement is sometimes credited with creating the field from a variety of strands of quasi contract and constructive trust, although it has roots in the late nineteenth century.[47] It straddled the law-equity divide and was a classic fusionist project in that sense. It is worth asking, though, whether the equitable character of these strands was sufficiently preserved.[48] This is a major issue in the field to this day, and we will not try to resolve it here. Suffice it to say that the innovation was in bringing the strands together. It is less easy to see the structure in the field if there is any.

The irony is that reductionist approaches to system threaten the guidance function of the law. Communicating duties such as those in trespass is only the beginning. A connected set of relatively stable concepts is important for the guidance function of law. As F.H. Lawson pointed out in the 1950s, our attitude to concepts is formed too much by a focus on litigation and not enough from the perspective of people planning their activities—and the lawyers advising them on how to go about them.[49]

C. The Realist Attack

Reductionist skepticism about system was most pronounced in Legal Realism and in some forms of Realism more than others. Jerome Frank and Felix Cohen can both be seen as among the more extreme skeptics of system, with different emphases. For Frank (at least the early Frank), judges do and should look at cases individually, with decision first and rationale afterward.[50] Abstract legal concepts, especially interconnected concepts, would play little role in this process. For Cohen, the attack on system was even more direct.[51] The kinds of abstract concepts that could hold a system together were "transcendental nonsense." For both Frank and Cohen, judges and others need to stick close to facts and to avoid airy abstractions.

The Realists left a mark on the Restatement process. From the second round of Restatements there was a shift away from rules and toward standards. One need not see this as a reaction to the Realist backlash. Instead, Realist ideas had a profound influence on legal thinking and the law itself, so it is no wonder that subsequent Restatements look more Realist, even if a hard-core Realist might still doubt the value of the enterprise as such.

---

[47] Andrew Kull, *James Barr Ames and the Early Modern History of Unjust Enrichment*, 25 Oxford J. Legal Stud. 297 (2005); *see also* Emily Sherwin, *A Short History of the Restatement of Restitution and Unjust Enrichment*, in this volume.

[48] For a variety of views, *see, e.g.*, Caprice L. Roberts, *The Restitution Revival and the Ghosts of Equity*, 68 Wash. & Lee L. Rev. 1027 (2011); Lionel Smith, *Common Law and Equity in R3RUE*, 68 Wash. & Lee L. Rev. 1185 (2011). The Restatement neither emphasizes nor completely effaces the law-equity distinction. *See* Restatement Third, Restitution and Unjust Enrichment § 4 (2011) ("Restitution May Be Legal or Equitable or Both": "(1) Liabilities and remedies within the law of restitution and unjust enrichment may have originated in law, in equity, or in a combination of the two. (2) A claimant otherwise entitled to a remedy for unjust enrichment, including a remedy originating in equity, need not demonstrate the inadequacy of available remedies at law.")

[49] F.H. Lawson, *The Creative Use of Legal Concepts*, 32 N.Y.U. L. Rev. 909 (1957).

[50] Frank, *supra* note 8.

[51] Cohen, *supra* note 20.

III. Managing the Common-Law System

At the time the first Restatements were in the works, a different kind of system was gaining favor in other fields.[52] Crucially, systems theory depends on a different notion of complexity from the one spelled out by the founders of the ALI and most contemporary legal commentators. In general systems theory, a system is a set of interconnected elements, and complexity stems from the dense interconnection of numerous elements.[53] These dense interconnections make the properties of the system difficult to trace to individual elements. Such properties are emergent. Immune responses in organisms, prices in markets, and consciousness in brains are all said to be emergent phenomena.[54] In light of this possibility, reductionism, while often useful, must be handled with extra care.

During the era of the first Restatements, commentators by contrast assumed that system meant deductive system. This is not purely a matter of caricature by the Legal Realists. Much of the Langdellian rhetoric harked back to efforts to put some kind of logical system into the law.[55] Although some of those earlier efforts, like some of the nineteenth-century systematizing, were less exclusively focused on "deductive" systems than is usually thought, it is true that Langdell followed some earlier thinkers in being rather overoptimistic in how "dense" a system could be found in the law.[56] Although Langdell's method was empirical in the sense of looking to appellate opinions rather than natural law axioms, he and his followers were optimistic that a small number of principles would get one a long way. Thus, even if law was not all about deduction, the kind of system that the so-called formalists were interested in was quite economical and tightly interconnected. As Paul Miller notes, there are many kinds of formalism, and it is not entirely unfair to see the formalists as too enamored of the more formal kinds of system.[57]

The reaction against this kind of dense formal system swept more broadly than it needed to. If formalists were too optimistic about finding system in the common law, the Realists were dead set against it. By touting the "facts" and favoring narrow and shallow—rather than interconnected—concepts, the Realists took more productive—and yes, more realistic—notions of system off the table as well.

System in law need not be deductive. That is, the interconnections between areas of law need not involve deduction.[58] Some systems are more loosely structured, and they

---

[52] See, e.g., LUDWIG VON BERTALANFFY, PROBLEMS OF LIFE: AN EVALUATION OF MODERN BIOLOGICAL THOUGHT (1952); Ludwig von Bertalanffy, An Outline of General System Theory, 1 BRIT. J. PHIL. SCI. 134 (1950); Warren Weaver, Science and Complexity, 36 AM. SCIENTIST 536 (1948); see also P.A. Lewis, Systems, Structural Properties, and Levels of Organisation: The Influence of Ludwig von Bertalanffy on the Work of F.A. Hayek, 34A RES. IN THE HIST. OF ECON. THOUGHT & METHODOLOGY 125 (2016).

[53] See, e.g., MELANIE MITCHELL, COMPLEXITY: A GUIDED TOUR (2011); HERBERT A. SIMON, THE SCIENCES OF THE ARTIFICIAL (2d ed. 1981).

[54] MITCHELL, supra note 53, at 4.

[55] M.H. Hoeflich, Law & Geometry: Legal Science from Leibniz to Langdell, 30 AM. J. LEGAL HIST. 95 (1986).

[56] Scott Brewer, Law, Logic, and Leibniz: A Contemporary Perspective, in LEIBNIZ: LOGICO-PHILOSOPHICAL PUZZLES: PHILOSOPHICAL QUESTIONS AND PERPLEXING CASES IN THE LAW 199 (Alberto Artosi, Bernardo Pieri, & Giovanni Sartor eds., 2013).

[57] Paul B. Miller, The New Formalism in Private Law, 66 AM. J. JURISPRUDENCE 175 (2021).

[58] See, e.g., Simon Deakin, Juridical Ontology: The Evolution of Legal Form, 40 HIST. SOC. RES. 170 (2015) (presenting system of defeasible concepts as able to coevolve with social and economic context); Lawson,

may also be less formal. For an example from daily life that nonetheless guides conduct, consider the cultural system of "common sense." As Clifford Geertz recognizes, the system of common sense is a "loosely connected body of belief and judgment."[59] As he also indicates, "[c]ommon-sense wisdom is shamelessly and unapologetically ad hoc."[60] And, while the system of common sense operates through epigrams, witticisms, proverbs, and the like—its content may even be inconsistent at times—common sense can still be understood in system terms.[61] We would by no means suggest that the system of the common law closely matches a system of common sense (for better or for worse). The point is that systems are not inevitably deductive in their implications, formal in their style, or fully elaborated in their content.

Indeed, system can involve defeasible concepts—concepts which are open-ended to a degree which allows for the resolution of internal contradictions.[62] Thus, possession can link areas of property law without one being able to deduce case results from abstract propositions. The law then employs a number of specialized notions of possession, namely, possession in fact and the right to possess, which do not require an explicit statement of a set of physical-control-related facts that will work for acquisition, ongoing trespass protection, adverse possession, leasing, bailment, and the like. Much can be supplied by social fact (what is control in various contexts), but the notion of possession does serve to connect the various areas loosely, and in the common law it forms a platform for ownership. Relativity of title, even in its more modest versions, relies heavily on the notion of possession.[63] As a matter of "style," the common law achieves a notion of ownership through "possession-plus," whereas the civil law does so through more direct notions of dominion.[64]

Where does this leave Restatements? The looseness of the system can be a great benefit to a Restatement to the extent that it partakes of the structure of the common law. However, the danger is that such a loosely interconnected system is easy to overlook—and to downplay or suppress—if one is accumulating a series of individual sections.[65] System is not to be found in an individual black-letter section or even a collection of such sections working additively. Rather it stems from the interaction of multiple sections. Such interactions are hard to evaluate on a section-by-section basis.

The question is whether the law has any internal structure, that is, pattern to its internal connections, and what functions those serve. The risk is that the structure and

---

supra note 49; Henry E. Smith, *Systems Theory: Emergent Private Law, in* THE OXFORD HANDBOOK OF THE NEW PRIVATE LAW 139 (Andrew S. Gold et al. eds., 2020); *see also* Albert Kocourek, *Formal Relation Between Law and Discretion*, 9 ILL. L. REV. 225, 238 (1914).

[59] *See* Clifford Geertz, *Introduction, in* LOCAL KNOWLEDGE: FURTHER ESSAYS IN INTERPRETIVE ANTHROPOLOGY 10 (3d ed. 2000).

[60] *See* Clifford Geertz, *Common Sense as a Cultural System, in* LOCAL KNOWLEDGE: FURTHER ESSAYS IN INTERPRETIVE ANTHROPOLOGY 90 (3d ed. 2000).

[61] *See id.* (describing these features).

[62] *See, e.g.*, A. SCOTT KELSO & DAVID A. ENGSTRØM, THE COMPLEMENTARY NATURE (2006); Deakin, *supra* note 58.

[63] *See* LUKE ROSTILL, POSSESSION, RELATIVE TITLE, AND OWNERSHIP IN ENGLISH LAW 127–53 (2021).

[64] Yun-chien Chang & Henry E. Smith, *An Economic Analysis of Civil versus Common Law Property*, 88 NOTRE DAME L. REV. 1, 14–15 (2012).

[65] Henry E. Smith, *Restating the Architecture of Property*, 10 MOD. STUD. IN PROP. L. 19 (Sinéad Agnew & Ben McFarlane eds., 2019).

process of a Restatement can dictate a skeptical answer to the functional value of internal structure. We think that internal structure has a great deal of functional value. How then can a Restatement respect that internal structure? Answering this question will often require something other than a direct, detail-by-detail correspondence between a Restatement and preexisting legal doctrine. The next section of this chapter will turn to this structural consideration. In the process, it also sheds light on Cardozo's concern: how to creatively combine certainty and flexibility.

IV. Restatements and Common-Law Architecture

Restatements can only sometimes respect structure by reflecting the details of the common law in their full complexity; a precise match is both costly to achieve and in some cases undesirable. Given both the goals and the capacities of Restatements, another approach is often needed. The common law's structure is nonetheless functionally valuable, and it can often be preserved in its general contours. The looseness of the common-law system permits a structural fit between Restatements and the law even where a precise conceptual fit is lacking. We turn to this possibility in the following.

A. Restatements and Simplification

Restatements are designed to articulate existing law, bring out its latent principles, and clarify the implicit connections between legal concepts and across doctrines. In doing so, a Restatement can only imperfectly fit the legal phenomena that it restates. Compare Jorge Luis Borges' example of a map as detailed as what it depicted: such maps are useless.[66] A Restatement must elide some cases and leave out some nuance if it is to avoid a level of complexity that would defeat the purpose. Indeed, if Restatements simply described every case in the common law, there would be little point in restating; the would-be user of a Restatement could simply consult the original legal materials directly.[67]

At the root of this problem is a fundamental trade-off between accuracy and manageability. According to what is sometimes referred to as Bonini's Paradox, as scientific theories more accurately reflect the phenomena they cover, they become less understandable—and as they become simpler, they become less accurate as a representation of reality.[68] Or as the poet-philosopher Paul Valéry captured this point

---

[66] *See* Jorge Luis Borges, *On Exactitude in Science*, *in* COLLECTED FICTIONS (Andrew Hurley transl., 1999).

[67] *See* William Lucy, *Method and Fit: Two Problems for Contemporary Philosophies of Tort Law*, 52 McGILL L.J. 605, 652 (2007) (noting that a theory which redescribes every detail of its object "runs the risk of being literally pointless").

[68] CHARLES P. BONINI, SIMULATION OF INFORMATION AND DECISION SYSTEMS IN THE FIRM 22–28, 136 (1963); JOHN M. DUTTON & WILLIAM H. STARBUCK, COMPUTER SIMULATION OF HUMAN BEHAVIOR 4 (1971) ("As a model of a complex system becomes more complete, it becomes less understandable. Alternatively, as a model grows more realistic, it also becomes just as difficult to understand as the real-world processes it represents.").

even earlier, "Everything simple is false. Everything which is complex is unusable."[69] What this counsels is neither despair nor indifference. One combination of simplicity and accuracy can be better than another—a theory can be needlessly complex or inaccurate—and which combination of the plausible candidates is the best will depend on the problem to be solved.

A concern for the Restatement project is thus to discard outlier cases and trivial variations in legal doctrine. Restatements are also designed to limit an increasing proliferation of legal rules and the sheer quantity of facts that can be relevant to legal outcomes.[70] In the codification setting, as F.H. Lawson noted, "it is felt that the law needs to be tidied up."[71] The same need for tidying up holds true for Restatements.[72] There is a trade-off, for losses in variation may mean lost opportunities for experimentation and, perhaps, a decrease in the benefits of a spontaneous order.[73] Yet the costs of this trade-off may be limited, depending on how determinate a Restatement's terms are and on how ready courts are to adopt a Restatement's guidance.

B. Restatements and Reform

Restatements have additional goals, and they cause Restatements to imperfectly fit doctrine for additional reasons. For example, a Restatement might try to speed up the process of the law's evolution, offering content that is expected to prevail eventually but which does not currently represent accepted doctrine. Or, a Restatement might endorse legal content designed to improve on the common law, irrespective of the direction the common law is evolving. For that matter, a Restatement might try to reconceptualize a field. In any of these cases, Restatements are doing more than tidying up legal doctrine; their interpretation adjusts that content in light of a substantive goal.[74]

---

[69] Paul Valéry, *Mauvaises Pensées*, in 2 ŒUVRES 783, 864 (1960) ("Ce qui est simple est toujours faux. Ce qui ne l'est pas est inutilisable."). For thoughts on how this challenge plagues Legal Realist thinking, *see* Andrew S. Gold & Henry E. Smith, *Sizing Up Private Law*, 70 U. TORONTO L.J. 489, 533 (2020).

[70] *See* G. Edward White, *The American Law Institute and the Triumph of Modernist Jurisprudence*, 15 LAW & HIST. REV. 1, 8 (1997).

[71] *See* F.H. Lawson, *A Common Law Lawyer Looks at Codification*, 2 INTER-AM. L. REV. 1, 1 (1960).

[72] *Cf.* American Law Institute, Report of the Committee on the Establishment of a Permanent Organization for the Improvement of the Law 71–78 (1923). Removing the factual complexities posed by cases is another form of tidying up. Note, however, that those factual complexities could matter for reaching the right result. *Cf.* JOHN GARDNER, FROM PERSONAL LIFE TO PRIVATE LAW 11 (2018) (suggesting the import of a detailed background story for adjudication).

[73] We do not deny that there is such a trade-off. For an argument that overreliance on Restatements can cut the common law off from its roots in the case law and thereby stunt its further developments, *see* Shyamkrishna Balganesh, Relying on Restatements (Feb. 15, 2022), 122 COLUM. L. REV. __ (forthcoming), https://ssrn.com/abstract=4037911. We will argue that attention to the right kind of system and the need for architectural fit can mitigate some of the problems Balganesh identifies.

[74] For helpful analysis of the degree to which Restatements have been reformist in their aims, *see* Merrill, *supra* note 46; John C.P. Goldberg, *Torts in the American Law Institute*, in this volume. Note also that Restatements might leave existing legal concepts largely intact while revising their overarching rationale. *See* Sherwin, *supra* note 47.

Where adopted, such changes can have multiple effects on the operation of a legal system. Ironically, efforts to create simplicity on a rule-by-rule basis—often evident in Restatement drafting—can produce unforeseen complexity at the system level. To take one area, collapsing law and equity such that rights are either directly in rem or in personam rather than more articulated—as with equitable rights as an overlay on legal rights such that they can be overcome by good faith purchase—leads to all sorts of complications in far-flung situations; these include whether trust beneficiaries can sue trespassers, whether occupants have a right to stay in premises on the strength of a relied upon promise, and what to do in cases of controversial potential "property" as with hot news and body parts.[75] The difficulty is that different parts of the system interact, sometimes in areas that are seemingly unrelated in their subject matter. Local features of the law, when scaled up, can also produce emergent properties. Changes to individual parts of a system, including a legal system, can thus have dramatic and often unforeseen ripple effects.

Where the law is modular, such effects can be limited in scope if changes are focused on particular modules. As one of us has noted:

> If interactions are organized even loosely into groups (modules, components), then some changes can happen internally to a module without uncontrollable ripple effects. Modules can be altered, or swapped. And as is well known from evolutionary theory, modularity can help evolution through a certain range: modularity can smooth evolution locally, but still leave the global maximum and other distant higher maxima out of reach.[76]

Such internal change, however, is not always what Restatements do. Like codifications, Restatements may also attempt wide-ranging reform, up to and possibly including some remodularization.[77]

Granted, the common law itself makes adjustments over time (indeed, this is how Restatements are incorporated into legal doctrine). Even with a strong system of precedent, the common law evolves to address new concerns and new insights, and it is able to do so without help from statutes and Restatements. The common-law techniques of distinguishing cases and extending holdings allow for an incremental but sometimes quite expansive revision to earlier legal concepts.[78] Overruling precedents allows for major revisions where case-by-case adjustments are inadequate. The

---

[75] See, e.g., Ben McFarlane, *Form and Substance in Equity*, in FORM AND SUBSTANCE IN THE LAW OF OBLIGATIONS 197 (Andrew Robertson & James Goudkamp eds., 2019); Henry E. Smith, *Equitable Meta-Law: The Spectrum of Property*, in EQUITY TODAY: 150 YEARS AFTER THE JUDICATURE REFORMS (Ben McFarlane & Steven Elliot eds., forthcoming).

[76] See Henry E. Smith, *Property as a Complex System*, at 7 (ms. on file with authors).

[77] See id. See also Henry E. Smith, *The Ecology of the Common Law*, 9 BRIGHAM-KANNER CONF. PROP. RTS. J. 153, 161 (2020).

[78] While revisions to the common law are famously slow, revisions may also be too fast or too frequent. See Frederick Schauer, *Do Cases Make Bad Law?*, 73 U. CHI. L. REV. 883, 906–08 (2006). To the extent Restatements freeze features of the common law in place, this consideration suggests that will not always be a weakness. On the possibility that legal concepts can still evolve while left in place, see Deakin, *supra* note 58, at 173–74 (discussing the open-endedness and "defeasibility" of legal concepts).

common law, however, is not an efficient mechanism for wholesale changes, and in some settings it is not well suited even for smaller-scale reforms.[79]

With this in mind, it is worth noting that there are other long-standing mechanisms for change apart from those built into conventional common-law reasoning. Restatements are one tool among others for adjusting the common law when its evolution is either too slow or to constrained in scope. Indeed, many of these alternatives have ancient precursors.[80] With adjustments for modern understandings, legal fiction, equity, and legislation each allow for interventions in the common law's application. These mechanisms offer important ways that the common law can be adjusted—both at the micro level and at the macro level—and understanding the Restatement's distinctive merits requires understanding these alternatives.

Despite some superficial similarities, Restatements do not fit within any of these categories. They are generally more wholesale in their operation than fictions or equity, much like legislation. Yet they leave the common law intact unless a court chooses to adopt their terms, and in this respect they are far less intrusive than statutory law. Moreover, Restatements are consciously designed to track the common law in many of its aspects, thus replicating legal features produced by a case-by-case, adjudicative process. Their production is also distinctive. Restatements are drafted collaboratively by practitioners, judges, and academics, and the Restatement drafting process may facilitate inquiries into macro-level questions that are unlikely to arise when courts decide a specific litigated case.[81]

Even the timing of Restatement revisions is unique: Restatements are commonly amended across entire fields of law, but such amendments may not occur for generations, thus permitting the common law to evolve for decades on its own.[82] Indeed, Restatements may both accelerate legal change, and then freeze it in place.[83] With enough time, Restatements can be overtaken by a layering of ex post case law, but in the initial years after a Restatement's adoption the law may be substantially influenced by direct interpretations of the Restatement's text. These distinctive features bring us again to the question of fit.

---

[79] One notable reason the common law is not suited for such wholesale changes is its polycentricity, in Polanyi's sense of the word. For helpful discussion, see Shivprasad Swaminathan, *What the Centipede Knows: Polycentricity and "Theory" for Common Lawyers*, 40 OXFORD J. LEGAL STUD. 265 (2020).

[80] See Joshua Getzler, *Historical Perspectives*, in THE OXFORD HANDBOOK OF THE NEW PRIVATE LAW 211, 215 (Andrew S. Gold et al. eds., 2020) (noting three prominent mechanisms for legal change in Gaius's work: fiction, equity, and legislation). *See also id.* n.13 (indicating the same trilogy is recognized in HENRY SUMNER MAINE, ANCIENT LAW (1st ed. 1861)).

[81] On the other hand, Reporters with divergent views sometimes pull Restatements in inconsistent directions, and a tendency to revise Restatements section by section can obscure interactions between legal concepts. On Reporters with divergent views, see Thomas W. Merrill & Henry E. Smith, *Why Restate the Bundle? The Disintegration of the Restatement of Property*, 79 BROOK. L. REV. 681, 701–02 (2014). On section-by-section revision, *see* Smith, *supra* note 65, at 30.

[82] The founders of the ALI apparently considered it a plus that the Restatements did not need revision as often as treatises. *See* White, *supra* note 2, at 11 (noting that treatises required constant updating).

[83] Statutes pose a variation on this concern. On the challenges posed by obsolescence and updating of codes, *see* Robert E. Scott, *The Uniform Commercial Code and the Ongoing Quest for an Efficient and Fair Commercial Law*, in this volume. Note also that a Restatement or its provisions may become canonical, with implications for how courts will interpret its guidance. On the potential canonical status of Restatement provisions, *see* Richard R.W. Brooks, *Canon and Fireworks: Reliance in the Restatements of Contracts and Reliance on Them*, in this volume.

C. Restatements and Architecture

Where Restatements are incorporated into legal reasoning, the law is a hybrid between a spontaneous and a made order.[84] As suggested earlier, the relationship between Restatements and case law is complex; Restatements reflect prior case law within the common-law tradition, but they also tidy up and rework that case law to render it more coherent, simple, fair, or efficient. Restatements are then subject to further common-law decision-making, often elaborated over a span of decades. We turn now to another way that Restatements can intersect with a spontaneous order.

Systems are often thought to be artificial, but they need not be. Systems can be organic. As one of us has noted, "[a] complex system can arise spontaneously or as a mixture of spontaneous and direct development."[85] The common law is hybrid in this way, and the more so in those areas where it shows the influence of a Restatement. Still, Restatements can reflect the common law's spontaneous order even if they are not examples of one. This follows naturally enough in situations where Restatements reject outlier cases or smooth out the rough edges of legal doctrine. Suppose that we are considering a more wholesale reform of a field's legal concepts. Can such a Restatement still reflect common-law doctrine? One might think that a fit criterion has little place in such contexts, since the Restatement at issue is substituting new concepts for old. That, however, is not quite true, for Restatements can fit the structure of common-law concepts and reasoning even in those cases where they do not fit the content of existing common law.

A comparison to interpretive legal theory may be helpful. As Stephen Smith notes, a legal interpretation need not perfectly match its subject matter. Instead, one might explain the law "using concepts that are recognizably 'legal' (or at least using concepts that, though more abstract than standard legal concepts, work through recognizably legal concepts in their explanation of particular rules and decisions) even if those concepts are not the same legal concepts that were employed by judges."[86] Such explanations are "in the right ball park."[87] From this perspective, the key question to ask is "whether the theorist's explanation is of the sort that, once translated into legal concepts, could be accepted by a court, even if no court has yet done so."[88] New Private Law scholarship often makes use of this approach.[89]

We think the "recognizably legal" category is important not only for explanatory theories but also for Restatements. In part, this is because Restatements are intended to influence judicial decisions; a recognizably legal account could have a better chance of being adopted by common-law courts. Yet there is also another reason. If a Restatement adopts recognizably legal concepts, this allows the Restatement to more

---

[84] F.A. Hayek, Law, Legislation and Liberty 39 (1976); Michael Polanyi, The Logic of Liberty: Reflections and Rejoinders 162–63, 185 (1951); P.A. Lewis, *Systems, Structural Properties and Levels of Organisation: The Influence of Ludwig von Bertalanffy on the Work of F. A. Hayek*, 34 A Res. in the Hist. of Econ. Thought & Methodology 125 (2016).

[85] *See* Smith, *supra* note 65, at 27. *See also id.* at 32.

[86] *See* Stephen A. Smith, Contract Theory 28–29 (2004).

[87] *See id.* at 29.

[88] *See id.* at 30.

[89] For discussion, *see* Andrew S. Gold, *Internal and External Perspectives: On the New Private Law Methodology*, *in* The Oxford Handbook of the New Private Law (Andrew S. Gold et al. eds., 2020).

closely fit the structure, or architecture, of existing common-law reasoning. Through an exploration of this fit we will be able to see how the architecture often serves a purpose that goes beyond the merits of individual "legal rules." And this architecture is consequential: even where it is suboptimal, significant deviations from this architecture come with a cost. One way or another, system effects are often unavoidable, and to be sensitive to these effects, common-law reasoners and Restatement drafters both need to take architecture into account.

Others have noted the importance of structure when assessing how well an explanatory theory fits the law as it currently is.[90] We suggest, however, that structure offers a dimension of fit that is relevant even when *reforming* the law. We will refer to this dimension as "architectural fit." Architectural fit is usually emphasized by theorists who want to understand the law accurately prior to making any changes. Yet it can matter for designing such changes as well. It is possible to be "in the right ballpark" when revising the law, and in particular, it is possible for a reform to be in the right ballpark because it matches the law's conceptual structure.

It is also possible for Restatements to diverge from this structure, and this divergence may come with costs. For example, consider the idea of an in rem right. In rem rights are a fundamental feature of property law, and on the conventional understanding they often involve rights over a "thing." While various accounts of in rem rights could be "in the right ballpark," removal of an in rem right's relationship to a thing flattens the law's architecture. The early Restatement treatment of in rem rights provides an illustration of what it means to ignore the common law's architecture in this way, and it is also an illustration of why this can be problematic.

As Reporter for the first Restatement of Property, Harry Bigelow determined that it should follow the typology of legal concepts developed by Wesley Hohfeld.[91] An in rem right that is disaggregated in Hohfeldian fashion, however, loses the delineation shortcut that the earlier, non-Hohfeldian picture offered.[92] This could have been avoided, and with good reason. There is another way to think about in rem rights that shows more sensitivity to law as a complex system.[93] Rather than emphasize numerosity (as Hohfeld did), one might follow Albert Kocourek in emphasizing indefiniteness. As Kocourek recognized, the facts that give rise to an in rem right do not serve to directly identify duty-bearers.[94] This indefiniteness comes with major practical benefits. It is much simpler from a legal design perspective to set up a right

---

[90] *See, e.g.,* JULES COLEMAN, THE PRACTICE OF PRINCIPLE: IN DEFENSE OF A PRAGMATIST APPROACH TO LEGAL THEORY 21 (2001) (indicating that the corrective justice account of tort law "seeks to show how the structural components of tort law are independently intelligible and mutually coherent in the light of a familiar and widely accepted principle of justice"); Benjamin C. Zipursky, *Civil Recourse, Not Corrective Justice,* 91 GEO. L.J. 695, 708 (2003) ("But even to identify when the law is applied, extended, revised, or rejected, we need to have some idea of what the law is. This requires identifying what concepts and principles structure tort doctrine.").

[91] *See* Merrill & Smith, *supra* note 23 at 697.

[92] *See* Brian Angelo Lee & Henry E. Smith, *The Nature of Coasean Property,* 59 INT'L REV. ECON. 145 (2012) (analyzing in rem rights in terms of a Coasean thought experiment).

[93] Although it is not clear that Hohfeld would have endorsed the bundle-of-rights picture of property, to the extent that the bundle conception has influenced the Restatements, this version of Hohfeld and Hohfeldianism does not permit connections to be drawn or generalizations to be stated in anything like a useful or intuitive form. J.E. PENNER, PROPERTY RIGHTS: A RE-EXAMINATION 43–56 (2020).

[94] *See* Albert Kocourek, *Rights in Rem,* 68 U. PA. L. REV. 322, 322 (1920).

against the world, communicated through a thing, than to spell out extensionally equivalent unital rights one by one. And delineation costs are not the only benefit; information costs are limited dramatically when in rem rights are taken as rights against the world at large.[95]

Architectural fit also has implications that extend well beyond in rem rights. A key architectural feature is the way the law makes use of interlocking concepts. For example, in tort law it matters how primary rights and duties, wrongs, secondary rights and duties, private rights of action, and remedies are each interconnected. Where these conceptual relations are left in place, it may be easier to forecast how changes to one concept will indirectly impact the application of another adjacent concept.[96] Not every impact can be foreseen even then. Even so, judges and regulated parties have good reason to care how a conceptual revision will ripple through the legal system. Focusing on problems case by case or rule by rule will not readily address system effects. Retaining a well-functioning conceptual structure permits some confidence that the ripple effects will be contained even where their details are hard to discern ex ante.

For example, consider how the Restatements have handled the notion of "duty" in negligence law. As John Goldberg notes, the Restatement (Third) of Torts, Section 6, places "duty" at the end of an "unless" clause, with the effect that "duty questions are questions about exemptions or immunities from liability."[97] The *Palsgraf* principle is likewise downplayed. Should that trouble us? Ironically, the problem here also involves Hohfeld. As Hohfeld well knew, shifting from one Hohfeldian incident to another can be consequential. If duty questions are treated instead in immunity terms, the conceptual structure of negligence law is changed. Indeed, for potential tortfeasors it may be considerably changed, given the guidance function of law. Goldberg suggests that, to the extent the Restatement excises duty from negligence law, it excises negligence law's "moral center."[98] That, we would suggest, constitutes a notable divergence from tort law's conceptual structure, its architecture. Goldberg also sees signs that the downplaying of duty analysis may lead courts to narrow the scope of negligence liability, rather than leave more negligence cases to juries as the Reporters apparently intended.[99] It should not be surprising if such conceptual shifts have unforeseen consequences.

Another, related reason for seeking architectural fit is that the common law's legal architecture will tend to track simple and generalizable moral norms, at least in broad

---

[95] The same holds true with appropriate adjustments for the corporation. If corporations are disaggregated as Hohfeld wished, they lose their corporate features; legal reasoning about corporations becomes, ironically, much more complex. *See* Gold & Smith, *supra* note 69, at 504.

[96] *See* Smith, *supra* note 65, at 32 ("The point of employing concepts in an architectural fashion is that the concept can link together and manage interactions in the system."). In theory, one might sidestep this concern by eliminating the connections between concepts. As one of us has noted, "Eliminating interlocking concepts means that advisors, Council members, and those voting at an annual meeting can evaluate sections in isolation without worrying about unseen effects." *See id.* But in practice, removing such conceptual linkages substitutes other types of complexity—potentially intractable types—for the kind posed by the law's existing architecture.

[97] *See* Goldberg, *supra* note 74, at 192 (citing RESTATEMENT (THIRD) OF TORTS: LIABILITY FOR PHYSICAL AND EMOTIONAL HARM §§ 6 & 7 (2010)).

[98] *See id*, at 195.

[99] *See id.*

outline. In private law settings, the "recognizably legal" is often a proxy for the "recognizably moral."[100] As we have noted in our prior work:

> The set of legal concepts benefits from its congruence with relatively simple local forms of conventional morality. Forms of morality that deal with what one individual owes another are well suited for the basic set up of a system of private law.[101]

These moral structures are frequently modular, comparatively straightforward in application, and accessible to both judges and private parties.[102] There are, moreover, multiple reasons to anticipate that legal systems will evolve toward such moral norms (if not to an optimal level, then at least to a point which avoids intractable complexity).[103]

A more wide-ranging structural feature is the way legal concepts carry over to new settings. As Simon Deakin notes, "concepts are transferable across different contexts."[104] This is a part of how concepts work within legal systems, where the notion of a wrong in tort law can influence the notion of a wrong in contract law, or the idea of standing in contract law may affect the idea of standing in corporate law. Or, to return to the idea of possession, maintaining some continuity in notions of possession across areas and situations is likely to keep property law closer to people's moral and social intuitions: coming up with tailored regulations for drone overflights and subsurface drilling does not exactly describe the role of common law courts or Restatements. And, as Jeremy Waldron emphasizes, it is therefore important to be able to "keep track" of the way that changes to a legal concept will influence its application elsewhere in the law.[105] Where concepts are treated as epiphenomenal or as ad hoc placeholders for whatever outcome is considered desirable on a case-by-case basis, the difficulty in keeping track can be insurmountable.

These system effects will not vanish by wishing them away, and, so long as legal systems evolve gradually (and through the decisions of multiple institutional actors), it is impossible to avoid the impact of transferable legal concepts. Even if a Restatement section assumes away an existing conceptual structure, it is a further leap to the idea that the common-law system already in place will neglect that structure. It is likewise

---

[100] Stephen Smith's work suggests another reason to care about the "recognizably moral", in light of the law's claim to authority. See SMITH, *supra* note 86, at 22–23.

[101] See Gold & Smith, *supra* note 69, at 504. See also Andrew S. Gold & Henry E. Smith, *Scaling Up Legal Relations*, in THE LEGACY OF WESLEY HOHFELD: EDITED MAJOR WORKS, SELECT PERSONAL PAPERS, AND ORIGINAL COMMENTARIES 419 (Shyamkrishna Balganesh, Ted Sichelman, & Henry E. Smith eds., 2022).

[102] To the extent these features are the product of a spontaneous order, they may also incorporate the informational benefits that spontaneous orders offer. As noted, we think the common law is a hybrid between a spontaneous order and artificial rules, but the artificial component can reflect structural features that evolved more organically.

[103] See Gold & Smith, *supra* note 69, at 511–13.

[104] See Deakin, *supra* note 58, at 180. There is an added complexity if such concepts are multifunctional. See id. For an example of how remedial concepts can be multifunctional, *see* ANDREW S. GOLD, THE RIGHT OF REDRESS 135 (2020).

[105] See Jeremy Waldron, *"Transcendental Nonsense" and System in the Law*, 100 COLUM. L. REV. 16, 47 (2000). Waldron goes further in arguing for the benefits of a "neutral matrix" by means of the law's conceptual structure. We are hesitant to endorse that view across the board, as it might require giving up the simple moral norms that provide much of the accessibility and modularity of common-law concepts.

difficult for drafters of one Restatement to know with certainty what conceptual structure will be adopted by drafters of a subsequent Restatement. The reality that Restatements are adopted piecemeal, with different Reporters seeking different policy goals, means that the transferability of concepts to new settings is more, not less, important.

None of this is an argument for resisting legal change. The structural interrelationship among legal concepts can be retained even where the content of these legal concepts is revised substantially. Indeed, the common law itself evolves through conceptual changes that preserve the law's architecture. This is possible, in part, because preexisting legal concepts are often mutable or "defeasible."[106] Concepts can evolve in various ways while leaving their overall structure intact; for example, legal concepts may be adjusted in their specifics while still remaining consistent with a more foundational concept.[107] Moreover, a legal system can translate concerns from the external, social environment into terms that fit the law's conceptual structure without having to give up that structure.[108] Our point, once again, is a point about architectural fit as elaborated in the context of reform.

In sum, architectural fit is desirable even where Restatements pursue wholesale reform of the common law.[109] Two dimensions of fit are usually emphasized by legal theorists: fit with the actual concepts used in the courts' judicial reasoning, and fit with ultimate case outcomes.[110] Architectural fit is a third dimension of fit, and unlike the first two it is available as a criterion for legal reform. Restatements that propose significant changes to the law will not fit the precise concepts that courts use nor the outcomes their decisions compel, yet such Restatements may still fit the law's conceptual structure. Indeed, Restatements may have an institutional advantage here; they may be better situated for providing an architectural fit than legislation.[111] In turn, this possibility brings us back to Cardozo. Recall Cardozo's concern that principles, rules, and concepts might lose their regenerative capacity if they were sufficiently degraded. Where Restatements preserve the structure of the law—even in the midst of reform—they may also preserve this regenerative capacity for future common law elaborations, extensions, and even Restatements themselves.

---

[106] *See* Deakin, *supra* note 58, at 180.

[107] *Cf. id.* at 173.

[108] *Id.* at 176. *See also* Waldron, *supra* note 105, at 21.

[109] Note that the import of architectural fit is not the only insight we can take from systems theory. For example, another, overlapping consideration is the interconnectedness of aspects of a legal system. Where these aspects are less interconnected, change will be easier. *See* Yun-chien Chang & Henry E. Smith, *Convergence and Divergence in Systems of Property Law: Theoretical and Empirical Analyses,* 92 S. CAL. L. REV. 785 (2019); Henry E. Smith, *The Persistence of System in Property Law,* 163 U. PA. L. REV. 2055 (2015); *see also* Henry E. Smith, *Systems Theory: Emergent Private Law, in* THE OXFORD HANDBOOK OF THE NEW PRIVATE LAW 151 (Andrew S. Gold et al. eds., 2020).

[110] *Cf.* Jody S. Kraus, *Philosophy of Contract Law, in* THE OXFORD HANDBOOK OF JURISPRUDENCE AND PHILOSOPHY OF LAW 687 (Jules Coleman & Scott Shapiro eds., 2002) ("[T]he criterion of fit with outcomes provides the dispositive constraint on legal interpretation for economic analysts, whereas the criterion of fit with stated judicial reasoning provides the dispositive constraint for deontic theorists.").

[111] In suggesting Restatements may have a comparative institutional advantage, we do not downplay the challenges they face in light of their procedural features. *See* Smith, *supra* note 65, at 29–31.

V. Conclusion

The common law has always been and still is at the heart of the Restatement program. The special challenges of the common law have to do with system and its lack, but sometimes not quite in the way that those working on Restatements had in mind. The ALI process favors some kinds of simplification, reform, and fit over others, and even within this wide range, architectural fit and a sensitivity to loose but interconnected system in the law has sometimes fallen by the wayside. If we can better appreciate the benefits and limits of system—and which kinds of nondeductive system are appropriate for the hybrid of spontaneous and made order that is the common law—we will be able to point Restatements in fruitful new directions.

Past and Present ALI Projects

(As of November 2022)

In this list, the first year in parentheses is the year of the first draft produced for the project or other initiation of the project. The concluding year is the year of publication of the final product or other conclusion of the project.*

ALI

THE AMERICAN LAW INSTITUTE

RESTATEMENTS OF THE LAW

- Agency (1923–1933)
  Agency (Second) (1952–1958)
  Agency (Third) (1995–2006)
- The Law of American Indians (2012–2022)
- Charitable Nonprofit Organizations (2014–2021)
  [a related project, Principles of the Law, Charitable Nonprofit Organizations, began in 2000 and ended in 2014]
- Children and the Law (2015–)
- Conflict of Laws (1923–1934)
  Conflict of Laws (Second) (1952–1971); Revisions (1985–1989)
  Conflict of Laws (Third) (2014–)
- Constitutional Torts (2022–)
- Consumer Contracts (2014–)
- Contracts (1923–1932)
  Contracts (Second) (1959–1981)
- Copyright (2014–)
- Corporate Governance (2019–)
- Employment Law (2000–2015)
- Foreign Relations Law of the United States (Second) (1954–1965)
  The Foreign Relations Law of the United States (Third) (1978–1987)
  The Foreign Relations Law of the United States (Fourth): Selected Topics in Treaties, Jurisdiction, and Sovereign Immunity (2012–2018)
- Judgments (1940–1942)
  Judgments (Second) (1969–1982)
- The Law Governing Lawyers (Third) (1986–2000)
- Liability Insurance (2010–2019) [formerly known as "Principles of the Law of Liability Insurance"]

- Property (1927–1944)

  Property (Second):
  - Donative Transfers (1977–1992)
  - Landlord and Tenant (1969–1977)

  Property (Third):
  - Mortgages (1988–1997)
  - Servitudes (1986–2000)
  - Wills and Other Donative Transfers (1991–2011)

  Property (Fourth) (2014–)

- Restitution (1933–1937)
  [Restitution (Second) (1981–1984) [discontinued]]
  Restitution and Unjust Enrichment (Third) (1997–2011)

- Security (1936–1941)
  Suretyship and Guaranty (Third) (1989–1996)

- Torts (1923–1939)
  Torts (Second) (1955–1979)
  Torts (Third):
  - Apportionment of Liability (1993–2000)
  - Defamation and Privacy (2019–)
  - Intentional Torts to Persons (2012–)
  - Liability for Economic Harm (2010–2020) [formerly "Economic Torts and Related Wrongs" and "Liability for Economic Loss" (2004–2007)]
  - Liability for Physical and Emotional Harm (1996–2012)
  - Miscellaneous Provisions (2019–) [formerly "Concluding Provisions"]
  - Products Liability (1991–1998)
  - Remedies (2019–)

- Trusts (1927–1935)
  Trusts (Second) (1952–1959)

  Trusts (Third) (1992–2012):
  - Prudent Investor Rule (1987–1992)

- Unfair Competition (Third) (1986–1995)

- The U.S. Law of International Commercial and Investor–State Arbitration (2007–)

  [formerly known as "Restatement of the Law Third, The U.S. Law of International Commercial Arbitration"; "Restatement of the Law, The U.S. Law of International Commercial Arbitration"; and "Restatement of the Law, The U.S. Law of International Commercial and Investment Arbitration"]

PRINCIPLES OF THE LAW

- **Aggregate Litigation** (2003–2010)

- **Compliance and Enforcement for Organizations** (2014–) [formerly known as "Compliance, Risk Management, and Enforcement" and as "Compliance, Enforcement, and Risk Management for Corporations, Nonprofits, and Other Organizations"]

- **Corporate Governance: Analysis and Recommendations** (1977–1994) [formerly known as "Principles of Corporate Governance and Structure: Restatement and Recommendations"]

- **Data Economy, Principles for a** (2018–) [joint project with the European Law Institute]

- **Data Privacy** (2013–2020) [formerly known as "Restatement of the Law Third, Information Privacy Principles"]

- **Election Administration: Non-Precinct Voting and Resolution of Ballot-Counting Disputes** (2010–2019) [formerly known as "Principles of the Law, Election Law" and "Principles of Election Law: Resolution of Election Disputes]

- **Family Dissolution: Analysis and Recommendations** (1989–2002)

- **Government Ethics** (2009–)

- **High-Volume Civil Adjudication** (2022–)

- **Intellectual Property: Principles Governing Jurisdiction, Choice of Law, and Judgments in Transnational Disputes** (2001–2008)

- **Policing** (2015–) [formerly known as "Principles of the Law, Police Investigations"]

- **Software Contracts** (2004–2010)

- **Student Sexual Misconduct: Procedural Frameworks for Colleges and Universities** (2015–) [formerly known as "Project on Sexual and Gender-Based Misconduct on Campus: Procedural Frameworks and Analysis"]

- **Transnational Civil Procedure** (1997–2006) [formerly known as "Transnational Rules of Civil Procedure"; cosponsored by the International Institute for the Unification of Private Law (UNIDROIT)]

- **Transnational Insolvency Project** [cosponsored by the International Insolvency Institute]:
  - ❖ **Principles of Cooperation Among the NAFTA Countries** (1993–2003)
  - ❖ **Global Principles for Cooperation in International Insolvency Cases, Report to ALI** (2006–2012)

UNIFORM COMMERCIAL CODE

Uniform Commercial Code (1942–1952) [with The Uniform Law Commission (also known as the National Conference of Commissioners on Uniform State Laws)]

[Articles 1 to 10: General Provisions, Sales, Commercial Paper, Bank Deposits and Collections, Letters of Credit, Bulk Transfers, Warehouse Receipts, Investment Securities, Secured Transactions, Effective Date and Repealer] *Revisions, Amendments, and Comments to the Uniform Commercial Code* (in chronological order):

- Changes and Modifications to the 1952 UCC (1952–1953)
- 1955 Supplement to the 1952 UCC (1954)
- 1958 Supplement to the 1957 UCC (1958)
- Revised Article 9 (Secured Transactions); 1972 Amendments to UCC (1967–1972) [including New Article 11: Effective Date and Transition Provisions]
- Revised Article 8 (Investment Securities); 1977 Amendments to UCC (1975–1977)
- [New] Article 2A: Leases (1986–1987)
- Permanent Editorial Board Commentaries and Reports (ongoing since 1987)
- Current Payment Methods:
  - ➤ [New] Article 4A: Funds Transfers (1988–1989)
  - ➤ Revised Article 3 (Negotiable Instruments) (1988–1990) [formerly "Commercial Paper"]
  - ➤ Revised Article 4 (Bank Deposits and Collections) (1988–1990)
- Repealer of Article 6 (Bulk Transfers) and Revised Article 6 (Bulk Sales) (1988–1989)
- Article 2 (Sales) Study Group (1988–1990) [Permanent Editorial Board study]
- Article 9 (Secured Transactions) Study Group (1989–1992) [Permanent Editorial Board study]
- Amendments to Article 2A (Leases) (1990)
- Revised Article 5 (Letters of Credit) (1991–1995)
- Revised Article 2 (Sales) (1992–1999) [new Drafting Committee appointed in 1999]
- Revised Article 8 (Investment Securities) (1992–1994)
- Revised Article 9 (Secured Transactions) (1993–1999)
- Revised Article 1 (General Provisions) (1996–2001)
- Revised Article 2A (Leases) (1996–1999) [new Drafting Committee appointed in 1999]
- Proposed Amendments to Articles 2 and 2A (Sales and Leases) (1999–2003) [formerly [New] Revised Articles 2 and 2A (Sales and Leases); withdrawn 2011]
- Proposed Revisions to Articles 3 (Negotiable Instruments) and 4 (Bank Deposits and Collections) (2000–2002) [formerly "Revised Articles 3, 4, and 4A"]
- Amendments to Article 7 (Documents of Title) (2000–2003)
- Article 9 Review Committee (2008–2010)
- Amendments to Article 9 (Secured Transactions) (2010)
- Amendment to Section 4A-108 (Relationship to Electronic Fund Transfer Act) (2012)

OTHER CODIFICATIONS, STUDIES, AND PROJECTS

- **Administration of the Criminal Law** (1930–1935)
  - Double Jeopardy (1931–1935)
  - Summoning Witnesses in One State to Testify in Another State (1930–1931)
- **Code of Criminal Procedure** (1924–1930)
- **Complex Litigation: Statutory Recommendations and Analysis** (1984–1994) [formerly known as "Preliminary Study of Complex Litigation"]

- Criminal Justice—Youth:
  - Youth Correction Authority Act/Program (1938–1940; 1944–1951)
  - Youth Court Act (1938–1941)
- Enterprise Responsibility for Personal Injury (1986–1991) [formerly known as "Compensation and Liability for Product and Process Injuries"; Reporter's Study issued]
- Federal Estate and Gift Tax Project:
  - Recommendations of The American Law Institute and Reporters' Studies (1961–1969)
  - Study on Generation-Skipping Transfers Under the Federal Estate Tax (1982–1984) [Discussion Draft issued]
- Federal Income, Estate and Gift Tax Project:
  - Income Tax Problems of Corporations and Shareholders (1954–1958) [with American Bar Association Section of Taxation; Report of Study issued]
  - Study of Definitional Problems in Capital Gains Taxation (1958–1960) [Discussion Draft issued]
- Federal Income Tax Project:
  - Integration of the Individual and Corporate Income Taxes (1989–1993) [Reporter's Study of Corporate Tax Integration issued]
  - International Aspects of United States Income Taxation:
    - ➤ Volume I: Proposals of The American Law Institute on United States Taxation of Foreign Persons and of the Foreign Income of United States Persons (1982–1987)
    - ➤ Volume II: Proposals of The American Law Institute on United States Income Tax Treaties (1987–1992)
  - Subchapter C: Proposals of The American Law Institute on Corporate Acquisitions and Dispositions and Reporter's Study on Corporate Distributions (1974–1982)
  - Subchapter J: Proposals of The American Law Institute on the Taxation of Trust and Estate Income and Income in Respect of Decedents (1979–1985)
  - Subchapter K: Proposals of The American Law Institute on the Taxation of Partners (1976–1984)
  - Subchapter C (Supplemental Study) (1986–1989) [Reporter's Study Draft issued]
  - Taxation of Private Business Enterprises (1994–1999) [formerly "Taxation of Pass-Through Entities"; Reporter's Study issued]
- Federal Judicial Code Revision Project (1995–2004)
- Federal Securities Code (1969–1980)
- Income Tax Project/Statute (1947–1954) [also known as "Federal Income Tax Statute"; 1954 Draft issued]
- Model Code of Evidence (1939–1942) [formerly known as "Code of Rules of Evidence" and "Code of Evidence"]
- [A] Model Code of Pre-Arraignment Procedure (1963–1975)
- [A] Model Land Development Code (1960; 1965–1976) [formerly known as "Public Control of Land Use and Land Planning"]
- Model Penal Code (1950–1962)
- Model Penal Code Commentaries (1976–1985) [2 parts]
- Model Penal Code: Sentencing (1999–)
- Model Penal Code: Sexual Assault and Related Offenses (2012–)
- Paths to a "Better Way": Litigation, Alternatives, and Accommodation (1986–1988) [Steering Committee Report and Background Paper published at 1989 *Duke Law Journal* 808 (1989)]
- Recognition and Enforcement of Foreign Judgments: Analysis and Proposed Federal Statute (1999–2006) [formerly known as "International Jurisdiction and Judgments Project"]

- Statement of Essential Human Rights (1942–1945)
- [A] Study of the Business of the Federal Courts (1931–1934) [with Yale School of Law]
- Study of the Division of Jurisdiction Between State and Federal Courts (1959–1969)
- Uniform Contribution Among Tortfeasors Act (1936–1939) [with National Conference of Commissioners on Uniform State Laws; formerly known as "Contribution Between Tortfeasors Act," "An Act on Contribution Among Tortfeasors," and "Contribution Among Tortfeasors Act"]
- Uniform Law of Airflight (1937) [with National Conference of Commissioners on Uniform State Laws and American Bar Association; formerly known as "Law of Airflight"]
- Uniform Property Act (1935–1938) [with National Conference of Commissioners on Uniform State Laws; formerly known as "Property Act" and "Law of Property Act"]
  - Accumulations Act (1938)
  - Perpetuities Act (1938)
- World Trade Law: The World Trade Organization (2001–2013) [formerly known as "Principles of Trade Law: The World Trade Organization"]:
  - WTO Case Law Analyses (2001–2013)
  - Legal and Economic Principles of World Trade Law, Report to ALI (2007–2013)

DISCONTINUED PROJECTS

Discontinued Restatements of the Law:
- Business Associations (1928–1933) [initially a non-Restatement project]
- Property Third: Joint Ownership (1996–1998)
- Restitution (Second) (1981–1984)
- Sales of Land (1935) [formerly known as "Vendor and Purchaser"]

Discontinued Principles of the Law:
- Government Access to and Use of (Personal) Digital Information (2006–2008)

Discontinued Uniform Commercial Code Projects:
- [New] Article 2B: Software Contracts and Licenses of Information (1995–1999) [formerly "Licenses"; not completed as part of the UCC; promulgated solely by the National Conference of Commissioners on Uniform State Laws as the "Uniform Computer Information Transactions Act"]
- Uniform New Payments Code (1977–1984) [formerly "New Payments Code" and "New Uniform Payments Code"; drafted under the supervision of the "3-4-8 Committee" of the Permanent Editorial Board; see also "Current Payment Methods"]

Discontinued Codifications, Studies, and Projects:
- American Law: A Moral Inventory (1949–1951)
- Taxation of Innovative Financial Products (1999–2000) [part of the Federal Income Tax Project]
- International Secured Transactions Project (1997–2001)

Notes

* For the older projects, this list shows the start date as the year in which the first draft in the project was produced for a meeting; thus, the first date shown in parentheses could well be a year or more after the project was approved, the Reporter appointed, and the work actually begun. For the more recent projects, the year in parentheses is the year in which the project actually began (and not the year of the first draft, which could be one or more years later).

In all projects, the concluding year shown in parentheses is the year that the final product in the project was published or, if the project was discontinued before a final ALI-approved product was accomplished, then the year shown is the year the project terminated, sometimes with publication of a Reporter's Study, Discussion Draft, or other work; an explanation in each such case is shown in brackets. In most cases, the official work in the project is published in the year following the Annual Meeting in which the work is finally approved by the Institute, and sometimes even later, due to the time necessary to get the manuscript revised, edited, and printed. If no concluding year is shown in parentheses, then the project is ongoing.

Index

For the benefit of digital users, indexed terms that span two pages (e.g., 52–53) may, on occasion, appear on only one of those pages.